Silent Films, 1877–1996

Silent Films, 1877–1996

A Critical Guide to 646 Movies

by
Robert K. Klepper

McFarland & Company, Inc., Publishers
Jefferson, North Carolina and London

Cover: **Lillian Gish in *Way Down East* (1920).**

Frontispiece: **Harold Lloyd and Jobyna Ralston in *The Kid Brother* (1927).**

All photographs are from the author's collection unless otherwise credited.

British Library Cataloguing-in-Publication data are available

Library of Congress Cataloguing-in-Publication Data

Klepper, Robert K., 1966–
Silent films, 1877–1996 : a critical guide to 646 movies / by Robert K. Klepper.
p. cm.
Includes bibliographical references and index.
ISBN 0-7864-0595-3 (casebound : 50# alkaline paper) ♾
1. Silent films—Reviews. 2. Video recordings—Reviews. I. Title.
PN1995.75.K57 1999
791.43'75—dc21 98-53004
CIP

Manufactured in the United States of America

McFarland & Company, Inc., Publishers
Box 611, Jefferson, North Carolina 28640

Dedicated in memory of Miss Kitty
[circa 1990–April 7, 1998]

The greatest cat who ever lived,
and cherished companion of the author
for the duration of the composition of
Silent Films on Video and *Silent Films, 1877–1996*
and to
Margaret Poppell,
my business communications teacher in high school

Acknowledgments

First and foremost, I would like to thank my parents, Kenneth H. and Altha A. Klepper, without whose help this author would never have written a first book, much less a second.

A great debt of gratitude is also due to the great film historian Anthony Slide, whom the late, great Lillian Gish referred to as "our foremost historian of silent films." Mr. Slide went through the manuscript meticulously, and saved this author from going into print with a number of potentially embarrassing errors.

Thanks are also due to Mr. Frank "Junior" Coghlan, who not only took the time from his busy schedule to write the foreword for this book, but also looked over the reviews of his films to make sure that everything was factually correct and in order. Diana Serra Cary, formerly known as "Baby Peggy" Montgomery, provided significant assistance with information and photos from her career as a silent era child star as well.

Film historian and MGM archivist Jeffrey Vance was very helpful on the comedy reviews especially.

Elaina Archer of the Mary Pickford Library deserves credit for having provided the author with screening copies of a number of rare Mary and Jack Pickford titles, and she was also kind enough to supply stills for use in the book, too. Without her significant assistance and cooperation, this book would not have been as complete. Ms. Archer also went through the reviews of the Pickford films evaluated, and made good suggestions that significantly improved the text of those reviews.

I am also grateful to David Shepard, who provided copies of several of the silent films he has done video productions of, as well as made suggestions for improving the text.

Marjorie Sweeney of Kino Video has provided a number of review copies of videos, as well as quite a few stills from the movies that they have released.

Serge Bromberg of Lobster Films in Paris provided a video copy of *Little Mary Sunshine* (1916), which is the only surviving work of child star Baby Marie Osborne known to exist. He has made it possible not only for this author to review the film, but for Ms. Osborne, now known as Marie Osborne Yeats, to see one of her films for the first time since 1923.

My best friend, Teresa Hunt, stayed up many a late night to watch films from Turner Classic Movies for me. She has come over to my house every Monday for the past four years and watched silents as a continuing tradition.

Sandra Birnhak and Wandjina of the Killiam Collection gave significant help, providing screening copies of a number of rare films in their collection. Jeff Hines and Nancy Hamlin of Critic's Choice Video also provided review copies of their silents on video, as did Jack Hardy of Grapevine Video and Chris Snowden of Unknown Video.

Lee Donahue of the Pensacola Public Library accessed several hard to find books for me through interlibrary loans.

The following others, listed in alphabetical order, have made important contributions and provided significant assistance as well: Jack Bona; the late David Bradley; Kevin Brownlow; Danny Burk; Charles Campbell; John Cavallo; Tony Crnkovich; Dennis Doros; Billy Doyle; Robert Edwards; Douglas Fairbanks, Jr.; Eve Golden; Jim Jorden; the late George Katchmer; Bob King; Ron Krueger; Mike Lentz; Bruce Long; Diane MacIntyre; Vladimir Malyshev of Gosfilmofond in Russia; Ernie Markinkovich; Henry Nicolella; director and actress Leni Riefenstahl of Germany; Jerry Rutledge; Kim Schweizer, John Sherwood; Jean Sperbeck; Gilda Tabarez; Edwin "Ned" Thanhouser; Tom Trusky; Martin Verlaan of the Netherlands; Edward Wagenknecht; Al Weissberg; Marie Osborne Yeats.

Contents

Foreword

I am pleased that Robert K. Klepper has asked me to write the foreword for his fine book. And well I should be, as like him, I am also an admirer of the silent era in motion pictures as I must have worked in at least 50 of them before being cast in my first "talkie," *The Girl Said No*, at MGM in 1930.

I worked in my first film, a silent of course, in 1920 when I was still only three years old. It was *Mid Channel*, which starred the fine actress Clara Kimball Young. It was made at her own studio in Edendale, Garson Studios, and was directed by her husband Harry Garson.

If the name Edendale puzzles you, it was where many of our early studios were located before moving to Hollywood, Culver City, and into Burbank in the San Fernando Valley.

Mack Sennett, Charlie Chaplin, Marshall Neilan, and of course Clara Kimball Young once had their studios located there. Edendale is no longer seen on the map of Los Angeles, but it was just north of where Sunset Boulevard crosses Glendale Boulevard near Echo Park.

After working as an extra in many films, I moved up to be a bit player with more important roles. Then, at the suggestion of the fine director Marshall Neilan, Cecil B. DeMille cast me to play a small role in his silent film, *The Road to Yesterday*. Evidently C.B. was impressed with my work as he signed me to a five year contract at his own studio in Culver City. I am still the only child actor C.B. ever had under a personal contract.

While I was under contract to Mr. DeMille, I worked in 15 films at his studio, and finally attained stardom rating in the last four of them.

At the many film festivals I attend around our great country, fans have asked me if we had to memorize lines in silent films. I say yes, sort of. We had a script with all the dialogue printed and we were supposed to say our lines as closely as possible so the other performers could give their proper reactions. If we made a minor mistake of a word or two, it did not cause an immediate retake, as it does today in today's talking films.

After the filming was completed and finally edited, then the people who wrote the printed titles that you once saw on the screen at your local theaters went to work. If we said something far removed from the printed titles it made us look rather stupid.

The next to last silent film I played in was *A Harp in Hock*. There I costarred with the fine actor Rudolph Schildkraut, the father of Joseph Schildkraut. The rather unusual title was because I was a "Harp," the nickname given to Irish people because of the beautiful golden harp encased on a field of green on the Irish flag of those days.

I played an Irish boy who sailed to America in ship steerage to join my mother who had preceded me to the United States. When I arrived at her humble dwelling I was saddened to find that she had just passed away.

Now being an immigrant boy without parents, I was destined to be placed in an orphanage. However, the nice Mr. Schildkraut then adopted me. Because he was a pawnbroker, I then became "A Harp in Hock."

The nice director of this film, Renaud Hoffman, even though it was a silent film, had me say my lines with an Irish brogue. Golly, how much more realistic can a director be in a silent motion picture?

I sure miss those "good old days."

Frank "Junior" Coghlan
Fall 1998

Introduction

This is the first time since the silent film era itself that a critical guide of this scope has been possible to write. Similar works on silent films were done in 1959 and 1980—in the days before video when a reviewer either had to have his or her own 16 mm or 35 mm prints to review, or be well connected enough with somebody at the major archives to be able to have the films screened for them. With the limited access to archive time and silent films, past reviewers have had to limit themselves to the greatest and most historically important films. An archivist is only going to spend so much time screening films for historians, so one has to make the best of the time available, thus forcing into a low priority the reviewing of "not so great" silents that nevertheless have historic significance. The video revolution has changed this, and it is now possible for a reviewer to watch hundreds of silent films at home, being able to screen and rescreen the film as many times as necessary to be able to write comprehensively about the particular film in question.

What you will find in this book are complete, detailed critiques of all types of silent films—from the very primitive films that came out in the late 1800s, "B" westerns, light comedies, and early documentaries to the great epics like *Intolerance* (1916) and *Napoléon* (1927). Some of the early pornographic films from the 1910s and 1920s are covered, as well as films dealing with all types of social issues including child labor, homosexuality, black civil rights, alcoholism, and drug addiction. Every type of film that existed in the silent era is represented in this book.

Before now, it would have been very difficult to do a comprehensive work with cast lists that included birth and death dates. There were no one-stop reference sources for that type of information before 1995, when two fine silent film player directories came on the market after decades of research had been put into them. Film historians Eugene Vazzana and Billy Doyle, respectively, published *The Silent Film Necrology* (McFarland, 1995) and *The Ultimate Directory of the Silent Screen Players* (Scarecrow, 1995). Doyle's book is used as the primary source for dates, and Vazzana's book is used as a secondary source, along with Ephraim Katz's 1994 *Film Encyclopedia* and Everett Grant Jarvis' 1996 edition of *Final Curtain*. The fact that the present work contains birth and death dates for most players and directors listed is attributable to these fellow film historians who did the research and worked years so that new historians like this author would have easy access to such information. If a birth or death date does not appear next to a name, one can assume that such information does not survive in the accessible historic record at the point of this writing.

This book covers silent films spanning 119 years—from the early experimental motion photography of Eadweard Muybridge in 1877 to the most recent silent film effort, *The Taxi Dancer* (1996). Some readers may question the value of including entries for some of the early experimental films which really require little commentary. The purpose of listing these early experimental films is to put in book form at a glance the types of subjects that were being filmed at the dawn of cinema, as well as who was directing, producing, and starring in the films. These early experimental films with running times under a couple of minutes should be accepted for what they are—early experiments with a new medium. The films did not really have enough substance to give a star rating to, so only the real standout early films with significant plot or story line are given quality ratings. If you do not see a star rating listed for a film, you can assume that the film was an experimental effort that should be taken and accepted for what it is. Most of the earliest films will not have star ratings. How can one very well rate Edison's *The Kiss* (1896), which has about a half minute close-up of a man and woman kissing?

The rating system used was:

☆☆☆☆	A masterpiece not to be missed
☆☆☆½	Excellent
☆☆☆	Good, solid entertainment
☆☆½	Not bad, but not one of the greats
☆☆	Fair, worth watching for historic value
☆½	Don't go out of your way for this one
☆	Poor or abysmal

A great deal of time and money went into the writing of this book to acquire the most representative sampling of silent films possible, from all different genres. One will see among the films reviewed some extremely rare titles that have not been covered in-depth since their original releases, if at all. It is the author's intention that this book provide information on what films are around, which of them are not as widely available as they should be, and which ones are not worthy of video release, while presenting a relatively comprehensive history of silent films.

Robert K. Klepper
Fall 1998

The Experimental Years (1877–1885)

The Motion Photography Experiments of Eadweard Muybridge

The first attempts to create the illusion of objects in motion date back to the 1830s, when William George Horner (1786–1837) invented the Zoetrope, which allowed animated drawings to be mounted on a wheel, creating the illusion of motion. Other similar inventions included the Phenakistoscope invented by Joseph Plateu (1801–1883) in 1832. Emile Reynaud (1844–1918) patented his Praxinoscope in 1877.

The year 1877 also marks the year that Eadweard Muybridge (1830–1904), formerly known by his given name of Edward Muggeridge, became the first person to attempt to create the illusion of motion with actual photographic images. Legend has it that Muybridge took on the task of experimental motion photography to settle an argument with California governor Leland Stanford concerning whether a horse ever had all four feet off the ground at the same time during a canter. Twenty-four still cameras were set up to take consecutive photos of the running horse, and thus the "motion picture" was born.

Among the subjects Muybridge photographed were nude and scantily clad men alone and in pairs wrestling, as well as nude and scantily clad women engaged solitarily in a variety of activities. While these early experiments do not technically qualify as silent films, they were among the origins of the art. Some of these early studies of an unidentified nude woman in motion are included in Kino Video's *The Movies Begin* video series, and are reviewed as follows:

1. **Woman Hopping on One Foot** (circa 1885)

Directed and Photographed by Eadweard Muybridge

This series of nine photos contains two sets of pictures—one set taken from the back, and the other from the front. They picture a barebreasted woman hopping up and down on one foot.

Experimental photography of a Horse in Motion by Eadweard Muybridge (1877).

2. Woman Jumping from Rock to Rock (circa 1885)

Directed and Photographed by Eadweard Muybridge

This series of 14 photos shows a barebreasted woman dressed in a translucent skirt as she jumps from one rock to another.

3. Woman Picking Up Skirt (circa 1885)

Directed and Photographed by Eadweard Muybridge

This series of six photographs records a barebreasted woman lifting her translucent skirt from the floor.

4. Woman Pouring from Jug (circa 1885)

Directed and Photographed by Eadweard Muybridge

This series of ten photos shows a nude woman picking up a jug and starting to pour from it. One would think that Muybridge would have been interested in capturing images of the water as it was being poured, but he was obviously more interested in photographing the woman's movements, and stopped short of showing the actual pouring.

5. Woman Setting Down Jug (circa 1885)

Directed and Photographed by Eadweard Muybridge

This series of 14 photos is of a nude woman shown from the back and from the front, holding a heavy jug over her head and setting it down.

6. Woman Sitting Down (circa 1885)

Directed and Photographed by Eadweard Muybridge

This series of 12 photos shows a barebreasted woman in a standing position first as she moves to sit down on the floor.

Eadweard Muybridge at right shaking hands with one of his male models, circa 1885.

7. **Woman Throwing a Baseball** (circa 1885)

Directed and Photographed by Eadweard Muybridge

This series of ten photos shows a nude woman as she picks up and then throws a baseball.

8. **Woman Turning and Walking Upstairs** (circa 1885)

Directed and Photographed by Eadweard Muybridge

This series of nine photographs features a nude woman walking to the foot of a staircase, turning, and proceeding up the stairs.

9. **Woman Walking Downstairs** (circa 1885)

Directed and Photographed by Eadweard Muybridge

This series of 11 photos shows a nude woman walking down a staircase.

Early Films: The 1890s

1894

10. Cockfight

Edison Kinetoscope Company; ***Directed by*** W.K.L. Dickson; ***Running Time:*** 44 seconds

The stars of this film are two birds engaged in a cockfight. Cockfighting, a once-popular spectator sport in which the birds often fought to the death of the loser, has since been banned in the United States and other countries as cruel and inhumane. This film does not show any gory sequences, and is limited to the two birds pulling some of each other's feathers.

11. Fred Ott's Sneeze

Edison Kinetoscope Company; ***Directed by*** W.K.L. Dickson; ***Running Time:*** 10 seconds; ***Cast:*** Frederick P. Ott (1860–1936)

This early film has two significant firsts to its credit. It was the first motion picture series to be registered with the Library of Congress for copyright purposes, and also was the first close-up, with Frederick P. Ott, one of the Edison scientists, sneezing as the camera rolls.

12. Glenroy Brothers Comic Boxing

Edison Kinetoscope Company; ***Directed by*** W.K.L. Dickson; ***Running Time:*** 26 seconds; ***Cast:*** The Glenroy Brothers

This peep show attraction features two brothers known as the Glenroys play-boxing in a boxing ring. No further information could be found on the subjects of this film.

13. Sandow the Strong Man

Edison Kinetoscope Company; ***Directed by*** W.K.L. Dickson; ***Running Time:*** 18 seconds; ***Cast:*** Eugene Sandow (1867–1925)

This film shows the world famous "strong man" Eugene Sandow flexing his muscles in a number of poses. Sandow was 27 at the time this film was shot. The film

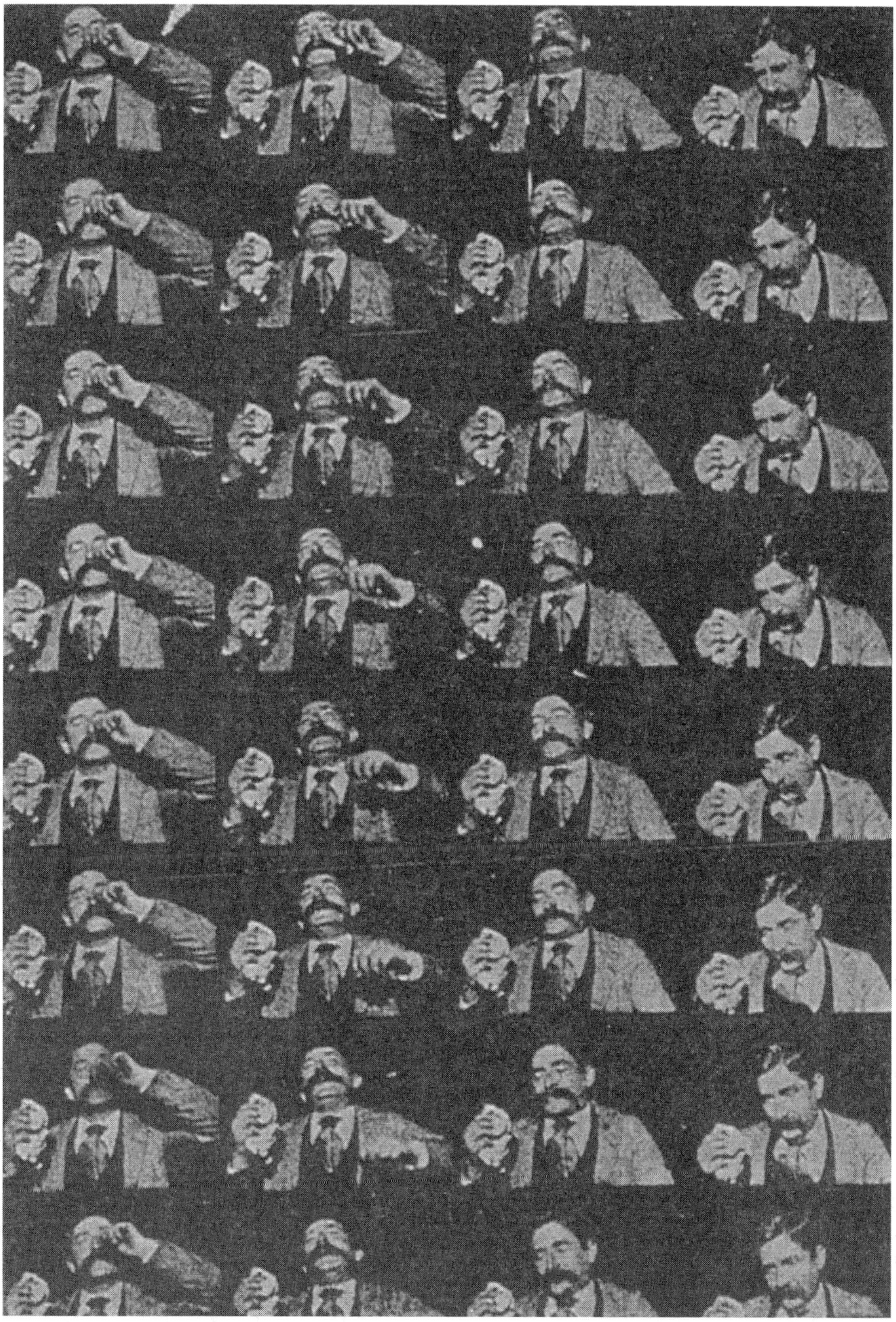

Fred Ott's Sneeze (1894)—the first copyrighted motion picture.

undoubtedly was among the first to attract a large female audience to the peep show parlors.

Sandow died at age 57 in 1925 of a brain aneurysm. The aneurysm was reportedly attributed to the strain of having lifted an automobile.

14. Serpentine Dances

[a.k.a. *Annabelle Serpentine Dance*]

Edison Kinetoscope Company; ***Directed by*** W.K.L. Dickson; ***Running Time:*** 37 seconds; ***Cast:*** Annabelle (1878?–1961) [a.k.a. Mrs. Annabelle Whitford Buchanan]

This film created a sensation when it was released to the peep show parlors, as it showed the famous dancer Annabelle doing one of her serpentine dances. What makes this an especially attractive film is the lush hand coloring that was used in it. Annabelle waved pieces of her dress on each side of her, forming circles, and each section of the dress was painted a different color. This film segment has stood the test of time for more than 100 years and is still a striking film to watch.

The film was directed by William Kennedy Laurie Dickson (1860?–1935), who directed most of Edison's early films through 1894.

1895

15. Arrival of the French Photographic Society

Produced by Louis Lumière/France; ***Running Time:*** 44 seconds

This film features the arrival of members of the French Photographic Society for a meeting. They are pictured walking off of a boat, with some of them waving or taking off their hats to the camera as they pass.

This film was developed and printed immediately upon exposure, and shown to the people who appeared in it at the meeting.

16. Arrival of Train

Produced by Louis Lumière/France; ***Running Time:*** 52 seconds

This film footage, taken in the south of France at Lyons, shows the arrival of a passenger train. The waiting passengers prepare to board as arriving passengers depart from the train.

17. The Barber Shop (circa 1895)

Edison Kinetoscope Company; ***Running Time:*** 45 seconds

This attraction shows a man at the barber shop getting a shave. It is interesting to note a sign advertising the cost for a shave and haircut at 5¢.

18. Childish Quarrel

Produced by Louis Lumière/France; Lumière Film #82; ***Running Time:*** 47 seconds

This film shows two fully dressed babies sitting in their high chairs quarreling over toys. This is as amusing to watch today as it was when it was originally filmed.

19. Children Digging for Clams

Produced by Louis Lumière/France; Lumière Film #45; *Running Time:* 45 seconds

This film features about a dozen or so people on a beach digging for clams. All of the ladies are dressed in full length dresses with feather hats. Those involved in the clam digging must lift the bottom of their skirts to keep them dry. The boys are fully clothed as well, complete with hats.

20. Demolition of a Wall

Produced by Louis Lumière/France; *Directed by* Auguste Lumière; *Running Time:* 1 minute, 21 seconds

This film records the demolition of a wall on the grounds of the Lumière factory. Early exhibitors amused audiences by running the film backwards upon its conclusion.

21. End of Work Shift, Lumière Factory

Produced by Louis Lumière/France; *Running Time:* 48 seconds

This film shows employees leaving the Lumière factory in France. The camera is set up in front of the doors to the factory, and the employees walk toward the camera. Knowing that they were being photographed, some of the employees staged various antics.

22. Feeding the Baby

Produced by Louis Lumière/France; *Running Time:* 36 seconds; *Cast:* Auguste Lumière (1862–1954); Mrs. Auguste Lumière; Their baby

For this film, Louis Lumière photographed his brother Auguste, and his wife feeding their baby at home.

23. Feeding the Doves (circa 1895)

Edison Kinetoscope Company; *Running Time:* 25 seconds

This film shows an unidentified middle aged woman throwing food to a flock of doves. The copy of this film evaluated had flash titles every few seconds with Thomas Edison's name on them, as what was presumably an antipiracy measure.

24. L'Arroseur Arrose

Produced by Louis Lumière/France; *Running Time:* 47 seconds

This is said to be the first fully staged fictional film shown to the public. It features a gardener watering his plants. Another man steps on his hose, and the gardener chases him off.

25. Lion, London Zoological Garden

Produced by Louis Lumière/France; Lumière Film #54; *Running Time:* 40 seconds

This film was taken on location at the London Zoological Gardens. It features a lion pacing up and down in his cage, and a zoo keeper feeding it. Unfortunately, this film does not show anything else of the gardens save for the cage and immediate vicinity.

26. Loading a Boiler

Produced by Louis Lumière/France; Lumière Film #20; ***Running Time:*** 42 seconds

This film is a demonstration of men aboard a ship loading a large steam boiler. This once rather insignificant film is an interesting piece of history, showing how jobs such as these were done 100 or more years ago.

27. Partie d'écarté

Produced by Louis Lumière/France; ***Running Time:*** 53 seconds

This film shows three men at a table playing cards and drinking wine. One of the men featured was Felicien Trewey, one of Europe's top vaudeville performers of the time.

28. Poultry Yard

Produced by Louis Lumière/France; Lumière Film #14; ***Running Time:*** 50 seconds

This early Lumière film shows two young girls feeding a flock of ducks and chickens in their yard.

29. Promenade of Ostriches— Paris Botanical Gardens

Produced by Louis Lumière/France; Lumière Film #4; ***Running Time:*** 49 seconds

After Thomas Edison had perfected his Kinetoscope in America, Louis Lumière (1864–1948) of France became inspired in 1895 to invent his Cinematograph.

This, among the first of the Louis Lumière films, was taken at the beautiful Botanical Gardens of Paris. The film shows one ostrich at the head of a line of people following in various types of vehicles, as well as on horseback and on elephants. The elegant clothing styles indicate that the people who appeared in this film were among Paris' elite crowd.

30. Rough Sea at Dover

Directed/Produced by Birt Acres and Robert W. Paul; ***Running Time:*** 32 seconds

Cinema pioneer Birt Acres (1854–1918) initially started working for the Edison Kinetoscope Company before going out on his own with Robert W. Paul (1869–1943).

This early collaboration of the two cinematographers shows a rough tide smashing against a wall, with a second shot concentrating on the swift current of what appears to be a river in a different, non-coastal location.

Among Acres' more notable projects, inaccessible for evaluation, are the *Oxford-Cambridge Boat Race* (1895) and *Inauguration of the Kiel Canal by Kaiser Wilhelm II* (1895).

After Robert W. Paul parted company with Acres in 1896, Acres dropped out of filmmaking.

31. Seminary Girls (circa 1895)

Edison Kinetoscope Company; ***Running Time:*** 33 seconds

This film shows four unidentified girls engaged in a pillow fight in their dorm room.

32. Swimming in the Sea

Produced by Louis Lumière/France; Lumière Film #11; ***Running Time:*** 54 seconds

This film was shot on a coastal location, and shows a number of men jumping from a pier into the water. The men's swimsuit styles are interesting to see over 100 years later.

1896

33. Carmaux: Drawing Out the Coke (circa 1896)

Produced by Louis Lumière/France; Lumière Film #122; ***Running Time:*** 38 seconds

This film was taken at a coal mine, and shows how piles of coal ashes are removed from their various storage areas and dissolved by spraying water on the piles.

34. The Derby

Produced by Robert W. Paul; ***Running Time:*** 37 seconds

This was Robert W. Paul's first solo production effort after having parted ways with Birt Acres. It documents a horse derby, showing a number of jockeys racing on horseback before a large audience. The surviving print material on this subject shows signs of decomposition, indicating that it was saved just in time.

35. Dragoons Crossing the Saône (circa 1896)

Produced by Louis Lumière; Lumière Film #186; ***Running Time:*** 44 seconds

This film shows a group of men crossing from one side of the Saône River to the other on horseback. The horses are submerged to the point that only the very tops of their backs and heads stay above water.

36. The Kiss

Edison Kinetoscope Company; ***Running Time:*** 22 seconds; ***Cast:*** THE WOMAN, May Irwin (1862–1938); THE MAN, John C. Rice (1858–1915)

This was the first film to be projected publicly on the big screen. At the time it came out, it shocked audiences, who felt that public displays of affection of this type were inappropriate. The man in this film, John C. Rice, died from Bright's disease in 1915 at age 57. (Bright's disease claimed film comedian John Bunny in 1915 as well.) May Irwin enjoyed a stage career as a comedienne for more than 50 years. When she died at 76, she left an estate worth over $100,000 to her surviving husband and son.

They are actually enacting a scene from the play *The Widow Jones.*

37. Leaving Jerusalem by Railway

Produced by Louis Lumière/France; ***Running Time:*** 48 seconds

This film was shot on location in Jerusalem, Israel, being the earliest existing footage of that area of the world. The camera was mounted on the back of a train, recording

May Irwin and John Rice enacting a scene from the play *The Widow Jones* in Thomas Edison's *The Kiss* (1896).

how everything looked as the back of the train passed the area being filmed. Some early historic buildings can be seen in the background.

38. **Photograph** (circa 1896)

Produced by Louis Lumière/France; Lumière Film #118; ***Running Time:*** 35 seconds

Photograph could be classified as among the earliest of slapstick comedies. A still photographer tries to prepare his client for a photo session, but the client keeps spoiling the shot by first blowing his nose, and then by moving, combing his hair, etc. The photographer's camera falls down, and he gives up on the session.

39. **Pompiers à Lyon** (circa 1896)

Produced by Louis Lumière/France; ***Running Time:*** 37 seconds

This film shows firemen racing to their destination on a city street. The fire trucks consist of horse-drawn carriages containing the firefighting equipment.

40. **Snowball Fight in Neige**

Produced by Louis Lumière/France; ***Running Time:*** 44 seconds

This film features a snowball fight on a city street in Neige. The surviving film material has suffered some scratches over the years and is not as pristine as most of the surviving Lumière material.

41. **Transformation by Hats, Comic View** (circa 1896)

Produced by Louis Lumière/France; Lumière Film #105; ***Running Time:*** 45 seconds

This film features an unidentified comedian changing his appearances over a dozen times by putting on different hats, wigs, and mustaches. This is an early example of pantomimic comedy. The film itself is not in as pristine condition as other Lumière films of the period but is still in relatively good shape.

1897

42. Arab Cortege, Geneva

Produced by Louis Lumière/France; Lumière Film #310; ***Running Time:*** 36 seconds

In 1897, Louis Lumière sent his staff to various locations around the world to take film footage. This film was shot on location in Geneva, Switzerland, showing what the busy streets of Geneva were like during the late 1890s.

43. New York: Broadway at Union Square

Produced by Louis Lumière; Lumière Film #328; ***Running Time:*** 38 seconds

This film shows footage taken of the busy intersection at New York's Broadway and Union Square. One sees streetcars, as well as a horse and buggy in the background. A number of pedestrians are also seen walking across the street.

44. New York, Brooklyn Bridge

Produced by Louis Lumière; Lumière Film #321; ***Running Time:*** 47 seconds

This film contains footage of New York's famous Brooklyn Bridge, still relatively new at the time this film was shot. Trains and street cars are shown traveling on the bridge, which looks much different now than it did a century ago.

45. Niagara

Produced by Louis Lumière; ***Running Time:*** 46 seconds

Niagara was shot on location in Niagara Falls, being the earliest existing footage of the famous tourist attraction. The film shows a stationary shot of the waters rushing down the falls, and an observation area can also be viewed.

46. Policemen's Parade—Chicago

Produced by Louis Lumière; Lumière Film #336; ***Running Time:*** 45 seconds

This film footage was taken on location in Chicago, and shows what appears to be the entire police force marching down one of Chicago's main streets in uniform. A horse and buggy follows the parade of officers.

47. President McKinley at Home [a.k.a. *Major McKinley at Home*]

American Biograph Company; ***Directed by*** W.K.L. Dickson; ***Running Time:*** 37 seconds; ***Cast:*** William McKinley (1843–1901) and his secretary

This footage of then-president William McKinley was shown in the first presentation of films produced by the American Biograph Company, where D.W. Griffith would start his film career in 1908. It shows McKinley walking with his secretary down the steps of his home and into the yard where the secretary gives him a paper to read. Upon reading the paper, McKinley takes off his hat and walks toward the camera.

According to Terry Ramsaye's 1926 book *A Million and One Nights*, this film had a closing shot of the American flag. This shot of the flag does not appear in the print of this film that was evaluated.

While this film may not look significant today, crowds packed the theaters to see McKinley's walk across his yard when it was originally screened.

1898

48. Come Along Do!

Produced by Robert W. Paul; ***Running Time:*** 44 seconds

This is another early example of Robert W. Paul's work. Paul patented a device known as the Theatregraph projector, which is also known as the Animatograph. Among his more notable films was an 1897 version of *The Last Days of Pompeii.*

Come Along Do! shows a man and a woman sitting outside a museum drinking a beverage, and then proceeding to the art section of the museum. The film is said to be the first to carry over action from one shot to another.

49. Dewar's It's Scotch!

Thomas A. Edison Company; ***Running Time:*** 51 seconds

This was the first advertising film, a promotion for Dewar's Scotch, which is still sold today. The film consists of four men in Scottish kilts dancing and making merry against the backdrop of a banner with the Dewar's logo on it. A century later, film ads for hard liquor are banned from the screen in most countries.

50. The Miller and the Sweep

Produced/Directed by G.[eorge] A.[lbert] Smith/England; ***Running Time:*** 40 seconds

This is among the earlier efforts of pioneer cinema innovator George Albert Smith (1864–1959). This film takes place on a farm, with a windmill as the prominent backdrop. A miller is seen walking out of the mill and toward the camera with a heavy bag of flour. He crosses paths with another man, and they fight and get flour all over each other. This was among the first films to break a single scene down into multiple shots.

51. Pack Train on Chilkoot Pass

American Biograph Company; ***Directed by*** W.K.L. Dickson; ***Running Time:*** 1 minute, 16 seconds

This film footage shows a long line of people and their horses traveling on a place called Chilkoot Pass. The surviving film has suffered scratches over the last century and is slightly faded, but still is quite watchable, showing beautiful mountain scenery in the background.

1899

52. The Kiss in the Tunnel

Produced/Directed by G.A. Smith/England; *Running Time:* 1 minute, 10 seconds; *Cast:* G.A. Smith (1864–1959); Mrs. G.A. Smith

This was among the first efforts to demonstrate continuity of action through the process of editing. A train is shown entering a tunnel. As the train has entered, the film cuts to a scene inside the train, showing the two featured passengers kissing. The film then cuts to a view from the train as it is emerging from the tunnel.
Director/producer Smith starred in this film with his wife.

53. The Kiss in the Tunnel
(1899 remake of previous entry)

Bamforth and Company/England; *Running Time:* 1 minute, 27 seconds

This film is a remake of G.A. Smith's film released earlier in the year bearing the same name. This version shows a train entering a tunnel from a distance, and then cuts to a male and female passenger on the train. The male takes a few drags from his cigarette, and then kisses his female companion. After the kiss, the train is shown arriving at a station. The film does not actually show the train exiting the tunnel, and is not as visually striking as G.A. Smith's original version of the film.

The 20th Century

1900

54. As Seen Through a Telescope

Directed/Produced by G.A. Smith; ***Running Time:*** 1 minute, 6 seconds

This film features another innovation by G.A. Smith known as the "point of view" shot. A second innovative technique used in this film is the use of highlighting scenes in a circle. This effect was accomplished by placing a black mask with a hole in it over the camera lens. It is a comedy showing a man with a telescope watching a man and a woman across the street. The observer gets a close-up view of the man tying the woman's shoe for her and patting her on the ankle, which was considered risqué at a time when a proper lady never exposed her ankles to men. Comedy comes into the picture when the couple pass by the observer, and the man rewards the voyeur with a rap on the head.

55. The Biter Bit

Bamforth and Company/England; ***Running Time:*** 1 minute, 9 seconds

This comedy shows a gardener watering flowers, with a prankster bending the hose and stopping the water flow. When the gardener looks at the opening of the hose to see what is wrong with it, the water is released, and he is squirted in the face. The gardener then evens the score.

This is a remake of an earlier Lumière comedy, and the only one of Bamforth's many remakes of other people's work that really improved on the original.

56. Grandma's Reading Glass

Directed/Produced by G.A. Smith; ***Running Time:*** 1 minute, 26 seconds

This film shows a boy with his grandmother's magnifying glass that she uses for reading, and shows the various objects as the boy would see them through the glass.

Various objects highlighted in this fashion are a close-up of the grandmother's eye and a cat.

This film is another of G.A. Smith's which experimented with his innovative point of view and circle shots.

57. How It Feels to Be Run Over

Hepworth Manufacturing Company/England; ***Directed by*** Cecil Hepworth; ***Running Time:*** 51 seconds

This is among the earliest surviving films of British producer and director Cecil Hepworth (1874–1953). The film shows a motor vehicle speeding right at the camera. At the implied point of impact, titles flash on the screen, one word at a time: "Oh! Mother! will be pleased." This is possibly the first film to use title cards in conveying part of the story line.

58. Ladies' Skirts Nailed to a Fence (circa 1900)

Bamforth and Company/England; ***Running Time:*** 1 minute, 12 seconds

This early comedy shows two older women bickering with each other next to a fence. Instead of moving the camera to the other side of the fence, the actresses were moved to the other side so that two pranksters could be seen nailing the women's skirts to the back of the fence. The women represented were suffragette activists.

59. Let Me Dream Again

Produced/Directed by G.A. Smith; ***Running Time:*** 1 minute, 7 seconds

This was the first film to use the technique of bringing the camera temporarily out of focus to indicate the transition from dream to reality. A man is shown having a jolly time drinking and laughing with a pretty girl. The camera is then brought out of focus to blur the image, and is refocused on the same man in bed with his glaring and angry not-so-attractive wife, adding a comedic element to the film.

60. Rough Sea (circa 1900)

Bamforth and Company/England; ***Running Time:*** 56 seconds

This was the Bamforth Company's remake of the 1895 film of the same title produced by the Birt Acres/Robert W. Paul partnership. Instead of showing the waves going against a wall, this remake shows the waves crashing against rocks on the beach. This remake has the camera fixed in a stationary position, as opposed to how the original progressed to another shot emphasizing the rushing current of the water.

61. Spanish Bullfight

Produced by Louis Lumière/France; ***Running Time:*** 48 seconds

This early footage records a bullfight shot on location in Spain. It is interesting to note that there were about a half-dozen fighters taking on one bull, with one of the fighters being on horseback.

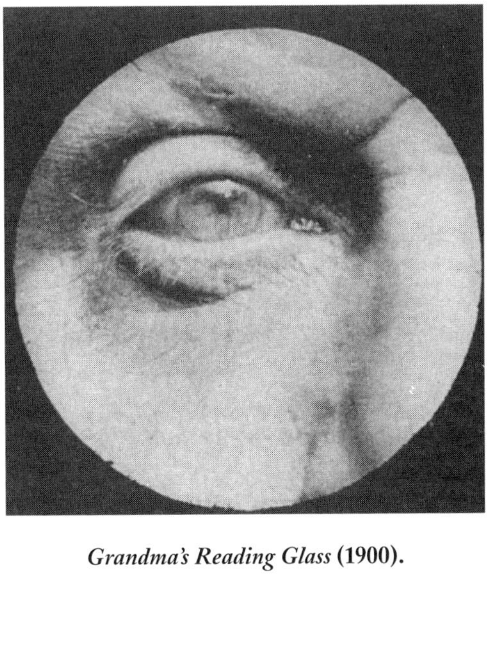

Grandma's Reading Glass **(1900).**

1901

62. The Big Swallow (circa 1901)

Williamson Kinematograph Company; ***Directed by*** James Williamson; ***Running Time:*** 1 minute

This film, one of the early efforts of cinema pioneer James Williamson (1855–1933), provides an early example of extreme close-up. It portrays a man coming closer and closer to the camera lens until only his mouth occupies the screen. The screen becomes black once the lens is totally engulfed, and then cuts to a shot of the camera disappearing into the dark. The man is then shown licking his lips as if he has just finished a meal.

The poor condition of the surviving print material on this subject does not detract from its amusement.

63. The Countryman and the Cinematograph

Produced by Robert W. Paul; ***Running Time:*** 25 seconds

This early effort is perhaps the first film to show a film being shown on screen. A country bumpkin is shown standing next to a movie screen and laughing at the different images as they appear.

64. Dream and Reality

Pathé Frères/France; ***Produced by*** Charles Pathé; ***Directed by*** Ferdinand Zecca; ***Running Time:*** 45 seconds

This film was Pathé's remake of the 1900 film *Let Me Dream Again.* Like its predecessor, it features a man drinking with a pretty girl, and then waking up to the reality of being in bed with his unattractive wife. Instead of bringing the film out of focus to indicate the transition from dream to reality, double exposure was used instead to show the pretty woman turning into the wife, and the man going from being dressed up in a suit to being in bed with his pajamas on.

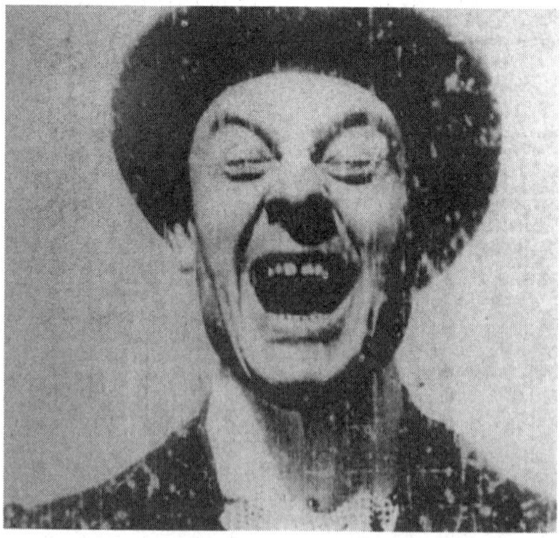

***The Big Swallow* (1901).**

65. Explosion of a Motor Car

Hepworth Manufacturing Company; ***Directed by*** Cecil Hepworth; ***Running Time:*** 1 minute, 29 seconds

This early film makes striking use of trick photography in depicting the explosion of an automobile. A car with passengers is seen driving down the road, and it suddenly explodes. A cloud of smoke appears, and a pile of scraps is shown in the car's place. A few seconds later, body parts (which are obviously stuffed props) fall out of the sky.

66. Fire!

Williamson Kinematograph Company; ***Directed by*** James Williamson; ***Running Time:*** 4 minutes, 43 seconds

This film expands on previous fire rescue films, which only showed fire trucks racing to a scene. This film includes as its introductory sequence a fire being spotted by a policemen, who reports it to the fire station. The fire trucks race to the scene, put out the fire, and are also shown rescuing three people.

This film shows that Williamson was ahead of most others in the field of motion pictures at the time, as there were succeeding fire films produced after this one that are not as elaborate.

67. History of a Crime

Pathé Frères; ***Produced by*** Charles Pathé; ***Directed by*** Ferdinand Zecca; ***Running Time:*** 5 minutes, 20 seconds

This early effort by the Pathé Frères Company is among the oldest of their extant productions. It portrays a man committing a robbery and murder. A shot of the relatives identifying his victim is shown, followed by the arrest of the murderer. The shots showing the murderer in his cell awaiting execution introduce one of the first attempts to simultaneously show a dream sequence. One sees the prisoner lying in bed, with flashbacks of his early childhood and adult life appearing on the screen above him. It is obvious that these flashback sequences were filmed on a stage that was incorporated into the prison wall above the prisoner. Once the prisoner wakes up, he is prepared for the guillotine. This guillotine sequence is graphic, showing the man's "head" actually being chopped off. The film further portrays the executioner picking the "head" out of the basket and throwing it into the coffin.

68. Stop Thief!

Williamson Kinematograph Company; ***Directed by*** James Williamson; ***Running Time:*** 1 minute, 57 seconds

This film features a chase sequence after a thief steals from a man walking down the street. The victim gives chase, and the thief hides in a barrel. Several dogs jump into the barrel with the thief, where he is apprehended as neighbors look on.

The camera mobility and pace featured in this film was far ahead of most other films of its time.

The Nickelodeon Age (1902–1911)

1902

69. A Trip to the Moon

Rating: ☆☆☆☆

Star Film Company of Paris; ***Directed by*** Georges Méliès; ***Based on Two Stories by*** Jules Verne *From the Earth to the Moon; Around the Moon*; ***Running time:*** 12 minutes

This is the most famous work of pioneering French film producer Georges Méliès (1861–1938). It is also perhaps the first science fiction film in motion picture history. At the time of its release, *A Trip to the Moon* was the most elaborate film spectacle the public had ever known. Press reports from Paris in September of 1902 described the film as "an unprecedented triumph."

The film portrays a voyage to the moon as anticipated in the mind of director Méliès—a full 67 years before such a voyage was actually accomplished. It shows the initial preparations and conflicts preceding the voyage. Then, an artistic looking moon with eyes, nose, and a happy face is pierced with the space capsule from earth, making the moon cry. This sequence of the actual travel of the earth capsule to the moon remains one of the most famous and most often shown sequences in motion picture history. It is featured in numerous retrospective film compilations.

Once the explorers get to the moon, Méliès creates a fascinating fantasy world. Stars are shown with people's faces in them, giving each star a unique personality. Umbrellas are shown elongating and turning into mushrooms. Strange creatures called Selenites inhabit the moon, and take the explorers prisoner to retaliate for their unwanted intrusion. It is only when one of the explorers discovers that hitting the Selenites with an umbrella causes them to explode that the expedition members are able to escape to their capsule and return to earth.

Méliès spent the enormous sum (at the time) of 10,000 francs to produce this film over a three-month period. It was an international sensation, and so much so that the film attracted unwanted attention from the Edison and Lubin companies, who widely pirated the film in the United States.

When *A Trip to the Moon* was originally shown, a narrator was on hand to explain what was happening in the film from a script that Méliès had prepared. This narration was restored to the new video version of the film in Kino's *The Movies Begin* series. This reviewer found the narration to be irritating and intrusive, but it was interesting to see the film as Méliès had intended for it to be seen.

A Trip to the Moon is a fascinating and highly imaginative fantasy/science fiction film. Nearly a century after its original production, it stands the test of time as one of the great artistic masterpieces of cinema.

A Trip to the Moon (1902).

While *A Trip to the Moon* has guaranteed its producer Georges Méliès a prominent place in motion picture history, many people forget about his older brother, Gaston Méliès, who ran the Star Film Company's American branch from 1903 to 1914. The elder Méliès died on the Isle of Corsica in 1915, and the few of his films that survived are archived in collections inaccessible to the general public, thus explaining why he has faded into film history as a footnote. Frank Thompson's book *The Star Film Ranch* gives a complete account of Gaston Méliès' career and serves to partially right the wrong done him.

1903

70. A Chess Dispute

Produced by Robert W. Paul; ***Running Time:*** 1 minute, 9 seconds

This film features two men playing chess, and then getting into an altercation. It was a "first" in showing most of the action occurring below the frame of the film. One does not actually see the men fighting, but instead sees hats and objects flying about, and an occasional head coming into view.

71. Daring Daylight Burglary

Sheffield Photo Company/Thomas A. Edison Studios; ***Running Time:*** 4 minutes

This film was the greatest success of England's Sheffield Photo Company, which specialized in still photography and dabbled for a brief period in film production.

Daring Daylight Burglary is an account of a burglar being confronted by a police officer, which culminates in a rooftop battle between the two, with the officer emerging victorious. The burglar manages to escape on a train, and the officer telegraphs a message to the next train station, where the would-be thief is apprehended.

When this film was originally released, an accompanying synopsis was given to audiences to explain what was happening in the film, as titles were not used at this point in cinema history. The film was distributed in the United States by the Edison

Company and is reported to have inspired Edwin S. Porter to make *The Great Train Robbery* (1903).

72. Desperate Poaching Affray

Produced by Haggar and Sons/Great Britain; ***Running Time:*** 2 minutes, 46 seconds

Desperate Poaching Affray is widely regarded as the film that helped to set the pattern for chase sequences in the movies. It shows thieves being chased by citizens and police into the woods, over fences, and across rivers. Some of the pursuers are shot by the fugitives, and an exciting hand-to-hand combat sequence is also included. The thieves cross the river only to be greeted by a dozen or so waiting police officers and citizens and apprehended.

73. Extraordinary Cab Accident

Produced by Robert W. Paul; ***Running Time:*** 49 seconds

This early comedy portrays a man being run over by a horse and carriage cab, feigning death, and then getting up and showing the police that the joke is on them.

74. From Show Girl to Burlesque Queen

American Mutoscope and Biograph; ***Running Time:*** 58 seconds

This blue movie features an attractive, fully dressed woman taking off her layers of clothes. When she gets down to her slip, she goes behind a dressing area, and the slip is shown being flung over it. The woman then emerges in a scanty burlesque outfit.

75. The Gay Shoe Clerk

Thomas A. Edison Studios; ***Directed by*** Edwin S. Porter; ***Running Time:*** 1 minute, 14 seconds

The male shoe clerk in this film steals a kiss from an attractive female customer as he is fitting her for new shoes. The woman's mother, sitting in a nearby chair, is enraged by the clerk's effrontery and hits him over the head several times with her umbrella. The woman and her mother then walk out of the store.

76. The Georgetown Loop [Colorado]

American Biograph Company; ***Running Time:*** 3 minutes, 5 seconds

This film was shot from the back car of a traveling train as it traveled around the settlement of Georgetown in Colorado. When the film opens, one sees mountains, and as the train rounds a turn, the front part comes into view. The audience proceeds to see close-up views of the mountains, and the buildings in the then-sparse settlement as they come into view, consisting mostly of wood-frame houses. The people in the front cars of the train waving to the camera give one an idea of the significance and excitement surrounding the filming of this footage.

77. The Great Train Robbery

Rating: ☆☆☆

Thomas A. Edison Studios; ***Directed by*** Edwin S. Porter; ***Running Time:*** 10 minutes; ***Cast:*** THE OUTLAW, George E. Barnes (1879–1926); A DANCE HALL GIRL, Marie Murray; MAN

The Great Train Robbery (1903).

WHO FALLS OFF HORSE, Frank Hanaway; BIT PART, G.M. "Broncho Billy" Anderson (1884–1971)

This was the most famous as well as the most financially successful film until D.W. Griffith's *The Birth of a Nation* was released in 1915.

Absent of titles, *The Great Train Robbery* is an action western featuring 24-year-old George E. Barnes in the leading role as the leader of a gang of outlaws. First, they break into the train station, kill the attendant, and blow up the safe to steal the money. The film progresses to a heist of the incoming train. All passengers are forced to come off the train, and are each individually robbed of their money. A fleeing passenger is shot dead in his tracks. The film culminates in a thrilling chase sequence in which the robbers are fleeing from the law on horseback.

Some of the original prints of this film contained hand-colored sequences. The dance hall sequence featured hand-colored banners and dresses. In some of the gunfight sequences, the clouds of smoke were hand colored orange. One sequence that was especially intriguing to audiences of the time was a medium close-up shot of George Barnes firing a shot at the audience. In the prints available for evaluation today, the sequence appears at the end of the film. When the film was originally released, some exhibitors placed this shot at the beginning of the film. This sequence was also hand colored in the color prints.

The Great Train Robbery has a number of "firsts" erroneously attributed to it. It was not the first western, having been predated by the 1898 Edison film *Cripple Creek Bar Room* and at least a couple of other 1890s western-themed films. Neither was it the first film to tell a narrative story, having been predated by Georges Méliès' *A Trip to the Moon* (1902), among others.

The Great Train Robbery stands as Edwin S. Porter's most famous achievement. Although Porter remained in the motion picture industry as a director and producer until the mid–1910s, he never managed to top the success of this film. Despite his subsequent lackluster career, this one film marked a milestone in motion picture history, and is the only film Porter needed to maintain a prominent place in the history of cinema.

78. Mary Jane's Mishap

Rating: ☆☆☆

Directed/Produced by G.A. Smith; ***Running Time:*** 4 minutes, 6 seconds; ***Cast:*** MARY JANE, Mrs. George Albert Smith

This is the most complex of G.A. Smith's early releases, using a number of special trick photography effects. In this film, Smith's wife plays a brazen maid trying to light the stove. The stove explodes, and the film cuts to a shot of the maid being blown up and out of the chimney. The film proceeds to a shot of Mary Jane's tombstone, which reads, "REST IN PIECES." When visitors come to the grave, double exposure is used to show Mary Jane's ghost rising out of the grave and scaring them away.

This was G.A. Smith's last film produced for wide distribution. He turned to private experimentation and invented the Kinemacolor process, which he patented in 1906.

79. Sick Kitten

Directed/Produced by G.A. Smith; ***Running Time:*** 53 seconds

This film is a remake of G.A. Smith's 1901 film *The Little Doctors*, the original negative of which were allegedly worn out due to the high demand for prints. It shows a little boy and girl spoon-feeding milk to a kitten. This was among the first films to show a change of camera position during an ongoing scene, cutting to a brief close-up of the kitten.

80. Skyscrapers of New York City from North River

American Biograph Company; ***Directed by*** W.K.L. Dickson; ***Running Time:*** 2 minutes, 50 seconds

This film features footage that was obviously filmed from a water vessel traveling down New York's North River. One can see dockside businesses such as the Pennsylvania Railroad Company, as well as some of New York's oldest skyscrapers in the background. The nearly three minutes of footage provides a fascinating look at New York City at the beginning of the 20th century.

81. Uncle Tom's Cabin

Rating: ☆☆

Thomas A. Edison Studios; ***Directed by*** Edwin S. Porter; ***Based on the novel by*** Harriet Beecher Stowe; ***Running Time:*** 16 minutes

This is the earliest film adaptation of Harriet Beecher Stowe's literary classic *Uncle Tom's Cabin*. Filmed during the experimental stages of film, it was among the first American films to tell a narrative story. The early narrative style was a bit different in these earliest motion pictures. The titles were used to sum up, in a few words, what the audience was about to see.

This film is stagy, with the sets consisting of painted backdrops as a general rule. But, the filmmakers experimented with some innovative trick photography. The race of the two ships was filmed using miniature models, which is obvious. The death of Little Eva is portrayed using double exposure photography to portray an angel coming from the sky and taking Eva's soul from her body into heaven.

As primitive as this production might seem today, it was extremely elaborate for the time that it was produced, being among the most innovative films of 1903. Its historic value alone makes it an interesting film to watch.

1904

82. Buy Your Own Cherries

Produced by Robert W. Paul; ***Running Time:*** 4 minutes, 18 seconds

This was perhaps the first film to touch on the subject of domestic abuse. A man comes home in a rage, and scares his children so that they huddle under the table. He gives his wife a threatening look, but then realizes that he is in the wrong. In this portrayed instance, the man atones by buying gifts for his wife and children, and they presumably live happily ever after.

83. The Cook in Trouble

Rating: ☆☆½

Star Film Company of Paris; ***Produced by*** Georges Méliès; ***Running Time:*** 4 minutes, 30 seconds

This comedy has as its main character a chef who makes an enemy of a sorcerer. The sorcerer produces a magic box from which devils emerge. The devils create chaos for the cook, pouring extra ingredients into the dinner he is preparing and running in and out of the stove. Simple special effects are prevalent in this film as the box disappears and reappears, as well as the devils. This one is still a lot of fun.

84. Fire in a Burlesque Theater

American Mutoscope and Biograph; ***Running Time:*** 41 seconds

This is one of the early and controversial blue movies that came out in the early 1900s, and appeared in peep show parlors. The footage consists of scantily clad women being rescued from a burning burlesque theater.

This film was obviously hurriedly put together, and there was no effort to conceal that the "theater" was actually a painted and decorated board.

While this film is very tame by today's standards, it was considered risqué at the time.

85. An Impossible Voyage

Rating: ☆☆☆½

Star Film Company of Paris; ***Produced/Directed by*** Georges Méliès; ***Running Time of Evaluated Footage:*** 6 minutes, 45 seconds

This was one of Georges Méliès' (1861–1938) more spectacular but less famous follow-ups to his classic *A Trip to the Moon* (1902). This film portrays a voyage to the sun, and is completely hand-colored in pastels. The film shows a train full of passengers flying to the sun. On their way, they pass a number of hand-colored stars and flaming comets. As they get close to the sun, the distant sun is shown moving closer and closer, with its rays rotating around it, showing its facial expressions as the flying locomotive nears it. The train flies into the sun's mouth, and the sun turns from yellow to red, spewing red smoke out its mouth.

Once the expedition members are on the sun, they climb into an ice box to deal with the searing heat. They end up frozen stiff until one of the explorers, who conveniently did not go into the ice box, thaws them out. The explorers decide they have had enough of the sun and head back to earth. The capsule drops into the earth's ocean, bringing the film to conclude with an animated underwater sequence.

Although this film is not as widely seen or talked about as its predecessor, *A Trip to the Moon* (1902), *An Impossible Voyage* is just as much an artistic masterpiece, and possibly more so because it features the beautiful and vibrant hand coloring that is not present in prints of *A Trip to the Moon*.

86. Troubles of a Manager of a Burlesque Show

American Mutoscope and Biograph; ***Running Time:*** 1 minute, 46 seconds

This comedy portrays a day in the life of the manager of a burlesque theater. Women are shown coming in for auditions. Two women are shown modeling burlesque outfits. The manager takes a liking to the second girl, who answers his advances by throwing a bottle of ink at him.

1905

87. Airy Fairy Lillian Tries on Her New Corsets

American Mutoscope and Biograph; ***Running Time:*** 57 seconds

This early blue comedy features a very fat, rotund woman trying to fit into a corset that is too small. A man playing her husband helps her to finally strap the corset on, and then falls onto the bed from the strain. Parody of Lillian Russell, who had gained a lot of weight at the time.

88. Ali Baba and the Forty Thieves *Rating:* ☆☆☆

Pathé Frères Company; ***Produced by*** Charles Pathé; ***Directed by*** Ferdinand Zecca; ***Running Time:*** 8 minutes, 18 seconds

This is actually a reissue of a Pathé film originally released in 1901, with hand coloring added. It is likely that this color reissue was Pathé's answer to Georges Méliès' hand-colored 1904 film *An Impossible Voyage*. Although this film did not feature special effects as elaborate as in Méliès' film, it offered an *Arabian Nights* fantasy complete with a harem of beautiful dancing girls. The pastel coloring is especially striking, and the film stands as a significant work of art despite its primitive narrative style.

89. An Interesting Story

Williamson Kinematograph Company; ***Directed by*** James Williamson; ***Running Time:*** 3 minutes, 50 seconds

This early farce shows a man who is so interested in the book he is reading that he does not pay attention to what he is doing. He spills coffee on himself, trips over a woman scrubbing floors, walks into a jump rope that children are playing with, and finally manages to run into a street paver, which rolls him flat. Two good samaritans literally blow him back up by using hand pumps and bring him back to life. The man dusts himself off and picks his book right up and starts reading again while walking down the street.

This is among the first comedy classics with a significant story line. Although the special effects of the man being pumped back up are primitive and not very convincing, it still stands the test of time as a fun and amusing comedy.

90. Rescued by Rover

Hepworth Manufacturing Company; ***Produced by*** Cecil Hepworth; ***Directed by*** Lewin Fitzhamon; ***Running Time:*** 6 minutes, 27 seconds; ***Cast:*** Family of Cecil Hepworth

If you thought Lassie was the screen's first famous collie, you are mistaken. Having made her film debut in 1942, Lassie was predated by 37 years with Rover, the family dog owned by producer Cecil Hepworth

Starring Cecil Hepworth's family, *Rescued by Rover* is the story of a baby who is kidnapped by an old woman, and is nowhere to be found. Fortunately, Rover picks up the scent of the woman and baby and leads the way for the rescue.

This film was highly innovative and advanced for its time, using sophisticated editing and intercutting techniques not typically found in other films of 1905.

Rescued by Rover **(1905).**

After 1904, Cecil Hepworth started delegating the directorial work on his films to staff and did not direct again until 1914.

91. Revolution in Russia

Pathé Frères; ***Produced by*** Charles Pathé; ***Directed by*** Ferdinand Zecca; ***Running Time:*** 3 minutes, 45 seconds

This is a recreation of the Russian battleship *Potemkin* revolution incident in Odessa, Russia—produced the same year it happened. The Pathé Company did a number of such reenactments of important news events, including the murder of Stanford White by Harry K. Thaw in 1906.

While the film starts out showing a real ship on a real river, the scenes showing the cannon explosions fired from the *Potemkin* are obviously staged with miniature sets. Other than its production values and length, this film's account of the *Potemkin*-Odessa incident is in conformance with Sergei Eisenstein's portrayal of the incident 20 years later in his masterpiece *Battleship Potemkin* (1925) [a.k.a. *Potemkin*].

92. The Whole Dam Family and the Dam Dog

Thomas A. Edison Studios; ***Directed by*** Edwin S. Porter; ***Running Time:*** 1 minute, 30 seconds

This was possibly the first film comedy with a play on words in its title much like many of the later Mae West films. In this film, the audience is introduced to the "Dam" family, along with the "Dam" cook and the "Dam" dog. The father's name is "I.B. Dam." The mother is "Mrs. Hellen Dam." Their children are "Jimmy Dam," "U.B. Dam," "I.P. Dam," and "Baby Dam." The whole film is shot in medium close-up, showing each member of the family for a few seconds, with their respective names appearing at the bottom of the screen.

Depending on how one interprets the names in this film, it can either be an innocent introduction to the family or a film bordering on what would have been considered vulgarity at the time.

1906

93. Aladdin and the Marvelous Lamp

Rating: ☆☆☆½

Pathé Frères; ***Produced by*** Charles Pathé; ***Directed by*** Ferdinand Zecca; ***Running Time:*** 11 minutes, 42 seconds

This was Pathé's follow-up to the successful hand-colored version of *Ali Baba and the Forty Thieves (1905)*. This early *Aladdin* adaptation shows him finding the magic lamp and demonstrating a number of impressive tricks with it. Servants appear and disappear at Aladdin's will. Staircases are turned into walls, and vice versa, and a person is even shown jumping toward a wall decoration and becoming part of it. Aladdin and the princess enjoy a luxurious life until the magic lamp is stolen by the villain of the story. The rest of the film details how the lamp is finally recovered, and justice is served.

The finale of the film showing Aladdin's triumph is especially elaborate, showing a group of beautiful dancing girls in a richly colored, ornately directed set.

Aladdin and the Marvelous Lamp demonstrates how far Zecca's technique had advanced since the production of *Ali Baba and the Forty Thieves*. The plot in this film is far more sophisticated, as are the special effects.

Aladdin and the Marvelous Lamp stands as a beautiful and fascinating work of art, which we are fortunate has survived for our enjoyment today.

94. The Dog and His Various Merits

Pathé Frères Company/France; ***Produced by*** Charles Pathé; ***Directed by*** Ferdinand Zecca; ***Running Time:*** 2 minutes, 6 seconds

This is one of the earliest surviving films of the motion picture company founded by Charles Pathé (1863–1957) in 1896. The film was directed by Ferdinand Zecca (1864–1947), who started in motion pictures as an actor in 1899 and began directing for Pathé in 1901.

The film explores and shows various dog tasks, such as running in a wheel to provide power for a machine, pulling its disabled and legless master in a box with wheels, herding sheep, and pulling a milk barrel mounted on wheels.

The trademark Pathé rooster appears in the opening titles.

95. The Dream of a Rarebit Fiend

Rating: ☆☆½

Thomas A. Edison Studios; ***Directed by*** Edwin S. Porter; ***Running Time:*** 5 minutes, 14 seconds

Based on a 1904 comic strip by Winsor McCay, this film portrays the dream of a drunk. As the drunk is on his way to bed, the film superimposes images of the drunk against a rocking background. The dream sequence shows the drunk having delusions of objects moving across the floor, and progresses to show three small devils hammering at the top of his headboard. The bed is then shown to bounce up and down and go into a fast spin, flying out the window.

For the shots of the man in the bed flying over the city, the bottom half of the screen contains footage of the city, while the top half—shot with a black background in a studio—contains the footage of the flying bed. Porter should have used a lighter background for the studio shots so that it would not be so obvious that the top half of the film was shot in a different location.

Despite the obviously primitive special effects, this film is still amusing to watch.

96. The Motorist

Rating: ☆☆☆

Produced by Robert W. Paul; ***Running Time:*** 2 minutes, 34 seconds

Of the Robert Paul films evaluated, this is the most imaginative and complex. It shows a bride and groom speeding down the street in their automobile, with the cop giving chase. The car is shown driving up the side of a building and into the air. The air journey shows the car driving on and around clouds, and jumping from one planet to the other. They reach Saturn, drive around the rings, and then fall over the edge and crash through the ceiling of the courtroom. Let off with a warning, they get into a slow-moving horse and carriage, which then magically turns into an automobile, and the chase ensues again.

This is Robert Paul's most sophisticated work, and an amusing film to watch over 90 years later.

97. San Francisco: Aftermath of Earthquake

American Biograph Company; ***Running Time:*** 1 minute, 21 seconds

This early Biograph newsreel footage provides candid documentation of the pandemonium in the aftermath of the great San Francisco earthquake of 1906. The first footage shows the still-raging fires that were triggered as a result of the earthquake. The film proceeds to show the piles of rubble that were once buildings, as well as the giant cracks in the streets, and the look of disparity on those who survived the disaster. It is also interesting to note a sign at a devastated business advertising jobs for men to help with reconstruction.

This film footage is highly compelling to watch even today, and provides documentation of the reality of the horrifying disaster that has gone down as one of the worst catastrophes in world history.

98. A Visit to Peek Frean and Company's Biscuit Works

Rating: ☆☆☆

Cricks and Martin/England; ***Directed/Produced by*** E.H. Cricks and H.A. Martin; ***Running Time:*** 11 minutes, 47 seconds

This early documentary takes one behind the scenes of a large biscuit factory in England, showing each step of the manufacturing process, from shoveling coal into the steam engines that provide power to the factory to the complete assembly line process to the preparation of biscuits for the various restaurant and prepackaged markets. Title cards are used in some parts of the film to explain which process one is about to see.

This film is fascinating as it shows the methods and machinery used in factories of the time. The documentary is well-produced and as thorough as many modern documentaries.

1907

99. Ben-Hur

Rating: ☆☆

Kalem; ***Directed by*** Sidney Olcott and Frank Oakes Rose; ***Produced by*** Marc Klaw and Abraham Erlanger; ***Adapted for Screen by*** Gene Gauntier; ***Based on the novel by*** Lew Wallace; ***Running Time:*** 12 minutes

This was the first screen adaptation of Lew Wallace's classic literary masterpiece, *Ben-Hur*. It uses extremely primitive techniques, comprised solely of distant shots. The film shows a scene reenacting the accident in which Ben-Hur drops a tile on Gratus' head. He is then taken and sentenced to the galleys. The film then skips to the chariot race. The sets, especially in the chariot race, are obviously painted wood backdrops.

Although this primitive *Ben-Hur* production is laughable today, it was considered quite elaborate for the time. It actually employed a few dozen people, as well as 16 horses for four chariots. The producers also obviously spent a lot of money on historically authentic costumes.

Unbeknownst to the Kalem Company at the time, this production of *Ben-Hur* would prove to be the most expensive one-reel film in cinema history. The issue of motion picture rights to novels had never before been addressed. Kalem was sued for copyright infringement by the estate of Lew Wallace. The case went to the U.S. Supreme Court, which ruled in the Wallace estate's favor, resulting in a judgment of $25,000 against Kalem.

This film has survived only in poor quality prints, but it is good that it is available for evaluation, if for nothing but posterity and historic value.

100. Le Chevale Emballe

Rating: ☆☆☆

Pathé Frères; ***Produced by*** Charles Pathé; ***Directed by*** Ferdinand Zecca; ***Running Time:*** 6 minutes, 44 seconds

This early comedy features a horse that is parked outside a building where bags of oats happen to be stored. The horse devours almost an entire bag of oats and then runs loose with the carriage he is pulling, wreaking havoc all over the town.

One segment of this film was reversed to create the illusion of the horse running backwards. This technique was used in a similar sequence in D.W. Griffith's *The Curtain Pole.*

101. The Golden Beetle

Rating: ☆☆☆☆

Pathé Frères/France; ***Directed by*** Ferdinand Zecca; ***Based on a Story by*** Segundo de Chomon; ***Running Time:*** 2 minutes, 37 seconds

This film stands as the greatest artistic achievement of pioneer director Ferdinand Zecca. With lavish production values and meticulous hand-coloring and other special effects, this film features a magician who sees a golden beetle crawling up the wall and turns it into a beautiful woman with wings. The winged woman appears above the cloud of smoke from which she has been produced, appearing to stand five feet or so above the ground. A fountain appears, and she sinks to the ground disappearing behind the fountain. The streams of water from the fountain are multicolored. The fountain goes on to give the illusion of fireworks being emitted, with the colors becoming brighter and brighter. This sequence leads into the winged woman appearing in a black and white circle surrounded by bursts of bright colors, dancing around and around. The artistic beauty of this sequence would be hard to surpass even with modern special effects equipment. When the circle breaks up, the winged woman appears in the air with two assistants at her side, who help her to devour the magician in a fire from the fountain.

If *The Golden Beetle* were to be shown in theaters today preceding the feature presentation, its artistic beauty would still put audiences in awe, and they would likely talk more about the introductory short than the featured attraction. It is a magnificent work of art that stands the test of time more than 90 years after its original production and release.

A 1911 Italian film called *The Golden Beetle* was not a remake of this film, but rather an early 60-minute feature about a murderer with a dual personality.

102. That Fatal Sneeze

Rating: ☆☆☆

Hepworth Manufacturing Company; ***Produced by*** Cecil Hepworth; ***Running Time:*** 5 minutes, 38 seconds

This comedy portrays a man who makes his wife sneeze by blowing pepper at her. To get revenge, the wife puts pepper in all of her husband's handkerchiefs, toiletry items and clothes while he is asleep. Once he wakes up, he sneezes so hard that the bed falls apart and the walls shake. Once outside, he proceeds to wreck the whole town with his sneezing, until he sneezes himself into oblivion.

In 1910 producer Cecil Hepworth patented a device called the Vitaphone, a primitive system for synchronizing films with sound from a phonograph. Hepworth remained active in the motion picture industry until the early 1920s, and made one last film in 1927.

1908

103. Magic Bricks

Rating: ☆☆½

Pathé Frères; ***Produced by*** Charles Pathé; ***Directed by*** Ferdinand Zecca; ***Running Time:*** 3 minutes, 10 seconds

This tinted and hand-toned film opens with two magicians appearing from a small box. The most visually stimulating trick shows the magicians setting up a pile of blocks, with each block being part of the moving image of a baby until all of the cubes come together for the full image. This appears to have been accomplished by having a mirrored surface on one side of the blocks. The blocks are then disassembled and reassembled to create the image of Pathé's trademark rooster.

The hand coloring in this film is not as vibrant as in earlier Pathé hand colored films. It is mostly tinted, with subtle tones added.

104. Moscow Clad in Snow

Pathé Frères; ***Produced by*** Charles Pathé; ***Directed by*** Ferdinand Zecca; ***Running Time:*** 7 minutes, 22 seconds

This film provides interesting wintertime footage taken on location in Moscow, Russia, during the Czarist regime. Pictures of the snow-covered Kremlin are featured, progressing to the rest of downtown Moscow. The film makes a special point to give emphasis to the booming fish and mushroom market that prevailed in Moscow during the winter months. People are shown walking through the snow-covered streets, as well as riding in horse-drawn sleighs. There are no automobiles present at this early point in Russia's history. Petrovsky Park is prominently featured, as is an aerial view of Moscow, which concludes this early documentary.

1909

105. The Red Man's View

Rating: ☆☆

Biograph; ***Directed by*** D.W. Griffith

This is a film featuring the story of an Indian couple peacefully enjoying the riverside when white men invade the territory and drive the whole tribe off of the land that they had settled. Once the Indians stake out another territory, they are driven off by yet another group of whites. This is a compelling social portrayal of the problems that existed between the Native American Indians and the white settlers during the first decade of the 1900s.

1910

106. Aeroplane Flight and Wreck

Running Time: 4 minutes, 9 seconds; *Cast:* THE PILOT, M. Cody

This film documents an early flight attempt by a pilot referred to only as M. Cody. Shown are the preparations for the flight as the airplane is procured from its special storage room and close-ups of the running engine as it is being started. The open, uncovered engine would certainly fail the flight safety standards of today.

The plane manages to hover off the ground for a short distance before it crashes. Pilot Cody is shown walking away from the wreck, having lost only his hat in the accident.

107. A Day in the Life of a Coal Miner

Rating: ☆☆☆½

Kineto Production Company; *Running Time:* 9 minutes

This eye-opening documentary portrays a day in the life of coal miners in 1910. Females actively worked in the coal mines of that era. Groups of women are shown pushing the coal-filled carts to their destinations and are also shown right beside the men in the mines.

It also delivers a prolabor social message. When the work day is over, the tired and haggard workers are shown in line collecting their pay checks. Their "light at the end of the day" shows the workers returning to run-down, barely inhabitable, company owned shanties. In contrast, the mine administrator is shown in his beautiful, lavishly furnished home sitting by a cozy fire with his family.

It was documentaries like this one, as well as Thanhouser's film of 1912 called *The Cry of the Children*, that led to the movement to reform labor practices in the United States and other countries around the world.

108. Frankenstein

Rating: ☆☆☆½

Thomas A. Edison Company; ***Directed by*** J. Searle Dawley; ***Running Time of Existing Footage:*** 12 minutes; ***Cast:*** DR. FRANKENSTEIN, Augustus Phillips (1874–19??); HIS FIANCEE, Mary Fuller (1888–1973); THE MONSTER, Charles Ogle (1865–1940)

This version of *Frankenstein* is on the American Film Institute's "Top Ten" list of titles desired for archival preservation. Only one print survived, and is in the hands of private collector Al Detlaff of Wisconsin. He has offered to sell the print to the archives, but none have thus far been willing or able to pay the reported asking price of $1 million.

Charles Ogle as *Frankenstein* (1910).

In reviewing an extremely rare, but poor quality and barely watchable, video version of *Frankenstein* that the owner of the print has made available to a few collectors, it was revealed that although this film is in some ways as primitive as most other films from 1910, it is, in many ways, very sophisticated for the time. Unfortunately, there are no close-up shots whatsoever in the film footage itself. This is surprising, as there are many close-up stills of Charles Ogle as the monster. The stills reveal an impressive makeup job that Ogle reportedly did himself—on par with some of the great makeup jobs that Lon Chaney, Sr., did for his characters. Ogle's monster is grotesque looking—far more so than Boris Karloff's 1931 rendition of the monster. There are some very good special effects for the time, especially in the scene in which the partially formed monster gradually materializes from a bubbling cauldron. The film shows the skeleton gradually forming flesh as it materializes.

This adaptation portrays Dr. Frankenstein as a man with a diabolical mind who deliberately creates an evil creature with some resemblance of human form. The monster attacks Dr. Frankenstein upon being created, seeing himself in the mirror and becoming appalled by what he looks like. The monster, jealous of Frankenstein's relationship with his fiancée, attacks the fiancée at night. Frankenstein comes to the rescue when he hears his bride-to-be's screams. He finds his own image in the bedroom mirror to be that of the monster he created. The power of love for his bride is overwhelming enough to dissolve the image, and Frankenstein and his fiancée get married and live happily ever after.

The reviews of this film upon its original release were very enthusiastic, and *Frankenstein* was a critical and box office success—perhaps among the most famous of all of the films produced by the Thomas Edison Studios. The film still holds up relatively well nearly 90 years after its original production.

109. In the Border States

Rating: ☆☆½

Biograph; ***Directed by*** D.W. Griffith

This film is set during the Civil War. The daughter of a Union soldier helps a Confederate hide from the Union Army. When the girl's father is captured by the Confederates, the same soldier she helped saves her father's life. This is an early example of how D.W. Griffith injected his pacifist viewpoints into his work, showing how decency prevails over war.

1911

110. Cinderella

Rating: ☆☆☆

Thanhouser; ***Directed by*** George O. Nichols; ***Running Time:*** 14 minutes, 23 seconds; ***Cast:*** CINDERELLA, Florence LaBadie (1888–1917); THE PRINCE, Harry Benham (1883–1969); ***Supporting Cast:*** Anna Rosemone, Frank H. Crane (1873–1948), Alphonse Ethier (1874–1943), Isabelle Daintry

This version of *Cinderella* was released just before Christmas of 1911, and stars Florence LaBadie in the lead role. LaBadie was at the top of every movie magazine's popularity contests of the early 1910s. She was the first of the really big female stars to die at the height of her career, having been killed in a car accident at age 29. In this adaptation of *Cinderella*, she is especially appealing.

This is a magical film, featuring simple but effective special effects. This is the earliest extant film adaptation of the fairy tale.

111. The Coffin Ship

Rating: ☆☆½

Thanhouser; ***Running Time:*** 14 minutes, 37 seconds; ***Cast:*** THE SHIP CAPTAIN, William Garwood (1884–1950); MARY, Marguerite Snow (1889–1958)

The Coffin Ship was preserved by the Nederlands Filmmuseum in The Netherlands. It stars William Garwood, who was one of the leading matinee idols of the early 1910s. By the 1920s, Garwood had faded into obscurity. His chronic alcoholism is likely what led to his demise in motion pictures, and it eventually caused his death from cirrhosis of the liver.

In this film, he plays a ship captain who falls in love with a girl named Mary, the daughter of a wealthy ship builder. They marry secretly, much to the disapproval of her father. While on a cruise, the ship on which the couple is traveling springs a leak. When they are rescued as the sole survivors, a reconciliation occurs.

112. Get Rich Quick

Rating: ☆☆½

Thanhouser; ***Running Time:*** 12 minutes, 46 seconds; ***Cast:*** CON ARTIST, Harry Benham (1883–1969); HIS WIFE, Marguerite Snow (1889–1958); DAUGHTER OF A POOR WIDOW, Marie Eline (1905–1981)

This is the story of a couple who are lured into a scam operation called the "Utopia Investment Corporation" and gain a great deal of wealth by dishonest means. Marie Eline, who was known and billed as "the Thanhouser kidlet," plays the daughter of one of the poor widows who has lost all of her money in the scam. She causes the couple to regret what they have done and return the money that they stole.

Marguerite Snow received wide critical acclaim for her performance, which *The Billboard* praised as "the most natural we have ever seen in a picture."

113. Only in the Way

Rating: ☆☆½

Thanhouser; ***Running Time:*** 12 minutes, 14 seconds; ***Cast:*** Marie Eline (1905–1981)

Marie Eline plays a girl whose beloved grandmother is scorned by her selfish daughter, who convinces her husband to put her in a nursing home so that she won't be in the way. The little girl runs away from home, leaving behind a note which says, "Grandma was in the way and I guess so am I. I am going to live with her." This makes the mother realize how selfish she has been, and the family is reunited as a result of the girl's demonstration of unconditional love.

114. She

Rating: ☆☆

Thanhouser; ***Running Time:*** 20 minutes; ***Cast:*** SHE WHO MUST BE OBEYED, Marguerite Snow (1889–1958); LEO, James Cruze (1884–1943); A LITTLE GIRL, Marie Eline (1905–1981)

This 1911 version of *She* is the earliest existing silent adaptation of the H. Rider Haggard fantasy novel of 1902. At least eight adaptations were made, but only this and the 1925 version remain from the silent era adaptations.

Produced by the Thanhouser Company, this version consists of two reels and is 20 minutes long. The story starts out in Ancient Egypt about 350 B.C. "She who must be obeyed" is the empress of a civilization on the tip of Africa. She possesses unique powers which allow her to maintain eternal youth and life by bathing in flames. Having been spurned by the man she has set her desires on, she strikes him dead. The wife of the stricken man avows that her son or one of her descendants will avenge the death of her husband.

This brings us up to 1885. Leo, a descendant, sets out for the African civilization to avenge his ancestor's death. All these years, "she who never dies" has kept the body of the man she loved and killed preserved. Believing Leo to be the reincarnation of the man who spurned her love, she destroys the body, with the hopes that she can once again convince Leo to bathe in the flames of eternal life with her. When demonstrating the flames, she shrivels up and dies instead of preserving her youth. Thus, Leo's ancestor is avenged after 2,000 years.

While the narrative style of this film is quite primitive compared to other Thanhouser films of the period, it is more elaborate than one would expect for the time.

115. Troublesome Secretaries

Rating: ☆☆☆

Vitagraph; Director Unidentified; ***Running Time:*** 8 minutes, 45 seconds; ***Cast:*** MR. HARDING, John Bunny (1863–1915); BETTY HARDING, Mabel Normand (1892–1930); ***Supporting Cast:*** Ralph Ince (1882–1937); James Morrison (1888–1974); Alec B. Francis (1867–1934)

This is one of Mabel Normand's earliest surviving films, and also one of the few films of John Bunny that has survived as well. The Vitagraph Company burned most of its negatives and prints of their early films to reclaim the silver from them, and therefore few of their films were preserved.

This is a romantic comedy in which John Bunny plays a feisty businessman whose daughter seems to detract his male secretaries from their work. He fires her fiancé, and tries a female secretary. Little does he know that the new secretary is a friend of Mabel's, who conspires with her to come onto her father, so that he'll give up on female secretaries. He finally asks a friend for advice and is told to hire a secretary over the age of 60. This would work, but the two scheming lovers get around that, too, by dressing Mabel's fiancé, Ralph, with a white wig and long beard, disguising him as an old man.

This is among the best of the surviving comedies from the earliest part of the 1910s, providing a great look at two early comedy legends. Mabel Normand later credited John

Bunny as one of the first stars to have really helped her in learning the motion picture business.

This is one of only four of the films of James Morrison known to survive. He was a major matinee idol of the 1910s and early 1920s, with this being among his first films. His other three known surviving films are *A Tale of Two Cities* (1911), *The Ten Commandments* (1923), and *Wine of Youth* (1925). He also played in the 1924 version of *Captain Blood*, a lost film that has been on the American Film Institute's "rescue list" for years.

Ralph Ince was the brother of Thomas H. Ince (1881–1924) and John Ince (1878–1947). He died at 55 in 1937 in a car accident in London.

116. The Two Orphans

Rating: ☆☆

Selig Polyscope Company; ***Directed by*** Otis Turner; ***Supervised by*** Kate Claxton; ***Based on the 1874 Play,*** *Les Deux Orphelines*; ***by*** Philippe d'Ennery and Eugene Cormon; ***Running Time:*** 32 minutes; ***Cast:*** HENRIETTE, Kathlyn Williams (1888–1960); LOUISE, Winifred Greenwood (1885–1961); CHEVALIER MAURICE DE VAUDREY, T.(homas) J.(ay) Carrigan (1886–1941); COUNT DE LINIERES, Charles Clary (1873–1931); PICARD [VALET TO CHEVALIER], Miles McCarthy (1874–1928); JACQUES FROCHARD, Leighton Stark (died 1924); PIERRE FROCHARD, James O'Burrell; MARQUIS DE PREALES, Rex Rosselli; THE DOCTOR, Frank Weed; LE FLEUR, Will [William] Stowell (1885–1919); ANTOINE, Tom I. Commerford (1855–1920); OFFICER OF THE GUARD, Louis Fierce (1852–1926); MARIANNE [AN OUTCAST], Adrienne Krowell (1892–1949); LA FROCHARD [THE HAG], Lillian Leighton (1874–1956); MADAM GIRARD, Vera Hamilton; COUNTESS DE LINIERES, Myrtle Stedman (1885–1938)

This was the second American film adaptation of the play *The Two Orphans*, and the oldest one available for evaluation. It was a three-reel production, released one reel at a time over a three-day period.

This version starts with a brief sequence of the two orphans as babies being given up by their parents with a note to whomever finds them. It then cuts to 18 years later, where the orphans are living in poverty. Louise is blind, and they travel to Paris in hopes of a better life. The movie follows the familiar plot, with Henriette and Louise becoming separated. Louise ends up at the mercy of La Frochard, a hag who forces her to beg in the streets to earn her keep. Eventually, the sisters are reunited.

This film was highly acclaimed when it was released. *Moving Picture World* stated that it was "a massive production" and "a triumph of the Selig Polyscope Company." Winifred Greenwood's performance was acclaimed as "a pretty bit of realistic acting."

In reevaluating this film today, one can conclude that it does have its flaws, but is not a bad production for the time. It is stagy, and the "outdoor" scenes were obviously filmed indoors. The two lead stars, Kathlyn Williams and Winifred Greenwood, were both very attractive at this stage in their careers. Unfortunately, the stiff directorial style provides little opportunity for either of them to demonstrate real acting ability. The only actress that really stands out in this film is Lillian Leighton, who made her film debut as La Frochard when she was 37. Her performance as the villainous hag makes a distinct impression.

This is perhaps the only surviving work of William Stowell. In 1919, while on his way to a location filming in South Africa, he was killed in a train accident at age 34. The director of this film, Otis Turner (1862–1918), died the previous year at 56.

For further information on the various other film adaptations of *The Two Orphans*, see the review herein of *Orphans of the Storm* (1921).

117. What Shall We Do with Our Old? *Rating:* ☆☆☆

Biograph; ***Directed by*** D.W. Griffith

This is a stinging indictment of age discrimination. The subjects of the story are an older woman, dying of tuberculosis, and her husband, who loses his job and is replaced by a younger man. Due to his age, the husband cannot find employment elsewhere. There is no money for medical care, and the couple faces starvation once their savings run out.

The situation portrayed in this film was not uncommon for the time. It was outcries such as the message in this film that eventually led to modern day Social Security programs.

The Golden Era of Silents (1912–1931)

1912

118. The Cry of the Children

Rating: ☆☆☆½

Thanhouser; ***Directed by*** George O. Nichols; ***Running Time:*** 29 minutes; ***Cast:*** ALICE (THE LITTLE GIRL), Marie Eline (1905–1981); THE WORKING MOTHER, Ethel Wright; THE WORKING FATHER, James Cruze (1884–1942); THE FACTORY OWNER'S WIFE, Lila H. Chester

Most people who watch educational television have probably seen clips from this film featured in many documentaries. This film is among the best of the non–Griffith dramatic shorts of the 1910s, and delivers a powerful message against the grueling conditions that impoverished children were forced to work under at the time.

Alice, the daughter of a factory worker, is singled out by her family as the one child who will be kept "out of the shadow of the factory." Due to the low salaries paid by the mill, the family falls upon hard times. The mill owner's wife takes a liking to the girl and offers to adopt her. The girl's father leaves the decision in Alice's hands, and she chooses to stay with her family. Then, the mill owner and his wife offer a nice sum of money, and Alice still refuses at first.

When the family becomes absolutely destitute, the girl finally relents and agrees to be adopted to help her family. When she goes to see the mill owner's wife, it seems that she has gotten over her whim for the child, and she nonchalantly waves her off and tells her that she doesn't want her anymore. In desperation, the child goes to work in the factory to help her family with extra income. She dies from overwork.

This is a truly eloquent statement of social commentary, and its punch is just as powerful today as it was more than 80 years ago. The film's use of symbolism makes it an artistic masterpiece as well. It stands as the most highly acclaimed and famous of all of the films produced by the Thanhouser Company.

John Bunny and Flora Finch in *A Cure for Pokeritus* (1912).

119. A Cure for Pokeritus

Rating: ☆☆☆☆

Vitagraph; ***Cast:*** John Bunny (1863–1915); Flora Finch (1869–1940)

This is probably the most famous and popular of the John Bunny/Flora Finch collaborations. John Bunny plays a husband who loses money in poker and promises his wife that he will never play again. Unable to resist temptation, he tells his wife that he is attending a church social function, and even shows her a fake invitation as proof. The wife pretends not to suspect, but Bunny gives himself away by talking in his sleep. Her suspicions confirmed, Finch conspires with her cousin Freddie to find "a cure for pokeritus." This is a truly hilarious comedy classic.

120. Dr. Jekyll and Mr. Hyde

Rating: ☆☆☆

Thanhouser; ***Directed by*** Lucius Henderson; Based on the Thomas Russell Stover stage play from Robert Louis Stevenson's novel; ***Running Time:*** 11 minutes, 31 seconds; ***Cast:*** DR. JEKYLL, James Cruze (1884–1942); HYDE, James Cruze/Harry Benham (1883–1969); HIS SWEETHEART, Florence LaBadie (1888–1917); LITTLE GIRL KNOCKED DOWN BY HYDE, Marie Eline (1905–1981)

This adaptation of *Dr. Jekyll and Mr. Hyde* was filmed in 1911 and released in January of 1912. Although James Cruze is widely credited as having been the sole player of the double role of Jekyll and Hyde, this is not entirely true. He played the Jekyll character throughout, but in some scenes the Hyde character was played by Harry Benham. This second of nine silent screen adaptations of this literary classic holds up well and is highly enjoyable to watch more than 85 years later.

121. Every Inch a Man

Rating: ☆☆½

Vitagraph; Director Uncredited; ***Running Time:*** 11 minutes; ***Cast:*** BOB, Wallace Reid

(1891–1923); HIS MOTHER, Rose Tapley (1881–1956); THE DETECTIVE, Robert Gaillord (1868–1941)

This is another of the rare Vitagraph films, which starred Wallace Reid when he was 21 years old. In the film, Reid plays Bob, the son in a family of farmers. He apprehends a cattle rustler and decides to pursue work as a detective. His father, not taking him seriously, sends him to a detective friend of his, telling him to scare Bob out of his ambition by explaining the dangers of the job. The detective stages a fake robbery, and Bob comes through with flying colors, proving himself perfectly capable of the job, and "every inch a man."

Wallace Reid was an imposing, tall figure, showing his strength by carrying two men tied together. It was films like this that gave him the image as an all–American boy.

Rose Tapley, who plays Bob's mother, was a veteran of the stage when she made her film debut at age 24 in 1905 with the Edison Company. Her film career lasted until 1931.

122. The Female of the Species

Rating: ☆☆

Biograph; ***Directed by*** D.W. Griffith; ***Cast:*** THE WIFE, Claire McDowell (1878–1966); HER SISTER, Mary Pickford (1892–1979); THE WIFE'S HUSBAND, Charles West (1885–1943); THE LONE GIRL, Dorothy Bernard (1890–1955)

This film was billed as a psychological drama. A group of people leave a deserted mining town and begin the long trek by foot through the hot desert. A husband tries to force himself on one of the female members of the party. The wife sees him with the other woman, and thinks that she instigated the situation. The husband suddenly dies. The wife and her sister blame the woman for it and are set on revenge. Then, they come across an orphaned Indian baby. Their common motherly instincts bring about a reconciliation.

123. Fine Feathers

Rating: ☆☆

Rex; ***Directed by*** Lois Weber; ***Running Time:*** 11 minutes; ***Cast:*** MIRA, Lois Weber (1879–1939)

This is the earliest of the Lois Weber shorts that is available for evaluation. Weber was one of the two most prominent female movie directors and producers of the silent era. In this film she plays Mira, a down-on-her-luck woman who is hired by an artist named Vaughn as a cleaning woman. She poses for one of his pictures, which receives wide acclaim. She takes the initiative in asking Vaughn to consider marrying her. He refuses at first, but after another successful portrait with his new model realizes how much he really does love her.

Lois Weber was known for being way ahead of her time in some of the social issues she dealt with in her films. She breaks tradition in this film by having the woman take the initiative and propose marriage. The print of this film that survived was a beautifully tinted 35 mm print.

124. Flo's Discipline

Rating: ☆☆☆

Universal/Victor; ***Directed by*** Harry Salter; ***Running Time:*** 10 minutes; ***Cast:*** FLO, Florence Lawrence (1886–1938); ASSISTANT PRINCIPAL, Owen Moore (1886–1939)

Florence Lawrence was one of the first major stars to become a box office attraction. She was the first "Biograph girl"—Mary Pickford's predecessor to the title. In 1910,

An original picture post card of Florence Lawrence from *Flo's Discipline* (1912).

she left Biograph to join Carl Laemmle's newly formed Independent Motion Picture Company (known as IMP), which evolved into Universal Pictures.

Flo's Discipline was one of a series of comedies in which Lawrence costarred with Owen Moore, who was at the time Mary Pickford's husband. In this film, Lawrence plays a school marm dealing with a group of rowdy boys who have left school in protest of her firing the assistant principal, played by Owen Moore. She deals with the problem by chasing the boys with a water hose into the ice house and locking them in.

This rare surviving example of Lawrence's work reveals her to be a radiant personality well suited to comedy. Sadly, she suffered severe burns in a studio fire in 1914, and spent a year recuperating before she tried returning for one film in 1916, which proved too much, as her recovery was not complete. She was relegated to extra work when she tried for a comeback in the early 1920s. By the 1930s, MGM, as an act of charity, put her on their payroll and used her in extra parts. In 1938 she committed suicide at age 52 by swallowing ant paste. Costar Owen Moore died of chronic alcoholism the following year.

Director Harry Salter (1886–1928) was Lawrence's first of three husbands. He died of influenza at age 41.

125. For His Son

Rating: ☆☆☆

Biograph; ***Directed by*** D.W. Griffith;

This was among the first films to deal head-on with the problem of drug addiction. A physician has a spoiled son, and in order to keep him supported in the lifestyle he wants to live in, he invents a soft drink laced with cocaine. The product is "Dopokoke" and takes off as more and more people become addicted. The money starts rolling in. Unfortunately, the son becomes an addict and dies from his addiction. Anybody who thinks that drug problems do not predate the 1960s should see this film.

126. From the Manger to the Cross

Rating: ☆☆½

Kalem; ***Directed by*** Sidney Olcott; ***Written by*** Gene Gauntier; Filmed on location in Egypt and Palestine; ***Running Time:*** 70 minutes; ***Cast:*** CHRIST AS A BOY, Percy Dyer; CHRIST, R. Henderson Bland (died 1941); THE VIRGIN MARY, Gene Gauntier (1880–1966); MARY MAGDALENE, Alice Hollister (1886–1973); MARTHA, Helen Lindroth (1874–1956); JOHN, Jack J. Clark (1876–1947); ANDREW, J.P. McGowan (1880–1952); JUDAS, Robert Vignola (1882–1953); LAZARUS, Sidney Baber

This was the first feature length biopic on the life of Christ. It was actually filmed on location in Bethlehem and Jerusalem. The executives of Kalem had been resistant to moving beyond one and two reelers and into features. It was with reluctance that they produced this, their one and only multireel film. This film, the one that they were so opposed to making, has been the most highly acclaimed of all of their films.

The story is simply told, with no fancy special effects. The story does move a bit slowly in parts, but is historically authentic. The title cards consist exclusively of quotations of the Judeo-Christian New Testament of the Bible. The authentic location settings are impressive, and the crucifixion sequence is well done. It is difficult to see Jesus' hands in the crucifixion, as the shots are rather distant. As far as can be determined, it appears that the producers properly placed the nails in the wrists, as they should have. Crucifixion portrayals in later silents erroneously place the nails through the center of the palms. After the death of Christ, the earthquake sequence is simply depicted. This sequence uses animation to feature the illusion of moving clouds, and the building that comes down is obviously a small-scale model.

At one point in this film's history, a resurrection sequence was spliced in from another film at the end of this movie. The new restoration of the film by David Shepard properly removes this resurrection sequence and ends the film where it originally ended. The then-common practice of filming nighttime sequences in broad daylight was also done when this movie was originally shot. The restored version corrected this problem by tinting the film and using blue for the night sequences.

This is one of the few films of Alice Hollister that is widely available on video. Hollister was actually the very first screen vamp, having played such a role in *The Vampire* (1913) a little over a year before Theda Bara sensationalized the "vamp" image in *A Fool There Was* (1914).

127. The Girl at the Cupola *Rating:* ☆☆☆

Selig Polyscope; Director Unidentified; ***Running Time:*** 12 minutes; ***Cast:*** JESSIE, Kathlyn Williams (1888–1960)

This is one of the few surviving films of Kathlyn Williams from the peak of her career. Made before her most famous role, *The Adventures of Kathlyn (1913)*, *The Girl at the Cupola* has Williams playing the daughter of a business owner whose factory is failing. Jessie's fiancé, Jack, a financial wizard, is brought in to help get the business back on its feet.

The first thing Jack does is cut back the work force, getting rid of the older workers and replacing them with younger, "more efficient" workers. All of the employees go on strike. As the new staff is brought in, Jessie is caught in the middle of a riot. She pleads with Jack, and the combination of her pleading and the workers striking results in the older workers getting pensions.

This film was an elaborate commentary on labor, one of the hottest social issues of the time. Nearly a hundred extras were featured in the strike sequence. Kathlyn Williams is appealing in the role, and *The Girl at the Cupola* provides a rare chance to see her in action.

Williams, whose career started in 1910 at age 22, remained a top star through the early 1920s. By the late 1920s she made a smooth transition into character roles. She made five talkies in the early 1930s and tried for a comeback in *The Other Love* (1947). This film proved to be her last, as shortly after completing it, she lost a leg in a car accident. She died from a heart attack in 1960 at age 72.

128. Love and Charity

Rating: ☆☆½

[a.k.a. *The Burglar's Dilemma*]

Reliance; ***Running Time:*** 10 minutes; ***Cast:*** THE BURGLAR, Henry B. Walthall (1878–1936)

This is a rare obscurity featuring a young looking Henry B. Walthall as an out-of-work father who has no money to buy his children Christmas gifts. As a last resort, he breaks into a house to steal gifts for his children. The father of the house catches him in the act, and the burglar relates his sad story. Instead of prosecuting him, the man has his wife go out to buy more gifts and invites the rest of the burglar's family to celebrate Christmas at their home.

This was yet another social commentary film dealing with unemployment and how it would drive otherwise honest people to steal out of desperation. It also implores the more fortunate to celebrate the spirit of Christmas by helping the downtrodden.

129. The Mender of Nets

Rating: ☆☆☆½

Biograph; ***Directed by*** D.W. Griffith; ***Running Time:*** 12 minutes; ***Cast:*** THE OLD LOVE, Mabel Normand (1892–1930); THE FIANCÉE, Mary Pickford (1892–1979); THE MAN, Charles West (1885–1943); A NEIGHBOR, Marguerite Marsh (1892–1925)

This is one of Mabel Normand's few extant dramatic films with the Biograph Company. In this film, Mary Pickford plays the lead as a net mender who becomes engaged to a man, only to find out that he has another girl on the side—played by Mabel Normand, whom it is hinted is pregnant with his child. Mary finds out what has happened, and gives the fiancé up so that he can do right by Mabel. The finale has a showdown between Mabel's brother and the meandering boyfriend.

This is an excellent melodrama—one of the best of its time—that provides a rare chance to see Mabel Normand and Mary Pickford together in one of their two appearances together on film. This film also features in a bit part Marguerite Marsh, who was the sister of Mae Marsh. Marsh also worked under the names of "Lovey" Marsh and Marguerite Loveridge. Marguerite Marsh was only 37 years old when she died of pneumonia in 1925, which was partially brought on by a nervous breakdown. Few of her films have survived, and only a couple of the Griffith films she starred in are available outside the archives.

130. The New York Hat

Rating: ☆☆☆½

Biograph; ***Directed by*** D.W. Griffith; ***Scenario by*** Anita Loos; ***Running Time:*** 13 minutes; ***Cast:*** THE DAUGHTER, Mary Pickford (1892–1979); THE MINISTER, Lionel Barrymore (1878–1954); ***Supporting Cast:*** Mae Marsh (1895–1968); Robert Harron (1893–1920); Dorothy Gish (1898–1968); Lillian Gish (1893–1993)

This is perhaps the most famous of the D.W. Griffith/Mary Pickford collaborations. *The New York Hat* also has a significant place in motion picture history as the first film scenario written by Anita Loos (1888–1981), who was paid $25 for this debut film script.

In this film, Mary Pickford plays the daughter of a tyrannical miser who has literally worked her mother to death. On her death bed, the mother gives the minister an envelope containing money that she had saved over several years, a couple of pennies at a time, with instructions that he use the money to buy her daughter some of the nice things that she had always been denied. Mary sees a hat from New York in a display window, and the minister buys it for her with the money that her mother had given him.

Rumors begin to circulate among the ignorant townspeople that the minister bought Mary the hat because he was interested in more than friendship. Mary's reputation is tarnished, and the minister is almost defrocked. It is only when the minister produces the letter from Mary's mother that the problem is straightened out, but by this time Mary's father has destroyed the hat that he automatically assumes is the gift of an illicit lover.

The New York Hat is a fabulous social commentary condemning those who are quick to judge others before they know the real facts. Mary Pickford gives a poignant performance—probably her best from her early years with D.W. Griffith—in the last film she completed with Griffith before going to Paramount.

131. The Petticoat Camp

Rating: ☆☆☆½

Thanhouser; ***Running Time:*** 14 minutes, 50 seconds; ***Cast:*** THE STRIKE LEADER, Florence LaBadie (1888–1917); HER HUSBAND, William Garwood (1884–1950); The Jordan sisters

This is a battle of the sexes comedy about a group of husbands and wives going on a camping trip. The women overwork themselves waiting on their husbands hand and foot while the husbands have fun fishing and hunting. Florence LaBadie convinces the other women to go on strike. They leave a note to the husbands saying they are on strike and camping out on the next island. The note is signed "your former slaves."

Pandemonium occurs when the husbands return from fishing and find that the women have left. The husbands try to travel to the "petticoat camp" of their wives to break the strike, but the wives are ready—with guns. The husbands finally surrender and call a truce. Features a special appearance by the Jordan sisters, who were highly acclaimed professional divers of the time. A delightful comedy.

132. Queen Elizabeth

Rating: ☆☆

Produced in Europe; ***Distributed in the U.S. by*** Adolph Zukor; "Famous Players in Famous Plays"; ***Directed by*** Louis Mercanton; ***Running Time:*** 52 minutes; ***Cast:*** QUEEN ELIZABETH, Sarah Bernhardt (1844–1923); ROBERT DEVEREAUX [EARL OF ESSEX], Lou Tellegen (1883–1934); COUNTESS OF NOTTINGHAM, Mlle. Romaine; EARL OF NOTTINGHAM, M. Maxudian

This is the photographed stage play that was partially responsible for helping to bring motion pictures out of the "nickelodeon" age. Adolph Zukor (1873–1976) thought that by getting some of the top and most respected stage stars to do pictures, he could attract the social upper classes to pictures at what were called the "legitimate" theaters of the time. The gamble paid off, and the success of this film was so phenomenal that Zukor used the profits to form the "Famous Players in Famous Plays" company, a forerunner of Paramount Pictures.

Sarah Bernhardt, the legendary stage actress, was 68 at the time that *Queen Eliz-*

abeth was filmed. She consented to do it partially because she considered it "my one chance at immortality." By this time, she had a wooden leg which made walking difficult and painful. If one looks closely, one can actually catch a glimpse of her wooden leg in the segment in which she is being lifted up and carried to see *The Merry Wives of Windsor*. In spite of such, she carried herself with incredible grace and dignity. In most of the scenes, her walks are very brief, or with another actor or actress holding her hand. In most of the scenes, she is pictured either sitting or standing. The only thing that she did wrong was in refusing to adapt her acting technique to motion pictures. On stage, one could hear the "golden voice," in which case her techniques were perfect. But, without the golden voice to accompany her acting, her performance appeared stiff and reserved.

The story of this film is rather interesting. Lou Tellegen plays the Earl of Essex, the man with whom Queen Elizabeth falls in love. When a fortune teller foresees death at the scaffold for Essex and an unhappy life for Elizabeth, Elizabeth is prompted to give Essex a ring. She promises that should he ever get into any trouble, the return of the ring to her would save him from the fate of the scaffold.

Essex engages in an adulterous affair with Mary of Nottingham. Mary's husband, the Earl of Nottingham, walks in on them and vows revenge. In league with Lord Bacon (another enemy of Essex), an anonymous letter accusing Essex of treason is written. Elizabeth at first dismisses the letter. But, when she, too, finds out about the affair, she reasons that if Essex could be unfaithful to her, he could also be unfaithful to his country. She signs his death warrant on charges of treason.

Elizabeth sends Mary of Nottingham to Essex for the ring, with intentions of granting him clemency. Unfortunately, the ring is intercepted by the Earl of Nottingham and thrown into the Thames River. Once Essex is executed, Elizabeth views the body and finds that the ring is missing, and that he had indeed intended to ask for clemency. The rest of her life is unhappy, thus proving the fortune teller correct.

This film used the most primitive of filming techniques, consisting almost exclusively of distant shots showing the entire stage setting. There are no close-up shots at all, which is a shame, as it would have been great to be able to get a good look at Bernhardt's face in a close-up shot. Despite its primitive techniques, it is an interesting film for its historic value, and the only one of Sarah Bernhardt's surviving films widely available on video. (*Camille* and other Bernhardt films do survive, but have not yet been made available on video due to concerns about their limited commercial appeal.) In a sense, *Queen Elizabeth* did in reality provide Bernhardt with a form of immortality. Although we unfortunately cannot hear the fabulous voice that was part of her fame, she can still be seen on video many decades after her death in 1923.

Lou Tellegen, the leading man in this film, is quite appealing as well. He was married to actress and opera diva Geraldine Farrar from 1916 to 1923. By the 1930s he was unable to find work and living in poverty. Distraught, he committed suicide by stabbing himself with a pair of scissors in 1934.

133. The Star of Bethlehem

Rating: ☆☆½

Thanhouser; ***Directed by*** Lawrence Marston; ***Production Supervised by*** Edwin Thanhouser; ***Scenario by*** Lloyd F. Lonergan; ***Running Time:*** 15 minutes, 13 seconds; ***Cast:*** MARY (MOTHER

Promotional poster reproduction from Thanhouser's *Star of Bethlehem* (1912) as the design of a 1996 Christmas card.

OF JESUS), Florence LaBadie (1888–1917); MICAH/JOSEPH, James Cruze (1884–1942); HEROD, William Russell (1886–1929); ANGEL GABRIEL, Harry Benham (1883–1969); GASPAR (ONE OF THE MAGI), Justus D. Barnes (1862–1946); MELCHIOR, Charles Horan (1882–1928); BALTHASAR, Riley Chamberlin (1854–1917); SCRIBE, Harry Marks; SCRIBE, N.W. Woods; SCRIBE, Lawrence Merton; PHARISEE/RABBI, David H. Thompson (1886–1957); PHARISEE/SCRIBE, Lew Woods; ROMAN MESSENGER, Joseph Graybill (1877–1913); SHEPHERD, Carl LeViness (1885–1964); SHEPHERD, Frank Grimmer

The Star of Bethlehem was released on Christmas Eve of 1912, being one of the most ambitious films of the year, with a cast of over 200 players. This early epic of the birth of Christ was originally over three reels long, but all that has survived is an edited version of 15 minutes duration. The special effects of the star were elaborate for the time. The scene of the birth of Christ is beautifully filmed, with angels shown in double exposure photography. Florence LaBadie is among the most attractive actresses to have played the Virgin Mary on screen.

134. An Unseen Enemy

Rating: ☆☆☆

Biograph; ***Directed by*** D.W. Griffith; ***Scenario by*** Edward Acker; ***Running Time:*** 11 minutes; ***Cast:*** OLDER SISTER, Lillian Gish (1893–1993); YOUNGER SISTER, Dorothy Gish (1898–1968); YOUNGER SISTER'S SWEETHEART, Robert Harron (1893–1920); OLDER BROTHER, Elmer Booth (1882–1915); ***Supporting Cast:*** Harry Carey, Sr. (1878–1947)

This film is historically significant as the film debut of Lillian and Dorothy Gish. They play adolescent girls recently orphaned by the death of their father. Their brother deposits a large sum of money in a safe, witnessed by their drunken maid. The girls, abandoned in the house alone, are held at gunpoint by the maid while a friend of hers breaks into the safe. Dorothy Gish is the one who shows the courage to get to a telephone and call for help as she is being shot at. In typical Griffith style, there is a suspenseful chase sequence as the older brother races to their rescue.

Supporting player Elmer Booth, a promising actor, was only 33 years old when he was killed in a car accident, three years after this film was made.

A beautifully restored version of this film with full orchestral score is available as part of a shorts compilation from Kino Video's D.W. Griffith video series.

135. The Water Nymph

Rating: ☆☆½

Keystone; ***Directed by*** Mack Sennett; ***Running Time:*** 7 minutes; ***Cast:*** Mack Sennett (1880–1960), Mabel Normand (1892–1930)

This film is regarded as the first of the Mack Sennett "bathing beauty" films. It is fun to see the 1912 fashion bathing suits. Mabel Normand is featured in what is historically among the first "one piece" bathing suits, which covered the whole body except the feet and arms. In this film, she is quite obviously doing a parody of champion swimmer Annette Kellerman (1888–1975). *The Water Nymph* is a charming look into the early days of Mabel Normand's career, before her life was plagued with personal problems.

136. What Happened to Mary? *Rating:* ☆☆☆

Episode Nine: A Way to the Underworld

Thomas A. Edison; Director Unidentified; ***Running Time of Episode:*** 11 minutes; ***Cast:*** MARY, Mary Fuller (1888–1973); MR. CRAIG [MARY'S UNCLE], Charles Ogle (1865–1940); HIS SON, Harry O'Moore; BILLY PEART [MARY'S FOSTER FATHER], William Wadsworth (1874–1950)

What Happened to Mary? was the screen's first chapter play, with a new episode released every month starting in July of 1912. The ninth of twelve episodes, released in early 1913, has fortunately survived and made it into the video market.

The episode starts with Mary having just testified against her uncle and his son, who misappropriated funds at the bank they worked in. They are sentenced to prison. In prison, the father and son are shown conspiring to cheat Mary out of her impending inheritance, trying to find a way to keep her from claiming it on her 21st birthday. The foster father from whom Mary has escaped is in on the plot, and fakes illness to get Mary to fall into a trap.

Each of these episodes was complete in itself, thus really classifying *What Happened to Mary?* not as a serial, but rather as a series of related films. In evaluating this chapter, the plot is really more interesting and intriguing than that of *The Perils of Pauline* (1914), which followed two years later.

This series was released as part of a promotion for *McClure's Ladies World Magazine*, which printed each of the stories before the screen adaptations appeared.

Mary Fuller's career started in 1907 with the Vitagraph Company, and lasted until 1917. Her role in this series really rocketed her to stardom. While she was still on top and highly popular, Fuller vanished without a trace. By 1920, the fantasy of what happened to Mary became a reality. Film historian Billy Doyle revealed the circumstances of Fuller's demise in the 1995 book, *The Ultimate Directory of the Silent Screen Players.* He relates that she fell in love with a man whose wife refused to give him a divorce, and had a nervous breakdown. She lived in quiet seclusion recovering at her mother's house in Washington, D.C. A comeback attempt in the late 1920s failed, and Fuller returned to her mother's home. The death of Fuller's mother in 1940 resulted in another breakdown, and in 1947 Mary's sister had her committed to a mental institution. She spent the last 25 years of her life there before her death in 1973 at age 85.

1913

137. Atlantis *Rating:* ☆☆☆

Produced in Denmark by Nordisk; ***Directed by*** August Blom; ***Screenplay by*** Karl Ludwig Schröeder and Axel Garde; ***Based on the Novel by*** Gerhardt Hauptmann; ***Photography by*** Johann Ankerstjerne; ***Running Time:*** 113 minutes; ***Cast:*** KAMMACHER, Olaf Fonss (1882–1949); DR. RASMUSSEN, Frederik Jacobsen; DR. SCHMIDT, Carl Lauritzen; INGIGERD, Ida Orloff; MISS BURNS, Ebba Thomsen; ARTHUR STOSS (THE ARMLESS MAN), Charles Unthan

This adaptation of *Atlantis* was based on the 1912 novel by Nobel Prize winner Gerhardt Hauptmann, whose writing was inspired by the *Titanic* disaster. It is one of the pre–World War I motion pictures turned out in Europe that demonstrated that Europe was far ahead of the United States in motion picture technology before suffering setbacks caused by World War I in 1914. This was nearly a two-hour feature, and much longer than the two best American offerings of the year: *Traffic in Souls* and *Judith of Bethulia.*

Atlantis is the story of a man whose wife is mentally ill. While lead character Kammacher's wife is in an asylum, he goes to Berlin and meets an attractive dancer named Ingigerd, who spurns him. While on a ship voyage, Kammacher falls asleep and has a dream about a walk through the lost continent of Atlantis. When he wakes up, there is chaos on board, as the ship he is on, the *Roland*, is sinking.

While the story development in this film is a bit on the slow side, it features some really interesting parts. The portrayal of the sinking ship is extremely well done, especially for 1913. Contrary to popular opinion, Lon Chaney was not the first actor to play an armless man, in *The Unknown* (1927). Charles Unthan, a real amputee, performs two routines in *Atlantis*, during which he types and writes with his toes, plays cards with his toes just as any other person would do with their hands and fingers, and a variety of other feats.

138. Barney Oldfield's Race for a Life

Rating: ☆☆☆☆

Keystone/Mutual; ***Directed by*** Mack Sennett; ***Running Time:*** 11 minutes; ***Cast:*** MABEL, Mabel Normand (1892–1930); BASHFUL SUITOR, Mack Sennett (1880–1960); VILLAINOUS RIVAL, Ford Sterling (1880–1939); HIMSELF, Barney Oldfield (1878–1946); ONE OF RIVAL'S HENCHMEN, Hank Mann (1887–1971)

This is one of the very best of the early Sennett/Normand shorts, which contains a plot that is stereotypical of early silents. Mabel plays a girl with two suitors. Mack Sennett plays the bashful suitor that she prefers, and Ford Sterling plays a rival suitor whom Mabel spurns.

To get even with Mabel, Sterling's character, with two henchmen, kidnaps Mabel and has her tied to the railroad tracks, while he comes at the damsel in distress with a train going full steam. It is up to Mack, with the assistance of champion race car driver Barney Oldfield, to rescue Mabel before the train runs her over.

This film features the tongue-in-cheek portrayal of Ford Sterling as the villain whose facial expressions are exaggerated, the damsel in distress, and the great rescue. This type of plot has been used in many modern-day depictions of silents. It is still a lot of fun to watch on home video today, and is good for many laughs—as much fun today as it was over 85 years ago.

139. Cohen Saves the Flag

Rating: ☆½

Keystone/Mutual; ***Directed by*** Mack Sennett; ***Running Time:*** 12 minutes; ***Cast:*** MABEL, Mabel Normand (1892–1930); COHEN, Ford Sterling (1880–1939); COHEN'S SIDEKICK, Hank Mann (1887–1971); ***Supporting Cast:*** Edgar Kennedy (1890–1948); Nick Cogley (1869–1936)

This is a period piece that appears to be set during the Civil War. It features a large cast for a one-reel comedy, with what looks like almost 100 players.

In this film, Mabel plays a friend of two soldiers who go off to war. One of the soldiers, Cohen, is mistakenly identified as a spy and sentenced to be shot. Mabel leads soldiers on horseback to save him at the last minute.

Of the earlier Mack Sennett films, this is among the more elaborately produced.

140. The Farmer's Daughters

Rating: ☆☆☆½

Thanhouser/Princess; ***Running Time:*** 15 minutes; ***Cast:*** MURIEL, Muriel Ostriche (1896–1989)

This delightful comedy is the best surviving example of the work of Muriel Ostriche. In it, she plays one of two daughters of a farmer. The farmer—without consulting his daughters—runs an ad looking for farm help, promising the privilege of courting his daughters as one of the fringe benefits of the job.

Muriel and her sister rebel, making themselves up to look as unattractive as possible. When the college boys arrive, they are driven like slaves at gunpoint.

The Farmer's Daughters is one of the best short comedies of the early 1910s. It is absolutely hilarious, and a great opportunity to see Ostriche at her best. Fortunately, this gem is scheduled for general release on video through Thanhouser Film Preservation at a future date.

141. Hide and Seek

Rating: ☆☆

Keystone/Mutual; ***Running Time:*** 6 minutes; ***Cast:*** Mabel Normand (1892–1930); Helen Holmes (1893–1950); Nick Cogley (1869–1936)

In this film, Mabel plays "hide and seek" with a little girl in the bank she is working at. The situation goes awry when the girl cannot be found, and it is believed that she has been locked in a time-release safe.

This film features exceptionally good footage of Mabel Normand. In addition, one can see Helen Holmes in one of her earlier roles before she became famous in the late 1910s and 1920s for her railroad serials.

142. A House Divided

Rating: ☆☆☆

Solax; ***Produced/Directed by*** Alice Guy-Blaché; ***Running Time:*** 13 minutes; ***Cast:*** WIFE, Marion Swayne; HUSBAND, Fraunie Fraunholz

This comedy short is one of the extremely rare surviving examples of the work of director Alice Guy-Blaché (1875–1968). Guy-Blaché was not only the first woman to direct a film, but was also the most prolific female director in cinema history, having over 400 shorts to her credit. She started directing films in 1896 for Léon Gaumont's company in France, making her debut with *The Cabbage Fairy* (1896). Guy-Blaché was also the first person to direct a sound film, having directed the films produced with Gaumont's early Chronophone invention, first demonstrated for the public in 1901. She married husband Herbert Blaché in 1907, and they cofounded the Solax Company in 1910, which had a four-year existence.

A House Divided is a divorce comedy featuring a quarreling couple who draw up a legal agreement to live "separately" in the same house. Neither the man nor wife is permitted to speak directly to the other, and must communicate by passing notes via the maid. Eventually, the couple decides that it is too much trouble to live "separately together" and decide that it is easier to reconcile.

This comedy, as well as Alice Guy-Blaché's other evaluated film, *Matrimony's Speed Limit*, holds up well even today.

143. The House of Darkness

Rating: ☆☆½

Biograph; ***Directed by*** D.W. Griffith; ***Cast:*** THE MENTAL PATIENT, Lionel Barrymore (1878–1954); THE NURSE WHO PLAYS THE PIANO, Lillian Gish (1893–1993); THE WIFE, Claire McDowell (1878–1966); THE DOCTOR, Charles Mailes (1870–1937)

The House of Darkness explores the possibility of music being useful in calming the disposition of the mentally disturbed. The story takes place in an insane asylum. Lillian Gish plays a nurse who plays the piano. A distressed inmate suddenly calms down when he hears the piano, but once out of hearing range, flies into another rage and escapes. He ends up at a doctor's house, where the wife is alone, and threatens her with a gun. She accidentally hits the piano keys in her terror, and the lunatic asks her to play and spares her life when she complies. The practice of playing the piano becomes a regular form of therapy and makes for much more pleasant surroundings in the "house of darkness."

144. How Men Propose

Rating: ☆☆½

Crystal/Universal; ***Directed/Produced by*** Lois Weber and Phillips Smalley; ***Running Time of Existing Material:*** 5 minutes, 27 seconds; ***Cast:*** GRACE DARLING, Margarita Fischer (1886–1975); A SUITOR, Chester Barnett (1885–1947)

This early comedy, one of the extremely rare surviving films of the Universal Pictures Company when it was in its infancy, features Margarita Fischer as an attractive woman who entertains three suitors. All of the suitors propose marriage, with engagement ring in hand, which she accepts from each.

At the end of the film, each man is given his ring back with a note revealing that the woman was only using them as part of a research project for an article on the different techniques that men use in proposing marriage.

This film is possibly the only surviving work of Margarita Fischer from the prime of her career.

145. A Japanese Idyll

Rating: ☆☆

Rex/Universal; ***Directed by*** Lois Weber; ***Running Time:*** 10 minutes; ***Cast:*** THE GIRL, Lois Weber (1879–1939)

This is another of the rare surviving early Universal films. In this film, Lois Weber plays a woman whose family is determined to marry her off to a wealthy suitor. She is in love with a poor man, and elopes with him.

The early Lois Weber shorts are about average in comparison with other shorts of the same time period. They do not feature any close-ups or other advanced techniques like those in the Griffith shorts, but are not nearly as primitive as the techniques used in films such as *Queen Elizabeth* (1912) with Sarah Bernhardt. The existing print of this film has the original and vibrant color tints, which are a thing of beauty in themselves.

146. The Jazz Band

[a.k.a. *The Ragtime Band*]

Rating: ★½

Keystone; ***Directed by*** Mack Sennett; ***Running Time:*** 12 minutes; ***Cast:*** THE GIRL, Mabel Normand (1892–1930); LEADER OF THE BAND, Ford Sterling (1880–1939); BAND MEMBER, Hank Mann (1887–1971)

Members of the band fight over Mabel, who is making her debut on Amateur Night. Among the acts featured this night are a woman doing the dance of Salome, as well as a hideous duo act. When the band takes its turn, the audience starts throwing things at the band, and they retaliate with a fire hose. Hank Mann's real name was David W. Lieberman.

147. Judith of Bethulia

Rating: ★★★

Biograph; ***Directed by*** D.W. Griffith; ***Adapted from the Play by*** Thomas Bailey Aldrich; Based on the apocryphal book of Judith; ***Running Time:*** 61 minutes; ***Cast:*** JUDITH, Blanche Sweet (1896–1986); NAOMI, Mae Marsh (1895–1968); HALOFERNES, Henry B. Walthall (1878–1936); A YOUNG MOTHER, Lillian Gish (1893–1993); NATHAN, Robert Harron (1893–1920); JUDITH'S MAID, Kate Bruce (1858–1946); A CRIPPLED BEGGAR, Dorothy Gish (1898–1968)

This was D.W. Griffith's first hour-long feature, and the last film that he directed for the Biograph Company. Budgeted originally at $18,000, the film ended up costing $36,000 to produce. After this film, Biograph opted to stick with one- and two-reel shorts, and Griffith moved on to the Mutual Film Company.

The two leading players in this film are Blanche Sweet and Henry B. Walthall. Blanche Sweet plays the title role of Judith, the ruler of the settlement of Bethulia, just outside of Jerusalem. Walthall plays Halofernes, whose armies are attempting to conquer Bethulia. Knowing that Bethulia cannot possibly stand up to Halofernes' powerful army, Judith makes the decision to infiltrate his camp by seduction. Once she gains his confidence, she starts to like him, and has second thoughts about killing him. But, she thinks about the suffering and misery he has inflicted upon her people, and she beheads him, thus winning victory for Bethulia.

This biblical epic is very well done. The sets and costumes are realistic and historically accurate. Blanche Sweet is excellent as the seductress who uses her beauty to save her people. Mae Marsh, the Gish sisters, and Robert Harron can all be spotted in bit parts in the film.

In 1917, Biograph did an expanded version of *Judith of Bethulia*, and rereleased it under the title *Her Condoned Sin*. This longer version of the film would turn out to be Biograph's last release, as the executives decided to take their money and get out of the movie business rather than try to compete in the increasingly more sophisticated motion picture medium. The original four-reel version—the version that Griffith intended for public viewing—is all that is widely available at present.

148. Matrimony's Speed Limit

Rating: ★★★

Solax; ***Produced/Directed by*** Alice Guy-Blaché; ***Running Time:*** 14 minutes; ***Cast:*** THE BUSINESSMAN, Fraunie Fraunholz; THE FIANCÉE, Marion Swayne

This is another of the extremely rare extant films of female director Alice Guy-

Henry B. Walthall and Blanche Sweet in *Judith of Bethulia* (1913).

Blaché (1875–1968). As one of Guy-Blaché's three Solax films known to survive, *Matrimony's Speed Limit* features a plot very similar to that in Buster Keaton's later comedy, *Seven Chances* (1925). In this film, lead actress Marion Swayne asks her fiancée to go ahead with their marriage, but he does not feel that the time is right. To speed things up, she sends him a telegram stating that his aunt has died and left him a fortune—provided that he is married by noon that day. When Fraunie gets the telegram, he finds he only has 12 minutes to get married. Frantically, he searches in vain for any woman he can find on the street to marry him. At the last minute, Marion and Fraunie finally catch up to each other. It is only after they are married that she tells him that the telegram was a hoax.

The subtlety of this sophisticated comedy was ahead of its time, and still holds up well today. New Line Cinema recently purchased the rights to a script for a new version of *Seven Chances* (1925), demonstrating that this type of marriage comedy has as much popular appeal today as when Guy-Blaché did *Matrimony's Speed Limit* 84 years ago.

149. The Quakeress *Rating:* ☆☆½

Broncho/Mutual; ***Produced by*** Thomas H. Ince; ***Directed by*** Charles Giblyn; ***Scenario by*** Richard V. Spencer; ***Running Time:*** 28 minutes; ***Cast:*** PRISCILLA, Louise Glaum (1900–1970); JOHN HART, Charles Ray (1891–1943); THE MINISTER, William Desmond Taylor (1872–1922)

This film has historic importance as the only known surviving film available outside the archives starring the ill-fated director William Desmond Taylor. (One other film starring Taylor is said to exist in the Library of Congress.)

In *The Quakeress*, Taylor plays a Puritan minister who is suitor to Priscilla, a Quakeress who rejects him. She takes John Hart, the schoolmaster, in as a boarder, and they become good friends. When her mother dies, Hart promises to look after Priscilla.

A set of blue laws are passed, making it illegal to skip Sunday services. Priscilla is arrested and brought to trial. John Hart is on the jury and is the one holdout for acquittal. The minister has Priscilla banished from the colony, and John Hart joins her. As they are on foot, they see that their colony is about to be attacked by savage Indians, and they go back to warn the colonists who had wronged them of the impending attack. During the raid, the minister is killed, and apologizes to Priscilla just before he dies.

While some photos reveal William Desmond Taylor to have been a nice looking and debonair man, the early klieg lights and black puritan wig he wore for this film are not kind to him; he looks every day of his 42 years. There is one point in his death scene during which one can catch a glimpse of his real hair underneath the disheveled wig.

In addition to allowing a look at Taylor, this film provides a chance to see Louise Glaum at age 13 (some sources give a birthdate of 1895; if they are right, she would have been 18)—before she started playing the vamp characters that she became so famous for in the late 1910s and early 1920s.

The Quakeress came out at a time when the reform and prohibition movements were gaining prominence in the affairs of the United States, and this film seems to be a stab at the modern-day Puritanism. Unlike D.W. Griffith, who generally preferred to do social message films set in current times, Thomas Ince preferred a more subtle approach, using past history to get his messages across.

Unfortunately, this important film remains extremely rare and is not widely accessible.

150. A Strong Revenge

Rating: ☆½

Keystone/Mutual; ***Directed by*** Mack Sennett; ***Running Time:*** 12 minutes; ***Cast:*** THE GIRL, Mabel Normand (1892–1930); A SUITOR, Ford Sterling (1880–1939); A RIVAL SUITOR, Mack Sennett (1880–1960)

Mack Sennett and Ford Sterling are both vying for Mabel's affections. The rivalry results in one of the rivals putting Limburger cheese into the other's shoes.

151. Traffic in Souls

Rating: ☆☆☆½

IMP/Universal; ***Directed by*** George Loane Tucker; ***Running Time:*** 88 minutes; ***Cast:*** MARY BARTON, Jane Gail (1890–1963); LORNA BARTON, Ethel Grandin (1894–1988); ISAAC BARTON, Fred Turner (1858–1923); LARRY BURKE (OFFICER 4434), Matt Moore (1888–1960); WILLIAM TRUBUS, William Welsh (1870–1946); TRUBUS' DAUGHTER, Irene Wallace; MRS. TRUBUS, Mrs. Hudson Lyston; BILL BRADSHAW, William Cavanaugh (1876–??); THE "GO-BETWEEN," Howard Crampton (1865–1922); INSPECTOR SMITH, Charles Burbridge (1849–1922); THE CADET, Arthur Hunter; A COUNTRY GIRL, Laura Huntley; THE EMIGRANT GIRL'S BROTHER, William Powers; MR. GESHAM, William Calhoun; BOBBY GESHAM, Arthur Stein; WIRELESS OPERATOR, George Loane Tucker (1872–1921); FIRST CABIN CADET, Walter McNamara; MRS. GESHAM, Sarah McVicker; SWEDISH GIRL, Gloria Nason; HER SISTER, Vera Hansey; TELEPHONE OPERATOR, Laura McVicker; MADAME F. FORSTER, Adele Graham; MADAME MCCARROL, Blanche Craig (1866–1940)

This is highly acclaimed director George Loane Tucker's only film known to survive in complete form. Other than this film, only four minutes of *The Miracle Man* (1919) are known to exist. *Traffic in Souls* was a feature filmed on a budget of $7,500—without the knowledge of Carl Laemmle and other Universal executives, who were focusing on low budget one and two reelers. The project was financed by King Baggot, Herbert Brenon, and by Tucker himself.

This is a controversial exposé of white slavery, which was rampant at the time. It shows how girls in foreign countries were lured into the slavery by promises of good jobs, and how they were bought, sold, and abused. One police officer named Burke busts a few of the slave traffickers when he witnesses two Swedish girls being taken in by scoundrels. Unfortunately, this bust only included those who were lower on the ladder of the ring. The girls freed from bondage are quickly replaced with others—one of whom is Lorna Barton, the daughter of a famous inventor, well-portrayed by the delightful actress Ethel Grandin. Barton also happens to be the fiancée of Officer Burke.

The gang is finally brought down when Mary Barton, Lorna's older sister, gets a job as a secretary with the reform and purity league, whose offices serve as a front for the higher-ups in the slavery ring. She gathers evidence using a then-new invention of her father's—a device that records dictagraph voice recordings on to a phonograph cylinder.

Traffic in Souls was a smashing box office success, having earned its investors $500,000 on their initial investment. As Universal's first feature length film, it is a very well-produced and powerful drama. This reviewer would go as far as to say that the story narrative is better even than that of D.W. Griffith's *Judith of Bethulia*, which came out the same year.

After the success of this film, George Loane Tucker produced and directed a number of films in England. He returned to the United States in 1917, where he made about half a dozen films, including *The Miracle Man* (1919), before his death in 1921. Since the vast majority of his work was done in the 1910s—the era of silent films which has had the poorest survival rate—none of his work was believed to have survived. It was in 1972 that a print of *Traffic in Souls* was finally found and made widely available to collectors by Blackhawk Films. Kino Video released the film on video in 1994. Seeing this film makes one wish that more of Tucker's work would turn up. This one film demonstrates that Tucker was one of the greats of the pioneering directors.

1914

152. Cabiria

Rating: ☆☆☆½

Itala Film; ***Directed by*** Giovanni Pastrone; ***Story by*** Gabriele d'Annunzio; ***Running Time:*** 77 minutes; ***Cast:*** MACISTE, Bartolomeo Pagano (1878–1947); CROESSA, Lydia Quaranta (1891–1928); ***Supporting Cast:*** Umberto Mozzato

Set in North Africa during the second Punic War in the time of Alexander the Great, *Cabiria* is a tale of the conflict between Rome and Carthage. The film starts with General Hannibal, the "Sword of Carthage," crossing the Alps to attack Rome. The home of Batto, a wealthy Roman Patrician in Sicily, is destroyed when a volcano erupts. Cabiria is Batto's only child, a daughter. The governess Croessa saves Cabiria, and they are the only survivors of the entire household. They are captured by pirates and sold separately

A shot from Italy's *Cabiria* (1914), which influenced the Babylon sets in D.W. Griffith's *Intolerance* (1916).

into slavery, with the rest of the film depicting Croessa's struggle to save Cabiria from being burned as a sacrifice to Pagan gods.

The first two really big epic features, *Quo Vadis?* (1912) and *Cabiria* (1914), were made in Italy. *Cabiria* featured thousands of extras, and an elaborate sequence of destruction during the volcano eruption sequence holds up well and is impressive to watch today. One setting showed a huge temple which was shaped like a lion, with extras walking up a staircase leading into the lion's mouth. These lavish sets were what inspired D.W. Griffith's Babylon story setting for *Intolerance* (1916). *Cabiria* was so popular in the United States that it was given a special screening in the White House.

Director Giovanni Pastrone (1883–1959) made his directorial debut in 1908, and was one of the leaders of the Italian cinema in its golden age from the early 1910s through the mid–1920s. Some sources state that Enrico Guazzone, who directed *Quo Vadis?* (1912), was a codirector on this film as well, but most sources list Pastrone only.

Bartolomeo Pagano, a former dock worker, plays the "gentle giant" who takes Cabiria under his wing after being given a magic ring by Croessa. Heroine Croessa is played by Lydia Quaranta who, with her two younger twin sisters Letizia and Isabella (1892–??), was one of a trio of sisters who were leading players in early Italian cinema.

Gabriele d'Annunzio was among Italy's most renowned writers of the period, and his work on *Cabiria* brought even more prestige to the production. This film is a monumental part of motion picture history that led the way for American directors such as D.W. Griffith to move beyond the one and two reelers and into feature films. It remains an interesting film to watch today, and is must-see viewing for serious film historians.

153. Cinderella

Rating: ☆☆☆½

Paramount; ***Directed by*** James Kirkwood; ***Running Time:*** 51 minutes; ***Cast:*** CINDERELLA, Mary Pickford (1892–1979); THE PRINCE, Owen Moore (1886–1939); FAIRY GODMOTHER, Georgeia Wilson; WICKED WITCH, Lillianne Leighton (1874–1956)

When Mary Pickford left the Griffith company after *The New York Hat* (1912), she went to Paramount Pictures. Her first five pictures for Paramount were directed by Edwin S. Porter (1870–1941). After *Tess of the Storm Country* (1914), Pickford worked in nine films under the direction of James Kirkwood, Sr. (1875–1963). *Cinderella* was Pickford's ninth feature film for Paramount, and her third under Kirkwood's direction. This is also one of the two features that Pickford costarred in with first husband Owen Moore.

Cinderella is among the rarest of the existing Pickford films. For years, it was not believed to have survived, but a print turned up in a Dutch archive in Amsterdam in the mid–1990s. The surviving print material is beautiful, with the color tints preserved as well. (It is said that a print of *Cinderella* with English titles is archived at the George Eastman House.)

This is a wonderful adaptation of the classic fairy tale, with some original elements that are unique to this version. In the magic sequences, the coach and footmen are gradually faded into the picture. The effect is not as striking as the special effects in the 1911 Thanhouser version of *Cinderella*, which just shows various objects appearing out of thin air, but it is interesting to see how this experimental effect came across. There is also a dream sequence that comes in after the ball sequence, in which Cinderella sees the clock about to strike midnight, with two midgets striking the bell and then proceeding to wreck the clock, with the hands and numbers scrambling around as the clock goes haywire.

Another interesting element in this version of *Cinderella* is that the wicked stepsisters (who were played by men in drag) consult a wicked witch and her midget thugs when they want to look beautiful at the ball. This element better defines the association of the ugly stepsisters with evil, contrasting them to the beautiful fairy godmother who helps Cinderella when she is left behind, dressed in rags.

Mary Pickford and Owen Moore had been married for four years when they made this film. It is also interesting to note that Owen Moore, who plays the prince in this *Cinderella* adaptation, was the brother of Tom Moore (1883–1955), who played the role of the prince 11 years later in *A Kiss for Cinderella* (1925).

Currently, all available copies of this film not held at the George Eastman House have Dutch titles, but the story is well-enough-told visually that the foreign titles do not detract from the enjoyment of the film. This is a good film with a classic story line, and was among the most popular of Pickford's earliest features. Hopefully, this version of *Cinderella* will eventually be made widely available on video and have the wider modern-day audience that it deserves.

154. The Decoy

Rating: ☆☆½

Thanhouser/Princess; ***Scenario by*** Philip Lonergan; ***Running Time:*** 16 minutes; ***Cast:*** MURIEL, Muriel Ostriche (1896–1989); JOHN HENDERSON/MR. VINCENT, Charles Horan (1882–1928); HIS WIFE, Marie Rainford; JANE PHELPS, Virginia Waite; A MILLIONAIRE, Morgan Jones (1879–1951); BOYD, A BUSINESSMAN AND MURIEL'S BOYFRIEND, Boyd Marshall (1885–1950)

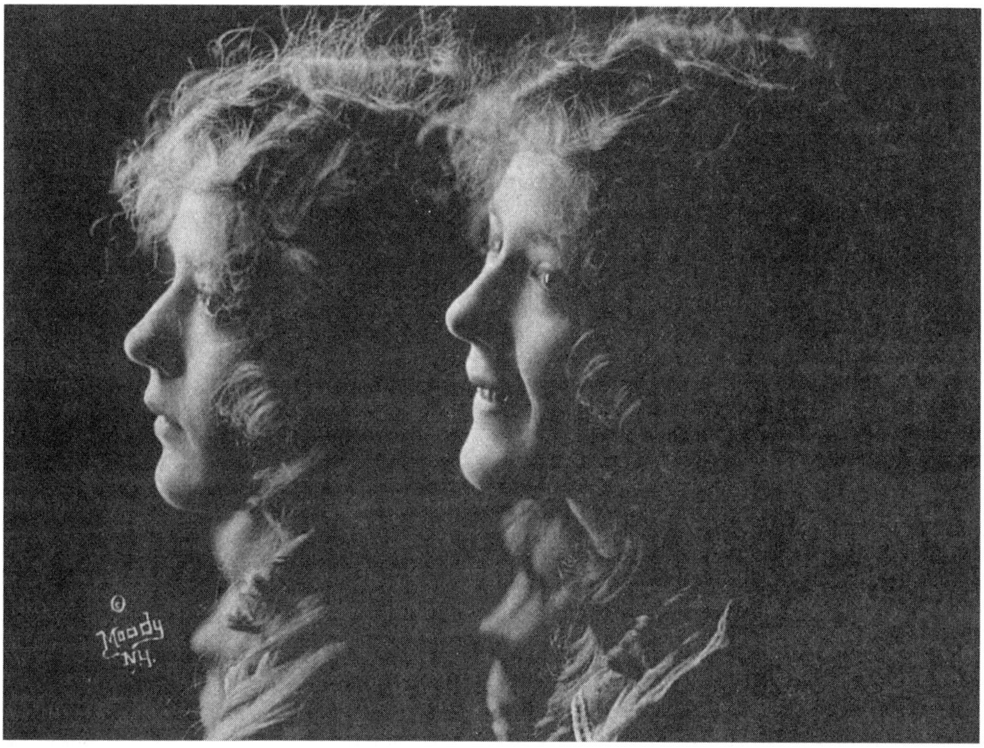

Mary Pickford, around the time that she appeared in *Cinderella* (1914).

This one-reeler is one of only two surviving films of silent screen actress Muriel Ostriche. Ostriche was at the height of her fame in 1913, and one popularity poll placed her second only to Alice Joyce. From 1915 to 1920 she was known not only for her work in films, but as the "Moxie girl" whose face adorned the Moxie soft drink advertisements. She married in 1921, and retired from films at that time.

In this film, Ostriche plays a country girl who visits with her city relatives. The aunt and uncle use her to lure wealthy patrons to their card sharking operation. Muriel ends up exposing the aunt and uncle, and marrying the undercover police investigator.

155. A Dog's Love

Rating: ☆☆☆

Thanhouser; ***Directed by*** John Harvey; ***Scenario by*** Nolan Gane; ***Running Time:*** 11 minutes, 12 seconds; ***Cast:*** BABY HELEN, Helen Badgely (1908–1977); HELEN'S FATHER, Arthur Bauer (1878–??); HELEN'S MOTHER, Ethyle Cook Benham; A VISITOR, Fan Bourke (1886–1959)

Animal lovers will especially love this film, which features "Baby Helen" Badgely, who was Marie Eline's successor to the throne of the "Thanhouser kidlet." In this film, she plays a poor little rich girl who has no friends, but finally finds companionship in the neighbor's dog, Shep, who is played by the animal star known as "the Thanhouser collie." Shortly after they have become friends, tragedy strikes when Helen is hit by a car. Shep summons help immediately, but Baby Helen dies later. The grieving dog refuses to eat and makes daily trips to the florist to put flowers on Helen's grave. The dog is consoled somewhat when Helen's ghost appears (filmed by using double exposure), demonstrating that her love for the dog went beyond life. Just when you start to cry, a title flashes on the screen which says, "Don't cry—it's only make believe," and shows Helen Badgely and her dog embracing in real life. This film really demonstrates what an emotional impact a mere 11 minutes of film can have.

156. Fatty and the Bathing Beauties *Rating:* ☆☆☆

Keystone/Mutual; ***Directed by*** Mack Sennett; ***Running Time:*** 10 minutes; ***Cast:*** FATTY, Roscoe Arbuckle (1887–1933); MABEL [A BATHING BEAUTY], Mabel Normand (1892–1930); "HANDSIM HARRY," Mack Sennett (1880–1960); KEYSTONE COP, Slim Summerville (1892–1946)

This is a short featuring Mabel Normand as a bathing beauty. "Handsim Harry" is a scoundrel making passes at the women. Fatty gets into a number of misadventures with Harry, and Mabel takes an unexpected ride in a hot air balloon, courtesy of Harry. Arbuckle's striped bathing suit is especially enjoyable, as are some of the other beachwear styles of the time.

157. A Fool There Was *Rating:* ☆☆½

Fox; ***Directed by*** Frank Powell; Based on Rudyard Kipling's 1897 poem, *The Vampire*; ***Running Time:*** 67 minutes; ***Cast:*** THE VAMP, Theda Bara (1885–1955); THE CHILD, Runa Hodges; THE WIFE (MRS. SCHUYLER), Mabel Frenyear; THE HUSBAND (MR. JOHN SCHUYLER), Edward José (died 1930); WIFE'S SISTER, May Allison (1890–1989); THE FRIEND, Clifford Bruce (1885–1919); ONE OF THE VICTIMS, Victor Benoit (1877–1943); THE DOCTOR, Frank Powell; DOCTOR'S FIANCEE, Minna Gale

This is one of only four Theda Bara movies in existence, and the only example of her extremely popular vamp movies that has survived. The only other Bara film widely available for evaluation is *The Unchastened Woman* (1925). *Madame Mystery* (1926), her last film, was originally two reels long, and currently exists only in the form of a one-reel version. *East Lynne* (1916), one of Bara's few nonvamp movies from the height of her career, is held in archives.

The story starts out with some shots of the happy family of the prosperous John Schuyler. We then see the vamp, Theda Bara, reading a newspaper article about how Schuyler is leaving on a cruise ship for an important assignment in Europe, and decides at this point that he will be her next victim. When her current victim sees her packing her clothes after having taken what she can get from him, she replies that it was simply a ruse to test his true love. In the process, she picks his pocket and takes his wallet. Once she boards the ship, he follows her. He has a gun and threatens her, and she just casually beats the gun down with a rose, and he turns the gun on himself. Just when his body is being carried off the ship, none other than John Schuyler is arriving. Bara's vamp wreaks havoc on Schuyler and his entire family. The movie ends with Theda pouring rose pedals all over Schuyler's body, and laughing at the demise of yet another victim.

Since this was Theda Bara's first film, produced at a time when the movies were still in their relatively primitive stages, it is not fair to judge Bara's performance. At some points in this film, she overacts to the point of being ridiculous. Nonetheless, it is an entertaining film, and gives us an idea of what her later films improved on as the film techniques become more polished.

This movie is often erroneously acknowledged as the first major vamp film. In actuality, the first vamp film came a year before this one, in 1913. Alice Hollister (1886–1973) played the leading role in the 1913 Kalem film *The Vampire*. (The original negative of this first vamp film is held at the George Eastman House.) Although Theda Bara was not technically the first vamp, she was by far the most popular and most famous, with many imitators including Betty Blythe and Virginia Pearson.

158. Hearts and Diamonds

Rating: ☆☆☆

Vitagraph; ***Running Time:*** 11 minutes; ***Cast:*** John Bunny (1863–1915); Flora Finch (1869–1940)

John Bunny plays a widower with three daughters who seeks to marry a wealthy widow, portrayed by Flora Finch. This film has a hilarious sequence at the beginning of the film, in which Bunny's daughters have a party with male guests, and Bunny bodily throws the guests out—one by one going down the line. He then packs his daughters off to their uncle's, thinking that the wealthy widow will be more attracted to a bachelor than a widower with daughters. Learning that the widow is an avid baseball fan, Bunny forms his own team. He starts the game by striking out, and it is humorous to see the tantrum he throws.

This is among the best of the Bunny/Finch films. John Bunny's brand of comedy was more situational than the slapstick that was so prevalent at the time.

159. His Trysting Places

Rating: ☆☆☆

Keystone/Mutual; ***Directed by*** Charles Chaplin; ***Edited and Titled by*** Sydney Chaplin; ***Running Time:*** 21 minutes; ***Cast:*** THE HUSBAND, Charles Chaplin (1889–1977); THE WIFE, Mabel Normand (1892–1930); CHARLIE'S BAR ACQUAINTANCE, Mack Swain (1876–1935); HIS WIFE, Phyllis Allen (1861–1938)

This is a marital comedy with Chaplin playing the lazy husband of Mabel. A trip to the drug store for a bottle for the baby results in a bar meeting with Mack Swain. Their coats get mixed up, and Chaplin returns home with a love note in his pocket, while Swain goes back to his wife with the baby bottle.

This is a hilarious situation comedy, with some slapstick as well. Chaplin and Normand made a good team on screen, and this is one of the better early comedies that Chaplin directed with Keystone.

There has been some question as to whether the proper title for this film is *His Trysting Place* or *His Trysting Places*. Most prints of the film available on video today use the singular form of the noun, but Chaplin scholars have determined that the plural form is the correct one.

160. The Locket

Rating: ☆☆

[a.k.a. *When She Was Twenty*]

Vitagraph; ***Running Time:*** 12 minutes; ***Cast:*** John Bunny (1863–1915); Flora Finch (1869–1940); Leah Baird (1883–1971); Robert Gaillord (1868–1941)

In this Bunny/Finch comedy, Leah Baird plays a woman who accidentally puts her locket with her portrait into Judge Jones' (played by Bunny) pocket instead of her own while riding in a trolley car. Interesting situations arise when Evelyn, wife of the judge (played by Finch), finds the locket in his pocket.

161. The Magic Cloak of Oz

Rating: ☆☆☆½

Oz Film Company; ***Directed by*** L. Frank Baum; ***Running Time:*** 37 minutes; ***Cast:*** FLUFF, Mildred Harris (1902–1944); TIMOTHY [BUD], Violet McMillan (1887–1953); NICKODEMUS, Fred Woodward

This is one of the three films produced by the Oz Film Company, and is one of the two directed by original "Oz" author L. Frank Baum (who died in 1919) after he fired J. Farrell MacDonald.

In this film, the enchanted fairies of the ancient forest have made a magic cloak that has the ability to grant one wish to whomever it is given. The moon instructs the fairies to give the cloak to the most unhappy person they can find, who happens to be Fluff, a girl who has just left the home that she loves.

The fairies give her the cloak, and her wish is to be happy again. Meanwhile, her friend Bud has been appointed the new king of Noland, after being the 47th person to enter the palace gates after the original king dies.

Another part of the story deals with Nickodemus—a live donkey played by Fred Woodward in costume—who is kidnapped by a gang of robbers. They have also kidnapped a little girl named Mary. While in the robbers' camp, Nickodemus encounters a lonely zoop, who is a gorilla-type character, as well as the lion. The zoop and lion fight with each other, and Nickodemus meets a friendly crow, who conspires with him to get the forest animals together against the gang of robbers.

Meanwhile, Fluff and King Bud are spending all of Noland's money on toys. Nickodemus and the animals rescue Mary from the robbers and return to Noland.

The villain of the story is Nixi, the queen of the kingdom of Ix, who is actually 683 years old. She has angered one of the higher powers and is forced to carry a mirror that reflects her true age. Queen Nixi steals Fluff's magic cloak to break the spell, and the fairies tell her that since she stole it, it won't grant her wish. Meanwhile, creatures known as the "Rolly Rogues"—big, fat, rotund beings that eat everything in sight—descent upon Noland, and King Bud and Fluff must recover the cloak to wish the Rolly Rogues away.

Although this film did not have the fancy special effects of *The Patchwork Girl of Oz*, it is in many ways an improvement over the debut film of the series. Under L. Frank Baum's direction, *The Magic Cloak of Oz* sports a simpler and more polished narrative style. Also, Baum realized the charm of Mildred Harris and gave

Segment from an original decomposing 35 mm nitrate print of Mabel Normand in Charlie Chaplin's *His Trysting Places* (1914).

her a much bigger role in this film than she had in the prior film. While J. Farrell MacDonald later did good directorial work, he was just really starting to learn film technique (as was everyone else) at this point in his career. L. Frank Baum, as the author of the "Oz" stories, knew exactly how he envisioned these films to look, and thus had an advantage over MacDonald.

For many years, none of the original Oz films were known to have survived. Prints were rediscovered by the American Film Institute in the early 1970s and rescued.

Unfortunately, the Oz films bombed at the box office, and the Oz Film Company was shut down after less than a year. It is hard to fathom why these films failed, as they stand the test of time and are a delight to watch 83 years after they were produced. It is fortunate that the three films survived and are all widely available on video.

162. The Man from Texas *Rating* ☆☆

Selig; ***Directed by*** Tom Mix?; ***Edited and Titled by*** Donald I. Buchanan; ***Running Time:*** 42 minutes; ***Cast:*** TEXAS, Tom Mix (1880–1940); MOYA DALTON, Bessie Eyton (1890–1965)

Western actor Tom Mix made his film debut in 1909, the year he won the national riding and rodeo championship. From 1911 to 1917, he directed and starred in over 100 films for Selig, and rose to fame as one of the most popular of all western film actors, at this time second only to William S. Hart and possibly William and Dustin Farnum.

The Man From Texas is one of Mix's earliest surviving films that is widely available for evaluation. In this film, he plays Texas, a man who is seeking revenge on Bill Hargreaves, his sister's husband who left her and caused her to commit suicide. In his search for his ex-brother-in-law, Texas encounters Moya Dalton, whom he rescues from Hargreaves before shooting him in self-defense. He falls in love with her, although she at first rejects him. He wins her in the end when he captures the cattle rustlers who target her ranch.

While the story of this film sounds like it would be interesting, as one of Mix's earlier efforts, it is a bit more slow paced than expected, and not nearly as polished as his later films of the 1920s. While not among Mix's best films, this film is worth watching for its historic value, and has some excellent footage of Bessie Eyton, who costarred with Mix in many of his early Selig westerns.

163. The Patchwork Girl of Oz *Rating:* ☆☆☆

Oz Film Company; ***Directed by*** J. Farrell MacDonald; ***Running Time:*** 62 minutes; ***Cast:*** THE "OZ" GIRL, Vivian Reed (1893–1989); DOROTHY, Mildred Harris (1902–1944); DANX, Pierre Couderc (1896–1966); OJO [MUNCHKIN BOY], Violet McMillan (1887–1953); UNC NUNKIE, Frank Moore (1880–1924); DR. PIPT [CROOKED MAGICIAN], Raymond Russell; JINJER, Juanita Hansen (1895–1961); MARGOLOTTE PIPT, Haras Dranet; MUEL [STRAY DONKEY]/WOOZY, Fred Woodward; ***Extras:*** Harold Lloyd (1893–1971); Hal Roach (1892–1992)

This was the first of the three "Oz" movies produced by the short-lived Oz Film Company that was established by L. Frank Baum (who died in 1919) for the purpose of producing movies based on his popular "Oz" novels.

The Patchwork Girl of Oz is a delightful story of a boy and his father going to Oz to escape poverty. The boy ends up working at the home of a magician, who is working to bring a patch doll to life for use as a slave. Ojo slips in some magic formulas that will give the doll the ability to rebel, thus foiling the magician's plans.

Somehow, Ojo's father, along with Dorothy and Danx, are turned into statues, and the quest is on for ingredients needed for the magic potion to bring them back to life. A number of obstacles are overcome in the course of the journey to acquire the ingredients.

While this film is somewhat primitive in technique, it is still a charming film. The trick photography showing the doll assembling itself, the cast disappearing into a wall and reappearing on the other side, and a table setting itself are quite impressive and well done for the time.

J. Farrell MacDonald, the director, apparently did not present this film in a manner that was satisfactory to producer L. Frank Baum, and was fired after completing it.

164. The Perils of Pauline *Rating:* ☆☆

Pathé/Eclectic; ***Directed by*** Louis Gasnier; ***Running Time of Available Footage:*** 200 minutes; ***Cast:*** PAULINE MARVIN, Pearl White (1889–1938); HARRY MARVIN, Crane Wilbur (1886–1973); KOERNER [SECRETARY/VILLAIN], Paul Panzer (1872–1958)

This early directorial effort by Louis Gasnier was the fourth serial made, and the most famous of them all. In addition, it is the oldest serial that is available on videocassette in semicomplete form, as all that is available on earlier serials is a random chapter or two. Originally filmed in 20 episodes, the versions of this serial that are widely available today contain nine chapters.

If you expect cliffhanger endings with Pauline tied to the railroad tracks (as was portrayed in the 1947 movie *The Perils of Pauline*), you will be disappointed to see that such does not happen in the available footage. *The Perils of Pauline* was produced before the cliffhanger format became commonplace in serials. If there was an episode in which Pauline was tied to the railroad tracks, it is not among the chapters that are available for evaluation. The perils of bombed ships, runaway hot air balloons, being trapped in a burning house, and a rigged auto race are among those resolved in these chapters.

In summary, *The Perils of Pauline* is about a wealthy orphan heiress who is currently living with her guardian and his son. Pauline and Harry Marvin are urged by the family to marry. The son, Harry, is more than willing, but Pauline is not. She first wants to have at least one year of freedom to experience exotic adventures to write about in a novel she is planning to write. Her guardian dies and leaves the responsibility of managing Pauline's fortune (until her marriage) to his secretary Koerner. Little does the father know that Koerner is an escaped prisoner being blackmailed. He is desperate for money and willing to stoop to any level to get it.

Throughout Pauline's adventures Koerner and his accomplice scheme to cause Pauline's death or "disappearance" in hopes of getting their grubby hands on the fortune with which Koerner has been entrusted. Therefore, the attempts to cash in turn "the adventures of Pauline" into "the perils of Pauline."

This is an important contribution to motion picture history, as it was the first serial to become a box office hit. It was also one of the more expensive undertakings of the time, costing $25,000 to produce. *The Perils of Pauline* established Pearl White as a major star. Although this reviewer was rather disappointed with the entertainment value of this serial, it is still one that every silent film buff should see.

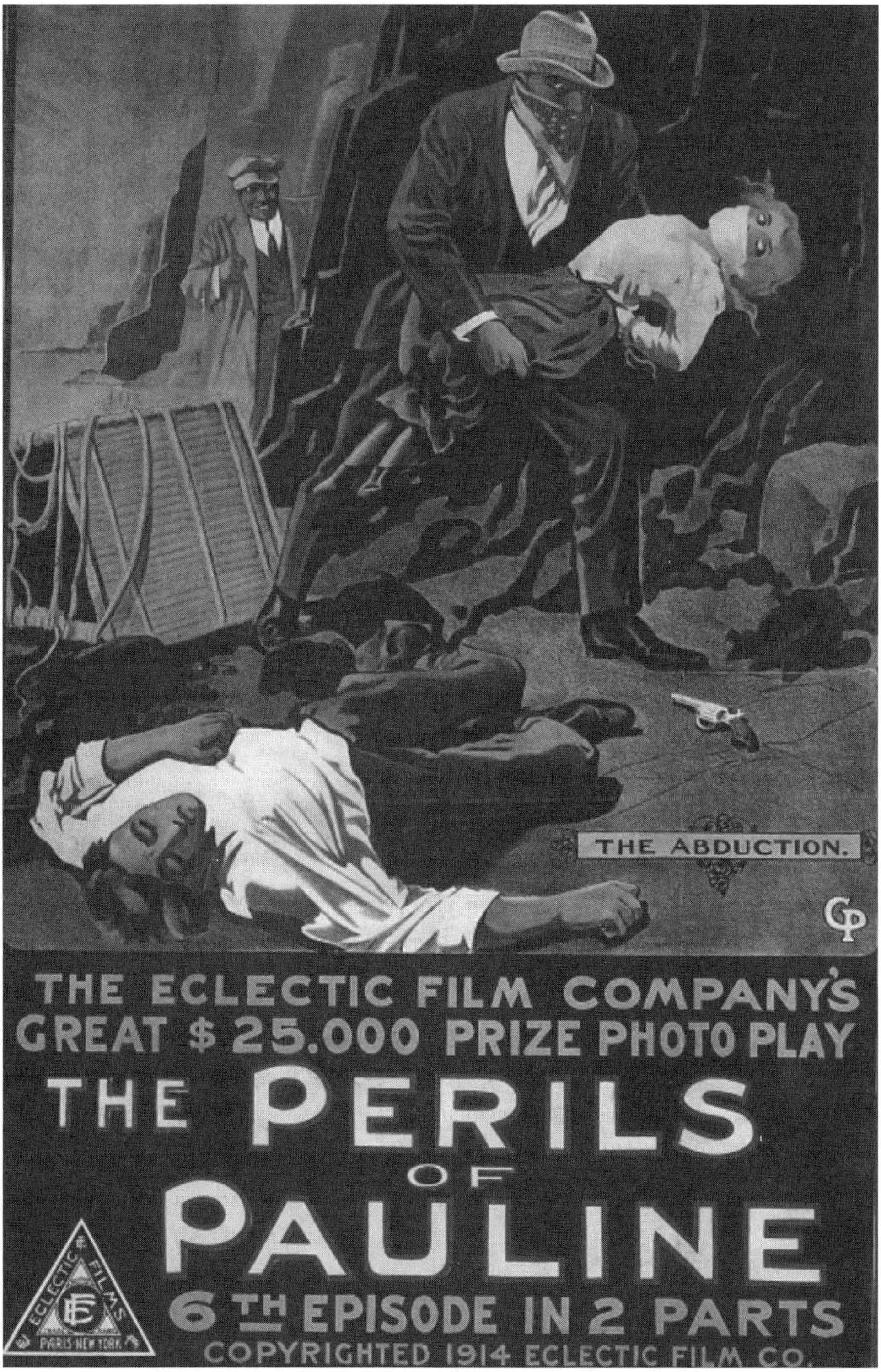

Advertisement for Pearl White's *The Perils of Pauline* (1914).

Some sources state that Milton Berle (born 1908) appeared in a bit part in this film at age 6, but this reviewer has not yet been able to spot him in any of the available chapters.

When interviews were conducted with people who grew up during the silent era, the vast majority said that the Pearl White serials made the greatest impressions in their memories. Much of Pearl White's work is known to exist in American and foreign archives. Unfortunately, very little of it has been made widely available to the public. Three of her early comedies for the Crystal Company are available, as well as her last film, *Terror* (1924). No Pearl White serials are available in complete form. Other than this fragmented version of *The Perils of Pauline*, the only other white serial footage available is a couple of chapters from her last serial, *Plunder* (1923), and a couple of episodes of *The Exploits of Elaine* (1915).

165. Rumpelstiltskin: A Fairy Story

Rating: ☆☆☆½

New York Motion Picture Company/Mutual; ***Directed by*** Thomas H. Ince; ***Running Time:*** 45 minutes; ***Cast:*** RUMPELSTILTSKIN, Clyde Tracy; POLLY CROW, Elizabeth Burbridge (1895–1987); PRINCE COLE, Kenneth Browne; JIM CROW (THE MILLER), J. Barney Sherry (1874–1944); CAPTAIN PILKIN, George Fischer; GOOD FAIRY, Margaret Thompson (1889–1969); KING COLE, Louis Morrison (1866–1946); SIMPLE SIMON, H.C. Kern (1894–1985)

This early adaptation of *Rumpelstiltskin* was produced during the transition period in which movie production was moving from the East Coast to the West Coast. At four reels, it was one of the longer films of 1914, when features were still in the experimental stages.

In this version of the classic fairy tale, Rumpelstiltskin is portrayed as a villain from the very beginning, turning a character named Simple Simon into a pig for mocking him. The dwarf then offers Jim Crow, the miller, a bag of gold for his daughter, Polly. The miller refuses, and Polly, in the meantime, has fallen in love with Prince Cole, the son of King Cole, and promises to meet him the next day. While waiting for her prince, Polly is kidnapped by Rumpelstiltskin. Simple Simon, as a pig, witnesses the act, is finally changed back by the good fairy, and leads the prince to Rumpelstiltskin's cave. The prince rescues Polly.

It turns out that King Cole's treasury is empty. Hearing of Rumpelstiltskin's magic powers, the king summons the dwarf. To get revenge on Jim Crow for refusing to sell Polly to him, the dwarf tells the king that the daughter has the ability to spin straw into gold. Polly is summoned by the king and ordered to perform the task. The lecherous dwarf then appears before her and offers to spin the straw into gold—in exchange for her first-born daughter. Having no other choice, she agrees to the pact. King Cole, meanwhile, has imprisoned his son due to his objections to the planned marriage. So, once Polly is freed, she goes to the good fairy, who gives her a magic carpet on which she and the prince can escape. When their first child, a daughter, is born, Rumpelstiltskin comes to claim the baby. In the end, Rumpelstiltskin is sentenced to spin straw into gold for the rest of his life.

Most of the performers in this film have been long forgotten by film historians. Clyde Tracy, who shares top billing with Elizabeth Burbridge, is not mentioned in any other film history books. His receiving top billing indicates that he was obviously a significant actor whose name was widely recognized at the time. His appearance as Rumpelstiltskin reminds one of Lon Chaney, Sr.'s, "Fagin" character in the 1923 version of *Oliver Twist*. Elizabeth Burbridge is listed under the nicknames of "Tommy" and "Betty" in various sources.

This film adaptation of *Rumpelstiltskin* is a delightful and magical film. It contains basic special effects that, although primitive, come across nicely. It is surprising that none of the video companies offer this public domain title on video. There are a few extremely poor quality video copies that circulate among a few private collectors, but they are barely watchable. *Rumpelstiltskin: A Fairy Story* is a title that deserves to be released in a better quality video format than what is currently available through private collectors. The original nitrate negative for this film is reportedly preserved in the Museum of Modern Art.

166. The Speed Kings

Rating: ☆☆

Keystone/Mutual; ***Directed by*** Wilfred Lucas; ***Running Time:*** 8 minutes; ***Cast:*** MABEL, Mabel Normand (1892–1930); A SPEED DEMON [FATHER'S CHOICE], Earl Cooper (1886–1965); THE SPEED KING [MABEL'S CHOICE], Teddy Tetzlaff (1883–1929); ***Supporting Cast:*** Barney Oldfield (1878–1946); Roscoe Arbuckle (1887–1933); Ford Sterling (1880–1939); Paul Jacobs

In this film, Mabel has two race car drivers as suitors. Her father prefers that she marry Earl Cooper. Mabel prefers Teddy Tetzlaff. As a result, her father tries to sabotage Teddy's car.

This is one of the earliest directorial efforts of Wilfred Lucas (1871–1940), whose career started as an actor with Biograph in 1907. He was best known for his acting. He played the title role in D.W. Griffith's *Enoch Arden* (1911), and also starred with Blanche Sweet in *The Lonedale Operator* (1911). Among the significant silent features he appeared in was Mary Pickford's *Dorothy Vernon of Haddon Hall* (1924).

167. The Spoilers

Rating: ☆☆☆

Selig; ***Directed by*** Colin Campbell; ***Produced by*** Colonel William N. Selig; ***Screenplay by*** Lanier Bartlett; ***Based on the 1906 Novel by*** Rex Beach; ***Photography by*** Harry W. Gerstad; ***Running Time:*** 98 minutes; ***Cast:*** ROY GLENNISTER, William Farnum (1876–1953); HELEN CHESTER, Bessie Eyton (1890–1965); ALEX MCNAMARA, Tom Santschi (1880–1931); CHERRY MALOTTE, Kathlyn Williams (1888–1960); BRONCHO KID, Wheeler Oakman (1890–1949); DEXTRY, Frank M. Clark (1857–1945); SLAPJACK, Jack F. McDonald (1880–??)

This was the first of five film adaptations (1914, 1923, 1930, 1942, and 1955) of Rex Beach's 1906 western classic, and it was acclaimed as the version most faithful to the novel—if not the best of the film adaptations. The film opens with Glennister and Cherry Malotte breaking up. Roy Glennister is the good buy, whose claim to a gold mine is brought into question. Cherry Malotte, owner of the local saloon, is still in love with Glennister, and proves to be his ally despite the fact that she is jealous of the friendship he has with Helen Chester. Malotte's card dealer, Broncho Kid, is in love with her, and, together with the corrupt gold commissioner McNamara, plots to seize Glennister's mine and frame him for murder. The situation comes to a head in a final showdown between Glennister and McNamara.

The Spoilers was one of the greatest critical and box office successes of the Selig Polyscope Company, featuring an all-star cast in the four main roles in the film. Serial queen

Kathlyn Williams of *The Adventures of Kathlyn* (1913) fame is unforgettable as Cherry Malotte in what is perhaps the finest role of her career. Bessie Eyton, whose career began in 1911, had no stage experience before entering films. Her role in this film and in Tom Mix's *In the Days of the Thundering Herd* (1914) made her one of Selig's most popular leading ladies. She stayed popular until the mid–1920s. The late 1920s and early 1930s saw Eyton in bit parts, and after a fight with her mother, she walked out of her house and was never heard from again. In 1996, film historian Billy Doyle finally found out the sad story of Eyton's last years. She died at 75 in a charity shelter in 1965, after having apparently suffered from years of chronic alcoholism.

Tom Santschi and William's Farnum's brawl sequence at the end of this film is widely acclaimed. Upon viewing this sequence, this reviewer was expecting a protracted knockdown, dragout, but it is actually a short sequence that falls far short of expectations and is disappointing.

Despite the disappointment of the brawl sequence and the primitive style of this film, this original screen version of *The Spoilers* is still a well done film worth seeing.

168. Tess of the Storm Country *Rating:* ☆☆☆

Paramount; ***Written, Photographed, and Directed by*** Edwin S. Porter; ***Based on the Story by*** Grace Miller White; ***Running Time:*** 80 minutes; ***Cast:*** TESSIBEL SKINNER, Mary Pickford (1892–1979); FREDERICK GRAVES, Harold Lockwood (1887–1918); TEOLA GRAVES, Olive Fuller Golden (1896–1988) [a.k.a. OLIVE CAREY, WIFE OF HARRY CAREY, SR.]; DADDY SKINNER, David Hartford (1873–1932); ELDER GRAVES, W. R. Walters; ***Supporting Cast:*** Lorraine Thompson; Louise Dunlap (1865–1940); Richard Garrick (1878–1962); Jack Henry; H. R. Macy; Eugene Walter (1874–1941); H. L. Griffith (1866–1926).

This first of four screen versions of *Tess of the Storm Country* has historic significance as the earliest surviving feature length Mary Pickford film. It was her fifth film for Paramount. *Tess* is also significant as the only extant feature length film directed by Edwin S. Porter (*The Count of Monte Cristo* [1913] was codirected with Joseph Golden). Furthermore, it is the only surviving feature length film of actor Harold Lockwood to survive. All that otherwise survives on Lockwood are a couple of shorts. He made over 150 films before his death at 31 in the Spanish flu epidemic. Thus, we have three rarities combined into this one film.

The story is familiar, and is detailed in depth in the review of Pickford's 1922 remake of *Tess*. The big difference with this adaptation is in Edwin S. Porter's directorial style. While he did a competent job in portraying the events in the story, he had not yet developed techniques for enhancing dramatic value and building suspense. It is these factors that made the 1922 version the superior of the two silent versions.

This was the film that really helped to boost Mary Pickford to major stardom in the motion picture industry being her first real box office blockbuster. Of the pre–1915 Paramount films available for evaluation, this, along with Pickford's *Cinderella* (1914), are by far the best.

Tess of the Storm Country was remade twice in the talkie era. The 1932 version was produced by Fox and directed by Alfred Santell, starring Janet Gaynor in the title role. In 1960, a version directed by Paul Guilfoyle and starring Diane Baker was released under the 20th Century–Fox banner. Neither of the two sound remakes are available on video. This original 1914 version is not yet available to the general public on video, either. It is certainly worth seeing for its historic value alone.

169. Tillie's Punctured Romance

Rating: ☆☆☆☆

Mack Sennett Company; ***Directed by*** Mack Sennett; ***Running Time:*** 73 minutes; ***Cast:*** THE CITY SLICKER, Charlie Chaplin (1889–1977); TILLIE BANKS, Marie Dressler (1869–1934); CHARLIE'S CITY GIRLFRIEND, Mabel Normand (1892–1930); TILLIE'S FATHER, Mack Swain (1876–1935); SOCIETY GUEST, Chester Conklin (1886–1971); CAFE OWNER, Edgar Kennedy (1890–1948); DETECTIVE, Charlie Chase (1893–1940); DETECTIVE, Charlie Murray (1872–1941); SOCIETY GUEST, Ford Sterling (1880–1939); NEWSPAPER BOY, Milton Berle (born 1908); ***Keystone Cops:*** Slim Summerville (1892–1946); Hank Mann (1887–1971); Roscoe Arbuckle (1887–1933); Eddie Sutherland (1897–1973)

This was the world's first feature length comedy, featuring an all-star supporting cast centered around Marie Dressler, the top billed star of the film. Dressler first acted on the Broadway stage in 1892 at age 22, and was by 1914 one of the premiere comediennes of the stage. *Tillie's Punctured Romance* was an adaptation of one of her popular stage plays.

In this film, she plays Tillie Banks, a poor and gullible farmer's daughter who is conned by Charlie, a dapper man from the city, into taking her father's mortgage money and going to the city. Once in the city, Charlie and Tillie run into Mabel, his girlfriend. Tillie gets drunk, and Charlie and Mabel abscond with her money. When Tillie can't pay the cafe check, she ends up in jail, and is riotously funny in her misadventures with the Keystone Cops while in her intoxicated state. She is released from jail when it is learned that her uncle is "Old Money" Banks, but cannot go back home without the mortgage money, with which Charlie and Mabel are having a grand time. So, Tillie takes a job as a scrubwoman to make back the money that she took from the farm.

As she is scrubbing floors, Charlie reads that Tillie has just inherited $3 million from her uncle, and he immediately comes back and rushes her to a pastor for a quick marriage ceremony. The fun in the film really starts when the newlyweds make their high society debut, with Charlie's girlfriend Mabel ending up as one of the servants!

As the first slapstick feature, *Tillie's Punctured Romance* remains one of the best and funniest. It stands as one of director Mack Sennett's (1880–1960) finest films. Charlie Chaplin's role as the city slicker is far more appealing to this reviewer than the "tramp" character he would invent the next year. It is refreshing to see Mabel Normand in her prime as well, at a time before numerous heartaches and tragedies entered her life.

Virtually every supporting player in this film went on to great success as comedians in their own right—including Charlie Chase, who can be seen as a detective sitting next to Chaplin and Normand in the theater sequence. Chase had a successful directing and acting career into the late 1930s, just before alcoholism led to his death at age 46 from a heart attack in 1940. His real name was Charles Parrott, which he sometimes used on screen, and his brother was comedy director Paul Parrott (1892–1939), also known as James Parrott.

Roscoe Arbuckle can be briefly glimpsed as a Keystone Cop during the finale of the film. Even the young 6-year-old boy who made a cameo as a newspaper boy went

Original promotional advertisement for *Tillie's Punctured Romance* (1914).

on to stardom—as famed television comedian Milton Berle, who still appears in occasional guest spots in television sitcoms today, over 83 years after his debut in *Tillie's Punctured Romance.*

The smashing success of this film resulted in two followups starring Marie Dressler: *Tillie's Tomato Surprise* (1915) and *Tillie Wakes Up* (1917). *Tillie's Tomato Surprise* is lost, but the latter sequel exists and is available from Grapevine Video. Eddie Sutherland, who played a Keystone Cop in this film, went on in 1928 to direct a remake for Paramount Pictures that starred W.C. Fields (1880–1946). The 1928 version was not nearly as successful as this original, and is now classified as a lost film.

This original version of *Tillie's Punctured Romance* remains the best slapstick comedy of the 1910s, and possibly of all time. It is still widely shown at film festivals today, as well as on television. It is also available in the video market. This slapstick masterpiece is one not to be missed.

170. Uncle Tom's Cabin *Rating:* ☆☆½

Thanhouser/Minot; ***Directed by*** William Robert Daly; ***Running Time:*** 42 minutes; ***Cast:*** UNCLE TOM, Sam Lucas (1840–1916); GEORGE HARRIS, Irving Cummings (1888–1959); CHLOE, Hattie Delaro (1861–1941); LITTLE EVA, Marie Eline (1905–1981); ***Supporting Cast:*** Walter Hitchcock (1872–1917); Paul Scarden (1874–1954)

This is the Thanhouser Company's adaptation of *Uncle Tom's Cabin*, which was filmed many times during the silent era. Unfortunately, only this version and Edison's 1903 version are widely available for evaluation on video.

This is not a bad adaptation for the time. The story starts on the plantation of George Shelby, the original owner of older slave Uncle Tom. Shelby, who is kind to his slaves, loses custody of Uncle Tom as well as the baby of George and Elizah Harris, a mulatto couple. His landlord has sold the mortgage on Shelby's plantation to an unscrupulous slave trader who demands ownership of Uncle Tom and the boy in exchange for not foreclosing on the mortgage. The elder Shelby's son, who likes Uncle Tom, promises to buy him back when he grows up and can make enough money.

The rest of the film portrays Uncle Tom's acquisition by the St. Clair family after rescuing Little Eva from drowning, and the subsequent deaths of the St. Clairs, which lead Tom to be auctioned off to yet another cruel plantation owner. It is this final plantation owner that orders Uncle Tom to whip a young slave, which he refuses to do. For this refusal, Tom is beaten, and is on his deathbed just as George Shelby's son has arrived to free him. The final shot of the film is a title card containing the Emancipation Proclamation.

Sam Lucas, who plays Uncle Tom, was the first black actor to play a major leading role in a motion picture feature. He had actually been a slave in his youth, having turned 21 at the start of the Civil War.

The actor who receives top billing is Irving Cummings. He entered films in 1909 after having toured with Lillian Russell's company on stage. By the early 1920s, he began directing silents, maintaining an active career through 1951, when he retired. No information could be located on the film's director, William Robert Daly.

Two other silent versions of *Uncle Tom's Cabin* were filmed in 1913 and 1927 for Universal Pictures. The 1913 version was produced when Universal was still referred to as IMP, and starred Harry Pollard (1879–1934) and his wife, Margarita Fischer (1886–1975). This first version is not known to exist. The 1927 remake was directed by Pollard, and also starred his wife Margarita Fischer. It had been filmed on a big budget, and on a lavish scale. It was possibly the ultimate silent adaptation of the film, but failed miserably at the box office. This 1927 version does still exist, and negotiations are underway for a possible video release in late 1998 or early 1999.

171. Under Royal Patronage

Rating: ☆☆½

Essanay; Director Unidentified; ***Running Time:*** 23 minutes; ***Cast:*** H.R.H. FRANCIS, Thomas Commerford (1855–1920); BARON SPITZHAUSEN, Lester Cuneo (1888–1925); PIERRE DE LA MARCHE, Arthur Stengard; COUNT KARL VON BLUMEN, E.H. Calvert (1863–1941); PRINCE PHILLIP, Bryant Washburn (1889–1963); RICHARD SAVAGE, Francis X. Bushman (1883–1966); H.R.H. FRIEDRICH, Charles Hitchcock; THE PRINCESS, Beverly Bayne (1893–1982); BARONESS KANN, Betty Scott; THE GIRL, Jane Paddock

This is one of the few surviving films that husband-wife team Francis X. Bushman and Beverly Bayne starred in together. They were the first important romantic team in films, as predecessors to Garbo and Gilbert, Gaynor and Farrell, and others. This film was made in the early days of their partnership, with their popularity reaching its peak from 1916 to 1918, after the couple left Essanay and went to Metro Pictures. They were married in 1918, but kept their marriage a secret so as not to possibly discourage fans. The marriage ended in 1924. It has been alleged that Bushman was a wife beater, and when Louis B. Mayer found out about it shortly after Bushman completed his role in *Ben-Hur*, he blacklisted him.

In this film, Beverly Bayne plays a princess who is obligated to either marry Prince Phillip or forfeit her allowance. Prince Phillip is in the same situation, being required to marry the princess whom he hardly knows and does not really want to marry. The prince sends a friend, played by Bushman, to take his place in the wedding ceremony and temporarily marry the princess until the prince's income is guaranteed. The princess does the same thing by sending a friend of hers to the wedding in her place. It turns out that the substitute spouses actually fall in love with each other, and the real prince and princess meet and fall in love as well. In the end, everyone is married to the right person.

This was not a bad film in comparison to other films of the same time period. It was originally released in 1914, and then rereleased in 1916, after Bayne and Bushman went to Metro Pictures. Bushman comes across well, and has an especially good side-profile shot in this film. Bayne appears on screen for only a short time, but also comes across well. What is really interesting is to see Bryant Washburn in his prime. He was also a leading matinee idol of the 1910s, and was 26 when he appeared in this, one of his extremely rare early films in existence. He later starred in a number of "B" pictures, westerns, serials, and action films from the mid–1920s through the 1940s. Another interesting player in this film is Lester Cuneo, who was married to Francelia Billington from 1920 to 1925, a period during which they appeared in a number of films as a husband and wife team. Francelia divorced Lester, and two days after the divorce was finalized, he committed suicide at age 37.

172. The Virginian

Rating: ☆☆☆

Paramount; ***Directed by*** Cecil B. DeMille; ***Based on the Novel by*** Owen Wister; ***Photography by*** Alvin Wyckoff; ***Art Direction by*** Wilfred Buckland; ***Running Time:*** 54 minutes; ***Cast:*** THE VIRGINIAN, Dustin Farnum (1874–1929)

In 1913, Cecil B. DeMille made his directorial debut with *The Squaw Man*, released early in 1914, which starred Dustin Farnum in the title role. This first DeMille feature is also said to be the first film produced on location in Hollywood. DeMille directed

Farnum again in the title role of *The Virginian*, which came out later in 1914 as DeMille's seventh film.

This was the first of at least four screen adaptations of Owen Wister's western classic. The familiar story has Farnum playing the Virginian, whose job it is to administer justice. His best friend Steve, despite warnings to the contrary, joins a gang of cattle rustlers. The gang hides out in the woods, where their fire gives them away. The leaders of the gang escape, leaving the others behind. The Virginian is forced to hang his own best friend in keeping with his word of honor, and is determined afterward to get the gang leaders at any cost.

One scene that was especially notable and innovative for the time was the hanging scene. DeMille's portrayal of the hanging showed only the shadows of the swinging corpses against the ground, without showing the actual dangling corpses. Of all of Dustin Farnum's roles, this is among his most famous.

While the 1929 film adaptation of *The Virginian* directed by Victor Fleming and starring Gary Cooper is the definitive and best film adaptation, this original is not bad—especially for the time—and is the better of the two silent adaptations. In 1994, American Movie Classics presented a beautiful, color tinted print of this film, with a new piano score.

1915

173. Alias Jimmy Valentine *Rating:* ☆☆☆½

World Film Company; ***Directed by*** Maurice Tourneur; ***Running Time:*** 64 minutes; ***Cast:*** Lee Randall/Jimmy Valentine, Robert Warwick (1878–1964); Rose Fay, Ruth Shepley (1892–1951); Bill Avery, Alec B. Francis (1867–1934); Red, John Hines (1895–1970); Doyle, Robert Cummings (1865–1949)

This was the fifth film that director Maurice Tourneur did in the United States. It is also one of the first two feature length gangster films, having been released the same year as Raoul Walsh's *Regeneration* (1915), reviewed elsewhere in this section.

Matinee idol Robert Warwick plays the lead role of Lee Randall, who is a respectable banker by day, but a gangster who goes by the alias of Jimmy Valentine at night. His double life catches up to him when he loses a cuff button during a burglary of a bank, which is traced to him. He is sentenced to ten years in Sing Sing. (The prison sequences were actually filmed on location at Sing Sing, with the cooperation of the prison warden and staff.) When the governor tours the prison, Valentine puts on an act and convinces him that he is innocent, securing a pardon. He returns to society and lives a straight, honest life, getting back into the banking business and achieving success as Lee Randall. Unfortunately, there is still an outstanding warrant for "Jimmy Valentine," which one detective Doyle is determined to serve. A situation arises in which a little girl is accidentally locked in one of his bank's vaults. If Lee Randall opens the vault and rescues her, he risks exposing his identity as "Jimmy Valentine," putting him in a precarious situation.

Robert Warwick is highly appealing in the lead role. He made very few silent films, as he was primarily a stage actor. However, once the talkie era began, he made a comeback in films, playing character roles in such classics as *I Am a Fugitive from the Chain Gang* (1932), *Cleopatra* (1934), *A Tale of Two Cities* (1935), *Romeo and Juliet* (1936), *The Prince and the Pauper* (1937), *The Awful Truth* (1937), *The Adventures of Robin Hood* (1938), *The Sea Hawk* (1940), and *Salome* (1953). This film also features one of the earliest film appearances by "John" Hines, before he became the popular comedian known as "Johnny" Hines.

In the early 1990s, the Library of Congress, in conjunction with the Smithsonian Institution, released a series of silents on video, which included this original version of *Alias Jimmy Valentine.* The print material used was a beautiful, multitinted print. The tints were used effectively, especially in scenes in which lights were being turned off and on.

Alias Jimmy Valentine is among the most famous of all gangster stories, having been remade several times. A man believed to have been Edward Sands burglarized the home of film director William Desmond Taylor (1872–1922) and left a note that was signed "Alias Jimmy Valentine."

None of the remakes of *Alias Jimmy Valentine* is available for evaluation, but this original is quite impressive, and it would be difficult to improve on an original that is so well done.

174. The Birth of a Nation

Rating: ☆☆☆☆

Epoch; ***Directed by*** D.W. Griffith; ***Assistant Director:*** Thomas E. O'Brien; Based on Thomas Dixon's 1905 novel, *The Clansman*; ***Screenplay by*** D.W. Griffith and Frank E. Woods; ***Photography by*** G.W. Bitzer; ***Assistant Cameraman:*** Karl Brown; ***Film Editor:*** James Smith; ***Costumes by*** Robert Goldstein; ***Running Time:*** 188 minutes; ***Cast:*** ELSIE STONEMAN, Lillian Gish (1893–1993); MARGARET CAMERON, Miriam Cooper (1894–1976); FLORA CAMERON AS A CHILD, Violet Wilkie; FLORA CAMERON, Mae Marsh (1895–1968); COLONEL BEN CAMERON, Henry B. Walthall (1878–1936); SILAS LYNCH, George Siegmann (1882–1928); GUS, Walter Long (1879–1952); TOD STONEMAN, Robert Harron (1893–1920); ABRAHAM LINCOLN, Joseph Henabery (1887–1976); PHIL STONEMAN, Elmer Clifton (1890–1949); MRS. CAMERON, Josephine Crowell (died 1934); DR. CAMERON, Spottiswoode Aitken (1868–1933); WADE CAMERON, André de Beranger (1895–1973); DUKE CAMERON, Maxfield Stanley; MAMMY (FAITHFUL SERVANT), Jennie Lee (1850–1925); GENERAL ULYSSES S. GRANT, Donald Crisp (1882–1974); GENERAL ROBERT E. LEE, Howard Gaye (died 1955); SENATOR CHARLES SUMNER, Sam DeGrasse (1875–1953); JOHN WILKES BOOTH, Raoul Walsh (1887–1980); A FALLEN UNION SOLDIER, Eugene Pallette (1889–1954); JAKE (FAITHFUL SERVANT), Ernest Campbell; A FEMALE SLAVE WHO MOCKS DR. CAMERON, Madame Sul-Te-Wan (1873–1959); A CLANSMAN, John Ford (1894–1973); CONFEDERATE SOLDIER/BAR PROPRIETOR, Elmo Lincoln (1889–1952); ELSIE STONEMAN'S ADMIRING HOSPITAL GUARD, William F. Freeman ***Other Extras in Bit Parts:*** Olga Grey (1897–1973); William De Vaull (1870–1945); Tom Wilson (1880–1965); David Butler (1895–1979); Pauline Starke (1900–1977); John McGlynn

This landmark film was based on material from two of the Reverend Thomas Dixon's books, *The Leopard's Spots* (1902) and *The Clansman* (1905). No copy of *The Leopard's Spots* could be located, but upon reading *The Clansman*, it was concluded that it was the prime source material for the film. Originally entitled *The Clansman*, the name of the film was changed to *The Birth of a Nation* at the suggestion of Thomas Dixon himself. He rightly stated that the film was too great and magnificent to be called just *The*

Promotional poster for D. W. Griffith's *The Birth of a Nation* (1915).

Clansman. The novel itself, though widely read at the time, was really no masterwork in its own right. Had it not been for *The Birth of a Nation*, the book itself would be all but forgotten as a minor novel today. But, the success of *The Birth of a Nation* will give *The Clansman* an immortal place in history. The book was reissued in 1971 by the University of Kentucky Press, and will likely be reissued again in the future.

The Birth of a Nation has many firsts to its credit. It was the first feature length motion picture produced in the United States to run more than two hours. It was the first movie to charge a $2 admission fee at the legitimate theaters—which would be equivalent to about $20 or $30 in 1990s dollars. It was also the first American film to be screened in the White House, a few months after Italy's *Cabiria* (1914). Most of all, it was the first film to really generate controversy, owing to what was perceived by many as racist overtones. When the film was originally released, it sparked near riots in many cities, thus causing D.W. Griffith to have to fight a few legal battles to allow its screening. Griffith's message to the censors was a pamphlet that he independently published called "The Rise and Fall of Free Speech in America," which featured a picture of the Statue of Liberty with her hands tied behind her back with reels of film. The NAACP vehemently protested upon this film's original release. The Ku Klux Klan, which had been dormant since the late 1870s, was resurrected, and still uses it as a propaganda film today. In recent years, there have been more protests against it, too. In the 1980s, a San Francisco screening sparked protests, and some of the protesters invaded the projection booth and destroyed the print while the screening was in progress. Turner Classic Movies canceled an airing of the film one week after a predominately black California jury rendered a "not guilty" verdict in the O.J. Simpson murder trial. It was eventually aired about three months later, after the controversy had a chance to die down some. More than 80 years after its original release, *The Birth of a Nation* remains one of the most controversial films in existence.

This film recreates the Civil War and Reconstruction eras, focusing on the viewpoint of the Southern states. The story starts out at the home of a Southern family (the Camerons) who are receiving friends from the North (the Stonemans) at their Piedmont, South Carolina, residence. As the story progresses into the Civil War, one sees the same friends facing each other on the battlefield. The battle scenes are very well done, and were shot at what is today the site of Universal Studios in California. Tom Wilson, who appeared as an extra in this film, threw grenades onto the battlefield to simulate the explosions. He released one of the grenades too late and suffered severe burns on his hands. The living conditions of the soldiers are portrayed with grim reality, most notably in the scenes in which they are shown with their daily rations of parched corn. The scene of dead soldiers on the battlefield preceded by the title "War's peace" is especially powerful.

The Lincoln assassination is especially well staged, and probably remains the best of all motion picture portrayals of the assassination. A replica of Ford's Theater was built using the original building plans. Griffith even found the play that Lincoln was watching, *Our American Cousin*, and staged the part of the play that was being performed when the assassination occurred.

As the film continues into the Reconstruction period, the audience is shown a portrayal of how the white South was crushed beneath the heels of the black South. The blacks rig elections, forcibly denying whites access to the ballot boxes. Black legislators are portrayed as unrefined, while passing laws that require whites to salute black officers on the streets, legalize interracial marriages, and so on. One of the most intense scenes of white victimization is the sequence in which Flora Cameron is approached by Gus, the renegade Negro army officer who attempts to rape her. Forced on top of a cliff, Flora threatens to jump if Gus comes closer. He does, and she makes good on her word, preferring death over the dishonor of rape. In actuality, Griffith played this sequence down compared to the way it appeared in Dixon's novel. In *The Clansman*, both Flora and her mother are actually gang-raped by four Negro officers, and commit suicide together rather than face the possibility of giving birth to illegitimate children who might have been conceived during the rapes. This is the incident that prompts Ben Cameron to form the Ku Klux Klan with the intent of rescuing whites from black terrorism. This positive portrayal of the Klan as heroes is what makes this film so controversial.

If one can put the racial overtones aside, this is quite probably the most accurate celluloid representation of Civil War times to exist. It was made only 50 years after the Civil War ended, when many people who had actually been through the war were still alive to give firsthand accounts. D.W. Griffith's own father had been a Confederate officer in the war. It remains one of the great box-office successes of all time, and revolutionized the entire cinema industry.

175. Burlesque on Carmen

Rating: ☆☆☆

Essanay; ***Written and Directed by*** Charles Chaplin; ***Photography by*** Harry Ensign; ***Running Time:*** 47 minutes; ***Cast:*** CARMEN, Edna Purviance (1894–1958); DON JOSÉ, Charlie Chaplin (1889–1977); REMENDEDO, Ben Turpin (1869–1940); MORALES, Leo White (1882–1948); VILLAS PASTIA, Jack Henderson (1878–1957); ESCAMILLO, John Rand (1878–1940); THE TRAMP, Wesley Ruggles (1889–1972); TRASQUITA, May White

This was Charlie Chaplin's last film for Essanay, in which he was teamed with legendary comedian Ben Turpin. In this *Burlesque on Carmen*, Chaplin parodies the two highly successful dramatic adaptations of the opera starring Geraldine Farrar and Theda Bara. Edna Purviance plays the title role in this film.

Chaplin as Don José makes a nice departure from his tramp character. One can see that underneath the unflattering tramp garb was an attractive man whose good looks were wasted for most of his career. Edna Purviance's real talent as a comic shines through, as she is seen parodying Geraldine Farrar's facial gestures and overacting as she is being glamorous and smoking a cigarette.

This film had footage added to it by the Essanay Company after Chaplin left, and he sued over the release of the altered version of the film and lost after a protracted battle.

This was among the first film parodies of a contemporary film, and is still fun to watch today.

176. Carmen

Rating: ☆☆☆

Paramount; ***Directed by*** Cecil B. DeMille; ***Scenario by*** William C. de Mille; ***From the Story by*** Prosper Merimeé; ***Art Direction by*** Wilfred Buckland; ***Photography by*** Alvin Wyckoff; ***Running Time:*** 59 minutes; ***Cast:*** CARMEN, Geraldine Farrar (1882–1967); DON JOSÉ,

Wallace Reid (1891–1923); ESCAMILLO, Pedro de Cordoba (1881–1950); MORALES, Billy Elmer (1869–1945); PASTIA, H.B. Carpenter (1875–1945); FRASQUITA, Jeanie MacPherson (1887–1946); MERCEDES, Anita King (1889–1963)

In 1915, two major, competing film versions of *Carmen* were released. The William Fox Company's version starred Theda Bara (1885–1955) in the lead role and was directed by Raoul Walsh (1887–1980). The Walsh-Bara version is lost. This Paramount version is quite good, with good performances by Geraldine Farrar and Wallace Reid in the leading roles. Farrar as Carmen overexaggerates a bit in some of her acting gestures, but delivers a much more natural performance than those exhibited by fellow stage stars Sarah Bernhardt and James O'Neill in their respective films. Wallace Reid, who was more experienced in film acting by this time, delivers an excellent performance as Don José. This film was one of Reid's earliest major roles in a feature length film.

***Top and above:* Geraldine Farrar in *Carmen* (1915).**

In comparing this version of *Carmen* to other surviving silent versions, it is far superior to the abysmal and overrated 1918 Lubitsch-Negri collaboration from Germany. Another version, *The Loves of Carmen* (1927), is reviewed elsewhere in this book. The 1927 version was very good, but DeMille's narrative style in this version is more straightforward and easier to follow.

David Shepard recently acquired this film from the George Eastman House where it had been archived, and released a beautiful, restored, and color tinted version on video through Kino.

177. The Cheat

Rating: ☆☆☆½

Paramount; ***Produced and Directed by*** Cecil B. DeMille; ***Screenplay by*** Hector Turnbull; ***Photography by*** Alvin Wyckoff; ***Art Direction by*** Wilfred Buckland; ***Running Time:*** 59 minutes; ***Cast:*** EDITH HARDY, Fannie Ward (1872–1952); DICK HARDY, Jack Dean (1875–1950); TORI, Sessue Hayakawa (1890–1973); JONES, James Neill (1860–1931); TORI'S VALET, Utake Abe; DISTRICT ATTORNEY, Dana Ong (1874–1948); MRS. REYNOLDS, Hazel Childers

In recent years since *The Cheat* has become widely available for evaluation, it has been highly acclaimed by film historians. James Card, in his book *Seductive Cinema*, refers to it as "a towering masterpiece of 1915."

The Cheat was among the first films to star highly renowned stage actress Fannie Ward, who was known for her youthful appearance. She was 43 when she made this film, but could have easily passed for someone 20 years younger.

In this film, she plays a woman who is happily married, but wants to live beyond her means. She is treasurer of the Red Cross fund, and takes $10,000 with the hope of gambling it to make extra money for herself, after which she intends to return the money. Things go wrong when she loses the money, and does not have it to return. She must find a way to replace it, or be subjected to scandal and a possible prison term. This is where "the cheat," played by Sessue Hayakawa, comes in. He offers to give her the $10,000 in return for her granting favors as his mistress. When she doesn't come through with the sexual favors and tries to pay back the $10,000 instead, he tries to rape her, and brands his mark of ownership into her shoulder. She shoots him in self defense. Her husband takes the blame, and his trial results in a thrilling courtroom finale.

Both Sessue Hayakawa and Fannie Ward received wide critical acclaim for their performances in this film, which was highly successful both with critics and at the box office. Hayakawa went on to form Haworth Pictures, his own production company that operated from 1918 to 1922. He won an Oscar nomination for his performance in *The Bridge on the River Kwai* (1957).

The Cheat is excellent melodrama and easily one of the top five films of 1915. The direction by Cecil B. DeMille is above reproach, and the actors are excellent as well. Fortunately, this title has been made available in a restored video version by Kino, and is well worth watching.

178. Crossed Wires

Rating: ☆☆☆

[a.k.a. *A Telephone Tragedy*]

Thanhouser; ***Directed by*** Frederick R. Sullivan; ***Scenario by*** Philip Lonergan; ***Running Time:*** 31 minutes; ***Cast:*** MRS. ANGELL (THE OLD WOMAN), Inda Palmer (1853–1923); WILL DRAKE,

Morris Foster (1889–1969); FLO DRAKE, Florence LaBadie (1888–1917); BENTON, Boyd Marshall (1885–1950); SUSAN WATSON, Ina Hammer (died 1953)

This is a mystery-suspense film about an older woman who is murdered just after writing her will. Once she realizes she has been poisoned, she tried to telephone for help. She reaches the police station and is able to utter only the words, "I'm dying, poisoned—Will Drake." The telephone operator mistakenly transfers the call to a wrong number, at which time she finishes the statement, saying that Will Drake had warned her about Susan, the housekeeper, who was the guilty party. Due to the error, the police assume that Will Drake is the murderer, and he is convicted and sentenced to death. Flo Drake, his sister, sets out to prove his innocence.

It is ironic that Inda Palmer, who played the murdered woman, died under mysterious circumstances in real life. In November 1923, her skeleton was found, and it was roughly estimated that she had been dead since that April.

179. Dawn and Twilight

Rating: ☆☆

Essanay; Director Unidentified; ***Running Time:*** 12 minutes; ***Cast:*** PIETRO, Francis X. Bushman (1883–1966); MARY, Ruth Stonehouse (1892–1941); HIS MOTHER, Helen Dunbar (1863–1933); DR. BURKE, Thomas Commerford (1855–1920); EDNA, Alice Miss; MARY'S MOTHER, Clare Smith

This is another rare surviving example of Francis X. Bushman's work from his heyday as a matinee idol. In this film, he plays a blind musician whose sight is restored, compliments of Mary, the girl in love with him who secretly pays $500 for the operation that he needs. Once Pietro gets his sight back, he spurns Mary and dates Edna, another girl he finds more attractive. He overworks his eyes, and loses his sight again, and Mary, heartbroken over his rejection, dies of a broken heart.

This is a romantic tragedy that was rather primitive in comparison to other dramas of the time, and the acting techniques are extremely overexaggerated. Nonetheless, it was these types of roles that brought Bushman fame in his early days—more than ten years before his greatest role as Messala in *Ben-Hur* (1927).

Leading lady Ruth Stonehouse began her career in 1910. She went on to do a number of popular serials and action films. She and Bushman were two of Essanay's most popular dramatic players, and they were teamed frequently in the early- to mid-1910s.

180. The Exploits of Elaine

Chapter Eight: "The Hidden Voice"

Rating: ☆☆½

Pathé/Eclectic; ***Directed by*** Louis Gasnier; ***Scenario by*** Charles Goddard, George B. Seitz; ***Story by*** Arthur B. Reeve; ***Running Time of Episode:*** 23 minutes; ***Cast:*** ELAINE DODGE, Pearl White (1889–1938); CRAIG KENNEDY, Arnold Daly (1875–1929); JAMESON, Creighton Hale (1882–1965); ***Supporting Cast:*** Sheldon Lewis (1868–1958); Edwin Arden (1864–1918); Ramon Owens; Lee Roy Barker; Bessie Wharton; William Riley

The Exploits of Elaine was the 14-chapter followup to *The Perils of Pauline* (1914). In this serial, Pearl White plays Elaine Dodge, who is on the trail of a villain known as "the clutching hand," the criminal who murdered her father to gain possession of incriminating papers that would reveal his identity. This episode shows her friend Arnold Daly, inventor of a device known as the "Vocaphone." Kennedy installs one of the Vocaphones in Elaine's house so that he can hear what is going on in case Elaine is in danger. Soon after, the clutching hand breaks into Elaine's house and steals vital documents. The Vocaphone alerts Kennedy to the fact that Elaine is in trouble so that he can notify her servants of her plight and they can rescue her from being killed by the clutching hand in the nick of time. (In the sequences portraying the communication over the Vocaphone, the words being said over the phone are superimposed in cursive writing on the screen to show the words as they are transmitted.)

This chapter of *The Exploits of Elaine* reveals that the production values were slightly more polished than in *The Perils of Pauline*, although the presentation of the chapters still had not yet progressed to the cliffhanger format. The superimposed words on the screen give it a more primitive appearance than it otherwise would have had.

Creighton Hale, who made his film debut in a supporting role in the 1914 serial *The Million Dollar Mystery*, had his first big role as White's leading man in *The Exploits of Elaine*. They teamed up in two more "Elaine" serials of 1915. *The New Exploits of Elaine* was a 10-chapter serial that put Pearl up against opium dealers. *The Romance of Elaine* was a 12-chapter serial that had Pearl's character joining the war effort against Germany.

181. Fatty and Mabel View the San Francisco World's Fair

Rating: ☆☆☆

Keystone; ***Directed by*** Mack Sennett; ***Running Time:*** 14 minutes; ***Cast:*** Mabel Normand (1892–1930); Roscoe Arbuckle (1887–1933)

In the early days, the Keystone Company did some films that were classified as "educational" pictures, and others categorized as "farce comedy" pictures. This is one of the few films from the educational genre that has survived. The film features Fatty Arbuckle and Mabel Normand, who were, at the time, the most popular comedy team in the movies. It shows them on a historical tour of the 1915 World's Fair held in San Francisco, seeing various historic sights and exhibits. It is ironic to see that one of the featured sites of the San Francisco tour is the St. Francis Hotel—where the Arbuckle-Rappe incident that ruined Arbuckle's career took place just six years later. This fascinating film is, fortunately, widely available on video.

182. Fatty and Mabel's Simple Life

Rating: ☆☆☆

Keystone/Mutual; ***Directed by*** Roscoe Arbuckle; ***Running Time:*** 12 minutes; ***Cast:*** FATTY, Roscoe Arbuckle (1887–1933); MABEL, Mabel Normand (1892–1930); MABEL'S FATHER, Joseph Swickard (1866–1940); THE LANDLORD'S SON, Al St. John (1892–1963)

This film features Mabel as a poor, but honest, farmer's daughter, whose sweetheart is Fatty. When Mabel's father can't pay the mortgage, the landlord promises to forgive the debt in return for Mabel marrying his son. When Mabel is introduced to "the lad of her father's choice," she refuses to marry him and is locked in her room. Fatty helps her escape, and a number of hilarious antics occur as Fatty and Mabel flee to get married before her father can marry her off to the landlord's son.

It was the Fatty and Mabel films like this one that sported the best story lines and plots of the early Keystone Comedies. This film is a prime example of Roscoe Arbuckle's substantial talent as a director. Of the Keystone Comedies evaluated, those directed by Arbuckle are the best.

183. Fatty's Plucky Pup [a.k.a. *Foiled by Fido*]

Rating: ☆☆☆½

Keystone/Mutual; ***Directed by*** Roscoe Arbuckle; ***Running Time:*** 23 minutes; ***Cast:*** FATTY, Roscoe Arbuckle (1887–1933); MABEL, Mabel Normand (1892–1930); FATTY'S PLUCKY PUP, Luke the dog

This is among the best of the highly popular "Fatty & Mabel" shorts. In the beginning, Fatty is shown as a careless son who manages to make a mess of everything. First, he sets his bed on fire with a cigarette. While the fire is raging, Fatty gets a small cup of water from the kitchen to put it out, stopping to comb his hair and take a sip of water in the process. Next, he tries to atone by hanging the laundry on the clothesline for his mother. On the way to the clothesline, he stumbles, dropping the clothes basket in the mud, and they are filthy by the time they reach the clothesline. Fatty tries to hose the dirt off, and ends up squirting his mother in the process. Then, while he is sidetracked talking to sweetheart Mabel, the dogcatchers are after his dog. He manages to foil the dogcatchers and get his dog back. To get even, he lets all of the dogs that have been captured loose. The last misadventure in the first reel consists of Fatty washing his dog in his mother's laundry tub.

Roscoe Arbuckle and Luke the dog in *Fatty's Plucky Pup* (1915).

Reel two is where the excitement begins. Fatty and Mabel go on an outing. Fatty is cheated out of his money on a rigged amusement game. He takes his money back from the con artists, who kidnap Mabel in retaliation. It is "Fatty's plucky pup" who finds Mabel and leads Fatty to rescue her in the nick of time. The dog, played by an animal star named Luke, does a number of amazing stunts, including jumping out a window.

This is a delightful comedy with a little bit of melodrama mixed in. Of all of the Keystone films evaluated, *Fatty's Plucky Pup* is among this reviewer's favorites.

184. A Free Ride

Rating: ☆

Gay Paree Picture Company; ***Directed by*** A. Wise Guy; ***Photographed by*** Will B. Hard; ***Titles by*** Will She; ***Running Time:*** 13 minutes; ***Cast:*** The "Jazz Girls"

Those who believe that hard core pornography came around in the 1960s obviously have not seen this, the oldest hard core pornographic film in existence. Some might question the purpose in including reviews of pornographic films in a book on the silent era. But, in order to give a complete and accurate history of the early motion pictures, it is imperative that all types of films available from the era be included—even if some of the films go against what would be classified as good taste. Vulgarity and pornography have been around since the beginning of photography and motion pictures, and it would be foolish to try to deny that they existed.

This film starts out with the "jazz girls" walking down a desolate road, with a man in a car pulling up to offer them a ride. A title card flashes with the reply, "No thanks—we are walking home from one now." They end up getting into the car and driving to a secluded spot. The film proceeds to show first the man, and then the women, urinating as the other parties watch what they are doing. Once they are all in the car again, they have a few drinks. The man asks to speak to one of the women alone, and the two fondle each other and ultimately have sex. After a while, the second girl masturbates while watching the other two have sex. After the couple finishes, the second girl has sex with the man. The man eventually engages in oral sex simultaneously with both women.

This pornographic film is explicit even by today's standards. Because it shows urination, it would be considered raunchier than today's porno films, which are governed by an "unwritten taboo" against showing such. Back in 1915, when pornography was totally illegal, there were no written or unwritten boundaries. If one was caught producing or showing hard core pornography, one was in major trouble, no matter how much or what type of sex was shown.

The production values of this sex film are poor. Although the film is explicit even by today's standards, it is so bad that it could hardly cater to the prurient interest.

The film credits listed in this book are exactly as they appear in the actual film, combining satire with the necessary anonymity needed in 1915.

185. Hearts in Exile

Rating: ☆☆½

Supreme Photoplays Corporation; ***Directed by*** James Young; ***Running Time:*** 60 minutes; ***Cast:*** ANNA IVANOVNA, Clara Kimball Young (1890–1960); PAUL PAVLOFF, Vernon Steele (1882–1955); MIKHAIL, Paul McAllister (1875–1955); SERGE KARTOFF, Claude Fleming (1884–1952); NICOLAI, Montague Love (1877–1943)

Hearts in Exile is one of only two widely available Clara Kimball Young features in which she was directed by her husband, James Young. During this period in Mrs. Young's career, she was among the most popular of the screen actresses, placing near the top in many fan magazine polls of the mid–1910s. Before reviewing this film, this reviewer anticipated a film to be appreciated solely for its rarity and historic value. It turned out to be a much better film than expected.

Anna Ivanovna is a young philanthropist in prerevolution Russia who finds joy in helping the poor and less fortunate. Paul Pavloff is a young, struggling doctor who takes an interest in the charity work to get to know Anna better. Mikhail is a nihilist whose home is a headquarters for the revolutionary movement, which had been underway in Russia since the mid–1900s. Sergei Kartoff is a wealthy and influential merchant who also develops an interest in charity work to get to know Anna. Montague Love, who specialized in villain roles, plays Nicolai, the chief of police.

Both Paul Pavloff and Sergei Kartoff propose to Anna. Although she loves Paul, she marries Sergei, who is able to provide much-needed financial assistance for her charity work. Following the marriage, Paul, Sergei, and Anna remain friends. Paul is later appointed as a professor at Moscow University. The plot thickens when Nicolai, who also has eyes for Anna, has Paul arrested as a nihilist, and Sergei arrested on trumped-up charges. Paul is sentenced to the provinces, and Sergei is sentenced to the dreaded Siberia. Out of love for Anna, Paul switches identities with Sergei, going to Siberia so that Sergei will end up in the provinces, which are easier to escape from. Anna goes to Siberia to join Sergei, only to find that Paul is there instead. A daring escape attempt provides the film's finale.

Hearts in Exile is interesting in that it provides documentation of America's perception of Russia while the country was still under the czarist dictatorship. It is obvious that the American people were sympathetic toward the revolutionists at the time—before the revolutionists went to the extreme left.

James Young, the director of this film, was born in 1878, the son of a Maryland senator. He was a stage actor when in 1910 he started making films for Vitagraph. He directed Clara in several films until they divorced in 1916. He went on to direct Theda Bara in *The Unchastened Woman* (1925) and Lionel Barrymore and Boris Karloff in *The Bells* (1926). While his surviving work indicates that he was not a great director, he was certainly competent. No record of his death has been found by film historians.

Clara Kimball Young demonstrates remarkable pantomimic ability in this film. She skillfully underplays the role, and can convey emotions with a mere glance of the eye or other subtle facial expressions.

186. Mabel and Fatty's Married Life *Rating:* ☆½

Keystone/Mutual; ***Directed by*** Roscoe Arbuckle; ***Running Time:*** 11 minutes; ***Cast:*** MABEL, Mabel Normand (1892–1930); FATTY, Roscoe Arbuckle (1887–1933)

This comedy starts with Mabel and Fatty peacefully reading a book in the park. An organ grinder's monkey gets obnoxious, and Fatty chases it away. Fatty and the organ grinder get into a big argument, and the organ grinder vows revenge. Once Fatty and Mabel get home, Mabel reads an article about a rash of house robberies. Fatty leaves the house for a while and comes back, with Mabel mistaking him for a burglar, shooting at him through the door when she hears his footsteps. When Fatty leaves again, the organ grinder shows up at the house. Mabel also hears suspicious noises in the house, and the Keystone Cops are called. When the cops arrive, the organ grinder is still banging on the door. It turns out that the noises Mabel was hearing were made by the monkey, which somehow got into the house. The organ grinder is reunited with his monkey, and all is well.

This is not among the best of the Mabel and Fatty shorts.

187. Mabel and Fatty's Wash Day

Rating: ☆☆☆½

Keystone/Mutual; *Directed by* Roscoe Arbuckle; *Running Time:* 11 minutes; *Cast:* FATTY, Roscoe Arbuckle (1887–1933); MABEL, Mabel Normand (1892–1930); MABEL'S DOG, Luke the dog

In this delightful romantic comedy, Mabel has a lazy husband who sits in bed and smokes all day while she works. Her neighbor Fatty's domineering wife makes him do all of the housework while she attends social functions. Mabel and Fatty meet while slaving over their laundry work, and find each other compatible company. When their respective spouses see this, they both get angry.

The two couples go on separate strolls. Fatty's wife falls asleep, and Mabel and her husband have a falling-out. Fatty and Mabel meet again, and go to an outdoor café to talk. Complications arise when Fatty takes his wife's purse to pay for the café bill. Mabel's husband walks past Fatty's wife with Mabel's purse, which the wife assumes is hers that he has stolen. This results in a riotous chase sequence and conclusion.

188. Mabel Lost and Won

Rating: ☆☆½

Keystone/Mutual; ***Directed by*** Mabel Normand; ***Running Time:*** 11 minutes; ***Cast:*** MABEL, Mabel Normand (1892–1930); HER FIANCÉ, Owen Moore (1886–1939); ***Supporting Cast:*** Mack Swain (1876–1935)

This is a delightful romantic comedy in which Mabel is engaged to Owen Moore, who also has another admirer. The vamp forces herself on to Owen, but all Mabel sees is her fiancé in the arms of the vamp. Eventually, the rival vamp is exposed as a mother of three, and Mabel and Owen reconcile.

This film demonstrates that Mabel Normand was not only a great actress, but a competent director as well.

189. Mabel, Fatty, and the Law

Rating: ☆☆☆☆

Keystone/Mutual; ***Directed by*** Roscoe Arbuckle; ***Running Time:*** 11 minutes; ***Cast:*** FATTY, Roscoe Arbuckle (1887–1933); MABEL, Mabel Normand (1892–1930); COUPLE #2, Al St. John (1892–1963) and Minta Durfee (1889–1975); ***Supporting Cast:*** Harry Gribbon (1885–1961); Frank Hayes (1871–1923)

This is a hilarious situation comedy which finds two couples on an innocent stroll in the park. All through the park are signs reading, "No spooning allowed." Couple number one consists of Fatty and Mabel. Couple number two is played by Minta Durfee and Al St. John. Fatty leaves Mabel alone on the park bench to go to the ice cream stand. Minta arrives at the same time, and they engage in some light conversation. The watchful eyes of the Keystone Cops—hidden in the trees to watch for spooning scofflaws—interpret this interaction as spooning, and the couple are arrested.

While Fatty and Minta are on their way to jail, Al St. John strikes up a conversation with Mabel. They, too, are arrested for spooning. It is riotously funny to see the couples when they meet at the jail house.

Minta Durfee was the real-life wife of Roscoe Arbuckle from 1908 through 1925. They separated in 1921, and legally divorced in 1925. Despite the separation, Durfee stood by Arbuckle through the entire ordeal of his tragedy with the Virginia Rappe incident. They remained on friendly terms even after their divorce. Durfee was also a good friend of Mabel Normand's, having started at the Keystone Company in 1913. Her last silent film appearance was in Normand's *Mickey* (1918), which is reviewed elsewhere in this book. Durfee returned for occasional bit parts in the talkie era clear into the 1960s. She had a prominent cameo in the highly popular comedy *The Odd Couple* (1968), as a waitress. Although she was 79 years old in this cameo role, she could have easily passed for someone in her middle 50s.

Mabel, Fatty, and the Law is most definitely a favorite comedy classic not to be missed.

190. Old Heidelberg

Rating: ☆☆

Triangle; ***Directed by*** John Emerson; ***Based on the W. Meyer-Forster novel; and the play by*** Richard Mansfield; Supervised by D.W. Griffith; ***Running Time:*** 34 minutes; ***Cast:*** PRINCE KARL, Wallace Reid (1891–1923); KATHY (THE WAITRESS), Dorothy Gish (1898–1968); LUTZ [VALET], Erich von Stroheim (1885–1957); ***Supporting Cast:*** Madge Hunt (1875–1935); Raymond Wells (1880–1941); Erik Von Ritzau (1877–1936); Harold Goodwin (1902–1987); Kate Toncray; Francis Carpenter

Old Heidelberg has historic significance as the only solo work (without sister Lillian) of Dorothy Gish that is available outside the archives and on video. It is also one of the first film appearances of Erich von Stroheim as an actor. It is stated in some sources that he also served as an assistant director on this film.

This first screen adaptation of the popular story of unrequited love between a prince and a barmaid has Wallace Reid well cast as the prince who studies at Old Heidelberg University, with Dorothy Gish as Katie Ruder. Erich von Stroheim plays the prince's valet, with his back so erect and stiff that one wonders how he could hold such a position for very long.

Dorothy Gish in the mid–1910s, around the time she appeared in *Old Heidelberg* (1915).

One aspect of this adaptation that is downplayed in the subsequent remakes is the portrayal of the prince and Katie as childhood friends. Katie's mother provides the motherly figure that the prince never had, but when he is seen playing with "commoners," he is admonished for it.

This film has a good, distinguished cast, and isn't a bad adaptation of the *Old Heidelberg* story. Unfortunately, the copies circulating on video are of poor quality, missing the opening titles, transferred at the wrong speed so that the film moves at an overly rapid and jerky pace, and has as musical accompaniment only a generic or universal organ score. The print is also worn, faded, and scratched. If this film could be seen at the correct speed, it would probably go over better. But, this film is at least available to the general public in some form, giving viewers an idea of what the film was like.

While Dorothy Gish gives a good dramatic performance in this film, it was before she branched out into comedy, which is what she was known for throughout the rest of her career. While most of Dorothy Gish's solo comedy work is lost, three of her comedies do survive, but none of them are widely available on video. One of her early comedies, *Gretchen the Greenhorn* (1916), exists on 3/4" video tape, as one was made for the 1995 Silent Film Festival in San Francisco. Film historian Randy Haberkamp has control over this master tape. Dorothy's *Nell Gwyn* (1926) is held at the George Eastman House, and *The Country Doctor* (1927) is currently archived at the Museum of Modern Art.

191. Pool Sharks

Rating: ☆☆½

Running Time: 8 minutes, 30 seconds; ***Cast:*** THE POOL SHARK, W.C. Fields (1879–1946)

This is the rare and obscure film debut of comedian W.C. Fields. Fields started in the entertainment business as a circus juggler in the 1890s as a teenager. He was a top vaudeville star before he was 20, and in 1905 made his first appearance on Broadway. He was 35 years old when this film was made.

Pool Sharks starts as a slapstick romantic comedy, with Fields and a rival fighting over a girl. They settle their score in a pool game, during which trick photography is used to simulate the illusion that Fields is doing the impossible. Each man tries to outdo the other by having a greater and more unusual feat. These pool tricks, though obviously faked, are nonetheless amusing to watch.

In the early part of the film, Fields has a confrontation with a boy, showing the beginnings of his usual trademark distaste for kids.

Pool Sharks was an "off the wall" debut for Fields, who still had black hair when he appeared in it. (It is believed that Fields made one other film around the time he did *Pool Sharks*, but such a film is not known to exist.) He did not make another film appearance until his cameo role nine years later in *Janice Meredith* (1924).

No further credits information appears in any of the currently available prints of *Pool Sharks*.

192. Regeneration

Rating: ☆☆☆

Fox; ***Directed by*** R.A. (Raoul) Walsh; ***Scenario by*** R.A. Walsh and Carl Harbaugh; Based on Owen Kildare's *My Mamie Rose*; ***Photography by*** Georges Benoit; ***Running Time:*** 71 minutes; ***Cast:*** OWEN (AGE 10), John McCann; JIM CONWAY, James Marcus (1867–1937); MAGGIE CONWAY, Maggie Weston (died 1926); OWEN (AGE 17), H. [arry] McCoy (1894?–1937); OWEN (AGE 25), Rockliffe Fellowes (1883–1950); SKINNY, William Sheer (died 1933); AMES [DISTRICT ATTORNEY], Carl Harbaugh (1886–1960); MARIE, Anna Q. Nilsson (1888–1974)

Regeneration is the earliest of Raoul Walsh's surviving directorial projects. (Some sources list the title of this film as *The Regeneration*, but the title in the film itself does not contain "*The*.") It is also one of the first two major gangster features of the silent era, coming out the same year as Maurice Tourneur's *Alias Jimmy Valentine* (1915).

Regeneration is the story of an underprivileged orphan of New York's Bowery slum district who becomes a gangster for lack of any other direction in his life. He eventually falls in love with wealthy socialite Marie, who convinces him to give up gangster life and work with her in charity work instead. Owen and Marie's newfound happiness is shattered when "Skinny," who was Owen's successor as gang leader and who at one time took the fall for him, comes to collect on the past favor.

Many of the sequences in this film were shot on location in New York's Bowery slum district lending an aura of authenticity to the film. The rest of the film was shot mostly in Fort Lee, New Jersey, where many films were shot in the early days before the mass migration to Hollywood.

In comparing *Regeneration* to Tourneur's *Alias Jimmy Valentine*, one sees that *Alias Jimmy Valentine* was a more entertaining film, but that *Regeneration* was actually a more realistic portrayal of gangster life. *Regeneration*'s sad ending is more in conformance with what would have really happened in 1915.

One of the film's most spectacular sequences is when a yacht catches on fire, and the mob of people are running for their lives. Among the extras whom Raoul Walsh used were prostitutes who wore no underclothes while working in the film. It is reported that Walsh brought in an artist to paint underclothes on the women.

Stage actor Rockliffe Fellowes gives a compelling performance in this film, which is one of his very few existing silents. Anna Q. Nilsson shines as leading lady Marie. Nilsson is probably best remembered for her role in *Seven Keys to Baldplate* (1917), and also she played herself in Gloria Swanson's *Sunset Boulevard* (1950). Harry McCoy worked in a number of Sennett comedies as a Keystone Cop, and was also reportedly Mabel Normand's first leading man. In addition, he directed some films and gained fame as a musical composer with his "Pagan Love Song." He was only 43 years old when he died of a heart attack. He was 26 when he played the 17-year-old Owen in this film.

Regeneration is a fine achievement, demonstrating that Raoul Walsh had exceptional talent from the very beginning of his film career.

193. A Small Town Bully

Rating: ☆☆☆

Keystone/Mutual; ***Directed by*** Mack Sennett; Adapted from *The Little Teacher*; ***Running Time:*** 20 minutes; ***Cast:*** MABEL [THE NEW TEACHER], Mabel Normand (1892–1930); MABEL'S FIANCE, Owen Moore (1886–1939); FATTY, Roscoe Arbuckle (1887–1933); FATTY'S CHUM, Mack Sennett (1880–1960); A HARASSED STUDENT, Harry McCoy (1889–1937)

This classic short finds Mabel as the new school teacher, with Arbuckle and Sennett playing two of her pupils who wreak havoc in the classroom. Arbuckle, with his "baby face," could easily pass for school age. Sennett, on the other hand, looks a bit preposterous playing such a role, but that is part of what makes this film so funny.

Mabel's fiancé, played by Owen Moore, is almost driven off by the rowdy pupils. Moore was, in reality, Mary Pickford's first husband from 1910 to 1920. Pickford allegedly divorced Moore because of his chronic alcoholism. He died at age 52.

Harry McCoy was the first leading man that Mabel Normand ever worked with. In this film, he plays the boy that Arbuckle and Sennett harass unmercifully. He died of a heart attack at age 48 in 1937.

This is among the funniest of the Mabel and Fatty shorts directed by Mack Sennett, and is highly recommended.

194. The Soap Suds Star

Rating: ☆☆

Thanhouser; ***Scenario by*** Lloyd F. Lonergan; ***Running Time:*** 14 minutes, 38 seconds; ***Cast:*** SOPHIE (THE STAR), Carey Hastings; THE HUSBAND, Reginald Perry

This is a comedy about a laundress and an actor who make it big on the vaudeville comedy circuit, but who are relegated back to the laundromat when their attempt at Shakespeare fails. This film gives an interesting historic perspective of vaudeville in the 1910s. No further information on either star could be found.

195. Son of Man

Rating: ☆☆½

Running Time: 68 minutes

This film is yet another of the early biographical pictures of the life of Jesus Christ. A print was sent to a convent in France in 1928, where each of the over 200,000 frames were individually hand-colored by the nuns.

The film starts out with Mary and Joseph's journey to Bethlehem to give birth to Jesus, and ends with the crucifixion and the resurrection. The sets and costumes for this production are relatively authentic-looking. The special effects showing the appearance of angels and Jesus walking on water are well done for the time. The resurrection sequence showing Jesus floating up to heaven in the midst of clouds combines some animation with the photography.

Although the narrative style of this film is rather primitive, it is an artistic accomplishment worth watching. The hand coloring is more vibrant in some scenes than in others, probably due to the age of the print when it was transferred to video.

Son of Man pales in comparison to later biographical films on Jesus Christ such as the 1927 *King of Kings*. But, when compared to other biographical pictures on Christ from the 1910s, this is the most artistic and innovative from that time period.

196. That Little Band of Gold

Rating: ☆½

Keystone/Mutual; ***Directed by*** Roscoe Arbuckle; ***Running Time:*** 21 minutes; ***Cast:*** MABEL, Mabel Normand (1892–1930); FATTY, Roscoe Arbuckle (1887–1933); ***Supporting Cast:*** Ford Sterling (1880–1939); Al St. John (1892–1963); Ethel Madison; May Emory; Phyllis Allen (1861–1938); Vivian Edwards; Dora Rodgers; Dixie Chene (1894–1972)

In this film, Mabel and Fatty are newlyweds. Fatty's mother-in-law hasn't a good word to say about him. The trio attend the opera, which bores Fatty. He is seen in the dining room with a vamp, and sparks fly.

While this film is more elaborately staged than most two-reel comedies of the time, for some reason it does not come together as well as most of the other Fatty and Mabel films. The story drags in spots, making this one of the weakest of the Normand-Arbuckle collaborations.

197. "The Wild Engine"

Rating: ☆☆☆½

An episode from *The Hazards of Helen*

Kalem; ***Directed by*** J.P. McGowan; ***Running Time:*** 19 minutes; ***Cast:*** HELEN, Helen Holmes (1893–1950); ***Supporting Cast:*** Jack Hoxie (1885–1965); Hoot Gibson (1892–1962)

This is one of 119 episodes of *The Hazards of Helen*, a series of highly popular railroad dramas produced by the Kalem Company in 1914 and 1915. Helen Holmes starred in the first 40 episodes, but left Kalem for greener pastures in 1915. The remaining episodes were filmed with Helen Gibson as the star.

When Kalem went out of business in 1917, they sold the negatives of *The Hazards of Helen* to the Aywon Distributing Company, which rereleased many of the episodes in 1919 under *The Adventures of Helen*.

In this episode, Holmes plays Helen, a school teacher who has been fired by the town elders for being too "frivolous." Disaster is in the making when a railroad car full of explosives is about to collide with a passenger train, and Helen, knowing immediately what to do, derails the explosive car and saves the day. This results in her being hired by the railroad company as a telegraph operator.

In her first day on the new job, a crisis pops up, with a wild train engine running loose after an accident, threatening to collide with another excursion train. Holmes races on a motorcycle to warn the excursion train of the impending disaster, and just as she is crossing the drawbridge, it is raised, sending Helen crashing on her motorcycle into the river. Undaunted, she makes a run for it on foot, and arrives just in time.

Upon evaluation of this episode of *The Hazards of Helen*, it appears far superior to the Pearl White serials that were being produced about the same time. One can see why Helen Holmes was among White's closest rivals in popularity. This reviewer was far more impressed with Holmes' early work than with White's.

Future western star Jack Hoxie is prominently featured as a supporting player at the beginning of his career, and future western star Hoot Gibson made his film debut in a small part as well.

Director J.P. McGowan (1880–1952) was married to leading lady Helen Holmes, and this series was among his first directorial projects.

198. Wished on Mabel

Rating: ☆☆☆

Keystone/Mutual; ***Directed by*** Roscoe Arbuckle; ***Running Time:*** 10 minutes; ***Cast:*** FATTY, Roscoe Arbuckle (1887–1933); MABEL, Mabel Normand (1892–1930)

This is a charming comedy in which Mabel and her mother go for a walk in the park. Mabel meets Fatty, and they go to walk while the mother is asleep on the bench. Meanwhile, while the mother is sleeping, her watch is stolen. The thief who stole it drops it, and Fatty finds it and gives it to Mabel as a gift. When Mabel's mother wakes up and discovers the theft, the Keystone Cops are called to the scene.

199. Young Romance

Rating: ☆☆☆

Jesse L. Lasky Company; ***Written by*** William C. de Mille; ***Directed by*** George Melford; ***Photographed by*** Walter Stradling; ***Art Direction by*** Wilfred Buckland; ***Running Time:*** 58 minutes; ***Cast:*** NELLIE NOLAN, Edith Taliaferro (1893–1958); TOM CLANCY, Tom Forman (1893–1926); JACK [TOM'S CHUM], Raymond Hatton (1887–1971); LOU [NELLIE'S CHUM], Florence Dagmar; COUNT SPAGNOLI, Al Garcia (1887–1938); THE MOTOR BOATMAN, Charles Wells; LANDLADY, Mrs. Lewis McCord (died 1917)

Young Romance is an obscure but interesting film. The leading characters in the story both work in separate sections of a large department store. Both are inspired separately by the same article to spend their hard-earned savings to live like high society elite figures for a week. Tom impersonates a count, and Nellie impersonates a wealthy society matron. They end up having a more adventurous time than they had planned on when Nellie is kidnapped and held for ransom.

This was the film debut of Edith Taliaferro. She received top billing in this film, which is her only work widely available for evaluation. Edith was the sister of silent screen actress Mabel Taliaferro (1887–1979) and the cousin of Bessie Barriscale (1884–1965). Edith gives a radiant performance, which whets one's desire to see more of her work.

Tom Forman is appealing as the leading man in this film. He later became a motion picture director after a stint in the armed forces during World War I. He committed suicide by shooting himself in 1926 when he was 33 years old.

The screenplay of *Young Romance* was written by William C. de Mille, who was the brother of Cecil B. DeMille. This screenplay is a good one, and demonstrates that William de Mille was talented in his own right. He later directed films on his own, although for some reason never achieved the fame of his brother. William spelled his surname with a lower case "d" and also put a space between "de" and "Mille."

Young Romance is a simple yet highly enjoyable film. It is available on laser disc, but has not yet been released on videocassette.

1916

200. Cenere *Rating:* ☆☆

Produced in France; ***Co-written and Co-directed by*** Eleanora Duse; ***Running Time:*** 30 minutes; ***Cast:*** CENERE, *Eleanora Duse (1859–1924)*

This film has its place in history as the one and only film of the great stage diva Eleanora Duse, who was perhaps Sarah Bernhardt's (1844–1923) closest rival. Duse helped to write and direct this film, but was not happy with how she came across on the silver screen. She withdrew *Cenere* from circulation and tried to have all prints of the film destroyed. She is quoted in one source as stating, "I made the same mistake that nearly everyone has made. But something quite different is needed. I am too old for it, isn't it a pity?"

This reviewer had the opportunity to see an extremely rare copy of this film, which is currently known to be available only with French titles. In watching the film, it is obvious that Duse, unlike her contemporaries of the stage, realized the differences between the stage and motion picture mediums, and adapted her acting style accordingly. Her technique is much more relaxed and far less stagy than the acting techniques demonstrated in the surviving work of Sarah Bernhardt and James O'Neill (1847–1920). Eleanora Duse deserves far more credit than she gave herself. Like many artists and actors, she was probably her own worst critic. It is extremely fortunate that she did not succeed in her mission to obliterate all copies of *Cenere*. With this one surviving example of her acting technique, her talent can be appreciated and admired more than seven decades after her death in 1924, granting Duse the form of immortality that she deserves.

If this film became available with English titles, a more engrossing story might be revealed, and the rating therefore might be higher under those circumstances.

201. Civilization

Rating: ☆☆☆

Thomas H. Ince Productions; ***Directed by*** Raymond B. West and Reginald Barker; ***Screenplay by*** C. Gardner Sullivan; ***Photography by*** Irvin Willat; ***Film Editor:*** LeRoy Stone; ***Running Time:*** 86 minutes; ***Cast:*** THE KING OF WREDPRYD, Herschel Mayall (1863–1941); QUEEN EUGENIE, Lola May (1891–1928); COUNT FERDINAND, Howard Hickman (1880–1949); KATHERYN HALDEMANN, Enid Markey (1896–1981); THE CHRIST, George Fisher (1891–1960); LUTHER ROLE (PEACE ADVOCATE), J. Frank Burke (1867–1918); THE PRIME MINISTER, Charles K. French (1860–1952); THE BLACKSMITH, J. Barney Sherry (1874–1944); HIS SON, Jerome Storm (1890–1958); HIS DAUGHTER, Ethel Ullman; A MOTHER, Kate Bruce (1858–1946); A YOUNG CHILD, Lillian Read; ***Extras:*** Alice Terry (1899–1987); Claire DuBrey (1892–1993)

Civilization was Thomas Ince's pacifist epic, which came out in early 1916. At this point, the American people were hoping to stay out of World War I. It was alleged that *Civilization* helped Woodrow Wilson be reelected president on a pacifist platform. *Civilization* was a box-office success due to the timing of its release. D.W. Griffith's *Intolerance*, released later in 1916, was a box office failure, as the tide of public opinion had by then turned more in favor of U.S. intervention on behalf of France against the German Kaiser Wilhelm II.

The lead character in this film is Count Ferdinand, a high ranking officer. His fiancée, who is opposed to war, pleads with him to speak out in favor of peace. Going against the tide, Ferdinand puts his reputation and life on the line for the cause of peace. His fiancée is played by none other than Enid Markey, who would play the screen's first "Jane" in *Tarzan of the Apes* (1918) two years later.

Civilization is lavishly staged, with impressive battle sequences. The horrors of war are graphically portrayed. One especially powerful sequence shows the troops marching off to war in "glory" with a man lamenting on how it is not right to be sending these young men to their deaths. Another is when Ferdinand sees visions of those who propagate war in hell.

Despite the sometimes stiff acting and directorial style, *Civilization* is an interesting film of significant historic value. It is compelling to watch in spite of its flaws.

202. Discontent

Rating: ☆☆½

Universal; ***Directed by*** Allen Siegler; ***Produced and Written by*** Lois Weber and Phillips Smalley; ***Running Time:*** 28 minutes; ***Cast:*** OLD MAN PEARSON, Ed Brown; HIS NEPHEW'S DAUGHTER, Marie Walcamp (1894–1936)

This film was written and produced by husband and wife team Lois Weber (1879–1939) and Phillips Smalley (1865–1939).

Ed Brown plays an old war veteran who gets tired of living in a veterans' home, and decides to move in with his wealthy nephew. Marie Walcamp plays the nephew's daughter. Things work out fine at first, until the uncle decides that the family should live according to the code of ethics he was required to live by years before. When he starts meddling into others' business, much friction is caused with all of the family members. He decides that despite the fancy home and other luxuries, he is much happier at the veterans' home with his friends.

This is the earliest example of Marie Walcamp's work that was available for evaluation. She started out at Universal under the direction of Henry MacRae in 1912, doing comedies and westerns until 1915. It was at this point that she starred in a number of films for Lois Weber and Phillips Smalley. Among the other Weber-Smalley films she starred in was the famous *Where Are My Children?* (1915), which dealt with the social issues of birth control and abortion. In 1916, she began a career in serials, which was successful for a few years, with Walcamp being on the same par as Pearl White and Ruth Roland. She was reteamed with Lois Weber again in 1921 for *The Blot*. She retired from the screen in 1927, and committed suicide by inhaling gas fumes in 1936. It was said that ill health was the reason for her suicide.

203. Easy Street

Rating: ☆☆☆

Lone Star/Mutual; ***Directed by*** Charles Chaplin; ***Photography by*** Roland Totheroh; ***Running Time:*** 23 minutes; ***Cast:*** THE DERELICT, Charlie Chaplin (1889–1977); THE MISSION WORKER, Edna Purviance (1894–1958); THE BULLY, Eric Campbell (1879–1917)

Easy Street was the ninth film that Charlie Chaplin did with the Mutual Film Company, as well as one of the best of his early slapstick shorts.

In *Easy Street*, Chaplin, a derelict, gets a job as a police officer and is assigned the most undesirable beat: Easy Street, the name of which defies its reputation as the roughest part of the slum area. Eric Campbell plays a bully who gives Chaplin an especially hard time, providing the film with its most amusing moments. Edna Purviance plays a charity worker who starts a mission on Easy Street once Chaplin's character gets the street cleaned up—more by chance than by Chaplin being a tough cop.

Eric Campbell, who was excellent at playing comedy "heavy" roles, is appealing in *Easy Street*, giving one of his best performances. This film is an entertaining comedy and would have been more so for this reviewer if it wasn't for the sterotypical "tramp" character that Chaplin started using regularly in 1915. The tramp character is an insulting and repulsive one, and this reviewer fails to see why it went over so big with the public.

204. Fatty and Mabel Adrift

Rating: ☆☆☆½

Keystone/Triangle; ***Directed by*** Roscoe Arbuckle; ***Running Time:*** 30 minutes; ***Cast:*** MABEL, Mabel Normand (1892–1930); FATTY, Roscoe Arbuckle (1887–1933); REJECTED SUITOR, Al St. John (1892–1963); MABEL'S FATHER, Frank Hayes (1871–1923); MABEL'S MOTHER, Mae Wells (1862–1941); FATTY'S DOG, Luke the dog ***Supporting Cast:*** Glenn Cavender (1883–1962); Wayland Trask (1887–1918); Joe Bordeaux (1886–1950); James Bryant

This was one of the last films to feature Mabel Normand and Roscoe Arbuckle as a team, as well as one of their best. In this film, Arbuckle plays a farmhand at the farm owned by Mabel's parents. He and Mabel decide to marry, with the blessing of Mabel's parents. One of the neighbors' sons is also infatuated with Mabel. When Mabel marries Fatty instead of him, he vows revenge.

The honeymoon of Mabel and Fatty is poignant as they start life in a new cottage purchased for them as a wedding gift. Their first meal is biscuits—which Mabel has overcooked and made hard. Seeing how distraught Mabel is, Fatty breaks the biscuit while she is not looking and eats it anyway. Fatty's dog, played by Luke, takes his place at the table with them. It is amusing to see Fatty fit the dog with a napkin just as if he was a human guest at the table.

Roscoe Arbuckle and Luke the dog prepare to eat Mabel Normand's first dinner as wife in *Fatty and Mabel Adrift* (1916).

At nightfall, Mabel and Fatty prepare for bed. Although they are depicted as a married couple, they sleep in separate beds. The scene with the goodnight kiss is poignant and well done. Mabel sleeps with Fatty's dog, while Fatty sleeps alone in his own bed. Then, Mabel's rejected suitor carries out his revenge.

Fatty, Mabel, and the dog wake up to see that their cottage has been pushed adrift. The whole house is flooded, and Fatty sends the dog with a note for Mabel's parents to rescue them. These flooded house sequences are especially well done, and classic clips from this sequence are routinely used in silent comedy documentaries.

In this film, Roscoe Arbuckle demonstrated that a man did not have to be handsome and debonair to be effective as a romantic leading man. He and Mabel Normand make such an excellent team in this film that one wonders what could have been if no scandals had occurred in the early 1920s, and they had been teamed up again for features. This film shows Mabel and Fatty at their best, before Mabel's tragic struggle with drug addiction and personal problems, and before the Virginia Rappe (1895–1921) incident ruined Arbuckle's career.

Al St. John, who plays the rejected suitor, was in reality Arbuckle's nephew. He played mostly in comedies through the late 1920s. He played a few dramatic roles in films such as *She Goes to War* (1929) before teaming with his uncle Arbuckle for the series of Vitaphone two-reelers that were completed just before Arbuckle's death in 1933. St. John worked in low budget westerns until 1950, when he retired.

Among the supporting cast members in this film is Wayland Trask, who would become one of many American celebrities to die from the Spanish influenza epidemic of 1918. He was 31.

205. Hell's Hinges

Rating: ☆☆☆½

Kay-Bee/Triangle; ***Directed by*** Charles Swickard and William S. Hart; ***Screenplay by*** C. Gardner Sullivan; ***Photography by*** Joseph August; ***Running Time:*** 50 minutes; ***Cast:*** BLAZE TRACEY, William S. Hart (1864?–1946); FAITH HENLEY, Clara Williams (1888–1928); REVEREND HENLEY, Jack Standing (1886–1917); SILK MILLER, Alfred Hollingsworth (1869–1926); A CLERGYMAN, Robert McKim (1886–1927); ZEB TAYLOR, J. Frank Burke (1867–1918); DOLLY, Louise Glaum (1900–1970); ***Extras:*** John Gilbert (1899–1936); Jean Hersholt (1886–1956)

Hell's Hinges is William S. Hart's most highly acclaimed western from the 1910s. Hart, a veteran of the legitimate stage, had played Messala in the 1899 tour of *Ben-Hur* at age 35. It was in 1910 that he became inspired to do westerns, and Thomas Ince, a former veteran of the stage himself and an old friend of Hart's, gave him his first chance at pictures in 1914. This was the beginning of a three-year partnership, which lasted until 1917 when Hart went into independent production. It is amazing that Hart was 50 years old before achieving fame as a motion picture actor—an age at which most stars were fading into character roles or into retirement.

Hart directs himself in his role as Blaze Tracey, an outlaw who lives in a western town in which a new church is being started. The saloon crowd objects to the church coming in, thinking that puritanical laws will be passed, and they use the new minister's chronic alcoholism in their efforts to shut the church down. Tracey is all for the saloon crowd's efforts until he meets the minister's sister and sees how sincere she is.

Tracey's friend, Silk Miller, is not as easily convinced, and continues his efforts to drive the church out of town by having Dolly, the town whore, to seduce the minister and get him drunk, thus forcing him into disgrace before his congregation. This is a good excuse to burn down the church, and a riot therefore ensues. Not only is the church burned to the ground, but the drunk minister is killed. Tracey seeks to avenge the minister's gentle sister, Faith, and since the saloon crowd burned down the church, he burns down the saloon!

Not only is *Hell's Hinges* one of the greatest films of the western genre, it is also historically important as the film debut of John Gilbert, who played an extra in the film that would put him on the road to stardom as one of the great romantic leads of the 1920s. Hart was so impressed with Gilbert in this film that he gave him an important role in *The Apostle of Vengeance* (1916) over the objections of producer Tom Ince.

Leading lady Clara Williams was married to film director Reginald Barker (1886–1945), who had directed Hart in some of his first films. Williams was only 40 when she died in 1928, following an operation for an unspecified illness.

Four of the other players died within 11 years of starring in this film. Jack Standing, who played the alcoholic minister, died at 31 in 1917. No cause of death has been

William S. Hart in *Hell's Hinges* (1916).

reported. Robert McKim died of a cerebral hemorrhage at age 40 in 1927. Alfred Hollingsworth died at 57 following a brief illness in 1926. J. Frank Burke died in 1918 at age 50 from arteriosclerosis.

206. Intolerance

Rating: ☆☆☆☆

Wark Producing Company; ***Directed and Written by*** D.W. Griffith; ***Assistant Directors:*** Allan Dwan, Erich von Stroheim, William Christy Cabanne, Tod Browning, Jack Conway, W.S.

The famous Babylon sets for *Intolerance* (1916) which have never been surpassed in any subsequent film in the 82 years since.

Van Dyke, Elmer Clifton, Monte Blue, Mike Siebert, George Siegmann; ***Photography by*** G.W. Bitzer and Karl Brown; ***Film Editors:*** James and Rose Smith; ***Titles by*** D.W. Griffith, Anita Loos, and Frank E. Woods; ***Set Design by*** Frank Wortman and Walter L. Hall; ***Research assistants:*** R. Ellis Wales, Joseph Henabery, Lillian Gish; ***Choreography of Dances by*** Ruth St. Denis; ***Costumes by*** Western Costume Company; ***Original Running Time:*** Approximately 8 hours; ***Running Time of Most Complete Existing Print:*** 210 minutes; ***Running Time of Most Complete Video Version:*** 177 minutes; ***Running Time of Most Video Versions:*** 170 minutes; ***Cast:*** *THE WOMAN WHO ROCKS THE CRADLE:* Lillian Gish (1893–1993); THE MODERN STORY: THE DEAR ONE, Mae Marsh (1895–1968); THE BOY, Robert Harron (1893–1920); THE DEAR ONE'S FATHER, Fred Turner (1858–1923); JENKINS, Sam DeGrasse (1875–1953); MARY T. JENKINS, Vera Lewis (1873–1956); THE FRIENDLESS ONE, Miriam Cooper (1894–1976); MUSKETEER OF THE SLUMS, Walter Long (1879–1952); THE KINDLY POLICE OFFICER, Tom Wilson (1880–1965); THE GOVERNOR, Ralph Lewis (1872–1937); ATTORNEY FOR THE BOY, Barney Bernard (1877–1924); THE JUDGE, Lloyd Ingraham (1874–1956); A WOMAN AT THE EMPLOYEES' BALL, Jennie Lee (1850–1925); THE PRIEST, Reverend A.W. McClure; PRISON GUARD, J.P. McCarthy (1865–1962); THE DEBUTANTE, Marguerite Marsh [a.k.a. Marguerite Loveridge] (1892–1925); OWNER OF CAR, Tod Browning (1882–1962); CHIEF DETECTIVE, Edward Dillon (1879–1933); BARTENDER, Billy Quirk (1873–1926); JENKINS' SECRETARY, Clyde Hopkins (1893–1958); THE WARDEN, William A. Brown; WIFE OF THE NEIGHBOR, Alberta Lee; THE VESTAL VIRGINS OF UPLIFT, Mary Alden (1883–1946); Eleanor Washington; Pearl Elmore (1879–??); Lucille Brown; Luray Huntley; Mrs. Arthur Mackley *THE JUDEAN STORY:* JESUS CHRIST, Howard Gaye (died 1955); MARY (MOTHER of Jesus), Lillian Langdon (1861–1943); Mary Magdalene, Olga Grey (1897–1973); Taller Pharisee, Gunther Von Ritzau; Shorter Pharisee, Erich von Stroheim (1885–1957); Bride of Cana, Bessie Love (1898–1986); Bridegroom, George Walsh (1889–1981); The bride's father, William H. Brown; A wedding guest, W.S. Van Dyke (1890–1943) *THE FRENCH STORY:* Brown Eyes, Margery Wilson (1897–1986); Prosper Latour, Eugene Pallette (1889–1954); Brown Eyes' Father, Spottiswoode Aitken (1868–1933); Brown Eyes' Mother, Ruth Handforth (1883–1965); The mercenary, A.D. Sears (1887–1942); King Charles IX, Frank Bennett (1890–1957); Duc d'Angou (effeminate heir), Maxfield Stanley; Catherine de Medici, Josephine Crowell (died 1934); Henry of Navarre, W.E. Lawrence (1896–1947); Marguerite of Valois, Georgia Pearce [alias used by Constance Talmadge] (1900–1973); Admiral Coligny, Joseph Henabery (1887–1976); A page, Chandler House (1904–1982); Catholic priest, Louis Romaine; Duc de Guise, Morris Levy; Cardinal Lorraine, Howard Gaye (died 1955) *THE BABYLON STORY:* The mountain girl, Constance Talmadge (1900–1973); The Rhapsode, Elmer Clifton (1890–1949); Belshazzar, Alfred Paget (died 1925); Princess Beloved [Attarea], Seena Owen (1894–1966); Nabonidus, Carl Stockdale (1874–1953); High Priest of Bel, Tully Marshall (1864–1943); Cyrus the Persian, George Siegmann (1882–1928); Mighty Man of Valour, Elmo Lincoln (1889–1952); The runner, Gino Corrado [a.k.a. Eugene Corey] (1893–1982); A boy killed in the fighting, Wallace Reid (1891–1923); Captain of the gate, Ted Duncan; Bodyguard to the Princess, Felix Modjeska (1887–1940); Judges, Lawrence Lawlore; George Fawcett (1860–1939); Old woman, Kate Bruce (1858–1946); Solo dancer, Ruth St. Denis (1878–1968); Slave, Loyola O'Connor (1880–??); Charioteer, James Curley; Babylonian dandy, Howard Scott; Auctioneer, Martin Landry; Brother of the mountain girl, Arthur Mayer; Gobryas (Lieutenant of Cyrus), Charles Van Cortland; Chief Eunuch, Jack Cosgrave (1875–1925); Girls of the marriage market, Alma Rubens (1897–1931), Madame Sul-Te-Wan (1873–1959), Ruth Darling (died 1918), Margaret Mooney; Girls in the orgy sequence, Mildred Harris (1902–1944), Pauline Starke (1900–1977), Carmel Myers (1901–1980), Winifred Westover (1899–1978), Jewel Carmen (1897–??), Eve Sothern, Natalie Talmadge (1899–1969), Carol Dempster (1901–1991), Ethel Grey Terry (1891–1931), Daisy Robinson, Anna Mae Walthall (1894–1950), Grace Wilson, Lotta Clifton; First Priest of Nergel, Ah Singh; Second Priest of Nergel, Ranji Singh; Charioteer of the Priest of Bel, Ed Burns; Second Charioteer of the Priest of Bel, James Burns (died 1975); Barbarian Chieftain, Charles Eagle Eye; Ethiopian Chieftain, William Dark Cloud; The Dancers, The Denishawn Dancers; *NOTEWORTHY EXTRAS:* Donald Crisp (1882–1974), Douglas Fairbanks, Sr. (1883–1939), Frank Campeau (1864–1943), Nigel De Brulier (1877–1948), Owen Moore (1886–1939), Wilfred Lucas (1871–1940), Tammany Young (1887–1936), Sir Herbert Beerbohm Tree (1853–1917), DeWolfe Hopper (1858–1935) *The Epilogue:* The two children, Francis Carpenter and Virginia Lee Corbin (1910–1942)

Intolerance is D.W. Griffith's answer to those who were offended by and criticized *The Birth of a Nation*. It has been regarded by many respected film historians as one of the greatest American films of all time—if not the greatest. The grandeur of this spectacle has never been topped. The cost of rebuilding the Babylon sets alone would be prohibitive. Few films can come even close to being worthy of comparison.

Intolerance consists of four separate but parallel stories portraying intolerance throughout four different ages of human history spanning approximately 2,500 years. The image of Lillian Gish rocking the cradle (in a blue tint in the color tinted versions) serves to link the stories. Some skeptics state that Griffith was unclear in defining the meaning of the interlinking image, but William M. Drew lays those arguments to rest quite easily in his 1986 book, *D.W. Griffith's Intolerance: Its Genesis and Vision.*

The four periods of history covered in *Intolerance* are the Babylonian (539 B.C.), the Judean (about A.D. 27), the Renaissance (1572 France), and modern day (1914 America). The audience is shown how intolerance has reared its ugly head in such destructive events as the greatest treason in history which resulted in the fall of Babylon due to intolerance of a newly introduced religion, the crucifixion of Jesus Christ, and the mass murder of many Huguenots in St. Bartholomew. The modern story shows how intolerance directly and indirectly ruined the lives of Americans in the early part of this century.

Originally shot for the unprecedented sum of $1.9 million (sources vary), *Intolerance* would probably cost upwards of $500 million to reshoot today if shot exactly as it was in 1916—with the massive sets, lavish costumes, and thousands of extras. D.W. Griffith financed the film himself, after buying out his skeptical financial backers with long-term notes, and using his profits from *The Birth of a Nation* to do so. Richard Schickel asserts in his book, *D.W. Griffith: An American Life*, that the production costs of *Intolerance* came to only about $386,000. This reviewer finds it hard to believe that Griffith could have possibly produced the film for less than $1 million even in 1916 dollars. Perhaps there were some undocumented expenses that were not included in the $386,000 figure. If Schickel's figure is indeed correct, then Griffith was an even greater genius for producing such an extravagant film for such an economical price. Griffith was a man who truly produced films for the sake of art, without the greedy profiteering attitude prevalent within most of the larger motion picture studios. At the box office, *Intolerance* lost a great deal of money, and the debts it incurred reportedly took years to pay off. Part of the reason for the financial failure was the timing of its release. In its first few months, *Intolerance* was outgrossing *The Birth of a Nation*. Unfortunately, by mid-1917, America was ready to enter World War I, and the box-office receipts for this pacifist film plummeted. While Griffith needed high box-office receipts for a few years (as *The Birth of a Nation* had) to recoup his costs, he only benefited from a few months of such. *Intolerance* grossed millions in Russia, but Griffith never saw a dime of the money it made in the Russian market.

The battle scenes and sets in the Babylon story are the most elaborate and historically realistic to date. Here the instruments of war are burning oil, bows and arrows, stones, and the large moving towers that were necessary for the offensive armies to climb up and over the 300-foot walls of Babylon (of which replicas were constructed). Decapitations, stabbings, and the other horrors of ancient war are graphically portrayed and grimly realistic.

The backdrop sets for the Babylon banquet hall are still the largest in Hollywood history to date, possibly equaled only by the castle set in Douglas Fairbanks, Sr.'s, 1922 production of *Robin Hood.* The size of the backdrop for the Feast of Belshazzar necessitated the invention of the modern day "crane shot." Another invention that is directly attributable to *Intolerance* is the first false eyelashes, which were created for the part of Princess Beloved. These first eyelashes were so cumbersome that Owen could only wear them a few hours at a time, as otherwise her eyes would swell shut.

With the possible exception of *The Birth of a Nation, Intolerance* was the greatest single advance in the motion picture medium, being to Hollywood what the 1969 moon voyage was to NASA.

The original running time of the director's cut of *Intolerance* was 8 hours. Lillian Gish stated that the full 8-hour version should have been released as it was, as valuable footage was lost forever in the editing process. The running time of the original theatrical release print was approximately 3 hours, 30 minutes. A restored print in the Museum of Modern Art comes close to this original length, but is inaccessible to the public. The most complete print that is widely available is one of 2 hours, 57 minutes, which was the version used for Kino's video release of *Intolerance*. Most available prints run 2 hours, 50 minutes. There were several different edit cuts of *Intolerance*. For example, there are three different ways in which the baby of the modern story's fate is presented. This is because Griffith shot extra footage for *The Mother and the Law* (1918), and this footage was spliced into later prints of *Intolerance*. In one print, the baby just disappears and is never mentioned again after he is initially taken away from his mother, played by Mae Marsh. In another print, the baby dies. In the print used for the Kino Video version, the baby is reunited with his mother. Kevin Brownlow produced in 1989 a version of *Intolerance* which had orchestral accompaniment by the great musician Carl Davis. This version was distributed on video in the United States by HBO Video, but has since gone out of print. *Intolerance* is a film that really must be seen with full orchestral accompaniment to be fully appreciated. The video versions with organ and piano scores simply do not do the film justice, and cannot be recommended. Some company hopefully will reissue Brownlow's production of the film.

207. Joan the Woman

Rating: ☆☆☆☆

Cardinal/Paramount; ***Directed by*** Cecil B. DeMille; ***Story and Scenario by*** Jeanie MacPherson; ***Art Direction by*** Wilfred Buckland; ***Photography by*** Alvin Wyckoff; ***Running Time:*** 138 minutes; ***Cast:*** JOAN OF ARC, Geraldine Farrar (1882–1967); ERIC TRENT, Wallace Reid (1891–1923); CAUCHON, Theodore Roberts (1861–1928); GEORGE DE LA TREMOILLE, Charles Clary (1873–1931); GENERAL LA HIRE, Hobart Bosworth (1867–1943); CHARLES VII, Raymond Hatton (1887–1971)

This was the first of Cecil B. DeMille's (1881–1959) super spectacles, filmed at a time when he was experimenting with different types of films. It was filmed on a grand scale, using thousands of extras just like D.W. Griffith's *Intolerance*. Until now, this epic has not received the proper recognition in film history books. This is due largely to the fact that until David Shepard took on *Joan the Woman* as a video release project, it had been archived at the George Eastman House and inaccessible for review. Since *Joan the Woman*'s profit margin was slim, it discouraged Paramount and DeMille from attempting further epics of this grandeur until the early 1920s.

This film came out during World War I, before the United States entered the war. The prologue shows a French soldier (also played by Wallace Reid) in a war trench, who sees a vision of Joan of Arc, telling him that now is the time—in service to the country that she died for nearly 500 years before—to right the wrong that he did to her in a past life by taking on a dangerous mission for the sake of France. The film then proceeds to the biography of "Joan the Woman," the great French martyr. The biography is divided into two epochs. The first shows how she led France to victory over the British

Geraldine Farrar plays Joan of Arc in Cecil B. DeMille's masterpiece, *Joan the Woman* (1916).

troops who had tried to invade and take over. The second epoch deals with how Eric Trent betrayed Joan to the British, who were determined to burn her as a witch in retaliation for her role in their defeat. The final sequence depicting the burning features hand-colored orange flames, and is especially impressive.

Geraldine Farrar gives a fabulous performance as Joan of Arc. Her acting technique was much more polished in this film than it had been in Carmen, as she was by this time more accustomed to motion picture work. Based on what has survived from 1916 and been available for evaluation, Farrar's performance was among the four or five best female performances of the year, coming very close to giving Mae Marsh a good run for her money on her *Intolerance* performance. Wallace Reid's performance as Eric Trent was easily the best male performance of the year based on what is available for evaluation. Through his subtle pantomime, one can see the anguish on his face as Joan, who twice saved his life, is burned. Among the supporting cast are the great character actor Hobart Bosworth and Theodore Roberts, who played Moses in the 1923 version of *The Ten Commandments*.

Two other biopics on Joan of Arc from the silent era are available for comparison. *The Passion of Joan of Arc* (1928) is a masterpiece in its own right, as it tells most of the story exclusively with facial close-ups. But, it covers only the trial, with hardly any account of the events leading up to the trial. *The Marvelous Life of Joan of Arc* (1928) is relatively well-done, but still pales in comparison to this version. *Joan the Woman* is by far the best film narrative of the life of Joan of Arc.

In this reviewer's opinion, *Joan the Woman* is Cecil B. DeMille's greatest film achievement. It was difficult to decide between *Joan the Woman* and *The King of Kings* (1927), but the artistry of the hand-colored flames in *Joan the Woman*, as well as the minor problems with historical authenticity in *The King of Kings*, put *Joan the Woman* over the top. It is high time that this artistic masterpiece received the recognition and acclaim that it deserves. Anyone who doubts Cecil B. DeMille's directorial ability will likely change his or her mind upon seeing *Joan the Woman*.

208. Little Mary Sunshine

Rating: ☆☆☆½

Balboa/Pathé; ***Directed by*** Henry King; ***Assistant Director:*** Alen Willey; ***Scenario by*** Daniel Whitcomb; ***Camera Operator:*** Harry W. Gerstad; ***Running Time:*** 45 minutes; ***Cast:*** LITTLE MARY SUNSHINE, Baby Marie Osborne (born 1911); BOB, Henry King (1886–1982); SYLVIA, Marguerite Nichols (190–1941); SYLVIA'S MOTHER, Mollie MacConnell (1865–1920); ORGAN GRINDER, Leon Osborne; HIMSELF, Pete the bear; ***Supporting Cast:*** Andrew Arbuckle (1887–1939)

From 1915 to 1919, Baby Marie Osborne starred in 22 films as a child. Of these 22 films, only *Little Mary Sunshine* is known to survive. This was the first in a series of eight *Little Mary Sunshine* films that Henry King directed and costarred with Baby Marie. Osborne was catapulted to stardom as perhaps the most popular child star of the late 1910s, paving the way for 1920s child stars Baby Peggy, Junior Coghlan, and Jackie Coogan.

According to Osborne, now known as Marie Osborne Yeats, this was the best of her films and her own personal favorite. Thus, it is fortunate that in this case the best representation of a star's work has been the one to survive.

Little Mary Sunshine is a delightful and charming film in which Osborne stars as a 4-year-old girl whose mother has died from years of abuse by her drunken father, and runs away from home. She is taken in by a man named Bob, who comes from a wealthy family, and is provided for in luxurious conditions. Bob is depressed, as his drinking and partying caused him to miss a date with his fiancée Sylvia, who has broken off their engagement. Little Mary Sunshine brings joy to her new household, and eventually Bob and Sylvia are reunited, adopting Little Mary as their own and living happily ever after.

One of the most amusing sequences is the one in which Little Mary sees a show bear that she and all of the other neighborhood kids admire. A dream sequence has Osborne bringing the bear home, where he gets into everything. We see him drinking a jug of milk, climbing across the bed that Mary is sleeping in, and finally being put into the bathtub which Mary fills to prepare to bathe him.

Little Mary Sunshine is a rarity in more ways than one. In addition to being Baby Marie Osborne's only surviving silent era work, it is the earliest of director and costar Henry King's work known to exist outside of the archives. This film reveals King to have been a dapper, attractive player, as well as a competent actor. He of course became famous on the basis of his abilities as a director, and some of his later films are reviewed elsewhere in this book.

Baby Marie Osborne, who played the title role in *Little Mary Sunshine* (1916), the first in a series of films directed by and co-starring Henry King.

Marguerite Nichols, who is appearing as fiancée Sylvia, would later become the wife of comedy producer Hal Roach (1892–1992). She was only 41 when she died of pneumonia. The organ grinder is played by Leon Osborne, who was the adoptive father of Marie, having taken her in when she was orphaned at the age of 11 days in real life. The Osbornes owned a traveling carnival, and among the animals in their entourage were a wildcat, a monkey, and a bear named Pete. Pete the bear, whom Marie was used to working with, played the bear in this film, which was the one and only film he starred in.

Once her career as a child star was over, Marie Osborne adjusted well to life away from the movies. In the early talkie era, she came back to do extra work, and ultimately was used as a stand-in for Ginger Rogers, Deanna Durbin, and Betty Hutton. In the 1950s, she began a successful 22-year career as a costume supervisor. She designed all of the costumes used by Elizabeth Taylor in *Cleopatra* (1963). After her retirement in 1976, she moved from Hollywood to San Clemente in Southern California, where she has lived happily since. Osborne maintains an active life at 86, making appearances at various film conventions from time to time, as well as visiting friends in Italy on a regular basis.

When this reviewer wrote to Osborne in 1997, she mentioned that she had not seen any of her silent films since 1923. Serge Bromberg of Lobster Films in Paris, France, was contacted and, upon learning of this situation, was kind enough to provide a video transfer of his print of *Little Mary Sunshine*. In early 1998, Marie Osborne Yeats at last saw one of her starring films again for the first time in 75 years.

The surviving print material is a beautiful, pristine, color tinted 35 mm print meticulously restored by Bromberg.

209. The Mystery of the Leaping Fish

Rating: ☆☆½

Triangle; ***Directed by*** John Emerson; ***Scenario by*** Tod Browning; ***Running Time:*** 19 minutes; ***Cast:*** SECRET SERVICE CHIEF I.M. KEENE, Tom Wilson (1880–1965); DETECTIVE COKE

ENNYDAY, Douglas Fairbanks, Sr. (1883–1939); INANE, Bessie Love (1898–1986); THE DRUG DEALER, A.D. Sears (1887–1942); FEMALE CONFEDERATE, Alma Rubens (1897–1931)

This early Fairbanks comedy has him playing Coke Ennyday, a cocaine addicted detective who is hired to investigate the mystery of some leaping fish that are used to smuggle in cocaine. Done totally tongue-in-cheek as a satire, Coke Ennyday is seen with a variety of gadgets, driving a checkered car and wearing checkered clothing. Bessie Love plays the girl who blows up the inflatable fish, not knowing the drugs are being smuggled in them. A blackmailer named Fishy Joe demands that the drug dealer either convince Love's character to marry him within the week, or he will tell all he knows. Alma Rubens plays a small part as the drug dealer's partner.

This comedy, with its satirical approach to drug abuse, would not have been allowed to be released in the era of the Hays office, which came about in the early 1920s after the Arbuckle and Taylor scandals. It would be 63 years before another satire on drugs would be released: *Cheech and Chong's Up in Smoke* (1979).

One of the attractions of this film is that it is one of the rare surviving examples of Alma Rubens' work. Although she is fully billed, viewers will be disappointed to see that her part is minor, and she only appears onscreen for a few seconds. It is ironic that she played a drug dealer in this film, and that she, in real life, became addicted to drugs in the 1920s, which led to her early death.

The script was written by film director Tod Browning (1882–1962) in the first years of his film career. This was the first of many popular satires that director John Emerson (1874–1956) and Douglas Fairbanks, Sr., would collaborate on in the late 1910s.

Despite the film's primitive production values, the satirical subject matter makes it far ahead of its time, and an enduring cult classic.

210. The Pawn Shop *Rating:* ☆

Lone Star/Mutual; ***Written and Directed by*** Charles Chaplin; ***Photography by*** Roland Totheroh; ***Running Time:*** 20 minutes; ***Cast:*** THE CLERK, Charlie Chaplin (1889–1977); THE GIRL, Edna Purviance (1894–1958)

This is one of the most popular of the Chaplin vehicles distributed through the Mutual Film Corporation. It is basically a silly, knockabout slapstick comedy with Chaplin working as a clerk in a pawnshop, where he unintentionally bungles everything.

This film contains the famous ladder sequence, as well as the sequence in which Chaplin unwittingly tears up a rare antique alarm clock brought in for appraisal. Edna Purviance is charming as Chaplin's coworker in the kitchen. Purviance is the redeeming factor in this vastly overrated film, which generally has no substance and shows Chaplin acting stupid.

211. Poor Little Peppina *Rating:* ☆☆☆½

Paramount; ***Directed by*** Sidney Olcott; ***Photography by*** Emmet Williams; ***Based on the Story by*** Kate Jordan; ***Running Time:*** 47 minutes; ***Cast:*** PEPPINA [LOIS TORRENS AS ADOLESCENT], Mary Pickford (1892–1979); HUGH CARROLL, Eugene O'Brien (1880–1966); BEPPO, Jack Pickford (1896–1933); VILLATO, Cesare Gravina (1858–1954?); ROBERT TORRENS, Edwin Mordant (1868–1942); MRS. TORRENS, Edith Shayne; LOIS TORRENS [AS A CHILD], Eileen Stewart; FRANZOLI SOLDO, Antonio Maiori (1869–1938); PIETRO, Ernesto Torti

This film was done during a period in which Mary Pickford was experimenting with various types of roles, before her resounding success in *The Poor Little Rich Girl* (1917) set a pattern of child roles for her. *Poor Little Peppina* sees Pickford in one of her popular "tomboy" roles, which Olive Thomas and Marion Davies later did successfully as well. In this film, Mary plays Peppina, a girl who was kidnapped from a good home by an escaped Italian Mafia murderer, and sold to a disreputable scoundrel. She is brought up as the sister of a boy named Beppo, played by her real life brother, Jack Pickford. The time comes when she is to marry the mobster who bought her, and, with the help of Beppo, she runs away disguised as a boy. She stows away on a ship, where she hides in the cabin of prominent attorney Hugh Carroll, who feeds her and provides partial fare to America. (She works a deal with one of the deck hands for the rest of her way to America.)

Once in America, Peppina is back into the hands of her original kidnappers, who are now running a counterfeiting racket. She is arrested when she unknowingly passes off one of the counterfeit bills, which leads into the resolution of the story.

Mary Pickford demonstrated good versatility in this role, showing early in her career that she could play any type of role given to her, and play it well. It was perhaps because she was so good in so many types of roles that Paramount at this point wasn't quite sure what to do with her. That question was answered with the runaway success of her child roles. She certainly was impressive, as at the time she did this film, she was making $4,000 a week, and just a few months later renegotiated a $10,000 per week contract with Paramount.

Before having seen this film, this reviewer had seen Jack Pickford only in some of his later films of the late 1920s, when he was in his early 30s, and had been through some hard times. Pickford was 20 when he made this film—at a time before he went through the tragedy of wife Olive Thomas' death. He looks fantastic in this film during happier times—the ultimate image of the all-American adolescent boy. By seeing Pickford in this film, one can see why he was chosen for the lead role in William Desmond Taylor's *Tom Sawyer* (1917) a year later.

Poor Little Peppina is also historically significant as the second film of matinee idol Eugene O'Brien. He was 35 when he abandoned a career in medicine to become a star, and he is appealing as the leading man in this film despite his middle age. This is also one of the earliest film appearances of Italian actor Cesare Gravina, who gained prominence as a character actor in Erich von Stroheim's films.

Although most of director Sidney Olcott's (1872–1949) films were mediocre efforts, this film is an exception. It was the second of two films that he and Mary Pickford collaborated on, and based on this film, it looks as if the two worked well together.

Poor Little Peppina has survived in excellent, pristine condition, and will hopefully be made more widely accessible in the future. It is a delightful film with excellent performances by both Mary and Jack Pickford. This is one of only two surviving features in which they can be seen together. A third film that starred all three Pickford siblings (Mary, Jack, and Lottie), *Fanchon the Cricket* (1915), was at one time classified as a lost film, but a print turned up in a foreign archive in the mid to late 1990s.

212. Snow White

Rating: ☆☆

Educational Pictures; ***Running Time:*** 47 minutes; ***Cast:*** QUEEN MARY, Aimee Erlich; THE KING, Pansy Grace Lichtenburg; ALICE THE WICKED PRINCESS, Ruth Richey

This early German silent version of *Snow White* is one with which very few people are familiar. It is not available on video from any company, and circulates only in a few private collections in the United States.

This adaptation departs a bit from the original story, with the good Queen Mary longing for a child. The fairies grant her wish, and Snow White is born. The evil Princess Alice wants the queen dead so that she can assume the throne. Alice poisons Mary, and assumes the throne when Snow White is 2 years old.

Eight years later, Queen Alice becomes jealous of Snow White's magnificent beauty. (The mirror effects showing Queen Alice seeking counsel are crude and not very convincing. Basically, the queen holds the mirror at an angle that allows Snow White to be seen in the background.) This version, the wicked queen demands that the huntsman kill Snow White, and bring back her blood-stained dress as proof of her death. When he is unable to go through with the murder, he uses the blood of a dove to stain the dress. As in the traditional versions of the story, Snow White takes refuge in the home of the dwarfs.

Once again, Queen Alice consults her mirror, and is told that Snow White is still the fairest of them all. She consults the wicked witch, who gives her a necklace that will close around Snow White's neck and strangle her. Alice dresses up as a peddler and convinces Snow White to wear the necklace. The dwarfs return from work to find her unconscious, and remove the necklace. With the help of the good fairies, she is revived. The fairies and dwarfs celebrate the revival with a feast. The queen consults her mirror and sees that she has been tricked again. At this point in the film, some footage is missing, and the story cuts to the queen bringing a poisoned apple to the cottage. This time, it appears that Queen Alice has succeeded in killing Snow White. The fairies and dwarfs take the body to its final resting place. But, Prince Paul asks if he can take it to his palace. The prince's huntsmen stumble, which dislodges the apple from Snow White's throat. Snow White and the prince marry. Alice is banished from the country, but is forgiven by Snow White. The final shot shows the seven dwarfs holding up signs with the words, "AND THEY LIVED HAPPY EVER AFTERWARD!" The seventh dwarf holds up the exclamation point.

This is an interesting version of *Snow White*—despite its stagy direction and primitive techniques and effects. One thing that is unique about this adaptation is that most of the titles have been written in poetic verse.

There have been at least six film adaptations of *Snow White*. The most famous of the silent versions was the version that Paramount released on December 25, 1916, which starred Marguerite Clark (1883–1940) in the title role. It was the Marguerite Clark version that inspired Disney's 1937 animated feature version. For years, the Clark version was believed lost. A print turned up extant in a European archive, and the George Eastman House has had a print since the early 1980s. The Disney Company restored the print, which is inaccessible to the general public on video.

213. The Social Secretary

Rating: ☆☆☆

Triangle; ***Running Time:*** 49 minutes; ***Cast:*** MAYME, Norma Talmadge (1897–1957); JIMMIE DE PUYSTER, Gladden James (1892–1948); ELSIE DE PUYSTER, Helen Weer; MRS. PEABODY DE PUYSTER, Kate Lester (1857–1924); COUNT LIMONITTIZZ, Herbert Frank (1885–1926); BIT PART, Erich von Stroheim (1885–1957)

This is one of the few extant films of Norma Talmadge that is available outside the archives for evaluation. Although Talmadge was primarily known for her work as a dramatic actress, this is a comedy with dramatic elements.

Norma Talmadge, star of *The Social Secretary* (1916).

Talmadge plays Mayme, a pretty secretary who has trouble keeping a job because many of her bosses make unwanted advances. The first job she quits is with the New York Purity League—where the director, an older man, makes advances. She slaps him in the face and quits on the spot. This was quite obviously a jab at the "reform" and "prohibition" movements that had gained so much momentum at this period in the late 1910s.

Mayme's problem is finally solved when an older couple advertises for an unattractive secretary, as their secretaries all seem to leave to get married. Mayme makes herself up to look prudish—with her hair in a bun, round spectacles, and a hideous outfit that looks like something out of the 1880s. Things get complicated when the young daughter of her employers becomes engaged to one Count Limonittizz, a scoundrel for whom Mayme once worked. Mayme comes out of disguise to show the De Puysters what a scoundrel the count is, and complications arise.

Despite the arrogant attitude that Norma Talmadge was said to have had offscreen, she is charming in this film. It whets one's desire to see more of her films. One of Talmadge's most highly acclaimed films, *Camille* (1927), does exist in the Raymond Rohauer collection. Unfortunately, the Rohauer estate has not made *Camille* accessible to the public on video or even in the form of a public screening.

The leading man in this film, Gladden James, was married to Marion Blackton, the daughter of J. Stuart Blackton, one of the founders of Vitagraph. Kate Lester, who was renowned as one of the great beauties of the stage, died a tragic death in 1924 at age 67. The death was caused by burns resulting from a gas stove explosion. J. Herbert Frank, who plays the contemptible count, had a personal life that was in some ways similar to the character that he portrayed in this film. He had been arrested numerous times for drug dealing. He committed suicide in 1926 by inhaling gas fumes. No further information could be found on Helen Weer.

The Social Secretary is a light, entertaining film that shows a lighter side of Norma Talmadge. She is absolutely delightful in this film, which is a must-see especially for Talmadge fans.

214. Sold for Marriage

Rating: ☆½

Triangle; ***Directed by*** William Christy Cabanne; ***Running Time:*** 43 minutes; ***Cast:*** MARFA, Lillian Gish (1893–1993); UNCLE IVAN, A.D. Sears (1887–1942); PETER, William Siebert; HER GRANDFATHER, Curt Rehfeld (1881–1934); HER AUNT, Pearl Elmore (1879–??); JAN, Frank Bennett (1890–1957); GEORG, William A. Lowery (1885–1941); NICHOLAS, Frank Brownlee (1874–1948); ***Supporting Cast:*** Olga Grey (1897–1973); Walter Long (1879–1952)

Every major movie player—no matter how stellar their career—has invariably had one or two bad films. In Lillian Gish's case, *Sold for Marriage* is one of her bad films, and *The Enemy* (1928; reviewed elsewhere in this book) is the other.

Sold for Marriage is one of a group of films that Lillian Gish starred in for William Christy Cabanne (1888–1950) after she had finished her cradle sequences for *Intolerance*. In her 1969 autobiography, she stated that she did not remember anything about the films she did for Cabanne, although she does discuss this period somewhat in her 1973 book *Dorothy and Lillian Gish*. When one sees this film, one can see why it was among those that Gish wanted to forget.

The plot itself was an interesting one—dealing with white slave trafficking. Gish plays Marfa, a girl being raised by her uncle and aunt in Russia. They are determined to marry her off to any unscrupulous suitor from whom they can get money. Marfa refuses, as she is in love with a poor man. She finally relents when a Russian official tries to rape her, and in the process of defending herself believes that she has killed him. She sees no choice but to flee the country with her aunt and uncle, who attempt to sell her into a "marriage market" now that they have her totally under their control.

Under D.W. Griffith's direction, this plot might have been made into a good film. But, the inept direction of William Christy Cabanne simply does nothing for it. In seeing this film, it appears as if the most primitive of directorial techniques were used. Basically, it consists of a few sequences hastily shot and spliced together with some title cards thrown in. The film simply does not give Gish any opportunity to act.

Among the other cast members are two of Gish's costars in *Intolerance*: Frank Bennett and Allan D. Sears. No further information is known on William Siebert.

Sold for Marriage illustrates that one cannot judge a player's career on the basis of a single film. Lillian Gish was among the greatest of the silent screen actresses, mainly because the vast majority of her work survives and is available for evaluation. Her reputation might be different had *Sold for Marriage* been her sole surviving film.

While *Sold for Marriage* is an abysmal film, it has fortunately survived as an example of Lillian Gish's work under Christy Cabanne.

215. Twenty Thousand Leagues Under the Sea *Rating:* ☆☆☆

Universal; ***Directed by*** Stuart Paton; ***Assistant Director:*** Martin Murphy; ***Screenplay by*** Stuart Paton; ***Based on Two Jules Verne Novels*** *Twenty Thousand Leagues Under the Sea, The Mysterious Island*; ***Photography by*** Eugene Gaudio; ***Assistant Photographers:*** Friend Baker, Milton Loryea; ***Art Direction by*** Frank D. Ormston; ***Technical Directors:*** H.H. Barter, James Milburn; ***Running Time:*** 100 minutes; ***Cast:*** CAPTAIN NEMO/PRINCE DAAKER, Allen Holubar (1890–1923); A CHILD OF NATURE/PRINCESS DAAKER, Jane Gail (1890–1963); PROFESSOR ARONNAX, Dan Hanlon; ARONNAX'S DAUGHTER, Edna Pendleton; NED LAND, Curtis Benton; LIEUTENANT BOND, Matt Moore (1888–1960); CYRUS HARDING, Howard Crampton (1865–1922); PENCROFT, Wallace Clark (1897?-1963); HERBERT BROWN, Martin Murphy; NEB, Leviticus Jones; CHARLES DENVER, William Welsh (1870–1946); PRINCE DAAKER'S DAUGHTER AS A CHILD, Lois Alexander (1891?-1968); MAJOR CAMERON, Joseph W. Girard (1871–1949); AS THEMSELVES, Ernest and George Williamson; ***Supporting Cast:*** Noble Johnson (1881–1978); Ole Jansen

This was the first feature length motion picture to feature underwater photography. The photography was made possible by the inventions of brothers Ernest and George Williamson, who appear in the film's prologue.

The first screen adaptation of Jules Verne's *20,000 Leagues Under the Sea* was a one-reeler produced by Biograph in 1905. This second screen adaptation actually included elements from two of Verne's works: *20,000 Leagues Under the Sea* and *The Mysterious Island.*

In this adaptation, Captain Nemo has a secret submarine that he has been using to get revenge against his enemy. The story is set shortly after the Civil War. Professor Aronnax and his daughter are sent on a mission to destroy the "monster of the sea." Their boat is attacked by Nemo's submarine, and the crew are taken as prisoners of Nemo. The "mysterious island" holds the secret for which Nemo is seeking revenge.

The underwater photography as seen through the "magic window" of Nemo's submarine is quite impressive. It is interesting to see the manner in which underwater photography was presented for the first time, as well as the early aquatic suits used for underwater exploration. These underwater sequences were filmed in the Bahamas. The film itself took two years to complete, with a lucrative budget for the time of $500,000.

Allen Holubar, who plays Captain Nemo, went on to become a significant director, best remembered today for his role in this film, as well as for directing *The Heart of Humanity* (1918). He was only about 33 years old when his life was cut short by pneumonia in 1923. As far as can be determined, this film is the only significant surviving work directed by Stuart Paton (1883–1944).

20,000 Leagues Under the Sea is a fascinating part of motion picture heritage, and a title that is fortunately widely available in a restored version on video. In addition to the excellent photography and engrossing storyline, the film is enhanced with color tinting. The restored video version from Kino features an impressive orchestra score.

216. The World and the Woman *Rating:* ☆☆☆½

Thanhouser/Pathé; ***Directed by*** W. Eugene Moore; ***Scenario by*** Philip Lonergan; ***Running Time:*** 66 minutes; ***Cast:*** MARY, Jeanne Eagels (1890–1929); JAMES PALMER, Thomas A. Curran (1879–1941); HARRY BRADLEY, Boyd Marshall (1885–1950); ANNA GRAHAM, Carey Hastings; DOT COLLINS, Ethelmary Oakland (1909–??); SAMUEL COLLINS, George L.

Jeanne Eagels, star of *The World and the Woman* (1916), her best surviving film work.

Mason; MARTHA COLLINS, Miriam Harris; JIM BAYLISS, Wayne Arey (1880–1937); JULIA BAYLISS, Grace de Carlton (1890–??)

The World and the Woman was the second film of legendary stage actress Jeanne Eagels. Two sources list this film as Eagels' film debut, but another indicates that Eagels made *House of Fear* (1915) prior to this film.

Eagels first gained wide acclaim on Broadway in her stage rendition of Somerset Maugham's *Rain*. She made only eight films—five from 1915 to 1918, and three more in the late 1920s. For her performance in *The Letter* (1929), she received an Academy Award nomination for Best Actress of 1928–29.

In *The World and the Woman*, Eagels plays a down-on-her-luck New York prostitute named Mary. James Palmer, a wealthy playboy, invites her to a party he is throwing in a posh restaurant, and offers her a job on his country estate as a servant. At first, she turns down the job, but then changes her mind and sees it as a possible way back into society. While working at the estate, she befriends the neighbors' daughter, Dot Collins. All is well until Palmer returns home, and makes it known to Mary that bedroom pleasures are also part of the job. Mary, having found renewed faith in God and herself when having attended church with the Collins family, resists with all her might and is saved only when guests walk in.

Looking for solace, Mary goes to the Collins' home, and is taken in as a live-in housekeeper and nanny. Mary once again finds happiness and self-worth. A catastrophe occurs when Dot Collins falls over a stair railing and is paralyzed. Through her faith in herself and God, Mary helps Dot to recover from her injuries through faith and prayer. She finds that she is able to help others as well, and becomes a renowned faith healer in the community. Then come the skeptics and the people who threaten to expose her past.

The World and the Woman shows Jeanne Eagels at her very best. Just by her acting, one can see the major difference as she transforms from a prostitute with no self-esteem to a woman who realizes her ability to love herself and others. Eagels delivers the performance of a lifetime, and in this film, one can see why she was such a highly renowned actress. In the final shots, Eagels looks breathtakingly gorgeous. Although Eagels' other surviving films (*Man, Woman, and Sin* and *The Letter*) are disappointing, she acquits herself well with this film, and it is this film by which Eagels should be judged.

1917

217. Babes in the Woods

Rating: ☆☆☆☆

Fox; ***Directed by*** Chester and Sidney Franklin; ***Screenplay by*** Bernard McConville; ***Based on the Fairy Tale,*** *Hansel and Gretel*; ***Running Time:*** 36 minutes; ***Cast:*** GRETHEL, Virginia Lee Corbin (1910–1942); THE ROBBER PRINCE, Violet Radcliffe (1908–1926?); HANSEL, Francis Carpenter; ***Supporting Cast:*** Buddy Messenger (1907–1965)

This is one of only a dozen or so pre–1920 Fox films known to survive. Originally filmed in six reels, a four-reel version is all that is available today.

This delightful adaptation of *Hansel and Gretel* starts out with Hansel and Grethel's (so spelled in the titles) wealthy father dying, and leaving everything to his two children. The stepmother and stepbrother hire two bandits to kidnap Hansel and Grethel and kill them in the Black Forest so that they can take their inheritance for themselves. One of the bandits kills the other and lets the children go. They come across the "castle" of the robber prince, which is a large tree. The robber prince and his bandits threaten the children, so the good fairy casts a spell to freeze them long enough for the children to escape.

The robber prince then enlists the help of the wicked witch in capturing the children. They are lured to the gingerbread house by the witch's dove. They are held prisoner by the witch, who locks Hansel in a room and orders Grethel to cook all of his meals to fatten him up so that the witch can eat him for breakfast. Grethel protests, saying that Hansel is too big to fit into the oven. So, the witch climbs into the oven herself to prove that she can fit into it, which gives Grethel the opportunity to push her in and escape with her brother. The good fairy uses her magic to produce a horse and carriage to transport the children to safety. But, the saga continues, with the robber prince still on their trail.

This film features a cast that is predominately made up of children (known as "The Fox Kiddies"). It is sad to note that two of the identifiable cast members, Virginia Lee Corbin and Violet Radcliffe, died at young ages (31 and 18, respectively).

Babes in the Woods is a wonderful and charming film, and it is fortunate that at least this four-reel version has survived. This gem is not to be missed.

218. The Clodhopper

Rating: ☆☆☆

Triangle; ***Directed by*** Victor Schertzinger; ***Running Time:*** 37 minutes; ***Cast:*** THE CLODHOPPER, Charles Ray (1891–1943); MARY MARTIN, Margery Wilson (1897–1986); ISAAC NELSON, Charles French (1860–1952); MRS. NELSON, Lydia Knott (1866–1955)

This film is acclaimed as among Charles Ray's best. Having been discovered on stage by Thomas Ince, Ray found his niche in playing innocent country bumpkins who triumph over the odds to gain prosperity and success. This film demonstrates that he played these parts very well. By 1920, Ray had amassed enough wealth as a popular star to form his own production company. Unfortunately, the types of roles he specialized in became less popular with the onslaught of the jazz and flapper eras. In an effort to change his image, he produced and starred in the expensive epic *The Courtship of Miles Standish* (1923), which failed miserably at the box office and put him out of independent production.

In this film, he can be seen at the height of his fame, playing a country boy whose father is a wealthy and abusive miser. The father forces him to do slave labor on the family farm for his board, clothes, and a dollar a week. The one time that his son does take a break to go to the carnival with his sweetheart, Mary, the father brutally beats him with a whip. The son decides that he has had enough, and goes to New York where he enjoys tremendous success as a dancer—making $10,000 a week. The time comes when the father's bank is in trouble, and the son has to decide whether or not to help him in his hour of need. Charles Ray gives a wonderfully and sensitively played performance, as well as demonstrating significant talent as a dancer.

Margery Wilson, who plays Ray's sweetheart, went into independent production later in her career as well. She was among the most significant female directors and producers of the early 1920s, but her accomplishments in this field are not well recognized because none of her production or direction work survives. Among her greatest achievements was *Insinuation* (1922), which was the first film to be made without the use of studios or sets—predating Italy's *The Bicycle Thief* (1947) by 25 years, which is often erroneously credited as the first such film. Wilson's only surviving work comes from early in her acting career and includes only this film, her part as Brown Eyes in *Intolerance* (1916), and William S. Hart's *The Return of Draw Egan* (1916), in which she played a supporting role. Of her three surviving films, this features the most footage of her, and she is a delightful presence.

Charles K. French, an accomplished character actor, gives a good performance as the miserly father. In most of his surviving work, he is generally relegated to the background and not very prominently featured, but this performance really gives one a chance to evaluate his acting ability.

This charming film provides the chance to see Charles Ray at his best, and is also a rare chance to see the lovely and talented Margery Wilson.

219. The Butcher Boy

Rating: ☆☆☆½

Comique/Paramount; ***Written and Directed by*** Roscoe Arbuckle; ***Story by*** Joe Roach; ***Edited by*** Herbert Warren; ***Photography by*** Frank D. Williams; ***Running Time:*** 19 minutes; ***Cast:*** FATTY THE BUTCHER, Roscoe Arbuckle (1887–1933); BUSTER, Buster Keaton (1895–1966); ALOYISIUS THE CLERK, Al St. John (1892–1963); MR. KLONDIKE THE STORE OWNER, Arthur Earle; AMANDA KLONDIKE, Josephine Stevens; MRS. DYDSTRUP, Agnes Neilson

This film is historically important as the film debut of Buster Keaton, when he was 21 years old. Keaton had been part of his father's vaudeville act up to this point. The act broke up as Joseph Keaton's alcoholism escalated. Buster's performance in this debut film occurs about six minutes into the movie. He plays a customer who orders a pound of syrup from Fatty, the butcher who is filling in while clerk Al[oyisius] is away on an errand. The syrup is dropped, and Keaton's foot is stuck in it. The film progresses as Fatty and Amanda, the store owner's pretty daughter, hook up—much to the chagrin of the returning clerk, who had previously laid claim to Amanda. The argument between Fatty and the jilted clerk escalates into a hilarious slapstick free-for-all, in which people are throwing bags of flour, pies, and everything else they can get their hands on to throw at one another. Mr. Klondike solves the problem by sending Amanda to a boarding school.

To get into the school to visit sweetheart Amanda, Fatty dresses as a woman in one of his classic performances as a female impersonator. Passing himself off as Amanda's cousin, he is admitted into the school. Things are fine until Al the clerk learns of Fatty's scheme, dresses like a girl, and is also admitted into the school. The sequences showing Arbuckle and St. John at the dinner table dressed as women are especially funny.

With this film's entertainment as well as historic value, it is a gem not to be missed.

220. Coney Island

Rating: ☆☆☆½

[a.k.a. *Fatty at Coney Island*]

Comique/Paramount; ***Produced by*** Joseph Schenk; ***Written by*** Roscoe Arbuckle and Herbert Warren; ***Directed by*** Roscoe Arbuckle; ***Photographed by*** George Peters; ***Running Time:*** 21 minutes; ***Cast:*** FATTY, Roscoe Arbuckle (1887–1933); THE LIFEGUARD, Buster Keaton (1895–1966); JILTED MAN, Al St. John (1892–1963); THE GIRL, Alice Mann; FATTY'S WIFE, Agnes Neilson; ***Supporting Cast:*** James Bryant; Joe Bordeaux (1886–1950)

This is a comedy that is appealing not only for its entertainment value, but for its significant historic interest. The film opens with a beautiful night shot of the Coney Island amusement park in its glory days, beautifully lit up in neon lights. This film finds Fatty involved in a number of misadventures at Coney Island. He breaks away from his wife on the beach, and meets a pretty girl to ride with in the amusement park. There are no swimsuits big enough for him when he decides to go for a swim, so he "borrows" a fat woman's swimsuit, and passes himself off as a woman. The situation gets a bit more complicated as Fatty's wife meets up with the boyfriend of the girl whom Fatty has stolen from him.

This is the best of the early legendary films pairing Buster Keaton and Roscoe Arbuckle. Arbuckle is hilarious, especially in his female impersonation sequence, helping make *Coney Island* one of the great classics of silent comedy shorts.

221. The Dinosaur and the Missing Link

Rating: ☆☆☆

Thomas A. Edison/Conquest Pictures; ***Directed by*** Willis O'Brien; ***Running Time:*** 3 minutes, 20 seconds

This is perhaps the most famous of Willis O'Brien's early Conquest shorts. It features the comedic adventures of Wild Willie, an ape man character made out of clay. He is shown in a wide variety of activities, from rowing a boat down a river to confronting a dinosaur. He is killed in the confrontation, thus comedically explaining where and how the "missing link" between humans and prehistoric animals disappeared.

All three of the Conquest shorts reviewed in this book are available on video, included at the end of Milestone Video's release of *The Lost World (1925)*.

222. '49–'17

Rating: ☆☆

[*Forty-Nine Seventeen*]

Universal; ***Scenario and Direction by*** Ruth Ann Baldwin; ***Based on a Story by*** William Wallace Cook; ***Photography by*** S.S. Norton; ***Running Time:*** 63 minutes; ***Cast:*** JUDGE BRAND, Joseph Girard (1871–1949); TOM REEVES, Leo Pierson (1888–1943); J. GORDON CASTLE, William J. Dyer (1881–1933); MA BOBBETT, Martha Witting (1863–1945) [a.k.a. Mattie

Davis Witting]; PA BOBBETT, George Pearce (1865–1940); PEGGY BOBBETT, Donna Drew; "GENTLEMAN JIM" RAYNOR, Jean Hersholt (1886–1956)

Lois Weber, Alice Guy-Blaché, and other female directors demonstrated that women were just as capable of turning out good movies as their male counterparts. Ruth Ann Baldwin did just that with *'49–'17*. Baldwin started her career as a journalist, and joined Universal as a scenario writer in 1915. In 1917, she directed two Universal westerns starring her husband, Leo Pierson. She did scenario writing until 1921, when she retired from screen writing. It is not known what happened to her after the movies, or when she died.

'49–'17 got passable reviews upon its original release. The film's plot has a retired judge whose desire is to use his retirement money to relive the glory days of the gold rush of 1849 by restoring Nugget Notch, an old, long-abandoned ghost town. In flashback, he explains to his secretary that part of his motivation in going back is to solve the mystery of what happened to his partner's daughter, who disappeared just a few days before they struck it rich.

The first task is to find people to populate and settle in the new town, and most of these new residents are recruited from the ranks of a traveling circus that has gone bankrupt. Jean Hersholt plays villain "Gentleman Jim" Raynor, a professional gambler who tries to blackmail the Bobbetts into giving him $10,000 once they find out that Peggy Bobbett is really the missing heiress, Lorena Adams, for whom the judge has been searching to give her her rightful share of the fortune. Failing in the blackmail attempt, Raynor holds up the town hall and robs everybody there.

This film is a grade "B" programmer western, and wasn't meant or anticipated to be any great classic. Director Baldwin did a competent job with what she had to work with, and *'49–'17* is comparable to other "B" pictures of the time.

223. A Girl's Folly

Rating: ☆☆☆

Paragon Films, Inc./World Film Corporation; ***Produced by*** William A. Brady; ***Directed by*** Maurice Tourneur; ***Running Time of Complete Version:*** 66 minutes; ***Running Time of Evaluated Edited Version:*** 29 minutes; ***Cast:*** KENNETH DRISCOLL, Robert Warwick (1878–1964); MARY, Doris Kenyon (1897–1979); VIVIEN CARLETON, June Elvidge (1893–1965); ANOTHER POPULAR STAR, Johnny Hines (1895–1970)

This is a fascinating early look at behind-the-scenes moviemaking. Robert Warwick plays matinee idol Kenneth Driscoll. Driscoll is admired by many women, including costar Vivien Carleton. While on location to shoot a cowboy film in rural New Jersey, Driscoll meets Mary, a starstruck country girl. He leads her on and encourages her to try to break into the movies. With high hopes, Mary goes to New York for a screen test. She bombs, but Driscoll offers to give her a life of luxury. The edited print that was evaluated implies that she accepts his offer, marries him, and lives happily ever after. However, the complete version has Mary consenting to be Driscoll's mistress, only to have her mother come onto the scene, confronting Driscoll on his intentions for her daughter.

In *A Girl's Folly*, one can see an indoor set being put together, as well as the interior of a studio as it was in 1917. There is also a sequence showing an editing room and some of the machinery used then in the moviemaking process. This is a historically valuable and important film. It was saved just in time, as nitrate decomposition is evident in parts of the film.

This is another one of the few silent films of Robert Warwick's available for evaluation. Shortly after this film, Warwick did a stint as an Army captain in World War I. Upon his return from the war, he worked mostly on stage through the rest of the silent era.

A Girl's Folly is the earliest performance of Doris Kenyon's that is widely available for evaluation. She was married to actor Milton Sills when he died unexpectedly in 1930. Her career in silents and talkies was successful through the end of the 1930s. She made a television comeback in the 1964 series *The Tycoon*. Johnny Hines, who has a minor role in this film, would later become a highly popular comedian in the 1920s under the direction of his brother, Charles Hines.

224. The Immigrant

Rating: ☆☆☆½

Lone Star/Mutual; ***Written and Directed by*** Charles Chaplin; ***Photography by*** Roland Totheroh; ***Running Time:*** 20 minutes; ***Cast:*** THE IMMIGRANT, Charlie Chaplin (1889–1977); A WIDOW, Edna Purviance (1894–1958); THE WAITER, Eric Campbell (1879–1917)

This Chaplin vehicle has historic importance for two reasons. It was reportedly the film that put Chaplin on the bad side of J. Edgar Hoover (1895–1972), the future director of the FBI. In the film, there is a sequence showing the immigrants approaching the Statue of Liberty. In the "land of liberty," the immigrants are shown being herded as cattle, with groups of them being roped off, shoved around, and so on. This was also the last film to star Eric Campbell, who died in an auto accident shortly after completing work in *The Immigrant*.

Charlie Chaplin, star of *The Immigrant* (1917).

On board the ship, Chaplin wins a lot of money at poker, and, upon hearing the story of a widow with a daughter and no money, slips most of his winnings into her pocket. A ship inspector sees him handling her pockets and the money, and automatically assumes that Chaplin is a pickpocket. Edna clears up the misunderstanding just as the boat is arriving.

Once the three arrive in America, Chaplin, broke and alone, struggles to find work. This leads into another of his best early sequences, when he is dining with Edna in the restaurant and can't pay the check. The imposing waiter (played by Eric Campbell) has viciously beaten a man for being 10 cents short, and the rest of the sequence centers around how the burly waiter is placated until, by a stroke of good luck, Charlie and Edna get job offers from another customer, who picks up the tab.

This film is by far the best of the Chaplin Mutuals, and is deserving of the high acclaim it received. The only sour note is the opening shot, which shows Chaplin's backside as he vomits over the side of the ship.

225. The Little American

Rating: ☆☆☆½

Paramount Artcraft; ***Directed by*** Cecil B. DeMille; ***Scenario by*** Cecil B. DeMille and Jeanie MacPherson; ***Photography by*** Alvin Wyckoff; ***Art Director:*** Wilfred Buckland; ***Running Time:*** 62 minutes; ***Cast:*** ANGELA MORE [THE LITTLE AMERICAN], Mary Pickford (1892–1979); KARL VON AUSTREIM, Jack Holt (1888–1951); COUNT JULES DE DESTIN, Raymond Hatton (1887–1971); ***Supporting Cast:*** Hobart Bosworth (1867–1943); Ben Alexander (1911–1969); Walter Long (1879–1952); Ramon Novarro [bit part] (1899–1968)

This was the second of two films that Mary Pickford starred in under Cecil B. DeMille's direction, while she was at Paramount. As her one wartime propaganda film, it was one of the great box-office successes of the year, as well as being a resounding critical success. DeMille was a director who knew better than possibly anyone else how to cater to the moviegoing public. With Pickford's status as the reigning queen of the American box office, the combination was unbeatable.

In this film, Pickford plays an American girl whose lover is half-German and half-American. He fights for the Germans; whereas she is traveling to France on the *Lusitania*—referred to as the "Veritania" in this film—to visit her aunt. The Germans sink the boat before Karl receives the note that this was the same ship on which his beloved is traveling. Angela is rescued and makes it to her aunt's home, to find that she has died, leaving her as head of the household. She nurses wounded soldiers at the house, doing her part in the war effort.

German troops invade her home, and Angela runs, being pursued by one of them, who tries to rape her until Karl—now the German Hun—recognizes her as Angela, his sweetheart from America. Once he realizes Angela's identity, he is immediately repentant.

DeMille, much in the same way that Griffith showed friends and cousins fighting on opposite sides of the Civil War in *The Birth of a Nation* (1915), shows friends and lovers on opposing sides in *The Little American*. But, in the case of this film, Karl defies his own country for the sake of Angela; whereas in *The Birth of a Nation*, the soldiers do their duty to their cause.

There is very little work from the year 1917 available for evaluation, but based on what is available, Mary Pickford gave what is possibly the best performance of 1917. It is highly charged and extremely emotional. When she is watching in horror as all of her possessions are being destroyed by the Germans, she makes viewers feel the same horror. When she looks with sympathy at the wounded soldiers, she makes the viewer ashamed not to share her sympathy. When she is shaking her fist at the Germans who have just sunk the *Veritania*, chastising them for attacking a ship with civilian women and children aboard, one's first instinct is to give her a standing ovation.

The only other performance of the year that might have rivaled Pickford's is possibly Theda Bara's in *Cleopatra* (1917), but since that film is lost, there is no way to fairly evaluate it. Bara certainly got publicity, and the film was a box-office sensation and highly acclaimed. But, none of Bara's better work has survived at all, and all that is left are her lesser films, and her very first, *A Fool There Was* (1914), in which her acting techniques are rather primitive.

Leading man Jack Holt also gives an outstanding performance. He started in films in 1915, and his first great roles were with Cecil B. DeMille, starting with *Joan the Woman* (1916). He is very convincing as the repentant Hun who would do anything to redeem himself for the lascivious effrontery he has committed on his sweetheart. Of his few surviving films, this is Holt's most impressive performance. On close inspection one can see an 18-year-old Ramon Novarro in a bit part as a cowering prisoner sentenced by the Germans to be shot.

With fine performances in the lead roles, and excellent direction by Cecil B. DeMille, *The Little American* (1917) ranks with D.W. Griffith's *Hearts of the World* (1918) as among the best of the World War I–era propaganda films.

226. The Mystery of the Double Cross *Rating: ☆☆☆*

Astra Studios/Pathé Exchange; ***Directed by*** William Parke; ***Story by*** Gilson Willets; ***Scenario by*** B. Millhauser; ***Running Time:*** 350 minutes; ***Cast:*** Miss Brewster, Mollie King (1898–1981); Peter Hale, Leon Bary (1880–1954); Bridgey Bentley, Ralph Stuart (1890–1952); ***Supporting Cast:*** Robert Broderick; Gladden James (1892–1948); Harry Fraser (1889–1974)

This was silent screen actress Mollie King's first serial, produced in late 1916 and released in early 1917. It was also the directorial debut of William Parke (1873–1941), who was active as a director until 1924 according to Weaver's *Twenty Years of Silents*. Ephraim Katz's *Film Encyclopedia* (1994 edition) lists Louis Gasnier (1875–1963) as having directed this serial, which has caused the historic record a bit of confusion. William Parke is listed as director on the film itself; if Gasnier had anything to do with the film, one can assume that he perhaps worked as an assistant director.

Leon Bary plays the male lead as Peter Hale, the son of a wealthy father who has just died. When the will is revealed, some strange conditions are attached to it. It states that son Peter is to inherit his fortune, provided that he marries a certain girl who has a tattoo of a double cross on her arm. If Peter does not marry this woman, the fortune goes to whomever does.

Instead of the cliffhanger format, this serial ends each of its 15 episodes with a question mark, challenging the viewers to solve the mystery of the woman with the double cross. This is a highly entertaining serial that encourages audience participation.

Mollie King had started out young in vaudeville, and was a veteran of the stage by the time she made her first three films for the World Film Company in 1916. She signed a contract with Astra Studios afterward, which resulted in her having this part in *The Mystery of the Double Cross*. Although she was popular as a film actress and could have continued her film career indefinitely, she did not care for films, and returned to the stage after only a dozen or so film appearances. Leading man Leon Bary is an obscure figure on which little is known except that he starred in a few western films.

An interesting aspect about this serial is its beginning. Mollie King is shown a letter telling her of the serial production planned, and is shown studying the story to prepare herself. The book with the script shows her walking in the book itself, inviting the audience to join her as she finds out more about the adventures she is supposed to reenact.

At nearly six hours, *The Mystery of the Double Cross* is a long serial, but well worth taking the time to watch.

227. The Outlaw and His Wife *Rating:* ☆☆☆½

Swedish Biograph Company; ***Directed by*** Victor Seastrom; ***Based on a Play by*** Johann Sigurjonsson; ***Photography by*** J. Julius; ***Running Time:*** 73 minutes; ***Cast:*** KARI [THE OUTLAW], Victor Seastrom (1879–1960); HALLA [HIS WIFE], Edith Erastoff (1887–1945); ARNES, John Ekman (1880–1949); BJORN BERGSTEINSSON, Nils Arehn

This film is set in Iceland during the 18th century. The leading characters are a wanted fugitive and his wife. This is the film that was the turning point in bringing the Swedish film industry around as a competitive force in the world market. It is also that film that solidified Victor Seastrom's reputation as a director and actor.

Seastrom directs himself as a man who escapes from jail on a charge of stealing food for his impoverished family. He gets work at a farm and falls in love with Halla, the widow who owns it. He is spotted by Halla's brother-in-law, who happens to be the bailiff. After revealing his past to Halla, they marry and escape to the mountains. They live a primitive but happy life for about five years, having a little girl. Then Kari's friend Arnes, now a fellow outlaw, comes onto the scene. He becomes jealous of Halla's and Kari's relationship.

Of the foreign silents produced in the 1910s that are available for evaluation, this is among the best. Victor Seastrom demonstrates that he was just as great an actor as director. Edith Erastoff, Seastrom's wife offscreen as well as in this film, also gives an excellent performance.

This film was beautifully restored by the Swedish Film Archive in 1986, with the original color tints and an orchestral score. It is available on video and is also occasionally shown on Turner Classic Movies.

228. The Poor Little Rich Girl *Rating:* ☆☆☆½

Paramount Artcraft; ***Directed by*** Maurice Tourneur; ***Assistant Director:*** M.M. Litson; ***Screenplay by*** Ralph Spence and Frances Marion; ***Based on the Novel by*** Eleanor Gates; ***Photography by*** John van der Brock and Lucien Andriot; ***Art Direction by*** Ben Carré; ***Running Time:*** 61 minutes; ***Cast:*** GWENDOLYN, Mary Pickford (1892–1979); HER MOTHER, Madeline Traverse (1875–1964); HER FATHER, Charles Wellesley (1873–1946); SUSIE MAY SQUAGGS, Maxine Elliott Hicks (1904–1997?); JANE (THE NURSE), Gladys Fairbanks; THE PLUMBER, Frank McGlynn (1866–1951); THE ORGAN GRINDER, Emile LaCroix; MISS ROYLE (THE GOVERNESS), Marcia Harris (1880–??); THOMAS (THE FOOTMAN), Charles Craig; POTTER (THE BUTLER), Frank Andrews; THE DOCTOR, Herbert Prior (1867–1954); JOHNNY BLAKE, George Gernon

This was Mary Pickford's third film for Paramount, and the first in which she deliberately played a child role. The previous two efforts for Paramount had not been as suc-

The Poor Little Rich Girl (1917).

cessful. The enormous success of this film was surprising to both Paramount and to Pickford, and gained her increasingly wide popularity.

In *The Poor Little Rich Girl*, Pickford plays Gwendolyn, a girl who has everything that money can buy—except love and attention from her parents. It is thought that perhaps a playmate might solve the problem of her loneliness, so Susie May Squaggs is introduced to her. Susie May turns out to be the typical arrogant brat who can't seem to carry on any conversation except about how much richer and superior her family is to Gwendolyn's. This was among the first film roles played by Maxine Elliott Hicks, who was 93 years of age when she reportedly died in 1997. Gwendolyn tells Susie what she thinks of her, and they have a hilarious confrontation. When Susie sits on her ice cream, she accuses Gwendolyn of messing up her dress on purpose, and Gwendolyn's punishment is that she has to wear boy's clothes, while giving Susie her best lace dress.

One night, the governess decides that she wants to go out instead of watching Gwendolyn, so she drugs her. Gwendolyn takes her recommended dose as instructed, but the governess does not believe that she took it, and gives her another dose. The label on the medicine specifically states that higher doses can be fatal. It is when Gwendolyn is in a coma that the highly amusing dream sequence occurs. Maurice Tourneur was especially innovative in staging this sequence. The governess appears as "the two-faced woman," and her image with a face on each side of her head twirls throughout the footage. In addition, "the silly ass" looks much like the donkey characters from L. Frank

Baum's "Oz" films of 1914. Double exposure of fairies is used artistically as well. At one point in the dream, Gwendolyn is tempted by the angel of death, who promises her eternal sleep.

This is a charming film, and one can see why it was so popular. To give the illusion of making Mary Pickford look smaller than she really was, oversized sets were built. This is among her best feature films. This is the film that paved the way to her stardom as "America's Sweetheart," whereas later films such as *Pollyanna, Tess of the Storm Country,* and *Little Annie Rooney* maintained this stature.

This was among the first film efforts of Ralph Spence (1890–1949), who would gain fame in the 1920s as one of the most popular title writers, having penned the title cards in a number of the successful MGM comedies of the period. It is also one of the earliest surviving films of director Maurice Tourneur (1873–1961).

The best of the supporting cast members would have to be Maxine Elliott Hicks. (Reportedly worked as an extra in an Edison film of 1914, according to Michael Ankerich's *Broken Silence.*) She is hilarious as the snooty Susie May Squaggs, and plays the part perfectly. *The Poor Little Rich Girl* was her fifth film, and the earliest of her work that survives. Hicks had the longest film career in motion picture history. Her film and television career spanned 80 years, from her first film appearance in 1917 in *The Crimson Dove*, to her most recent television guest appearance in a 1994 episode of the *Murphy Brown* television series. This is five years longer than Lillian Gish's 75-year film career, which started in 1912 and ended with *The Whales of August* in 1987.

229. Prehistoric Poultry: The Dinornis or Great Roaring Whiffenproof

Rating: ☆☆☆

Thomas A. Edison/Conquest Pictures; ***Directed by*** Willis O'Brien; ***Running Time:*** 2 minutes, 20 seconds

This is another of the early experimental stop-motion photography films of Willis O'Brien (1886–1962). This film opens with a shot of a dinornis, the prehistoric ancestor of the modern day chicken. A comedic element comes into the picture as a clay man leads a dinosaur out of his cave, and his wife hits him on the head, making him see stars. A rival suitor is shot into the sky with a sling shot.

While these types of special effects are done mostly with computers today, they were shot frame by frame in the early days of stop-motion photography. Work began on the Conquest Pictures in the early 1910s, but the three reviewed in this book were not released until 1917, giving one an idea of how much time it took to produce these early shorts of less than five minutes footage.

This comedy short remains an entertaining conversation piece today.

230. R.F.D. 10,000 B.C.

Rating: ☆☆☆

Thomas A. Edison/Conquest Pictures; ***Directed by*** Willis O'Brien; ***Running Time:*** 4 minutes, 23 seconds

This is one of the more complex of the early Conquest pictures produced by Willis O'Brien (1886–1962) in the Edison Studios. It is a comedy satire featuring a day in the life of a prehistoric caveman.

The film shows a prehistoric mailman carving a valentine to his sweetheart before delivering the mail on a dinosaur drawn carriage. He gets into trouble when he delivers the wrong valentine to his girl, and is shown having the top part of his body separated from the bottom half, with the legs running to reattach to the top.

The Conquest shorts were the beginning of O'Brien's stop-motion photography experiments, and after the release of the three Conquest Pictures reviewed in this book, he started work on *The Lost World* (1925).

231. A Tale of Two Cities *Rating:* ★★★★

Fox; ***Adaptation and Direction by*** Frank Lloyd; ***Based on the 1859 Novel by*** Charles Dickens; ***Photography by*** Billy Foster and George Schneiderman; ***Running Time:*** 80 minutes; ***Cast:*** CHARLES DARNAY/SYDNEY CARTON, William Farnum (1876–1953); LUCIE MANETTE, Jewel Carmen (1897–??); DEFARGE, Herschel Mayall (1863–1941); MADAM DEFARGE, Rosita Marstini (1887–1948); MANETTE, Joseph Swickard (1866–1940); JARVIS LORRY, Mark Robbins (1868–1931); ***Supporting Cast:*** Florence Vidor (1895–1977); Charles Clary (1873–1931); Ralph Lewis (1872–1937); William Clifford (1877–1941); Olive White (?1880–1960); Willard Louis (1882–1926); Harry De Vere (1870–1923)

For years, it was believed that none of the big Fox epics from the 1910s had survived. This version of *A Tale of Two Cities* turned up in the Killiam archives in the late 1990s, and was released to the public on video through Critic's Choice in late 1997. This entry is the earliest feature film directed by Frank Lloyd that is widely available for evaluation.

There were at least six screen adaptations of *A Tale of Two Cities*—in 1911, 1917, 1935, 1958, 1980, and 1991. Although none of these films were bad adaptations, the 1917 and 1935 versions are the best of the lot. The 1911 was good for the time it was released, but the movies were still in the very primitive stages at the time. The 1958, 1980, and 1991 versions would all get solid three-star ratings, as opposed to the four-star ratings for the two preferred versions.

This adaptation features William Farnum in a double role as both Charles Darnay, aristocrat, and Sydney Carton, attorney. Both are in love with Lucie Manette during the French Revolution, and have a strong resemblance to one another. When Darnay is denounced as an aristocrat because of his cruel father's actions years before toward Lucie Manette's father, he is sentenced to the guillotine. Carton shows his love for Lucie by switching places with Darnay in prison, thus making the ultimate sacrifice at the guillotine so that Lucie and Darnay can escape and be happy together.

The sequence portraying the storming of the Bastille was lavishly staged on a level comparable to the battles in *Intolerance* (1916) and *Joan the Woman* (1916). The setting is huge, and there are thousands of extras used.

One thing that Lloyd does differently in his adaptation is soften the blow as Sydney Carton is executed. Instead of showing the guillotine blade coming down, the film shows him being brought before the guillotine, and then portrays his last thought, cutting to a shot of happy couple Lucie and Darnay a few years into the future with their son Sydney.

There is evidence indicating that William Desmond Taylor (1872–1922) worked in some capacity on this film. *The Motion Picture Studio Directory* for 1918 and 1920 lists this film as a title that Taylor directed. *The Motion Picture Studio Directory* for 1921 states that he acted in the film. In looking over the film carefully several times, this reviewer was unable to spot Taylor in the cast, which would lead one to guess that if Taylor worked on the film, it was in an assistant directorial capacity.

232. Tom Sawyer

Rating: ☆☆☆☆

Paramount; ***Directed by*** William Desmond Taylor; ***Scenario by*** Julia Crawford Ivers; ***Photography by*** Homer Scott; ***Based on*** Mark Twain's 1876 Classic; ***Running Time:*** 59 minutes; ***Cast:*** TOM SAWYER, Jack Pickford (1896–1933); BECKY THATCHER, Clara Horton (1904–1976); HUCKLEBERRY FINN, Robert Gordon (1895–1971); AUNT POLLY, Edythe Chapman (1863–1948); JOE HARPER, Antrim Short (1900–1972); ALFRED TEMPLE, Carl Goetz; ***Supporting Cast:*** Alice Marvin; George Hackathorne (1896–1940); Helen Gilmore (1862–1936)

Tom Sawyer is significant as one of the greatest successes of Jack Pickford's film career, as well as one of the rare surviving films of William Desmond Taylor (1872–1922). It is the first of three screen adaptations that Taylor directed based on Mark Twain's classics, *Tom Sawyer* and *Huckleberry Finn*. When Julia Crawford Ivers finished the adaptation from *Tom Sawyer*, it was determined that there was enough material for two five-reel films. So, the novel was broken down into two movies. The followup, *Tom and Huck* (1918) (a.k.a. *The Further Adventures of Tom Sawyer*) is not known to survive. It used most of the same players as the first film. The final entry in the trilogy, *Huckleberry Finn* (1920), does exist but is held in archive by the George Eastman House. This third entry was directed by Taylor, but used an entirely different cast except for Edythe Chapman.

This first screen adaptation of *Tom Sawyer* is absolutely delightful, with Jack Pickford at his best as the appealing, boyish figure who has a penchant for mischief. What one sees of the early Jack Pickford is a far cry from the bland figure seen in most of his later films after 1920, when the ravages of alcoholism—as well as the tragic death of his wife, Olive Thomas—had taken away his charm and charisma.

Jack Pickford, star of *Tom Sawyer* (1917), his greatest role.

This adaptation, some of which was filmed on location in Hannibal, Missouri, starts with Tom being presented as the boy who is *not* a model child, and progressing to show him in a confrontation with Alfred Temple, who does fit the image of a model school boy. Tom's misadventures include his hoodwinking a neighborhood boy into doing his whitewashing so that he can go fishing with Joe and Huck. Then, the introduction of Becky Thatcher, whom Tom gets into trouble at school over, is made. The film's final adventure is the portrayal of the celebrated incident in which Tom, Huck, and Joe get tired of their lives at home, running away on a river raft. This adaptation ends with the return of the boys to their home church, where the townspeople are worried sick about them. *Tom and Huck* (1918) presumably picks up the story where this one leaves off.

Jack Pickford perfectly fits the image of the quintessential, all–American adolescent boy, having been a perfect choice for this lead role as Tom Sawyer. Robert Gordon as Huck also gives a distinctive flair to his part. Clara Horton at age 13 is delightfully charming as Becky Thatcher. This role is one of only two of her films known to survive. At age 8, she was known as "the Eclair kid" at the Eclair Film Company. Her popularity in shorts for companies like Powers and Universal from 1915 to 1917 resulted in her being chosen for *Tom Sawyer* as Jack Pickford's leading lady, as well a few roles opposite Charles Ray and Cullen Landis. By the mid–1920s, her popularity had waned, and after a few unsuccessful "flapper" roles, she faded into obscurity. Fortunately, her one major role that survives is that which is acclaimed as her best.

A few 16 mm prints were sold many years ago by Film Classic Exchange. The copy reviewed for this book came from the Mary Pickford Library. *Tom Sawyer* is a truly delightful experience. It was released on video in September 1998. This is an important piece of Americana that deserves to be brought out of obscurity and into the limelight.

Director William Desmond Taylor played an important part in the careers of both Jack and Mary Pickford in the late 1910s. In Jack's case, this was the third of seven films he starred in under Taylor's direction, and the only one of the seven known to survive. The second film they did just before *Tom Sawyer* was an adaptation of *Jack and Jill* (1917), which is unfortunately lost. Their final collaboration, *Mile-A-Minute Kendall* (1918), also starred Lottie Pickford (1895–1936). Taylor's next three projects were with Mary Pickford. Unfortunately, none of these three collaborations between the two are known to survive in complete form. Their first collaboration, *How Could You, Jean?* (1918) is believed to be totally lost. *Johanna Enlists* (1918) is missing a reel. *Captain Kidd, Jr.* (1919) is missing three of its five reels. After Mary Pickford left Paramount for First National, Taylor's next project was *Anne of Green Gables* (1919) with Mary Miles Minter.

Judging from the two Taylor-directed films available for evaluation, this reviewer sees masterful directorial ability, and concludes that the rest of his surviving work deserves to be revived and brought out of obscurity. At least five of his films are known to survive in complete form: *Tom Sawyer* (1917); *Huckleberry Finn* (1920), *Nurse Marjorie* (1920), *The Witching Hour* (1921), and *Morals* (1922).

1918

233. All Night

Rating: ☆☆☆

Universal/Bluebird; ***Directed by*** Paul Powell; ***Running Time:*** 57 minutes; ***Cast:*** Richard Thayer, Rudolph Valentino (1895–1926); Elizabeth Lane, Carmel Myers (1901–1980); Colonel Hudson Lane, Wadsworth Harris (1862–1942); Bill Harcourt, Charles Dorian (1891–1942); Harcourt's wife, Mary Warren; Jim Bradford, William J. Meyer

This is one of the extremely rare early Valentino films for Universal, of which the only print was believed to be held at the George Eastman House. Fortunately, another print turned up in a private collection, and in 1997, this film was put out on video by Grapevine and made widely available to the public for the first time in nearly 80 years.

It is interesting to see Valentino in a light romantic comedy as opposed to the heavy romantic dramas that he was known for, showing another side of Valentino that modern day audiences haven't been exposed to in recent years. In *All Night*, Valentino plays Richard Thayer, who is in love with Elizabeth Lane and intends to propose to her, but hasn't had the courage. His friends, the Harcourts, work out a plan whereby they will invite Elizabeth to dinner, and Richard will conveniently stop by.

The simple plan goes haywire when Bill Harcourt has fired all of his household staff, and is expecting a visit from a potential investor without whose money he will go bankrupt. So, the Harcourts pose as servants, and Richard and Elizabeth pose as the Harcourts. When investor Jim Bradford arrives, he turns out to be a pushy eccentric who decides to stay all night. Posing as a married couple when they are not, Bradford becomes insistent at bedtime, demanding the "couple" go to bed. This is impossible, as Elizabeth has to be home by 11:00 P.M., and certainly cannot share the same bed with a man she isn't really married to and keep her reputation intact. It is fun to see how the awkward situation is finally resolved.

All Night turned out to be a much better film than expected on evaluation, and it is fortunate that this rare early Valentino title has finally been released on video after nearly 20 years.

234. Amarilly of Clothes Line Alley *Rating:* ☆☆☆

Paramount Artcraft; ***Directed by*** Marshall Neilan; ***Based on a Story by*** Belle K. Maniates; ***Photography by*** Walter Stradling; ***Screen Adaptation by*** Frances Marion; ***Running Time:*** 54 minutes; ***Cast:*** AMARILLY JENKINS, Mary Pickford (1892–1979); GORDON PHILLIPS, Norman Kerry (1889–1956); TERRY MCGOWAN, William Scott; DAVID PHILLIPS, Herbert Standing (1846–1923); AMARILLY'S MOTHER, Kate Price (1872–1943); AMARILLY'S BROTHER, Wesley Barry (1907–1994); MRS. DAVID PHILLIPS, Ida Waterman (1852–1941); JOHNNY WALKER, Fred Goodwins; COLETTE KING, Margaret Landis (1890–1981); SNITCH MCCARTHY, Tom Wilson (1880–1965)

This was the fourth of seven films that Mary Pickford starred in under the direction of Marshall Neilan, right after *Stella Maris* (1918) was released. It was also the fourth film of actor Norman Kerry, right at about the time when he helped his friend Rudolph Valentino (1895–1926) break into the movies. In this film, Pickford plays a poor girl from the slums who is taken in by a rich philanthropist, Mrs. Phillips. Amarilly and Phillips' nephew, Gordon, start dating, but disaster strikes when Mrs. Phillips invites Amarilly's family for a high society tea party. The party is a disaster, but Gordon still is attracted to Amarilly, and wants to "educate" her in the ways of high society. Tragedy strikes when Terry McGowan, Amarilly's suitor from her own neighborhood and social class, is shot by stray gunfire. As he is recovering, Amarilly grows to like him, and decides to marry the man who loves her as she is, and doesn't require her to change.

This is a film that departs from the expected ending by having Amarilly becoming disillusioned with her prince charming, and finding that she would be happier with someone from her own social class. Instead of marrying into money, she chooses a man that she can build a more laid-back, middle class life with.

Kate Price is pleasing, as usual, as Amarilly's poor but honest and caring mother. Margaret Landis, who plays the society girl whom Mrs. Phillips wants her nephew to marry, was the sister of actor Cullen Landis (1895–1975).

While this was not among Pickford's more successful films with Paramount, it is nevertheless a delightful and highly enjoyable film. In some ways, it is one of Pickford's more realistic films in that she doesn't marry prince charming and live happily ever after in wealth, but abandons him for a man closer to her heart.

235. The Blue Bird

Rating: ☆☆☆☆

Paramount; ***Directed by*** Maurice Tourneur; ***Screenplay by*** Charles Maigne; ***Based on the play by*** Maurice Maeterlinck; ***Photography by*** John van der Brock; ***Art Direction by*** Ben Carré; ***Running Time:*** 75 minutes; ***Cast:*** TYLTYL, Robin MacDougall; MYTYL, Tula Belle (born 1909); DADDY TYL, Edwin E. Reed; MUMMY TYL, Emma Lowry; GAFFER TYL, William J. Gross (1837–1924); GRANNY TYL, Florence Anderson (1882–1962); BERLINGOT, Edward Elkas (1862–??); BERLINGOT'S DAUGHTER, Katherine Bianchi; FAIRY BERYLUNE, Lillian Cook (1898–1918); DOG [TYLO], Charles Ascot; CAT [TYLETTE], Tom Corless; FIRE, S. E. Popapovitch

At last, Maurice Tourneur's finest surviving work, *The Blue Bird*, has made it into the video market—courtesy of Kino Video. This is the first and best of three film versions of the allegorical masterpiece by author Maurice Maeterlinck (1862–1949). Maeterlinck was the recipient of the 1911 Nobel Prize for Literature, and *The Blue Bird* (written in 1908) and *Pelléas et Mélisande* (written in 1892) were the primary Maeterlinck works for which he won this recognition.

The Blue Bird was first performed in France under the title of *L'Oiseau bleu* in 1908, and the play had its American debut in 1910. Maeterlinck published a sequel to *The Blue Bird*, called *The Betrothal*, in 1919. As far as can be determined, *The Betrothal* was never adapted as a play or a movie; it was released as a novel only, but was still popular, having gone through several printings. It is included with the 1995 reprint of *The Blue Bird* that is still in print in 1998.

The acclaim for this silent version of *The Blue Bird* has been enthusiastic. Edward Weitzel of *The Moving Picture World* said it portrays "the simplicity of childhood and the wisdom of a deep but kindly philosophy ... [will] appeal to every mind." *Photoplay* regarded it as "one of the most important productions ever made ... so beautiful ... that it stings the senses, awakening in the spectator esthetic emotions so long dormant." In *Fifty Great American Silent Films* (Dover, 1980), Edward Wagenknecht stated, "If Maurice Tourneur's productions of [*The Blue Bird*] and *Prunella* had met the success they deserved, they might have pointed the way to a 1920s in which the screen might have been decorated by something better than sheiks and flappers and flaming youth."

Of the three film adaptations of *The Blue Bird*, this original version is by far the most faithful to the original story. It features the characters of fire, water, milk, bread, and other elements omitted from the 1940 remake, and not dealt with as effectively in the 1976 remake. This version features the Palace of Night, which is left out of the 1940 remake. In addition, the original has Tyltyl as the dominant older brother, as he was originally referred to in Maeterlinck's novel and play adaptation. The 1940 remake, tailored for Shirley Temple (born 1928), turned her character of Mytyl into the dominant, older sibling. The only major departure from the novel in this silent adaptation is that Light and the Fairy Berylune are combined into one character.

This original adaptation features elaborate tinting and toning, and these original tints were restored to the film at the George Eastman House in 1990. This was clearly a director's film, as it featured no big name stars like the remakes. Of all of the silents directed by Maurice Tourneur that are currently available for evaluation in complete form, this is by far his greatest masterpiece. The 1940 remake features Shirley Temple, Nigel Bruce, and Laura Hope Crews in its cast; the 1976 remake features big name stars Jane Fonda, Elizabeth Taylor, Ava Gardner, and Cicily Tyson. While the 1940 version is positively delightful, Tourneur's version is still the best despite the lack of big name stars. The 1976 version proved to be disappointing upon evaluation.

Lillian Cook, who plays Fairy Berylune, might have become a big star had she lived longer. She was extremely appealing and delightful in *The Blue Bird*, which is her only known surviving work. She died at age 19 in 1918 shortly after this film's release, but no cause of death could be found in the major player directories and reference sources. If Lillian Cook had lived longer, she might have gone on to enjoy the same level of stardom that was attained by Mary Pickford, Marguerite Clark, Mary Miles Minter, Vivian Martin, the Gish sisters, and others.

The Blue Bird is a masterpiece that every silent film buff should have a copy of. This is by far the best film of 1918, possessing an artistic charm that hasn't since been equaled.

236. The Eyes of Julia Deep

Rating: ☆☆½

Mary Miles Minter, star of *The Eyes of Julia Deep* (1918).

American Film Company; ***Directed by*** Lloyd Ingraham; ***Running Time:*** 56 minutes; ***Cast:*** JULIA DEEP, Mary Miles Minter (1902–1984); TERRY HARTRIDGE, Alan Forrest (1884–1941); LOTTIE DRISCOLL, Alice Wilson (1888?-1944); TIMOTHY BLACK, George Periolat (1873–1940); MRS. TURNER, Ida Easthope; MRS. SARAH LOWE, Eugenie Besserer (1868–1934); SHERIFF PLUMMET, Carl Stockdale (1874–1953)

For over 70 years, this was the only Mary Miles Minter film that was widely available for evaluation. In the introductory title cards on the video release, it had been acclaimed as one of Minter's last and best films for the American Film Company. Within the last year, two more of Minter's films have become available for evaluation. *The Ghost of Rosy Taylor* (1918), which was also produced by American Film Company, is by far superior to *The Eyes of Julia Deep*, and reviewed elsewhere in this book. The third Minter film that is widely available is *Nurse Marjorie* (1920), produced by Paramount Realart and directed by William Desmond Taylor. Of the three, *The Eyes of Julia Deep* is the weakest, owing mostly to the inferior directorial style of Lloyd Ingraham.

In this film, Minter plays Julia Deep, a girl who keeps irresponsible playboy Terry Hartridge from killing himself once he has squandered the last of his substantial inheritance. He gets a job at the same department store that she works at, and they pool their earnings in a "co-op" arrangement. They decide to get married—much to the disapproval of Timothy Black and Sarah Lowe, a couple determined to stop the marriage from happening.

This is a light romantic film of which the story is charming. Unfortunately, Lloyd Ingraham's directorial style does little to bring out the personalities of the cast members. It is saved from the abyss only by the presence of Mary Miles Minter, whose personal charm brings the film above Ingraham's stultifying direction, and gives it appeal.

Alan (also spelled "Allan" in some sources) Forrest was Minter's leading man in this film and many others. Minter considered him as one of her favorite leading men to work with. He was married to Lottie Pickford (Mary's younger sister) from 1922 to 1928. Alice Wilson was also known under the names of Alice Houghton and Alice Browning. She was married to Tod Browning. No further information could be found on Ida Easthope. Carl Stockdale had costarred in a number of Minter's films for American and was a good friend of Minter's mother, Charlotte Shelby.

Although *The Eyes of Julia Deep* is probably among the worst of the Mary Miles Minter films, its rarity as one of her few extant films gives it appeal. In spite of its poor direction and photography, it sports a good storyline and cast, which makes it worth watching.

237. The Ghost of Rosy Taylor

Rating: ☆☆☆½

American Film Company; ***Directed by*** Edward S. Sloman; ***Running Time:*** 47 minutes; ***Cast:*** RHODA ELDRIDGE, Mary Miles Minter (1902–1984); MRS. HERRIMAN-SMITH, Marian Lee; JEANNE DUVIVIER, Helen Howard (1899–1927); CHARLES ELDRIDGE/JOSEPH SAYLES, George Periolat (1873–1940); MRS. SULLIVAN, Kate Price (1872–1943); JACQUES LECLERE, Alan Forrest (1884–1941); MARIAN WATKINS, Ann Schaefer (1870–1957)

The Ghost of Rosy Taylor is one of only six Mary Miles Minter films known to survive, and one of only three available for evaluation outside the archives. In this film, Minter plays Rhoda Eldridge, a girl in France whose father has died. Shortly after his death, she learns that all of his savings had been invested in a shipping company that has gone bankrupt, leaving her penniless.

Rhoda comes to America with $17 in her pocket and desperate to find honest work. Sitting on a park bench, she finds an envelope addressed to a woman named Rosy Taylor. In the envelope is money with instructions for Taylor to report for a house cleaning job. She goes to Taylor's house to return the money and envelope, only to find out that Taylor died. Rhoda then assumes Rosy Taylor's identity, and takes the cleaning job for herself. When the owner of the house, Jeanne DuVivier, arrives, she is aware that Rosy Taylor is dead, and upon seeing that someone is in the house, believes that the house is haunted by "the ghost of Rosy Taylor."

Upon seeing this film, it is far better than *The Eyes of Julia Deep*, the only Mary Miles Minter film that had been widely available for evaluation until recently. This is partly because Minter worked under the direction of Edward S. Sloman, and because the story itself had more substance and provided better opportunities and situations for

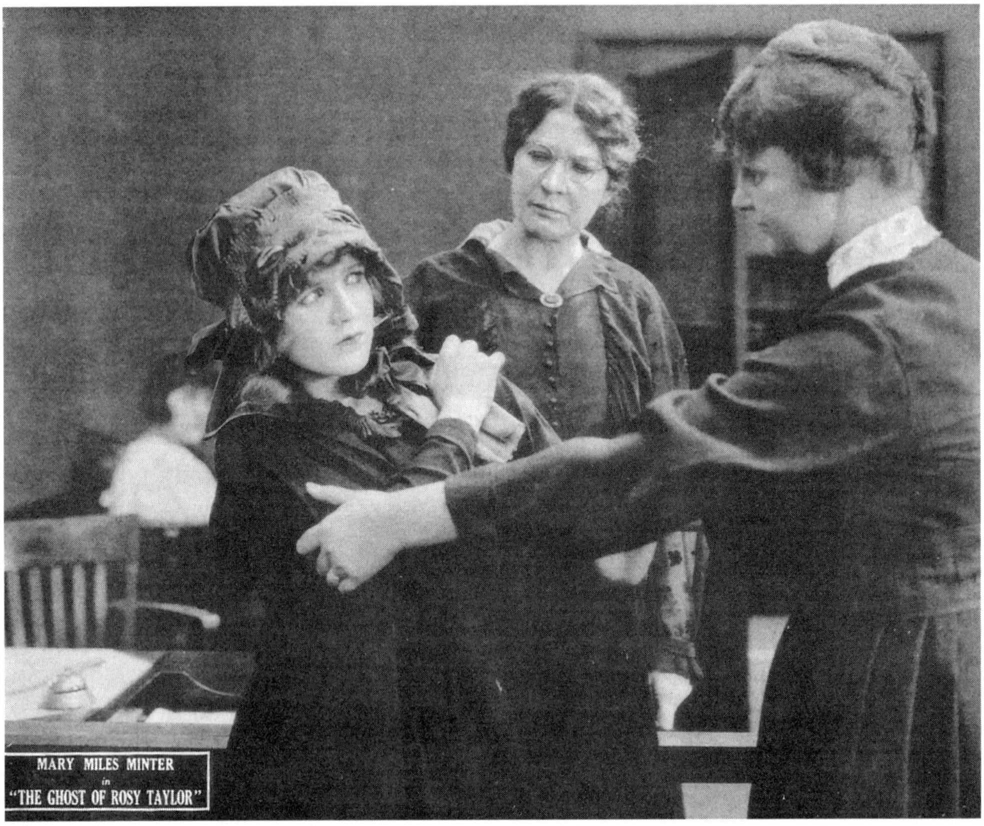

Original lobby card featuring Mary Miles Minter in *The Ghost of Rosy Taylor* (1918), the best of her three films currently available on video.

Minter's acting ability to be demonstrated. The sequence in which she is escaping from a girl's reformatory is especially good. Another sequence in which Minter looks especially appealing is when she tries on a fancy lace dress that Ms. DuVivier has given to "Rosy Taylor," and determines to bask in elegance for one hour—even if she has to scrub floors extra hard to make up for it.

Edward Sloman (1885–1972), the director, is one who had been all but forgotten by film historians because very little of his work has survived. It was only when historian Kevin Brownlow took an interest in his work that his name came back into the limelight. Although Sloman stated that he and Minter were professionally incompatible, he got a much better performance from her than Lloyd Ingraham did in *The Eyes of Julia Deep*. His superior directorial ability also made a difference in the performance of George Periolat. In *The Ghost of Rosy Taylor*, Sloman succeeds in bringing out the various unique traits in each actor's personality.

Edward Sloman also added a nice touch to this film in the sequences in which the house was allegedly "haunted," showing a hand rattling a chain to provide somewhat of a horror atmosphere. His only silent films widely available for evaluation on video are *Surrender* (1927), in which he got a superior performance out of Mary Philbin, and *His People* (1925).

George Periolat, who played Charles Eldridge/Joseph Sayles, was ill for three years prior to his death. When he was found dead in his home, the circumstances were mysterious, as he died from arsenic poisoning. Kate Price (Mrs. Sullivan) was best known for her role in the late 1920s film series *The Cohans and the Kellys*. She was the sister of Jack Duffy, and the aunt of Mary Charleston. Ann Schaefer (Marian Watkins) was the aunt of Jane and Eva Novak.

Based on what survives and is available for evaluation of Mary Miles Minter's work for the American Film Company, *The Ghost of Rosy Taylor* is her best surviving work from this earlier period in her career.

238. Good Night, Nurse!

Rating: ☆☆☆

Comique/Paramount; ***Produced by*** Joseph Schenk; ***Written and Directed by*** Buster Keaton and Eddie Cline; ***Technical Director:*** Fred Gabourie; ***Photography by*** Elgin Lessley; ***Running Time:*** 17 minutes; ***Cast:*** FATTY, Roscoe Arbuckle (1887–1933); SANITARIUM DOCTOR, Buster Keaton (1895–1966); A SANITARIUM PATIENT, Alice Lake (1895–1967); SANITARIUM WORKER, Al St. John (1892–1963); SANITARIUM NURSE, Kate Price (1872–1943); ***Supporting Cast:*** Joe Bordeaux (1886–1950); Joe Keaton (1867–1946)

This comedy finds Fatty committed to a sanitarium for an alcoholism cure. He escapes with an attractive patient played by Alice Lake. She wants to go back to the sanitarium, as she is attracted to the doctor, played by Keaton. Fatty has eyes for her, and disguises himself as a nurse to join her. The nurse's outfit that Fatty steals belongs to a nurse played by Kate Price, who immediately notices her missing uniform on Fatty, and exposes him. On his second escape attempt, Fatty unwittingly becomes involved in a marathon for heavyweights. He wins the race, only to find the men from the sanitarium by his side to take him back. The film then shows Fatty waking up after an operation—revealing the experience to be a dream.

This is one of the few films of Alice Lake that is available for evaluation. Having gained great popularity in comedy shorts in the 1910s, she was eventually starring in features for Metro Pictures in the 1920s. By the late 1920s, her popularity had waned, and she was relegated to roles in minor productions until her retirement from the screen in 1935. Her eyes were of two different colors—one brown and one grey.

Ironically, the two main stars in this film about alcoholism would, in real life, struggle with the disease. Arbuckle suffered most of his adult life from alcoholism, which possibly contributed to his early death from a heart attack at age 46. Keaton's battle with alcoholism caused him some very bleak times in the early 1930s, but he recovered from the affliction by going through an alcohol rehabilitation program.

239. Hearts of the World

Rating: ☆☆☆½

D.W. Griffith, Inc./Paramount Artcraft; ***Directed by*** D.W. Griffith; ***Scenario by*** M. Gaston de Tolignac; ***English Translation by*** Captain Victor Marier; ***Running Time:*** 119 minutes; ***Cast:*** THE GRANDFATHER, Adolphe Lestina; THE MOTHER, Josephine Crowell (died 1934); THE GIRL [MARIE STEPHENSON], Lillian Gish (1893–1993); THE BOY [DOUGLAS GORDON HAMILTON], Robert Harron (1893–1920); FATHER OF THE BOY, Jack Cosgrave (1875–1925); MOTHER OF THE BOY, Kate Bruce (1858–1946); LITTLEST BROTHER, Ben Alexander (1911–1969); OTHER BROTHERS, M. Emmons and F. Marion; THE LITTLE DISTURBER, Dorothy Gish (1898–1968); MONSIEUR CUCKOO, Robert Andersen (1890–??); VILLAGE CARPENTER,

Lillian Gish in *Hearts of the World* (1918).

George Fawcett (1860–1939); VON STROHM, George Siegmann (1882–1928); INNKEEPER, Fay Holderness; DEAF/BLIND MUSICIAN, L. Lowy; A POILU, Eugene Pouyet (1883–1950); FRENCH PEASANT GIRL, Anna Mae Walthall (1894–1950); A REFUGEE, Yvette Duvoisin; FRENCH MAJOR, Herbert Sutch (1884–1939); GERMAN SERGEANT, George Nichols (1864–1927); REFUGEE MOTHER, Mrs. Mary McConnell Gish (1860–1948); A DANCER, Mary Hay

(1901–1957); A HUN, Erich von Stroheim (1885–1957); MAN WITH WHEELBARROW/VILLAGER IN STREETS, Noel Coward (1899–1973); ***Cast Of Prologue***: HIMSELF, David Wark Griffith (1875–1948); HIMSELF, British Prime Minister David Lloyd George

This was a propaganda film that D.W. Griffith produced as his part in the war effort. Griffith, as is well known, was an ardent pacifist, and would later come to regret making *Hearts of the World*, and produced *Isn't Life Wonderful?* (1924) as atonement six years later.

The film begins with a prologue, showing D.W. Griffith on location in a British trench 50 yards from enemy lines. The prologue ends with a shot of Griffith shaking hands with British Prime Minister David Lloyd George.

The story, set in France, opens with a depiction of peaceful life in 1912. Robert Harron plays the male lead, an aspiring writer whose sweetheart is the girl played by Lillian Gish. Dorothy Gish plays "the little disturber," who would very much love to be courting the aspiring writer herself. She flirts with him while fighting off unwanted attention from a suitor in whom she is not interested. Once she realizes that she cannot have the man she wants, she wants the man that she can get, nicknamed Monsieur Cuckoo.

Everyone's quaint, peaceful lives are thrown into disarray when war is declared. The boy gives up his writing aspirations to go to battle, leaving sweetheart Marie behind, who is in the village when it is taken over by German troops. The film proceeds to show the barbaric and cruel treatment that the citizens of the captured village endure under German control, showing wartime France in all its glamour, glory, and destruction. Some of the battle scenes in this film consist of actual footage that was taken of the war as it was in progress.

As much as Griffith himself hated this film, he did a superb job with it. In addition, the film consists of an excellent cast, featuring many prominent motion picture players who would go on to even greater success. Lillian Gish as leading lady Marie is flawless in this film—especially during the sequence in which she and leading man Robert Harron are trapped in a room about to have its door broken down by the German Huns. Dorothy Gish as the little disturber provides excellent comedy relief, as well as a thrilling sequence in which she saves the lives of the two lead players. Dorothy steals the show in every single sequence in which she appears. Mrs. Mary Gish, mother of the Gish sisters, has a small part in the film, as does Anna Mae Walthall, the sister of Henry B. Walthall. Erich von Stroheim's cameo as a German Hun established his acting career as a lecherous "man you love to hate," which evolved into his significant directing career. Child star Ben Alexander makes a significant appearance as the boy's charming youngest brother. At the beginning of the film, one can see a very young 19-year-old Noel Coward making his film debut as a man pushing a wheelbarrow toward the camera. Coward went on to great fame as a playwright in the 1920s and 1930s, and penned the script for *Cavalcade* (1933), the 1932-33 Academy Award winner for Best Picture.

Hearts of the World stands as the best of all of the surviving World War I films produced while the war was in progress. It has just the right blend of comedy courtesy of Dorothy Gish (without going to the extreme like Raoul Walsh's *What Price Glory?* did), as well as intense melodramatic characteristics. Nearly 80 years later, it is still a compelling film to watch.

240. Johanna Enlists

Rating: ☆☆☆

Paramount; ***Directed by*** William Desmond Taylor; ***Photography by*** Charles Rosher; ***Scenario by*** Frances Marion; ***Based on*** "The Mobilizing of Johanna" ***by*** Rupert Hughes; ***Running Time of Surviving Footage:*** 67 minutes; ***Cast:*** JOHANNA RANSALLAR, Mary Pickford (1892–1979); HER MOTHER, Ann Schaefer (1970–1957); HER FATHER, Fred Huntley (1864–1931); PRIVATE VIBBARS, Douglas MacLean (1890–1967); LT. FRANK LEROY, Emory Johnson (1894–1960); AN OFFICER, Monte Blue (1890–1963); COLONEL ROBERTS, Wallace Beery (1885–1949); MAJOR WHOPPINGTON, John Steppling (1870–1932).

This is one of three films that Mary Pickford starred in under the direction of William Desmond Taylor (1872–1922), which were also the last films that Pickford made for Paramount before going to First National. This is the only one of the Taylor/Mary Pickford collaborations to survive in relatively complete form; it is missing one reel. *How Could You, Jean?* (1918) is not known to survive at all. Only two reels of *Captain Kidd, Jr.* (1919) are known to survive, and are held by private collector Rusty Castleton.

This is also one of only three extant films of actor Douglas MacLean. *The Home Stretch* (1921) is the only MacLean film known to survive in complete form. He also appeared with Pickford in *Captain Kidd, Jr. Johanna Enlists* is also one of the three earliest Wallace Beery films known to survive, having been made shortly after *Teddy at the Throttle* (1917) and *The Little American* (1917), which are Beery's earliest surviving films.

In *Johanna Enlists*, Mary Pickford plays a farmer's daughter whose parents are abusive. She prays for a good man to bring her out of her life of drudgery. Lo and behold, the 143rd California Field Artillery passes through, needing a place to rest for a few days. Douglas MacLean plays injured soldier Private Vibbars, whom Johanna allows to sleep in her bed while she sleeps with her dog in the dog's bed. They fall in love, and after a number of complications, they get married and live happily ever after.

Mary Pickford did this as one of her films promoting the war effort, and was named an honorary colonel of the 134th California Field Artillery, who play themselves in supporting roles. Of the three William Desmond Taylor films evaluated, *Johanna Enlists* is probably the weakest of the three, but not a bad film by any means. Considering the rarity of the films of William Desmond Taylor and Douglas MacLean, it is well worth watching. It is reportedly scheduled for video release at a later date.

241. Little Miss Hoover

Rating: ☆☆½

Paramount; ***Directed by*** John S. Robertson; ***Running Time:*** 64 minutes; ***Cast:*** ANN CRADDOCK, Marguerite Clark (1883–1940); MATTHEW BARRY, Alfred Hickman (1872–1931); ADAM BALDWIN, Eugene O'Brien (1880–1966); WILLIAM CRADDOCK, Forrest Robinson (1858–1924); POLLY BEASLEY, Frances Kaye; UNCLE CRADDOCK, Hal Reid (1862–1920)

Little Miss Hoover is a film that draws interest primarily due to its star: Marguerite Clark. Clark was an actress whose popularity at one time rivaled Mary Pickford's. In a 1918 poll conducted by *Motion Picture* magazine, Pickford led the voting with 158,000 votes, with Clark coming in second with 138,000 votes.

For many years, none of Marguerite Clark's films were known to have survived. It was not until the 1980s that some of her films began to turn up. Two reels of *Prunella* (1918), which is acclaimed as Clark's best film, are known to survive in the National Film Archive in London. Clark's versions of *Snow White* (1916) survives in archives in the

United States. *Mrs. Wiggs of the Cabbage Patch* was released on video August 1998. *Little Miss Hoover* is one of Clark's two surviving works that is widely available for evaluation outside of the archives, having been transferred from the Library of Congress to film historian Richard A. Davis of Maryland.

If one is judging *Little Miss Hoover*'s entertainment value, it is probably the weakest of Marguerite Clark's surviving work. But, if one is looking at historic value, it is the most interesting. This is a World War I propaganda film in which Clark plays Ann Craddock, a woman from a wealthy family who is seeking to do her part in the war effort. She finally decides to raise chickens to provide food to the Allied countries. When she gets home to her grandfather's house, she is told that they have lost everything they own—except for half ownership in a farm that is maintained by her great uncle. The great uncle and grandfather have been estranged for more than 50 years—since they fought on opposite sides in the Civil War. Having no other choice, Ann convinces her father to try to make up with his brother. So, in a sense, it was war that separated the family, and war that once again brings them together.

Throughout the film, the Craddocks go through various tribulations and obstacles in making their farm a success. A subplot occurs with one of the male characters being branded a "slacker" who will not enlist in the armed forces and do his part for the Allied cause.

In this film, Marguerite Clark's beauty shows, but her acting ability is not particularly extraordinary. It is not fair to judge her on the basis of this film, as it departs from the type of roles for which she was generally remembered. Even the reviews of the time for this film were mixed—without near the enthusiasm as for Clark's other work.

The leading man in this film is Eugene O'Brien, a popular matinée idol of the time. O'Brien started his career as a doctor, which he abandoned to pursue an acting career. He was leading man opposite many of the great actresses such as Norma Talmadge, Mary Pickford, and Gloria Swanson. He retired from the screen in 1928, as the talkie era was beginning to take over. Supporting player Hal Reid was the father of Wallace Reid. No further information could be found on Frances Kaye.

Although *Little Miss Hoover* is not the best of Marguerite Clark's surviving films, it is one worth watching.

242. Little Orphant Annie *Rating:* ☆☆☆

Selig-Pioneer; ***Directed by*** Colin Campbell; ***Running Time:*** 57 minutes; ***Cast:*** ANNIE, Colleen Moore (1900–1988); DAVE JOHNSON, Tom Santschi (1880–1931); AN UNCOOPERATIVE ORPHAN, Ben Alexander (1911–1969); James Whitcomb Riley (1853–1916) as himself ***Supporting Cast:*** Harry Lonsdale (died 1923); Eugenie Besserer (1868–1934); Doris Baker; Lillian Wade; Lillian Howard; Lafayette McKee (1872–1959)

Little Orphant Annie is the earliest Colleen Moore performance that is widely available for evaluation. The film opens with a shot of James Whitcomb Riley, the author of the original "Little Orphant Annie" story, reading the book to a group of children. The story is a charming one, telling of how Annie, a teenage orphan, was forced to live with her evil aunt and uncle, her only surviving relatives. Later, her "knight in shining armor," Dave Johnson, manages to get the caretakers of a local orphanage to take her in, and threatens the uncle with bodily harm if he dares lay another hand on Annie again.

Annie, as the oldest orphan, entertains the younger children with her stories of witches and goblins. She even uses her goblin stories to get the younger kids to do as they are supposed. One obstinate orphan who refuses to say his nightly prayers is told of how the goblins will take him away—never to be seen again. The child star is played by Ben Alexander, who would later become famous in the *Dragnet* television series of the 1950s. Since this film was released during World War I, it contains a segment at the end featuring the tragedy of how Annie's friend, Dave Johnson, is called away to fight in the war.

Little Orphant Annie is a delightful, magical story, featuring entertainment as well as historic value. Of the films produced by the Selig Company, this one has the best production values of any that have been evaluated to date. The trick photography showing the goblins flying around is innovative for the time and well done. In addition, the goblin costumes are just as adorable as they are scary. Colleen Moore shines in the title role, of which type would have typically starred Mary Pickford or Mary Miles Minter. It is interesting to see Moore in such a role of demure innocence—a far cry from her flapper image of the 1920s. Western fans will enjoy seeing Tom Santschi in a rare and early nonwestern role as Annie's knight in shining armor.

In addition to the good cast and production values, this adaptation of *Little Orphant Annie* is the only film adaptation of the story in which the original author, James Whitcomb Riley, directly participated. Riley died shortly after his footage was shot, but before the film's release. The movie was dedicated to him in the introductory titles. Even for those who are not silent film fans per se, if they enjoy the story of "Little Orphant Annie," they will find this early adaptation of interest. For silent film fans, *Little Orphant Annie* is truly a rare gem not to be missed, and a chance to see Colleen Moore as you have never seen her before.

243. Lucky Dog

Rating: ☆☆½

Directed by Jess Robbins; ***Running Time:*** 16 minutes; ***Cast:*** THE TENANT, Stan Laurel (1890–1965); THE THIEF, Oliver Hardy (1892–1957)

This rare comedy short was the first that Laurel and Hardy appeared in together, long before they officially became a team in the late 1920s. Stan Laurel got top billing as a down-on-his-luck tenant who has just been evicted by his landlady. Oliver Hardy plays a thief and scam artist. Laurel finds an orphaned dog, hoping to enter him in a dog show and win some money. The show, wreaked by chaos, is a disaster, but Laurel returns a dog to its wealthy and attractive female owner.

Once at the lady's house, Ollie, who previously tried to mug Stan, resurfaces as a swindler whose plans are ultimately foiled.

This comedy was better than average slapstick for the time. This reviewer found it to be much better than originally expected. In addition to good entertainment, the coincidental pairing of Laurel and Hardy makes this film a fun curiosity piece as well.

Director Jess Robbins is an obscure figure in film history, and no further information could be found on him, except that he directed a few films with Charlie Chaplin earlier in his career, as well as a few films with Baby Peggy Montgomery in the early 1920s.

244. The Lure of the Circus *Rating:* N/A

Universal; ***Directed by*** J.P. McGowan; ***Story by*** William Wing; ***Scenario by*** Hope Loring; ***Running Time of Reconstructed Version:*** 54 minutes; ***Cast:*** EDDIE SOMERS, Eddie Polo (1875–1961); MALCOLM SOMERS, Charles H. Mailes (1870–1937); STEVE HARDEN, Frederic Starr (1878–1921); HOWARD MASON, Fred Montague (1864–1919); BROCK, James Gordon (1871–1941); RICHARD VAN NORMAN, Duke R. Lee (1881–1959); DYNAMITE DAN, Andrew Waldron (1847–1932); NAN HARDEN, Molly Malone (1895 or 1897–??); REYNOLDS, Sydney Deane; SILENT ANDY, Noble Johnson (1881–1978); ALICE PAGE, Eileen Sedgwick (1898–1991)

Among silent film actors, the films of Eddie Polo are the rarest. Not one single silent film of Polo's survives in complete form. His films are even rarer than those of Olive Thomas, who has partial prints of three of her films in existence, but, like Polo's work, nothing in complete form.

All that has survived of Polo's silent era work is eight reels of *The Lure of the Circus*, which was originally 36 reels long, filmed in 18 chapters. The surviving footage was discovered in Amsterdam, Holland. Blackhawk Films reconstructed a version of the serial with titles to bring continuity to the surviving film footage, which provides the viewer with an idea of what the serial was like when it was originally released.

Polo was a former circus acrobat who was known for his death-defying stunt work. His career in serials began in 1915 and was steady through the end of the silent era. With Charles Hutchison, he was among the most popular of the male serial actors. Other than bit parts in four talkies in the early 1940s, no other example of Polo's film work survives.

In this serial, Polo played Eddie Somers, part owner and trapeze artist of the Great Western Circus who is not only fighting to keep his share of the circus but trying to protect his father, who has struck it rich on a land deal that yields oil, from swindlers scheming to get the deed out from under him. According to Blackhawk's explanatory titles, among the perilous situations Eddie Somers endures are battles with a lion and a leopard, attacks with bullets and knives, and dangerous motorcycle stunts.

Weaved into the serial is a mystery surrounding the missing niece and heir of Steve Harden, one of the wealthy oil business owners from whom Eddie's father leases land. Molly Malone, in one of her rare surviving film appearances, plays Nan Harden, a cousin of the missing niece. Eileen Sedgwick, another popular serial star who made her serial debut in this film, plays the niece and heiress. The titles by Blackhawk explain that the reason for creating the impostor role is because Molly Malone as Nan Harden had an appendicitis attack, and her recovery time required Eileen Sedgwick to be written into the script to replace Malone and to explain Malone's absence from the latter half of the film. Molly Malone's bout with appendicitis turned out, in essence, to be Eileen Sedgwick's big break.

Unfortunately, most of Polo's really exciting stunts are not among those in the surviving footage. Among the surviving scenes is a segment in which Polo takes on a gang of thugs, and picks one man up over his head and throws him across the room before diving from a window and into the water. Also included are a thrilling motorcycle chase, a car chase, and impressive trapeze stunts in the circus footage.

There are some scenes also which exploit Polo's muscular physique, which was also one of the factors of his popularity. Like Francis X. Bushman, Sr., Polo had an exceptional side profile.

In addition to this film's importance as the only surviving footage from the height of Polo's career, this footage from *The Lure of the Circus* is also the only known surviving footage of Eileen Sedgwick. Sedgwick went on from this serial debut to star in nearly a dozen more silent serials, as well as numerous action pictures, all of which are believed lost. Her popularity for a time rivaled Ruth Roland's and Pearl White's.

245. Mickey

Rating: ☆☆☆

Mabel Normand Feature Film Company/Western Import Company; ***Produced by*** Mack Sennett; ***Directed by*** F. Richard Jones; ***Based on a Story by*** J.G. Hawks; ***Photography by*** Hans F. Koenekamp; ***Running Time:*** 93 minutes; ***Cast:*** MICKEY, Mabel Normand (1892–1930); REGGIE DRAKE, Lew Cody (1888–1934); TOM RAWLINS, Tom Kennedy (1885–1965); MRS. GEOFFREY DRAKE, Laura LaVarnie (1853–1939); HERBERT THORNHILL, Wheeler Oakman (1890–1949); ELSIE DRAKE, Minta Durfee (1889–1975); MINNIE HA HA, Minnie; JOE MEADOWS, George Nichols (1864–1927); THE BUTLER, William Colvin (1877–1930)

This film has historic significance as the one and only title produced by Mabel Normand's own independent studio. While it was made in 1916 and ready for release in 1917, *Mickey* was not released until 1918 due to court battles over control of the film. Triangle Films said they had control, as Mack Sennett was under contract to them at the time he produced it; Mack Sennett tried to claim control, as the film was produced for a company outside of Triangle. Then, the Aitken brothers, who produced many of the Triangle films, borrowed a lot of money, using *Mickey* as collateral, bilking Triangle stockholders out of a great deal of money. Bickering and arguing over ownership caused numerous delays in release, and no exhibitor would touch it until all of the legal technicalities were resolved. When it was finally released, *Mickey* was one of the biggest box office hits of the time, grossing millions when it had reportedly cost only $150,000 to produce. Unfortunately, Mabel Normand, who should have had control over the film, reportedly never saw much of the money that the film made. *Mickey* was plagued with numerous problems, and what should have been a fabulous financial success for Normand turned out to be her biggest headache.

This was the first of Normand's Cinderella-type features, with the mixture of comedy and drama that Mabel wanted for her films. In this early classic dramatic comedy, Normand plays Mickey, a poor orphan who goes to live with rich relatives who treat her like a slave. The relatives change their tune when they find out that Mickey is heiress to a gold mine that has just struck a fortune.

A subplot centers around Mabel's leading man, played by Wheeler Oakman, whom Mabel saves from losing everything he has by substituting as a horse jockey. He in turn saves her from falling for a scoundrel out to marry her for her money.

This film has some great sight gags and sequences, although it is a bit slow-moving in parts. Normand is especially charming during the scenes in which she is protecting her dog from animal control officers. This film is also significant as Minta Durfee's last and best surviving silent era role. She is very attractive in her role as one of Mickey's snobbish relatives, and is a competent actress who deserves a more prominent place in film history. She was the wife of Roscoe Arbuckle, and although they separated after the 1921 scandal, they parted on amicable terms. She stood behind him throughout the ordeal of the trials, and he kept her supported in comfort long after they were divorced. Durfee came back to do occasional character roles with one bit part in the 1930s, another in *How Green Was My Valley* (1943), and a few in the 1960s. When she made an unbilled cameo as a waitress in *The Odd Couple* (1968), she was almost 80 years old, but could have easily passed for someone in her early 50s.

Mickey was Mabel Normand's own personal favorite of her films. It was a pity that she did not get proper financial and emotional satisfaction out of the film. While this reviewer prefers some of Normand's other films over *Mickey*, it is still a relatively entertaining film despite its slow pace and not always coherent storyline. Normand does have some of her most poignant and charming scenes in this film.

246. The 1918 [Nineteen-Eighteen] Maxwell *Rating:* N/A

Produced by Harold S. Arnold Maxwell Agency; ***Running Time:*** 9 minutes, 30 seconds;

This early commercial advertisement shows the 1918 Maxwell automobile in a showroom just before it is to be taken on an endurance demonstration. The car is driven through a shallow river, a desert with rough terrain, and even over large boulders. An onscreen, signed affidavit states that through the course of filming, there were no mechanical breakdowns, demonstrating the durability of the Maxwell automobiles.

If one does not take theatrical movie trailers into consideration, this is one of only a very few commercial advertisements from the silent era that have survived.

247. Out West *Rating:* ☆☆

Comique/Paramount; ***Written and Directed by*** Roscoe Arbuckle; ***Scenario by*** Natalie Talmadge; ***Edited by*** Herbert Warren; ***Photography by*** George Peters; ***Running Time:*** 14 minutes; ***Cast:*** FATTY, Roscoe Arbuckle (1887–1933); SALOON OWNER, Buster Keaton (1895–1966); A ROWDY CUSTOMER, Al St. John (1892–1963); THE GIRL, Alice Lake (1895–1967)

This comedy finds Buster Keaton as a saloon proprietor in the wild, wild west. Shootings are so common in the saloon that Keaton has an automatic drop chute in the floor with which to dispose of the bodies. The saloon is held up by robbers, and sharpshooter Fatty comes into town, cleans out the robbers, and becomes the new bartender. Alice Lake's character comes into the saloon, and is relentlessly harassed by a rowdy customer portrayed by Al St. John. Fatty tries to knock Al out, but he is so drunk that he is not even aware that a dozen beer bottles have been broken over his head. Finally, Fatty and Buster find his weak spot and tickle him, throwing him out of the bar. He vows revenge.

This is not among the better Keaton-Arbuckle collaborations.

248. A Romance of Happy Valley *Rating:* ☆☆½

D.W. Griffith, Inc./Paramount Artcraft; ***Directed by*** D.W. Griffith; ***Story by*** Captain Victor Marier; ***Photography by*** G.W. Bitzer; ***Running Time:*** 57 minutes; ***Cast:*** OLD LADY SMILES, Lydia Yeamans Titus (1866–1929); JOHN L. LOGAN JR., Robert Harron (1893–1920); MRS. JOHN LOGAN SR., Kate Bruce (1858–1946); JOHN LOGAN SR., George Fawcett (1860–1939); JENNIE TIMBERLAKE, Lillian Gish (1893–1993); MR. TIMBERLAKE, George Nichols (1864–1927); VINEGAR WATKINS, Adolphe Lestina; JUDAS, Bertram Grassby (1880–1953); A NEGRO FARM HAND, Porter Strong (1879–1923)

For many years, this film was believed to have been lost. A print turned up in a Russian archive in 1971.

This is a romantic drama in which John Logan, Jr., a poor country boy who is dissatisfied with farm life, determines to better himself in the city. He goes to New York, chancing all. Jennie Timberlake, whose parents own an adjoining farm, wants more than anything for the younger Logan to take notice of her. When the community finds out about his intentions, they try to dissuade him. The preacher of the local church even makes it a point to sermonize on the "cities of sin," comparing New York to Sodom and Gomorrah.

Despite all of this, Logan goes to New York and gets a job in a toy factory. He is barely making enough for bare necessities, but is determined to succeed—working on toy inventions in his spare time. Meanwhile, his parents suffer financial woes that put their farm in danger of foreclosure. The girl he left behind is so lonely and dejected that she makes up an imaginary "other man"—in this case a scarecrow. These scenes by Gish are especially poignant.

This film features one of Robert Harron's best post-*Intolerance* performances. It was also one of the last films in which he starred. In 1920, he was at a hotel in the city where *Way Down East* was premiering. He was found shot in his hotel room, and died a couple of days later. The official conclusion was that he had accidentally dropped the gun, which made it go off, but some sources allege that he committed suicide.

249. Shoulder Arms

Rating: ☆☆☆½

Charles Chaplin/First National; ***Written and Directed by*** Charlie Chaplin; ***Running Time:*** 40 minutes; ***Cast:*** THE GIRL, Edna Purviance (1894–1958); THE DOUGHBOY, Charlie Chaplin (1889–1977); CHARLIE'S COMRADE, Sydney Chaplin (1885–1965); THE KAISER, Sydney Chaplin; SMALL GERMAN OFFICER, Loyal Underwood (1893–1966); THE WHISKERED GERMAN SOLDIER, Henry Bergman (1868–1946); THE KAISER'S GENERAL, Henry Bergman; A BARTENDER, Henry Bergman; DUMB GERMAN WOODCUTTER, Tom Wilson (1880–1965); AMERICAN OFFICER, Albert Austin (1885–1953); CLEAN SHAVEN GERMAN SOLDIER, Albert Austin; BEARDED GERMAN SOLDIER, Albert Austin; CROWN PRINCE, Jack Wilson (1881?-1931)

Shoulder Arms was the biggest box office comedy hit of 1918. In this film, Charlie Chaplin plays a soldier for the allied cause. He takes on a dangerous espionage mission, the first part of which he accomplishes a number of heroic deeds disguised as a tree. When he is "unmasked," he escapes to the home of a German girl. When she is arrested for assisting the allied forces, it is up to Chaplin to rescue her.

Of Chaplin's films of the 1910s, this is among the best. He gives a great acting performance, using a number of different disguises. In addition, his brother, Sydney Chaplin, plays a double role, and triple roles are taken on by Henry Bergman and Albert Austin. These actors are so convincing that one is not able to tell that the same actor is playing the various parts until the end credits.

In addition to Chaplin's hilarious sequence disguised as a tree, he also finds subtle ways to make fun of the German forces when he is disguised as a German officer. Of all of the war comedies of the silent and talkie eras reviewed herein, this is the best. This is definitely a film not to be missed by Chaplin fans, and its satire on World War I and Germany is of historic interest as well.

250. A Society Sensation

Rating: ☆☆☆

Universal; ***Directed by*** Edmund Mortimer; ***Story by*** Hapsburg Liebe; ***Photography by*** William S. Cooper, O.S. Zangrilli; ***Titled and Edited by*** J.E. Robbins; ***Running Time:*** 20 minutes; ***Cast:*** Richard Bradley, Rudolph Valentino (1895–1926); Margaret Fairfax, Carmel Myers (1901–1980); Harry Hannibal Fairfax, Alfred Allen (1866–1947); Just Mary, Zasu Pitts (1898–1963)

Of Rudolph Valentino's eleven films made before 1920, this is one of only four known to survive. This is one of the rare subjects he did in his early days with Universal. He started his career as an extra in *Alimony* (1918), a part that his friend Norman Kerry helped him to get.

In this film, Carmel Myers is the leading player as a country hick who finds out that she is a duchess, and is sent to New York among high society people to properly play her part as a member of royalty. She makes a good impression on society matron Mrs. Bradley, by saving her son, Richard, from drowning in the ocean when his legs cramp up. There is an instant attraction between the two, but he is reluctant to ask her to marry him because she is a duchess. Meanwhile, Margaret receives word that she is not a duchess after all.

Things get more complicated as Margaret's country suitor tries to kidnap her and force her to marry him. This time, Richard Bradley saves the day. After her rescue, Margaret finds out that she really is a duchess after all, and she and Bradley live happily ever after.

While this was basically a routine, nonextravagant programmer, it is still a fun, light, romantic melodrama. Carmel Myers is a delight as the leading lady. Valentino in his first starring role to actually hit the screen, makes a good debut. This was also the fourth film appearance of Zasu Pitts, who plays the country girl who is interested in Margaret's country suitor, who does not return her admiration. She only appears on screen for a few seconds but has full billing and exudes a comedic aura as a woman who would likely keep her husband walking a fine line.

This is one of the first films of director Edmund Mortimer (1875–1944), who went on to direct mostly railroad dramas and westerns. *A Society Sensation* is not only historically important, but entertaining as well. Fortunately, it is widely available on video on various Valentino compilation tapes on the market.

251. The Star Prince

Rating: ☆☆☆½

Little Players' Film Company of Chicago; ***Directed by*** Madeline Brandeis; ***Running Time:*** 61 minutes; ***Cast:*** Zoe Rae; Dorphia Brown; John Dorland; Edith Rothschild; Marjorie Claire Bowden

As far as can be determined, this is the only surviving work of the Little Players' Film Company of Chicago, as well as the only surviving work of female director Madeline Brandeis (1898–1937), who was 19 at the time of production. She did a few more films in the early 1920s for the Hodkinson Company, none of which are known to exist. Brandeis was only 39 when she was killed in a tragic car accident in Hollywood, California, in 1937. Unfortunately, no further information could be found on any of the cast members.

The Star Prince is a charming and delightful story of a boy who is found in the woods by a woodcutter just after a falling star is seen in the area. The boy thinks that since he was brought from a star, he is superior to all of the other kids. The day comes when his real mother, a poor beggar, comes into the forest, and the boy leads the other kids to throw stones at her. He spurns his mother when he finds out who she is, saying she is an embarrassment to him and that he wants nothing to do with her. A fairy witnesses this foul deed, and turns the "star prince" into an ugly beggar in raggedy clothes with a big nose. Realizing that he has been punished for being cruel to his mother, the boy sets out to find her to ask her forgiveness, braving a number of obstacles in his search. Among those characters causing complications along the way are a wicked witch and a wicked dwarf.

It is obvious that director Brandeis was an animal lover. One charming sequence features two bears in a situation in which one is trying to rescue the other. A deer is shown nursing her baby fawns, and a trapped squirrel is featured being freed by the star prince. The scenes with the squirrel were filmed using an early stop-motion photography technique.

With all of the parts being played by children, *The Star Prince* is an intriguing, unique film that promotes the importance of being kind to others. It has become one of this reviewer's very favorites, and is highly recommended as a family film that can be enjoyed by persons of all ages.

252. Stella Maris

Rating: ☆☆☆☆

Paramount Artcraft; ***Directed by*** Marshall Neilan; ***From the Novel by*** William J. Locke; ***Scenario by*** Frances Marion; ***Art Direction by*** Wilfred Buckland; ***Photography by*** Walter Stradling; ***Running Time:*** 99 minutes; ***Cast:*** STELLA MARIS/UNITY BLAKE, Mary Pickford (1892–1979); JOHN RISCA, Conway Tearle (1878–1938); LOUISA RISCA, Marcia Manon [a.k.a. Camille Ankewich] (died 1973); AUNT GLADYS LINDEN, Josephine Crowell (died 1934); SIR OLIVER BLOUNT, Herbert Standing (1846–1923); LADY BLOUNT, Ida Waterman (1852–1941)

Before this reviewer saw *Stella Maris,* he believed Lillian Gish's turn in *Hearts of the World* to be the best actress performance of 1918. Seeing Pickford's riveting double role in this film changed that perception. Pickford's performance in this film at least makes it a draw between the two for best actress of 1918, based on surviving material evaluated. While Gish gave a highly charged, emotional performance in *Hearts of the World* that cannot be criticized on any grounds, Pickford rises to meet the challenge with the added accomplishment of playing a dual role, which is territory that Gish never explored.

This is one of Pickford's more serious and intense films, in which there is never an idle second. In Pickford's role as Unity Blake, she plays a poor orphaned girl who is taken in by Louisa Risca, a brutal, abusive alcoholic whose husband has just left her because of her drinking, and who beats Unity almost to death. Risca's husband, John, feels partially to blame, and his aunt takes Unity in, where she lives in comfort, and very much adores both John Risca and his love interest, Stella Maris, whom Pickford also plays.

As Stella Maris, Pickford's role is that of a wealthy, privileged girl who is crippled, and has been sheltered from the harsh realities of the outside world. She is the exact opposite of Unity Blake in many ways. The use of split screen photography allows Pickford to appear as both characters simultaneously.

Top: Mary Pickford as Stella in *Stella Maris* (1918). *Bottom:* Mary Pickford as Unity Blake in *Stella Maris* (1918).

Through an operation, Stella regains the ability to walk. At about the time when her relationship with John begins to blossom, his wife gets out of prison, and is the only factor standing between his and Stella's happiness. Unity Blake, out of love for John and Stella—the only people who have ever been kind to her—makes the ultimate sacrifice so that John and Stella can live happily and in peace.

Conway Tearle plays the male lead in this, his seventh film, made four years after his debut in 1914. In his films of the 1920s he looks a bit old for leading male roles, but he is in his prime in this film, giving the best of his evaluated performances and looking strikingly attractive at age 39. By the mid–1920s, he started looking his age.

Marcia Manon gives an exceptional performance as the alcoholic, brutal wife who terrorizes everyone in her path. The scene in which she is beating Unity senseless leaves the viewer utterly outraged. Unfortunately, information on this fine supporting actress is scarce.

In addition to the fine performances, this was director Marshall Neilan's finest film of those that have been evaluated. Under his direction, Pickford not only gave one of the best performances of her career, but was also gorgeously photographed. The close-ups of her face in the impressive early sequences as Stella are the most beautiful this reviewer has ever seen of Pickford.

In the past, many historians have compared Mary Pickford to Mary Miles Minter (1902–1984). This reviewer, in *Silent Films on Video*, compared their performances in *The Eyes of Julia Deep* (1918) and *My Best Girl* (1927), which in hindsight wasn't really an appropriate comparison. The ultimate Pickford-Minter comparison would be Pickford's *Stella Maris* to Minter's *Anne of Green Gables* (1919). Both films called for the lead actress to play an "ugly duckling" and a swan. While Pickford played both these roles, Minter's part as Anne Shirley called for her to be transformed into a beautiful, radiant girl over time. Both films are truly among the best of each actress, as opposed to the previous comparison this reviewer made. Since *Anne of Green Gables* (1919) is probably lost forever, there is no way that a really fair modern-day comparison between the two can be made, and each actress should be appreciated in her own right.

Stella Maris is a true masterpiece of romance and tragedy, and is one that all Pickford fans should see. It is moving and highly recommended.

253. Step Lively

Rating: ☆

Rolin/Pathé Exchange; ***Director:*** Uncredited; ***Photography by*** Walter Lundin; ***Titles by*** H.M. Walker; ***Running Time:*** 10 minutes; ***Cast:*** The Boy, Harold Lloyd (1893–1971); Billy Bullion, Harry "Snub" Pollard (1889–1962); Miss Flighty, Bebe Daniels (1901–1971)

Harold Lloyd plays a man who has just been kicked out of his boarding house for nonpayment. Snub Pollard plays a food vendor. Harold steals a sausage, which is in turn stolen from him by a dog. The dog leads him to Miss Flighty's house. Harold and the dog foil a robbery attempt, and Harold gets the girl. This is typical knockabout slapstick.

Credits information is scarce on most of the earliest of the Lloyd shorts. The directors of the shorts were not credited, but most were directed by Harold Lloyd, Hal Roach, Alf Goulding, or G.W. Pratt, although it is not known who directed which shorts.

254. Tarzan of the Apes *Rating:* ☆☆☆

National Film Corporation of America; ***Directed by*** Scott Sidney; ***Based on*** Edgar Rice Burroughs' novel; ***Running Time:*** 63 minutes; ***Cast:*** TARZAN AS A BOY, Gordon Griffith (1907–1958); TARZAN AS A MAN, Elmo Lincoln (1889–1952); JANE PORTER, Enid Markey (1896–1981); BINNS, Thomas Jefferson (1856–1932)

This is the famous first of many screen adaptations of Edgar Rice Burroughs' classic novel. Burroughs and Bill Parsons formed the National Film Corporation for the purpose of producing this film. During the middle of production, Burroughs sold his rights to production control to Parsons. Scott Sidney (1872–1928) was hired to direct the film, and later specialized in comedy. At the time of his death in 1928, he owned 25 percent of the Christie Comedies.

Of the *Tarzan* films, this original version was the most faithful to Burroughs' novel, although Parsons made departures once Burroughs sold out artistic control to him. Child star Gordon Griffith plays Tarzan as an adolescent, whose English parents died when he was a boy, and who was raised by Kala, an ape that had just lost her baby and adopted Tarzan instead. Thomas Jefferson plays Binns, a man who traveled with the Greystoke family when they came to the jungle, and who was the only human contact that the young Tarzan had. Jefferson is best remembered for having played the title role in both the 1914 and 1921 screen adaptations of *Rip Van Winkle*, based on the popular play by his father, Joseph Jefferson (1829–1905).

Elmo Lincoln plays the adult Tarzan, in his most famous role. As king of the jungle, he saves expedition members Jane Porter and her maid from a lion. (It is reported that the lion was upset at the time, and actually attacked Lincoln, who killed the lion in self-defense.) Tarzan falls in love with Jane, who is played by Enid Markey in her most famous role. At first, he follows his acquired ape instincts and forces himself on her, but she scolds him and he redeems himself. Jane decides to stay with Tarzan, and this serves as the end of the film.

Although Elmo Lincoln was not among the better looking Tarzans, he was the most realistic, despite the fact that Burroughs did not feel that he fit the image that he had in mind when creating the character. Lincoln plays the title role again in the followup to this film, *The Romance of Tarzan* (1920). Two more followups were made with other actors, but Lincoln returned to play the role one more time in the serial *The Adventures of Tarzan* (1921). Enid Markey plays Jane in the first sequel as well, but retired from the screen shortly after. In the 1940s, Markey returned to play character roles in a few films, and starred in a few television comedies of the 1960s. She was highly appealing as the screen's first "Jane," and was, in this reviewer's opinion, the best-looking "Jane" ever to grace a screen. When *Tarzan of the Apes* opened in 1918, it was both a critical and box office success, having been one of the first films to gross over $1 million upon its initial release. It remains one of the most widely seen silents today, being frequently shown on television, as well as widely available on the video market.

255. The Tenth Symphony *Rating:* ☆☆☆½

Produced in France; Pathé Frères; ***Directed by*** Abel Gance; ***Running Time:*** 89 minutes; ***Cast:*** EVE DINANT, Emmy Lynn; FRED RYCE, Jean Toulout (1887–1962); ENRIC DAMOR, M. Severin-Mars (1873–1921); CLAIRE DAMOR, Nizan

This is Abel Gance's (1889–1981) earliest film available for evaluation, directed when he was only 28 years old. It was both a critical and commercial success in Europe, and was completed just before Gance was drafted to serve in World War I. (Gance took advantage of his military service to film battle scenes for his pacifist film, *J'accuse* [1919].)

In this film, Eve Dinant, an aristocrat, is taken for a ride by Fred Ryce and his sister, who are trying to get their hands on her fortune. Driven to near insanity, she finally kills the sister, and Ryce blackmails her into giving him a large sum of money to remain silent.

Later, Eve marries the prominent composer Enric Damor, a great admirer of Beethoven. His daughter by a previous marriage, meets up with none other than Fred Ryce, and they become romantically involved. Eve must remain silent, but Damor notices her anxiety and believes she is having an affair. His distraught feelings over his wife prove the inspiration for his masterpiece, "The Tenth Symphony." Karma eventually catches up to the despicable Ryce.

This film features many innovative cinema techniques that were so prevalent in Gance's films. One of the most impressive sequences shows a woman dancing against a background of trees, with these images presented in an early letterbox format. The top and bottom borders of the picture contained six silhouetted images of a dancing woman in a gown, with the colors of the images constantly interchanging with one another.

In 1988, French film historian Bambi Ballard produced a beautifully restored version of this film, with an excellent full orchestral score, as well as the original tinting and hand colored sequences. This restoration is available on video, but only in France with French titles. This is a film that deserves an American video release with English titles.

256. The Whispering Chorus *Rating:* ☆☆☆½

Paramount Artcraft; ***Directed by*** Cecil B. DeMille; ***Scenario by*** Jeanie MacPherson; ***From the Novel by*** Perley Poore Sheehan; ***Photography by*** Alvin Wyckoff; ***Running Time:*** 81 minutes; ***Cast:*** JOHN TREMBLE, Raymond Hatton (1887–1971); JANE TREMBLE, Kathlyn Williams (1888–1960); JOHN TREMBLE'S MOTHER, Edythe Chapman (1863–1948); GEORGE COGGESWELL, Elliott Dexter (1870–1941); TREMBLE'S FRIEND, Noah Beery, Sr. (1882–1946); CHIEF MCFARLAND, Guy Oliver (1878–1932); E.P. CLUMLEY, Tully Marshall (1864–1943); MOCKING FACE, Gustav Von Seyffertitz (1863–1943); EVIL FACE, Walter Lynch; GOOD FACE, Edna Mae Cooper (1900–1986); GIRL IN SHANGHAI DIVE, Julia Faye (1893–1966)

The Whispering Chorus is presented in a style that deviates from the film that Cecil B. DeMille (1881–1959) was typically remembered for, being a bit more lurid and morbid in its presentation of the seedy side of life. Raymond Hatton plays John Tremble, a bookkeeper who is unhappy with the modest wages he receives, and becomes convinced that there is no hope for improvement in what he sees as a dreary, humdrum life. The "whispering chorus" is the thoughts of evil and good, portrayed through double exposure as the faces of the various influences on Tremble's decision making. The evil force wins, convincing Tremble to embezzle $100 in company money to buy some of the luxuries and necessities that he wants for his wife and mother. The next day, the newspaper headlines tell of an oncoming audit of the company's books. The audit is totally unrelated to the small amount that Tremble embezzled, but his conscience gets the best

A scene from *The Whispering Chorus* (1918) featuring Raymond Hatton.

of him. He panics, and switches identities with a dead man, thus making it appear as if he were murdered by higher-ups in the company for refusing to embezzle money for bribes.

This is good artistic work by director Cecil B. DeMille, in some ways reminding one of Edgar Allan Poe's literary classic, *The Tell-Tale Heart*. It is also the best showcase available to date of the talents of Raymond Hatton and Kathlyn Williams. Hatton's transformation from a respectable family man to a disfigured and haggard fugitive is very convincing and well portrayed. He later starred in a number of Paramount comedies opposite Wallace Beery, and in the talkie era was featured in a number of westerns. Kathlyn Williams, best known for her performance in *The Two Orphans* (1911) and the early Edison serial *The Adventures of Kathlyn* (1913), gives a skillfully underplayed performance as Tremble's goodhearted wife.

257. Why Pick on Me?

Rating: ☆½

Rolin/Pathé Exchange; ***Director:*** Unidentified; ***Photography by*** Walter Lundin; ***Titles by*** H.M. Walker; ***Running Time:*** 10 minutes; ***Cast:*** THE BOY, Harold Lloyd (1893–1971); THE GIRL, Bebe Daniels (1901–1971); HARRY HAM, Harry "Snub" Pollard (1889–1962)

This comedy was filmed on Coney Island. Harold is trying to court Bebe, but is having bad luck. Bebe encourages him to throw a horseshoe over his shoulder. He breaks a storefront window, which leads the cops to chase him all over the amusement park. Snub Pollard plays Bud Ham, the husband of Ethel Egg. This is not among the better Lloyd shorts, but the Coney Island footage is of historic interest.

1919

258. Back Stage

Rating: ☆☆☆

Comique/Paramount; ***Written and Directed by*** Roscoe Arbuckle; ***Scenario by*** Jean Havez; ***Running Time:*** 19 minutes; ***Cast:*** FATTY, Roscoe Arbuckle (1887–1933); A STAGE HAND, Buster Keaton (1895–1966); ANOTHER STAGE HAND, Al St. John (1892–1963); "CLEOPATRA," Alice Lake (1895–1967); CLEOPATRA'S RIVAL, Molly Malone (1895 or 1897–??); THE STRONG MAN, John Coogan (1880–1935)

Back Stage was the first of the Paramount Arbuckle comedies to be shown with color tinting. Unfortunately, black and white copies are the only ones currently available on video. It was also the first of the last three films that Arbuckle and Keaton were paired in before going their separate ways. Keaton had been called to served in World War I after completion of *The Cook* (1918), and this was the first film he made upon his return from the war.

This film finds Fatty and Buster working for a theatrical company. The strong man, an arrogant character who thinks that the whole company depends on him, is the star of the show. The effort is made to put him in his place when he goes too far with throwing his weight around. He convinces all of the actors to quit the show, leaving Fatty, Buster, and other stage help to do the show on their own. (The burly "strong man" is played by John Coogan, the father of legendary child star Jackie Coogan. He was killed in a 1935 automobile accident, in which son Jackie was the only survivor.)

Working with the few crew members that are left, this show features Alice Lake doing a hilarious parody on Theda Bara's *Cleopatra* role, with Arbuckle as leading man. This parody on Theda Bara was possibly Alice Lake's most notable performance, ensuring her a permanent place in motion picture history. The next act features Arbuckle and Keaton together for a segment called "snow serenade." Everything that could possibly go wrong does—unintentionally turning the production into a comedy that the audience loves. This success puts the "strong man" into a rage.

Molly Malone plays the actress who comes onto the scene as Cleopatra's rival. There were two actresses named Molly Malone who worked in the silent era, and they are often confused with each other. Molly Malone appeared in this film and in *The Lure of the Circus* (1918); the other Molly Malone (1889–1952) was known as Mrs. Edith Greaves and did a few bit parts in some movies under the name of Molly Malone. The Molly Malone who played in this film was the sister of film actress Violet Malone. Film historian Billy Doyle cleared up the mystery of the two Molly Malones, making it possible to at last set the record straight.

259. Back to God's Country

Rating: ☆☆☆½

Shipman-Curwood Productions; ***Distributed in the U.S. by*** First National; ***Directed by*** David M. Hartford; ***Scenario by*** Nell Shipman and James Oliver Curwood; ***Photographed by*** Joseph B. Walker and Dal Clawson; ***Running Time:*** 73 minutes; ***Cast:*** DOLORES LEBEAU, Nell Shipman (1892–1970); BAPTISTE LEBEAU, Roy Laidlaw (1883–1936); PETER BURKE, Wheeler Oakman (1890–1949)/Ronald Byram (died 1919); RYDAL, Wellington Playter (1879–1937); RYDAL'S SIDEKICK, Charles Murphy (1881–1942); "SEALSKIN" BLAKE, Charles Arling (1880–??); MURDERED MOUNTIE, William G. Colvin (1877–1930)

Based on *Wapi the Walrus*, a novel by James Oliver Curwood, *Back to God's Country* is the earliest of Nell Shipman's starring features known to survive. It is her most highly acclaimed starring feature, made just before she became one of the most significant female film producers of the silent era. Long thought to have been lost, *Back to God's Country* was rediscovered and restored from two incomplete prints in 1985. With this film's rediscovery, it has the distinction of being Canada's oldest surviving feature film. Recently, the Canadian postal service issued a movie centennial series of stamps, and *Back to God's Country* is among the films featured in this series.

In this film, Shipman plays a woman named Dolores LeBeau, who lives contentedly in the wilderness with her father. Among the costars in these wilderness sequences is Cubby the Bear, played by the animal star Brownie. Wapi, a killer great dane trained and tamed by the female heroine, plays a significant role at the end of the film. Some of the animal actors featured in this sequence practically steal the show in the sequences in which they appear. In addition, these opening sequences include some nude shots of Shipman showering in a waterfall. These nude shots created quite a bit of controversy when the film was originally released, but they were presented in very good taste.

While living in the wilderness, Dolores LeBeau takes a liking to Peter Burke, a ranger played in the opening sequences by Wheeler Oakman and later in the film by Ronald Byram. (Byram appears in the winter sequences at the end of the film, which were filmed first. He died of pneumonia shortly after having completed these sequences, and was replaced by Oakman for the rest of the film. The footage of him reveals he had

THE MOVING PICTURE WORLD
421
July 24 1920
DON'T BOOK
"BACK TO GOD'S COUNTRY"
Unless
You want to prove that the Nude is NOT Rude
Is the Nude Rude?
September Morn

Nell Shipman's brief nude sequence caused a furor with *Back to God's Country* (1919), which is her best surviving work.

a great deal of potential.) All is well until a murderous bandit named Rydal kills LeBeau's father. Following the murder, Dolores and Peter Burke move to the city and marry. The whole time, Dolores longs to go back to the wilderness she had grown so comfortable in, so the couple boards a cruise ship for the purpose of returning to their wilderness home. Once they are far enough out to sea that they can't turn back, Dolores discovers that the captain of the ship is none other than Rydal, her father's murderer.

In addition to an engrossing story line, *Back to God's Country* features wonderful cinematography. The waterfall and wilderness shots rival the highly acclaimed, Academy Award winning cinematography in *Tabu* (1931). Seeing this film with the original color tints enhances the beauty of the photography that much more.

Nell Shipman demonstrates wide versatility and talent in this film. The sequences in which she attempts to rescue her father from the torrential current of the river are death defying. The winter sequences were filmed in temperatures of -60°F. It is hard to believe that any acting and directing crew would work under such hazardous conditions for the sake of a film. Ronald Byram's death from pneumonia demonstrates that the crew of this film did indeed work under these conditions, and that a life was lost in the process.

260. Broken Blossoms *Rating:* ☆☆☆☆

D.W. Griffith, Inc./United Artists; ***Directed and Written by*** D.W. Griffith; ***Based on The Chink and the Child by*** Thomas Burke; ***Photography by*** G.W. Bitzer and Karl Brown; ***Special Effects by*** Henrik Sartov; ***Film Editor:*** James Smith; ***Technical Adviser:*** Moon Kwan; ***Cast:*** LUCY BURROWS, Lillian Gish (1893–1993); THE YELLOW MAN, Richard Barthelmess

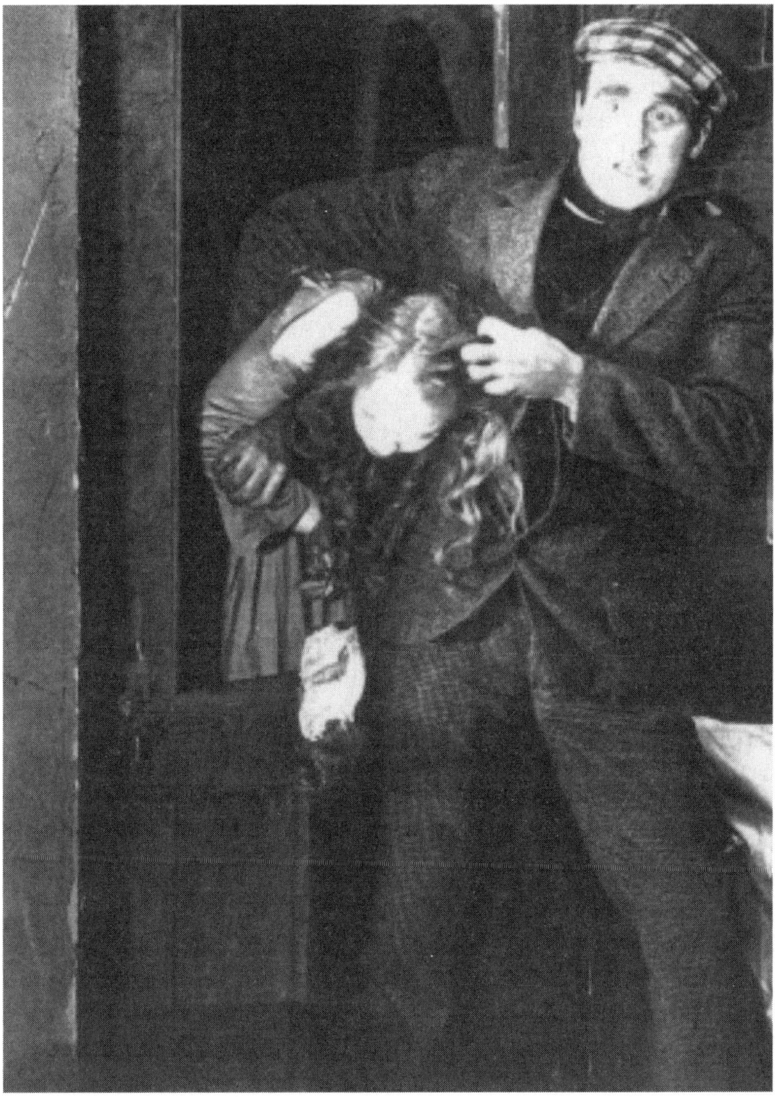

Lillian Gish and Donald Crisp in the horrifying closet sequence in *Broken Blossoms* (1919).

(1895–1963); BATTLING BURROWS, Donald Crisp (1882–1974); HIS MANAGER, Arthur Howard (1889–1942); EVIL EYE, Edward Peil (1883–1958); THE SPYING ONE, George Beranger (1895–1973); THE PRIZEFIGHTER, Norman Selby a.k.a. "Kid McCoy" (1873–1940)

Broken Blossoms has been widely acknowledged as one of the great masterpieces of silent drama. It was filmed in 18 days with a small budget and no retakes. Lillian Gish's performance as the abused 15-year-old Lucy Burrows is widely acclaimed as the greatest dramatic performance in the history of cinema. It is a miracle that Gish was able to do this part at all. At the time of filming, she was extremely ill with Spanish influenza, the wide-ranging epidemic that killed more people than World War I.

The film opens with a shot of a seemingly quiet night with the boats gliding in the harbor of the limehouse district of London. The scene shifts to China's busy streets, where a native observes discord and rowdiness among American sailors, and decides to spread the message of the gentle Buddhist philosophies beyond China's frontiers. In the London limehouse district, he encounters prejudice and bigotry, scorned as "the Chink storekeeper." At one of the households near the seemingly calm harbor in the opening shot, Lucy Burrows is the abused daughter of Battling Burrows, a champion prizefighter and brute. He is a drunk whose heavy drinking forces a life of poverty, and Lucy's life is so miserable with his demands and abuse that she has to force a smile with her fingers when her father demands it. Seeing no hope for her situation, she looks for a way out. A friend tells her not to get married, and judging by her miserable marriage with a slave driving husband and several kids, it appears to be sound advice. The prostitutes of the street warn her against their lifestyle, leaving nowhere else to turn.

After yet another brutal beating at the hands of her father, Lucy falls into the doorway of the Chinese man's shop. He takes her in, giving her the only kindness she has ever known in her life. Unfortunately, a friend of her father's finds out she is there, and the father rushes over immediately after the conclusion of his fight to "assert his parental rights."

Once Battling gets Lucy home, he throws her on the bed and prepares to beat her. Lucy locks herself in the closet, and what follows is one of the greatest dramatic and emotional performances ever committed to celluloid. As Battling Burrows is breaking the door down, Lucy is running around in circles aimlessly like a caged and threatened animal, looking in vain for an escape in a state of delirium. The despair on her face and in her body language is utterly realistic.

Gish's death scene in this film is also among the best in motion picture history—rivaled only possibly by her death scene in *La Bohème* (1926). She was an artistic genius at pantomime, and it is in this film that she demonstrates it perhaps better than in any of her other films except for possibly *The Wind* (1928).

This was also the film that really made Richard Barthelmess a star. He gives an impressive performance, although he does overact a bit in the sequence in which he comes back to find his room trashed and Lucy gone.

This is also perhaps the greatest performance ever given by Donald Crisp. In real life, Donald Crisp was said to have been a mild-mannered man with a heart of gold. To play such a sadistic brute in this film must have been a real challenge.

Broken Blossoms, with its small cast and modest settings, is an exact contrast to Griffith's previous epics *The Birth of a Nation* and *Intolerance*, which feature large casts and elaborate sets. Its elaborate tinting is wonderful to behold, and the film is at its best now that David Shepard has produced a restored version with the original color tints and with the original orchestral score that D.W. Griffith had commissioned for this film. It is an artistic masterpiece not to be missed.

Broken Blossoms was remade as a talkie in England in 1936. Although D.W. Griffith was originally slated to direct the remake, the deal fell through, and John Brahm directed it. The remake is static, and in some parts seems to drag. Dolly Haas puts her heart and soul into the role of Lucy, but she cannot be expected to measure up to Lillian Gish. In the remake's favor, this reviewer feels that Emlyn Williams does a better job as the Chinese storekeeper than Richard Barthelmess.

261. Bumping Into Broadway

Rating: ☆☆½

Rolin/Pathé Exchange; ***Directed by*** Hal Roach; ***Photography by*** Walter Lundin; ***Titles by*** H.M. Walker; ***Running Time:*** 21 minutes; ***Cast:*** THE BOY, Harold Lloyd (1893–1971); THE GIRL, Bebe Daniels (1901–1971); THE DIRECTOR, Harry "Snub" Pollard (1889–1962); BEARCAT THE LANDLADY, Helen Gilmore (1862–1936) ***Supporting Cast:*** Noah Young (1887–1958); "Freddie" Newmeyer (1888–1967); Charles E. Stevenson (1887–1943); Sammy Brooks; Gus Leonard (1856–1939)

This comedy begins with Bebe Daniels as an aspiring actress, and Harold Lloyd as an aspiring writer, living in New York to make their dreams of Broadway stardom become reality. The extreme poverty they live in while paying their dues is presented in a humorous and amusing fashion. They both live in the same boarding house, and are both $3.75 behind on their rent. The landlady gives them both notices that say, "Pay up, get out, or be locked in." Harold generously uses his own rent money to pay up Bebe's rent. He then goes through a major ordeal dodging the landlady and her burly collector to hitch a ride to Broadway in an effort to sell his play.

Neither Bebe nor Harold has any luck in a Broadway career, so Bebe, in desperation, is lured to an illegal gambling establishment by a scoundrel. Harold follows, ready to rescue her if something should go wrong. In a stroke of luck, Harold ends up winning a great deal of money—just as the place is being raided by the cops.

Bumping into Broadway is quite possibly based on real-life experiences of many actors before striking it rich in Hollywood. Many paid hard dues with minor touring shows in similar conditions to the poverty portrayed in this film before getting their lucky breaks. Helen Gilmore is excellent as the abrasive landlady demanding her money. She is not to be confused with a silent screen actress of the same name who was born circa 1900, and died in 1947.

This is among the last, as well as one of the best, collaborations of Harold Lloyd and Bebe Daniels, produced just as Lloyd's pictures were becoming more polished and sophisticated.

262. The Cabinet of Dr. Caligari

Rating: ☆☆☆½

Decla Film-Gesellschaft/Berlin, Germany; ***Directed by*** Robert Wiene; ***Story and Screenplay by*** Carl Meyer, Hans Janowitz; ***Design:*** Herrmann Warm, Walter Reimann, Walter Rohrig; ***Photography by*** Willy Hameister; ***Running Time of New Kino Restoration:*** 71 minutes; ***Cast:*** DR. CALIGARI, Werner Krauss (1884–1959); CESARE [THE SOMNAMBULIST], Conrad Veidt (1893–1943); ***Supporting Cast:*** Friedrich Feher; Lil Dagover (1894–1980); Hans Heinz von Twardowski (1898–1958); Rudolph Lettinger (1865–1937)

In this reviewer's previous book, *Silent Films on Video*, this film was described as boring, incoherent, and disappointing. This was correct based on what was available for evaluation at the time. The copy reviewed was the old Kino version, which was the best copy available. In 1995, David Shepard produced a new restoration of the film for Kino. This new version reveals that the film has not been fairly evaluated, as all previously available prints were truncations of the film as it was meant to be seen. This new restoration contains a great deal of footage that was not present in the previously available prints, thus accounting partially for the incoherence of the print evaluated before. In addition, the new restoration features the original art deco titles designed to match the decor of

A promotional poster for the American release of *The Cabinet of Dr. Caligari* (1919).

the particular part of the film being seen, as well as a proper translation. This proper translation also plays a big part in making the film more coherent. Previous prints were in black and white, missing footage, poorly translated, and taken from negatives that were shot from inferior angles, thus cutting out a lot of important details in the picture itself.

The Cabinet of Dr. Caligari, properly presented, is a highly artistic and intriguing film. Werner Krauss gives a great performance as the deranged head of a mental institution. He has a fascination with somnambulists—people with a disorder in which they are constantly asleep. Conrad Veidt plays Cesare, a somnambulist who has recently been admitted to Caligari's asylum. Caligari tours with Cesare, exhibiting him in "freak shows" at local fairs. A series of strange murders begins to occur, bringing an aura of mystery to the story.

This is a film widely recognized for its macabre set design. The sets are oddly shaped in deco style, emphasizing every shadow as a significant part of the appearance of the locale. To design sets such as these took sheer genius, making *The Cabinet of Dr. Caligari* the defining German expressionist film.

This movie is also notable as the second screen appearance of actress Lil Dagover. It was the beginning of international fame for Dagover, and she maintained an active motion picture career through 1979, just one year before her death.

Werner Krauss, whose career began in 1914, was the leading interpreter of German expressionist cinema, having starred in over 100 silent films. He later starred in propaganda films during the Nazi regime, and was designated as "actor of the state."

Although Conrad Veidt had starred in notable films such as *Opium* (1918) and *Different from the Others* (1919), it was his performance in *The Cabinet of Dr. Caligari* that solidified his reputation as an actor. It was turns in this film and *The Student of Prague* (1926) that led to his being recruited by Hollywood's Universal Studios in 1927. He returned to Germany in 1929, but when the Nazis came to power, he fled to England with his Jewish wife and became a British citizen in 1939. He starred in a number of American talkies from 1940 until his death in 1943 from a heart attack. The most notable of these later talkie performances was in *Casablanca* (1943).

If not previously impressed with *The Cabinet of Dr. Caligari*, viewers should consider getting a copy of the new restoration and giving it another chance. There is a vast improvement in seeing it properly presented.

263. Different from the Others *Rating: ☆☆☆*

Produced by Magnus Hirschfeld/Germany; ***Directed by*** Richard Oswald; ***Running Time of Currently Available Version:*** 23 minutes; ***Approximate Running Time of Original Release:*** 60 minutes; ***Cast:*** PAUL KORNER, Conrad Veidt (1893–1943); FRANZ BOLLECK, Reinhold Scheunzel; KURT SIVERS, Fritz Schulz; SEX THERAPIST, Magnus Hirschfeld

Different from the Others, of which only a fragment survives, proves that the silent era films dealt with all of the same controversial issues that today's films deal with—even the taboo subject of homosexuality. To boot, the leading player in the film was Conrad Veidt, one of the most famous of all German actors, who had just completed work on *The Cabinet of Dr. Caligari* (1919). Director Richard Oswald (1880–1963) was a prominent director as well, having directed such other notable pictures as *The Picture of Dorian Gray* (1917), *Around the World in Eighty Days* (1919), *Lucretia Borgia* (1922), and *The Hound of the Baskervilles* (1929). When the Nazis took over Germany, Oswald moved to England, France, and, after a time, settled in the United States in the 1940s.

In this film, Conrad Veidt plays Paul Korner, a highly regarded and successful gay concert pianist. He goes to a ball, where he is offered a walk home by a scoundrel who hints that he is gay and interested in him. Once they get to Korner's house, Franz Bolleck blackmails him into giving him money, threatening to expose him for violating Statute 175 if he does not comply.

Korner, while enduring Bolleck's blackmail, falls in love with one of his music students. They are happy together until Bolleck presses for more and more money. Finally, Korner gets tired of Bolleck's games, and charges him with blackmail. The courts send Bolleck to prison on the blackmail, but both Bolleck and Korner are each sentenced to an additional three months on Statute 175 violations as well.

The fragment of footage available for evaluation stops with Korner coming back from prison to find that his contracts have been terminated as a result of the publicity of his homosexuality. He takes a lethal dose of pills and commits suicide, and there is footage of Magnus Hirschfeld giving a speech, pleading for tolerance of the "third sex" and abolition of Statute 175.

Gay activist and film historian Vito Russo put together a presentation of *Different from the Others* with an introduction and concluding comments that was aired on cable television in the late 1980s. He explains that the missing footage of the film included sequences of Korner's lover at his casket, vowing to have Statute 175 removed from the books. Further footage showed prominent gay figures appearing in chains of bondage, who are freed when a hand erases Statute 175 from the books. This presentation has never been released on video. The only people who have the film on video are those who taped it when it originally aired.

Magnus Hirschfeld, the film's producer and star, was head of the Institute of Sexology in Berlin. When this film was originally released, it got good critical reviews and was moderately successful at the box office—despite sabotaging from gay bashers who threw stink bombs and even fired sniper bullets into audiences. By 1920, the film was banned in many cities, and could only be viewed by psychology professionals. In 1930, Hirschfeld was forced to flee for his life to France as the Nazis gained power in Germany. In 1933, the Nazis raided Hirschfeld's library, and burned all of his work, including the last complete prints of *Different from the Others*.

For the next 43 years, it was believed that this film had been completely obliterated from existence by the Nazis. Fortunately, a partial print turned up in a Ukrainian archive in 1976, and from this newly rediscovered print material came the 23 minute version of the film.

Different from the Others is a historic milestone, having been the first film to present a positive viewpoint on gay liberation. It provides the first screen depiction of a gay bar, with Conrad Veidt playing a gay role—all 50 years before the 1969 Stonewall riots, which marked the beginning of the gay liberation movement in America.

In a recent article on Conrad Veidt that appeared in *The Silent Film Monthly* in 1997, there was not a single word mentioned about his gay role in *Different from the Others*. It is time that this film be documented and recognized in publications outside of those that deal exclusively with gay history.

264. Don't Change Your Husband *Rating:* ☆☆½

Paramount Artcraft; ***Directed by*** Cecil B. DeMille; ***Screenplay by*** Jeanie MacPherson; ***Photography by*** Alvin Wyckoff; ***Art Direction by*** Wilfred Buckland; ***Running Time:*** 84 minutes;

Cast: LEILA PORTER, Gloria Swanson (1897–1983); JAMES DENBY PORTER, Elliott Dexter (1870–1941); "TOODLES" THOMAS, Julia Faye (1893–1966); THE BISHOP, Theodore Roberts (1861–1928); MRS. HUCKNEY, Sylvia Ashton (1880–1940); SCHUYLER VAN SUTPHEN, Lewis J. Cody (1888–1934)

This was the first of the marital comedies on which Cecil B. DeMille and Gloria Swanson collaborated. Swanson graduated from Sennett comedies and independent productions to land a contract with Paramount Artcraft, where DeMille put her on her way to stardom.

Gloria Swanson, star of *Don't Change Your Husband* (1919), the first of many marital comedies that she and Cecil B. DeMille collaborated on.

In *Don't Change Your Husband*, Elliott Dexter was the leading man. He made his film debut in 1915 after a career in vaudeville and on the legitimate stage. Dexter starred mostly in light romantic dramas like this one and Mary Pickford's *Romance of the Redwoods* (1917), and also had a part in the 1918 version of *The Squaw Man*. He retired from films after 1925.

Dexter and Swanson play Leila and James Porter, a couple whose marriage is becoming less satisfactory to the wife. At an anniversary party, their friend Mrs. Huckney brings along her nephew, Schuyler Van Sutphen. Leila decides to stay at Mrs. Huckney's for a few days, and decides that perhaps she would be more content divorcing her husband and marrying Von Sutphen, who turns out to be a spendthrift and squanderer of money (a typical role for Lew Cody, who was typecast as a scoundrel throughout most of his career). She soon finds out that perhaps her first husband's annoying habits weren't so bad after all.

Don't Change Your Husband was the film that established the genre of future DeMille-Swanson films that would be among Paramount's biggest moneymakers, and is still amusing to watch today. Despite the fact that this film has been public domain for a few years, it has not yet been widely released on video. While it isn't much different from the other DeMille-Swanson comedies that are prevalent on the market, its historic importance as the introductory entry of the genre makes it worth having.

265. Don't Shove *Rating:* ☆☆

Rolin/Pathé Exchange; Director Uncredited; ***Photography by*** Walter Lundin; ***Titles by*** H.M. Walker; ***Running Time:*** 9 minutes; ***Cast:*** THE BOY, Harold Lloyd (1893–1971); THE GIRL, Bebe Daniels (1901–1971)

This short features Harold at a birthday party thrown for Bebe Daniels. He has a bully as a rival, who gives chase. The rival offends a man whose little brother knocks him out. The little brother then teaches Harold to box. Just as Harold perfects his technique, he accidentally hits a cop, who chases him into a skating rink. The skating rink so happens to be where everybody at Bebe's party congregates afterward. A champion roller skater performs an act, and Harold attempts to outdo him to impress Bebe, but he bombs. He then enters a hurdle race conducted on skates in an effort to redeem himself. By a stroke of luck, he wins and gets the girl.

Don't Shove was quite obviously inspired by Charlie Chaplin's *The Rink* (1916). Although well done, it is not as good as Lloyd's later shorts, in part because he was trying to copy Chaplin.

266. Eyes of Youth

Rating: ☆☆☆½

Garson/Equity; ***Directed by*** Albert Parker; ***Screenplay by*** Charles Whittaker; ***Based on the Stage Play by*** Max Marcin and Charles Guernon; ***Photography by*** Arthur Edeson; ***Running Time:*** 84 minutes; ***Cast:*** GINA ASHLING, Clara Kimball Young (1890–1960); HINDU DISCIPLE, Vincent Serrano (1866–1935); KENNETH ASHLING, Gareth Hughes (1894–1965); RITA ASHLING, Pauline Starke (1900–1977); ASA ASHLING, Sam Sothern (1865–1920); PETER JUDSON, Edmund Lowe (1890–1971); ROBERT GORING, Ralph Lewis (1872–1937); LOUIS ANTHONY, Milton Sills (1882–1930); CLARENCE MORGAN, Rudolfo Valentino (1895–1926); PAOLO DE SALVO, William Courtleigh (1867–1930); ***Supporting Cast:*** Edward M. Kimball (1859–1938)

Eyes of Youth is by far the best surviving film work of the great Clara Kimball Young, produced while she was still on top, just before her career began to falter in the early 1920s. It was produced by Harry Garson (1882–1938), her former agent and second husband, whom she married after her 1916 divorce from James Young.

In this film, Young plays Gina Ashling, a woman who has some hard decisions to make in a very short time. Her father's business is failing, and he wants her to marry Mr. Goring, the chairman of the financial institution to which he owes money, who has promised financial help in return for Gina's hand in marriage. Another suitor tells her it is her duty to remain with her family, and to wait for him to move up within the ranks at the bank in which he works. She could also go to Paris and become an opera singer. All of these options counter what she really wants to do in her heart: marry Peter Judson, the man she really loves, and go to South America with him to do a charity irrigation project.

A Hindu spiritualist, who has come from the Middle East to America seeking a pure and innocent heart to help, meets Gina and provides her with the opportunity to look into the future with a crystal ball to see the outcome of each option she is deciding upon.

Clara Kimball Young gives a magnificent performance. When one sees her rescuing a tailless dog from two boys who are harassing it, she wonders why there is so much cruelness and unhappiness in the world, wanting to find a way to help. She looks straight into the camera with her emotional eyes, showing how powerfully her emotions come across the screen. The emotional depth of Young's acting is equaled only by Lillian Gish and a handful of other actresses.

In addition to Clara Kimball Young, *Eyes of Youth* features several other luminary actors of the screen—some before they made it big, and some riding the crest of stardom. Rudolph Valentino, billed as "Rudolfo" in this film, plays a villainous gigolo who, in league with bank financier Goring, is having an affair behind Gina's back with another woman, sets her up to look like an adulteress, giving her husband grounds for divorce so that he can marry the other woman. It was this role that would later influence June Mathis (1889–1927) at Metro Pictures to insist that Valentino play the male lead in *The Four Horsemen of the Apocalypse* (1921), his first really big break. Indirectly, *Eyes of Youth* was the film that made Valentino a major star.

This was Edmund Lowe's fifth film, made four years after his 1915 debut. It is his earliest surviving work, done seven years before *What Price Glory?* (1926), his most famous silent era film. Lowe worked in films steadily through 1960.

Milton Sills, a popular screen hero, rose to prominence in *Patria*, a 1916 serial, and this is his earliest work available outside the archives. His career lasted until his sudden death in 1930, with *The Sea Hawk* (1924) being his most famous film.

Gareth Hughes made his film debut in this film, and found later success as leading man to such stars as Marguerite Clark and Pola Negri. He also played in *The Christian* (1923), a much coveted lost film. In the 1930s, Hughes abandoned Hollywood's glitz and glamour, and became a Catholic Priest working with Native Americans.

Pauline Starke, a Griffith protégé who stars as the younger Ashling sister, went on to significant success, and the Griffith character actor Ralph Lewis is great as the despicable Robert Goring.

Eyes of Youth was remade, again under the direction of Albert Parker (1887–1974), as *The Love of Sunya* (1927), one of Gloria Swanson's independently produced films for United Artists. While Swanson's version was stylized and sophisticated, Young's original still has a slight edge over the Swanson version. One unique artistic touch the original has is the fourth path, in which Gina waits for Louis Anthony and stays with her family while working as a schoolteacher before she is fired. The sequences in the schoolroom provide some great comedy relief, especially where the mischievous student sticks his tongue out at his classmates. In addition, this original version presents Gina Ashling as a warm, emotional, and compassionate person, which is lost with Gloria Swanson's suave sophistication. The original has Rudolph Valentino, who is a great asset to any film in which he appears.

Eyes of Youth is a fine film featuring a magnificent cast. It is highly recommended for its entertainment as well as historic value.

267. From Hand to Mouth

Rating: ☆☆☆½

Rolin/Pathé Exchange; ***Directed by*** Alf Goulding; ***Photography by*** Walter Lundin; ***Titles by*** H.M. Walker; ***Running Time:*** 17 minutes; ***Cast:*** THE BOY, Harold Lloyd (1893–1971); THE CHILD WAIF, Peggy Cartwright (1912); THE GIRL, Mildred Davis (1901–1969); THE KIDNAPPER, Harry "Snub" Pollard (1889–1962)

From Hand to Mouth was the first Lloyd comedy to feature Mildred Davis as the leading lady. Davis took over after Bebe Daniels left and went to Paramount to work for Cecil B. DeMille. In this film, Davis plays a wealthy heiress who has until midnight to provide the documentation necessary to claim her fortune. Harold is a down-on-his-luck guy who has befriended a homeless waif. A dog brings Lloyd and the waif a bundle of money, and they immediately go to the grocery store to stock up on food. Unfortunately, the money turns out to be counterfeit. In a panic, the food is dropped, and the storekeeper demands payment. Mildred's car drives by, and she sees what is going on and generously pays the money owed.

Lloyd, out of desperation, becomes unwittingly involved with a band of thieves. His first assignment is to break into a house and open the door for the thieves. He gets into the house, and instead of opening the door has a generous meal. The owner of the house is none other than Mildred, who walks in on Lloyd during his feast. The bad guys finally get into the house, and the ashamed Harold tries but fails to stop them from kidnapping her, which they are hired to do to prevent her from claiming her inheritance in time. Harold follows the thugs to their hideout, and tries to alert the police. Failing to get any policeman's attention, he resorts to hitting the officers and having them pursue him, getting the entire police force into the chase by the time they reach the hideout.

Of the Lloyd shorts evaluated by this reviewer, this is the best that he did in the 1910s. There was only one technical problem. The deadline for Mildred to claim her inheritance was clearly stated in the titles at 12:00 midnight. Yet, when Lloyd rescues her in the nick of time, it is broad daylight in the outdoor scenes. It is possible that this film was originally color tinted, in which case these scenes would have been presented in a blue tint. But, the black and white prints on video today are not tinted.

Mildred Davis was a wonderful choice as Lloyd's new leading lady, and makes a good debut in this film. In addition, child actress Peggy Cartwright is charming as well. In many of the existing prints of *From Hand to Mouth*, her name is misspelled as "Courtwright." Cartwright worked in films from 1919 to 1924, with *From Hand to Mouth* being among the first. She was married to character actor Bill Walker until his death, and currently lives in Canada.

268. The Greatest Question *Rating:* ☆☆½

D.W. Griffith, Inc./First National; ***Directed by*** D.W. Griffith; ***Story by*** William Hale; ***Scenario by*** S.E.V. Taylor; ***Photography by*** G.W. Bitzer; ***Running Time:*** 73 minutes; ***Cast:*** NELLIE JARVIS, Lillian Gish (1893–1993); JIMMY HILTON, Robert Harron (1893–1920); MRS. HILTON, Eugenie Besserer (1868–1934); MR. HILTON, George Fawcett (1860–1939); JOHN HILTON, Ralph Graves (1900–1977); ZEKE, Tom Wilson (1880–1965); MARTIN CAIN, George Nichols (1864–1927); MRS. CAIN, Josephine Crowell (died 1934)

This was one of D.W. Griffith's potboilers, which helped to finance his better and more expensive productions. The story is an interesting one, with Lillian Gish playing Nellie Jarvis. She is an orphan who witnessed a murder as a child, and ends up going to work for the murderers as an adult. After a horsewhipping from Mrs. Cain (for accidentally breaking a plate), the memory of the murder comes to mind, and it is at this point that Jarvis realizes that she is working for the same people who committed the murder she witnessed so many years ago.

While this film is not a great melodrama, it is a good one, with especially fine performances by Lillian Gish and Josephine Crowell.

269. Heart o' the Hills *Rating:* ☆☆☆½

First National; ***Directed by*** Sidney Franklin; ***Photography by*** Charles Rosher; ***Based on a Story by*** John Fox, Jr.; ***Art Direction by*** Max Parker; ***Screen adaptation by*** Bernard McConville;

Running Time: 67 minutes; ***Cast:*** MAVIS HAWN, Mary Pickford (1892–1979); JASON HONEYCUTT (AS A BOY), Harold Goodwin (1902–1987); JASON HONEYCUTT (AS A MAN), Allan Sears (1887–1942); GRANDPOP JASON HAWN, Fred Huntley (1864–1931); MARTHA HAWN, Claire McDowell (1878–1966); STEVE HONEYCUTT, Sam DeGrasse (1875–1953); COLONEL PENDLETON, W.H. Bainbridge (1853–1931); GRAY PENDLETON, "Jack" Gilbert (1899–1936); MARJORIE LEE, Betty Bouton; MORTON SANDERS, Henry Herbert (1879–1947); JOHN BURNHAM, Fred Warren (1880–1940)

Heart o' the Hills is one of three movies that Mary Pickford starred in under the banner of First National Pictures, after she left Paramount and before becoming a cofounder of United Artists.

The story takes place in the mountains of Kentucky, with Mary Pickford as hillbilly Mavis Hawn, whose main goal is to improve her gunshot accuracy in order to get revenge on her father's murderer. Her abusive mother, Martha Hawn, is contemplating marrying Steven Honeycutt, who makes a regular practice of beating his son, Jason. Mavis' and Jason's common problems at home bring them together as best friends. They try to marry, but cannot obtain a marriage license on account of Mavis' age, of which she says, "I aim to be 13 on the 30th or 40th of May."

The plot progresses as Morton Sanders, a coal mining prospector, tries to drive Mavis off of her land. She organizes a group of fellow mountaineers, using white robes and hoods as disguises to drive out Sanders and his henchmen. One of Sanders' people shoots at one of the riders, and other shots are fired, one of which kills Sanders. Having been seen hiding one of the night rider costumes, Mavis becomes the prime suspect. It is interesting to see how the situation plays out.

In addition to being Mary Pickford's last film before going into independent production, *Heart o' the Hills* is also historically significant in that it features John Gilbert in a very early appearance, when he was still billed as "Jack" Gilbert in the credits.

Heart o' the Hills is entertaining fare, and was a most appropriate subject for Pickford to end her contract career.

270. His Royal Slyness *Rating:* ☆☆½

Rolin/Pathé Exchange; ***Directed by*** Hal Roach; ***Photography by*** Walter Lundin; ***Titles by*** H.M. Walker; ***Running Time:*** 19 minutes; ***Cast:*** THE AMERICAN BOY, Harold Lloyd (1893–1971); PRINCESS FLORELLE, Mildred Davis (1901–1969); PRINCE OF ROQUEFORT, Harry "Snub" Pollard (1889–1962); KING LOUIS XIVIIX, Gus Leonard (1856–1939); COUNT NICHOLA THROWE, Noah Young (1887–1958); THE PRINCE/HAROLD'S DOUBLE, Gaylord Lloyd (1888–1943)

This is a comedy taking place on the island of Thermosa. A Harold Lloyd lookalike is a prince who wants to marry a woman of whom his royal family disapproves. Harold takes his place when recruited to bid for the hand of Princess Florelle, so that the real prince can marry the woman he loves.

Despite bumbling a few times in his new role as Prince, Harold's charm wins the hand of the princess over his rival, the Prince of Roquefort. Then, the real prince arrives, and exposes Harold as an impostor. By this time, the monarchy is being overthrown by revolutionists, who declare Harold their president. Harold wins back the princess, who now serves as first lady.

This is a delightful parody of European aristocracy.

271. In Wrong

Rating: ★★★

First National; ***Written and Directed by*** James Kirkwood; ***Photography by*** Sol Polito; ***Art Titles by*** Ferdinand Earle; ***Running Time:*** 81 minutes; ***Cast:*** JOHNNY SPIVINS, Jack Pickford (1896–1933); MILLIE FIELDS, Marguerite de la Motte (1902–1950); MRS. SPIVENS, Edythe Chapman (1863–1948); MORGAN COLEMAN, George Dromgold (1894–1948); BANK PRESIDENT, Hardie Kirkland (1868–1929); JOHNNY'S COWORKER, Robert Gordon (1895–1971); MILLIE'S RIVAL, Clara Horton (1904–1976)

When Mary Pickford left Paramount and signed with First National, one of her stipulations was that brother Jack was provided a lucrative contract as well. *In Wrong* is the only one of the Jack Pickford–First National collaborations known to survive. Upon evaluation, it can be concluded that Jack Pickford's fast-lane lifestyle was just beginning to catch up with him. There are still shades of the boyish charm present in his two earlier films evaluated, but one can tell that there is a difference in his persona. The death of Olive Thomas a year later took away what bit of charismatic charm was left.

In Wrong is historically significant as one of the last two films directed by James Kirkwood (1875–1963) before he went into acting. Kirkwood and Jack Pickford were close drinking buddies, and thus Kirkwood was chosen by the Pickford family to direct these final two projects, as he had trouble finding directorial work elsewhere.

It features a delightful story, with Jack Pickford playing adolescent Johnny Spivens, who is just coming of age into manhood. The girl he has a crush on is Millie Fields, daughter of the boarding house owner in the small town they live in. Spivens desperately tries to prove himself, but it seems everything that can possibly go wrong does. When rival suitor Morgan Coleman arrives from New York, things really go awry. Coleman is the typical dapper gentleman, who always seems to be one step ahead of Johnny. He has charm, good looks, and polished manners. It seems Coleman is always in the right place at the right time, while Johnny, despite his efforts to compete, always misses the boat. Just as he has given up hope and is starting to go off to try to prove himself elsewhere, a group of bandits rob the local bank, and Johnny redeems himself by catching the robbers that everybody else failed to catch. He wins the respect of the locals, and ultimately gets the girl, as well as a better job than the grocery store job from which he was fired.

In Wrong is notable as the earliest known surviving work of Marguerite de la Motte, who had made her debut a year earlier at 17 in *Arizona* (1918). She is a delight, and one can see why Douglas Fairbanks, Sr., used her in his early features—most notably in *The Mark of Zorro (1920)*. She is at her best in *In Wrong*. Robert Gordon, Clara Horton, and Edythe Chapman, who all previously costarred with Jack Pickford in *Tom Sawyer*, also costar in *In Wrong*. Edythe Chapman again plays Jack's mother, and Clara Horton has a supporting role as Millie's rival for Johnny's attentions early in the film. Robert Gordon, most famous as the first "Huckleberry Finn," plays Johnny's coworker at the grocery store.

This is a light, enjoyable romantic story, and one of the last of Jack Pickford's better starring films toward the end of one of the happier periods in his life. It is well worth seeing for the rare chance to see him while he was still at a high point in his career, as well as for the rare opportunity to see Clara Horton at work. Fans of Marguerite de la Motte will also find her at her best in this earliest extant example of her work.

272. Just Neighbours

Rating: ☆☆

Rolin/Pathé Exchange; Director Uncredited; ***Photography by*** Walter Lundin; ***Titles by*** H.M. Walker; ***Running Time:*** 9 minutes; ***Cast:*** THE BOY, Harold Lloyd (1893–1971); THE NEIGHBOUR, Harry "Snub" Pollard (1889–1962); THE BOY'S WIFE, Bebe Daniels (1901–1971)

This film features Lloyd and Pollard as close neighbours. They get into an argument, leading into a slapstick free-for-all fight. Then, one of Pollard's children is in the middle of the street blocking traffic in a dangerous intersection. The neighbours stop fighting to save the child, and all is well again.

This is an entertaining effort, but very simple and does not provide much opportunity to demonstrate any of the cast members' talents.

273. Leaves from Satan's Book

Rating: ☆☆

Nordisk Films/Denmark; ***Directed by*** Carl-Theodore Dreyer; ***Scenario by*** Edgar Hoyer; ***From a Novel by*** Marie Corelli; ***Running Time:*** 133 minutes; ***Cast:*** **Part One:** SATAN, Helge Nissen; JESUS CHRIST, Halvard Hoff; JUDAS ISCARIOT, Jacob Texiere; **Part Two:** SATAN, Helge Nissen; DON GOMEZ DE CASTRO, Hallander Hellemann; ISABELLA, Ebon Standin; DON FERNANDEZ, Johannes Meyer; JOSE, Nalle Halden; COUNT MANUEL, Hugo Bruun; **Part Three:** SATAN, Helge Nissen; MARIE ANTOINETTE, Tenna Frederikson Krafft; COUNT DE CHOMBORD, Viggo Wiehe; COUNTESS DE CHOMBORD, Emma Wiehe; LADY GENEVIEVE DE CHOMBORD, Jeanne Tramcourt; THE PEOPLE'S COMMISSAR, Emil Helsengreen; JOSEPH, Elith Prio; **Part Four:** SATAN, Helge Nissen; SIRI, Clara Wieth; CORPORAL MATTI, Christian Nielsen; NAIMI, Karina Bell

This film is a profile of how Satan exerted his evil influence in various ages of human history. Each story is told individually, as opposed to the style of D.W. Griffith's *Intolerance*, which intercut the stories in a parallel fashion.

The first story portrays how Satan influenced Caiaphus to bring about the crucifixion of Jesus Christ. Part two takes place in 16th century Spain, at the height of the infamous Spanish Inquisition. This part portrays Satan taking the role of the Grand Inquisitor. Part three is set during the French Revolution of 1793. It portrays Satan as having a hand in the revolutionists' going too far with the guillotine executions that they carried out. The final story takes place in Finland in 1918, and is primarily an anti–Communist and antilabor message, which caused quite a bit of controversy.

The sequences of this film are generally well done. The costumes and sets appear to be historically authentic, with good acting performances to boot. The mistake that Dreyer made with *Leaves from Satan's Book* was in trying to emulate another director's style. He fell far short of accomplishing the effect that D.W. Griffith achieved in *Intolerance*. Carl-Theodore Dreyer (1889–1968) did much better with *The Passion of Joan of Arc* (1928), the film widely acclaimed as his masterpiece. For *Passion*, he used the unique style of telling his story almost exclusively in facial close-ups. He demonstrated with *The Passion of Joan of Arc* that he had the creativity to develop his own unique style, and did not need to rely on doing inferior imitations of other directors' work.

274. Lightning Bryce

Rating: ☆☆☆

Arrow; ***Directed by*** Paul C. Hurst; ***Story by*** Joe Bandt; ***Scenario by*** Harvey Gates; ***Running Time:*** 300 minutes; ***Cast:*** LIGHTNING BRYCE, Jack Hoxie (1885–1965); KATE ARNOLD, Anna

Little (1890–1984); THE MYSTERY WOMAN, Jill Woodward; POWDER SOLVANG, Paul Hurst (1888–1953); ***Supporting Cast:*** True Boardman (1881–1918); Ben Corbett (1892–1961); Walter Patterson; George Champion; Slim Lucas

When Jack Hoxie costarred with William S. Hart in *Blue Blazes Rawden* (1918), his casting in westerns became a pattern, and established the genre for which Hoxie was to become one of the most popular stars of the 1920s. This serial, *Lightning Bryce*, was the first of his western serials, and was the film that made him a leading star in his own right as opposed to the supporting roles he had previously played. While Hoxie never learned to read or write, he had a handsome physique, and a good talent for impressive stunts and entertainment. (Among the impressive stunts that Hoxie performs in *Lightning Bryce* is being pulled off a horse while traveling at a high rate of speed.) While he was popular, he was not paid what he was really worth. His lack of business acumen to negotiate salaries with studios resulted in his making $1,000 per week at his prime, when other stars of comparable popularity were making ten times that amount.

Lightning Bryce is a 15-chapter serial in which Hoxie plays the son of a man who has found hidden treasure, but has died and left him a pocket knife with a string wrapped around it on which the directions to the treasure are written. Ann Little (billed as "Anna" Little in the credits) plays Kate Arnold, the daughter of Bryce's father's partner who is believed to have been killed by Bryce's father for his half of the stake in the treasure. The serial follows the couple's adventures as they try to find the ancient treasure while fending off corrupt lawmen and outlaws who will do anything they have to do to get their hands on the knife and string's instructions. Meanwhile, there is a "mystery woman" who always seems to be around to rescue Bryce and Arnold just when the calamities they face seem hopeless.

Jack Hoxie, star of *Lightning Bryce* (1919), the only silent western serial known to survive in complete form.

This is widely acclaimed as the best of the silent western serials, so it is fortunate that this happens to be the one silent western that survives in complete form. It is action packed fun, and widely available for viewing on video.

Jack Hoxie's popularity continued through the 1920s, and he made a successful transition to talkies before retiring in 1933. He had a brother, Al Hoxie (1901–1982), who also starred in westerns, but always lagged behind Jack in success and popularity. After his retirement from the movies, Jack toured around the country in western rodeo shows, and even had his own show for a while. He made his last public appearance in 1959, and died at age 80 from leukemia in 1965.

Leading lady Ann Little had made her film and serial debut in *The Black Box* (1915). She did a number of other serials during her career, as well as westerns and some of Wallace Reid's race car films of the late 1910s and early 1920s. She maintained an active life after her retirement from films, and even appeared at the 1980 Cinevent Convention when she was 90. She died four years later at 94.

275. Love's Prisoner

Rating: ☆☆

Kay-Bee/Triangle; ***Directed by*** Jack Dillon; ***Running Time of Surviving Footage:*** 47 minutes; ***Cast:*** NANCY, Olive Thomas (1894–1920); THE DETECTIVE, Joe King (1883–1951); TWIST, William V. Mong (1875–1940)

Of all the major silent film actresses, Olive Thomas' films are probably the rarest. Not one single film starring Thomas is known to exist in complete form. As is well known, Thomas died at the height of her career in Paris in September 1920. She had taken mercury while on her honeymoon with Jack Pickford. It is not known whether her demise was an accident or suicide. Her death was the first of the really big scandals to rock Hollywood, just a year before the Arbuckle-Rappe incident of 1921. Among the three Olive Thomas titles of which footage is known to survive is *Beatrice Fairfax* (1916), a serial which was Thomas' debut and which costarred Marion Davies. It is missing the entire first chapter, as well as footage throughout. *An Even Break* (1917) is missing the second of five reels. *Love's Prisoner* is the most complete of Thomas' surviving titles, with all but the last few minutes intact.

In *Love's Prisoner*, Olive Thomas plays the daughter of a poor, but honest, reformed criminal. Owing to his past reputation, the father is railroaded by the police for a crime he did not commit, and dies in prison. Thomas' character, Nancy, determines to rise out of poverty with honest work, and gets a job as a sales girl in a coffee shop. While working at this job, she meets a wealthy aristocrat from England, and eventually marries him. With her new wealth, Nancy resolves to help the poor. When her husband dies, she is left only with the American mansion, as the English estates and assets are left to his nephew. Having no means to support the maintenance of her mansion, she turns to stealing jewels to support the mansion and to continue her charity work. The missing few minutes of the film are summed up in title cards.

In the opening sequences of this film, Thomas is rather plain looking, and it is hard to fathom why she was acclaimed as one of Hollywood's most beautiful actresses. But, in the ballroom sequences later in the film, Thomas looks absolutely exquisite in her evening gown, fanning herself with a white feather fan. It is her appearance in these sequences that demonstrates that still photos simply do not do her justice compared to what she looks like in film footage. In addition, it shows what a refreshingly natural disposition Thomas displayed as an actress. She had a radiant quality about her personality, and expressed herself beautifully.

Although *Love's Prisoner* is probably not among the best of Olive Thomas' films, it is extremely fortunate that her work can be accessed at all. (In the case of Ruth Clifford, born in 1900, none of her work is available outside the archives.) It is truly a pleasure to see Thomas in action, and one wonders how far she might have gone as an actress if she had not died so young.

Olive Thomas with Jack Pickford, a few months after Thomas appeared in *Love's Prisoner* (1919).

276. Male and Female

Rating: ☆☆½

Paramount; ***Directed by*** Cecil B. DeMille; ***Scenario by*** Jeanie MacPherson; ***From J.M. Barrie's Play** The Admirable Crichton*; ***Photography by*** Alvin Wyckoff; ***Art Direction by*** Wilfred Buckland; ***Production Manager:*** Howard Higgin; ***Film Editor:*** Anne Bauchens; ***Running Time:*** 116 minutes; ***Cast:*** LADY MARY LASENBY, Gloria Swanson (1897–1983); WILLIAM CRICHTON, Thomas Meighan (1879–1936); TWEENY, Lila Lee (1905–1973); EARL OF LOME, Theodore Roberts (1861–1928); EARNEST WOOLEY, Raymond Hatton (1887–1971); LADY AGATHA LASENBY, Mildred Reardon; BABYLONIAN KING'S FAVORITE, Bebe Daniels (1901–1971); SUSAN, Julia Faye (1893–1966); BUTTONS, Wesley Barry (1907–1994)

Male and Female was the last film that Cecil B. DeMille directed in the 1910s, and was his biggest box-office hit of that decade. During this decade, DeMille experimented with several types of films, and it was his social comedies that performed best at the box office. This social comedy had been preceded by *Don't Change Your Husband* (1919) and *For Better for Worse* (1919).

Male and Female explores what would happen if the various social classes were equalized by depicting a wealthy and aristocratic family being shipwrecked with their servants on a desert island. It is interesting to see who pairs up with whom once social status and money are no longer factors in their everyday lives.

This film is especially notable because it contains two of Gloria Swanson's most famous sequences. The first is the celebrated sequence showing Swanson taking a bath in a lavish sunken tub that she walks down into. This film also contains the sequence showing Swanson's encounter with a lion in the Babylonian flashback.

This page and following: *Male and Female* (1919) starring Gloria Swanson.

Male and Female was not among DeMille's more remarkable artistic accomplishments. Much of the credit for this film's enormous box-office success is attributable to the cast featured. Thomas Meighan had just been skyrocketed to stardom overnight a few months earlier in George Loane Tucker's mega-hit, *The Miracle Man* (1919). In addition, Gloria Swanson and Bebe Daniels brought a lot of drawing power to the film as well. Daniels had just finished her contract as Harold Lloyd's leading lady. Gloria Swanson was at her prettiest in this film, and never looked better. Another thing that helped this film's box-office success was the time at which it was released. The world had just been through the first world war, and was tired of having serious social issues thrown back into their faces again at the theaters. Light romantic comedies became far more popular with moviegoers during this period than serious dramatic epics. DeMille gave the public what they wanted, which resulted in his having one of the longest careers of any motion picture director.

This film benefits greatly from being viewed in a good quality print with proper musical accompaniment. The print that was reviewed a few years ago was an edited, mediocre quality copy with a generic score that was not appropriate for the film, thus providing a negative first impression. Kino Video recently released a restored version, complete and of excellent quality, with the original color tints and an orchestra score performed in accordance with the original release. Seen in its proper format, *Male and Female* is quite enjoyable and entertaining despite its flaws.

277. The Miracle Man *Rating:* N/A

Paramount Artcraft; ***Directed and Written by*** George Loane Tucker; ***Based on the Story by*** Frank Packard ***and Stage Play by*** George M. Cohan; ***Titles by*** Wid Gunning; ***Photography by*** Philip E. Rosen and Ernest G. Palmer; ***Original Running Time:*** Approximately 70 minutes; ***Running Time of Surviving Footage:*** 4 minutes; ***Cast:*** "THE MIRACLE MAN," Joseph J. Downing (1848–1928); TOM BURKE, Thomas Meighan (1879–1936); THE FROG, Lon Chaney, Sr. (1883–1930); ROSE, Betty Compson (1897–1974); THE DOPE, J.M. Dumont (1879–1959); RICHARD KING, Lawson Butt (1883–1956); CLAIRE KING, Elinor Fair (1903–1957); MR. HIGGINS, F.A. Turner (1858–1923); RUTH HIGGINS, Lucille Hutton

This is probably the second-most coveted of the lost films of Lon Chaney, Sr., following *London After Midnight* (1927). Only four minutes of this film currently survive. The surviving footage is a segment that was copied for a 1930s Paramount one-reel short subject while it was still extant. It is the only footage of any of director George Loane Tucker's (1872–1921) films that survives, other than his 1913 feature *Traffic in Souls*. After *The Miracle Man*, Tucker lived to make only one more film before his death from an unspecified illness in 1921 at age 49.

Betty Compson, leading lady of *The Miracle Man* (1919), a film of which only 4 minutes survive.

The surviving footage shows Betty Compson, Thomas Meighan, and Chaney plotting their next scam, in which Chaney's character is to play a "cripple" who miraculously is healed by a fake faith healer, and bilking the audience out of donations. The rest of the footage shows the healing scene, with Chaney manipulating his joints back into place and walking as part of the act. The unexpected happens, as a boy who is really crippled runs up to the altar, throwing down his crutches on the way there. This one surviving sequence from *The Miracle*

Man is excellent, and whets one's appetite for another miracle—a rediscovery of a complete print of the whole film.

Although Chaney had been in films since 1914 with moderate success, *The Miracle Man* was the film that really got him noticed. Betty Compson and Thomas Meighan also significantly boosted their careers as a result of their performances in this film.

The Miracle Man was remade as a talkie in 1932, starring Hobart Bosworth as the faith healer. This remake does survive in complete form. It starts off well enough, but drags out for about the last 30 minutes, and gets boring at the end. Considering the acclaim received by the original production, one could guess that it was probably a good, solid film all the way through, without the last 30 minutes dragging on forever. Also, without Chaney as the cripple, it surely can't be as good as the original must have been.

278. Mrs. Wiggs of the Cabbage Patch *Rating:* ☆☆☆½

Paramount; ***Directed by*** Hugh Ford; ***Scenario by*** Eve Unsell; ***Based on the Novel by*** Alice Hegan Rice; ***Photography by*** William Marshall; ***Running Time:*** 48 minutes; ***Cast:*** MRS. NANCY WIGGS, Mary Carr (1874–1973); LOVEY MARY, Marguerite Clark (1883–1940); BILLY WIGGS, Gareth Hughes (1894–1965); MAGGIE DUNCAN, Gladys Valerie; TABITHA HAZY, Vivia Ogden (died 1952); ASIA WIGGS, May McAvoy (1901–1984); HIRAM STUBBINGS, Robert Milash (1885–1954)

For many years, classic film fans have lamented over the unavailability of Marguerite Clark's silent films. Until the early 1980s, none of Clark's work were known to exist at all. Then, *Little Miss Hoover* (1918), a World War I propaganda film Clark played in, turned up. Within the next few years, two more complete Clark films—*Mrs. Wiggs of the Cabbage Patch* and *Snow White* (1916)—turned up, as well as two reels from the highly acclaimed Maurice Tourneur masterpiece, *Prunella* (1918). *Little Miss Hoover* was released on video in 1996 by private collector Richard A. Davis.

Thanks to Unknown Video, Clark's *Mrs. Wiggs of the Cabbage Patch*, which was acclaimed as one of Clark's better and more popular films, is available on video. This marks the first time in nearly 80 years that any of Clark's most coveted films have been widely accessible to the general public.

The first screen version of this classic that this reviewer saw was the 1934 Paramount sound remake, which was utterly delightful, featuring Zasu Pitts and W.C. Fields, respectively, as Tabitha Hazy and Hiram Stubbins. It was a lot different in its presentation of the story than this original silent version. Both versions are equally as wonderful and charming in their own respective ways.

This silent version starts out at an orphanage, with Clark as Lovey Mary, a teenaged orphan who looks after the younger orphans. Maggie Duncan, the oldest of the orphans, throws her weight around, and Lovey Mary goes to bat when witnessing Maggie's cruel treatment. Eventually, Maggie leaves the orphanage, but returns a couple of years later to drop off her baby son, whom she is unable to care for as a single, unmarried mother. Lovey Mary and the son Tommy form a close friendship, and when word comes a few years later that mother Maggie is returning to claim her son, the two make the great escape to the Wiggs' cabbage farm, where the little fugitives are taken in. The story continues as Lovey Mary, Tommy, and the other characters overcome various adversities to eventually live happily ever after.

One aspect that gives this 1919 film an edge over the 1934 version is that it has five really outstanding cast members, as opposed to two in the 1934 version. In seeing Marguerite Clark in one of her best roles, one can definitely understand why she was so popular, ranking with Lillian Gish, Mary Miles Minter, and Clara Kimball Young as among Mary Pickford's closest rivals in popularity polls of the late 1910s. It is hard to believe that Clark was 36 years old when she played this teenage girl. She easily passed for a girl in the 14–16 year range, and played the part with a unique sense of grace, charm, and innocent appeal. Clark became one of this reviewer's favorites after watching *Little Miss Hoover* (1918), which, as stated above, isn't even among her stronger films. Seeing Clark in *Mrs. Wiggs* elevates her status even higher (and makes one long even more to see Clark in *Snow White* [1916] and the surviving footage of *Prunella* [1918]). It is also good to see another example of the work of prominent character actress Mary Carr, who specialized in playing motherly figures, having her greatest success in the original *Over the Hill and to the Poorhouse* (1920). Surprisingly, Carr was only about 9 years older than Clark was when this film was made, but with Carr's ability to look much older than 45, and Clark's ability to pass for 20 years younger than 36, they were convincing as orphan and adoptive mother. Gareth Hughes had his first really important leading role as Clark's leading man in this film, which came out the same year that he played a really supporting role in Clara Kimball Young's *Eyes of Youth*. May McAvoy can be briefly seen as Asia Wiggs in one of her earliest film appearances, which is the earliest McAvoy footage currently known to survive. McAvoy and Hughes both starred two years later in the lead roles in *Sentimental Tommy* (1921), a triumphant success which was among their most highly acclaimed performances. A year before Vivia Ogden (whose first name was misspelled as "Vivian" in the titles) meddled in the life of Lillian Gish as the busybody gossip Martha Perkins in *Way Down East* (1920). She played the comedic role of "old maid" Tabitha Hazy in this film, looking for love in the personal ads, and ending up with one Hiram Stubbins, played by Robert Milash, who first appeared in films around 1900 for the Edison Company.

This is a great addition to the list of silents now widely available on video, having been the most important new video release of 1998.

279. True Heart Susie *Rating:* ☆☆½

Paramount Artcraft; ***Directed by*** D.W. Griffith; ***Scenario by*** Marion Fremont; ***Running Time:*** 63 minutes; ***Cast:*** TRUE HEART SUSIE, Lillian Gish (1893–1993); WILLIAM, Robert Harron (1893–1920); WILLIAM'S FATHER, Wilbur Higby (1867–1934); SUSIE'S AUNT, Loyola O'Connor (1880–??); THE STRANGER, George Fawcett (1860–1939); BETTINA, Clarine Seymour (1898–1920); BETTINA'S AUNT, Kate Bruce (1858–1946); BETTINA'S CHUM, Carol Dempster (1901–1991); SPORTY MALONE, Raymond Cannon (1893–1977)

This is a romantic drama loosely based on the Dora/Agnes story in Charles Dickens' *David Copperfield*. Although not considered to be among Griffith's best films, it is a good film—better than Griffith potboilers like *The Greatest Question* (1919) and *One Exciting Night* (1922).

Lillian Gish plays Susie, an innocent country girl who is in love with William. She sacrifices a great deal to send him to college, selling her cow and other possessions to raise the money—unbeknownst to him. At college, William forgets Susie, and becomes infatuated with a girl named Bettina. They marry, much to Susie's heartbreak. The marriage goes awry with Bettina running around and partying with her college friends, and not giving much consideration to her husband. Through it all, Susie never betrays Bettina's escapades to William, and true love eventually wins out.

If acted and directed by any other crew, this story would have been largely inconsequential. But, with Griffith's sensitive directorial style and excellent performances from Lillian Gish, Robert Harron, and Clarine Seymour, it works well.

This was one of the earlier roles played by Carol Dempster, who started with the Griffith Company in a bit part in *Intolerance*.

True Heart Susie is widely available on video, but only in fair quality copies. The print used for this review was obviously transferred at a higher rate of speed than which the film was intended to be seen. This is a film that could benefit greatly from being presented in a better quality format with a nice music score.

280. Victory *Rating:* ☆☆☆

Paramount Artcraft; ***Directed by*** Maurice Tourneur; ***Based on a Story by*** Joseph Conrad; ***Adapted by*** Stephen Fox; ***Photographed by*** René Guissart; ***Scenic Effects by*** Floyd Mueller; ***Running Time:*** 51 minutes; ***Cast:*** AXEL HEYST, Jack Holt (1888–1951); ALMA, Seena Owen (1894–1966); SCHONBERG, Wallace Beery (1885–1949); MR. JONES, Ben Deeley (1878–1924); RICARDO, Lon Chaney, Sr. (1883–1930); PEDRO, Bull Montana (1887–1950)

The story for this film takes place on the island of Samburen in the Dutch East Indies. Jack Holt, who is best remembered for his numerous western roles, plays the leading role of Axel Heyst. Heyst is the wealthy grandson of a famous author and lives in seclusion on the island of Samburen. On a last visit to a neighboring island to close out his final business affairs, he attends a show at a hotel. Alma, traveling with the show, is the "patsy" of the touring company, not treated well by her boss and coworkers. Heyst, feeling sorry for her, takes her to his island to get her away from the bad company that she has gotten mixed up into.

Wallace Beery plays Schonberg, an old enemy of Heyst's who owns the hotel on the neighboring island. A gang of three thugs comes to his hotel to stay, and to get revenge on Heyst, Schonberg directs them to Heyst's residence, telling them that he has a stash of money hidden. Heyst and Alma are now the prime targets of the gang of three headed up by a man simply known as "Mr. Jones."

Although this film is not among Maurice Tourneur's (1873–1961) best, it is an intriguing film with an interesting cast. What makes it especially appealing to silent film fans is that it is among the rarest of the existing films of Lon Chaney, Sr. In *Victory*, Chaney plays Jones' knife-throwing sidekick Ricardo, who attempts to betray his boss to escape with Alma. Seena Owen plays the female lead of Alma in one of her very few extant films. Ben Deeley, who plays the head of the gang, was married to actress Barbara LaMarr. He died in 1924 at age 46 from pneumonia. LaMarr's death followed in 1926, when she was only 29. She is discussed in further detail in *The Prisoner of Zenda* (1922), reviewed elsewhere in this book.

The print of *Victory* seen by this reviewer is a very contrasty copy that circulates on video among a select group of private collectors. Mint condition, 35 mm nitrate material does survive in the Library of Congress, but Paramount Pictures has not released it on video nor let anyone else do anything with it. *Victory* is in the public domain, but since the print material was reportedly donated by Paramount, they have control over it, and it cannot be accessed without their permission.

281. Within Our Gates

Rating: ☆☆☆

Oscar Micheaux Productions; ***Directed by*** Oscar Micheaux; ***Running Time:*** 78 minutes; ***Cast:*** SYLVIA LANDRY, Evelyn Preer (1896–1932); DR. V. VIVIAN, Charles Lucas; ALMA PRICHARD, Flo Clements; CONRAD DREBERT, James D. Ruffin; LARRY PRICHARD, Jack Chenault; PHILIP GENTRY, William Smith; GERALDINE STRATTON, Bernice Ladd; ELENA WARWICK, Mrs. Evelyn; JASPER LANDRY, William Stark; MRS. LANDRY, Mattie Edwards (1866–1944); PHILIP GRIDLESTONE, Ralph Johnson; EFREM, E.G. Tatum; EMIL LANDRY, Grant Edwards; ARMAND GRIDLESTONE, Grant Gorman

Within Our Gates is the oldest feature film known to survive that was directed by an African American. Long thought to be lost, a print was discovered in Spain in the late 1980s. The Library of Congress released the title on video in conjunction with the Smithsonian Institute in 1994.

This film is the story of a mulatto woman, Sylvia Landry, and her struggle to finance a school for black students in central Mississippi. With the state willing to spend only $1.49 per year to educate each black student, the money runs out. As a result, Sylvia travels north to seek private funding from wealthy philanthropists. Having no luck in getting help, she ends up in the hospital where she meets a wealthy socialite named Elena Warwick, a kindhearted woman in her 70s who promises help. In deciding how best to help the cause of educating blacks, Warwick consults Geraldine Stratton, a bigoted friend of hers from the South. Ms. Stratton advises Warwick against giving money to the school, using the argument that blacks don't really want an education, and should be kept in their place. Warwick thinks over the matter, and decides to pledge ten times the amount she had originally promised. All is well with the school until Sylvia's cousin, Larry Prichard, asks her to marry him, and she refuses. He threatens to tell the school lies about her past, and she heads north again.

The flashback sequences for *Within Our Gates* are most compelling. In these sequences, a black man is falsely accused of murder, which results in his entire family being hunted down like animals in the swamps by a lynch mob. Efrem, the black servant responsible for the accusation, betrays his own race in order to curry favor with the whites. Eventually, he is beaten to death by the mob, which is reported in the newspapers as an "accidental" death. These sequences showing the lynching of an entire black family for a crime the father did not commit are just as powerful as some of the sequences in the more recent and highly acclaimed *Mississippi Burning* (1988).

History has demonstrated that this portrayal was not exaggerated or exploited at all. In 1923, four years after *Within Our Gates* was released, the notorious "Rosewood massacre" occurred in Central Florida. What happened in this case was that a woman in a nearby white settlement claimed to have been raped by a black man who lived in the black township of Rosewood. A mob of people attacked the entire settlement, murdering nearly all of the black residents of that community. The only survivors of the massacre were the few blacks who were able to escape to the home of a white man, which was the only building spared. *Within Our Gates* documents the black viewpoint of a shameful period in American and human history, and is an extremely vital part of American film history.

In addition to showing how bigoted whites hurt blacks, director Micheaux does not hesitate to show how some of the blacks caused misery to people of their own race. One example is the aforementioned character of Efrem, who carried tales to the whites about his fellow blacks to curry favor. Another example is in the character of "Old Ned," an elderly black preacher who convinces his congregation that, if they stay in their place, they will to go to heaven, and more blacks than whites will end up in eternal paradise. A later sequence shows that Ned has a conscience, and knows that what he is doing is wrong. It is simply his way of being more accepted by the white community even though he is preaching against his own convictions.

Oscar Micheaux (1884–1951), who directed, wrote, and produced *Within Our Gates*, was the most prolific of the early black motion picture producers. From 1919 to 1930, he produced and directed at least 25 silents, and nearly a dozen talkies from 1931 to 1948. Of his silents, only two are known to survive: *Within Our Gates* and *Body and Soul* (1924). Micheaux was born in 1884, less than 20 years after his parents had been freed from slavery by the Emancipation Proclamation.

Evelyn Preer, who plays the lead role, was hailed as "the foremost dramatic actress of the colored race." Born in 1896, she was 23 when she starred in *Within Our Gates*. She died in 1932 at age 36 from pneumonia. Little is known about any of the rest of the cast members from this milestone in film history, except that Mattie Edwards was a prolific character actress who lived to be 78 years old.

Although *Within Our Gates* was obviously produced on a low budget and left a couple of loose ends in the script (for example, what happened to Emil Landry when he rode away from his family's lynching on his horse?), it is, in general, a well produced film with significant dramatic and historic value.

282. A Woman in Grey

Rating: ☆☆☆½

Serico Producing Company; ***Directed by*** James Vincent; ***Screenplay by*** Walter Richard Hall; ***Edited and Titled by*** Joseph White Farnham; ***Photography by*** George Coudert; ***Running Time:*** 200 minutes; ***Cast:*** RUTH HOPE [THE WOMAN IN GREY], Arline Pretty (1885–1978); WILFRED AMORY, John Heenan; TOM THURSTON, Henry G. Sell (1889–??); PAULA WYNNE, Margaret Fielding (1895–1974); J. HAVILAND HUNTER, Fred Jones; MISS TRAILL, Ann Brody (1884–1944)

This is the best of the few silent serials that have survived in complete form. It is filled with mystery, suspense, and nonstop action, as well as thrilling stunts. This 15-chapter serial is among the last of the really complex adult serials before the genre was simplified to cater more to an adolescent crowd in the early 1920s. *A Woman in Grey* is a fine example of the famous cliffhanger serials at their best.

Arline Pretty plays the title role as a mysterious woman who shrouds her identity in secrecy. Leading man Henry Gsell (billed in this film as "Henry G. Sell") plays Tom Thurston, who has just purchased the old Amory homestead belonging to the father of his boss, Wilfred Amory. The house, said to be haunted, has a secret cache of treasure, which can be found only by obtaining the "Amory code," a secret message that tells where the treasure is hidden. When Thurston goes to the house, he finds "the woman in grey," who is also interested in the mystery surrounding the house. Little do they know that there is someone else lurking in the house who also wants to discover the secret of the missing treasure, and will go to any lengths to get it—even murder.

This serial is action packed without a single dull moment, as Arline Pretty endures falling out windows and off bridges, close calls with quicksand and a speeding locomotive, a narrow escape from a burning house, and other near fatalities.

Director James Vincent (1882–1957) began his career as an actor, playing opposite such actresses as Theda Bara (1885–1955). According to Eugene Vazzana's *Silent Film Necrology*, Vincent was elected president of the Motion Picture Director's Association, an office that was also held at one time by William Desmond Taylor (1872–1922).

Leading man Henry Gsell had become widely known in two Pearl White serials before he starred in this one. An attractive Arline Pretty lived up to her name, and made over two dozen films from 1915 to 1928. As far as can be determined, *A Woman in Grey* is her only surviving work other than *The Primrose Path* (1925) in which she has a minor supporting role. Character actress Ann Brody, who plays Ruth Hope's companion-guardian, had an active career in films as a motherly type. Her most famous other films were *Mrs. Wiggs of the Cabbage Patch* (1919) with Marguerite Clark and Josef Von Sternberg's lost film, *The Case of Lena Smith* (1929) with Esther Ralston.

This is the surviving classic of its genre, and is highly recommended. Fortunately, it is widely accessible on video.

1920

283. The Deerslayer

Rating: ☆☆

Produced in Germany; Mingo Pictures; ***Running Time:*** 62 minutes; ***Cast:*** AN INDIAN, Bela Lugosi (1882–1956)

This silent version of *The Deerslayer* is one for which information is scarce. In the print that is widely available, there are no opening credits, except for the title of the film. According to the 1953 book *A Pictorial History of the Silent Screen*, the film was produced by Mingo Pictures. Other sources indicate that it was produced in Germany.

This adaptation of the James Fenimore Cooper story is obviously filmed on a low budget, but the film itself is not quite as bad as one would expect. The worst thing about it is the amateurish title composition. An example of the contents of one of the most ludicrous titles is as follows:

> Deerslayer name for boy.
> You got big eye.
> Right name is Hawkeye.
> Hawkeye! Ugh. Now I die.

The one aspect that really gives this film an important place in motion picture history is the fact that it features one of the earliest film appearances of Bela Lugosi. This is the earliest Lugosi vehicle widely available for evaluation. The first few times that *The Deerslayer* was reviewed, it was difficult to spot Lugosi. Finally, Professor Robert D. Stock of the University of Nebraska pointed out that he appears as an Indian companion of the deerslayer about 22 minutes into the film. Once Lugosi was pointed out, it was hard to imagine how anybody could have missed his profile. The sequence takes place in a river raft, and Lugosi's one "spoken" title is "The water moves." One can catch a few more glimpses of Lugosi throughout the film following this sequence.

As mediocre as this adaptation of *The Deerslayer* is, Lugosi's brief appearance makes it worth watching as a curiosity piece.

284. Dr. Jekyll and Mr. Hyde

Rating: ☆☆☆½

Paramount Artcraft; ***Directed by*** John S. Robertson; ***Screenplay by*** Clara S. Beranger; ***Based on the Story by*** Robert Louis Stevenson; ***Photography by*** Roy F. Overbaugh; ***Running Time:*** 76 minutes; ***Cast:*** HENRY JEKYLL/EDWARD HYDE, John Barrymore (1882–1942); MILLICENT CAREW, Martha Mansfield (1899–1923); RICHARD LANYON, Charles Lane (1869–1945); GEORGE CAREW, Brandon Hurst (1866–1947); JOHN UTTERSON, J. Malcolm Dunn (1867–1946); EDWARD ENFIELD, Cecil Clovelly (1891–1965); GINA, Nita Naldi (1897–1961)

Robert Louis Stevenson's *The Strange Case of Dr. Jekyll and Mr. Hyde* was filmed at least nine times in the silent era alone. The first adaptation came out in 1908, and was produced by the Selig Polyscope Company. The earliest existing version is the 1912 Thanhouser version, reviewed elsewhere in this book. In 1920, three versions were filmed. Louis B. Mayer's Pioneer Company did a competing version starring Sheldon Lewis, which received mixed reviews. In addition, a comedy parody was filmed as well, which starred Hank Mann. It is this 1920 version with John Barrymore that is not only the most highly acclaimed silent version, but considered by many critics to be the best version ever filmed in any era of cinema history.

John Barrymore turns in a stellar performance in the lead role as the mild mannered Dr. Jekyll, whose scientific experiments bring out the loathsome beast in him known as Mr. Hyde. If the Academy Awards had been around in 1920, Barrymore would have received at least a nomination for Best Actor. It is a performance that he would come close to equaling only twice—in *The Sea Beast* (1925) and *Don Juan* (1926).

The leading lady is played by Martha Mansfield. Mansfield is appealing not only for her beauty, but for her very competent, underplayed performance. She was starting to gain significant stature as a motion picture actress when tragedy struck in 1923. While she was working in *The Warrens of Virginia* (released in 1924), somebody carelessly dropped a lighted match near her dress, which erupted into flames. After a week of pain and agony, she died from the severe burns that she suffered. As far as can be determined, *Dr. Jekyll and Mr. Hyde* is her only surviving work.

Appearing as Gina, a dancer that the evil Hyde has a fling with and terrorizes, is Nita Naldi, known for the vamp roles that she played. This was Brandon Hurst's first major film role. He went on to play character parts in several other important films, some of which are reviewed elsewhere in this book. Nita Naldi is discussed at length in the review of *Blood and Sand* (1922).

Kino Video has released a beautifully restored, color tinted copy of this classic on video, which is highly recommended.

285. Excuse My Dust

Rating: ☆☆½

Paramount Artcraft; ***Directed by*** Sam Wood; ***Based on*** *The Bear Trap* ***by*** Byron Morgan;

John Barrymore and the ill-fated Martha Mansfield in a scene from *Dr. Jekyll and Mr. Hyde* (1920).

Screenplay by Will M. Ritchey; ***Photography by*** Alfred Gilks; ***Art Direction by*** Wilfred Buckland; ***Running Time:*** 47 minutes; ***Cast:*** TOODLES WALDEN, Wallace Reid (1891–1923); DOROTHY WARD WALDEN, Anna Little (1890–1984); J.D., Theodore Roberts (1861–1928); TOM DARBY, Guy Oliver (1878–1932); MAX HENDERSON, Otto Brower (1895–1946); PRESIDENT MUTCHEN, Tully Marshall (1864–1943); RITZ, Walter Long (1879–1952)

By 1919, Paramount realized what a hot property they had on their hands with Wallace Reid, as any picture with his name in the cast was a guaranteed box-office success. The executives were determined to milk as much out of Reid's name as they could, and rushed him from one picture to another. During the filming of *Valley of the Giants* (1919), Reid was in a train accident and suffered a head injury. In order to keep Reid working and profitable, Paramount did not wait for his head injury to heal. Instead, they had doctors administer morphine so that Reid could keep working and churning out films. Paramount was concerned more with the quantity of Reid films they could produce than the quality of the productions.

Among Reid's popular vehicles in the 1918–1921 time period were his race car movies. In *Excuse My Dust*, a sequel to *The Roaring Road* (1919), Toodles Walden has married sweetheart Dorothy, whose love he won in the preceding film. The Darco race car company for which he works has him testing a new car engine they have developed, and a rival company called Fargot is trying to get their hands on the secret behind the new engine, willing to use whatever deceptive means they have to accomplish it.

In this film, one can see how the fast paced lifestyle and morphine addiction were starting to catch up to Reid. Dark circles were beginning to appear under his eyes, and his face was beginning to look gaunt to the point that at just the right angle, one could see the outline of Reid's cheek bone.

Excuse My Dust has significant historic importance as the second directorial project of Sam Wood (1883–1949), who had started out as an assistant director in 1915 before being promoted to director in late 1919. Under his capable direction, *Excuse My Dust* turned out to be a relatively good film—especially considering the fact that it was obviously a rush job. Wallace Reid and serial heroine Anna Little head up a good cast. Among the standout supporting cast members are Tully Marshall and Walter Long, playing the dishonest scoundrels with the competing Fargot race car company.

286. Get Out and Get Under *Rating:* ★★★½

Rolin/Pathé Exchange; ***Directed by*** Hal Roach; ***Photography by*** Walter Lundin; ***Titles by*** H.M. Walker; ***Running Time:*** 25 minutes; ***Cast:*** THE BOY, Harold Lloyd (1893–1971); THE GIRL, Mildred Davis (1901–1969); THE RIVAL, Fred McPherson; A CURIOUS CHILD, Ernie "Sunshine Sammy" Morrison (1912–1989)

This classic comedy opens with a dream sequence in which Mildred, the girl to whom Lloyd is about to propose, has married another man. Lloyd wakes up when Mildred, the director of an amateur play he is to star in, calls to tell him that he is running late. In his haste to get to the play on time to play the "masked prince," he encounters one problem after another, and everything that can go wrong, does.

This film is especially notable for the classic sequence in which Lloyd is trying to fix his broken-down Model T, only to have a curious black boy hindering his work in every way imaginable—even dropping ice cream on Lloyd's spectacles. This boy is played by none other than Ernie "Sunshine Sammy" Morrison, who was one of the first players signed for Hal Roach's "Our Gang" comedies.

Get Out and Get Under is among Harold Lloyd's best short comedies, as well as one of the most enduring of all silent comedy classics.

287. Haunted Spooks

Rating: ☆☆☆

Rolin/Pathé Exchange; ***Directed by*** Hal Roach and Alf Goulding; ***Photographed by*** Walter Lundin; ***Titles by*** H.M. Walker; ***Running Time:*** 20 minutes; ***Cast:*** THE BOY, Harold Lloyd (1893–1971); MILDRED HILLARY, Mildred Davis (1901–1969); THE UNCLE, Wallace Howe; A BLACK SERVANT'S CHILD, Ernie "Sunshine Sammy" Morrison (1912–1989)

In this film, Mildred Davis plays Mildred Hillary, the granddaughter of a wealthy southern colonel who has just died. Mildred gets the entire estate—provided that she and her husband live in the family mansion for one year. Failure to keep this condition of the will gives the entire estate to the girl's uncle.

The first problem is in finding Mildred a husband. Harold is at this time vying for the hand of another girl, losing her to another rival. He is heartbroken, and attempts suicide by drowning. The plan is foiled when he jumps off the bridge and finds that the water is only ankle deep. He then tries jumping in front of a car. The car so happens to be carrying Mildred's lawyer and a minister, who promptly recruit Harold as a man that Mildred can marry. The marriage is the easy part.

Staying in the mansion for a full year becomes difficult, partially because Mildred's scheming uncle and his girlfriend plot to scare the newlyweds off so that he can inherit the estate. In addition, numerous freak coincidences result in an even scarier atmosphere. Eventually, the scheming uncle and girlfriend are exposed, and foiled in their attempt to inherit the estate.

This is a hilarious "spook" comedy, and quite possibly the forerunner of such later "old house" horror comedies as *The Bat* (1926) and *The Cat and the Canary* (1927). Mildred Davis is delightful in the lead role, and an appealing leading lady. In addition, "Sunshine Sammy" Morrison is wonderful as the little boy who manages to get into everything.

288. High and Dizzy

Rating: ☆☆☆½

Rolin/Pathé Exchange; ***Directed by*** Hal Roach; ***Photographed by*** Walter Lundin; ***Story by*** Frank Terry; ***Titles by*** H.M. Walker; ***Running Time:*** 25 minutes; ***Cast:*** THE BOY, Harold Lloyd (1893–1971); HIS FRIEND, Roy Brooks; THE GIRL, Mildred Davis (1901–1969); HER FATHER, Wallace Howe

This Lloyd classic provides yet another of many stabs at prohibition. Lloyd plays a young medical doctor who gets drunk from drinking home-brewed beer. He checks into a local hotel to sober up. When he finally gets a room, he is shocked to see a pretty patient whom he admired in his office earlier in the day walking outside his window, which is several stories from the ground floor. Lloyd, in trying to steer the sleepwalking beauty inside, gets locked out in the process. He finally finds an open window after a few mishaps, which happens to be the girl's. When Harold is in her room, her father knocks at the door. The only way to save the situation is for the couple to get married before letting the girl's father in. A minister staying in the room below conducts the marriage ceremony from his window.

This "thrill comedy" is a classic, and provided audiences with a small taste of what was to come in *Safety Last* (1923) a few years later.

289. The Jungle Princess

Rating: ☆☆½

Warner Brothers; ***Directed by*** E.A. Martin; ***Story by*** Frederic Chapin; ***Running Time of Feature Version:*** 51 minutes; ***Cast:*** PRINCESS LOLA, Juanita Hansen (1895–1961); JACK, George Cheseboro (1888–1959); ***Supporting Cast:*** Frank Clark (1857–1945); Hector Dion (1881–??)

This is the only significant serial work of Juanita Hansen known to survive, as her roles in the 1914 "Oz" movies were smaller supporting roles, as was her work in *Martyrs of the Alamo* (1915). All of her other work is lost.

The Jungle Princess is a condensed feature version of a 31-reel serial that was originally released under the title of *The Lost City*. It was Hansen's first real hit, and she gained wide popularity in the early 1920s.

In *The Jungle Princess*, Hansen plays Princess Lola from the South African province of Wanda. She has been kidnapped and is held prisoner by villain Madros in the jungle, given the choice of either marrying him or being a slave. She endures a number of dangerous situations at the hands of Madros, including being trapped in a pit with lions and leopards. There is some good stunt work as leading man Jack rescues Lola from the pit in his airplane, with Hansen getting into the plane while it is still flying. There is plenty of action as Madros continues his relentless pursuit of Lola, recapturing her so that he can marry her and force her father, ruler of Wanda, to recognize him.

While this film is a bit on the campy side, with some especially ludicrous sounding titles and overexaggerated expressions on Hansen's part, it is an enjoyable film and a good opportunity to see Hansen in her glory days.

Hansen's career lasted until 1923, when she became addicted to drugs and alcohol, and was arrested for drug possession, which hit the front page of newspapers worldwide. Hansen managed to overcome her drug and alcohol problems. While she could have gone back into film work and been welcomed with open arms, Hansen instead chose to start the Juanita Hansen Foundation for drug dependency treatment.

290. Just Pals

Rating: ☆☆☆

Fox; ***Directed by*** Jack Ford; ***Story by*** E. McDermott; ***Scenario by*** Paul Schofield; ***Photography by*** George Schneiderman; ***Running Time:*** 49 minutes; ***Cast:*** BIM, Buck Jones (1889–1942); VILLAGE SLEUTHHOUND, Johnny Cookie; MARY BRUCE, Helen Ferguson (1901–1977); HARVEY CAHILL, William Buckley; A HOBO [THE BOY], George Stone; DR. WARREN STONE, Edwin B. Tilton (1859–1926)

Just Pals is one of the earliest directorial works of director John Ford (1895–1973) that is widely available for evaluation. (Ford's *Straight Shooting* [1917] is also available on video.) He started directing westerns in 1917 when he was only 22 years old. Born Sean O'Feeney, he followed brother Francis Ford (1882–1953) into the motion picture profession, and directed under the name of Jack Ford until 1923, when he took the name of John Ford.

This is also one of the earliest of the popular Buck Jones westerns. Jones entered the movie business in 1917 as a stunt man and extra, and started getting lead roles in 1919. He was among the most popular of western stars in the 1920s, and made a successful transition to serials in the talkie era. He maintained an active career until his tragic death in a Boston nightclub fire in 1942.

In *Just Pals*, he plays Bim, the town bum who really doesn't like to take responsibility, and does odd jobs when he needs money for food, sleeping in hay lofts or wherever he can. Despite his laziness, he is goodhearted and honest to a fault. He takes in a runaway boy, and finally realizes he needs to start taking some responsibility. He never went to school himself, but at the urging of the pretty schoolteacher, he sends the boy to school.

Complications arise when the school teacher's beau, Harvey Cahill, is about to be audited on his job as bank cashier, and asks her if he can borrow the school's memorial fund that she is in charge of to mask his shortage, promising to return it within 10 minutes if it is called for. When the trustees call for the fund, Cahill is nowhere to be found, and it is up to Bim to recover the money. Throughout a number of complications, he is falsely accused of a robbery, and is about to be lynched.

Just Pals is a light, entertaining effort that is highly enjoyable. It is not a great masterpiece, but just good, clean fun. It has a simple but interesting story line as well as good melodramatic highlights interspersed with occasional comedy relief. Buck Jones is a competent, appealing actor, and one can see why he was popular with western fans, although not as flashy in his stunt work as Tom Mix and Ken Maynard. Juvenile actor George Stone has been erroneously confused with George E. Stone (1903–1967), who made his debut in *7th Heaven* (1927). For the George Stone in *Just Pals* to have been the same person, he would have been 17, and couldn't have possibly been older than 8 or 9 when he appeared in this Jack Ford production.

291. The Last of the Mohicans

Rating: ☆☆☆☆

Associated Producers; ***Directed by*** Clarence Brown and Maurice Tourneur; ***Running Time:*** 72 minutes; ***Cast:*** Cora Munro, Barbara Bedford (1903–1981); Uncas, Albert Roscoe (1888–1933); Magua, Wallace Beery (1885–1949); Alice Munro, Lillian Hall (1896–1959); Major Heyward, Harry Lorraine (1866–??); Hawkeye, James Gordon (1871–1941); A Marauding Indian (bit part), Boris Karloff (1887–1969)

This 1920 adaptation of *The Last of the Mohicans* has stood the test of time as the most highly and consistently acclaimed screen version of any of James Fenimore Cooper's literary works.

For many years, this version was all but forgotten. It was in the early 1990s that the George Eastman House restored this film from the original nitrate negative. This complete, restored, and tinted version was very well received during a 1994 revival on American Movie Classics. Seeing this film in its restored format is a fascinating experience. At 72 minutes the film is short and to the point, and contains nonstop action. In some ways, this movie is actually better than Cooper's 1826 novel. Whereas Cooper's novel goes into long, boring descriptions, the movie depicts the action as it occurs. The titles are kept to a minimum, and say only enough to clarify what is happening as it happens. The cinematography is breathtaking, as everything is photographed from just the right angles to enhance the beauty of the location shots, and also features some shots of the people in silhouette.

Among the more impressive sequences in this film are two savage Indian attacks, and the sequence in which Cora Munro has a standoff with Magua at the edge of a cliff. The first finds the Munro sisters, Uncas, Hawkeye, and Great Serpent in a cave taking on Magua and his entire tribe of Indians. The second is when the Huron Indians, at the instigation of the French and under the influence of alcohol, attack the village within the British Fort William Henry. At one point in this sequence, an Indian finds a woman and her baby hiding in what is left of a covered wagon. The Indian takes the baby and throws it into the air, killing it. This was "borrowed" from a sequence in *The Heart of Humanity* (1918), in which Erich von Stroheim as a German Hun throws a baby out of a window. One of the final sequences departs a bit from the original Cooper story, and emulates the attempted rape sequence that Mae Marsh did in D.W. Griffith's *The Birth of a Nation* (1915). This is the scene featuring the standoff with Magua, which leads into the climax of the film.

Clarence Brown (1890-1987) and Maurice Tourneur (1873–1961) are credited as codirectors. Three sources have varying accounts of who did what, and why. One says that Tourneur dropped out of the directorial process early in the film due to illness; another says that it was an injury that caused him to drop out. Another source states that Tourneur did most of the directorial work, with Clarence Brown acting only as assistant director. Tourneur most likely did most of the preliminary work in planning the scenario, and dropped out partway through the production process. Upon Tourneur's departure, Clarence Brown finished the direction of the film in accordance to Tourneur's instructions.

In addition to this film's entertainment and high production values, it is a historically significant film in light of five of its cast members. The most famous of these five are Oscar winning actor Wallace Beery and, in a bit part, Boris Karloff. Barbara Bedford, Albert Roscoe and Lillian Hall turn in fine performances in the leading roles.

Barbara Bedford was a prolific actress who seemingly disappeared after her last cameo film roles in the 1940s. It was when her silent films such as *Cradle of Courage* (1920) and *Tumbleweeds* (1925) with William S. Hart; *Mockery* (1927) with Lon Chaney, Sr.; *Souls for Sale* (1923); and *The Last of the Mohicans* became widely available that historians began wondering what ever became of her. It was only recently discovered that Bedford's first marriage to Albert Roscoe ended in divorce in 1930. In 1940, she married Terry Spencer, an actor-director who was involved in production of "B" movies at the time. With his death in 1954, she moved to Jacksonville, Florida, where she worked in retail sales under the name of Violet Spencer. Of Bedford's available silent films, her performance as Cora in *The Last of the Mohicans* is by far the best. In this film, Bedford was able to display a wide range of emotions—from the happily contented, docile atmosphere at the beginning of the film, to the terrifying climax of the standoff with Magua. None of the other Bedford films available for evaluation allow her to demonstrate the full range and depth of her acting talents.

Albert Roscoe began his acting career at age 12 in 1900 on the stage, as *Little Lord Fauntleroy*. The height of his screen career was in the late 1910s, during which he was working for Fox Film Company. His most significant and historically important roles were as Theda Bara's leading man in films such as *Camille* (1917), *Cleopatra* (1917), and *Salome* (1918). Unfortunately, none of the Bara-Roscoe collaborations are known to survive. He died in 1933 at age 45, three years after Barbara Bedford divorced him.

Lillian Hall is often confused with a British silent film actress named Lillian Hall-Davis (1897–1933). She started in films in the late 1910s, with her first major role as a supporting player in Norma Talmadge's *Safety Curtain* (1918). She won wide critical acclaim as "Beth March" in a 1919 version of *Little Women*. Her role as Alice Munro in *The Last of the Mohicans* is acclaimed as her best work, and is also the one of her major films known to survive. She remained a popular actress until 1924, when she gave up her screen career to marry actor Glenn Tryon. After the Tryon's divorce, she never remarried, and was known as Lillian Tryon. She committed suicide in 1959.

Considering the historic importance of *The Last of the Mohicans* as the best example of the work of three significant silent era players, it is a film that every silent film aficionado should see. Many critics and historians qualify it as one of the great masterpieces of silent film.

292. The Love Flower

Rating: ☆☆☆

United Artists; ***Adapted and Directed by*** D.W. Griffith; ***From a Story by*** Ralph Stock; ***Photography by*** G.W. Bitzer; ***Running Time:*** 104 minutes; ***Cast:*** MARGARET BEVAN, Carol Dempster (1901–1991); JERRY TREVETHON, Richard Barthelmess (1895–1963); THOMAS BEVAN, George MacQuarrie; CRANE THE DETECTIVE, Anders Randolph (1870-1930); CLARA BEVAN, Florence Short (1893–1946); CLARA'S LOVER, Crawford Kent (1881–1953)

The Love Flower is one of the "forgotten Griffiths" that has not been highly acclaimed in the past. It was one of the potboilers that Griffith produced at low cost to finance his major epics. Some positive commentary was found in Joe Franklin's 1959 book, *Classics of the Silent Screen*. He states that "[Carol Dempster] was flawlessly photographed and looked stunningly beautiful throughout. She came to life for perhaps the first time."

This film is a melodrama in which the character of Thomas Bevan gets into an altercation with his wife's lover when he walks in on them. The lover is accidentally shot and killed in the process. The detective Crane, who knew Bevan from his only other prior offense of a bad check, is on the case. Bevan and his daughter escape to a remote island in the South Seas (which was actually filmed on Florida's East Coast). Here, father and daughter enjoy a measure of contentment, although always fearful of strangers.

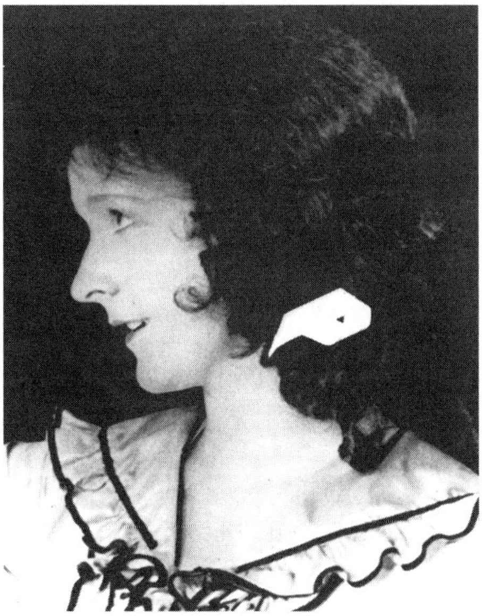

Carol Dempster, D.W. Griffith's protege and star of *The Love Flower* (1920).

About 34 minutes into the film, Richard Barthelmess' character enters. He is Jerry, a young adventurer who comes to the island and of whom Margaret Bevan is at first leery, but then grows to like. Their blossoming romance is dealt a blow when Detective Crane arrives on the island to extradite her father. Jerry, not knowing what Crane's purpose is, leads the detective to Bevan. Margaret thinks that Jerry was a spy who deliberately betrayed them, and now looks upon him as an enemy until he can prove otherwise.

This film does drag in spots, but generally sports a good and interesting melodramatic storyline. Some of the Florida location footage is gorgeous, owing partially to the superior camerawork of G.W. "Billy" Bitzer (1872–1944). Carol Dempster and Richard Barthelmess deliver wonderful performances. George MacQuarrie also turns in an excellent performance as the fugitive father. Unfortunately, no further information on MacQuarrie could be located. Florence Short was the sister of actress Gertrude Short. Anders Randolph, known primarily for his roles as a lecherous villain, plays a different type of villain in this story. In this film, he acts as an officer of the law carrying out the duties assigned to him, unaware of the circumstances under which Clara Bevan's lover was killed.

Part of the reason that this film has not been highly acclaimed in the past could be that the public expected too much from Griffith. He set such high standards with such masterworks as *The Birth of a Nation* (1915), *Intolerance* (1916), and *Broken Blossoms* (1919) that any film that fell short of these unusually high standards was considered inferior by comparison. But, it is worth noting that very few other directors in the entire history of motion pictures ever managed to produce anything comparable to the Griffith masterworks. *The Love Flower* demonstrates that even Griffith's "programmers" were well produced and entertaining films of good quality.

293. The Mark of Zorro

Rating: ☆☆☆½

United Artists; ***Directed by*** Fred Niblo; ***Screenplay by*** Elton Thomas (a.k.a. Douglas Fairbanks); ***Based on*** *The Curse of Capistrano* ***by*** Johnston McCulley; ***Photography by*** William McGann and Harry Thorpe; ***Art direction by*** Edward Langley; ***Running Time:*** 91 minutes; ***Cast:*** ZORRO/DON DIEGO VEGA, Douglas Fairbanks, Sr. (1883–1939); LOLITA, Marguerite de la Motte (1902–1950); SERGEANT GONZALEZ, Noah Beery, Sr. (1882–1946); DON CARLOS PULIDO, Charles H. Mailes (1870–1937); CAPTAIN JUAN RAMON, Robert McKim (1886–1927); GOVERNOR ALVARADO, George Periolat (1873–1940); FRAY FELIPE, Walt Whitman (1859–1928); DON ALEJANDRO, Sidney De Grey (1886–1941); ***Extras:*** Milton Berle (born 1908); Noah Beery, Jr. (1913–1994)

This was Douglas Fairbanks, Sr.'s, first big feature film, as well as one of his best. It was his first major release under the banner of United Artists, which he had cofounded in 1919 with future wife Mary Pickford, Charlie Chaplin, and D.W. Griffith.

Based on *The Curse of Capistrano*, this original Zorro adaptation is a fast-paced action movie without a single dull moment. It seems that Fairbanks is always up to something in one of the two roles he plays. As Don Diego Vega, he is always trying to make up new card or handkerchief tricks, or trying to make himself look as uninteresting, klutzy, and frail as possible to mask his second identity as Zorro.

As Zorro, Fairbanks accomplishes some marvelous stunts in his efforts to bring the tyrannical governor and his corrupt henchmen to justice. He swings from trees into building windows, jumps from roof to roof, and even jumps over tables and other large objects. It took quite an acrobat to pull off the stunts he did, and few people since have been able to pull off comparable stunt work.

Marguerite de la Motte plays the female lead in this film, and this is the role that she is probably best remembered for. In real life, she was married to actor John Bowers (1884–1936). Bowers committed suicide by drowning himself in the ocean. It is alleged in some sources that John Bowers' drowning was the inspiration for the story, *A Star Is Born* (1937, 1954, and 1980). But, because *What Price Hollywood?* (1932), produced four years before Bowers' suicide, has the same type of story, brings this assertion into doubt.

Many readaptations of Zorro have been made, some of them quite good. Included among the later adaptations have been action serials, comedy parodies, and, of course, the famous 1940 talkie remake starring Tyrone Power, Jr. (1913–1958). As good as some of the remakes have been, none manages to recapture the zest and pace of this original silent adaptation, which remains the definitive screen adaptation of the story.

294. The Married Virgin

Rating: ☆☆½

Produced/Directed by Joseph Maxwell; ***Screenplay by*** Hayden Talbot; ***Running Time:*** 60 minutes; ***Cast:*** COUNT ROBERTO, Rudolph Valentino (1895–1926)

This was the first major role that Rudolph Valentino played, in early 1918. It was independently produced and directed by Joseph Maxwell (1871–1930), who paid Valentino $50 per week for his work. Since Maxwell hadn't paid his cameramen, they sued, and release of the film was held up until 1920. Before *The Married Virgin*, Valentino had bit parts in *Patria* (1916) and *Alimony* (1918), which his friend Norman Kerry (1889–1956) helped him to secure.

In this film, Valentino plays a suave, debonair Italian count who plots with his girlfriend to get money out of the wealthy McMillan family. First, he finds an incriminating gun that belongs to Mr. McMillan, the father, and tries to blackmail him into giving him $100,000. This doesn't work, so he schemes to marry McMillan's daughter as a way to get his hands on the money.

Although this is a good melodrama and provides Valentino with a good part, he was hesitant to accept the role, for fear that he would be typecast as a villain and gigolo. This did happen, but one can see why movie producers offered him such excellent villain roles as in this film and *Eyes of Youth* (1919). Other than *A Society Sensation* (1918) and *All Night* (1918), Valentino was stuck in villain roles until his big break in *The Four Horsemen of the Apocalypse* (1921).

Director Joseph Maxwell is an obscure figure on whom no further information could be found. He died in 1930 at age 59 from an intestinal ailment.

295. Number, Please

Rating: ☆☆☆

Rolin/Pathé Exchange; ***Directed by*** Hal Roach and Fred Newmeyer; ***Photographed by*** Walter Lundin; ***Titles by*** H.M. Walker; ***Running Time:*** 21 minutes; ***Cast:*** THE BOY, Harold Lloyd (1893–1971); THE GIRL, Mildred Davis (1901–1969); THE RIVAL, Roy Brooks; A COP, Charles Stevenson (1887–1943); LITTLE BOY, Ernie "Sunshine Sammy" Morrison (1912–1989)

This film finds Harold Lloyd in an amusement park. He sees a pretty woman with her friend and dog. The dog gets away, and Lloyd sees recovering the dog as a way to get to know the girl better. He goes through great lengths to capture the dog, but his rival picks the dog up and hands him to Mildred, making it look as if it was he who went through the effort to rescue him. Nonetheless, Harold finds a way to introduce himself. Mildred has two passes to ride in the hot air balloon, and tells Harold and the rival that the first one to get her mother's consent to go on the ride can ride with her. The race is on, and Lloyd, being at a disadvantage when the rival has an automobile to go to Mildred's mother's, decides to phone the mother instead. First, all of the public phone booths have lines of people waiting to get in. Once he finally finds a vacant phone, he forgets the phone number, then has to hunt for it, and then has problems getting the necessary nickel for the call, and finally has trouble with the operators providing the correct connection. His call is just too late, as the rival has already received the necessary permission. So, Harold races to beat the rival back to Mildred, having a number of complications that delay him.

The story line on *Number, Please* is not as strong as on other Lloyd shorts of the period, but it is filled with a number of hilarious sight gags, and is quite enjoyable.

296. Nurse Marjorie *Rating:* ☆☆☆

Paramount Realart; ***Directed by*** William Desmond Taylor; ***Photoplay by*** Julia Crawford Ivers; ***Photographed by*** James C. Van Trees; ***Art Direction by*** Una Mason Hopkins; ***Running Time:*** 88 minutes; ***Cast:*** NURSE MARJORIE/LADY MARJORIE KILLONAN, Mary Miles Minter (1902–1984); DUKE OF DONEGAL, Arthur Hoyt (1874–1953); DUCHESS OF DONEGAL, Vera Lewis (1873–1956); LORD DOUGLAS FITZTREVOR, Frank Leigh (1876–1948); JOHN DANBURY, Clyde Fillmore (1875–1946); DICK ALLEN, Frankie Lee (1912–1977?); ANDREW DANBURY, George Periolat (1873–1946); ANDREW DANBURY'S WIFE, Mollie MacConnell (1865–1920)

When Mary Miles Minter went to Paramount Realart, her first four films were under the direction of William Desmond Taylor (1872–1922). The first of these four was *Anne of Green Gables* (1919), which is widely acclaimed as the greatest success of Minter's career. Their next three collaborations were *Judy of Rogue's Harbor* (1920), *Nurse Marjorie* (1920), and *Jenny Be Good* (1920). *Nurse Marjorie* is the only one of the four collaborations known to survive. Judging by synopses and write-ups of the other Taylor-Minter collaborations, *Nurse Marjorie* is probably the worst of their four films. The story is weaker than the other three, and a big disappointment is that there are no shots of Minter with her hair down, which is how she looks prettiest. (Even with her hair up, Minter certainly wasn't unattractive.) In reading early interviews with Minter, it sounds like this was the type of project that she wanted to do. She had expressed a desire to get away from the "little girl" roles and go into more mature roles. So, one can assume that she asked Taylor and Paramount to use her in this type of film.

In *Nurse Marjorie*, Minter plays Lady Marjorie Killonan, whose family is made up of Irish and British aristocracy. She "snubs the snobs" by going to work as a nurse, known as Nurse Marjorie rather than by her royal title.

While working as a nurse, she receives politician John Danbury as a patient. He expresses interest in her, but she does not want him to be attracted to her on the basis of her heritage of nobility and aristocracy. So, she leads him to believe that she comes from an impoverished family of fish market owners—to test and see if Danbury's love will transcend through the image of poverty that she puts forward. Some of what she puts Danbury through in the test is hilarious.

In this production, Minter was working with her friend, William Desmond Taylor, a highly competent director with whom she got along well. Her performance is nat-

Original lobby card from *Nurse Marjorie* (1920), the only surviving collaboration of director William Desmond Taylor and actress Mary Miles Minter. This photo features Minter with child actor Frankie Lee.

ural and skillfully underplayed. By this point in her career, she had blossomed into a much more polished actress than what is indicated in her earlier surviving films for American. As far as Mary Miles Minter's performance is concerned, *Nurse Marjorie* is the best of the three examples of her work evaluated, even if the film itself is not quite as charming as *The Ghost of Rosy Taylor* (1918).

Now that *Nurse Marjorie* is widely available for evaluation on video, the arguments denigrating Minter's acting ability will be laid to rest. When one sees the film, it is obvious that Minter had talent to match her good looks. Had it not been for the William Desmond Taylor murder scandal, Minter would have likely been mentioned in the same breath as Lillian Gish, Mary Pickford, Gloria Swanson, Norma Talmadge, and the other first ladies of the silent screen.

This is the only film of those directed by William Desmond Taylor that has become widely available to the general public. He was one of the up and coming directors, serving as president of the Motion Picture Director's Guild, when he was murdered on February 1, 1922. His murder was never solved, although different theories have been put forth over the years. Among his most famous films were the 1915 serial *The Diamond from the Sky*, *Anne of Green Gables* (1919), *Tom Sawyer* (1917), and *Huckleberry Finn* (1920). The latter two films do exist, but are held in archives and are inaccessible to the public.

The male lead in this film is Clyde Fillmore. Mary Miles Minter's sister, Margaret Shelby (1900-1939), was married briefly to a grandson of former U.S. president Millard Fillmore, but Clyde Fillmore, who was also known as Clyde Fogle, was in no way related to the former U.S. president. Vera Lewis was the wife of silent screen actor Ralph Lewis. Child actor Frankie Lee was the older brother of Davey Lee, also a juvenile actor of the silent era. Frankie made dozens of films in the late 1910s to mid–1920s, but only two are known to survive. The other surviving Frankie Lee film is *Daddy Long Legs* (1919) with Mary Pickford.

Other than the three Mary Miles Minter films reviewed in this book, three other surviving titles could not be evaluated. Historians who have seen *A Cumberland Romance* (1920) have had mixed opinions. Edward Wagenknecht writes that it is a beautiful film from what he remembers of having seen it in 1920. The stills are certainly appealing. Scott Eyman, author of the 1990 biography of Mary Pickford, went into a tirade about how Minter came off as white trash, but that if the film had been a Pickford film, she wouldn't have come off the same way. This reviewer finds Wagenknecht's appraisal to be the more credible of the two. Mary Pickford was a delightful actress in her own right, but so was Minter. Minter simply did not have the good fortune to get as many good roles as Pickford, and her two most highly acclaimed films—*Anne of Green Gables* (1919) and *The Trail of the Lonesome Pine* (1923)—are lost. Since Pickford owned most of her films, most of her work survives, including her best films. Mary Pickford's own opinion of Minter was obviously one of respect, as it was she who recommended Minter to Adolph Zukor as her successor when she left Paramount.

297. One Week

Rating: ☆☆☆☆

Buster Keaton Productions/Metro; ***Directed by*** Buster Keaton and Eddie Cline; ***Running Time:*** 18 minutes; ***Cast:*** THE GROOM, Buster Keaton (1895–1966); THE BRIDE, Sybil Seeley (1900–1984); A NEIGHBOUR, Joe Roberts (1870–1923)

One Week has historic significance as the first film that Buster Keaton independently produced on his own. It is among the best of the Keaton shorts. It is also the first film in which Keaton was injured, having suffered a fall that caused both arms and his lower back to swell to twice their normal size, which took several weeks of recovery.

In this film, Keaton plays a newlywed who has received a "do it yourself" house kit, which is supposed to be able to be assembled within seven days. A number of obstacles cause endless problems with the assembly of the house, including sabotage by a neighbour, who changes the numbers on the various parts of the house. Once Keaton finally gets the house done, a storm wreaks the housewarming party, blowing the house around and around. Finally, the couple gives up and abandons the house.

One sequence in this film resulted in *One Week* almost being banned in areas. In a bathtub sequence, leading lady Sybil Seeley is shown bathing, and just as she moves to get out of the bathtub, a hand is shown covering the camera lens.

The sequence in which Keaton injured himself appears at the beginning of the film, when he falls from the second story of the house after sawing the board off that he is sitting on. The hole where he was supposed to land had straw and foam, covered with grass, which was intended to cushion Keaton's fall. Instead, he fell right through the protective materials, and landed at the bottom of the hole with full force.

Unfortunately, no further information could be found on Sybil Seeley. She played the leading lady in four of Keaton's shorts of the early 1920s, but seems to have faded into obscurity afterward.

One Week is widely acclaimed as one of the best starring debuts of any lead actor.

298. The Penalty

Rating: ☆☆☆½

Goldwyn Pictures; ***Directed by*** Wallace Worsley; ***Screenplay by*** Charles Kenyon; ***Based on the Novel by*** Gouverneur Morris; ***Photography by*** Don Short; ***Film Editor:*** Frank E. Hull; ***Running Time:*** 77 minutes; ***Cast:*** BLIZZARD, Lon Chaney, Sr. (1883–1930); DR. FERRIS, Charles Clary (1873–1931); ROSE, Ethel Grey Terry (1891–1931); DR. WILMOT ALLEN, Kenneth Harlan (1895–1967); BARBARA FERRIS, Claire Adams (1898–1978); LICHTENSTEIN OF THE SECRET SERVICE, Milton Ross; FRISCO PETE, James Mason (1889–1959); BARBARA NELL, Doris Pawn

The Penalty was the film which established Lon Chaney as a star of endurance. Chaney's great success with *The Miracle Man* (1919), a year earlier, was to establish him as a major player. *The Penalty* demonstrated that Chaney was more than a one-hit wonder.

In *The Penalty*, Chaney plays a mob boss who controls the San Francisco underground. He has two main items on his agenda: to carry out his plan to loot San Francisco and take over entirely, and to get revenge on the doctor who erroneously amputated his legs when he was a boy.

To play this role as a double amputee, Chaney used a leather harness to strap his lower legs tightly behind his thighs. He performs some incredible stunts—from falling off a platform and landing on his knees, to walking up and down stairs, with the aid of crutches.

In addition to Chaney's phenomenal acting and interesting story line and plots, *The Penalty* features good production values under the direction of Wallace Worsley, as well as a good supporting cast to boot. The role of Barbara Ferris, the attractive daughter of Dr. Ferris, is played by Claire Adams, who is perhaps best remembered as a leading lady in such westerns as *Just Tony* (1922) opposite Tom Mix.

Film historian Michael Blake, recognized as the foremost Chaney expert in the world, states that, "*The Penalty* remains one of Chaney's most impressive character performances."

299. Pollyanna

Rating: ☆☆☆½

United Artists; ***Directed by*** Paul Powell; ***Running Time:*** 61 minutes; ***Cast:*** POLLYANNA, Mary Pickford (1892–1979); JIMMY BEAN, Howard Ralston (1904–1992); REVEREND JOHN WHITTIER, J. Wharton James; AUNT POLLY, Katharine Griffith (1876–1921); NANCY THING, Helen Jerome Eddy (1897–1990); OLD TOM, George Berrell (1849–1933); JOHN PENDLETON, William Courtleigh (1867–1930); DR. CHILTON, Herbert Prior (1867–1954)

Released in January, 1920, *Pollyanna* was the first Mary Pickford film to be released through United Artists. Of all of her films, this ranks among the most memorable, along with *The Poor Little Rich Girl* (1917) and *Rebecca of Sunnybrook Farm* (1917).

Based on the popular 1913 story by Eleanor Porter, this is the classic story of Pollyanna, an orphaned girl adopted by her cold, mean-spirited Aunt Polly, who is also

Mary Pickford as *Pollyanna* (1920).

wealthy. Polly feels it her "duty" as an aunt to adopt Pollyanna. When she arrives, she is shown to her room: the attic which is sparsely furnished with a bed only. Polly is crying because she knows she is not wanted by her aunt, and the maid starts crying, too. A title card flashes onto the screen with Mary Pickford saying, "What are you crying for? She's not YOUR aunt."

A while later, Pollyanna runs into Jimmy Bean, who has escaped from the nearby orphanage. She suggests that the come home to see if her Aunt Polly will adopt him, too. Of course, she refuses. On the sly, Pollyanna lets Jimmy stay in the basement. Eventually, the aunt finds him and wants him to leave, until Pollyanna asks, "How would you like to be an orphaned boy and get thrown out in the rain?" It is at this point that Aunt Polly's heart seems to soften, as she tells Pollyanna to get a quilt so that a bed can be made for him.

Throughout the course of the movie, Pollyanna plays the "glad game," in which she always finds a silver lining to every possible situation, no matter how bleak. In commenting on her Aunt Polly, she says, "Well, I'm glad she isn't twins." With the glad game, Pollyanna spreads joy and cheer to everyone with whom she comes into contact. She even uses her charm to convince Mr. Pendleton to adopt her friend, Jimmy, and give him a permanent home. Then, disaster strikes when she sees a car speeding toward a little girl. In saving the girl's life, Pollyanna is struck. Many of the people whom she cheered up try to cheer her up. Even her Aunt Polly realizes how important Pollyanna has become to her.

The performances of Mary Pickford and Howard Ralston are what really gives this film its charm. This movie probably contributed most to Mary Pickford's reputation as "America's Sweetheart."

Howard Ralston was the younger brother of silent screen actress Esther Ralston (1902–1994). In an interview with historian John Cavallo in the late 1980s, he stated that he was 13 at the time he was in *Pollyanna*, and that Mary Pickford was 26. He also relates how Charlotte Smith (Mary's mother) was constantly on the set. When asked how he liked playing in *Pollyanna,* he stated that he preferred being on the production end of films, and worked in this capacity for a number of stage productions. He stated that his sister Esther was the only real artist in the family. His performance in *Pollyanna* demonstrates that he certainly underestimated his own acting ability, and that he could have been a successful actor if he had chosen to pursue such as a career.

In 1960, the Walt Disney Company produced a successful remake of *Pollyanna* with Haley Mills in the title role. As wonderful as this remake was, the definitive image of *Pollyanna* for many will always be Mary Pickford in her frilly dress, with her blonde curls coming down on each side of her illuminating smile.

300. The Scarecrow

Rating: ☆☆☆½

Buster Keaton Productions/Metro; ***Directed by*** Buster Keaton and Eddie Cline; ***Running Time:*** 18 minutes; ***Cast:*** THE BOY, Buster Keaton (1895–1966); THE GIRL, Sybil Seeley (1900–1984); THE BOY'S ROOMMATE, Joe Roberts (1870–1923); THE GIRL'S FATHER, Joseph Keaton (1867–1946)

This is another of Buster Keaton's first independent productions, again using Sybil Seeley as his leading lady.

The Scarecrow starts with the sun rising at the modest one-room home of Buster and his roommate. They are so poor that they can't afford to put money in the gas meter, and Buster gets around this by putting a piece of string on the coin so that he can pull the coin out when the gas comes on. (Chaplin later did a variation of this in *The Kid* [1921].) When Buster and Joe sit down to dinner, another dig at prohibition is made when the father states that his stomach is as empty as a saloon. What makes this dinner sequence a classic is a string contraption that is over the dining table with salt, pepper, and other amenities that Buster and Joe might need, and which can be accessed by pulling a string instead of having to have someone pass it.

Sybil Seeley plays a rich farmer's daughter on whom Buster and Joe have set their sights. When the rival suitors arrive, a dog is turned loose on them, and there follows an excellent chase sequence as Keaton flees from the mad dog. He finally makes friends with the dog and they shake paws. (This gag was used later in *The Three Ages* (1923), in which Keaton befriends a lion and shakes hands with him.) He then hides from the girl's father by posing as a scarecrow, which is where this film's title comes in.

While this film is not among Keaton's masterpieces, it is most definitely among the classics.

301. Sex

Rating: ☆☆½

J. Parker Read, Jr./Thomas Ince Productions; ***Directed by*** Fred Niblo; ***Screenplay by*** C. Gardner Sullivan; ***Photography by*** Charles Stumar; ***Edited by*** Ralph Dixon; ***Art Direction by*** W.L.

Heywood; ***Running Time:*** 80 minutes; ***Cast:*** ADRIENNE RENAULT, Louise Glaum (1900–1970); PHILLIP OVERMAN, William Conklin (1872–1935); MRS. PHILLIP OVERMAN, Myrtle Stedman (1888–1959); DICK WALLACE, Irving Cummings (1888–1959); DAISY HENDERSON, Peggy Pearce (1894–1975)

The title for this film alone guaranteed that it would be one of the box-office sensations of 1920. To boot, the film's star, Louise Glaum, had become a popular vamp. Glaum's popularity in 1920 nearly rivaled that which Theda Bara had in the late 1910s.

Critical reception to *Sex* was mixed. Some reviewers called it immoral, while others lauded its message in showing that Glaum's vampish behavior came back to haunt her, as when she was ready to settle down, another vamp took her fiancé away from her—just as she had done to others.

While only a few censorship boards insisted on cutting some sequences, many areas would not allow the film's release under its original title. Among the alternate titles were *The Spider Woman* and *Sex Crushed to Earth.*

The film opens with some good atmospheric shots showing Louise Glaum as Adriennne Renault being lowered to the stage in an elaborate giant spiderweb as part of her ritzy cabaret act. Another member of the cast is young and naive Daisy Henderson, whom Adrienne corrupts over time, which eventually leads to her own "creation" doing to her what she taught her.

Irving Cummings plays opposite Louise Glaum as the man whom she finally falls for and is ready to settle down. He starred in only a few more films after this one before switching to a directorial career. His most famous silent directorial project was *The Johnstown Flood* (1926), an early, highly acclaimed Janet Gaynor vehicle which is held in archives and is inaccessible to the public. In the talkie era, Cummings directed some of Shirley Temple's best-loved films, including *Curly Top* (1935), *The Poor Little Rich Girl* (1936), and *Little Miss Broadway* (1938).

302. Something New

Rating: ☆☆½

A Nell Shipman Production; ***Directed by*** Nell Shipman; ***Scenario by*** Nell Shipman; ***Photographed by*** Joseph B. Walker; ***Running Time:*** 50 minutes; ***Cast:*** THE WRITING WOMAN, Nell Shipman (1892–1970); BILL, Burt Van Tuyle (died 1951); SID BICKLEY, L.M. Wells (1862–1923); GORGEZ, William McCormack

Something New has historic significance as being among the few silents directed and produced by a woman. Nell Shipman coproduced, codirected, and costarred with Burt Van Tuyle in this drama-comedy which featured the 1920 Maxwell as one of the heroes of the film. *Something New* was the second film that Shipman independently produced, after completing her leading role in *Back to God's Country* (1919) and her directorial debut with *A Bear, a Boy, and a Dog* (1920). *Something New* was a feature shot when Shipman was "between films" and waiting to start work on *The Grub Stake* (1922). It started out as a 10–minute commercial advertisement for Maxwell automobiles, which expanded into a 5-reel feature.

The movie starts with Nell Shipman playing an authoress who is out of new ideas and looking for "something new." Her inspiration comes when she sees two men betting on a race to see if a car can outperform a horse and buggy. The story progresses to Mexico, where Shipman is arriving from San Diego to spend time with her uncle. Burt

Van Tuyle plays Bill, a friend of the uncle's who owns a new Maxwell that the uncle dismisses as an "ornamental contraption." The man and his niece proceed by horse and buggy to a ranch, where they continue the journey to the uncle's Blue Lotus mine on horseback. The film then cuts to "Hell's kitchen," the hangout of Gorgez, who leads a band of outlaws. They are staking out the Blue Lotus as their next hit.

The bandits reach the mine, tie up the uncle, and kidnap Nell. The rest of the movie consists of one big chase sequence, which starts when Bill receives word of the attack sent in a message via Laddie, the dog star of the movie. He sees the Maxwell as the only hope of reaching the mine in time to help.

Throughout the course of the filming, the Maxwell is shown going over rocks that are its size and greater; through fields, cactuses, and rough desert terrain. In actuality, three transmissions were ripped out of the car during the course of the filming, and had to be replaced.

Something New is an interesting and enjoyable piece of film heritage. It shows how strong a personality Nell Shipman was to be able to endure working under such horrible conditions on location in the Mojave Desert, where the majority of the movie was filmed.

303. Suds

Rating: ☆☆☆

United Artists; ***Directed by*** Jack Dillon; ***Screenplay by*** Waldemar Young; ***Based on the Stage Play 'Op o' Me Thum by*** Frederick Fenn and Richard Bryce; ***Photography by*** Charles Rosher; ***Cast:*** AMANDA AFFLICK, Mary Pickford (1892–1979); HORACE GREENSMITH, Albert Austin (1885–1953); BENJAMIN PILLSBURY JONES, Harold Goodwin (1902–1987); MADAME JEANNE GALLIFILET DIDIER, Rose Dione (1875–1936); THE ARCHDUKE, Darwin Karr (1875–1945)

This was Mary Pickford's second film for United Artists, and was a rather unglamorous role that was not as well received as many of her other features. Despite its less than expected box-office totals, *Suds* remains a film that holds up well, and is probably better appreciated today than when it was originally released.

In this film, Pickford plays a London laundress named Amanda for whom everything seems to go wrong. She is the brunt of her coworker's jokes, who call her "Sudsie." She maintains that when wealthy customer Horace Greensmith asks her out over them, she'll have the last laugh. And, eventually, she does.

A subplot centers around the pony named Lavender that is used for laundry deliveries. Because the pony is old, it does not make it up a steep hill, and the owners of the laundromat determine to sell it to a glue factory, and Amanda saves her friend from its fate by buying it from the factory. She keeps the pony in her apartment, and disaster occurs when Lavender wrecks the place, and Amanda is kicked out by the landlord. Fortunately, both she and the horse are taken in by a rich philanthropist, and Amanda discovers her dream man Horace to be one of her new coworkers.

One of the most amusing parts of this film is a fantasy sequence in which Amanda dreams that she is the wealthy princess, whose suitor is Horace, a commoner—reversing the situation. There are some beautiful shots of Pickford in these sequences.

In Pickford's autobiography, she relays how the studio searched for weeks to find an emaciated looking pony for the role of Lavender. When they found Lavender, he was kept at Douglas Fairbanks' stables, where he was well fed, becoming so healthy that he had to be made up to look more like what he was supposed to look like for the role. Pickford herself applied the makeup to the pony.

Suds was the first film that Mary starred in after becoming Mrs. Douglas Fairbanks, Sr.

304. Terror Island

Rating: ☆☆☆

Paramount Realart; ***Directed by*** James Cruze; ***Based on a Story by*** Arthur B. Reeve and John W. Grey; ***Screen Adaptation by*** Walter Woods; ***Photography by*** William Marshall; ***Art Director:*** Wilfred Buckland; ***Running Time of Surviving Footage:*** 64 minutes; ***Approximate Running Time of Original Release:*** 88 minutes; ***Cast:*** HARRY HARPER, Harry Houdini (1874–1926); TOM STARKEY, Jack Brammall; JOB MORDAUNT, Wilton Taylor (1869–1925); GUY MORDAUNT, Eugene Pallette (1889–1954); CAPTAIN MARSH, Edward Brady; BEVERLY WEST, Lila Lee (1905–1973); STELLA MORDAUNT, Rosemary Theby (1885–??)

This was the third of Harry Houdini's six films, and one of only two known to survive. *Terror Island* is not known to survive in complete form. The print evaluated is missing reels 3 and 4 of its original 7 reels. Fortunately, the missing 2 reels do not detract much from the story, and the surviving footage is coherent and easy to follow.

In *Terror Island*, Houdini plays a scientist who has invented a submarine that can reach depths previously unattainable by humans. His first mission is to search for lost treasure off the African coast, with the intention of donating the proceeds to benefit poor children. Job Mordaunt is determined to have the treasure for himself, and will do anything to get it. Mordaunt's niece, Beverly West, is a friend of Harry's, and helps to thwart her uncle's scheme.

In one scene, one can see Houdini escaping from a contraption that has him hanging by the neck. Another impressive scene has him escaping from a locked safe that is submerged under water.

Of the two surviving Houdini films, this is the one to see. It is far superior to *The Man from Beyond* (1922), with a good storyline and the real chance to see Houdini perform the type of stunts you would expect from a man with his reputation.

It is interesting to see Eugene Pallette in a film from this period. At this point, he had just started to noticeably put on weight, but was not yet up to the 300-plus pounds that he would later attain by the mid–1920s. This is also one of the few extant silent films with actress Rosemary Theby. Theby was married to director-actor Harry C. Myers (1882–1938). Her career started at Vitagraph in 1910, and lasted into the mid–1930s. When her husband died in 1938, she was listed as his only survivor, but what happened to her after that point has remained a mystery that film historian Billy Doyle has been attempting for years to solve.

305. Twisted Souls

Rating: N/A

Based on a Story by Charles Fulton Oursler; ***Directed by*** George Kelson; ***Running Time of Extant Footage:*** 2 minutes, 47 seconds; ***Cast:*** THE MURDERER, Howard Thurston (1869–1936); A HINDU PHILOSOPHER, Tarah Ben Mahamet; ***Supporting Cast:*** Eric Mayne (1865–1947); Evelyn Sherman (1882–1974); Miriam Nesmith

Twisted Souls was a film that was apparently never released to the public. Only a fragment of the film survives today.

Howard Thurston, a highly renowned magician, played a man who murdered his best friend, a Hindu philosopher, who tried to keep him from doing a bad deed.

The surviving footage is from a point after the murder, during which Thurston is shown agonizing before his friends over what he has done. The murder victim reappears as a ghost that haunts his murderer.

One of the supporting cast members in this film is Eric Mayne, who was a highly acclaimed Shakespearean actor. No further information could be found on any of the other cast members.

Judging from what survives, it appears that *Twisted Souls* would have been an interesting and intriguing film if it had been released. Just at the end of the surviving film fragment is a macabre window setting shaped like a skull.

306. Way Down East

Rating: ☆☆☆☆

D.W. Griffith, Inc./United Artists; ***Directed by*** D.W. Griffith; ***From the Stage Play by*** Lottie Blair Parker; ***Scenario by*** Anthony Paul Kelly; ***Running Time of 1930 Re-issue Evaluated:*** 110 minutes; ***Cast:*** ANNA MOORE, Lillian Gish (1893–1993); DAVID BARTLETT, Richard Barthelmess (1895–1963); LENNOX SANDERSON, Lowell Sherman (1888–1934); SQUIRE BARTLETT, Burr McIntosh (1862–1942); MOTHER BARTLETT, Kate Bruce (1858–1946); KATE [THE YOUNG NIECE], Mary Hay (1901–1957)/Clarine Seymour (1898–1920); MARIA POOLE, Emily Fitzroy (1860–1954); HI HOLLER, Edgar Nelson; SETH HOLCOMB, Porter Strong (1879–1923); MARTHA PERKINS, Vivia Ogden (died 1952); ECCENTRIC AUNT, Florence Short (1893–1946); MRS. TREMONT, Josephine Bernard; DIANA TREMONT, Mrs. Morgan Belmont (1894–1945); SECOND TREMONT SISTER, Patricia Fruen; A DANCING GIRL AT THE BARN DANCE (BIT PART), Norma Shearer (1900–1983)

Lillian Gish braving the blizzard in *Way Down East* (1920).

Way Down East was adapted from an old stage play, and when D.W. Griffith paid $175,000 for the screen rights to it, Hollywood was shocked. With the Griffith touch, he added the famous and spectacular ice floe sequence to the film, making it one of his most successful films—both with the critics and at the box office. He turned an antiquated play into a blockbuster.

The story is one that starts out

slowly, introducing and establishing the characters. The film gradually moves faster and faster, building up to an explosive climax. The great Lillian Gish plays Anna Moore, who is tricked into a mock marriage by Lennox Sanderson, who has his way with her and forgets her. Anna gives birth to his child, who dies soon after birth. She is thrown out of the boarding house by her puritanical landlady, and is left to face the cruel world alone. Finally, she finds work as a maid at the estate of Squire Bartlett, one of the richest farmers in the area—who also is puritanical in his beliefs. The estate happens to be across the street from the country home of none other than Lennox Sanderson, who makes threats to expose Anna's past if she does not leave. At the urging of David Bartlett, the son of the squire who is in love with her, Anna stays and becomes a beloved member of the family. Then comes the day when Martha Perkins, the town gossip, finds out about Anna's past. In the closing sequences of the film comes the big confrontation, which results in Anna being thrown out into the snowstorm, leading to the sequence finding Lillian Gish as Anna trapped on a block of ice that edges closer and closer to a waterfall. This ice floe sequence is one of the most famous sequences in the entire history of motion pictures. When Lillian Gish's passing was recognized at the 1994 Academy Awards ceremony, it was this scene that was chosen for screening.

This snowstorm sequence was the real thing. Griffith actually had his crew wait for a real blizzard to hit before filming the blizzard scenes. In one shot, one can actually see real icicles forming on Lillian Gish's eyelashes. Lillian Gish stated that the hand that she allowed to drag in the icy cold water while on the ice floe still bothered her at times many decades afterward.

D.W. Griffith was injured in the course of filming the ice floe sequence. The dynamite blast used to break up the solid river ice went off sooner than expected, catching Griffith before he had the chance to attain a safe distance. While Griffith was treated at the hospital for his injuries, Elmer Clifton directed the rest of the ice floe sequence. It has also been stated that Clarine Seymour, who had originally been slated to play Kate, the young niece, died from pneumonia during filming. Another source states that Seymour died from an intestinal infection that was unrelated to the extremely cold conditions in which she was working. Mary Hay replaced Seymour when she died, but since the winter sequences could not be redone, one can still see some footage of Seymour taken at a distance during some of the table scenes. If one looks closely, one can catch a glimpse of Norma Shearer in a single close-up as a girl dancing at the barn dance on Christmas Eve. Lowell Sherman, who plays villain Lennox Sanderson, was almost ruined about a year after this film was produced. He had attended the infamous Arbuckle party at the St. Francis Hotel in San Francisco, at which Virginia Rappe died. Sherman's name was dragged through the newspapers with the headlines of the Arbuckle scandal, which initially tarnished his reputation with the public. Fortunately, his career managed to survive the bad press.

The only things that mar this film at all are some of the hokey comedy relief sequences. Griffith had wrestled with the idea of including these sequences, and decided that since audience members who had seen the play would expect to see these sequences in the movie version, he should include them. Griffith's first instinct was right, as the comedy sequences are the only flaws in what is otherwise a great film.

Way Down East was remade in 1935, with Henry Fonda playing the leading male role. Margaret Hamilton played gossip Martha Perkins. This remake was not highly acclaimed at all, and is but a footnote in film history. Upon evaluating the remake, this reviewer determined that although it certainly didn't equal Griffith's original version, it really wasn't as bad as some critics have said it was. It gets a solid three-star rating in comparison to the four stars that the silent version gets.

307. Why Change Your Wife? *Rating:* ☆☆☆

Paramount; ***Directed by*** Cecil B. DeMille; ***Story by*** William C. de Mille; ***Scenario by*** Olga Printzlau, Sada Cowan; ***Photography by*** Alvin Wyckoff; ***Art Director:*** Wilfred Buckland; ***Running Time:*** 77 minutes; ***Cast:*** ROBERT GORDON, Thomas Meighan (1879–1936); BETH GORDON, Gloria Swanson (1897–1983); SALLY CLARK, Bebe Daniels (1901–1971); RADINOFF, Theodore Kosloff (1882–1956)

This is among the best and most popular of the marriage comedies that DeMille and Swanson collaborated on, with Thomas Meighan again as leading man.

In *Why Change Your Wife?*, Swanson plays Beth Gordon, the typical nagging wife who tells her husband his faults and shortcomings, and is always getting onto him over his wine cellar, being a supporter of prohibition. Husband Robert starts dating another woman, Sally Clark, whom he meets at a ladies' clothing store while buying a dress for his wife.

Robert divorces Beth, and she thinks that if being modest and conservative was what turned her husband off, she'll show the world how wild she can be. Meanwhile, when Robert is married to Sally, he finds out that she, too, can be a bit of a nagger. In the end, everybody pairs up with their original spouses again.

Not only is this film a good opportunity to see Swanson, but it is also among the best performances of Bebe Daniels' career.

1921

308. The Affairs of Anatol *Rating:* ☆☆

Paramount; ***Directed by*** Cecil B. DeMille; ***Based on the Play by*** Arthur Sonair; ***Photography by*** Alvin Wyckoff, Karl Struss; ***Art Direction by*** Paul Iribe; ***Running Time:*** 94 minutes; ***Cast:*** ANATOL DE WITT SPENCER, Wallace Reid (1891–1923); VIVIAN, Gloria Swanson (1897–1983); EMILIE DIXON, Wanda Hawley (1895–1963); GORDON BRONSON, Theodore Roberts (1861–1928); MAX RUNYON, Elliott Dexter (1870–1941); JONER ELIOT, Monte Blue (1890–1963); ANNIE, Agnes Ayres (1896–1940)

This is yet another of the fidelity comedies that Gloria Swanson starred in under Cecil B. DeMille. It is a much coveted title for collectors, as it features the ill-fated Wallace Reid opposite Swanson. The two play newlyweds for whom all is going well until Anatol runs into an old girlfriend from middle school. Wanda Hawley plays Emilie Dixon, a girl who depends for her living on sugar daddy Gordon Bronson, a wealthy business executive. Anatol determines that Emilie needs help, and lets her move in with them until she can get back on her feet. This is where the trouble starts.

While *The Affairs of Anatol* features an appealing cast, it is not among the better DeMille-Swanson romantic comedies, being overlong and drawn out. One aspect that is appealing about this film is the rich tinting and toning in color prints. The film is tinted green, with some red tinted sequences. On some of the green tinted art titles, the roses are hand colored red.

309. The Blot

Rating: ☆☆☆½

Lois Weber Productions/F.B. Warren Corp.; ***Written and Directed by*** Lois Weber; ***Advisory Director:*** Phillips Smalley; ***Prepared for the Screen by*** Marion Orth; ***Photographed by*** Phillip DuBois and Gordon Jennings; ***Lighting by*** H.H. Harrod; ***Running Time:*** 90 minutes; ***Cast:*** PROFESSOR GRIGGS, Philip Hubbard; HIS WIFE [AMELIA], Margaret McWade (1872–1956); HIS DAUGHTER, Claire Windsor (1897–1972); HIS PUPIL [PETER OLSEN], Louis Calhern (1895–1956); THE OTHER GIRL, Marie Walcamp (1894–1936)

This is a beautifully portrayed and sensitively directed film from Lois Weber (1879–1939), one of the most prominent female motion picture producers in the history of cinema.

In this film, Louis Calhern plays a college student from a wealthy family who falls in love with the daughter of one of his college professors. It is through this relationship that his eyes are opened to "the blot"—the ridiculously low salaries paid to college professors, which provided only a bare existence.

Claire Windsor gives a fabulous portrayal as the daughter of the impoverished professor. The anguished look in her eyes well conveys her embarrassment at the old, worn out shoes she wears, as well as over the poverty that is apparent in her household. Windsor is so compelling that one cannot help but to share her anguish. Marie Walcamp, who plays the "other girl," was in the mid–1910s one of Pearl White's closest rivals in serials, which is what she was primarily known for before teaming with Lois Weber and Phillips Smalley. None of her serial work for Universal is known to survive. One other feature directed by Weber and starring Walcamp, *Where Are My Children* (1916), does survive in the Library of Congress archives, and is reportedly slated for video release at a future date. Walcamp's demise was a tragic one, as she committed suicide by inhaling gas fumes in 1936, when she was 42 years old.

The Blot was at one point believed to be lost. A nice print turned up, though, and was restored by Anthony Slide and Robert Gitt in 1973. Kevin Brownlow did a production featuring an orchestral score by Carl Davis in the early 1990s. Of the Lois Weber productions evaluated, *The Blot* is by far the best, and is highly recommended.

310. Camille

Rating: ☆☆½

Metro; ***Directed by*** Alla Nazimova and Ray C. Smallwood; ***Art Direction by*** Natacha Rambova; ***Photography by*** Rudolph Verquist and Paul Ivano; ***Running Time:*** 64 minutes; ***Cast:*** MARGUERITE GAUTIER, Alla Nazimova (1878–1945); ARMAND DUVAL, Rudolph Valentino (1895–1926); NICHETTE, Patsy Ruth Miller (1904–1995); GASTON RIEUX, Rex Cherryman (1898–1928); PRUDENCE, Zeffie Tilbury (1863–1950)

This was Alla Nazimova's modern day rendition of Alexandre Dumas' classic, *Camille*, which Rudolph Valentino starred in between work on *The Four Horsemen of the Apocalypse* (1921) and *The Conquering Power* (1921) for Rex Ingram. This was the last film that Nazimova starred in for Metro, as differences over artistic issues resulted in her contract not being renewed when it expired.

It was during the filming of *Camille* that Valentino had his troubles with first wife Jean Acker (1893–1978), and that he met Natacha Rambova (1897–1966), whom he later married. This was also the film debut of Patsy Ruth Miller, who was 16 at the time she played a lead supporting role in this film.

When this modernization of *Camille* was released, the reviews were mixed. Some critics praised Nazimova and the highly stylized sets of Natacha Rambova. Others panned the adaptation as gaudy and ludicrous. In evaluating the film today, one has to give art director Rambova her due credit for her vision as an artist. The deco sets are beautiful, and the ultra modern design was far ahead of its time. Although Rambova may have influenced her future husband Valentino to make some bad business decisions, her talent as an artist cannot be denied.

While Ray C. Smallwood (1887–1964) is generally credited as the director of this film, cameraman Paul Ivano (1900–1984) stated in interviews that Alla Nazimova did most of the directorial work herself, with Smallwood simply being an assistant.

In this adaptation, Nazimova plays the lead role as Marguerite Gautier, a highly attractive call girl who is living it up, knowing that her time is limited. Rudolph Valentino plays Armand Duval, the young law student who becomes smitten with the "lady of the camellias." He asks Marguerite to marry him, but when his father finds out, he objects to his son's marriage to a woman with such a notorious reputation. While she is sincere, Marguerite, at the urging of Armand's father, turns him off, making him think that she was a gold digger interested only in money. It is not until she is on her deathbed from tuberculosis that Armand finds out the truth.

A subplot has Rex Cherryman playing Armand's best friend, Gaston, who falls in love with Nichette, who worked with Marguerite's dress shop. While Patsy Ruth Miller's part is a small one, she makes a nice impression in her debut. Actor Cherryman (born in the United States and reportedly engaged at one point to Barbara Stanwyck) is an obscure figure on whom no other screen credits could be found outside of this film. He died in 1928 from septic poisoning in France, in his late twenties or early thirties.

While this adaptation of *Camille* is not by any means a dramatic masterpiece, Alla Nazimova and Rudolph Valentino give good performances. The talents of Valentino and Nazimova, coupled with Natacha Rambova's skillful artistry in set and costume design, make this film an artistic accomplishment worthy of respect.

311. The Conquering Power *Rating:* ☆☆☆☆

Metro; ***Directed by*** Rex Ingram; ***Based on*** *Eugenie Grandet* ***by*** Honoré de Balzac; ***Screenplay by*** June Mathis; ***Photography by*** John F. Seitz; ***Running Time:*** 89 minutes; ***Cast:*** CHARLES GRANDET, Rudolph Valentino (1895–1926); EUGENIE GRANDET, Alice Terry (1899–1987); VICTOR GRANDET, Eric Mayne (1865–1947); PERE GRANDET, Ralph Lewis (1872–1937); PERE GRANDET'S WIFE, Edna Demaury; NOTARY CRUCHOT, Edward Connelly (1855–1928); HIS SON, George Adkinson; THE ABBE, Willard Lee Hall (1863–1936); MONSIEUR DES GRASSINS, Mark Fenton (1866–1925); HIS WIFE, Bridgetta Clark; ADOLPH, Ward Wing (1893–1945); NANON, Mary Hearn; CORMOILLER, Eugene Pouyet (1883–1950); ANNETTE, Andrée Tourneur

This was Rex Ingram's follow-up to the highly successful *Four Horsemen of the Apocalypse*. As in its predecessor, the lead roles are played by Alice Terry and Rudolph

Rudolph Valentino in *The Conquering Power* (1921).

Valentino. This would be the last film that Valentino would make at Metro; despite the phenomenal success of *Four Horsemen*, Louis B. Mayer refused to give Valentino the raise that Valentino felt he deserved.

In *The Conquering Power*, Valentino plays a man whose father, financially ruined, commits suicide. He is sent to his rich uncle Pere's to live. The uncle is a greedy miser who cares nothing about anyone but himself and making more and more money.

Charles Grandet falls in love with cousin Eugenie, who also loves him. Previously unknown assets of Charles' father are found, but Pere Grandet fails to inform his nephew of that fact, and keeps everything for himself. Charles, believing he is penniless, makes his own fortune in the West Indies. Pere is eventually killed by ghosts of people he has wronged, who, in the powerful climactic sequence, crush him with a vault of his own gold. The conquering power of love eventually brings Eugenie and Charles back together again.

Ralph Lewis is excellent as the greedy, domineering, deceitful miser, and played a similar role three years later in *Dante's Inferno* (1924). The haunted vault sequence is especially good, with Lewis playing the part of the man whose karma has come to roost most effectively. The hands of the ghosts are especially macabre. Director Ingram must have believed in ghosts or was fascinated by them, as several of his films feature them.

Valentino's good looks are exploited in a variety of settings. The island setting has him sporting facial stubble. The final sequences show him sporting a distinguished beard and mustache.

Alice Terry gives one of her best performances in *The Conquering Power* as well. The scene in which she is terrified of her father, who flies into a tirade after he finds out she has given the gold coins he gave her to Charles, is especially good, and brings Terry's talent to its fullest potential.

The Conquering Power is another example of a great film that almost didn't survive. The one surviving print is scratched in parts, but is in otherwise good shape. It has been shown a few times with a new piano score on Turner Classic Movies.

312. Dream Street

Rating: ☆☆☆

United Artists; ***Produced and Directed by*** D.W. Griffith; ***Screen Adaptation by*** Roy Sinclair; ***Based on*** *Gina of Chinatown* and *The Sign of the Lamp* ***by*** Thomas Burke; ***Running Time:*** 134 minutes; ***Cast:*** GYPSY FAIR, Carol Dempster (1901–1991); JAMES "SPIKE" MCFADDEN, Ralph Graves (1900–1977); BILLIE MCFADDEN, Charles Emmett Mack (1900–1927); SWAY WAN, Edward Peil (1883–1958); GYPSY'S FATHER, W.[illiam] J. Ferguson (1845–1930); SAMUEL JONES, Porter Strong (1879–1923); TOM CHUDDER, George Neville (1865–1932); POLICE INSPECTOR, Charles Slattery; MINISTER OF GOOD WORDS, Tyrone Power, Sr. (1869–1931); EVIL INFLUENCE, Morgan Wallace (1881–1953)

When *Dream Street* was in production, D.W. Griffith (1875–1948) had initially done some synchronized sound experimentation by filming a sound prologue in which he introduced the film. This sound prologue still exists, but was not used in the final version. Griffith came to the conclusion that sound would be suicidal to his career. He reasoned that it would cost him the foreign, non–English speaking audiences. When the silents were produced, there were sets of titles made for the specific language of the countries to which the prints were going.

For this film, Griffith turned again to the works of Thomas Burke, author of *The*

Chink and the Child, on which his critical and financial success *Broken Blossoms* was based. This story also takes place in the Limehouse district of London. Carol Dempster portrays Gypsy Fair, a beautiful and talented dancer, to whom two brothers are attracted. Billie McFadden, the less attractive of the two brothers, has the better personality, and is a talented writer. His attraction to Gypsy is a genuine, wholesome love. Spike McFadden is the better looking of the two brothers, with a good singing voice. Unfortunately, he has an abysmal personality. His attraction to Gypsy is physical only. Sway Wan is a scoundrel who owns an illegal smuggling and gambling establishment in the Chinese district. He makes advances towards Gypsy, who turns him in to a police inspector. This results in a raid, and incurs the wrath of Wan, who vows vengeance against Gypsy and anyone with whom she is associated.

Later in the story, Spike McFadden reforms, and the good in him overcomes his evil impulses, making a likable man out of the character previously loathed by Gypsy. Billie McFadden sees them together, revealing how the jealousy causes the evil impulses in him to overtake the good side. He commits a murder, and the reformed Spike takes the blame for him.

Not only does this film feature an excellent storyline, but excellent performances by the three main cast members. As far as can be determined from available reference material, this was the film debut of Charles Emmett Mack. Judging from the other films of his evaluated—*America* (1924), *The Unknown Soldier* (1926), *The Devil's Circus* (1927), *Old San Francisco* (1927), and *The First Auto* (1927)—this first performance was his best. Ralph Graves gives a remarkable performance, especially in the sequences during which the good side of him struggles against his evil impulses. He also is marvelous in the courtroom sequence. But, the star of the show is most definitely Carol Dempster as the innocent heroine caught in the middle of the jealousy, revenge, and betrayal of those surrounding her. The more this reviewer saw of Carol Dempster in this film, the more my admiration and respect for her as an actress grew. Her performance in *Dream Street* is better than some of the Oscar-winning performances in film history.

The villain of the story is Edward Peil, whom fans will remember from his role as "Evil Eye" in *Broken Blossoms*. Peil went on to play villain roles in many westerns. Among the supporting cast members who especially stand out is Morgan Wallace. As the unmasked evil influence, his gruesome appearance reminds one of Lon Chaney's "Quasimodo" character in *The Hunchback of Notre Dame* (1923) filmed two years later. It would be interesting to find out if Chaney saw this film, and modeled his makeup partially after Wallace's. This is a powerful saga of the neverending struggle of good versus evil. Griffith's only major blunder was in trying to inject double meanings by following the progress of the dim and or illuminating stars in the sky.

313. The Four Horsemen of the Apocalypse *Rating:* ☆☆☆☆

Metro; ***Directed by*** Rex Ingram; ***Based on the Novel by*** Vicente Blasco Ibañez; ***Adaptation by*** June Mathis; ***Running Time:*** 132 minutes; ***Cast:*** JULIO DESNOYERS, Rudolph Valentino (1895–1926); MARGUERITE LAURIER, Alice Terry (1899–1987); JULIO'S FATHER, Joseph Swickard (1866–1940); ***Supporting Cast:*** Jean Hersholt (1886–1956); Alan Hale (1892–1950); Wallace Beery (1885–1949); Nigel de Brulier (1877–1948); Noble Johnson (1881–1978); Bowditch Turner (1878–1933); Pomeroy Cannon (1870–1928); Mabel van Buren (1878–1947)

Rudolph Valentino as Julio in *The Four Horsemen of the Apocalypse* (1921).

This was Rudolph Valentino's first really big box-office hit. Screenwriter June Mathis (1889–1927), then one of the most powerful female executives in Hollywood, remembered having been impressed upon seeing Valentino in *Eyes of Youth* (1919), and insisted, over the reservations of Louis B. Mayer, that he play the male lead in this film. *The Four Horsemen* was a risky proposition at the time, because the public had tired of war films when World War I was over, and it was not certain that America was ready for another such film yet. The original negotiations between Louis B. Mayer (1885–1957) and author Blasco Ibañez for the screen rights to his novel called for him to receive a percentage of the film's box-office earnings. However, once Mayer realized what a box-office hit he had on his hands, he bought Ibañez out for a flat sum, saving Metro a lot of money in royalty payments that would have otherwise been due to Ibanez.

The Four Horsemen is historically important for the famous tango sequence that Valentino did for the film, which started a worldwide tango fad. In this film, Valentino plays Julio, a spoiled artist who is supported by exceedingly wealthy parents. Alice Terry plays Marguerite, the married woman with whom Julio falls in love and has an affair. Nigel de Brulier has an important part as the man who prophecies from the Book of Revelations in the Bible that worldwide suffering will occur with the coming of the four horsemen of the apocalypse, representing conquest, war, pestilence, and death. This prophecy comes to light with the arrival of World War I, which shatters the luxurious lifestyles of Julio and Marguerite. Marguerite goes into service as a nurse, taking care of her now-blind husband. Julio, not wanting initially to face the horrors of war, realizes that he must do his part, and enlists as a French soldier.

Under the masterful direction of Rex Ingram, *The Four Horsemen of the Apocalypse* was an artistic masterpiece, as well as one of the top five grossing films of the silent era. It was remade in 1962 under the direction of Vincente Minnelli (1903–1986). The remake can't even come close to equaling the artistic mastery of the original.

Kevin Brownlow's Photoplay Productions did a beautiful restoration on this film, restoring the color tints and adding a full orchestral score by Carl Davis. There are some striking two-tone sequences in the film, and one impressive sequence has the French national anthem playing while the tints alternate between blue, white, and red—the three colors of the French flag.

Leading lady Alice Terry married Rex Ingram in 1922, and starred in many of his subsequent films.

As a war film, this is first rate. The only minor flaw is that the editing could have been tighter, as the film is a little bit overlong. Despite this flaw, the film was Rex Ingram's first big success as well as Valentino's, and established him as one of the world's premier directors. Erich von Stroheim hailed Ingram as the greatest of all directors.

This first war film of the 1920s still remains the best. Not even *The Big Parade* (1924) or *Wings* (1927) quite manages to surpass it in terms of artistic value and quality.

314. The Goat

Rating: ☆☆☆½

Metro; ***Written/Directed by*** Buster Keaton and Malcolm St. Clair; ***Running Time:*** 23 minutes; ***Cast:*** THE "FUGITIVE," Buster Keaton (1895–1966); POLICE CHIEF'S DAUGHTER, Virginia Fox (1902–1982); POLICE CHIEF, Joe Roberts (1870–1923); DEADSHOT DAN, Malcolm St. Clair (1897–1952)

This comedy classic finds Buster Keaton in a case of mistaken identity. He has managed to get himself in front of the camera just as a photo is being taken of "Dead Shot Dan," a fugitive wanted for murder. The chase is on as Keaton runs from the law. There are some great sequences in the chase as Keaton finally finds refuge in the home of the leading lady of the film, who is revealed to be the daughter of the police chief who is relentlessly pursuing him.

This is one of two Keaton films that Mal St. Clair codirected after leaving the Mack

Sennett Company, where he started out in 1915 as a gag writer, and by 1919 was directing.

The leading lady, Virginia Fox, later became known as Virginia Fox Zanuck, the wife of producer Darryl F. Zanuck. She had started in pictures as one of Sennett's bathing beauties. Joe Roberts, who plays the burly, imposing police chief, died at age 53, only two years after this film was made.

For many years, *The Goat* was rarely seen. Fortunately, it was brought out of obscurity by being included with *The Three Ages* (1923) in Kino's "Art of Buster Keaton" video series.

315. Hail the Woman

Rating: ☆☆☆☆

Thomas H. Ince/Associated Producers; ***Directed by*** John Griffith Wray; ***Screenplay by*** C. Gardner Sullivan; ***Photographed by*** Henry Sharp; ***Running Time:*** 78 minutes; ***Cast:*** JUDITH BERESFORD, Florence Vidor (1895–1977); DAVID BERESFORD, Lloyd Hughes (1897–1958); OLIVER BERESFORD, Theodore Roberts (1861–1928); MRS. BERESFORD, Gertrude Clarke; NAN HIGGINS, Madge Bellamy (1899–1990); ODD JOBS MAN [NAN'S STEP-FATHER], Tully Marshall (1864–1943); WYNDAM GRAY, Edward Martindel (1873–1955); RICHARD STUART, Charles Meredith (1894–1964); MRS. STUART, Mathilde Brundage (1859–1939); THE BABY, Eugenia Hoffman; DAVID JR., Muriel Frances Dana

This story takes place in Massachusetts, in a town called Flint Hill near Plymouth Rock. It compares Flint Hill of 1921 to the puritan Plymouth Rock of 300 years earlier. The family portrayed is the Beresfords, whose father is a hard-line conservative preacher who believes that a woman's place is in the home to take what a man says as gospel. The elder Beresford demands that his son follow in his footsteps. It turns out that his son has secretly married a poor girl named Nan Higgins. When Higgins' stepfather finds out that Nan is carrying David Beresford's child, he goes to his father, demanding that David marry her (which nobody else knows has already happened). The elder Beresford refuses, reasoning that it would affect his son's future career in the ministry. So, he pays Higgins' stepfather $1,000 to send Nan away and keep quiet, so as not to disgrace the family name and interfere with the career decision he has made for his son. David fails to speak up and say that he is married to Nan, and the alcoholic stepfather takes her home to beat her. She shows her stepfather the marriage certificate, but he scoffs at it as a forgery and burns it. Nan runs away with no place to go, and ends up living alone in poverty to raise her and David's child the best way she can.

Judith Beresford, the sister of David, is ordered by her father to marry a man of his choosing, one for whom she does not care. When she befriends a progressive-minded man, the chosen fiancé sees her talking, and holding the man's cigarette for him. The fiancé tells the father that she is a loose woman who was smoking in another man's house. The father automatically accepts this as truth. Florence Vidor is great when she gets in his face and asks him if he will forgive her as he forgave her brother. Then she suggests that possibly the other man could pay him off as he did Nan's father. This infuriates the father, and he disowns her.

When Judith is forced to leave home, she does charity work in a nearby city. In the course of her work, she comes across Nan, who is dying. She adopts Nan's and David's baby boy and cares for him. Matters come to a head when she falls in love with the son

Florence Vidor, who gave an electrifying performance in *Hail the Woman* (1921).

of a woman who is chairperson of the missionary board to which her brother is applying for a foreign missionary post. It is thrilling to see the close-minded, chauvinistic, and judgmental Oliver Beresford put in his proper place.

Like *Way Down East*, *Hail the Woman* gets across the point that men and women should share the burden equally when they conceive children. *Hail the Woman* goes further than *Way Down East*, and challenges other chauvinistic and hypocritical attitudes as well. It is more "in your face" with its messages. Although *Hail the Woman* does not have the ice floe spectacle that *Way Down East* did, and was filmed on a lower budget, it is in many ways a better melodrama. It does not contain anything like the comic relief attempts that marred *Way Down East*. In addition, the story grips the audience from the start, never letting up at any point of its duration. *Way Down East* is slow moving well past the first third of the film, and does not really start getting interesting and exciting until almost halfway through.

Based on the work of director John Griffith Wray (1896–1929) that is available for evaluation, this was his very best film, as well as one of his first. (With the excellent manner in which he handled social issues in this film, it makes one long for a print of *Human Wreckage* (1923), which he directed for Dorothy Davenport Reid, and which starred Bessie Love, to turn up.) Although Wray's 1923 *Anna Christie* was more highly acclaimed than *Hail the Woman*, it is this reviewer's opinion that *Hail the Woman* is the superior of the two. Wray was only 25 years old when he directed it. He died in 1929 at the age of 33. He is often confused with character actor John Wray (1888–1940), who made his film debut in *New York Nights* (1929) the year that director Wray died.

In addition to Wray's excellent direction, this film sports fabulous performances by its cast members. Madge Bellamy turns in her greatest performance of all of her evaluated films. She demonstrates great depth and emotional range in this film, which was one of the few to provide her with a role worthy of her talent. She was also one of the most beautiful actresses ever to grace the silver screen. In an interview with film historian William M. Drew, she stated, "I rarely had a good dramatic part. Just about the only one I had was in *Hail the Woman*, one of my first pictures." This film was also host to the best performance of Florence Vidor's career. She was truly terrific as the daughter rebelling against and challenging her arrogant and hypocritical father. This evaluation is based on her available films, but one longs to see what she did in the Academy Award nominated *The Patriot* (1928), one of the most sought of the lost films.

For years, *Hail the Woman* was believed lost. Eileen Bowser of the Museum of Modern Art located a worn print in a foreign archive in the 1970s. This film was accessed from a one-time PBS showing as part of the "Lost and Found" series that aired many years ago. It is one of this reviewer's "top ten" of the silent era.

316. The Kid

Rating: ☆☆☆☆

Charles Chaplin/First National; ***Written and Directed by*** Charles Chaplin; ***Assistant Director:*** Charles Riesner; ***Photography by*** Rollie H. Totheroh; ***Running Time of Edited Version:*** 52 minutes; ***Cast:*** THE MAN, Carl Miller (1893–1979); THE WOMAN, Edna Purviance (1894–1958); THE CHILD, Jackie Coogan (1914–1984); A TRAMP, Charles Chaplin (1889–1977); THE POLICEMAN, Tom Wilson (1880–1965); THE BULLY, Charles Riesner (1887–1962); A CROOK, Albert Austin (1885–1953); A WOMAN, Nellie Bly Baker (1894–1985?); LODGING HOUSE PROPRIETOR, Henry Bergman (1868–1946); A FLIRTING ANGEL, Lita Grey (1908–1995); AN ANGEL (BIT PART), Esther Ralston (1902–1994); THE DEVIL (DREAM SEQUENCE), Jack Coogan (1880–1935); PICKPOCKET IN FLOPHOUSE, Jack Coogan ***Extras:*** Raymond Lee (1910–1974); Phyllis Allen (1861–1938)

In *Silent Films on Video*, this film is acclaimed as Chaplin's comedy masterpiece over all of his other silent comedies. This review will explain why and how this conclusion was arrived at.

There is no way that anybody can deny that Charlie Chaplin was a genius of phenomenal proportions. The man composed his own music; wrote, produced, and directed his own films; and developed and performed his own unique style of pantomime and slapstick comedy. He is probably the most imitated motion picture performer of all time. Even the great Harold Lloyd started out primarily as a Chaplin imitator in the character of "Lonesome Luke" before developing his own unique characterization. All of the Chaplin features contained a unique blend of comedy, drama, and social commentary. There are two words to explain what gives *The Kid* the edge over Chaplin's other silent films: Jackie Coogan.

The movie opens with Edna Purviance portraying a woman being discharged—alone—from the local Charity Hospital with a baby in her arms, scorned by the hospital officials for her "sin" of being a single mother. Having no means to support the baby, she leaves him in a fancy luxury car, hoping that he will be taken in by a wealthy family. Unknown to the woman, the car is stolen by bandits, with the baby inside. The baby ends up abandoned in a poor neighborhood, and is found by none other than the tramp, portrayed by Chaplin. The tramp takes the baby in and raises him as his own in the best way he can with his limited resources.

The story cuts to five years later, when Jackie Coogan is introduced into the story as "the kid." Here, we see the various escapades of the tramp and adopted son, as they work together mending broken glass. Coogan as the kid breaks windows, and Chaplin as the tramp conveniently comes along with tools and materials to repair them. They always manage to stay a step ahead of the police officer who is on to their scam.

By this time, the child's mother has attained a position of vast wealth as an opera singer. Unbeknown to the star, she does charity work in the very same neighborhood in

Charlie Chaplin and Jackie Coogan in *The Kid* (1921).

which her son, whom she obviously longs for, is currently living. All proceeds as usual with the tramp and the boy until the boy becomes ill, and the doctor brings him to the attention of the local orphan asylum, insisting that a poor tramp with no money is unfit to provide for a child. The sequence of the forced removal of the boy from the home is one of the most compelling and tear-jerking sequences on film. It is this sequence that provides the usual Chaplin social commentary—a damning indictment of the "proper care" provided by the orphan asylums of the time. The tramp and the boy escape and are on the run for most of the rest of the film, which shows them in a variety of humorous situations.

Jackie Coogan's compelling, heartwarming, and heartbreaking performance, as well as his mischievous nature, catapulted him to instant stardom in his own right. He was the first male child star to achieve such a degree of stardom.

In praising Coogan and Chaplin, it would be a travesty to overlook the fine dramatic performance given by Edna Purviance as the child's mother. Purviance was Chaplin's leading lady in virtually all of his films from 1915 through 1923. She is discussed at length in the review herein of *A Woman of Paris* (1923). The flirting angel in the dream sequence was played by Lita Grey, who would end up marrying Chaplin in 1924, and divorcing him three years later. Charles Riesner's last name is spelled Reisner in the titles of this film, as well as in many sources. Chaplin scholars have determined that the proper spelling is with the "i" before the "e," which is the spelling that is used throughout this book.

This review was based on the video release put out by CBS/Fox, which is an edited version. The complete version of this film, available only on laserdisc, contains more footage of Edna Purviance and Carl Miller at the beginning, and also shows them running into each other again toward the end of the film after they both have become successful.

As the feature length debut of Jackie Coogan as well as the first feature film directed by Charlie Chaplin, *The Kid* is a film of great historic importance, one that every silent film enthusiast should see.

317. La Terre

[a.k.a. *The Earth*]

Rating: ☆☆☆

S.C.A.G.L. Productions/France; ***Directed by*** Andre Antoine; ***Based on Emile Zola's The Earth***; ***Photographed by*** Rene Guychard, Rene Gaveau; ***Assistant Directors:*** Georges Denola, Julien Duvivier; ***Running Time of Surviving Footage:*** 96 minutes; ***Cast:*** PÈRE FOUNAN, Armand Bour; JEAN, Rene Alexandre; FRANÇOISE, Germaine Rouer; LOUIS [BOUTEAU], Jean Herve; HYACINTHE [JESUS CHRIST], Milo; OLYMPE [THE PEST], Berthe Bovy; LISE, Jeanne Briey; LACOGNETTE, Jeanne Grumbach; THE SHEPHERD, Emile Desjardins; BEEU, Max Charlier; NENESSE, René Hieronimus; ***Supporting Cast:*** Armand Numes; Léon Malavier

This foreign classic was all but forgotten and believed lost. A partial print was found in Russia's Gosfilmofond Archives, and beautifully restored by Kevin Brownlow and Photoplay Productions of England in the early 1990s. It was originally filmed around 1919 or 1920, and released in Europe in 1921.

The story centers around the main character, Père Founan, who gives his hardearned home and land to his selfish children, with the provision that he is to be provided for until his death. The children are losers who mistreat him and fail to live up to their end of the bargain. He is eventually tired of the abuse, and goes off to die. The final title states that only the earth is immortal.

This film is well-acted and photographed. What is left of it is in beautiful, pristine condition, and some of the later sequences are color tinted. Since it is incomplete, it is advisable to read the book for better comprehension. Although not yet released on video in the United States, *La Terre* is aired from time to time on Turner Classic Movies.

318. Leap Year

Rating: ☆☆

[a.k.a. *Should a Man Marry?*; *Skirt Shy*; *This Is So Sudden*]

Paramount; ***Directed by*** James Cruze; ***Running Time:*** 50 minutes; ***Cast:*** STANLEY PIPER, Roscoe Arbuckle (1887–1933); PHYLLIS BROWN, Mary Thurman (1894–1925); JEREMIAH PIPER, Lucien Littlefield (1895–1960); DORIS KEENE, Harriet Hammond; IRENE RUTHERFORD, Maude Wayne (1895–1983); SCOTT TRAVIS, Clarence Geldart (1867–1935); MRS. TRAVIS, Winifred Greenwood (1885–1961); TOMMY BLAINE, Allen Durnell; MOLLY MORRIS, Gertrude Short (1900–1968); MUMFORD (STAN'S VALET), John McKinnon

Leap Year is the only one of Roscoe Arbuckle's completed Paramount features that is widely available for viewing. *The Life of the Party* (1921) and a feature remake of *Brewster's Millions* (1921) are known to survive, but the Paramount Company has not teamed with any of the video companies to make them widely available on video. There was such a furor with the public over the Arbuckle-Rappe incident that none of the features was ever released in the United States.

In *Leap Year*, Arbuckle plays Stanley Piper, the nephew of millionaire Jeremiah Piper, and the heir to his fortune. It seems that Stanley can't keep out of trouble with women. So, he is sent to the Catalina resort, which is supposedly devoid of women.

It seems that Stanley has a stuttering problem which can be relieved only by having a drink. In the early days of prohibition, the word "water" appeared in parentheses next to the word "drink" in the title card, and was underlined. On this "womanless" resort, Stanley makes the mistake of striking up seemingly innocent conversations with three different beauties, who all mistakenly think that he has proposed marriage to them. So, his next problem is how to convince these three women NOT to marry him, so that he can propose marriage to his father's nurse, Phyllis Brown, who is really the woman of his dreams. He tries a number of different things to free himself from the possibility of trigamy—from playing sick to playing dead. There are quite a number of funny moments in Arbuckle's escapades to pursue the woman he truly wants to marry.

While *Leap Year* does have its moments, it is not among the best examples of Arbuckle's surviving work. This is partly because *Leap Year* was made after Arbuckle had signed his multimillion dollar contract with Paramount. His salary was costing the studio so much money that the executives wanted to make sure that they milked as much money as possible from Arbuckle's name—thereby churning out Arbuckle features as fast as they could, concentrating on quantity rather than on quality. Nonetheless, *Leap Year* is a relatively decent comedy feature, which is of historic interest not only as one of Arbuckle's unreleased features, but for the film's other personnel.

Lucien Littlefield was a prominent character actor with a distinguished career that began in 1913. He often portrayed older men, although he himself was not, in actuality, as old as he looked. Mary Thurman was an attractive actress who started her career as one of Mack Sennett's bathing beauties in 1916 at age 20. Her hair was cut much in the style of Colleen Moore and Louise Brooks. She is truly delightful in *Leap Year*, the one example of her work available for evaluation. One wonders how far she might have gone if she had not died at age 30 in 1925 from bronchial pneumonia. Gertrude Short began her career in the 1913 version of *Uncle Tom's Cabin*. Her role in the cult classic *Reefer Madness* (1937) gives her a permanent place in motion picture history. No information could be found on Harriet Hammond or Maude Wayne, two of the other beauties in the supporting cast. Winifred Greenwood, who plays a conservative, prudish woman in this film, first rose to fame in westerns produced by the Star Film Ranch in Texas, owned by Gaston Méliès, the brother of the highly acclaimed French film pioneer Georges Méliès. By 1913, she was one of the top female stars at the American Film Company.

After *Leap Year*, which was never released in the United States, Roscoe Arbuckle was forced to retire from the screen, as most theaters refused to run his films. The only work he could get was as a director, and he had to direct under the alias of "William Goodrich." He did make a comeback in a series of sound shorts for the Vitaphone Company in the early 1930s. Unfortunately, the comeback came too late. He died in 1933 at age 47 of a heart attack after the completion of the sixth short in the series. Having viewed five of these last six shorts, it is easy to conclude that if Arbuckle had lived, he would have once again finally enjoyed success as a talkie era comedian.

319. The Love Light

Rating: ☆☆☆½

United Artists; ***Written and Directed by*** Frances Marion; ***Photographed by*** Charles Rosher and Henry Cronjager; ***Art Directed by*** Stephen Goosson; ***Running Time:*** 79 minutes; ***Cast:*** ANGELA CARLOTTI, Mary Pickford (1892–1979); MARIA, Evelyn Dumo; GIOVANNI, Raymond Bloomer; THE SPY, Fred Thomson (1890–1928); FATHER LORENZO, Albert Prisco; ANTONIO, Georges Rigas (1890–1940); MARIO, Edward Phillips (1899–1965)

This was the second of three films directed by Frances Marion (1886–1973), and the only one of the three that survived. In *The Silent Feminists*, Anthony Slide stated of *The Love Light* that "The direction is faultless, as good as the work of the male directors who had earlier worked with Pickford." In *Moving Picture World*, Louis Reeves Harrison writes, "the atmosphere provided by director Frances Marion leaves nothing to be desired in the way of artistic backgrounds."

For this film, director Marion cast her husband, Fred Thomson, as the German spy who passes himself off to lead character Angela as a deserter. Angela falls in love with and marries him secretly, providing him with a hiding place in her cabin across the river from the lighthouse that she oversees outside her small Italian village. The spy goes across the river to the lighthouse, and he and Angela communicate through light signals, thus being the "love light" referred to in the title. When Angela finds out that her husband used these signals in the German attack in which her brother was killed, she turns him over to the authorities.

The Love Light features an intriguing and interesting plot, and makes use of beautiful scenery, featuring expert cinematography. It even has a gripping boat disaster as a finale to boot. The acting performances by Pickford and Thomson are first class. This was Thomson's film debut, and he is shown to be a handsome, appealing, and talented actor. Unfortunately, only two of his other films survive: *A Chapter in Her Life* (1923), in which he starred under another female director, Lois Weber, and the 1924 western *Thundering Hoofs*. He was only 38 when he died from tetanus complications in 1928. He is not to be confused with musical writer Fred Thompson (1884?–1949), who authored *Rio Rita* (1929).

With its historic value as Frances Marion's only surviving directorial work as well as one of the few examples of Fred Thomson's work in addition to being his debut, *The Love Light* is well worth seeing. Unfortunately, it has not yet been released on video. However, the Mary Pickford Library has been working to make more of the Pickford films accessible, and there is a good chance that it will be released on video sometime in the future.

320. Molly O'

Rating: ☆☆☆½

Mack Sennett Company/First National; ***Directed by*** F. Richard Jones; ***Original Running Time:*** Approximately 71 minutes; ***Running Time of Surviving Footage:*** 57 minutes; ***Cast:*** MOLLY O'DAIR, Mabel Normand (1892–1930); ***Supporting Cast:*** George Nichols (1864–1927); Eugenie Besserer (1868–1934); Anna Hernandez (1867–1945); Jack Mulhall (1887–1979); Albert Hackett; Jacqueline Logan (1902–1983); Ben Deeley (1878–1924); Eddie Gribbon (1890–1965); Carl Stockdale (1874–1953); Lowell Sherman (1888–1934); Gloria Davenport

Molly O' was filmed in early to mid–1921, and released in December of that year. It was the first film that Mabel Normand made as her comeback upon recovering from her ordeals with drug addiction that had plagued her during the time that she was with Sam Goldwyn's company.

For many years, *Molly O'* was believed to have been lost, as the only known print had disintegrated in the vaults of the American Film Institute in the 1960s before it could be copied. A relatively complete print (missing reel 3 of 7 reels) of *Molly O'* turned up in 1996 at the Gosfilmofond Archives in Moscow, Russia. An extremely rare video copy of this film reveals that *Molly O'* is probably the best of Mabel Normand's surviving feature films. Normand looks fabulous, indicating that her vibrancy and energy had returned following her drug addiction.

In this film, Mabel plays a character named Molly O'Dair, a Cinderella-type character who scrubs floors and washes clothes for a living. She falls in love with a man from high society, whom her parents greatly disapprove of, as they feel that she should not marry into an aristocratic family. She goes to a masked ball, where she has a wonderful time with the man she admires. Unfortunately, when she arrives back home, her infuriated father is waiting, and kicks her out. Having no place else to go, she finally consents to go with a villainous suitor, played by Lowell Sherman, out of desperation. She ends up with the suitor on a dirigible blimp, which culminates in a chase sequence that takes place in the air, with her "prince charming" catching up to the dirigible in a seaplane in an attempt to rescue Molly from the clutches of the villain. This air chase sequence was filmed in Pensacola, Florida, and is one of the most thrilling chase sequences in the history of the cinema.

In seeing this film, it is obvious that Mabel's career was back on the right track, as this is her best surviving work. Unfortunately, a couple of months before the release of this film, the notorious Roscoe Arbuckle/Virginia Rappe incident hit the newspapers.

Arbuckle had starred in many early shorts with Mabel from 1914 to 1916. Two other scandals shortly followed in which Mabel's name was indirectly linked, but this was played up to the fullest by yellow journalists. The first of these two incidents was the murder of William Desmond Taylor on February 1, 1922. Mabel was the last person known to have held a conversation with Taylor. The way that the yellow journalists presented the story tarnished Normand's reputation, and ruined the career of Mary Miles Minter as well. Approximately a year later, scandal erupted again when Mabel attended a party of Courtland Dines'. Normand's chauffeur shot and injured Dines in a heated, drunken argument. The fact that he was on Mabel's payroll dragged her name through the yellow journals again, which effectively ended her career. She made a bit of a comeback in the late 1920s with Hal Roach, but it was too late. Normand contracted tuberculosis, from which she died in 1930.

Hopefully, this excellent Normand vehicle will eventually be made widely available to the public now that it has been recovered from "lost" status.

321. The Nut

Rating: ☆☆☆

United Artists; ***Directed by*** Theodore "Ted" Reed; ***Story by*** Kenneth Davenport; ***Scenario by*** William Parker, Lotta Woods; ***Photographed by*** Harry Thorpe; ***Art Director:*** Edward Langley; ***Running Time:*** 77 minutes; ***Cast:*** CHARLIE THE INVENTOR, Douglas Fairbanks, Sr. (1883–1939); ESTRELL WYNN, Marguerite de la Motte (1902–1950); ***Supporting Cast:*** William Lowery (1885–1941); Gerald Pring; Morris Hughes; Barbara LaMarr (1896–1926); Sidney De Grey (1886–1941); ***Notable Cameo:*** Mary Pickford (1892–1979)

The Nut was Douglas Fairbanks' follow-up to *The Mark of Zorro* (1920), and the last of his silent comedy satires that made him so popular in the late 1910s. In this film, he plays a wacky inventor who has fallen in love with Estrell Wynn, a charity worker trying to get the "big money" people interested in her cause. Charlie tries to help people to generate interest in the cause, but manages to have a number of blunders and setbacks, although all turns out well in the end.

It has been erroneously stated in the past that Charlie Chaplin (1889–1977) played a cameo role in the impersonation show sequence. This was actually a Chaplin lookalike. If one looks closely, the profile is definitely not Chaplin's. Mary Pickford did make a cameo appearance, and she can be easily spotted in the audience during the impersonation show.

One of the factors that draws historic interest to this film is the appearance of Barbara LaMarr in the cast. Her part in the film is little more than a bit part, and there is only a couple of minutes' footage in which she appears, with no really good close-up shots.

The Nut is a light, entertaining film replete with a number of good sight gags.

322. Orphans of the Storm

Rating: ☆☆☆☆

D.W. Griffith/United Artists; ***Directed by*** D.W. Griffith; ***Adapted from the Play by*** Adolphe d'Ennery; ***Running Time:*** 150 minutes; ***Cast:*** LOUISE GIRARD, Dorothy Gish (1898–1968); HENRIETTE GIRARD, Lillian Gish (1893–1993); CHEVALIER DE VAUDREY, Joseph Schildkraut (1895–1964); DANTON, Monte Blue (1890–1963); COUNT DE LINIERES, Frank Losee (1856–1937); COUNTESS DE LINIERES, Catherine Emmett (1882–1960); MARQUIS DE

PRAILLE, Morgan Wallace (1881–1953); MOTHER FROCHARD, Lucille LaVerne (1869–1945); JACQUES FROCHARD, Sheldon Lewis; PIERRE FROCHARD, Frank Puglia (1892–1975); PICARD, Creighton Hale (1882–1965); JACQUES FORGET-NOT, Leslie King (1876–1947); ROBESPIERRE, Sidney Herbert (died 1927); KING LOUIS XVI, Leo Kolmer; THE DOCTOR, Adolphe Lestina; SISTER GENEVIEVE, Kate Bruce (1858–1946); A STARVING PEASANT, Flora Finch (1869–1940)

Orphans of the Storm was the last of D.W. Griffith's blockbuster epics. It is also the last film collaboration of D.W. Griffith and Lillian Gish, who left Griffith's company after ten years to star in *The White Sister* (1923) with Inspiration Pictures under the direction of Henry King.

The core story that *Orphans of the Storm* was based on was a stage play produced in 1874 called *Les Deux Orphelines*, written by Adolphe Philippe d'Ennery and Eugene Cormon. When the stage play premiered in New York in 1875, Kate Claxton starred as Louise, and also owned the American rights to the play. The play's original storyline was basically that of a baby from a wealthy family named Henriette, who is left on the doorstep of the home of a poor couple, who have a daughter named Louise. As the girls get older, Louise eventually goes blind, and the deaths of the parents leave the two girls orphaned. The sisters are separated, and Louise is taken in by a hag who forces her to beg in the streets to earn her keep. After enduring a number of calamities, the girls are eventually reunited.

There were at least three American film adaptations of the play, and one French film version. The French version, *Les Deux Orphelines* (1910), was directed by Albert Capellani. The first two American versions were filmed by the Selig Polyscope Company. The first 1908 version was a one-reeler lasting about 12 minutes. Very little is known about this lost version. Selig's second adaptation in 1911 was three reels long, and is reviewed elsewhere in this book. In 1915, Fox Film Company did a version which was directed by Herbert Brenon (1880–1958). It starred none other than Theda Bara (1885–1955) as Henriette, and an actress named Jean Sothern (1895–1924) as Louise. It was filmed partially in Quebec, and did well with the critics, but poorly at the box office. The story just did not have quite enough substance to be a real hit as a movie.

In 1921, D.W. Griffith (1875–1948) gave the story the twist that it needed—by having it take place in the middle of the French Revolution. By doing this, he was able to include spectacular mob scenes, as well as a social message. Griffith got across the point that the French revolutionists rightly overthrew a bad government, but allowed tyrannical mob rule to take over, equivalent to what happened in Russia after their 1917 revolution. He warns the Americans with their good government against confusing fanatics with leaders, and possibly making the same mistakes made in France and Russia.

Recently, this film was finally restored using an orchestra score based on the score that D.W. Griffith originally commissioned for the film, and with the original color tints as well. Seeing the restored version enhances the experience of this film a great deal, and is highly recommended. For further commentary on *Orphans of the Storm*, see this author's previous book, *Silent Films on Video.*

323. Outside the Law *Rating:* ☆☆☆

Universal; ***Written and Directed by*** Tod Browning; ***Scenario by*** Tod Browning and Lucien

Lillian and Dorothy Gish in *Orphans of the Storm* (1921).

Priscilla Dean, star of *Outside the Law* (1921), in one of her popular lost serials.

Hubbard; ***Titles by*** Gardner Bradford; ***Art Director:*** E.E. Sheeley; ***Running Time:*** 75 minutes; ***Cast:*** MOLLY MADDEN, Priscilla Dean (1896–1987); "SILENT" MADDEN, Ralph Lewis (1872–1937); CHANG LOW, E.A. Warren (1874–1940); AH WING, Lon Chaney, Sr. (1883–1930); "BLACK MIKE" SYLVA, Lon Chaney, Sr. (1883–1930); "DAPPER BILL" BALLARD, Wheeler Oakman (1890–1949); KID ACROSS THE HALL, Stanley Goethals

Outside the Law was the first of what would turn out to be eight screen collaborations between director Tod Browning (1882–1962) and actor Lon Chaney. This was filmed after Chaney's success with *The Miracle Man* (1919), but before he had ascended to the level of stardom that would later win him top billing in his films. Top billing for *Outside the Law* went to Priscilla Dean, who became enormously popular in 1917 after having played the heroine in Universal's serial *The Gray Ghost*. As far as can be determined, this film and a featurized version of *The White Tiger* (1923) remain her only surviving films. Dean was married to costar Wheeler Oakman in real life.

Lon Chaney plays two roles in this film, both as Ah Wing, the Chinese servant of Chang Low, and as mobster "Black Mike." The movie is set in the Chinatown district of San Francisco. Priscilla Dean plays Molly Madden, the daughter of "Silent" Madden, a mob boss attempting to go straight. The gang led by "Black Mike" fears that Madden will tell what he knows about them, and frame him for a shooting. Molly loses faith in the law, and engineers a jewelry robbery with Dapper Bill. They get away with the robbery, but have to constantly look over their shoulders, living a life "outside the law" which constantly has to be shrouded in secrecy. An exhilarating shootout provides the climactic finale for the film.

For many years, *Outside the Law* was believed to be yet another of many lost Universal Pictures films. A print turned up in the early 1980s. It was saved just in time, as the final reel suffered severe deterioration before being acquired for preservation. The film is still watchable despite the decomposition.

Outside the Law remains an excellent gangster drama, and holds up well today. Lon Chaney's double role is interesting to see, and Priscilla Dean's more-than-competent performance makes one wish more of her work had survived.

324. The Sheik

Rating: ☆☆½

Paramount; ***Directed by*** George Melford; ***Running Time:*** 80 minutes; ***Cast:*** AHMED BEN HASSEN (THE SHEIK), Rudolph Valentino (1895–1926); DIANA MAYO, Agnes Ayres (1896–1940); SIR AUBREY, Frank Butler (1890–1967); MUSTAPHA ALI, Charles Brindley (1880–1946); ZILAH, Ruth Miller (1903–1981); GASTON, Lucien Littlefield (1895–1960); RAOUL DE ST. HUBERT, Adolphe Menjou (1890–1963); OMAIR (THE BANDIT), Walter Long (1879–1952)

The Sheik was the first film that Rudolph Valentino starred in for Paramount Pictures. This was a highly successful film, and transformed Valentino into a major sex symbol overnight. Women in the audiences fainted during this film. The word "sheik" was to become a household word, and was part of the usual teenage lingo for an entire generation. In addition, a new fashion trend was started and sheik outfits became the "in" thing to wear.

In watching *The Sheik*, one can see that it obviously has flaws. The script is a bit hokey, and is sometimes downright ridiculous and preposterous. In some sequences, Valentino's leers at Agnes Ayres are way overexaggerated (partially because Valentino was actually squinting, being extremely nearsighted). Valentino himself hated the film, but one cannot very effectively argue with success.

Despite the film's flaws, it featured good art direction, costumes, and sets. It also featured an impressive supporting cast. Agnes Ayres is gorgeous in this role, and it is surprising that she did not enjoy a more prominent career than she did after her appearance in *The Sheik*. Among the supporting players is Adolphe Menjou, who would go on to win an Academy Award nomination for Best Actor in *The Front Page* (1931).

Agnes Ayres, Valentino's leading lady in *The Sheik* (1921).

There is one error regarding the cast credits of this film which has appeared in print time and time again. This film has been erroneously listed in the filmography of Patsy Ruth Miller (1904–1995). However, an actress named Ruth Miller (1903–1981), who was William Boyd's first wife for a couple of years in the 1920s, and who is of no relation to Patsy Ruth Miller, appears in a bit part in the beginning of this film. Since Patsy Ruth Miller did make her film debut as a supporting player in the Nazimova-Valentino version of *Camille* (1921), historians over the years have simply made the assumption that Ruth Miller and Patsy Ruth Miller were one and the same person. Even though it did not appear that the woman in *The Sheik* looked like Patsy Ruth Miller, the fact that the part is that of an Arabian woman would lead people to rationalize that Patsy Ruth Miller was made up to look Arabian, thus explaining the altered appearance. It was not until Patsy Ruth Miller's last interview of 1995 became public that the record was really set straight.

With *The Sheik's* importance in motion picture history as the film that established Rudolph Valentino as Hollywood's most legendary male sex symbol, it is one that all movie enthusiasts should see.

325. That Girl Montana

Rating: ☆☆☆

Jesse D. Hampton/Pathé Exchange; ***Directed by*** Robert Thornby; ***Based on a Story by*** Marah Ellis Ryan; ***Screen Adaptation by*** George H. Plympton; ***Photography by*** Lucien Andriot; ***Film Editor:*** K.E. Anderson; ***Running Time:*** 67 minutes; ***Cast:*** MONTE [MONTANA RIVERS], Blanche Sweet (1896–1986); DAN OVERTON, Mahlon Hamilton (1880–1960); LEE HOLLY, Edward Peil (1883–1958); AKKOMI, Charles Edler (1864–1942); JIM HARRIS, Frank Lanning (1872–1945); MRS. HUZZARD, Kate Price (1872–1943); MAX LYSTER, Jack Roseleigh (1887–1940); LOTTIE, Claire DuBrey (1892–1993)

This is one of the independent features that Blanche Sweet did after she left Paramount in 1917. For years, this film had been forgotten until Grapevine Video brought it back in 1997. This film is a major find, as it is much better than one would expect. In some ways, this reviewer liked it better than Sweet's most highly acclaimed surviving work, *Anna Christie* (1923). This film had more punch and action than *Anna Christie*, which was a much heavier film.

In this light western, Sweet plays Montana Rivers, a girl who is brought up by outlaw Lee Holly and disguised as a boy. When Holly is caught cheating at poker in the saloon, he barely escapes with his life, and Montana seeks help from an Indian friend who places her with a friend of his, Dan Overton. Overton has a kindly woman named Mrs. Huzzard to take her in.

While at a party, Montana is confronted by Jim Harris, who is Overton's partner in a mine claim who was victimized by her former guardian and recognizes her as Holly's "male" sidekick. She finally convinces Harris that she did not participate in her guardian's crimes willingly, and they become friends, with him giving her a third share in the gold mine.

Dan and Montana gradually fall in love, but there is an obstacle to their getting married: Lottie, the wife who deserted Dan to become a prostitute, comes back when she finds out he has struck it rich. There are a number of unexpected twists and thrills as the rest of the story unfolds.

This is an exciting, action-packed film with a good, solid storyline, complemented by especially good performances from Blanche Sweet and Mahlon Hamilton in the lead roles. Mahlon Hamilton never looked better, and Blanche Sweet looks better in this film than she did in some of her earlier films with D.W. Griffith in the early 1910s. Supporting player Claire DuBrey gives an exceptional performance as well as Overton's wife-turned-prostitute who comes back to haunt him. Edward Peil, who is best remembered for playing Chinese villains in two Griffith features, is at first hard to recognize as outlaw Lee Holly. Kate Price, as usual, is charming in her motherly character of Mrs. Huzzard.

Director Robert Thornby's (1888–1953) career spanned from 1916 to 1926. The most famous film he worked on was *Lorna Doone* (1922) as an assistant to Maurice Tourneur.

326. The Three Musketeers

Rating: ☆☆☆½

United Artists; ***Directed by*** Fred Niblo; ***Photography by*** Arthur Edeson; ***Based on the Novel by*** Alexandre Dumas; ***Scenario by*** Edward Knoblock; ***Scenario Editor:*** Lotta Woods; ***Art Director:*** Edward M. Langley; ***Technical Director:*** Frank England; ***Master of Costumes:*** Paul Burns; ***Set Design:*** Harry Edwards; ***Film Editor:*** Nellie Mason; ***Running Time:*** 118 minutes; ***Cast:*** D'ARTAGNAN, Douglas Fairbanks, Sr. (1883–1939); LOUIS XIII, Adolphe Menjou (1890–1963); ANNE OF AUSTRIA, Mary MacLaren (1896–1985); CARDINAL RICHELEAU, Nigel de Brulier (1877–1948); DUKE OF BUCKINGHAM, Thomas Holding (1880–1929); CONSTANCE, Marguerite de la Motte (1902–1950); DE TREVILLE, Willis Robards (1873–1921); ROCHEFORT, Boyd Irwin (1880–1957); MILADY DE WINTER, Barbara LaMarr (1896–1926); FATHER JOSEPH, Lon Poff (1870–1952); D'ARTAGNAN'S FATHER, Walt Whitman (1859–1928); BONACHTEAU, Sidney Franklin (1870–1931); BERNAJOUX, Charles Belcher (1872–1943); PLANCHET, Charles Stevens (1893–1964); ATHOS, Leon Bary; PORTHOS, George Siegmann (1882–1928); ARAMIS, Eugene Pallette (1889–1954)

The Three Musketeers was the first of Douglas Fairbanks' really big epics, and one of his best films as well. The film also has historic interest as being the first major role of Barbara LaMarr, whose early death from drugs at 29 has given her a legendary status.

Lavishly produced, the dresses worn by Barbara LaMarr and Marguerite de la Motte for this film were actual antique dresses from the time period portrayed. The French village sets were painstakingly modeled for authenticity to correlate with the time and place portrayed as well.

The film starts off a bit slow, but none of the footage would be classified as idle. Every foot is put to good use in establishing the various characters and other aspects that are necessary to develop the plot.

Douglas Fairbanks does a good job as D'Artagnan, a poor man of noble blood who quests to claim the privileges to which he is entitled, and to fight tyranny and corruption. Barbara LaMarr's part as Milady de Winter, who is in league with Richeleau, gives us the first really good look at her acting talent, and she lives up to her reputation as "the girl who was too beautiful," and was a highly competent actress to boot.

Fairbanks does some excellent swashbuckling stunts in this film, even if he doesn't really look French. Character actor Nigel De Brulier had one of the best roles of his career as Richeleau, the cardinal who seeks to betray Louis XIII. Marguerite de la Motte is also good as the damsel in distress.

This second of at least eight screen adaptations of the Dumas classic is widely acclaimed as the best of the serious film adaptations.

327. Tol'able David

Rating: ☆☆☆½

Inspiration Pictures/First National; ***Directed by*** Henry King; ***Scenario by*** Edmund Goulding and Henry King; ***Based on a Short Story by*** Joseph Hergesheimer; ***Photographed by*** Henry Cronjager; ***Edited by*** Duncan Mansfield; *Running Time:* 78 minutes; *Cast:* DAVID KINEMON, Richard Barthelmess (1895–1963); ESTHER HATBURN, Gladys Hulette (1896–1991); LUKE HATBURN, Ernest Torrence (1878–1933); ISKA HATBURN, Walter P. Lewis (1866–1932); "BUZZARD" HATBURN, Ralph Yearsley (1896–1928); NEIGHBOR HATBURN [ESTHER'S GRANDFATHER], Forrest Robinson (1858–1924); ROSE KINEMON, Patterson Dial (1902–1945); JOHN GALT, Lawrence Eddinger

Tol'able David won *Photoplay Magazine*'s 1922 Medal of Honor as outstanding film of the year. It is widely acclaimed as one of Richard Barthelmess' best performances, if not the very best. It was his first film after having left the D.W. Griffith Company. *Tol'able David* is also among the best achievements of director Henry King (1886–1982).

In this film, Barthelmess plays David Kinemon, a young adolescent living in rural Virginia, who is desperately trying to show both his love interest and his family that he is worthy of being regarded as a man. Gladys Hulette is the leading lady, playing Esther, a girl living with her grandfather Hatburn. The two Hatburns' lives are complicated when their contemptible cousins escape from jail and take over the Hatburn household. The most brazen of the three villains is Luke Hatburn, very well-played by Ernest Torrence in his film debut. It was Torrence's performance in this film which established him as one of the ultimate villain players of the silent screen.

David is thrust into manhood in a fashion different from any he had expected. The evil Hatburns kill his father and dog, and severely injure his brother, making him the new head of his household. David takes his brother's place as the town mail carrier, and the Hatburn brothers steal the mail. This results in the climactic sequence in which David takes on the brothers and settles the score.

Director Henry King was provided with a $250,000 budget for *Tol'able David*, but spent only $86,000 to complete the picture.

D.W. Griffith had the first option for the screen rights to this film, but passed it over, prompting Richard Barthelmess to move to Inspiration Pictures where he could make this film that he wanted as his next starring vehicle. Director Henry King expanded on a screen treatment which had been put together by Edmund Goulding (1891–1959), who would later become a famous director in his own right.

It is odd to note that while the two leading players lived full lives, most of the supporting players were dead within a dozen years of this film's completion. Walter P. Lewis and Forrest Robinson were in their 60s when they died, as they were close to that age when they appeared in the film. Ralph Yearsley committed suicide when he was 31 years old in 1928. Ernest Torrence was 54 when he died. In addition, Patterson Dial, who had a small role as David Kinemon's sister-in-law Rose, was 43 years old when she died in 1945.

While *Tol'able David* fell short of this reviewer's expectations based on its past acclaim, it is still a highly entertaining melodrama. The acting performances by Richard

Barthelmess and Ernest Torrence are flawless, and Henry King's achievement as director is significant.

A high quality copy of *Tol'able David* was released on laser disc in 1997, and on videotape in early 1998 by Kino.

328. Too Wise Wives

Rating: ☆½

Lois Weber Productions; ***Produced, Directed, and Adapted by*** Lois Weber; ***Story by*** Lois Weber and Marion Orth; ***Photographed by*** William C. Poster; ***Running Time:*** 79 minutes; ***Cast:*** MARIE GRAHAM, Claire Windsor (1897–1972); DAVID GRAHAM, Louis Calhern (1895–1956); SARA DALY, Mona Lisa; JOHN DALY, Phillips Smalley (1865–1939)

Too Wise Wives parallels two households. The Grahams are a well-off couple, with Mrs. Graham as the perfect, attentive model disposition of domesticity. The other couple are the Dalys, who are richer, and the wife not as attentive and caring, but who seems to have her husband pay more attention and appreciate her more.

Basically, this is a subtle satire on the role a wife should play. The film crawls along at the pace of a turtle, with nothing significant ever really happening. The cumbersome production's duration of 79 minutes seems like an eternity.

Of all of the Lois Weber films evaluated, this is the worst and least entertaining, despite Claire Windsor's emotional and sensitive performance. It is a good film to watch if you should ever run out of sleeping pills.

329. The Wandering Jew [a.k.a. *The Life of Theodor Herzl*]

Rating: ☆☆☆

Fox and Penser; ***Directed by*** Otto Kreisler; ***Titled and Edited by*** Charles Penser and Emil K. Ellis; ***Running Time:*** 75 minutes; ***Cast:*** THE WANDERING JEW, Rudolph Schildkraut (1862–1930); KING DAVID, Joseph Schildkraut (1895–1964); DR. THEODORE HERZL, H. Bath; BARON HIRSCH, Thomas Morley; POPE LEO XII, David Putnam; TORQUEMADO, Tom Pearson; SULTAN OF TURKEY, James Battle

This is the earliest American film credit of the great actor, Rudolph Schildkraut. Schildkraut started his show business career as part of Max Reinhardt's Berlin stage company, and later appeared on Broadway, becoming among the most renowned of stage actors. His first films were made in Germany in the 1910s.

Although Schildkraut was given top billing, his part is actually a minor one. He appears in the prologue as the biblical banished Jew condemned to wander the desert and wastelands. As brief as his role was, he certainly had a commanding presence, and one understands why he was so highly acclaimed.

This prologue leads into a biographical story on Theodor Herzl, the founder of modern day Zionism. It starts with his childhood, showing how he as a child read about the persecution of his ancestors, and was determined to reclaim Israel as a home country for the oppressed Jewish segment of society. It shows how he witnessed a Jew being beaten and dragged through the streets, as well as other unjust persecutions of the Jewish people. As Herzl reflects on the discrimination he has suffered in college and in the job market, the movie shows flashbacks to the earliest days of Jewish persecution, and it is in these segments that Rudolph Schildkraut's son, Joseph, appears as King David.

While *The Wandering Jew* moves slowly and drags in some segments, it is in general a fascinating account of both Jewish history and the life of Herzl, portraying his life story as well as the last hours before his death in 1904. Among the other incidents portrayed are the infamous Dreyfus case in France, which was the catalyst that sent Herzl into action. It ends with closing shots of prominent Jews Albert Einstein and Dr. Chaim Weizman, followed by a shot of the American flag with a plea for Americans to help the oppressed Jews of the time in their quest for a home country.

330. What Happened to Rosa?

Rating: ☆☆☆

Goldwyn Pictures; ***Directed by*** Victor Schertzinger; ***Running Time:*** 41 minutes; ***Cast:*** MAYME LADD/ROSA ALVARO, Mabel Normand (1892–1930); ***Supporting Cast:*** Hugh Thompson (1887–??); Doris Pawn; Tully Marshall (1864–1943); Eugenie Besserer (1868–1934); Buster Trow; Adolphe Menjou (1890–1963)

From 1918 to 1921, Mabel Normand starred in 16 films for the Samuel Goldwyn Company. It was during this period in her life that she was going through a series of tragedies. She had a horrible drug addiction problem, as well as an unhappy personal life in general. In *What Happened to Rosa?*, it is obvious that Normand was in extremely poor health. She was bone thin, had circles under her eyes, as well as gaunt facial features—looking constantly tired. Those who have not yet seen this film will be shocked when they see Mabel for the first time. *What Happened to Rosa?* was the last of the 16 films that Mabel starred in for the Goldwyn Company, and the only one of these Goldwyn films known to survive.

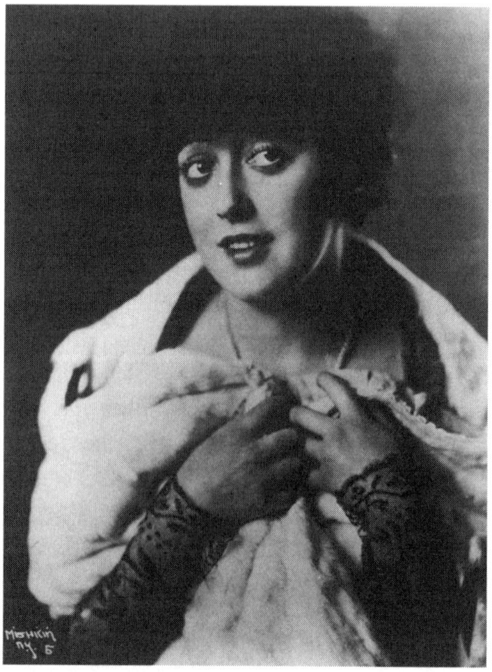

Mabel Normand around the time she was working for Goldwyn Pictures, star of *What Happened to Rosa?* (1921), the only surviving Goldwyn/Normand collaboration.

In this rare film, Mabel plays a shop girl named Mayme Ladd, employed at Friedman's Department Store. In search of adventure and some kind of escape from the drudgery of daily life, she visits a fortune teller. This fortune teller, portrayed by Eugenie Besserer, convinces her that the spirit of Rosa Alvaro, an exotic Spanish dancer, is within her. She predicts that if Mayme lets the spirit of Rosa Alvaro show, she will soon meet a dark-complected man of her dreams. When Mayme arrives home, she starts dressing the part of Rosa Alvaro. One of her coworkers walks in on her, and a title card flashes onto the screen which says, "Mayme Ladd, have you gone cuckoo?"

The next night, Mayme attends a costume party on a yacht called the *Mandalay*. She dresses up as none other than Rosa Alvaro, exotic Spanish beauty queen.

She meets a man named Dr. Drew, who falls for her. Unfortunately, Rosa does not think that she can win her man as Mayme Ladd, shop girl. Just before the coworkers identify who she really is, she takes off the Spanish clothes and jumps into the water, making everybody think that she drowned herself. Meanwhile, Dr. Drew searches frantically for Rosa. Her coworkers show up at Mayme's house, and find her peacefully sleeping in bed, telling them that she had never been aboard the *Mandalay* for the party. Her next idea is to somehow get into Dr. Drew's office, so that she can see him again. She dresses up like a roughed-up boy, and pretends to have an accident so that she will be taken to the doctor's office. Here, Mayme finds the Spanish clothes, which had been returned to the doctor as the only trace of Rosa Alvaro. She cleans herself up, puts on the Spanish clothes, and hopes that she can finally be reunited with the doctor.

Despite the fact that Normand was at the height of her drug addiction problems when this film was made, her delightful pantomimic ability still manages to come through. It shows that even at her most vulnerable, when Mabel was given good material to work with, her delightful pantomimic ability is still apparent. After *What Happened to Rosa?* was made, Normand left the Goldwyn Company, and managed to successfully kick her drug habit. She went back to the Mack Sennett Company, filmed *Molly O'*, and seemed to be on the brink of a great comeback before her name had been tarnished by the yellow journalists in the aftermath of two scandals in which her name had been linked.

1922

331. Big Stakes

Rating: ☆☆½

Clifford S. Elfelt Productions; ***Directed by*** Clifford S. Elfelt; ***Based on High Stakes by*** Frank Howard Clark; ***Photography by*** Clyde DeVinna; ***Art Direction by*** Arthur Allene; ***Running Time:*** 59 minutes; ***Cast:*** JIM GREGORY, J.[ames] B. Warner (1895–1924); MERCEDES ALOYEZ, Elinor Fair (1903–1957); MARY MOORE, Wilamae Carson; BULLY BRAND, Les Bates (1877–1930); SKINNY FARGO, H.S. Karr; EL CAPITAN MONTOYA, Robert H. Gray; PASCAL, Adelbert [a.k.a. Ethelbert] Knott (1859–1933)

This film is notable as one of two extremely rare surviving films of cowboy star James B. Warner, who was only 29 years old when he died in 1924.

Big Stakes is a western romantic comedy centering around Mercedes Aloyez, whose father has promised her hand in marriage to scoundrel El Capitan Montoya, whom she doesn't love. El Capitan's plans are spoiled when Jim Gregory becomes a rival suitor whom Mercedes prefers. El Capitan has Jim and his fat sidekick "Skinny" Fargo kidnapped and brought to his lair, where a Mexican jumping bean race is used to settle the score. The stakes are high, with the winner marrying Mercedes, and the loser allowing himself to be bitten by a poisonous reptile whose bite is fatal.

A subplot centers around Bully Brand, a repulsive outlaw who forces his affections on pretty waitress Mary Moore, who wants nothing to do with him. As the leader of the Night Riders, a gang wearing white sheets much like the old Ku Klux Klan costumes, Brand tries to force Moore to marry him, and it is up to Jim and Skinny to come to her rescue.

While the production values in this film aren't great, *Big Stakes* is a film that provides an interesting storyline, good comedy relief, nonstop action, and the rare chance to see J.B. Warner in action. Warner was a tall, lanky cowboy with rugged good looks. No cause for his death at 29 could be found in any reference sources.

Les Bates makes a good villain as Bully Brand. He was 45 when he appeared in this film, eight years before his death at 53 in a car accident in 1930.

332. Blood and Sand

Rating: ☆☆½

Paramount; ***Directed by*** Fred Niblo; ***Film Editor:*** Dorothy Arzner; ***From the Novel by*** Vicente Blasco Ibañez; ***Screen Adaptation by*** June Mathis; ***Photography by*** Alvin Wyckoff; ***Running Time of Complete Version:*** 79 minutes; ***Cast:*** JUAN GALLARDO, Rudolph Valentino (1895–1926); CARMEN, Lila Lee (1905–1973); WIDOW GALLARDO, Rosa Rosanova (1869–1944); MARQUIS DE MORAINA, George Periolat (1873–1940); DONA SOL, Nita Naldi (1897–1961); PLUMITAS THE BANDIT, Walter Long (1879–1952); ENCARNACION, Rosita Marstini (1887–1948); DON JOSE [MANAGER], Fred Becker (1882–1966); PHILOSOPHER, Charles Belcher (1872–1943)

This classic original film version of Ibañez's classic *Blood and Sand* was Rudolph Valentino's follow-up to *The Sheik* (1921), the film that made him an international sex symbol overnight. He plays Juan Gallardo, an impoverished adolescent who rises to fame and fortune as Spain's premier bullfighter. He marries his neighborhood sweetheart, Carmen, and they live in luxury and bliss until Gallardo is vamped by Dona Sol. He neglects his wife who truly loves him, and the heavy partying with Dona, who comes from a wealthy family and is simply amusing herself by using Gallardo as a boy toy, leads him to alcoholism. The alcoholism ultimately causes Gallardo to make a fatal error in what is to be his final bullfight.

As opposed to subsequent versions of *Blood and Sand*, this version has a parallel story which compares the life of Plumitas, who makes his living by terrorizing and killing people, to that of Juan Gallardo, who makes his living by killing bulls. The film gets across the inhumanity of bullfighting very effectively.

Dorothy Arzner's (1900–1979) editing of the bullfight sequences impressed the Hollywood moguls, and started her on the way to a directorial career. Unfortunately, neither of the two existing silents that Arzner directed are available for evaluation, but *The Wild Party* (1929), an early talkie she directed, is a bit disappointing. Arzner was openly lesbian, and the first female member of the Director's Guild of America.

Nita Naldi's role as the vamp of the story is her most famous. Sadly, her career ended with the advent of talkies, and she reportedly died a drug addict in a New York skid row hotel when she was in her early 60s.

This film also gave a significant boost to the career of Lila Lee, who plays Valentino's wife Carmen. Ms. Lee was married to James Kirkwood, Sr. She was the mother of James Kirkwood, Jr., the famous gay playwright who co-authored *A Chorus Line*.

While *Blood and Sand* is no great masterpiece, dragging in some spots and downright corny in others, its historic importance makes it a film well worth watching. In 1923, Stan Laurel did a hilarious parody of this film called *Mud and Sand*, which is reviewed elsewhere in this book.

333. Day Dreams

Rating: ☆☆☆

Joseph M. Schenk/First National; ***Written and Directed by*** Buster Keaton, Eddie Cline; ***Running Time of Surviving Footage:*** 21 minutes; ***Cast:*** THE BOY, Buster Keaton (1895–1966); THE GIRL, Renée Adorée (1898–1933); HER FATHER, Joe Roberts (1870–1923)

Day Dreams is a rare Keaton short which survives only in fragmented form. David Shepard produced a restoration of the film for Kino Video in 1995, using the available footage, linking titles, and stills from the missing sequences.

This film finds Keaton trying to win the hand of the girl he loves, by proving himself to her father. He vows to either make good in the big city, or return and shoot himself. He writes letters back to the girl which are deceptive and give the impression that he is having one success after another. His first job is in a hospital—a dog and cat hospital doing the most menial jobs, and still failing. He writes that due to an accident, he left the hospital to clean up on Wall Street. In actuality, he is sweeping Wall Street as a janitor. This sequence provides some hilarious slapstick sequences. He gets tired of Wall Street and decides to pursue his artistic talents. He is actually working in a second-string theater production, and fails in that production as well.

Keaton ends up being chased by the police for the finale. This leads into an especially good chase sequence, with Keaton performing a variety of impressive stunts. One is when he is shown hanging onto the back of a street car with his hands, hanging above the street in a horizontal position. He finally ends up caught in the paddle wheel of a steam boat. Having thoroughly failed, he mails himself back to his sweetheart and her father's house, conceding defeat. He tries to follow through on his promise to kill himself, and the father readily provides the gun. Keaton fails even in the suicide attempt, shooting and missing.

This film is especially important to film history as one of the first films of actress Renée Adorée, and the oldest of her films that is widely available for evaluation.

334. Down to the Sea in Ships

Rating: ☆☆☆

Whaling Film Corporation; ***Directed by*** Elmer Clifton; ***Scenario by*** John L.E. Pell; ***Photography by*** A.G. Penrod; ***Running Time:*** 84 minutes; ***Cast:*** PATIENCE MORGAN, Marguerite Courtot (1897–1986); THOMAS DEXTER, Raymond McKee (1892–1984); WILLIAM MORGAN, William Walcott; DOT MORGAN, Clara Bow (1905–1965); JIMMY, James Turfler; SCUFF SMITH, Leigh R. Smith (1889–1958); JAKE FINNER, Patrick Hartigan (1881–1951); SAMUEL SIGGS, J. Thornton Baston (1892–1970); TOWN CRIER, Curtis Pierce; "HENRY" CLARK, Ada Laycock; THUNDERBOLT BILL, William Cavanaugh (1876–??); A PLAYING CHILD (BIT PART), Anita Fremault (1915–1970)

This was the first major film production and direction effort by Elmer Clifton (1892–1949), just after he completed work as an assistant director for D.W. Griffith's *Way Down East* (1920). It is also historically significant as Clara Bow's film debut at age 16. (Bow's previous small part a year earlier in Christy Cabanne's *Beyond the Rainbow* (1921) ended up on the cutting room floor.) In addition, Anita Fremault, later known as Anita Louise, made her debut as an extra in this film.

Produced on location on a low budget in New Bedford, Massachusetts, this film is centered around the whaling industry, set in the early 1800s. The plot centers around villain Samuel Siggs' scheme to marry Patience Morgan, the daughter of wealthy shipowner William Morgan, for the sole purpose of taking his enterprise out from under him. Film star Raymond McKee plays the male lead as Thomas Dexter, who has true love for Patience, and seeks to rescue her from the clutches of Siggs. He must overcome the fact that the elder Morgan disapproves of him because of his religion and the fact that he is not a whaler, as well as the fact that Siggs has done a snow job on Morgan and made him like him.

With an interesting historical storyline and plot, *Down to the Sea in Ships* is a movie that captures and keeps the attention and is an enjoyable small-scale epic. Clifton demonstrates that he is a highly competent director—especially to turn out this type of film on the minuscule budget with which he reportedly worked.

Viewers will be shocked when they see Clara Bow in this debut film for the first time. At age 16, she could have passed for a child of 12, with her youthful baby face and straight black hair coming down to her shoulders. Her sequences as the mischievous younger Morgan sister provide excellent comedy relief, as does the brief sequence in which Anita Fremault appears.

Leading lady Marguerite Courtot is perhaps best remembered for her serial work in the late 1910s, most notably in the lost serial *Bound and Gagged* (1919). She only made a couple more films after *Down to the Sea in Ships* before retiring from the screen. As far as can be determined, this, along with one or two obscure shorts, is the only surviving work from her 10-year career spanning from 1913 to 1923.

335. The Electric House

Rating: ☆☆☆☆

Joseph M. Schenk/First National; ***Directed and Written by*** Buster Keaton, Eddie Cline; ***Running Time:*** 23 minutes; ***Cast:*** THE "ELECTRICIAN," Buster Keaton (1895–1966); ***Supporting Cast:*** Virginia Fox (1902–1982); Joe Roberts (1870–1923); Joe Keaton (1867–1946); Myra Keaton (1877–1955); Louise Keaton (1901–1981)

This is a delightful comedy which finds Keaton as a recent graduate of the People's University. His real major was in botany, but he is handed a certificate of electrical engineering instead. He is placed in a job that requires him to "electrify" a house. The owners of the house find quite a few surprises in store once the "electrification" is done. For starters, the electric staircase malfunctions, pushing both the owner and Keaton out a window and into a pool. In actuality, something went wrong in the filming of this sequence, and Keaton was actually thrown about 12 feet into the air, and suffered a broken leg. The actual sequence in which he breaks his leg is kept intact in the film, as well as in the video version. Keaton was unable to work for four months after this accident, having had to wait for his leg to heal before returning to work.

Other gadgets in the electric house include an electric pool table, dinner server, and dishwasher. It is interesting to note that the only one of these machines that is commonplace in residences in the 1990s is the dishwasher. A number of hilarious incidents occur when the electrical devices begin to malfunction.

The Electric House is among Keaton's best shorts, and is highly recommended.

336. Foolish Wives

Rating: ☆☆☆

Universal; ***Written and Directed by*** Erich von Stroheim; ***Assistant Directors:*** Edward A. Sowders, Jack R. Proctor; ***Photography by*** Ben Reynolds, William Daniels; ***Sets by*** Elma Sheely,

Richard Day; ***Titles by*** Marion Ainslee, Walter Anthony; ***Film Editor:*** Arthur Ripley; ***Running Time of Current Restoration:*** 107 minutes; ***Cast:*** ARTHUR HUGHES, Rudolph Christians (1869–1921); HELEN HUGHES, Miss DuPont (1894–1973); PRINCESS OLGA, Maude George (1888–1963); PRINCESS VERA, Mae Busch (1901–1946); COUNT SERGIUS [THEIR COUSIN], Erich von Stroheim (1885–1957); MAID, Dale Fuller; BUTLER, Al Edmondson (1896–1954); COUNTERFEITER, Cesare Gravina (1858–1954?); MARIAN [COUNTERFEITER'S DAUGHTER], Malwing Polo; ALBERT I [PRINCE OF MONACO], C.J. Allen

This was Erich von Stroheim's third directorial project for Universal Studios, where his debut, *Blind Husbands* (1919), and the lost film *The Devil's Passkey* (1920) were also filmed.

The success of von Stroheim's first two features resulted in his being given free reign over this third production, and an unlimited budget. For *Foolish Wives,* von Stroheim built a replica of Monte Carlo on the Universal lot, copying every minute architectural detail of the buildings of the early 1920s Monte Carlo. This was Universal's first really lavish grand production, reportedly costing over $1 million. Depending on which figures one believes for the cost of D.W. Griffith's *Intolerance* (1916), this was possibly the first film to cost over $1 million. Von Stroheim was so meticulous with details that he insisted on real caviar as a prop, and also insisted on using authentic replicas of Monaco's currency, having real counterfeit money printed up, as opposed to using play money as the studios normally used. This reportedly caused problems, as the extras were trying to cash this counterfeit money in at banks for American currency, and a few succeeded before the banks discovered what was going on.

Set against the fast casino life of Monte Carlo, *Foolish Wives* is the story of a fake Russian count and his two cousins, princesses Vera and Olga, who scheme to bilk a wealthy American couple out of their money. Along the way, "Count" Sergius manages to have affairs with the American wife of the ambassador he is trying to bilk, as well as a maid, a counterfeiter's daughter, and other women.

The original director's cut of this film was 21 reels long, or a little over three hours. Universal Pictures cut approximately one-third of the length from the film, and the censors in some areas cut still more footage. The film as released was a major box-office hit, and turned a comfortable profit, as well as establishing Universal as one of the major studios on a par with Paramount and Metro.

Over the years, *Foolish Wives* was further truncated as it was reissued, and for more than 40 years the film was seen only as a seven reel version. In the early 1970s, footage of the film was recovered from archives all over the world, and the film, although still not quite the complete version as released, was restored by Arthur Lennig to a fairly comprehensive approximation of the film as audiences saw it upon its original release. This restored version is the most complete version available, and was released by Kino Video with an excellent piano score.

337. Grandma's Boy *Rating:* ☆☆☆½

Associated Exhibitors/Pathé; ***Directed by*** Fred Newmeyer; ***Story by*** Hal Roach, Sam Taylor, Jean Havez; ***Photographed by*** Walter Lundin; ***Edited by*** T.J. Crizer; ***Titles by*** H.M. Walker; ***Running Time:*** 48 minutes; ***Cast:*** GRANDMA'S BOY, Harold Lloyd (1893–1971); HIS GIRL, Mildred Davis (1901–1969); HIS GRANDMA, Anna Townsend (1845–1923); HIS RIVAL,

Charles Stevenson (1887–1943); THE ROLLING STONE, Dick Sutherland (1881–1934); SHERIFF OF DABNEY COUNTY, Noah Young (1887–1958)

This comedy finds Harold Lloyd playing a meek weakling who has no self-confidence. His chief rival for the affection of his girl is a typical bully who will run over anybody and stoop to any level to make himself prevail. Lloyd's grandmother, trying to give him more confidence, tells him a story about how his grandfather, who was once like him, became a decorated Confederate hero. This flashback sequence has Lloyd playing his grandfather, and Anna Townsend playing a gypsy who gives him a magic charm.

The time comes when the sheriff enlists the aid of every man he can possibly deputize to capture a formidable fugitive called "the rolling stone." With his good luck charm in hand, "grandma's boy" succeeds in doing what an army of deputies couldn't—capture the fugitive. Upon achieving this feat, Lloyd and his rival have a major last confrontation, in which the bully ultimately gets his just desserts.

Although Harold Lloyd is the undisputed star of this show, Anna Townsend as his grandmother is delightful, and steals every scene that she appears in. She did a cameo role in *Safety Last* (1923) just before her death at 78. It is a shame that she did not live long enough to play more major roles such as in this film.

The director of this film was Fred Newmeyer (1888–1967), a former professional baseball player who entered films in 1913 as an extra with Universal Pictures. He collaborated on a number of Lloyd's best films from 1921 to 1925, and also worked with such actors as Richard Dix and W.C. Fields. He retired from film work in 1936.

This classic has been available on video in the past, but only in average quality format. This is a title that deserves a high quality, legitimately produced video release.

338. The Man from Beyond *Rating:* ☆½

Houdini Picture Company; ***Written and Produced by*** Harry Houdini; ***Directed by*** Burton King; ***Running Time:*** 59 minutes; ***Cast:*** HOWARD HILLARY, Harry Houdini (1874–1926); FELICE STRANGE, Nita Naldi (1897–1961)

This is one of the rare surviving films in which the famed magician Harry Houdini produced and starred. In this film, he plays a man who is brought back to life after being frozen for 100 years. He sets out on a mission to rescue the great-granddaughter of his fiancée from marrying a disreputable scoundrel.

When he tells his story, he is believed to be insane, and escapes from a mental institution, hoping to be able to convince Felice, her family, and authorities of the truth.

While this story of reincarnation sounds like it would be an interesting one, it falls far short of expectations. It moves slowly, and there is hardly any of the great stunt work that one would expect of Houdini. One sees a rather unremarkable stunt in a sequence which has Houdini wriggling out of a straitjacket to effect his escape from the mental asylum. In addition, the finale has a good rescue sequence in which Houdini braves a rushing current to Felice's runaway boat before it plummets over a waterfall. This sequence, although good, is an obviously inferior imitation of the ice floe sequence in *Way Down East* (1920).

While *The Man from Beyond* is an interesting curiosity piece just for the chance to see one of Houdini's few surviving films, it will prove disappointing to most viewers.

339. Manslaughter

Rating: ☆☆☆½

Paramount; ***Directed by*** Cecil B. DeMille; ***Adaptation by*** Jeanie MacPherson; ***From the Novel by*** Alice Duer Miller; ***Running Time:*** 100 minutes; ***Cast:*** LYDIA THORNE, Leatrice Joy (1893–1965); JIM DRUMMOND [POLICEMAN], Jack Mower (1890–1965); BOBBY DORSET, Casson Ferguson (1891–1929); STEPHEN ALBEE, John Miltern (1870–1937); DANIEL J. O'BANNON, Thomas Meighan (1879–1936); EVANS, Lois Wilson (1894–1988)

Before reviewing this film, this author was warned not to waste the effort, as *Manslaughter* was one of DeMille's worst films, and not worth bothering with. Needless to say, this film turned out to be far better than expected. Revealed are the best performances seen to date on three major silent film players—Leatrice Joy, Thomas Meighan, and Lois Wilson. To boot, the film itself wasn't bad at all.

Leatrice Joy gives an exceptional performance as Lydia Thorne, a rich heiress who lives life in the fast lane, and with her connections and money, always manages to buy her way out of trouble. She parties heavily, thinking of nothing or nobody but herself and the moment's pleasure. A friend of hers, District Attorney Daniel O'Bannon, tries to get her to slow down, but to no avail.

Lois Wilson plays Evans, who is Lydia Thorne's maid. Her son becomes ill, and has to go to California for a lifesaving operation. Evans steals some of Lydia's jewels and pawns them to get the money, as she has been brushed off every time she has tried to ask for an advance on her pay. Evans is arrested, and Lydia promises to testify in court to keep her from going to prison, but is too hung over and misses the court date. Evans is sentenced to four years.

The time comes when Lydia gets into a situation that she can't buy her way out of. She is caught speeding again, and in the process of ditching the pursuing motorcycle cop causes an accident that kills him. Her friend, Daniel O'Bannon, has even put his foot down this time, and he as prosecuting attorney sends the woman he loves to prison. Once Lydia gets to prison, she sees none other than Evans, the maid that she let go to prison by breaking her promise.

This is the very finest performance of Leatrice Joy's career. Ms. Joy actually sat in on a real trial to make herself familiar with people's actions in the type of situation she was portraying. Her delirium sequence in prison is especially powerful and moving.

Thomas Meighan as O'Bannon also gives an excellent performance as the D.A. who sends Lydia to prison, and then handles his grief by turning to alcohol and going on a downhill run just as Lydia is starting to find peace within herself.

Lois Wilson as maid Evans also gives an exceptional performance that hasn't been ade-

Thomas Meighan, leading man of *Manslaughter* (1922), an underrated DeMille classic.

quately noted by critics. She stated in interviews later in her life that working on *Manslaughter* was one of her fondest memories from her career.

340. My Wife's Relations *Rating:* ☆☆☆½

Comique/First National; ***Written/Directed by*** Buster Keaton and Eddie Cline; ***Running Time:*** 25 minutes; ***Cast:*** THE HUSBAND, Buster Keaton (1895–1966); THE WIFE, Kate Price (1872–1943); ***Supporting Cast:*** Monte Collins (1856–1929); "Wheezer" Dell; Tom Wilson (1880–1965); Joe Roberts (1870–1923)

This classic "in-laws" comedy was said to have been inspired by Buster Keaton's marriage to Natalie Talmadge (1899–1969), which lasted from 1921 to 1933.

Keaton's character is whisked off the street by the character of the pleasantly plump comedienne Kate Price, who takes him in front of the judge whose window Keaton's character has just accidentally broken. The judge, speaking no English, assumes he is to marry the couple, which he does. This is where the real fun begins.

It turns out that Keaton's new in-laws are roughnecks, who treat Keaton as substandard. The bedroom sequence with Keaton and Kate Price is hilarious, with the wife breaking a vase full of water on the husband's head as only Price can do. (Price should have been as highly renowned a comedienne as Marie Dressler [1869–1934].) The in-laws continue to treat Buster like a patsy until they discover that he has inherited a large sum of money—or so they think.

Although this is one of Keaton's more overlooked films, it is a delightful comedy. With Keaton and Price in the lead roles, there was no way it could miss the mark.

341. Nanook of the North *Rating:* ☆☆☆

Revillon Pictures/Pathé Exchange; ***Directed by*** Robert N. Flaherty; ***Running Time:*** 64 minutes

Filmed on a $50,000 budget on location in Northern Canada, *Nanook of the North*—the first feature length documentary to have a wide theatrical release—documents the life of an Eskimo family living on the outskirts of Hudson Bay. The head of household featured is Nanook, nicknamed "The Bear," who struggles against the harsh and brutal forces of nature in an effort to eke out a bare survival for himself and his large family. The film opens with a shot of Nanook rowing his kayak down the bay. Once he reaches his destination in this vessel that looks barely big enough for one person, one is shocked to see several members of his family, packed into the bottom of the kayak like sardines, emerging from below. Hunting and fishing techniques are graphically shown, and the plight of inadequate food supplies is emphasized in a scene during which Nanook is so hungry that he catches a walrus, and actually cuts a few bites on the spot and eats them raw.

While this film is a bit slow paced, and some may find it tedious to sit through, one must keep in mind that entertainment was not the underlying purpose of the film. Robert Flaherty accomplishes what he set out to do—document the harsh reality of Eskimo life as it was in the early 1920s.

In reality, Nanook ultimately lost his struggle for survival. He died from starvation shortly after *Nanook of the North* was released.

342. Nosferatu

Rating: ☆☆

Produced in Germany; ***Directed by*** F.W. Murnau; ***Screenplay by*** Henrik Golden; ***Based on the Novel, Dracula, by*** Bram Stoker; ***Photographed by*** Fritz Arno Wagner; ***Costumes and Sets by*** Albin Grau; ***Running Time:*** 79 minutes; ***Cast:*** COUNT ORLOK, Max Schreck (1879–1936); HUTTER, Gustav von Wangenheim (1895–1975); ELLEN, Greta Schroeder; HARDING [A SHIP BUILDER], G.H. Schnell (1878–1951); RUTH [HIS SISTER], Ruth Landshoff; PROFESSOR SIEVERS, Gustav Botz; KNOCK [A HOUSE AGENT], Alexander Granach (1890–1945); PROFESSOR BUHVER, John Gottowt (died 1934); CAPTAIN, Max Nemerz; FIRST SAILOR, Wolfgang Heinz; SECOND SAILOR, Albert Venohr

This film was the first screen adaptation of Bram Stoker's *Dracula*. In order to avoid paying royalties to the Bram Stoker estate, Murnau changed some character and location names. Despite the changes, he was still sued by the Stoker estate for copyright infringement, and the courts ruled in the estate's favor. In 1925, all copies of *Nosferatu* were pulled from distribution. A few copies of the film made their way into private hands, and it is because of these bootleg copies that *Nosferatu* is available for evaluation today.

***Nosferatu* (1922) featuring Max Schreck as Count Orlak.**

While this film has received consistent praise over the years, this reviewer fails to see why. Granted, Murnau did a great job in creating a horrific atmosphere, and Max Schreck's ghoulish appearance as Orloc is impressive. But, the narrative style is rather poor, and the film drags in many spots. In some parts, the story is barely coherent.

In this reviewer's opinion, *Nosferatu* is the weakest of all of the evaluated films directed by F.W. Murnau.

343. Oliver Twist

Rating: ☆☆☆½

Associated Producers/First National; ***Directed by*** Frank Lloyd; ***Produced by*** Sol Lesser; ***Screen Adaptation by*** Frank Lloyd and Harry Weil; ***From the Novel by*** Charles Dickens; ***Photographed by*** Glen MacWilliams and Robert Martin; ***Art Direction by*** Stephen Gooson; ***Costumes by*** Walter Israel; ***Running Time:*** 74 minutes; ***Cast:*** OLIVER TWIST, Jackie Coogan (1914–1984); FAGIN, Lon Chaney Sr. (1883–1930); MR. BUMBLE, James Marcus (1867–1937); MRS. CORNEY, Aggie Herring (1876–1939); NOAH CLAYPOOL, Lewis Sargent (1903–1970); CHARLOTTE, Joan Standing (1903–1979); MONKS, Carl Stockdale (1874–1953); JACK DAWKINS, Edouard Trebaol; CHARLEY BATES, Taylor Graves; BILL SIKES, George Siegmann (1882–1928); NANCY, Gladys Brockwell (1894–1929); MR. BROWNLOW, Lionel Belmore (1868–1953); MRS. BALDWIN, Florence Hale; GRIMWIG, Joseph Hazelton (1853–1936); MRS. MAYLIE, Gertrude Claire (1852–1928); ROSE, Esther Ralston (1902–1994)

This was the third major silent adaptation of *Oliver Twist*, having been preceded by a 1912 short produced by Cecil Hepworth (1874–1953), and a 1916 feature adaptation which starred Marie Doro (1882–1956). Neither of the two previous versions are accessible for evaluation, but judging from the stills of the 1916 version, Marie Doro simply does not fit the expected image of *Oliver Twist* as does Jackie Coogan, despite her prior stage success with the role.

This film features the directorial talents of Frank Lloyd (1887–1960), along with an all-star cast headed up by Coogan. Coogan is a delight in the title role of the poor orphaned boy who actually is not as poor as his half-brother, Monks, would have him believe.

In the beginning of the film, Coogan's Oliver is in one of the deplorable workhouses for orphaned children. When he dares to ask for a second serving of gruel, he is farmed out to an undertaker, whose two other employees are arrogant and nasty toward Oliver. When Oliver is pushed too far and justifiably puts Noah Claypool in his place, he is told that he will be sent back to the orphanage from which he came. Oliver runs away to London, walking the entire 75 miles over seven days. This is where he is taken in by the old scoundrel Fagin, who uses younger boys to commit robberies for him. On his first "job," Oliver is caught while the other boys escape. The victim is the kindly and rich Mr. Brownlow, who takes Oliver in as his own. All is well until Fagin has Oliver kidnapped and brought back. The rest of the film deals with how Monks and Fagin are finally brought to justice, and how Oliver finds out his real identity as wealthy heir to a fortune.

In addition to a charming and impeccable performance by Jackie Coogan as Oliver, Lon Chaney is impressive as the scoundrel Fagin. This role as Fagin was among Chaney's best, ranking right up with his costumes and performances in *The Hunchback of Notre Dame* (1923) and *The Phantom of the Opera* (1925).

Among the impressive supporting player performances in this film are those by Gladys Brockwell, George Siegmann, and Esther Ralston. Gladys Brockwell's performance as Wendy, the prostitute who sacrifices her life to free Oliver from the bondage of Fagin, is excellent. Former Griffith player George Siegmann turns in a good villain performance as Bill Sikes, Fagin's henchman who murders Wendy. Esther Ralston's role as Rose was among her earliest billed roles, done before she had really hit stardom. In addition, one will recognize Carl Stockdale in the role of Monks. Stockdale was an important character actor in a number of films for the Flying A/American Film Company in the late 1910s, and went on into the talkie era to work in a number of westerns and "B" pictures.

At least four talkie remakes of *Oliver Twist* were filmed. The first of these was the 1933 version starring Dickie Moore (born 1925). The most highly acclaimed of the talkie versions is the 1948 version which, in this reviewer's opinion, pales in comparison to this 1922 silent adaptation.

This film adaptation remains arguably the definitive version of Charles Dickens' classic, and is highly recommended. A beautiful, color tinted video version with organ score is available from Kino Video.

344. One Terrible Day

Rating: ☆☆☆½

Hal Roach/Pathé Exchange; ***Supervised by*** Charles Parrott [Charley Chase]; ***Directed by*** Robert F. McGowan, Tom McNamara; ***Story by*** Hal Roach and Tom McNamara; ***Titles by*** H.M. Walker and Tom McNamara; ***Running Time:*** 15 minutes; ***Cast:*** **"Our Gang":** Jack Davis (1914–1992); Mickey Daniels (1914–1970); Ernie "Sunshine Sammy" Morrison (1912–1989); Jackie Condon (1918–1977); Farina Hoskins (1920–1980); Peggy Cartwright (born 1912); Twins Weston and Winston Doty (1913–1934); ***Supporting Cast:*** JAMES [CHAUFFEUR], William Gillespie (1894–??); BUTLER, Charles Stevenson (1887–1943); OFFICER, Wallace Howe; CARLENE CULPEPPER, Helen Gilmore (1862–1936); ALVIRA, Clara Guiol; COOK, Ed Brandenberg; SECRETARY, Lincoln Stedman (1906–1948)

This was the fourth "Our Gang" silent filmed, and was actually the first of the series to be released to theaters. (The first film produced, entitled *Our Gang* [1922], is lost.) It opened to wide critical acclaim, and its success resulted in the *Our Gang/Little Rascals* films being produced for 22 more years. The timeless talkie episodes are still widely syndicated on cable television today, and many of the silents are generally available on video.

This was a good episode with which to introduce "Our Gang," featuring the gang on an outing at the country estate of a rich philanthropist. Havoc starts at the beginning of the trip, with the kids taking forever to get loaded into the car, as each invited kid invites their friends to come along, as well as a dog that rides on the back of the car. A tire goes flat in the middle of a busy intersection, and while the cop is trying to help change the tire, the kids are running all over the place, and the philanthropist's pet monkey squirts the cop in the eye with oil.

Once the party finally gets to the estate, the kids use a fountain as a swimming hole, and proceed to let all of the farm animals out. One especially cute sequence shows 2-year-old Farina walking into the kitchen which is swarming with ducks and geese, some of which are bigger than he. As the day finally ends, the tire goes flat yet a second time, just as the kids are leaving the farm.

At least three of the original "Our Gang" cast members got their starts in Harold Lloyd's movie shorts. These are Mickey Daniels, Peggy Cartwright, and "Sunshine Sammy" Morrison. A fourth member was Jack Davis, who was the younger brother of Lloyd's soon-to-be wife, Mildred Davis.

The Doty twins, who appeared in some of the early "Our Gang" shorts, met tragic deaths in 1934. They were killed in a catastrophic flood together at age 20. Lincoln Stedman died at age 41 in 1948, but no cause of death was listed in any of the player directories. He was the son of screen actress Myrtle Stedman.

The theme used in this film of the lovable kids wreaking havoc for the high society crowd was used in many more of their films to come.

345. The Paleface

Rating: ☆☆☆½

Comique/First National; ***Directed by*** Buster Keaton and Eddie Cline; ***Running Time:*** 20 minutes; ***Cast:*** THE PALEFACE, Buster Keaton (1895–1966); THE INDIAN CHIEF, Joe Roberts (1870–1923)

This has not been among Buster Keaton's more highly acclaimed films. Larry Edwards' biography on Keaton describes *The Paleface* as "Buster's weakest of the silent film era." Upon evaluating *The Paleface*, this reviewer concludes that if this was Keaton's weakest silent film, he simply did not do a bad picture in the 1920s. Some of his entries of the late 1910s with Roscoe Arbuckle were much weaker than *The Paleface*, which this author found thoroughly enjoyable.

The storyline of this film has a big oil company swindling an Indian tribe out of their land. The Indian chief instructs his tribe members to kill the first white man that appears on their property, which happens to be Buster's character. Buster does a number of good slapstick gags while fleeing for his life from the enraged Indians. He finally joins the Indian tribe, and leads them to stage a protest at the oil company's corporate office.

This film is memorable in that Keaton did a stunt which required him to fall 85 feet from a cliff using a blanket as a parachute. He allegedly broke bones during this stunt, adding to his status of eventually having reportedly broken every bone in his body. Another good stunt has him sliding down a steep slope and onto the top of a coconut tree.

Why this wonderful, solid comedy has been panned by critics in the past as Keaton's worst silent is inconceivable to this reviewer, who ranks *The Paleface* as one of the better comedy shorts of the silent era.

346. Pay Day

Rating: ☆☆☆

Charles Chaplin/First National; ***Directed by*** Charles Chaplin; ***Running Time:*** 22 minutes; ***Cast:*** THE HUSBAND, Charlie Chaplin (1889–1977); THE WIFE, Phyllis Allen (1861–1938); THE FOREMAN'S DAUGHTER, Edna Purviance (1894–1958)

This slapstick comedy features Chaplin as a construction worker. On his first pay day, he goes out with his drinking buddies, and gets into a variety of misadventures— much to the chagrin of his stern, domineering wife.

Pay Day was among Chaplin's best and funniest shorts. He also manages to inject some social commentary, portraying people going to the local speakeasy and drinking alcohol, although prohibition had been law for the two years prior to the making of this film.

347. The Primitive Lover

Rating: ☆☆½

First National; ***Directed by*** Sidney Franklin; ***Running Time:*** 68 minutes; ***Cast:*** PHYLLIS GRAHAM, Constance Talmadge (1900–1973); HECTOR TOMLEY, Harrison Ford (1884–1957); DONALD WALES, Kenneth Harlan (1895–1967); "ROARIN' BILL" RIVERS, Joe Roberts (1870–1923); PEDRO, Charles Stevens (1893–1964); CHIEF BLUEBOTTLE, Chief Big Tree (1865–1967); MRS. GRAHAM, Mathilde Brundage (1859–1939); JUDGE HENSEED, George Pierce; MR. GRAHAM, Frederic Vroom (1857–1942)

The Primitive Lover earns its place in movie history as one of the few extant comedies of Constance Talmadge, the sister of Norma (1897–1957) and Natalie (1899–1969). Of the Talmadge trio, it was Constance who had a flair for comedy. Her first really big break was in D.W. Griffith's *Intolerance* (1916), in which she played the mountain girl in the Babylon story. She put a bit of a comedic, mischievous spin on the role, playing it to the hilt. This role alone gives her a lasting place in motion picture history.

In *The Primitive Lover*, Talmadge plays Phyllis Grahame, who is contemplating a divorce from her husband, Hector Tomley. The movie opens with our couple on a raft, following a shipwreck. Accompanying the couple is novelist Donald Wales. Due to the short supply of food, Wales nobly sacrifices himself—concluding that two's company, but three's a crowd. Then the screen focuses on the last page of a book—revealing the prologue to have been a novel that Phyllis has been reading.

Harrison Ford, star of *The Primitive Lover* (1922).

The trouble starts when Phyllis asks her husband if he loved her enough to sacrifice his own life if they were stranded with three people, with enough food for only two. The husband tells her he wished she would stop imagining herself as the heroine of every trashy novel she reads. In this case, the novel in question had been written by Donald Wales, a novelist who had allegedly died on a safari, and to whom she was once engaged.

Matters are complicated when the dead comes back to life. Donald Wales, former and supposedly deceased fiancé of Phyllis, shows up at her parents' house alive and well. It seems that his death was faked as a publicity stunt to promote his new novel. In order to save his marriage, Hector takes Phyllis to a deserted area so that she can experience what it is really like. This film was directed by Sidney Franklin (1893–1972). Franklin codirected many films with his brother, Chester (1890–1948) from 1915 to 1918 before directing films on his own. Among the most significant films directed by

Sidney Franklin are *The Guardsman* (1931), for which Alfred Lunt was nominated for Best Actor of 1931–32, and for which his wife Lynn Fontanne (Lunt) was nominated for Best Actress, and *The Good Earth* (1937). As a producer, Sidney Franklin oversaw the productions of such films as *Waterloo Bridge* (1940), *Mrs. Miniver* (1942), and *The Yearling* (1947).

Harrison Ford's career began in 1915, and lasted through the end of the silent era. He made only one talkie, in 1932. He is perhaps best remembered for the series of bedroom comedies he starred in with Marie Prevost in the late 1920s. Ford is not in any way related to the modern day Harrison Ford who starred in the *Star Wars* movies of the 1970s and 1980s.

Kenneth Harlan was a prolific matinee idol whose career started in 1917 and lasted until 1944. His uncle, Otis Harlan (1865–1940), also starred in silent films and provided the voice of "Happy" in Walt Disney's 1937 version of *Snow White and the Seven Dwarfs*.

Charles Stevens was the grandson of the famous Apache chief, Geronimo. George Pierce was known primarily for his career in vaudeville as part of the teams of "Russell and Pierce" and "Pierce and Armstrong."

348. The Prisoner of Zenda

Rating: ☆☆☆½

Metro-Goldwyn; ***Directed by*** Rex Ingram; ***Based on the Novel by*** Anthony Hope; ***Screen Adaptation by*** Mary O'Hara; ***Photography by*** John F. Seitz; ***Film Editor:*** Grant Whytock; ***Running Time:*** 113 minutes; ***Cast:*** RUDOLF RASSENDYLL/THE PRISONER OF ZENDA, Lewis Stone (1879–1953); THE QUEEN, Alice Terry (1899–1987); ***Supporting Cast:*** Ramon Novarro (1899–1968); Robert Edeson (1868–1931); Stuart Holmes (1884–1971); Malcolm McGregor (1892–1945); Barbara LaMarr (1896–1926); Edward Connelly (1855–1928); Lois Lee; John George (1898–1968); Snitz Edwards (1862–1937)

Among the most coveted films that languished unseen in the MGM vaults for years were the early films of director Rex Ingram. In 1994, Turner Classic Movies restored three of these films and aired them with new piano scores. *The Prisoner of Zenda* (1922) aired the same night as *The Conquering Power* (1921), and *Mare Nostrum* (1925) was aired later in the year.

This was the first of four major feature film versions of Anthony Hope's classic. The story is a familiar one, with Lewis Stone playing a double role as Rudolf Rassendyll, who impersonates his cousin, the rightful ruler of a small British colony, when the cousin's brother, Grand Duke Michael, drugs him on his coronation day so that he can be crowned king instead. Needless to say, the Grand Duke is rather shocked when the "king" shows up.

Complications arise as Rassendyll falls in love with the queen, who actually likes Rassendyll better than the real husband, whom she married so that the public would tolerate him with her as his queen.

While Ramon Novarro received top billing in this film, he actually plays a supporting role as one of the king's supporters who fights for him. Lewis Stone is the real star of the film. Although he does a good job, his appearance (he looks 20 years older than his actual age of 43) just doesn't fit with the role he is playing. Ramon Novarro probably would have been better for the title role, but he was just starting to become an established name at the time the film was produced. What is really interesting about this film is that it is the only one of Barbara LaMarr's really big roles that is available outside the archives. She gives a truly wonderful performance as the girlfriend of Duke Michael, who turns on him to help free the king from his prison cell. There are some excellent close-ups of LaMarr as well.

While this silent version of *The Prisoner of Zenda* is an excellent adaptation, it was slightly outdone by the 1937 version. The 1937 version was a slightly better executed film, and featured Ronald Colman in the title role, who was more suited for the part than Lewis Stone was in the original. While the 1937 version won an Academy Award for Best Interior Decoration and was nominated for Best Score and is the definitive talkie version of this classic, this 1922 version comes in a close second, and is far superior to either the 1952 or 1979 remakes. It is interesting to note that Lewis Stone, star of this adaptation, came back 30 years later to play a small part as a cardinal in the 1952 version. It was his second to last film, made just a year before he died in 1953.

349. Robin Hood

Rating: ☆☆½

United Artists; ***Directed by*** Allan Dwan; ***Photographed by*** Arthur Edeson; ***Scenario by*** Elton Thomas; ***Scenario Editor:*** Lotta Woods; ***Art Direction by*** Wilfred Buckland; ***Costumes by*** Leisch; ***Research Director:*** Dr. Arthur Woods; ***Technical Director:*** Robert Fairbanks; ***Film Editor:*** William Nolan; ***Running Time:*** 141 minutes; ***Cast:*** EARL OF HUNTINGDON/ROBIN HOOD, Douglas Fairbanks, Sr. (1883–1939); RICHARD THE LION HEARTED, Wallace Beery (1885–1949); PRINCE JOHN, Sam DeGrasse (1875–1953); LADY MARION FITZWALTER, Enid Bennett (1893–1969); SIR GUY OF GISBOURNE, Paul Dickey (1882–1933); SHERIFF OF NOTTINGHAM, William Lowery (1885–1941); KING'S JESTER, Roy Coulsoh (1890–1944); MARION'S SERVING WOMAN, Billie Bennett (1874–1951); PRINCE JOHN'S HENCHMEN, Merriel McCormack (1893–1953) and Wilson Benge (1875–1955); FRIAR TUCK, Willard Louis; LITTLE JOHN, Alan Hale, Sr. (1892–1950); WILL SCARLETT, Maine Geary (1898 1946); ALLAN-A-DALE, Lloyd Talman

Of three possible film topics that Douglas Fairbanks was considering in 1921—*The Virginian, Monsieur Beaucaire*, and *Robin Hood*—it was *Robin Hood* that ultimately won out. Part of what helped *Robin Hood* to be the prevailing topic was that Fairbanks' brother, Robert (1880–1948), got Douglas into the sport of archery.

Budgeted at $750,000, *Robin Hood* is probably most famous for the mammoth castle set that was built for it. Most sources state that the sets for this film were as big or even bigger than the Babylon set in D.W. Griffith's *Intolerance*. Nonetheless, when *Robin Hood* was in production, the castle set was the foremost tourist attraction in Hollywood. It was actually bigger than any of the authentic 12th century European castles after which the set was modeled.

Robin Hood might have been among Fairbanks' biggest films as far as size of production, but it was not among his best. This is in part due to Allan Dwan's directorial style. Dwan may have been among the top pioneering directors, but there were few really remarkable successes among the over 50 films he directed. Those of his films that were great successes—*Wildflower* (1914), *Panthea* (1916), *Zaza* (1923), *Manhandled* (1924), and a handful of Fairbanks films—were successes that depended on the stars of the films for their vast box-office appeal. One prime example of Dwan's unremarkable directorial style is in the first sequence of the film, in which Fairbanks as Lord Huntingdon proves himself as victor in a sword duel on horseback. This sequence spends a good 13 minutes preparing for the event, which should have been done in a minute or so. Of the 16 minutes showing the preparation, battle, victory, and recognition, only a couple of minutes have any real flair to them. This plodding directorial style drags what should have been a 90 minute epic into nearly 2½ hours.

What saves the film from the abyss are its awe-inspiring sets, as well as the excellent stunt work of Fairbanks, and good character performances—especially on Wallace Beery's part as Richard the Lion Hearted, the rightful ruler of Nottingham, and with the highly dependable Fairbanks supporting actor Sam DeGrasse as the tyrannical Prince John. In addition, Enid Bennett was probably the most attractive of all of the women who ever played Lady Marion.

Among Fairbanks' impressive stunts in the film is the famous sequence in which he slides down a huge tapestry.

Despite its flaws, *Robin Hood* was a resounding box-office hit. While it is not a film totally without merit, it still doesn't hold a candle to *The Adventures of Robin Hood* (1938), the early Technicolor remake directed by Michael Curtiz and starring Errol Flynn, which remains the definitive adaptation of this adventure classic.

350. The Ropin' Fool

Rating: ☆☆☆½

Pathé; ***Directed by*** Clarence Badger; ***Running Time:*** 18 minutes; ***Cast:*** "ROPES" REILLY, Will Rogers (1879–1935); THE GIRL, Irene Rich (1891–1988); THE STRANGER, John Ince (1878–1947); THE FOREMAN, Guinn "Big Boy" Williams (1899–1962); THE MEDICINE DOCTOR, Russ Powell (1875–1950); THE SHERIFF, Bert Sprotte (1870–1949)

This is a classic two-reeler in which Will Rogers performs some of the most amazing rope tricks ever caught on film. Some of the tricks featured are throwing a "figure eight" around a horse, lassoing a rat with a piece of string, tying a knot simply by throwing a rope with one hand and dropping it, as well as lassoing circles around himself and playing jumprope. Rogers learned his initial rope tricks from a former Negro slave, and even performed at the 1894 World's Fair as a teenager. This film has historic importance as one of the first to use slow motion photography. (Some of the more complicated tricks were filmed in slow motion to dispel any possible speculation that the roping tricks had been faked.)

Although lasso competitions at modern rodeos are still popular, none of the feats seen at these rodeos can come close to matching even the simplest of the rope tricks that Will Rogers performs in this film. This is a true classic that no western buff should be without, and is available on video.

351. Shadows

Rating: ☆☆☆

Preferred Pictures/Al Lichtman; ***Directed by*** Tom Forman; ***Adapted by*** Eve Unsell and Hope Loring; ***Running Time:*** 69 minutes; ***Cast:*** DANIEL GIBBS, Walter Long (1879–1952); SYMPATHY GIBBS, Marguerite de la Motte (1902–1950); NATE SNOW, John Sainpolis (1873–1946); YEN SIN, Lon Chaney, Sr. (1883–1930); MISTA BAD BOY, Buddy Messenger (1907–1965); JOHN MALDEN, Harrison Ford (1884–1957)

This was the directorial debut of actor Tom Forman (1892–1926). Forman is not to be confused with another western cowboy star named Tom B. Forman (1891–1951). In

Will Rogers, the popular star of *The Ropin' Fool* (1922).

Shadows, Lon Chaney plays Yen Sin, a Chinese man who is shipwrecked in a small, conservative town in which he is scorned as a "heathen." He befriends minister John Malden and his wife. The situation becomes complicated when Malden is sent a letter from his wife's first husband, stating that he is not dead as was believed, but very much alive and well, thus making Sympathy Gibbs a bigamist. Another professing "Christian," Nate Snow, blackmails Malden into paying him off to keep silent about Daniel Gibbs' still being alive. An interesting twist comes at the end of the film during which the Chinese heathen, on his deathbed, forces Nate Snow to make a startling confession before witnesses.

Lon Chaney's performance as the stoop-shouldered Yen Sin is remarkable in this story, showing how racism and religious intolerance causes a village to scorn a hard-working, good-hearted man who never hurt anybody, while looking up to a white man who hides behind the Bible while doing evil deeds on the side.

Director Tom Forman committed suicide at the age of 34 with a gun in 1926, four years after *Shadows* was released. Harrison Ford gives a competent performance in the male lead role, as does Marguerite de la Motte in the lead female role. Buddy Messenger was 14 when he played the role of the fat, mischievous boy who befriends Yen Sin. Among the other films he played in were *Babes in the Woods* (1917) and *Treasure Island* (1918). Walter Long plays the role of the despicable Daniel Gibbs, whom Sympathy was forced to marry by her father before his death.

Although *Shadows* is not among Lon Chaney's more written-about films, his Chinese "heathen" is among his more memorable disguises.

352. Sodom and Gomorrah

Rating: ☆☆☆☆

SACHA Films/Germany; ***Directed by*** Michael Kertesz (Curtiz); ***Photography by*** Gustav Ucicky; ***Set Design by*** Julius Von Borsody; ***Architects:*** Hans Rolic, Stephen Wesseley; ***Produced by*** Arnold Pressburger; ***Running Time:*** 96 minutes; ***Cast:*** JACKSON HARBER, George Reimers (1870–1936); EDWARD HARBER, Walter Slezak (1902–1983); MISS MARY CONWAY, Lucy Doraine; MRS. AGATHA CONWAY, Erika Wagner; PRIEST OF CAMBRIDGE COLLEGE, Michael Varkonyi (1891–1976) [known as Victor Varconi in the United States]; HARRY LIGHTON, Kurt Ehrle

This is the earliest surviving work of director Michael Curtiz, who gained fame in America with such classics as *The Mystery of the Wax Museum* (1933), *Captain Blood* (1935), *The Adventures of Robin Hood* (1938), *Casablanca* (1942), and *Mildred Pierce* (1945). He also helmed the great underrated epic *Noah's Ark* (1929), which is reviewed elsewhere in this book, and which features many similarities to this film.

The story opens with a shot depicting chaos on the London Stock Exchange. Jackson Harber, in one move, has caused thousands of people to lose their entire fortunes. Among those hit hard with the market collapse is the Conway family. Agatha Conway is pressuring her daughter, Mary, to marry the elder Harber for his money. Harber's son, who is studying to be a minister, arrives at his father's posh estate with his tutor. He tries to talk sense into Mary, comparing her lifestyle to the biblical Sodom and Gomorrah.

This film was for many years believed to have been lost. It was rediscovered and restored as a joint project of various German and French archives.

Sodom and Gomorrah is a significant artistic accomplishment, filmed on a lavish and colossal scale. One especially good sequence takes place at the engagement party of Harber and Conway. It shows people dancing in the vast garden of the Harber estate, with the dancers twirling umbrellas that alternate between the colors of black and white. The interior sets feature art deco design.

The most impressive sequences occur in the dream sequences depicting the destruction of Sodom and Gomorrah. These sequences used thousands of extras, and mammoth sets were built to resemble the ancient temples. The sequences start with a demonstration of Pagan worship at the huge temple of Astarte, and take us through the biblical account of the destruction of Sodom and Gomorrah. A major revolt against the tyrannical queen of Astarte is depicted, with massive mob sequences that are just as impressive as those in *Intolerance* (1916), and which are quite obviously modeled after them. Once the battles are over, God destroys what is left of Sodom and Gomorrah. The scene showing Lot's wife, Leah, turned into a pillar of salt is convincing and well done.

It was on the basis of *Sodom and Gomorrah* and *Moon Over Israel* (1924) that the American studios were impressed enough with Michael Curtiz to bring him over from Europe. When one sees both *Sodom and Gomorrah* and *Noah's Ark*, many similarities between the two are present. Both interweave a modern story with a biblical story. *Sodom and Gomorrah* is the better of the two, partially because it is not hampered with the talking sequences that Warner Bros. was forced to add to *Noah's Ark*.

Until two years ago, this film was available in the United States only with French or German titles. This reviewer asked the French Honor Society of Pensacola (Fla.) High School to take on the translation as a class project. Video dealer Peter Kavel put new English titles on the film once the translation was completed, thus making an English version of this film widely available for the first time in over 70 years.

Of the foreign silent epics, this is among the most impressive.

353. Tess of the Storm Country *Rating: ☆☆☆☆*

United Artists; ***Directed by*** John S. Robertson; ***Photographed by*** Charles Rosher and Paul Eagler; ***Scenario by*** Elmer Harris; ***From a Novel by*** Grace Miller White; ***Running Time:*** 137 minutes; ***Cast:*** TESSIBEL SKINNER, Mary Pickford (1892–1979); FREDERICK GRAVES, Lloyd Hughes (1897–1958); TEOLA GRAVES, Gloria Hope (1899–1976); BEN LETTS, Jean Hersholt (1886–1956)

Tess of the Storm Country was the only film that Mary Pickford ever remade. Her first version was released in 1914, and was among the first and most successful films she made under contract to Paramount. In the opening titles of this remake, Pickford states that the "Tess" character was her very favorite of all the roles she had played, and that she desired to take advantage of the improved conditions of motion picture production to remake it, at the request of her fans. The original film was directed by Edwin S. Porter, and was impressive enough that it was included in the 1980 book *Fifty Great American Silent Films, 1912–1920*. This remake, only recently made available for evaluation on video, is also excellent, and is acclaimed by historians who have seen both versions as far superior to the original. It runs over two hours, twice as long as the original.

In this film, Pickford plays Tessibel Skinner, the daughter of a poor family of squat-

Tess of the Storm Country (1922).

ters and fishermen, whose shacks are at the base of the wealthy estate of one Elias Graves. The elder Graves finds the squatters repulsive, and is looking for a way to drive them off the property. He has a son named Frederick Graves, who is not a snob like his father, and a daughter named Teola. Frederick befriends Tess and her father, "Daddy" Skinner. Teola is being courted by Dan Jordan, of whom her father disapproves. In order to make points with the elder Graves, Jordan relentlessly tries to drive the squatters out of the area. When he tries to keep Daddy Skinner from using his fishing net, he is shot and killed by Ben Letts, but Tess' father is wrongly accused of the crime. Things really get complicated for Teola Graves, who was made pregnant by Jordan before he died. Fearing discovery of the baby by her judgmental father, Teola asks Tess to keep the baby for her. When Frederick returns to see Tess, he assumes that the baby is hers. So, on top of an erroneous murder conviction pinned on her father, Tess is falsely accused of being an unwed mother. The ultimate insult is when it is falsely stated that the father was Ben Letts, the revolting villain of the story.

The plot of this movie is very intriguing, and since it deals with the issue of conception of a child before marriage, was controversial for its time. Its message is a strong one, showing examples of one household in which traditional values are preached, but not practiced, and the other household in which these morals are practiced, but not preached.

In addition to the capable direction by John S. Robertson (1878–1964) and superior performance by Pickford, this version of *Tess of the Storm Country* has a fine supporting cast. Lloyd Hughes, who plays the male lead as Frederick Graves, was in many important films of the silent era, but for some reason was never able to attain the superstar status of leading men like Ramon Novarro, Rudolph Valentino, and John Gilbert. Gloria Hope, who plays the sister of Hughes' character, was in reality Mrs. Lloyd Hughes. *Tess of the Storm Country* was among Hope's last films, as she curtailed her film work once she and Hughes were married. Some of her other important roles were in D.W. Griffith's lost silent feature, *The Great Love* (1918), and in Universal Pictures' 1919 version of *The Outcasts of Poker Flat*. Jean Hersholt turns in a fine performance as the unredeemable villain, Ben Letts. This role was among Hersholt's first important parts, just after a supporting role in *The Four Horsemen of the Apocalypse* (1921).

Of all of the Mary Pickford silents currently available for evaluation, this is one of the favorites that stands out from the rest.

354. Toll of the Sea

Rating: ☆☆½

Technicolor/Metro; ***Directed by*** Chester M. Franklin; ***Story by*** Frances Marion; ***Photography by*** J.A. Ball; ***Running Time of Surviving Footage:*** 41 minutes; ***Cast:*** LOTUS FLOWER, Anna May Wong (1905–1961); ALLEN CARVER, Kenneth Harlan (1895–1967); BARBARA CARVER, Beatrice Bentley; LITTLE ALLEN, Baby Moran; GOSSIP, Etta Lee (1906–1956); GOSSIP, Ming Young

This was the first major multi-reel motion picture to be filmed entirely in the two-strip Technicolor process. Originally, the film was about an hour long, but some footage was edited from some of the later release prints. In addition, when *Toll of the Sea* was procured for restoration, it was missing the last few minutes. So, film historian and preservationist Robert Gitt took an original, antique two-strip Technicolor camera, shot some scenes on the beach and some new titles, and restored the ending to a status close to the original.

As an adaptation of the opera *Madama Butterfly*, *Toll of the Sea* stars Anna May Wong as a naive Chinese girl who meets Allen Carver, a traveling military American, has a common law marriage with him, and gives birth to his son. While Carver intended to legally marry Lotus Flower and take her with him on his next cruise, he decides after being ridiculed by his fellow shipmates to leave her behind, promising to come back.

Lotus Flower waits in vain for a few years, with no word, although trying to keep up appearances in the face of other women who had been abandoned by their "husbands," and who jeer, "I told you so!"

Carver, at the insistence of his new white American wife, finally gets around to coming back to China to tell Lotus Flower that he is not coming back to marry her. Lotus Flower gives custody of their son to Carver's new wife, after which she commits suicide by drowning herself in the ocean.

Unlike some of the later silent Technicolor features which had more subtle color to look more reserved, this film exploited the Technicolor process to the hilt. Beautiful Chinese flower gardens with bright and varied colors are featured. A three-color beach ball is shown, and there is also a scene in which a black and white photograph is shown to emphasize the contrast between the color and the black and white.

Director Chester M. Franklin (1890–1954) started out his career as a cartoonist with the Sennett Company in the mid–1910s before directing films with his more famous

Anna May Wong, star of *Toll of the Sea* (1922), the first multi-reel Technicolor film to receive a wide theatrical release.

brother Sidney (1893–1972). In 1917, he was drafted into World War I, after which he began his solo directing career in 1921. His 22-year-old wife, Ruth Darling (1896–1918), who had played a bit part in D.W. Griffith's *Intolerance* (1916), was killed in a tragic car accident in 1918.

This is Anna May Wong's fourth film, and the earliest of her films known to survive. She was only 17 when she made *Toll of the Sea*, which proved to be the role that was her big break.

Kenneth Harlan as leading man was competent, but not extraordinary. Unfortunately, no further information could be found on the supporting cast members.

This is a title that is widely available in the public domain video market, and is worth taking the time to see for the early Technicolor, even if it isn't a particularly great film in itself.

355. The Trap

Rating: ☆☆☆½

Goldwyn Pictures; ***Directed by*** Robert Thornby; ***Screenplay by*** Lon Chaney, Sr., Lucien Hubbard, Irving Thalberg, Robert Thornby; ***Running Time:*** 45 minutes; ***Cast:*** GASPARD, Lon Chaney, Sr. (1883–1930); BENSON, Alan Hale, Sr. (1892–1950); THALIE, Dagmar Godowsky (1896–1975); THE BOY, Stanley Goethals; THE TEACHER, Irene Rich (1891–1988); THE FACTOR, Spottiswoode Aitken (1868–1933); THE PRIEST, Herbert Standing (1884–1955); POLICE SERGEANT, Frank Campeau (1864–1943)

The Trap is one of the rare surviving examples of Lon Chaney's work for the Goldwyn Pictures Company. It is historically significant as the first Chaney vehicle to use the billing "man of a thousand faces" in its promotional literature.

In this production, Chaney plays Gaspard, a hard-working but illiterate man who has been legally cheated out of his ownership of a prosperous mine by swindler Benson. Once Gaspard no longer has title to the mine, his girlfriend, Thalie, marries scoundrel Benson, which sets the good-natured Gaspard on the war path for revenge. He frames Benson for an attempted murder, resulting in a long prison sentence, during which Gaspard gets custody of the son of his adversary and former sweetheart. Gaspard grows to become attached to the boy, and fears losing him when he learns that Benson is about to be released from prison. He sets a trap for Benson, intending for him to be attacked by a wolf upon his return. The plan goes awry when the boy is headed into the trap intended for his father.

Chaney's role in *The Trap* provided an excellent showcase for his talents, and the formula used in this film set a pattern that would be prevalent in a number of his future collaborations with Tod Browning.

In addition to Chaney, Alan Hale gives the best performance of any of his films evaluated. He is most impressive as the conniving Benson, whom audience members will agree deserves whatever bad karma he gets from his misdeeds. Irene Rich also provides a charming presence as the school teacher who encourages Gaspard to learn how to read. Dagmar Godowsky, who was known for "vamp" roles, plays Gaspard's meandering sweetheart in one of her few extant films.

Director Robert Thornby (1888–1953) showed promise with his work on *The Trap*, and should have had a more prominent place in motion picture history than he did.

356. Witchcraft Through the Ages [a.k.a. *Haxan*]

Rating: ☆☆☆

Svensk Filmindustri/Sweden; ***Written and Directed by*** Benjamin Christensen; ***Photography by*** Johann Ankerstjerne; ***Art Direction by*** Richard Louw; ***Running Time of Original Release:*** 94 minutes; ***Running Time of 1966 Narrated Version Evaluated:*** 76 minutes; ***Cast:*** SATAN, Benjamin Christensen (1879–1959); THE WITCH, Maren Pedersen; FAT MONK, Oscar Stribolt; THE NUN, Clara Pontoppidan; THE KLEPTOMANIAC, Tora Teje (1893–1973); THE YOUNG MONK, Elith Pio; CHIEF INQUISITOR, Johs Andersen; ***Supporting Cast:*** Karen Winther; Poul Reumert; Astrid Holm; Alice O'Fredericks; Frederick Christensen; Elizabeth Christensen

This was the third film directed by Benjamin Christensen, and the major success that got the critics to take notice of him. It has become, in recent years, a cult classic, with many referring to it as the weirdest and most bizarre film of all time. In 1966, a new reissue was done with narration by author William Burroughs. This is the version that was evaluated for this book, although the original silent version does still exist, and is available from Grapevine Video.

In this semidocumentary, director Christensen presents religious hypocrisy in a most unflattering light, showing the persecution of witchcraft throughout various times in human history. The first segment shows engravings and illustrations from the middle ages, picturing how demons in hell were tortured and punished, and witches casting spells to yield cows milkless, cause shoes to be painful for enemies, and the ritual of witches consummating their relationship with Satan by kissing his derriere.

The second segment is where the actual film depiction begins, by showing witches as they make brew from a corpse from the gallows, as well as frogs, snakes, and cat excrement. This mixture makes a love potion designed to make a monk fall in love with the first woman he sees upon drinking it. On the night of the witch's coven, a witch is shown to cast a spell on an outsider which makes him unable to close his mouth.

The film progresses to Satan, and the many different forms of seduction he takes. Director Christensen himself plays the leering, tongue-wagging devil. One scene shows Satan seducing an old, poor woman by dropping coins on her as she sleeps, and then having the coins fly up out of her reach. This is among the impressive special effects sequences contained in the film.

After the depiction of Satan and his disciples as believed to be by those who lived during the Middle Ages, the film depicts the horrors of those persecuted for witchcraft under the Spanish Inquisition. It shows how the accusations come about, the trials, as well as the torture sessions designed to force the accused to confess and name names.

Witchcraft is then portrayed in a modern setting, showing how women affected with kleptomania and sleepwalking are dealt with. It shows the poor ones ending up in an asylum, and the rich going to an elaborate sanitarium where they have therapeutic showers.

There are many graphic scenes depicting nudity, morbidity, and brutality. These graphic scenes resulted in the film being banned in many countries for years. The film offended many Catholics with its unflattering portrayal of that religion, as well as its scenes showing nuns engaged in a number of sacrilegious and immoral acts.

Because of the special effects and striking visual impact, director Christensen was awarded a contract with UFA Studios in Germany, and then was recruited by MGM in Hollywood, where he remained until 1929 before going to Denmark, where his career continued in sound films until 1939.

Witchcraft Through the Ages remains an interesting oddity, but its graphic nature still might offend some, and is not recommended for conservative or younger viewers.

1923

357. Adam and Eva

Rating: N/A

Cosmopolitan/Paramount; ***Directed by*** Robert G. Vignola; ***Running Time of Surviving Footage:*** 12 minutes; ***Cast:*** EVA KING, Marion Davies (1897–1961); ADAM SMITH, T. Roy Barnes (1880–1937)

This is one of the lost films (only a couple of fragments survive) of Marion Davies that was distributed through Paramount Pictures. Davies plays Eva, the daughter of a wealthy father, James King, who owns the King Rubber Company. T. Roy Barnes plays Adam Smith, who is the company's South American representative, dreading to go back to the loneliness. He comments on King's delightful family, and King tells him if he thinks his family so wonderful, they should trade places.

King leaves Adam in charge of his family, with a modest monthly allowance while he takes his place in South America.

The missing footage had Adam telling the family that their father has lost everything and is ruined, and he makes them think they have to move out of their Long Island mansion and to a country farm, where he puts them to work. Once the family is brought down to earth, the father returns, and Adam reveals that the whole story was a fake. Although Eva is at first furious, she and Adam reconcile and live happily ever after.

It is regretful that this film is for the most part lost, as the surviving footage and stills indicate that it was a delightful comedy. What is left of the film gives only a titillating taste of the complete film, with the first few minutes and some of the last few minutes being all that is intact.

358. Anna Christie

Rating: ☆☆☆

Thomas H. Ince/First National; ***Directed by*** John Griffith Wray; ***From the Play by*** Eugene O'Neill; ***Adapted to the Screen by*** Bradley King; ***Photographed by*** Henry Sharp; ***Running***

Time: 94 minutes; *Cast:* ANNA CHRISTIE, Blanche Sweet (1896–1986); MAT BURKE, William Russell (1886–1929); CHRIS CHISTOPHERSON, George F. Marion, Sr. (1860–1945); MARTHY, Eugenie Besserer (1868–1934); ***Supporting Cast:*** Ralph Yearsley (1896–1928); Chester Conklin (1880–1959); George Siegmann (1882–1928); Victor Potel (1889–1947); Fred Kohler (1888–1938)

This was the first film adaptation of Eugene O'Neill's highly popular and successful play, as well as the only film adaptation of any of O'Neill's work that he personally saw and approved of. In addition, it contains the best surviving work of three of the players who appeared in it—Blanche Sweet, William Russell, and Eugenie Besserer.

For many years, this film was believed to have been lost. Blanche Sweet, the leading star, personally helped to recover a print that turned up in a foreign archive. She also assisted in translating the Russian titles into English.

In this film, Sweet plays the abandoned daughter of a ship captain who is reunited with her father for the first time since childhood. Eugenie Besserer plays Marthy, the town drunk who is her father's current girlfriend.

Anna goes to sea with her father, and falls in love with a seaman named Mat Burke. Her father disapproves, as he does not want her to marry someone who would be like he was. Finally, she tells both men the truth about what her life as a prostitute had been like. This revelation of having been a prostitute sends Burke into a rage, but they all eventually reconcile.

This film was among Blanche Sweet's greatest successes after leaving D.W. Griffith's company in 1914, and is by far her best surviving work. If the Academy Awards had been around in 1923, she would likely have been nominated for Best Actress. She had been considered to play the role again in MGM's 1930 remake, but the role ended up going to Greta Garbo as her first talking picture.

William Russell gives a fine performance as Mat Burke in his best surviving film. His only other surviving work includes *Star of Bethlehem* (1912), a Thanhouser production in which his role was minor; fragments of *The Blue Eagle* (1926); and a couple of silent westerns. Russell had been a good friend and roommate of William Desmond Taylor. His life was cut short by pneumonia when he was only 42 years old in 1929.

Eugenie Besserer is excellent as the character of Marthy, and this is the best work of the films of hers available for evaluation. Marie Dressler played this role in the 1930 remake.

Chris Christopherson was played by George F. Marion, Sr., who would be the only cast member of this original version to play the same role again in the 1930 version. He was a major producer on Broadway in addition to his film work. His son, George F. Marion, Jr. (1899–1968) wrote titles for films such as *Irene* (1925), *It* (1927), *Mantrap* (1926), *The Eagle* (1925), and *Son of the Sheik* (1926).

It is extremely fortunate that the foreign archives saved this film, and that Blanche Sweet took the initiative to recover it and assist in its English restoration. Considering Eugene O'Neill's own opinion of this adaptation, it is the definitive film version of the play, and highly recommended.

359. Captain January

Rating: ☆☆☆½

Principal/Universal; ***Directed by*** Eddie Cline; ***Based on the Story by*** Laura E. Richards; ***Screen-***

play by Eve Unsell and John Grey; ***Photographed by*** Glen MacWilliams; ***Running Time:*** 62 minutes; ***Cast:*** CAPTAIN JANUARY, "Baby Peggy" Montgomery (born 1918); DADDY JUDKINS, Hobart Bosworth (1867–1943); THE AUNT, Irene Rich (1891–1988); ***Supporting Cast:*** Lincoln Stedman (1906–1948); Harry T. Morey (1873–1946); Barbara Tennant (1892–??); John Merkyl (1885–1954); Emmett King (1865–1953)

For the first time since the 1920s, it is once again possible to see the complete version of Baby Peggy's original silent version of *Captain January*. Jack Hardy of Grapevine Video painstakingly accomplished a restoration project which entailed putting together a complete copy from two different existing prints. The print of the complete version was missing some of the introductory titles. The other print was a truncated version, which had the original intro titles intact. The best elements from each of these prints were used for a restored video version.

The story of *Captain January* is a charming one. Baby Peggy plays a little girl who is orphaned when her parents are killed in a shipwreck. She is washed ashore in a trunk, and adopted by Jeremiah Judkins, an elderly, kindly lighthouse keeper. "Daddy Judkins" names the child "Captain January," teaching her his trade as a lighthouse keeper and boat navigator. In addition, he teaches her from the Bible, Shakespeare, and the dictionary. They become very close as father and adopted daughter. They work together, play together, and plan together, taking care of each other. For extra money, they fish for lobsters to save money toward their dream of one day sailing the seven seas together.

All is well for the first five years—until busybody meddlers from the nearby town of Fair Harbor try to separate them, claiming that the kindly Mr. Judkins is not qualified to care for a child properly. This effort is instigated by George Maxwell, a politician who is an old enemy of Judkins. The kindly minister Elliott staves off the effort to have Captain January placed in an orphanage, but her biological aunt and uncle find her. Judkins' failing health convinces him to agree to give the orphaned child up, although he loves her as his own and is heartbroken. Captain January runs away from her aunt and uncle's home, which leads into the resolution of the story.

Baby Peggy, leading star of *Captain January* (1923), doing an imitation of Pola Negri in an earlier film parody.

The director of *Captain January* was Eddie Cline (1892–1961), who directed several of Buster Keaton's early silents, as well as many W.C. Fields talkies. The excellent direction of Cline is complemented by a fabulous cast headed up by Baby Peggy in the title role. Hobart Bosworth was an ideal choice for the role of Jeremiah Judkins.

One of the attributes that made the Charlie Chaplin films so popular was

Chaplin's ability to make a person laugh one minute, and cry the next. In this respect, Chaplin has nothing over Baby Peggy, who is able to perform the same feat without resorting to some of the crudeness which was so prevalent in the Chaplin comedies.

A prime example of Baby Peggy's comedic talent in this film is a sequence during which her dog and pelican are fighting, and she shakes her finger at both animals, chastising them for their inability to love one another. Baby Peggy pulls off this sequence in a way that cannot possibly be imitated as effectively by any other star in Hollywood history—child or adult. The insight and intelligence demonstrated by the then 4-year-old Baby Peggy are phenomenal. It is no surprise that she grew up to be one of the world's most highly acclaimed historians of western Americana and early Hollywood history.

Captain January is wholesome entertainment that can be enjoyed by the whole family.

360. The Covered Wagon

Rating: ☆½

Paramount; ***Directed by*** James Cruze; ***Adaptation by*** Jack Cunningham; ***From the Novel by*** Emerson Hough; ***Photographed by*** Karl Brown; ***Running Time:*** 97 minutes; ***Cast:*** WILL BANION, J. Warren Kerrigan (1879–1947); MOLLY WINGATE, Lois Wilson (1897–1988); SAM WOODHULL, Alan Hale, Sr. (1892–1950); JACKSON, Ernest Torrence (1878–1933); JIM BRIDGES, Tully Marshall (1864–1943); MRS. WINGATE, Ethel Wales (1878–1952); MR. WINGATE, Charles Ogle (1865–1940); DUNSTON, Guy Oliver (1878–1932); JED WINGATE, Johnny Fox

Started as a minor programmer western, *The Covered Wagon* was expanded during the course of production by director James Cruze (1884–1942), who turned it into the first high budget western epic. The western genre, which had been beginning to lose popularity, was provided a boost by the release of this film. In addition, the film was James Cruze's first great success as a director, and is the film for which he is most widely remembered. *The Covered Wagon* also proved to be the big break that got actress Lois Wilson noticed by the public.

For *The Covered Wagon*, over 3,000 extras were used. The Conestoga wagons were authentic originals from the time period portrayed, as were many of the other props.

The story of the film takes place in 1848, with a caravan of people from Kansas City and other parts of the Midwest traveling westward to start pioneer

Lois Wilson, female lead of *The Covered Wagon* (1923), the film that provided her first big break.

settlements in Oregon. The film is a semidocumentary portraying the hardships faced during these pioneering trips, the rivalries within the members of the caravan, and the Indians' efforts to stop the pioneering settlers from invading what they felt was rightfully their territory.

Despite *The Covered Wagon*'s stellar cast and high past acclaim, the film when reviewed today falls far short of expectations. This is in part due to the stultifying directorial style of James Cruze. The sequence showing the pioneers dealing with the obstacle of a flooded river was well done, but the snowstorm sequences and Indian attack, which had the potential to be key sequences in the film, are far too downplayed. If this had been a film directed by someone like Maurice Tourneur or D.W. Griffith, the Indian sequences would have been spectacular, and focused in the middle of the action rather than giving a distant view for most of the sequence's all-too-short duration. Even Fred Niblo had sense enough to turn over the big pirate attack sequence in *Ben-Hur* (1927) to director B. Reeves Eason, who specialized in action sequences.

The much-hyped snow sequence is a big disappointment. It does not even look like snow is on the ground—just a few snowflakes flying around in the air. When this reviewer read about this snow sequence, what was expected was something like the blizzard scene in Griffith's *Way Down East* (1920) or in Clarence Brown's masterful epic, *The Trail of '98* (1929).

Despite James Cruze's plodding directorial style, the film might have been more appealing if it had been engraced with the charm of Mary Miles Minter (1902–1984), who had been first choice for the role of Molly Wingate. This is not to say that there was anything wrong with Lois Wilson's performance in the part, but Minter had a certain charm about her that was inimitable. While it has been erroneously stated (even by this author) in the past that Minter's mother, Charlotte Shelby, vetoed the role because it was a western, this cannot possibly be the case, as two of Minter's last three films were westerns. It is more likely that Shelby objected to Minter playing the role because it had originally been intended to be simply a routine programmer, and she had no idea at the time of the epic scale by which *The Covered Wagon* would be filmed.

While it is nice to have *The Covered Wagon* on video, the film is extremely disappointing and vastly overrated. If Paramount Home Video was going to provide only a limited number of its silents for the video market, they would have done a far greater service by releasing Herbert Brenon's *A Kiss for Cinderella* (1925) with Betty Bronson instead of *The Covered Wagon*, which is a classic bore.

361. The Extra Girl

Rating: ☆☆☆

Mack Sennett Productions/Associated Exhibitors; ***Directed by*** F. Richard Jones; ***Running Time:*** 69 minutes; ***Cast:*** SUE GRAHAM, Mabel Normand (1892–1930); DAVE GIDDINGS, Ralph Graves (1900–1977); PA GRAHAM, George Nichols (1864–1927); AARON APPLEJOHN, Vernon Dent (1895–1963); MA GRAHAM, Anna Hernandez (1867–1945); T. PHILLIP HACKETT, Ramsey Wallace; HIMSELF, William Desmond (1878–1949); ***Supporting Cast:*** Charlotte Mineau; Elsie Tarron (1903–1990); Charles K. French (1860–1952); Mary Mason (1911–1980); Max Davidson (1875–1950); Louise Carver (1868–1956); Carl Stockdale (1874–1953); Harry Gribbon (1885–1961); Billy Bevan (1887–1957); André de Beranger (1895–1973)

This was Mabel Normand's last feature length film. While it was completed in

Mabel Normand, star of *The Extra Girl* (1923).

1922, Mack Sennett delayed its release until late 1923, to give the William Desmond Taylor scandal time to blow over. The strategy paid off, and *The Extra Girl* had good box-office receipts in the United States, and was a sensation abroad, despite mixed critical reviews.

In this film, Mabel plays Sue Graham, a girl who tries to make it in Hollywood. She ends up working in the costume department. She is given a screen test, but everything goes wrong that possibly can, and she bombs. Meanwhile, her parents have entrusted their life savings to a swindler, and it is Sue's longtime beau Dave Giddings from back east who saves the day.

While *The Extra Girl* as a whole was only a fair to good film, it is famous for the lion sequence, which provided Mabel's best moments ever on screen. In this sequence, Mabel is walking what she thinks is a dog. Pandemonium occurs when she figures out that she actually is walking a lion, and the lion chases her and the rest of the crew all over the studio. She ends up being driven into a closet, trying to fight the lion off with a feather duster. It is this classic sequence that brings the film up to a good, solid three-star rating.

It was during the filming of this lion sequence that Mabel was injured. The first take with the lion had gone fine, but director Jones ordered a retake. He stumbled and frightened the lion, causing it to spring at Mabel. To top things off, Jones went at the lion with a pitchfork, but accidentally stabbed Mabel with it instead.

Normand looks tired and a bit gaunt in this film, although not as bad as she looked in *What Happened to Rosa?* (1921). She was under a lot of stress at the time, having just completed a long recovery from a broken collarbone that resulted from a horse riding accident in 1922. She became friends with a male hospital patient, whose wife found out that they were friends, filed for divorce, and named Mabel as a correspondent. This incident came on the heels of the Taylor scandal. Nonetheless, Normand's career was back on the right track with *The Extra Girl*, and she would have been back on top if it hadn't been for her chauffeur dragging her name into yet another scandal when he shot Courtland Dines at a party in 1923. Normand did not star in another film until 1926, when Hal Roach hired her to do a series of shorts.

362. The Hunchback of Notre Dame

Rating: ★★★★

Universal; ***Directed by*** Wallace Worsley; ***Adaptation by*** Perley Poore Sheehan; ***Scenario by***

Edward T. Lowe, Jr.; ***Based on*** Victor Hugo's masterpiece; ***Photography by*** Robert Newhard; ***Art Direction by*** E.E. Sheeley and Sidney Ullman; ***Running Time:*** 103 minutes; ***Cast:*** QUASIMODO, Lon Chaney, Sr. (1883–1930); ESMERALDA, Patsy Ruth Miller (1904–1995); PHOEBUS, Norman Kerry (1889–1956); CLOPIN, Ernest Torrence (1878–1933); MADAM DE GONDELAURIER, Kate Lester (1857–1924); JEHAN, Brandon Hurst (1866–1947); GRINGOIRE, Raymond Hatton (1887–1971); LOUIS XI, Tully Marshall (1864–1943); DOM CLAUDE, Nigel de Brulier (1877–1948); KING'S CHAMBERLAIN, Edwin Wallock (1877–1951); JUSTICE OF THE COURT, John Cossar (1858–1935); MONSIEUR NEUFCHATEL, Harry L. Van Meter (1871–1956); GODULE [ESMERALDA'S MOTHER], Gladys Brockwell (1894–1929); MARIE, Eulalie Jensen (1884–1952); FLEUR DE LYS, Winifred Bryson (1892–1987); MONSIEUR LE TORTERU, Nick de Ruiz; CHARMOLA'S ASSISTANT, W. Ray Meyers; JOSEPHUS, William Parke, Sr. (1873–1941)

Filmed on a budget of over $1 million, this was one of the grandest and most expensive productions made by Universal Pictures in the 1920s. The exterior of France's mighty Notre Dame cathedral were reconstructed at full size, as were many entire Parisian streets. With adjustments for inflation, it is said that to remake *Hunchback* exactly as this original was made would cost over $80 million.

While *Orphans of the Storm* (1921), a comparable epic set in France, was clearly associated with its director, D.W. Griffith, *Hunchback* was clearly an actor's film. Lon Chaney, Sr., carries the entire film, and carries it well. Director Wallace Worsley, Sr. (1878–1944), previously worked with Chaney on *The Penalty* (1920) at Sam Goldwyn's Company, and these two collaborations are, as far as can be determined, Worsley's only surviving work. It is reported that William Wellman (1896–1975) worked as an assistant director of the climactic mob finale.

To create his gruesome illusion as Quasimodo, the hunchback, Chaney had a 70-pound harness strapped to his back, which was so heavy that it was impossible for him to stand upright with it on. He was only supposed to wear the harness for 15 minutes at a time, but he often went over that time if he was involved in the middle of a scene that was going well. On top of all of this, he wore a hot, uncomfortable rubber suit with thick hair glued onto it. He deformed his face using mortician's wax, as well as a painful device to hold his mouth open. Chaney himself was solely responsible for his own makeup, demonstrating that not only was he among the greatest actors in history, but also possibly the greatest makeup artist who ever lived. Chaney himself wrote the entries for makeup in *Encyclopedia Britannica*.

While *The Miracle Man* (1919) brought Chaney to a prominent status as an actor, it was his role in *Hunchback* that catapulted him to superstar status. Patsy Ruth Miller's part of Esmeralda was her first really big role, and remains the role for which she is most remembered. She gives an excellent performance as the gypsy dancer who is terrified of Quasimodo on first glance, but then comes to understand and feel sorry for him as a tortured human being with the same emotions as anybody else.

Among the impressive supporting performances are those of Ernest Torrence and Gladys Brockwell. Torrence plays Clopin, the leader of the peasants who is planning a revolution against the aristocrats, and who is insanely jealous of Esmeralda's love for aristocrat Phoebus, well portrayed by Norman Kerry in one of his more outstanding roles. Gladys Brockwell gives a highly intense performance as the poor peasant who seeks vengeance on the gypsies who kidnapped her baby years before, directing her anger at

Esmeralda until she figures out, just before she collapses and dies, that she is in fact her kidnapped daughter. Brockwell is, in this reviewer's opinion, among the best character or supporting actresses of the 1920s.

As many times as this film has been remade, none of the remakes holds a candle to this original. Charles Laughton (1899–1962) came closest with his 1939 portrayal. Some critics have rated Laughton's version as superior to Chaney's, but this reviewer considers the 1923 version as the definitive one.

363. Little Old New York

Rating: ☆☆☆

Cosmopolitan/Goldwyn; ***Directed by*** Sidney Olcott; ***Running Time:*** 106 minutes; ***Cast:*** PATRICIA O'DAY, Marion Davies (1897–1961); LARRY DELAVAN, Harrison Ford (1884–1957); ROBERT FULTON, Courtenay Foote (died 1925); WASHINGTON IRVING, Mahlon Hamilton (1880–1960); CORNELIUS VANDERBILT, Sam Hardy (1883–1935); JOHN JACOB ASTOR, Andrew Dillon (1883–1934); HENRY BREVOORT, George Barrand; FITZ GREENE HALLOCK, Norval Keedwell; PHILLIP SCHUYLER, Riley Hatch (1862–1925); REILLY, Charles Kennedy (1871–1950); CHANCELLOR LIVINGSTON, Thomas Findlay (1873–1941); DELMONICO, Charles Judels (1882–1969); BULLY BOY BREWSTER, Harry Watson (1876–1930); BUNNY, Spencer Charters (1875–1943); HOBOKEN TERROR, Louis Wolheim (1880–1931); JOHN O'DAY, J.W. Kerrigan (1884–1964); PATRICK O'DAY, Stephen Carr (1906–1986); MRS. SCHUYLER, Marie R. Burke; BETTY SCHUYLER, Mary Kennedy; RACHEL BREWSTER, Elizabeth Murray (1871–1946); ARIANA DE PUYSTER, Gypsy O'Brien

Little Old New York is among Marion Davies' early comedy efforts with the Cosmopolitan Film Company. In the beginning of the film, one can see Marion Davies as a poor Irish woman, with beautiful blonde curls surrounding her stunningly gorgeous facial features. Her brother, Patrick O'Day, has just been named sole heir of their deceased uncle's vast fortune, but must travel to New York in America by a certain time to claim the inheritance. Upon the ship's arrival in New York, one sees Marion's character with bobbed hair dressed as a boy, with her father in tow. Patrick O'Day is not among them, and Marion's character assumes his identity. (In the early 1920s, many female actresses played "tomboy" roles—including Mary Pickford, Olive Thomas, Dorothy Devore, etc. Marion does a fabulous job in this particular role.)

The new "Pat" falls in love with the cousin who should have inherited his father's estate had "Patrick O'Day" been unable to claim his inheritance. The story is set in the late 1790s, and it is Marion's character of Pat who generously guarantees the money for her cousin's share in Robert Fulton's then-experimental steamboat. Her cousin's fiancée and she clash, and Marion is absolutely hilarious with her pantomime of various facial expressions, as well as wisecracks aimed at the fiancée.

Davies carries the entire film, and demonstrates very well that she was to comedy what Lillian Gish was to drama. It is really unfortunate that William Randolph Hearst steered Davies away from comedy and into drama. Based on the few silent Davies comedies available for viewing, it is obvious that witty and pantomimic comedy was her true talent. Virtually all, if not all, of the Davies comedies are preserved in archives and in existence, but all but a precious few are inaccessible to the public.

Among the more hilarious sequences in this film is when Pat plays the harp and sings, deliberately trying to drown out the singing and piano playing of her cousin's fiancée. In addition, it is amusing to see her making faces behind the fiancée's back at a social gathering. Nobody can pull off these types of facial expressions like Marion Davies.

Although this film starts out slow, it gets really good once the basis for the story is developed. It is a delightful, entertaining film that fortunately is widely available on video. Highly recommended.

364. Mud and Sand

Rating: ☆☆☆½

Amalgamated/Metro; ***Directed by*** Gil Pratt; ***Photography by*** Irving Ries; ***Running Time:*** 26 minutes; ***Cast:*** RHUBARB VASELINE, Stan Laurel (1890–1965)

By the early 1920s, comedy parodies of many of the most successful big pictures were commonplace. A great many of these parodies are unfortunately lost, but fortunately, *Mud and Sand*, a hilarious parody on Valentino's *Blood and Sand* (1922) is among the survivors.

Stan Laurel plays Rhubarb Vaseline, the bullfighter who starts in amateur shows with his friend Sapo, and whose parents complain that all they get out of him is bull. Rhubarb's mother starts to change her attitude when she hears the chinging of the change in the purse he has won.

Rhubarb's childhood sweetheart is renamed sweet Caramel in this parody, and the vamp Dona Sol becomes Filet de Sole.

One of the funniest sequence in the film is the dressing sequence. Laurel wraps his satin belt in such a fashion that he falls right out the window and onto the horse he is riding to the bullfight. He is also shown licking a lollipop behind his dressing area, and slicking his hair down with axle grease, getting more on his white shirt than in his hair.

The ending is especially funny. At the beginning of the bullfight, the bull is shown munching on grass, too busy to be bothered with the matador trying to arouse a response. Finally, Filet de Sole throws a brick at the back of Rhubarb's head, and when he hits the ground, he is shown being buried with mud and sand. The moral of the story is, "If you want to live long—and be happy—cut out the bull!"

This is one of those cases in which the parody is actually better than the film that is the subject of the parody. It is truly a side-splitting comedy that will have viewers laughing all the way through.

365. Our Hospitality

Rating: ☆☆☆☆

Buster Keaton Productions/Metro; ***Directed by*** Buster Keaton and Jack Blystone; ***Story by*** Jean Havez, Clyde Bruckman, Joseph Mitchell; ***Art Director:*** Fred Gabourie; ***Lighting:*** Denver Harmon; ***Photography by*** Elgin Lessley, Gordon Jennings; ***Costumes by*** Walter Israel; ***Running Time:*** 73 minutes; ***Cast:*** JOSEPH CANFIELD, Joe Roberts (1870–1923); CANFIELD'S SONS, Ralph Bushman (1903–1978) and Craig Ward; THE PARSON, Monte Collins (1856–1929); THE ENGINEER, Joe Keaton (1867–1946); THE AUNT, Kitty Bradbury; THE GIRL, Natalie Talmadge (1899–1969); WILLIE MCKAY [AGE 1], James Keaton (born 1922) billed as Buster Keaton, Jr.; WILLIE MCKAY [AGE 21], Buster Keaton (1895–1966)

This was Buster Keaton's parody of the famous Hatfield-McCoy family feud, at a time when "family feud" films were popular. The film is also historically significant in that it features three generations of the Keaton family: Buster Keaton and wife Natalie

Talmadge; Keaton's father, Joe Keaton; and Keaton's infant son, James Keaton, who was billed as Buster Keaton, Jr., in this film's credits.

Set in 1810, the film's prologue shows an account of how Willie McKay's father was killed by one of the Canfields when he was a year old, as part of an ongoing feud between the two families. The story cuts to New York City 20 years later in 1830, with settings remodeled after portraits from the time and place depicted. Keaton travels back to Rockville, the site of the feud, to claim his father's estate. While there, he meets the attractive daughter of the Canfield family, totally oblivious to the fact that she is from the family with which his own family has its ongoing feud. This puts him right into the home of the family that he was warned to stay away from. Joe Keaton plays the father who, with his two sons, are out to get McKay.

Two of the life threatening situations that Buster Keaton acted out turned out to be almost fatal in reality. The first of these occurs when Keaton is shown falling in a train car and crashing into a rough river current headed toward a waterfall. Keaton had a wire attached to him while braving the rocky river, but the security wire broke, sending him totally out of control. He saved himself by grabbing tree limbs that he was lucky enough to pass by, and he suffered severe bruises and scrapes from the rocks that he went over in the river. This sequence appears in the film exactly as it really happened, adding more of a sense of spontaneity to the film in knowing that this situation was the real thing. Keaton reportedly spent weeks recovering from the injuries he suffered in this incident.

Natalie Talmadge gets into a boat to rescue Keaton, and loses control, with Keaton having to pull off another dangerous stunt to rescue his rescuer. Keaton is hanging from a tree limb that juts out over the edge of the waterfall, and has to swing out and grab Talmadge just as she is going over the falls. Keaton reportedly inhaled so much water as he was swinging in the middle of the waterfall that he lost consciousness.

Of all of Keaton's feature films, *Our Hospitality* ranks with *The General* as one of his very best. Fortunately, it is widely available on video, and is just as thrilling and entertaining to watch now as it was when it was originally released.

Natalie Talmadge, at the time this film was made, was Keaton's wife. Ralph Bushman appeared in this film at age 20 as one of the Canfield sons, before he started billing himself as Francis X. Bushman, Jr., to capitalize on his famous father's name.

366. The Pilgrim

Rating: ☆½

First National; ***Written and Directed by*** Charles Chaplin; ***Photography by*** Roland Totheroh; ***Running Time:*** 47 minutes; ***Cast:*** THE PILGRIM, Charles Chaplin (1889–1977); THE HEAVY, Charles Riesner (1887–1962); THE KID, "Dinky Dean" Riesner (born 1918); DEACON, Mack Swain (1876–1935); ELDER, Loyal Underwood (1893–1966); DAUGHTER, Edna Purviance (1894–1958); MOTHER, Kitty Bradbury; HUSBAND, Sydney Chaplin (1885–1965); WIFE, Mae Wells (1862–1941); SHERIFF, Tom Murray (1874–1935)

The Pilgrim was Chaplin's last film for First National, with which he was still committed to make a few more pictures after forming United Artists.

In this work, Chaplin plays an escaped convict who masquerades as a preacher in a small town. He gets into a variety of misadventures, with the best sequences occurring when he goes to the home of a member of the congregation. While there, he is constantly tormented by their little boy, with some riotously funny moments in these sequences. Eventually, the law catches up with Chaplin and he flees to Mexico.

While this film portrays an interesting idea that could have had real potential as a satire on small-town religious hypocrisy, Chaplin's style has him coming off simply as a blithering idiot acting stupid. In this reviewer's opinion, Buster Keaton could have turned *The Pilgrim* into one of the great comedy masterpieces of all time if he had done it instead of Chaplin.

Child actor Dean Riesner is the one and only redeeming factor in the whole film. As the brat wreaking havoc, he brings to the film the only sequences that provide any amusement at all to this reviewer. He was easily the best supporting actor of 1923.

367. A Pleasant Journey

Rating: ☆☆☆

Hal Roach/Pathé Exchange; ***Directed by*** Robert F. McGowan; ***Titles by*** H.M. Walker, Tom McNamara; ***Story by*** Hal Roach; ***Running Time:*** 13 minutes; ***Cast:*** **"Our Gang":** Ernie "Sunshine Sammy" Morrison (1912–1989); Mickey Daniels (1914–1970); Jack Davis (1914–1992); Jackie Condon (1918–1977); Farina Hoskins (1920–1980); Joe Cobb (born 1917); Mary Kornman (1915–1973); Winston Doty (1913–1934); ***Supporting Cast:*** TILFORD THE BACHELOR, William Gillespie (1894–??); DRUNK SALESMAN, Roy Brooks; TRAIN PASSENGER, George K. French (1883–1961); PORTER, Ernie Morrison, Sr.; PHYSICIAN, Wallace Howe; CAB DRIVER, Sam Lufkin (1891–1952); Monty O'Grady; Richard Daniels; CONDUCTORS, Charley Young and Charles Stevenson (1887–1943); OFFICERS, Charles Stevenson and Charles Bachman; PEDESTRIAN, Robert McGowan (1882–1955); POLICE CHIEF, Lincoln Stedman (1906–1948); Pete the dog (1923–1930)

This was the eleventh "Our Gang" short to be released. In this episode, some members of the gang decide to run away by hopping a train to San Francisco. Ernie Morrison and Farina stay behind and try drumming up business for Ernie's shoe shining service. Little Farina, presented as a girl in this episode, helps Ernie by painting pedestrian's shoes white, so that Ernie can then solicit business from them. They get into trouble when Farina paints the shoes of policemen lined up for uniform inspection.

The runaway boys are discovered and sent back home. Farina, Ernie, dog Pete, and some other kids take the place of the runaways, wreaking havoc for their fellow train passengers. Pete the dog makes an early appearance in this film, and is actually shown closing a window with his teeth. All of the "Our Gang" players are charming and adorable, but Farina steals the show.

368. Plunder

Rating: N/A

Pathé; ***Directed by*** George B. Seitz; ***Written by*** Bertram Millhauser; ***Running Time of Evaluated Footage:*** 17 minutes; ***Cast:*** PEARL, Pearl White (1889–1938); MR. JONES, Warren [a.k.a. William] Krech (1894–1948); ***Supporting Cast:*** Harry Semels (1887–1946); Tom McIntyre; J. Elwood Poole; William Naly (died 1929); Charles Revada

In 1919, Pearl White left the Pathé company to pursue a contract with Fox, where she wanted to get away from serial work and star in features. After 11 of these features were made without succeeding as well as hoped, White returned to Pathé to do *Plunder*, which was her last serial, and acclaimed as her best.

All that is available from *Plunder* for evaluation is a compilation of excerpts put out by Blackhawk Films.

Pearl White, the alluring star of *Plunder* (1923), her last serial.

In *Plunder*, originally released in 15 episodes, Pearl is the part owner of a New York City skyscraper which is said to have buried treasure beneath it. With the aid of a man named Mr. Jones, Pearl withstands a number of perilous situations at the hands of the villains, who will stop at nothing to get Pearl out of the way so that they can have her stock in the building and ultimately the treasure.

The footage evaluated is impressive—much more so than any other Pearl White footage evaluated. One scene has Pearl lured to a morass, where she is trapped in quicksand. With one bullet left in her gun, she shoots down a vine with which she pulls herself out. Further outtakes show her taking on two villains in hand-to-hand combat, and surviving an underground explosion that happens while she and Jones are trying to recover the hidden treasure.

During the filming of *Plunder*, tragedy struck one of Pearl's stunt doubles, John Stevenson. He was doing a segment in which he was to jump from the top of a moving bus to an elevated track. He lost his grip, and fell to his death.

If the evaluated excerpts from *Plunder* are any indication of what the serial as a whole was like, the high acclaim is well justified. After completing this serial, White went abroad to France to live.

369. Rosita

Rating: ☆☆☆☆

United Artists; ***Directed by*** Ernst Lubitsch; ***Assistant Director:*** James Townsend; ***Photography by*** Charles Rosher; ***Scenario by*** Edward Knoblock, Norbert Falk, Hans Kraly; ***From the Play***, *Don Cesar de Bazan* ***by*** William Cameron Menzies; ***Running Time:*** 88 minutes; ***Cast:*** ROSITA, Mary Pickford (1892–1979); DON DIEGO DE BAZAN, George Walsh (1889–1981); THE KING, Holbrook Blinn (1872–1928); THE QUEEN Irene Rich (1891–1988); ROSITA'S MOTHER, Mathilde Comont (1886–1938); ROSITA'S FATHER, George Periolat (1873–1940)

Rosita has notoriety as the one Pickford feature that Mary herself absolutely hated. This was in part due to the fact that she didn't like working with director Ernst Lubitsch (1892–1947), who directed *Rosita* as his first American film upon emigrating from Germany. Based on Lubitsch's other silent era work, this reviewer was fully prepared to side with Pickford. Most of Lubitsch's silent era output was atrocious—especially *Gypsy Blood* (1919) and *Eternal Love* (1929). *So This Is Paris* (1926) and *The Student Prince in Old Heidelberg* (1927) were technically well produced, but nothing extraordinary. Frankly, this reviewer found *The Student Prince in Old Heidelberg* rather boring.

It is hard to understand why Pickford so despised *Rosita*, an utterly delightful film and the only one of Ernst Lubitsch's available silents to possess any real merit. It is a masterpiece, as well as being Pickford's most lavishly produced film, featured elaborate sets and art direction by William Cameron Menzies, being the fifth and earliest surviving film on which he worked.

Pickford plays Rosita, an impoverished street singer who is arrested when singing songs protesting the King of Seville's policies. The lyrics to these songs are absolutely hilarious. George Walsh gives one of his best performances as Don Diego, who keeps Rosita from being assaulted by one of the king's henchmen, and is sentenced to death for murder. While Don and Rosita are in jail, thcy fall in love. The king is taken by Rosita, releasing her from prison and putting her up in lavish surroundings as his mistress. The story reaches a fabulous climax after a number of intriguing plot twists and turns.

Among the supporting players, Mathilde Comont is the real standout. She is hilarious as Rosita's fat, unrefined mother. Holbrook Blinn, who plays the king, was killed just five years after starring in this film in 1928 at age 56 after falling from a horse.

Since its original release, few people have seen *Rosita*. Mary Pickford prohibited the film from being restored or publicly shown while she was alive. In the 1980s, a foreign print of *Rosita* was discovered and shown at one of the big film conventions. In 1997, a restoration with English titles was completed. *Rosita* is slated for video release in the future, and is a film not to be missed when it does become available.

370. Roughest Africa

Rating: ☆☆☆½

Hal Roach/Pathé Exchange; ***Running Time:*** 17 minutes; ***Cast:*** PROFESSOR STANILAUS LAUREL, Stan Laurel (1890–1965); HIS PARTNER, James Finlayson (1887–1953)

This teaming of Stan Laurel and James Finlayson has them on a movie-shooting expedition in Africa. A number of funny situations and antics are portrayed. Some of the best include a monkey dropping a coconut on Stan's head, and a bear that follows Finlayson everywhere he goes. While Finlayson is fleeing from the bear, a giant ostrich is chasing Stan. The finale has Stan being chased by a pack of lions, escaping to his car only to find a skunk in it. Of the comedies that Stan Laurel starred in during his solo career, this is a classic and among the best.

371. Rudolph Valentino and His 88 American Beauties

Rating: ☆☆☆

Directed by David O. Selznick; ***Running Time:*** 9 minutes; ***Cast:*** PAGEANT HOST, Rudolph Valentino (1895–1926); FIRST PLACE WINNER, Norma Niblock [Miss Toronto]; SECOND PLACE, Eugenia Gilbert [Miss Los Angeles]; THIRD PLACE, Reba Owen [Miss New York]; FOURTH PLACE, Mildred Adams [Miss Baltimore]; FIFTH PLACE, Gloria Heller [Miss Wichita, Kansas]

This was one of the first two films that David O. Selznick (1902–1965) did when he was 21 years old, the year that his father, movie mogul Lewis J. Selznick (1870–1933), went bankrupt. David Selznick went on to become one of Hollywood's most powerful producers, turning out such masterpieces as *King Kong* (1933) and *Gone with the Wind* (1939).

During Rudolph Valentino's contractual dispute with Paramount, he and Natacha Rambova made their money by touring the country and making personal appearances. Sometimes, they did tango dance presentations together. Valentino also judged a series of 88 beauty pageants in the United States and Canada. The winners of each of the 88 pageants competed in a final competition at Madison Square Garden in New York, and this film contains the footage from that pageant.

The second place winner, Eugenia Gilbert, actually did go on to star in a few films in the late 1920s.

372. Safety Last

Rating: ☆☆☆☆

Hal Roach/Pathé Exchange; ***Directed by*** Fred Newmeyer and Sam Taylor; ***Assistant Director:*** Robert A. Golden; ***Story by*** Hal Roach, Sam Taylor, and Tim Shelan; ***Photographed by*** Walter Lundin; ***Edited by*** T.J. Crizer; ***Titles by*** H.M. Walker; ***Running Time:*** 72 minutes; ***Cast:*** THE BOY, Harold Lloyd (1893–1971); THE GIRL, Mildred Davis (1901–1969); THE COP, Noah Young (1887–1958); THE PAL, Bill Strother; THE KID, Mickey Daniels (1914–1970); THE GRANDMA, Anna Townsend (1845–1923); THE FLOORWALKER, Westcott B. Clarke (1886–1959)

Safety Last is, in this reviewer's opinion, the best comedy of the silent era. Although many historians consider Lloyd's 1927 film *The Kid Brother* to be Lloyd's masterpiece, this film gets the nod due to its spectacular "human fly" sequence. Most people, if shown a still from *The Kid Brother*, would not recognize it. However, most people recognize the famous still of Lloyd perilously hanging by the hands of the clock in *Safety Last*. It is perhaps the most famous sequence in the history of silent comedy, with the possible exception of sequences in Chaplin's *The Gold Rush* (1925) or Keaton's *The General* (1927) and *Steamboat Bill, Jr.* (1928). Not only does the climb sequence have appeal, but some of the situations leading to the famous climb are hilarious as well. Some examples are when Lloyd fakes an injury to be transported to the hospital by ambulance, stopping the ambulance driver once he is close to the department store at which he is late to work. In addition, there is the hilarious sequence in which Lloyd tries to sneak into work undetected.

The storyline of this film is about a young man from a small town trying to make good in the big city. His girl, played by Lloyd's real-life wife Mildred Davis, promises to marry Lloyd once he has made good. One sees Lloyd making ends meet as a store clerk, trying to present to his girl an image of wealth. He spends his entire week's pay and sells his phonograph to buy her an expensive necklace, dodging the landlord whom he hasn't paid. Davis reasons that since Lloyd is doing so well, she will pay him a surprise visit. Lloyd has to do some acting to pull off the false illusion that he is general manager of the department store, as opposed to a struggling counter clerk.

The "human fly" sequence comes about when Lloyd overhears the real general manager's conversation in which he pledges $1,000 to anybody who can come up with an idea to promote the store. This is when Lloyd proposes that a "human fly" spectacle be staged at the department store building. Of course, Lloyd's intentions are to have his roommate, who is experienced in such spectacles, to do the stunt. Lloyd offers the roommate half of the $1,000, and he readily accepts. Unfortunately, the roommate has a disgruntled cop on his trail, and Lloyd ends up having to do the stunt himself—until the pal can "ditch the cop," which never happens.

Harold Lloyd in the famous "human fly" sequence of *Safety Last* (1923).

When watching the famous climb, one knows that this is the real thing, with minimal trick photography. The building was situated above a tunnel on one side, giving the illusion that Lloyd was slightly higher up than he really was. Nets and platforms were available to catch Lloyd if he fell, but otherwise the stunt was performed as it appears. What is really unbelievable is that Lloyd did these amazing stunts with his thumb and forefinger missing from his right hand. They had been blown off during a 1920 photo session in which the "fake" bomb with which Lloyd was lighting his cigarette turned out to be an actual explosive. Knowing this information makes this feat even that much more impressive.

This would be the last film to star Mildred Davis, who married Lloyd and gave up her motion picture career at his insistence. This was also the last film appearance of Anna Townsend, who died at 79 shortly after her bit part in *Safety Last* was filmed.

This is an all-time comedy classic, and a must for all comedy fans who have not yet seen it. A restored version with an orchestral score by Carl Davis was released by HBO Video in the early 1990s, but is unfortunately out of print at the time of this writing.

373. Salome

Rating: ☆☆½

Alla Nazimova/United Artists; ***Directed by*** Charles Bryant and Alla Nazimova; ***Costumes and Sets Designed by*** Natacha Rambova; ***Running Time of Most Available Versions:*** 38 min-

utes; ***Cast:*** SALOME, Alla Nazimova (1878–1945); KING HEROD, Mitchell Lewis (1880–1956); WIFE OF HEROD, Rose Dione (1875–1936); JOHN THE BAPTIST [JOKANAAN], Nigel De Brulier (1877–1948); NARRABOTH, Earl Schenk (1889–??); NAMAAN THE EXECUTIONER, Frederick Peters (1884–1963); NARRABOTH'S BLONDE FRIEND, Arthur Jasmina

Salome was the last in a series of films independently produced and financed by Alla Nazimova, who had notoriety as an openly lesbian actress. Originally running at about an hour in length, the only versions of the film widely available today are less than 40 minutes long. The complete version docs exist in an archive in the northeastern United States, but has heretofore been inaccessible. The original is reportedly elaborately tinted and toned.

Alla Nazimova doing the "dance of the seven veils" in *Salome* (1923).

Even in the truncated versions that are widely available, this is an interesting film, as it is alleged by many sources to feature an exclusively homosexual cast. Many of the prominent cast members of the film do dress in an openly gay fashion, but it is highly unlikely that Nazimova went down the line in casting auditions and inquired of each's sexual orientation. Nonetheless, the film was greatly influenced by gays, and featured gays prominently in its cast—perhaps the first such film in America to receive a wide theatrical release. This film adaptation of *Salome* was based on the play by Oscar Wilde. Wilde originally wrote the play in French, hoping that the French actress Sarah Bernhardt (1844–1923) would be interested in it. Bernhardt did not do the play, and it was translated into English. Lord Alfred Douglas, who was Wilde's gay companion at the time in 1895, did the translation, which featured sketched illustrations by the renowned artist Aubrey Beardsley. It was upon the Beardsley sketches that Natacha Rambova based her costume and set designs. At the time that Rambova worked on this film, she was Mrs. Rudolph Valentino.

The plot of the film is a relatively simple one. Nazimova plays the lead role of Salome, who is the daughter of the wife of King Herod. Herod, being an incestuous pervert, falls in lust with stepdaughter Salome. He makes an offer to give her anything she asks, in return for her performance of a dance routine, which would symbolize submission to him. She initially refuses.

The film progresses as Salome visits the dungeon in which John the Baptist, also referred to as Jokanaan, is held prisoner for having denounced Herod in his sermons. She becomes enamored with Jokanaan, who wants nothing to do with her. So, she reasons that if he won't let her kiss him while he is alive, she will have him executed and kiss him when he is dead. Thus, she consents to dance for Herod. This provides the highlight of the film, the dance of the seven veils. This sequence features some exotic costume styles that were way ahead of their time. The dress worn by Nazimova in this sequence looks more like something that would be worn in current times.

Upon completing the dance, Salome informs Herod of the price: the head of John the Baptist on a silver platter. Herod, who believes Jokanaan to be the Messiah, is terrified with the thought of carrying out such an order, but keeps his word. Once Salome kisses the severed head, Herod orders her execution. The end of the movie consists of a black shade being lowered over a title card which says, "And there was none in the world so black as the name of Salome."

Salome failed miserably at the box office, and Nazimova lost most of the $500,000 she had put into it, thus putting an end to her independent producing career. Nonetheless, it is a film of vital historic importance, as it is one of only two of Nazimova's silents known to survive. Seeing the complete version with its original tints and tones would probably add a great deal to this film's artistic value.

374. Save the Ship

Rating: ☆☆½

Hal Roach/Pathé Exchange; Director Unidentified; ***Running Time:*** 9 minutes; ***Cast:*** Stan Laurel (1890–1965)

This rare and obscure early Stan Laurel short features him as a member of a party who lives in a tent mounted on a raft. A number of slapstick gags are performed as one disaster after another occurs.

The girl on the "ship" accidentally spills gunpowder, and the tent/raft is blown up and sinks. A rescue boat that saves Laurel and another passenger also sinks.

375. Scaramouche

Rating: ☆☆☆½

Metro; ***Directed by*** Rex Ingram; ***Scenario by*** Willis Goldbeck; ***Photography by*** John F. Seitz; ***Edited by*** Grant Whytock; ***Running Time:*** 97 minutes; ***Cast:*** QUINTIN DE KERCADIOU, Lloyd Ingraham (1874–1956); ALICE DE KERCADIOUS [HIS NIECE], Alice Terry (1899–1987); ANDRE-LOUIS MOREAU, Ramon Novarro (1899–1968); MARQUIS DE LA TOUR D'ARYR, Lewis Stone (1879–1953); COUNTESS DE PLOUGASTEL, Julia Swayne Gordon (1878–1933); CHEVALIER DE CHABRILLANE, William Humphrey (1874–1942); PHILLIPE DE VILMORIN, Otto Matiesen (1893–1932); DANTON, George Siegmann (1882–1928); CHAPELIER, Bowditch Turner (1878–1933); BINET, James Marcus (1867–1937); CLIMENE BINET, Edith Allen; POLICHINELLE, John George (1898–1968); KING'S LIEUTENANT, Willard Lee Hall (1863–1936); LE REVOLTE, Rose Dione (1875–1936)

This film has a significant place in film history as Ramon Novarro's first big leading role. Set during the French Revolution, *Scaramouche* is a costume drama with Novarro as Andre-Louis Moreau, an aristocrat who is searching for his family, just coming out of law school. Lewis Stone plays the evil Marquis de la Tour d'Aryr, who abuses his powers as an aristocrat, killing anyone who so much as dares to disagree with him. When the Marquis kills his best friend, Andre-Louis goes on the war path against him, becoming a leader in the revolution movement. He becomes a fugitive sentenced to death, and joins a theater troupe under the name of Scaramouche while learning swordsmanship to take revenge on the Marquis and the unjust government that refuses to prosecute him.

This epic of the French Revolution came out just over a year after D.W. Griffith's *Orphans of the Storm* (1921), and the two are often compared. While Griffith focused primarily on the victims of the aristocrats, this film deals with the struggle of a nobleman against his aristocratic heritage, while trying to save his mother and the woman he loves from being swept up by the revolution. Like Griffith's film, this one features a top notch cast, huge mob scenes, and extraordinarily lavish costumes. While Griffith's film has a last-minute rescue attempt, Ingram's has a different type of twist—with Novarro's character finding out that the man he seeks revenge on is actually his own father!

Ramon Novarro makes an excellent impression in his first major role, which paved his way for stardom. Lewis Stone is especially good as the despicable Marquis.

Unfortunately, this fine film has not yet been made widely available in the United States. The copy evaluated for this review came from French television, with English titles and French subtitles. This is a film that is most deserving of a wider American audience.

Scaramouche was remade as a talkie in 1952, starring Stewart Granger (1913–1993) in the title role. This version was excellent, and actually had better executed and more elaborate swashbuckling sequences than this original. However, once one has seen Ramon Novarro in the title role, even Stewart Granger doesn't quite measure up. Novarro *is* Scaramouche, whereas Granger comes across as Stewart Granger giving a good performance as Scaramouche.

376. Soul of the Beast

Rating: ☆☆½

Thomas H. Ince/Metro; ***Directed by*** John Griffith Wray; ***Photographed by*** Henry Sharp;

Madge Bellamy with Los Angeles Zoo elephant Anna May in *Soul of the Beast* (1923).

Edited by Ralph H. Dixon; ***Running Time:*** 63 minutes; ***Cast:*** RUTH LORRIMORE, Madge Bellamy (1899–1990); PAUL NADEAU, Cullen Landis (1895–1975); CAESAR DURAND, Noah Beery, Sr. (1882–1946); JACQUELING BOUSSUT, Vola Vale; SILAS HAMM, Bert Sprotte (1870–1949); OSCAR THE ELEPHANT, Anna May (from the Los Angeles Zoo)

In this film, Madge Bellamy plays a circus performer whose best friend is an elephant named Oscar. When a storm hits and destroys the circus, it is Oscar who saves her, and they end up in the forest. In this remote area, she attracts a suitor, played by Cullen Landis, as well as the attention of the villain of the story, played by Noah Beery, Sr.

The story and script in this film leaves a bit to be desired, as it drags in some parts. But, it has some great moments. The storm sequence is impressively staged. Oscar the Elephant, played by Anna May of the Los Angeles Zoo, is very well trained, and brings some charming moments to *Soul of the Beast*. One of the funniest is when Oscar is outside the window of the tavern frequented by the villains, and he uses his trunk to drink the beer behind the villains' backs, making them think that the person sitting next to them is pilfering their drinks.

Madge Bellamy, the star of this film, was one of the most beautiful women ever to grace a screen, and there are some excellent shots of her in this film that bring out her beauty to the fullest. She was a very talented actress as well, but very feisty. She was the first choice for the role of Esther in *Ben-Hur* (1927), as well as for the lead in *7th Heaven*

(1927), but her refusal to bow down to the tyrannical studio heads of the time caused her trouble in getting the great roles for which she was considered.

This is the earliest appearance of Cullen Landis that is widely available on video. Landis made history in 1928 by starring as the male lead in *Lights of New York* (1928), the first all-talking picture.

Noah Beery, Sr., gives a usual good performance as an especially despicable villain in this film, going so far as to shoot Paul Nadeau's pet rabbit and have it served to him for dinner.

Although this film is relatively standard fare, the charm of Oscar the Elephant, as well as the grace, talent, and beauty of Madge Bellamy, put it over.

377. Souls for Sale

Rating: ☆☆☆

Goldwyn Pictures; ***Written and Directed by*** Rupert Hughes; ***Photographed by*** John Mescall; ***Running Time:*** 79 minutes; ***Cast:*** REMEMBER STEDDON, Eleanor Boardman (1898–1991); ROSINA TEELE, Mae Busch (1901–1946); LEVA LEMAIRE, Barbara LaMarr (1898–1926); FRANK CLAYMORE, Richard Dix (1893–1949); TOM HOLBY, Frank Mayo (1889–1963); OWEN SCUDDER, Lew Cody (1888–1934); REVEREND JOHN STEDDON, Forrest Robinson (1858–1924); MRS. STEDDON, Edith Yorke (1867–1934); COMIC OF THE COMPANY, Snitz Edwards (1862–1937); ASSISTANT DIRECTOR, William Haines (1900–1973); MISS TWEEDY, Dale Fuller; A "WANNA BE" ACTRESS, Eve Sothern; CASTING DIRECTOR, Roy Atwell (1879–1962); LADY JANE, Aileen Pringle (1895–1989); LORD FRYINGHAM, William Orlamond (1867–1957); **Cameos as themselves**, Erich von Stroheim (1885–1957); Charlie Chaplin (1889–1977); Frank Claymore; T. Roy Barnes (1880–1937); Zasu Pitts (1898–1963); Marshall Neilan (1891–1958); Clair Windsor (1897–1962); Raymond Griffith (1887–1957); Hobart Bosworth (1867–1943)

Souls for Sale is an all-star extravaganza that was for many years believed lost. A print turned up in the 1970s, and the film was aired on a "Lost and Found" series on PBS. It is one of the very few extant films produced by the Goldwyn Company before their merge with Metro Pictures and Louis B. Mayer to form MGM. Director Rupert Hughes (1872–1956) was the uncle of the famous billionaire, aviator, and movie executive Howard Hughes (1905–1976).

This was the third film for both Eleanor Boardman and William Haines, who both broke into Hollywood by winning a "new faces" contest. Boardman plays the leading role of Remember Steddon, a naive country girl who marries an attractive suitor. As suitor, Owen Scudder put on a totally different personality from the one he exhibited once he and Remember were married. While on the train, Remember realizes her mistake, and jumps off the train while her new husband is asleep. She is deserted in the desert, where she is found and rescued by matinee idol Tom Holby.

Remember sets herself on a dream of becoming a great actress. She is finally awarded a screen test, which she bombs. However, Frank Claymore, a director, sees that she realizes how bad her screen test looked, and decides to give her a chance. Throughout her experience in Hollywood, a number of celebrities are shown at work, which provides a fascinating inside look at Hollywood in the early 1920s.

All is well, and Remember gets a number of breaks and rises quickly to stardom. Then, her "husband" sees her on screen, and decides to cash in on her success.

This was Eleanor Boardman's first really big role, and she makes an impressive appearance in it. Her leading man is Richard Dix, who had just gained fame as the hero of the modern segment in *The Ten Commandments* (1923). William Haines at this point was still playing smaller roles, as his role in the film was little more than a brief cameo. *Souls for Sale* is one of the very few extant films of several different players, including Aileen Pringle, Lew Cody, and Barbara LaMarr.

This is a unique part of film heritage, and it is fortunate that it has been recovered. Perhaps *Hollywood* (1923), another lost all-star extravaganza of the period, will turn up.

378. The Ten Commandments *Rating:* ☆☆☆

Paramount; ***Directed by*** Cecil B. DeMille; ***Assistant Director:*** Cullen Tate; ***Story by*** Jeanie MacPherson; ***Art Direction by*** Paul Iribe; ***Photographed by*** Bert Glennon, Peverel Marley, Archibald Stout, and J.F. Westerberg; ***Technical Director:*** Roy Pomeroy; ***Edited by*** Anne Bauchens; ***Running Time:*** 146 minutes; ***Cast:*** **THE PROLOGUE:** MOSES, Theodore Roberts (1861–1928); RAMESES THE PHARAOH, Charles De Roche (1880–1952); MIRIAM [SISTER OF MOSES], Estelle Taylor (1894–1958); WIFE OF PHARAOH, Julia Faye (1893–1966); SON OF PHARAOH, Terrence Moore; AARON [BROTHER OF MOSES], James Neill (1860–1931); DATHAN THE DISCONTENTED, Lawson Butt (1883–1956); THE TASKMASTER, Clarence Burton (1881–1933); THE BRONZE MAN, Noble Johnson (1881–1978); **THE MODERN STORY:** MRS. MARTHA MCTAVISH, Edythe Chapman (1863–1948); JOHN MCTAVISH, Richard Dix (1893–1949); DAN MCTAVISH, Rod LaRocque (1896–1969); MARY LEIGH, Leatrice Joy (1893–1965); SALLY LUNG, Nita Naldi (1897–1961); REDDING [AN INSPECTOR], Robert Edeson (1868–1931); THE DOCTOR, Charles Ogle (1865–1940); THE OUTCAST, Agnes Ayres (1896–1940)

In the wake of the several scandals during the early 1920s which rocked Hollywood, studios scrambled to clean up the silver screen image. This provided incentive for Cecil B. DeMille and Paramount to try a religious epic filmed on a lavish scale. This was the first time since DeMille's *Joan the Woman* (1916) that such a lavish epic was considered. Thus, this original silent version of *The Ten Commandments* was produced. The prologue section featured massive sets, and the sequence depicting the journey of the Israelites to the Red Sea was filmed in two-strip Technicolor. Paramount released this title on video in 1987, and although the Technicolor sequence was not restored to its original condition, some of the greens and reds are still apparent in the now-faded print that was used in the video transfer.

In this prologue, Rameses the Pharaoh of Egypt is depicted as a tyrant who uses the Israelites as slaves who are treated no better than common animals. Even a person's death was no excuse for not working to build the magnificent towers that the Pharaoh wants built. The prologue progresses to the arrival of Moses onto the scene, who demands that the Israelites be freed from their bondage. He tells the Pharaoh that if the Israelites are not freed, God will take the lives of all first-born Egyptians, in addition to the other nine plagues previously inflicted upon the Egyptians for noncompliance with the orders to free the Israelites. Once the prophecy of the death of Rameses' son is realized, Rameses tells Moses to gather his people and get out of Egypt. This leads to the famous Technicolor sequence of the migration to and across the Red Sea. The special effects used to depict the parting of the Red Sea are marvelous, and actually better in this original version than in the 1956 remake of the film.

Cecil B. DeMille in 1923, around the time he was directing *The Ten Commandments* (1923).

Once the Israelites are safely across the Red Sea, Moses then goes into the mountains of Sinai, during which time he receives the Ten Commandments from God. The special effects used to depict the delivery of the commandments to Moses are well done, but this reviewer concedes that DeMille did do a better job with this sequence in his 1956 remake. While Moses is receiving the commandments, the other Israelites are busy corrupting themselves with orgies and constructing a golden calf for use as an idol. In typical DeMille fashion, the orgy sequence is lavish, condemning the debauchery but showing it first. After showing Moses throwing the Ten Commandments down in a rage, the movie fades into the Modern Story.

The Modern Story brings us to the home of the McTavish family, circa 1923. Martha McTavish is a devout follower of the Ten Commandments and the Bible, reading them to both of her sons on a daily basis. One son, John McTavish, follows these teachings. The other son, Dan McTavish, rebels against his mother's religious teachings. He breaks every law of God and man as he sees fit for the sake of making money and becoming rich. As a result of his sins, his mother is killed when a church wall that his company has constructed falls down and crushes her—because the son knowingly defied the construction codes to save money. He also ends up contracting leprosy from his adulterous mistress, well-played by Nita Naldi. He shoots Sally Lung upon being told that she has given him leprosy. DeMille's technique in showing this murder is unique. One does not actually see Sally die, but instead sees the curtain that she is clutching torn from the ceiling one ring at a time.

Upon comparing the two versions of *The Ten Commandments*, one discovers that the original is the one true version of the classic. The "remake" would have been more appropriately titled *The Life and Times of Moses*. Whereas this original focuses on the

Ten Commandments, how they came about, and the consequences of breaking such during both biblical and modern times, the "remake" focuses solely on the biography of Moses, not even mentioning the Ten Commandments until close to the finale, thus not having much to do with the Ten Commandments at all.

This film does have its flaws—especially in the modern segment. It does not meet the exceptional standards of other DeMille epics such as *Joan the Woman* (1916) and *The King of Kings* (1927), but is still a well-done biblical epic, and one of the better such epics in motion picture history.

379. The Three Ages

Rating: ☆☆☆½

Joseph Schenk/Metro; ***Directed by*** Buster Keaton and Eddie Cline; ***Story and Titles by*** Clyde Bruckman, Joseph Mitchell, Jean Havez; ***Photographed by*** William McGann and Elgin Lessley; ***Art Direction by*** Fred Gabourie; ***Running Time:*** 63 minutes; ***Cast:*** THE FAITHFUL ADMIRER, Buster Keaton (1895–1966); THE ADVENTURER, Wallace Beery (1885–1949); THE GIRL, Margaret Leahy (1902–1967); THE GIRL'S MOTHER, Lillian Lawrence (1868–1926); THE GIRL'S FATHER, Joseph Roberts (1870–1923); ***Supporting Cast:*** Blanche Payson (1881–1964); Lionel Belmore (1868–1953); Horace Morgan

This film was Buster Keaton's first feature length film. It is a unique contribution to motion picture history as a parody of D.W. Griffith's *Intolerance* (1916).

The Three Ages opens in much the same manner as *Intolerance*, with the camera focused on a book entitled *Three Ages* opening up. The theme is slightly different; rather than dealing with intolerance through different ages of history, love is the chosen theme which is demonstrated not to have changed throughout the Stone Age, the Roman Age, and the Modern Age. Each interlinking story features Keaton and nemesis Wallace Beery as rivals fighting for the affection of the same girl. The girl's parents always seem to favor Beery over Keaton. After being put to the test in a variety of challenges, Keaton always manages to emerge victorious in the end.

This hilarious movie finds Keaton in a variety of misadventures. During the Stone Age, he is challenged to a duel with clubs. When it is discovered that he cheated by wedging a stone into his club, Keaton is sentenced to take a tour of the neighborhood tied to the tail of an elephant which drags him all the way. The Roman Age finds Keaton challenged to a chariot race. Keaton shows up in a dog sled. After a number of mishaps, Keaton manages to catch up, but loses the race by a hair, and is thrown into a dungeon with a lion. Leave it to Keaton to make friends with the "vicious" lion, who waves goodbye when Keaton is rescued. The Modern Age finds Keaton pitted against Beery on opposite positions in a football game, and then in jail after bootleg whiskey is planted on his person. While at the police station, Keaton discovers some revealing facts about Beery's past, and must find a way out of jail and to the wedding before the marriage vows take place.

In the modern sequence especially, Keaton performs a number of remarkable stunts. These stunts were all performed by Keaton himself, who rarely, if ever, used a double. Another interesting sequence in the Stone Age segment is the early use of trick photography during a brief sequence in which Keaton rides on the back of a dinosaur.

The Three Ages was for many years believed to have been lost. One print turned up, but unfortunately had some severe nitrate decomposition. David Shepard of Film Preservation Associates repaired some of the damage where he could. Unfortunately, some parts of the chariot race were too severely damaged to salvage, and had to be cut.

This is a delightful and witty comedy—and even more so when one has seen *Intolerance* and knows what is being parodied.

380. The Untameable

Rating: ☆½

Universal; ***Directed by*** Herbert Blaché; ***Story by*** Gelett Burgess; ***Scenario by*** Hugh Hoffman; ***Photographed by*** Ben Kline; ***Film Editor:*** R.A. Roberts; ***Art Director:*** E.E. Sheeley; ***Running Time:*** 51 minutes; ***Cast:*** Joy Fielding, Gladys Walton (1903–1993); Chester Arnold, Malcolm McGregor (1892–1945); Ah Moy, Etta Lee (1906–1956); Dr. Copin, John Sainpolis (1873–1946)

The Untameable is a rather silly movie in which Gladys Walton plays Joy Fielding, a wealthy schizophrenic patient with two personalities: one being good, gentle, and kind; the other being a rude and obnoxious vamp who indulges in a number of vices. Malcolm McGregor is the leading man as Chester Arnold, who ends up in a car accident and is a "patient" in the same place as Joy. He falls in love with the good side of Joy. It turns out that Joy's "split personality" is the result of an evil doctor who is hypnotizing her as a scheme to tap into her vast wealth.

This film has historic significance as the only one of Gladys Walton's films that is widely available on video. Walton's film career began in 1920 at Universal. She was known primarily for a number of circus pictures she made with the company. She did not particularly care for acting, as the hours were long and she was never given a break. *The Untameable* was the last picture that Walton worked on for Universal when she took a vacation to Hawaii. When she returned, Universal docked her for three weeks' salary, and she walked out on the contract. After a few independent productions, Walton retired from the screen permanently.

At least one of Walton's circus pictures does exist, as she told a friend of this reviewer that she had a copy when she was still alive. It is not known what happened to the film after Walton's death.

Malcolm McGregor, the leading man in this film, was an appealing actor who starred in a number of films, but never achieved superstar status. He was killed in a fire in 1945 at age 52.

Director Herbert Blaché (1882–1953) was the husband of famed film pioneer Alice Guy-Blaché (1875–1968). Based on Herbert's and Alice's extant work available for evaluation, it appears that Herbert's work was far inferior to his wife's. However, Herbert's *Brats* (1919), starring Alla Nazimova, was highly acclaimed. Since his most highly acclaimed work no longer survives, it is not fair to judge him by this and other inferior examples which have been among those of his films to survive.

381. The White Rose

Rating: ☆☆☆½

D.W. Griffith/United Artists; ***Directed by*** D.W. Griffith; ***Running Time:*** 98 minutes; ***Cast:*** Bessie "Teasie" Williams, Mae Marsh (1895–1968); Marie Carrington, Carol Dempster (1901–1991); Joseph Beaugarde, Ivor Novello (1893–1951); John White, Neil Hamilton (1897–1984); Apollo, Porter Strong (1879–1923); Auntie Easter, Lucille LaVerne (1869–1945)

The White Rose was the first that Mae Marsh starred in for D.W. Griffith since 1916, when she signed with Goldwyn Pictures. In this film, she plays a poor orphan named Bessie Williams, who is just getting out of the orphanage and into the real world. She gets a job as a hostess in a hotel-restaurant, where she is encouraged to flirt with the male customers to increase sales. She meets a young minister who is on vacation, and falls in love with him. Because of her flirtatious reputation, he thinks he is but one of many casual encounters, and goes back to his home—unaware that Bessie is pregnant with his child, and that he had been her first and only intimate partner.

In a fashion similar to the story of *Way Down East*, Bessie is turned out and ostracized. Having no way of getting another job, she collapses from hunger and a nervous breakdown. Through a twist of fate, the dying girl is finally taken in by two black servants who happen to work for the wealthy Carrington estate, where the wedding preparations for Marie Carrington and the minister, Joseph Beaugarde, are taking place.

Although there is no way that Mae Marsh could have ever topped her excellent performances in *The Birth of a Nation* (1915) and *Intolerance* (1916), she gives a wonderful performance in this film. Of her 1920s films that are available for evaluation, this is the best.

The minister, Joseph Beaugarde, is played by Ivor Novello. Of his three silents that are available for evaluation, his performance in this film is the best. In this film, he is able to demonstrate depth in a wide range of emotional portrayals. The sequence in which he first learns that he has a son by Bessie is well-played, as well as when he is on the pulpit preaching, tormented by his conscience.

Carol Dempster, who plays Marie Carrington, the fiancée from an "old money" family of Louisiana plantation owners, has never looked lovelier than in this film. There are excellent shots in this film in which she is stunningly attractive.

Neil Hamilton got his first big break in this film, playing John White, a poor man from a stereotypical "white trash" family who is determined to rise above his heritage, and who is in love with Marie Carrington. Before playing in *The White Rose*, Hamilton had been a highly successful fashion model, having had a few occasional appearances in minor films. He made a good enough impression in this first part for D.W. Griffith that he played the male lead in two subsequent Griffith films, and was one of Paramount's most popular leading men in the late 1920s.

Although Lucille LaVerne's part in this film was a minor one, it is unique in that she plays the part of a sympathetic and kind servant who is one of the few that is not judgmental toward Bessie Williams. In *Orphans of the Storm*, she had played a villain role. For Walt Disney's 1937 version of *Snow White*, she provided the voice of the wicked witch. This role in *The White Rose* was closer to her actual generous personality. When LaVerne heard in 1924 that D.W. Griffith was having financial problems, she sent him a check for $50,000.

The White Rose is an excellent melodrama, as well as a chance to see several significant film players in some great roles.

382. The White Sister *Rating:* ☆☆☆☆

Inspiration Pictures/Metro; ***Produced by*** Charles H. Duell; ***Directed by*** Henry King; ***From the Novel by*** F. Marion Crawford; ***Scenario by*** George V. Hobart and Charles Whittaker; ***Titles*** *by* Will M. Ritchey and Don Bartlett; ***Photographed by*** Roy Overbaugh; ***Edited by*** Duncan Mansfield; ***Art Direction by*** Robert M. Haas; ***Running Time:*** 110 minutes; ***Cast:*** ANGELA CHIAROMONTE, Lillian Gish (1893–1993); GIOVANNI SEVERI, Ronald Colman (1891–1958); MARCHESA DI'NOLA, Gail Kane (1887–1966); MONSIGNOR SARACIUESSA, J. Barney Sherry (1874–1944); PRINCE CHIAROMONTE, Charles Lane (1869–1945); MADAME BERNARD, Juliett la Violette; UGO SEVERI, Sig. Serena; DERAND, Alfredo Bertone (died 1927); COUNT DEL FERICE, Ramon Ibañez; ALFREDO, Alfredo Martinelli

This was the first film that Lillian Gish made after departing the D.W. Griffith Company, and was also the greatest post–Griffith success that she had. It was filmed in Italy at a cost of $279,000. It was so lavishly produced that when director Henry King and producer Charles H. Duell screened it for First National, they were under the impression that it had cost $2 million to make and would not release such an expensive production. King and Duell decided to play it in one theater in New York. It made such an impression where it played that Metro Pictures picked it up for distribution. With a box-office gross of $4 million, it was highly profitable.

In *The White Sister*, Lillian Gish plays Angela Chiaromonte, a woman whose wealthy father has died, and whose half-sister Marchesa obtains the estate by fraudulent means, kicking Angela out of the house. Angela's fiancé, Giovanni Severi, is called off to war, and reported to have died. Upon hearing the news, she enters a convent in his memory.

It turns out that Giovanni had been taken as a war prisoner in a desert, and has been imprisoned all this time. He escapes and returns to Angela, and tries to get her to renounce her vows, leave the convent, and marry him. A volcano erupts, and Giovanni gallantly sacrifices his life to warn and save the other people in the area.

In filming the volcano sequences, Henry King and the cameraman actually went down into a real volcano to photograph the boiling lava. In addition, the flood sequences which follow the eruption of Mt. Vesuvius are impressive as well.

This was the first major film role for Ronald Colman, who was discovered by Henry King and Lillian Gish while he was touring with a stage production. He went on to great success in both the silent and talkie eras. He was nominated for a 1929 Best Actor Academy Award for his performances in *Bulldog Drummond* and *Condemned*, and again in 1942 for *Random Harvest*. He won the Oscar in 1947 for his performance in *A Double Life*.

The White Sister was remade as a talkie in 1933, but did not achieve the success of this original silent version.

383. A Woman of Paris

Rating: ☆☆☆☆

Charles Chaplin/United Artists; ***Written and Directed by*** Charles Chaplin; ***Running Time:*** 80 minutes; ***Cast:*** MARIE ST. CLAIR, Edna Purviance (1894–1958); HER STEP-FATHER, Clarence Geldert (1867–1935); JEAN MILLET, Carl Miller (1893–1979); HIS MOTHER, Lydia Knott (1866–1955); HIS FATHER, Charles French (1860–1925); PIERRE REVEL, Adolphe Menjou (1890–1963); FIFI, Betty Morrissey (1908–1944); PAULETTE, Malvina Polo; AN ORPHAN, Frank "Junior" Coghlan (born 1916); TRAIN STATION WORKER, Charlie Chaplin (1889–1977)

This was Charlie Chaplin's one and only serious drama which he wrote and directed, but did not star in. He makes only a brief, unbilled cameo appearance as a train station porter for a duration of a few seconds on screen. It was his first feature for United Artists,

Edna Purviance mourns the passing of her former lover. Lydia Knott as the mother of the boy looks on.

and was unfortunately unsuccessful at the box office. While this reviewer does not like Chaplin's "tramp" character, and the fact that Chaplin himself departed from the "tramp" character for this film indicates that he wanted to move away from it, the public clamored for the tramp, and did not support *A Woman of Paris*, which did not feature the tramp.

Set in France, *A Woman of Paris* is subtitled a drama of fate. Edna Purviance is, in her last major role, Marie St. Clair, a young woman from an unhappy home who decides to elope with Jean Millet, an aspiring artist from a poor family. When the two lovers are scheduled to meet at the train station, Jean's father dies suddenly from a heart attack, and he doesn't make it. Marie goes to Paris alone, and becomes the mistress of Pierre Revel, a wealthy businessman. Torn between a life of luxurious wealth and her true love for Jean, she hesitates to give up her easy life, and Jean, desperate to win Marie back, commits suicide in the lobby of the ritzy hotel where Marie and Pierre are dining. Wracked with guilt, Marie abandons her life of luxury to redeem herself through service.

This is an excellent, heartrending romantic drama that really demonstrates what Charlie Chaplin was capable of doing. It is a pity that he did not do more dramatic films of this sort. *A Woman of Paris* is the best film that Chaplin ever directed, and makes one wish he hadn't stopped at one dramatic effort. It is, in this reviewer's opinion, Chaplin's masterpiece even over his comedy masterpiece, *The Kid* (1921), as well as one of the better romantic tragedies in cinema history. It pulls at the heartstrings and also has light, subtle comedy that doesn't detract from the dramatic value of the film.

Edna Purviance's performance in the lead role as Marie is easily one of the best performances by a female in 1923. Unfortunately, that same year, she attended a party on the yacht of Courtland Dines, a millionaire playboy. Her best friend, Mabel Normand, was also at the party. Apparently, Mabel's chauffeur was using the alias of Joe Kelly, got into an argument with Dines, and shot him, causing a relatively minor wound. The press had a field day, blowing the whole incident out of proportion, tarnishing the reputations of both Normand and Purviance. The incident ensured that Mabel would not recover from the damage of the William Desmond Taylor murder scandal of a year earlier, and resulted in Purviance never having another starring role in an American film after *A Woman of Paris*. (Purviance starred in the 1926 French film, *Education du Prince*.)

Carl Miller is appealing in the lead male role of Jean, but unfortunately little is known about his life after the mid–1920s, except that he was living in Honolulu, Hawaii, when he died in 1979. Child star Frank "Junior" Coghlan made one of his first film appearances in a cameo as an orphan at the end of the film.

In 1976, Chaplin at age 87 reedited *A Woman of Paris* slightly, and composed a new music score for it, being his last creative project before his death.

1924

384. Aelita: Queen of Mars

Rating: ☆☆☆

Mezharspom U.S.S.R.; ***Directed by*** Yakov Protazanov; ***Based on novel by*** A. Tolstoy; ***Photographed by*** Yuri Ahelyabuzhsky and E. Shoneman; ***Sets by*** Sergei Kozlovsky, Alexandra Ester, Isaac Kabinovich, Victor Simo; ***Adaptation by*** Fydor Olsep, Alexei Faito; ***Running Time:*** 111 minutes; ***Cast:*** CHIEF ENGINEER LOSS, N.M. Tseretelli; NATASHA [LOSS'S WIFE], Valentina Kuinzhi; GUSSEV, Nikolai P. Batalov (1899–1937); SPIRIDINOV, N.M. Tseretelli; AELITA, U.I. Solnetseva; IHOSHKA [HER MAID], A.F. Pergonets; TUSKUB [RULER OF MARS],

K.V. Eggert; Gor, U.A. Zavadsky; Masha [nurse], V.G. Orlova; Erlich, T.N. Poly; Elena, N.M. Tretiakova

This innovative, early science fiction fantasy film features the story of an engineer who finds out that his wife is having an affair. He kills her for the transgression, and moves to Mars. With the film's status as the first science fiction film produced in the Soviet Union, it is a landmark in cinema history. Its futuristic image of Mars resembles modern depictions on film.

Although *Aelita*'s first hour or so is rather slow-moving, developing the characters on Earth and Mars, it is well worth sticking with. It starts to get really interesting after the first hour.

Director Yakov Protazanov (1881–1945) began his film career in 1905 as an actor, with his directorial debut coming in 1909. He directed three films during the early 1920s when he had moved to France, and *Aelita* was the first film he directed upon his return to the Soviet Union. Among his other notable films was a 1915 version of *War and Peace*. He made his last film in 1943, two years before his death.

Aelita: Queen of Mars doubled not only as entertainment, but as a Communist propaganda film, too. A revolt much like the Bolshevik Revolution of 1917 is staged on Mars. Its message emphasizes support for space technology, alluding to the possibility that the Communist revolution be taken beyond planet Earth.

385. America

Rating: ☆☆☆☆

D.W. Griffith/United Artists; ***Directed by*** D.W. Griffith; ***Running Time:*** 141 minutes; ***Cast:*** Nancy Montague, Carol Dempster (1901–1991); Nathan Holden, Neil Hamilton (1897–1984); Captain Walter Butler, Lionel Barrymore (1878–1954)

When *America* was first reviewed, the version evaluated was a truncated version, which was stretch-printed and heavily edited, with all of the titles removed and replaced with voice-over narration. In addition, the film was presented in black and white, as opposed to the original which was color tinted. Needless to say, the truncated version was not particularly impressive. But, once Kino Video made a restored version of the film, with color tints, original titles, and orchestra score based on the original score that Griffith had commissioned for the film, it was like watching an entirely different movie.

America is among the finest of the Revolutionary War epics. Basically, the movie moves from the original resistance of the Minute Men to the British "regular" troops, all the way through to the surrender of Cornwallis. Vivid reenactments of Paul Revere's famous ride are featured, as is the battle of Bunker Hill, Valley Forge, and the Cherry Valley massacre. An underlying romantic story serves as an excellent subplot. Nathan Holden, portrayed by Neil Hamilton, is a farmer and one of the leaders of the resistance to the Mother Country. He falls in love with Nancy Montague, a "Tory" from an extremely wealthy family.

This film, upon its release, was a critical success, and did relatively well at the box office. Unfortunately, like *Intolerance*, the film cost so much to make that the good box office showing simply did not recoup Griffith's production costs. William K. Everson has referred to *America* as "one of Griffith's most impressive and handsomely mounted spectacles." *America* was Griffith's most impressively staged historic epic since *Orphans of the Storm* (1921).

In addition to having D.W. Griffith as director and producer, this film featured an excellent cast as well. Carol Dempster was very good, and this was probably Neil Hamilton's greatest performance. Although Hamilton is best remembered by modern-day fans for his role as "Commissioner Gordon" in the *Batman* television series of the 1960s, it is this performance that should be his most memorable. In addition, Lionel Barrymore gives an especially impressive performance as the villain of the story, Captain Walter Butler, who was responsible for the Cherry Valley massacre.

Seen in its proper format, *America* can now be appreciated not only for its fabulous entertainment value, but as a good way to recall the events of the American Revolution as well. Highly recommended.

386. The Big Parade

Rating: ☆☆☆☆

MGM; ***Directed by*** King Vidor; ***Story by*** Laurence Stallings; ***Scenario by*** Harry Behn; ***Titles by*** Joseph W. Farnham; ***Settings by*** Cedric Gibbons, James Basevi; ***Wardrobe by*** Ethel P. Chaffin; ***Photography by*** John Arnold; ***Film Editor:*** Hugh Wynn; ***Running Time of Original Release:*** 142 minutes; ***Running Time of 1931 Reissue Evaluated:*** 123 minutes; ***Cast:*** JAMES APPERSON, John Gilbert (1899–1936); MELISANDE, Renée Adorée (1898–1933); MR. APPERSON, Hobart Bosworth (1867–1943); MRS. APPERSON, Claire McDowell (1878–1966); JUSTYN REED, Claire Adams (1898–1978); HARRY, Robert Ober (1881–1950); BULL, Tom O'Brien (1890–1947); SLIM, Karl Dane (1886–1934); FRENCH MOTHER, Rosita Marstini (1887–1948)

The Big Parade was the film that established director King Vidor (1894–1982) as one of the greats. It was a hard idea to sell, as it wasn't known if the public would be ready to support another war film, since there were so many done during World War I, and the public was heartily sick of seeing war on the screen. The smashing success of Rex Ingram's *The Four Horsemen of the Apocalypse* (1921) gave MGM and King Vidor the confidence to take the gamble, and the gamble paid off big. *The Big Parade* was one of the top five grossers of the silent era.

John Gilbert gave the best performance of his career—as well as one of the best performances of 1924—as spoiled rich kid James Apperson, who lives a life of luxury on his father's wealth. He thinks work is what other people do while he is in the barber shop getting a shave. His father finally lays down an ultimatum, and insists that James take a job in his factory. Before he can report to work, the nation enters World War I, and he enlists at the urging of girlfriend Justyn Reed. The only side of war that Apperson knows is the glory and victory parades. Once he ends up in France, he at first sees a rather carefree attitude. He still doesn't get it, and falls in love with a French girl, Melisande.

The cold, harsh reality of war brutally hits when James' regiment is called for its first combat situation. The sequence showing his truck pulling out—with Melisande running behind to have what may be one last kiss—is a classic powerhouse of emotion and sadness. It is this segment which is often used in film history documentaries.

The battle scenes in this film are brilliantly executed. While it may not be obvious when first watching the film, Vidor did some elaborate choreography in the initial combat sequence. Every step, every shot, and every falling corpse was perfectly timed to coincide with the accompanying music.

Karl Dane, who plays Apperson's Army sidekick, Slim, provides nice touches of

John Gilbert, star of *The Big Parade* (1924), which catapulted him to stardom.

comedy relief without getting too hokey. But, even amusing Slim is killed in the war, thus shocking the audience back into cold reality.

While a few subsequent war films like *All Quiet on the Western Front* (1930) come close to equaling *The Big Parade* in quality, none have ever surpassed it. *The Big Parade* (1924) and *The Four Horsemen of the Apocalypse* (1921) remain the masterpieces of the genre by which all others will be measured.

The Big Parade was reissued with a synchronized score and sound effects in 1931, with tighter editing. In comparing the complete original and reissue versions, the reissue is actually a slight improvement as it cuts out a few minutes of extraneous footage that slowed down the pace of the film.

387. Body and Soul

Rating: ☆☆☆½

Micheaux Film Corporation; ***Directed by*** Oscar Micheaux; ***Running Time:*** 79 minutes; ***Cast:*** THE REVEREND/HIS BROTHER, Paul Robeson (1898–1976); THE GIRL, Mercedes Gilbert (1894–1952); HER MOTHER, Julia Theresa Russell; FORMER JAILMATE OF THE REVEREND, Lawrence Chenault; SPEAKEASY PROPRIETOR, Marshall Rodgers; TWO PIOUS LADIES, Lillian Johnson and Madam Robinson; CHURCH ELDERS, Chester A. Alexander and Walter Cornick

Body and Soul, produced in Harlem, was the film debut of Paul Robeson, who is perhaps best remembered for his performance in the 1936 version of *Show Boat*. All of the major and minor roles except one were played by blacks. One black actor was made up to look white. The only white actor played a street vendor who sold spoiled food to poor blacks in the ghettos of Atlanta. This in itself was a subtle statement of social commentary.

Robeson plays a corrupt reverend who fleeces his entire congregation, and even accepts bribes from speakeasies as "hush" money. Trusted by a young girl's mother, he makes inappropriate sexual advances to the daughter when he is left alone with her, and steals the money that the mother had painstakingly saved for a home. The girl, knowing that her mother would never believe the truth about what the reverend did, runs away to Atlanta, leaving her mother to believe that she stole the money from the family bible. It is only when her mother finds her daughter living in poverty that she is finally convinced of the truth.

In the 1920s when this film was made, many blacks depended on their church leaders as among the few role models they had to look up to. *Body and Soul* explores the danger that occurs when a corrupt person attains such a position in the community. When Oscar Micheaux originally released this film, the censors refused to allow its release with

Paul Robeson, star of *Body and Soul* (1924), as he appeared at the height of his career in the mid–1930s.

such a negative portrayal of religious figures. Therefore, Micheaux was forced to tack a happy ending on, portraying the nightmare as a dream.

While this is a rather grim and depressing film, it is important in documenting what the black audiences of the 1920s were concerned with, and the issues that were being portrayed for this sect of the population.

The leading lady is Mercedes Gilbert, who gives a compelling performance. Unfortunately, no further information could be found on any of the supporting players.

Paul Robeson, the lead actor, was a highly intelligent man, having earned a law degree at Rutgers University. He had acted in some stage plays at the Harlem YMCA. Based on his success, he was personally requested by Eugene O'Neill to star in his plays *The Emperor Jones* and *All God's Chillun Got Wings*. He enjoyed significant success on Broadway and in the movies from the 1920s through the 1940s. Unfortunately, his left wing political leanings resulted in his being blacklisted in the United States. In the early 1960s, he toured Europe, but poor health caused him to retire to Harlem, where he died at the age of 78.

This is a film of significant historic interest. It was well received when a restored version was presented in 1997 on American Movie Classics as part of Black History Month.

388. Dante's Inferno

Rating: ☆☆½

Fox; ***Directed by*** Henry Otto; ***Modern Story by*** Cyrus Wood; ***Screen Adaptation by*** Edmund Goulding; ***Photographed by*** Joseph August; ***Running Time:*** 57 minutes; ***Cast:*** MORTIMER JUDD, Ralph Lewis (1872–1937); MRS. JUDD, Winifred Landis; ERNEST JUDD, William Scott; MISS VERNON (THE NURSE), Pauline Starke (1900–1977); EUGENE CRAIG, Joseph Swickard (1866–1940); MISS CRAIG (HIS DAUGHTER), Gloria Grey (1909–1947); DR. JOSEPHS, Lorimer Johnston (1858–1941); DANTE, Lawson Butt (1883–1956)

This version of *Dante's Inferno* is partly based on the original Dante's *Inferno* literary classic as translated by Gustave Dore, and interweaved with a modern story. The screenplay was written by Edmund Goulding (1891–1959), who would later direct such films as *Love* (1927), *Grand Hotel* (1932), and *Dark Victory* (1939).

Ralph Lewis plays the lead role of Mortimer Judd, a tyrannical and wealthy entrepreneur/slum lord with a heart of stone. This man is so cold that when he learns his wife is ill, he shrugs his shoulders and states, "Only the wives of rich men can afford to be ill." In addition, he ignores the pleas of his son, Ernest Judd, to provide fire protection for the residents of the tenements they own.

The original Dante's *Inferno* story comes into play when a neighbor of the Judds, Eugene Craig, appeals to the elder Judd for help. It seems Judd sits on a board which will decide whether to force Mr. Craig into bankruptcy, with Judd's vote being the swing vote. In reply to his plea for help, Judd replies, "I cut the word 'help' out of my vocabulary 20 years ago, and it has paid me well." Eugene Craig sends Judd a copy of Gustave Dore's translation of the book, Dante's *Inferno*. Judd reads the book, and falls asleep in the process. His dream brings the vision of his being taken on a tour of hell by Dante, thus bringing *Dante's Inferno* into the story.

The hell sequences graphically show the various punishments for specific misdeeds. The red tints in the tinted print emphasize the fiery atmosphere that much more. Some of the sequences created controversy, as they featured players clad in body stockings which gave the illusion of nudity. It is obvious that no expense was spared in the art direction, as the sets and costumes are quite impressive.

Although this film falls a bit short of a masterpiece, it is interesting to see the visual interpretations of hell, and there is some good special effects cinematography as well. Its historic value as one of the very few pre–1925 Fox silents available to us makes it especially appealing.

389. The Desert Secret

Rating: ☆☆☆

Kenneth J. Bishop/Madoc Sales Company; ***Written and Directed by*** Fred Reel, Jr.; ***Photographed by*** E.J. Zerr; ***Running Time:*** 54 minutes; ***Cast:*** BUD LAWLER, Bill Patton (1894–1951); DOLLY MADISON, Pauline Curley (born 1904); MONTY, Lew Meehan (1890–1951)

Pauline Curley, leading lady of *The Desert Secret* (1924), a good Bill Patton western.

This is one of the starring films of popular "B" western actor Bill Patton. It is also significant as one of the few extant films of silent screen actress Pauline Curley. Curley's most famous role was as a Russian princess in Herbert Brenon's *The Fall of the Romanoffs* (1918), a lost film that she starred in at 14. She was 20 when she did *The Desert Secret*. Now known as Pauline Peach, she is 93 at this writing and living in Southern California.

Patton plays Bud Lawler, who has just struck gold with a friend of his. The friend is an alcoholic, who has a propensity for telling too much. Lawler encounters Dolly Madison on his way into town to buy supplies, while she is trying to fix her Ford. The villain of the story is Monty, who owns the only store in Caliente. He has been searching for years for the gold that Bud and his friend just struck.

Pauline Curley is excellent in portraying the girl who gets Bud out of a number of scrapes. At one point, she drives her Ford right into the saloon to effect a rescue.

This western sports a good plot and story line. It features a number of good, old-fashioned barroom brawls to boot. In addition to these attributes, the film is worth watching and having for the rare chance to see the delightful Pauline Curley.

390. The Family Secret

Rating: ☆☆☆½

Century/Universal; ***Directed by*** William Seiter; ***Based on the Augustus Thomas Play,*** *The Burglar*; from *Editha's Burglar* ***by*** Frances Hodgson Burnett; ***Screenplay by*** Lois Zellner; ***Photographed by*** John Stumar; ***Running Time:*** 70 minutes; ***Cast:*** PEGGY HOLMES, "Baby Peggy" Montgomery (born 1918); MARGARET SELFRIDGE (HOLMES), Gladys Hulette (1896–1991); GARY HOLMES, Edward Earle (1882–1972); SIMON SELFRIDGE, Frank Currier (1857–1928); TOMASO SILVANO, Cesare Gravina (1858–1954?); UNCLE MOSE, Martin Tucker; AUNT MANDY, Elizabeth Mackey; NURSE SNEED, Martha Mattox (1879–1933); MISS ABIGAIL SELFRIDGE, Lucy Beaumont (1873–1937)

Just as Jackie Coogan was the first male child actor to achieve superstar status, Baby Peggy was the first female to achieve such stature as a child. Rough estimates indicate that during her film career, Baby Peggy earned somewhere in the neighborhood of $2 to $3 million (1920s dollars). After her movie career ended, she enjoyed a successful vaudeville career in which she was earning $2,000 per week. These days, Baby Peggy is known as Diana Serra Cary, a prominent author and historian of western Americana and early cinema.

Baby Peggy Montgomery, star of *The Family Secret* (1924), posing with a "Baby Peggy" doll in New York at the height of her career.

The story of this film centers around a woman named Margaret Selfridge, the daughter of a prominent "old money" family. She falls in love with average working man Gary Holmes, and marries him in secret—knowing that her father would never approve of the marriage, but hoping that once they were married for a while, that he would come around and accept it. When Mr. Selfridge finds out, he is enraged, as he thinks that Holmes married Selfridge for money. He orders him out of the house, but when he returns to see his wife and baby, has him arrested for burglary and sent to prison.

Four years pass, and Baby Peggy comes into the picture. Here we see her get into a variety of misadventures and comedy situations. One of the first, and a favorite, sequence is when the prudish Nurse Sneed sits Baby Peggy down for a story reading. While the nurse is reading, Baby Peggy is shown mocking every gesture and expression of the nurse. Slyly, she puts a doll in her place in the chair, and sneaks down to the kitchen where she gets into everything—literally. When Sneed figures out that she has been conned, she comes to the kitchen looking for Peggy, who is hiding behind the maid's dress. When Peggy sees the nurse, she climbs into the flour bin and hides. She is finally caught when she comes up long enough to raid the chocolate cookie dough. Another interesting aspect about this sequence is that it provides a refreshingly positive portrayal of the black servants in their efforts to protect Peggy from the prudish and sometimes abusive nurse. They also buy her a train set for her birthday, which none of the other household members bothered to observe.

The story progresses as Mr. Selfridge begins to soften his attitude, and realizes his error in separating his daughter from her husband. He gets off to a good start in making his amends by firing the nurse who was so mean to his granddaughter. Along the way, Baby Peggy charms us through some fabulous sequences, including one in which she chastises a police officer for taking an apple from a curbside market display. She discards a banana peel which the officer slips on. She then takes the apple away from him and says, "I told you God would punish bad little boys!"

Meanwhile, Peggy's father is released from prison, but is unable to find a job. In desperation, he resorts to committing a burglary. The house he chooses happens to be the Selfridge's vacation home. It is interesting to see how everything works out in the end.

In addition to Baby Peggy, this film features a fine supporting cast as well. Gladys Hulette, who plays Peggy's mother, had a long and distinguished career, which started in 1909 at Vitagraph when she was 13. Edward Earle started at the Edison Company in 1916. Martha Mattox is best remembered for her portrayal as the sinister housekeeper in *The Cat and the Canary* (1927).

While *Captain January* (1923) is the most famous of Baby Peggy's surviving films that are available for evaluation, *The Family Secret* really showcases her talents the best, as it provides the funniest situations. It is a delightful film, and a fine example of Baby Peggy at her best.

391. Fast Company

Rating: ☆☆☆½

Hal Roach/Pathé Exchange; ***Directed by*** Robert McGowan; ***Titles by*** H.M. Walker; ***Story by*** Hal Roach; ***Running Time:*** 12 minutes; ***Cast:*** **Our Gang:** Mickey Daniels (1914–1970); Joe Cobb (born 1917); Farina Hoskins (1920–1980); Jackie Condon (1918–1977); Jack Davis (1914–1970); Ernie "Sunshine Sammy" Morrison (1912–1989)

This is a film that just twenty years ago in 1977 was unavailable for evaluation. Leonard Maltin's 1977 book, *Our Gang: The Life and Times of the Little Rascals*, covered this film on the basis of reviews of the time and plot synopses because it could not be accessed. Fortunately, this is one "lost" film that has turned up and is now widely available to the public on video. It was the 16th of the "Our Gang" films released.

While *Fast Company* was originally released as a two-reeler, all that has survived is a truncated one-reel version from which most of the titles have been cut. This episode has Mickey Daniels trading places with a lonely rich boy who is staying at a posh hotel. The rest of the gang joins him, and they get into a variety of misadventures, terrifying the high society types and wreaking general havoc.

Joe Cobb, the much-loved fat toddler who appears as part of "Our Gang" in *Fast Company* (1924).

Joe Cobb steals the show as the centerpiece in the jungle room of the hotel, sitting in a stew pot while the others play like they are cannibals. Cobb gets out, and little Farina takes his place in the pot. Cobb then proceeds to try to break open a coconut, squirting coconut juice all over the place. Needless to say, many repairs are needed after the gang gets through.

In addition to the gang of kids, they bring along a goat with them, who runs around the hotel in a white sheet, terrorizing the housekeepers who think it is a ghost. The final shot shows the kids after they are thrown out of the hotel, sick to their stomachs after having smoked a "peace pipe."

While this film, when originally released, got the rave reviews it deserved, in these times of "political correctness," it would draw criticism. Its portrayal of the black servants being scared of the moving white sheet would be criticized, as would the sequence of the gang smoking peace pipes, which would draw fire from antismoking advocates despite the fact that the scene shows them sick at the end from the smoking.

392. Fifty Thousand Dollar Reward

Rating: ☆☆☆

Clifford S. Elfelt/Davis Distributors; ***Directed by*** Clifford S. Elfelt; ***Assistant Director:*** Jack Pierce; ***Story/Scenario by*** Frank Howard Clark; ***Photography by*** Bert Longenecker; ***Running Time:*** 43 minutes; ***Cast:*** TEX SHERWOOD, Ken Maynard (1895–1973); CAROLYN JORDAN, Esther Ralston (1902–1994); ANTHONY JORDAN, Bert Lindley (1873–1953); BUCK SCOFIELD, Edward Piel (1883–1958); MA MILLER, Lillianne Leighton (1874–1956); PA MILLER, Charles Newton (1874–1926); ASA HOLMAN, Frank Whitson (1877–1946); ELI HIGGINS, William Moran; SNOWBALL, Ananias Berry; FRECKLES, Augusta Aim; ***Follies Girls:*** Olive Trevor; Fern Lorraine; Edith Flynn; Katherine DeForrest; Grace Fay; Nancy Zann

Ken Maynard, star of *Fifty Thousand Dollar Reward* (1924), was known for his elaborate stunt work.

After having played some small parts in some early Fox westerns of 1923 as well as his cameo in *Janice Meredith* (1924), western star Ken Maynard starred in a few films for Clifford S. Elfelt and the Davis Distributing Company. While most of these early westerns were low budget productions, Maynard made a distinct impression with his excellent stunt work and riding skills, and by 1926 signed with First National where he was making $40,000 to $60,000 a picture.

This is one of the best of Maynard's earlier films with Davis and Elfelt, full of action and amazing stunts. In it, Maynard plays Tex Sherwood, a man who comes into a small Montana town to claim title to land that his father left him. There happens to be a price on his head of $50,000, as the land that he actually owns the title to is land that entrepreneur Asa Holman has claimed using a forged title for use as farming land,

and has already commissioned a $1 million dam irrigation project which makes the land that much more valuable.

Esther Ralston is the leading lady and daughter of the contractor whose livelihood depends on completion of the dam project by a certain time. Edward Peil plays villain Buck Scofield, the outlaw hired by Holman to get Sherwood out of the way, as well as to delay the dam project so that the Jordans won't complete it by the agreed deadline, and therefore not have to be paid the bonus of $100,000 which is the only profit Carolyn's father will make.

Among the impressive stunts that Ken Maynard does in the grand finale is one in which he pulls up on horseback beside a runaway carriage, gets onto one of the horses from his horse, and stands with one foot on each of two horses as he takes control of the carriage. This is one of the most impressive stunts ever portrayed in the history of western films, and *Fifty Thousand Dollar Reward* would be worth seeing for this stunt alone. One can definitely see why the world was so impressed with Maynard and how he became so popular.

This film provides a great chance to see Maynard at his best—before his alcoholism escalated, eventually ruining his career and reducing him from a popular millionaire western star to a man who depended on the charity of others for the bare existence he had during his final years.

393. Girl Shy

Rating: ☆☆☆

Harold Lloyd Corporation/Pathé; ***Directed by*** Fred Newmeyer and Sam Taylor; ***Assistant Director:*** Robert A. Golden; ***Story by*** Sam Taylor, Ted Wilde, and Tim Whelan; ***Titles by*** Thomas J. Grey; ***Photography by*** Walter Lundin and Henry N. Kohler; ***Editor:*** Allen McNeil; ***Production Manager:*** John L. Murphy; ***Technical Director:*** William MacDonald; ***Art Director:*** Liell K. Vedder; ***Running Time:*** 87 minutes; ***Cast:*** HAROLD MEADOWS, Harold Lloyd (1893–1971); MARY BUCKINGHAM, Jobyna Ralston (1900–1967); JERRY MEADOWS, Richard Daniels; RONALD DEVORE, Carlton Griffin (1893–1940); THE TRAIN CONDUCTOR, Charles Stevenson (1851–1929); ***Supporting Cast:*** Joe Cobb (born 1917); Mickey Daniels (1914–1970); Jackie Condon (1918–1977)

This romantic comedy has Harold Lloyd playing a tailor's apprentice who is also an aspiring writer. He is not a hit with the women, but the book he is writing is about the secrets of attracting them. The book relays torrid past affairs of his which are, in reality, merely fantasy.

He meets a rich girl on the way to take his book to the publisher, and his stuttering problem complicates the process of trying to strike up a conversation. He overcomes this obstacle, and makes an impression on the girl, but then finds it difficult to live up to the reputation he has established for himself. One funny sequence has him sitting on a turtle, and as he talks to the girl, the turtle walks toward the lake while he is talking.

When Harold returns to the publishers to see what they think of his book, he is the laughing stock of the company. One of the women jokingly asks for his autograph. Feeling like a failure, he gives up all hope of ever moving up in the career world or getting the girl of his dreams.

Turnabout is the order of the day when one of the editors convinces the publisher to publish Harold's book as a joke—under the title *The Boob's Diary*. The publishers send him an advance royalty check of $3,000. When Harold receives it, he expects a rejection slip, and tears the envelope up without opening it. His boss realizes that the envelope contains a check, and he and Harold piece it back together.

A newspaper article reveals to Harold that his girl is about to marry a bigamist, and the chase is on to stop the wedding in time. This chase sequence is a classic, and was one of the clips that became a part of the *Harold Lloyd's World of Comedy* series of the early 1960s. During the scene in which he is hanging on for dear life to a fire hose as it is unrolling, Lloyd reportedly fell and suffered injuries as a result. Another remarkable scene has Harold dangling from a rod that protrudes from the top of the trolley car as it is moving at a high rate of speed. As far as chase sequences go, this is definitely one of the best in comedy history.

Although *Girl Shy* as a whole isn't among the best of Lloyd's features, it is still good, solid entertainment. The chase finale alone is enough to give it status as a classic not to be missed.

394. Going to Congress

Rating: ☆☆☆☆

Hal Roach/Pathé Exchange; Director Unidentified; ***Running Time:*** 19 minutes; ***Cast:*** ALFALFA DOOLITTLE, Will Rogers (1879–1935); ***Supporting Cast:*** Marie Mosquini (1902–1983)

Going to Congress was the first in a series of three political satire comedies that Will Rogers did in 1924. He became so popular that people were actually encouraging him to run for president. In this film, Rogers plays a country hick who runs for Congress and wins. Among some of the witty political quips he comes up with are the following:

> Q: See where they're going to give the soldiers their bonus in Spring?
> A: Sorry to hear that. It means a late Spring.
> Q: Do you think Ford ought to run?
> A: Yes, I think they all OUGHT to run.

The film has Doolittle giving simple, appealing campaign speeches, as well as a hilarious debate against his opponent. The opponent talks about how the country needs lower taxes, help for the poor, etc. Rogers gets up and explains that what the country really needs is rain, and that if elected, he will make sure that we get it. He wins the election on that basis.

On his trip to Washington, Doolittle gets in a number of other witty political cracks, including some hilarious ones alluding to the Teapot Dome scandal, which was the political hot potato of the time.

Going to Congress is a masterpiece of political satire. It is a film that should be required watching in American history classes, and shows why Will Rogers was possibly the most popular man in America during the mid–1920s until his death in 1935. It is hilariously funny, sidesplitting satire at its best.

395. Greed

Rating: ☆☆☆☆

MGM; ***Directed by*** Erich von Stroheim; ***Assistant Directors:*** Eddie Sowders and Louis Germonprez; ***Screenplay by*** Erich von Stroheim; ***Based on Frank Norris' 1899 Novel, McTeague***; ***Directors of Photography:*** Ben F. Reynolds, William H. Daniels; ***Art Direction by*** Richard

A promotional poster for Erich von Stroheim's masterpiece, *Greed* (1924), featuring Gibson Gowland in the title role of Frank Norris' *McTeague*, upon which the movie was based.

Day and Erich von Stroheim; ***Editing:*** E. von Stroheim, Rex Ingram, June Mathis, Joseph W. Farnham; ***Settings by*** Cedric Gibbons; ***Running Time of Director's Cut:*** Approx. 480 minutes; ***Running Time of Currently Available Versions:*** 133 minutes; ***Cast Members Appearing In Final Cut:*** McTeague, Gibson Gowland (1877–1951); Trina Sieppe, Zasu Pitts (1898–1963); Marcus Schouler, Jean Hersholt (1886–1956); McTeague's mother, Tempe Piggott (1884–1962); Dr. "Painless" Potter, Erich von Ritzau (1877–1936); Hans Sieppe, Chester Conklin (1886–1971); Mrs. Sieppe, Sylvia Ashton (1880–1940); August Sieppe, Austin Jewell; Max and Moritz Sieppe, Oscar and Otto Gotell; Selina, Joan Standing (1903–1979); Charles W. Grannis, Frank Hayes (1871–1923); Miss Anastasia Baker, Fanny Midgeley (1879–1932); Maria Miranda Macapa, Dale Fuller; Mr. Heise, Hughie Mack (1884–1927); The minister, William Barlow (1852–1937); The man from the lottery company, Lon Poff (1870–1952); The Sheriff of Placer County, Jack McDonald (1880–??) ***Cast Members Deleted from Final Cut:*** McTeague, Sr., Jack Curtis (1880–1956); Uncle Rudolph Oelbermann, Max Tryon; Zerkow the junk dealer, Cesare Gravina (1858–1954); Mrs. Heise, Elizabeth "Tiny" Jones (1875–1952); Mr. Ryer, J. Aldrich Libbey (1872–1925); Mrs. Ryer, Rita Revela; Joe Frenna, Sol S. Simon (1864–1940); The photographer, Hugh J. McCauley; The palmist, William Mollemhauer; Cribbens [a prospector], James Fulton

Greed is recognized by film critics the world over as Erich von Stroheim's undisputed masterpiece. It is also ranked as one of the greatest films in the entire history of the cinema. Originally, *Greed* was intended to be a faithful adaptation of Frank Norris' 1899 novel *McTeague*, acclaimed by literary critics as a minor classic. Von Stroheim's original cut was approximately 8 or 9 hours in length. He cut this length himself to a little over 5 hours, hoping to show it in two parts with an intermission. His old nemesis, Irving Thalberg, who had fired him from Universal, was now head of production at MGM. Thalberg refused to let the film be released at the length of 5 hours. So, von Stroheim sent the film to his good friend director Rex Ingram. Ingram's editor, Grant Whytock, cut the film to approximately 3¼ hours. Ingram admonished von Stroheim, stating that if he cut another foot from the film, he would never speak to him again. Unfortunately, Irving Thalberg and Louis B. Mayer took the decision out of von Stroheim's hands. They took *McTeague* away from him, handed it to editors June Mathis and Joseph W. Farnham, and renamed the new 2¼ hour version *Greed*.

Only approximately ten people saw the complete version of *Greed* as Erich Von Stroheim had intended it to be seen. The original production featured hand applied gold coloring of the scenes with gold coins, brass, gold silverware, etc. In addition, the train coming during the rain storm is hand-colored red at the front, to symbolize a demon. This hand-coloring does not exist in current prints, either. Furthermore, the scenes of the greedy hands playing in the money, as well as the huge hand squeezing the life out of Trina and her husband, were originally filmed in 2-strip Technicolor, which has not been preserved. All of those who did see the original *McTeague* walked out exhausted, convinced that they had seen the greatest film ever made up to that time. The technology exists today to at least restore the Technicolor and hand-colored sequences to an approximation of what they were meant to be, but such has not as yet been done. It has been persistently rumored (insubstantiated) for years that a 5½ hour version of *Greed* exists in a private collection.

Even in its edited and truncated format (which von Stroheim disowned and refused to watch), *Greed* has stood the test of time as one of the greatest dramatic masterpieces in the entire history of cinema. If one watches the movie before having read the book, it is impossible to tell that parts of the story were left out. This would indicate a masterful editing job on the part of June Mathis and Joseph Farnham. It is only upon reading the novel that one discovers that Maria, the housekeeper, was supposed to develop into a significant character, and that the characters Miss Baker, Old Grannis, and junk dealer Zerkow are totally lost. The only remaining footage in which one can catch a brief glimpse of Miss Baker and Old Grannis is at the foot of the stairs, when the neighbors and lottery officials are waiting to break the good news that Trina has just won $5,000 in the lottery. They were originally supposed to have their own subplot, paralleling how their modest attitudes and lifestyles made their budding romance prosper into happiness, while the greed of Trina McTeague and junk dealer Zerkow ruined their respective marriages and resulted in their deaths. The junk dealer Zerkow is completely eliminated from the final cut of the film. He was supposed to have married housekeeper Maria Macapa, believing the pathological lies she told of the existence of a valuable gold dinner set in her family to be true, with the story escalating into beatings and finally murder to force Maria to tell him the location of the nonexistent gold dinnerware. The remaining stills of these sequences indicate that Cesare Gravina gave a powerful and chilling performance as Zerkow, and would have had a much greater place in film history if some of his footage had made it into the final cut. The only part of the subplots left is one of the linking images of hands admiring a gold platter set, which was supposed to be used to precede the segments in which this subplot dealt with. This interlinking device from this subplot is now haphazardly and randomly included in a few parts of the film. Despite the editing of these important subplots, what survives of this film is a chilling portrayal of how Trina McTeague's greed and obsession with money led to the downfall of herself, her husband, and her cousin Marcus Schouler.

The three main characters are excellently played. Zasu Pitts, whose talent was mostly wasted in trite comedies, demonstrates in this one major dramatic part that she had what it took to do serious drama work worthy of high critical acclaim. Based on what has been available for evaluation, Pitts' performance in *Greed* was the best dramatic performance by a female in the year of 1924. This one part qualifies her as one of the great dramatic actresses of silent motion pictures. Gibson Gowland was also excellent in the lead part of McTeague, and it is surprising that he did not go on to further stardom in pictures after this role. Jean Hersholt is remarkable in the second male lead role, and this is the role that really established his reputation as a major film player.

The actors, actresses, and entire crew worked under grueling conditions with infinite determination to complete this work of art. One of the cooks with the crew died, and other crew members were hospitalized while doing the Death Valley sequences. Jean Hersholt spent months in the hospital recovering from painful sunburn blisters that had actually formed under his skin rather than above it.

The MGM officials falsely claimed that *Greed* "cost a fortune and lost a fortune." In actuality, it did turn a small profit, having grossed a little more than the $470,000 it cost to make. It probably would have done better if it had been properly promoted, which Irving Thalberg refused to do.

In objectively trying to evaluate how successful *Greed* might have been in its complete form, this author has concluded that possibly the ultimate version would have been the 3¼ hour version that Grant Whytock and Rex Ingram presented for Erich von Stroheim's approval. Von Stroheim was willing to go with this version, as it still contained most of his subplots. At 3¼ hours, it would have been a great compromise between what von Stroheim had originally intended, and what Irving Thalberg eventually had it cut down to. A single motion picture production of the original five hours in length that von Stroheim wanted would likely have been cumbersome as too much of a good thing. At 3¼ hours, it would have been tightly edited, and still included enough to satisfy one's desire for the subplots that were in the book. *The Birth of a Nation* was highly successful at this approximate length, and so likely would *Greed* have been if released at this length.

396. He Who Gets Slapped

Rating: ☆☆☆☆

MGM; ***Directed by*** Victor Seastrom; ***Adapted from*** Leonid Andreyev's play; ***Translated by*** Gregory Zillboorg; ***Screenplay by*** Victor Seastrom and Carey Wilson; ***Settings by*** Cedric Gibbons; ***Costumes by*** Sophie Wachner; ***Photography by*** Milton Moore; ***Film Editor:*** Hugh Wynn; ***Running Time:*** 71 minutes; ***Cast:*** PAUL BEAUMONT, Lon Chaney, Sr. (1883–1930); BEZANO, John Gilbert (1899–1936); CONSUELO MANCINI, Norma Shearer (1900–1983); MARIE BEAUMONT, Ruth King; BARON REGNARD, Marc McDermott (1881–1929); TRICAND, Ford Sterling (1880–1939); COUNT MANCINI, Tully Marshall (1864–1943)

He Who Gets Slapped was the very first release of the newly formed MGM company. MGM pulled no punches with this debut release, having brought prestigious Swedish director Victor Seastrom over from Europe, and cast three of the biggest stars of the time in the lead roles—Lon Chaney, Norma Shearer, and John Gilbert.

In this film, Chaney plays Paul Beaumont, a man who, under the sponsorship of a wealthy benefactor, makes important scientific discoveries. Not only does benefactor Baron Regnard steal the credit for his discoveries for himself, but he steals Beaumont's wife from him, too. The title *He Who Gets Slapped* comes from the incident in which Beaumont tells the audience that the discoveries were his, and the Baron slaps him, with the audience laughing.

Cheated out of both a promising scientific career and his wife, Chaney's character becomes a clown named "he," making his living being slapped and laughed at before an audience.

John Gilbert plays Bezano, a trapeze artist with the circus, and Norma Shearer plays Consuelo, the daughter of a wealthy count who works with the circus, and whom Chaney's character falls for, although Consuelo falls in love with Bezano, forming another sticky love triangle.

He Who Gets Slapped gets really interesting when, years later, the baron comes to one of the circus shows, and "he" and the baron meet face to face for the first time in years. It seems that the baron has divorced his wife, and has his sights set on Consuelo. With his wealth, Consuelo's father agrees to the marriage. This leads into a confrontation, which provides the thrilling finale for the film.

Marc McDermott, who played Baron Regnard, was killed five years after he appeared in this film, in 1929, having been shot by a murderer right at his own front gate.

While all of Chaney's evaluated silents for MGM were good (with the exception of *Mockery* [1927]), director Victor Seastrom's allegorical style of presenting this story makes *He Who Gets Slapped* the only Chaney/MGM vehicle that really qualifies for masterpiece status. It is a magnificent artistic achievement.

Although Turner Entertainment has not released this film on video yet, *He Who Gets Slapped* was restored with an orchestral score and sound effects and has aired occasionally on Turner Classic Movies.

397. Hold Your Breath

Rating: ☆☆☆½

Christie/Hodkinson; ***Directed by*** Scott Sidney; ***Running Time:*** 31 minutes; ***Cast:*** FREDDIE, Walter Hiers (1893–1933); MABEL, Dorothy DeVore (1899–1976); MARY, Priscilla Bonner (1899–1996); JACK, Jimmy Harrison (1908–1977); THE CITY EDITOR, Lincoln Plumer (1875–1928); MILLIONAIRE BLAKE, Tully Marshall (1864–1943); A BUSINESSMAN, Max Davidson (1875–1950)

When one sees this film, it makes a person wonder why Dorothy DeVore is little more than a footnote in film history. While it is true that only two of her films are widely available for evaluation, these films demonstrate that her talent as a comedienne was a talent to be reckoned with. And, her two-film survival rate is greater than that of many other actresses who are more widely written about—such as Olive Thomas, Lillian Hall, Martha Mansfield, Ruth Clifford, and others.

In *Hold Your Breath*, DeVore plays Mabel, whose sister-in-law has just spent her and her husband's savings on oil stock. Mabel has been fired from her job, and her brother Jack has been laid off from his job as well. So, she takes a job as a newspaper reporter. She fails to make the mark in her new career, but is given one last chance—if she can get an interview with an eccentric millionaire that no other reporter has been able to. She at first has the same luck as her predecessors, but with her wit and charm finally manages to accomplish the impossible—only to have a monkey climb through the window and take a $50,000 bracelet belonging to millionaire Blake, who suspects her of stealing it. The monkey climbs out the high rise window with the bracelet, and Mabel gives chase in a sequence that resembles the "human fly" sequence in Harold Lloyd's *Safety Last* (1923).

The human fly sequence in this film is not quite as well photographed as Harold Lloyd's was in *Safety Last*, and it is obvious that a double was used for the most dangerous stunts. Nonetheless, it has comparable gags, and is thrilling to watch. Dorothy DeVore deserves a much more prominent place in film history.

398. Hot Water

Rating: ☆☆☆☆

Harold Lloyd Corporation/Pathé; ***Directed by*** Fred Newmeyer and Sam Taylor; ***Assistant Director:*** Robert A. Golden; ***Story by*** Sam Taylor, Thomas J. Grey, Tim Whelan, John Grey; ***Titles by*** Thomas J. Grey; ***Photography by*** Walter Lundin and Henry N. Kohler; ***Editor:*** Allen McNeil; ***Technical Director:*** William MacDonald; ***Running Time:*** 60 minutes; ***Cast:*** HUBBY, Harold Lloyd (1893–1971); WIFEY, Jobyna Ralston (1900–1967); HER MOTHER, Josephine Crowell (died 1934); CHARLEY, HER OLDER BROTHER, Charles Stevenson (1887–1943); BOBBY, HER YOUNGER BROTHER, Mickey McBan

This is a classic "in-laws" comedy farce, and is also said to have been a spoof on D.W. Griffith's *One Exciting Night* (1922).

In *Hot Water*, confirmed bachelor Harold's heart has been stolen by Jobyna Ralston, and they are newlyweds. Along with the girl comes her family—a domineering, back-seat driving mother aptly played by Josephine Crowell, a lazy older brother-in-law, and a bratty little brother-in-law.

Among the classic sequences is the one in which Harold is given a long grocery list by his wife, and is trying to balance everything on his way to a crowded street car. To complicate matters, he wins a live turkey in a raffle, and has that to contend with as well. To boot, he gets thrown off the street car halfway home, and has to walk the rest of the way.

The new car Harold has been waiting eagerly to surprise Jobyna with finally arrives, and what was planned as a romantic test drive for hubby and wifey becomes a family affair at the insistence of the mother-in-law. Mother-in-law's back seat driving and interference causes one calamity after another until the brand new car is finally destroyed, and the family must be towed home in what is left.

At the end of a perfectly rotten day, Harold drinks to relieve the tension, and ends up coming home drunk—in a house headed by the mother-in-law, one of the strongest supporters of prohibition one can find anywhere. This leads into the riotously funny "haunted house" sequence.

Josephine Crowell as the mother-in-law does in *Hot Water* what Anna Townsend did for *Grandma's Boy* (1922); she steals the show in virtually every sequence she appears in.

Hot Water is ***the*** quintessential "in-law" comedy of all time, and among this reviewer's favorites.

399. Isn't Life Wonderful? *Rating:* ☆☆☆½

D.W. Griffith/United Artists; ***Directed by*** D.W. Griffith; ***Running Time:*** 118 minutes; ***Cast:*** INGA, Carol Dempster (1901–1991); PAUL, Neil Hamilton (1897–1984); ***Supporting Cast:*** Erville Anderson; Helen Lowell (1866–1937); Marcia Harris (1880–??); Frank Puglia (1892–1975); Lupino Lane (1892–1959)

Isn't Life Wonderful? was D.W. Griffith's last independently produced silent film, before he went to work at Paramount Studios. Griffith, an ardent pacifist, made this film in part to atone for *Hearts of the World* (1918), an anti–German propaganda film he made during World War I.

The story of *Isn't Life Wonderful?* takes place in post-war Germany, circa 1923. Griffith opens with a portrayal of how war may have seemed glorious to the imperialistic leaders and profiteers in Germany, but brought about horrible conditions for the civilians. A stinging title flashes onto the screen with the two words, "War's harvest!" preceding long lines of homeless Polish refugees walking long distances and waiting for days to get shelter. Once the people receive room assignments, shown are the harsh conditions they live under in these overcrowded buildings in which each person receives a daily ration of one potato each.

The story then zeroes in on the trials and tribulations of the family of a professor. Carol Dempster plays the female leading role as Inga, an orphan. Neil Hamilton plays the male lead, Paul. Their performances are especially moving as we see that the Germans that the world hated so much had inhabitants including innocent people who suffered not only under the rule of the Kaiser, but under the sanctions imposed by the allied countries afterward. We see the trials and tribulations that their love endures.

One of the most famous sequences occurs when Inga is shown waiting in the food lines. She has rounded up all of the money she can from every family member, in hopes of being able to purchase the rare commodity of meat. While she stands in the long lines, the price of food steadily goes up, and by the time her turn comes, her money will buy only a loaf of bread.

The basic message that Griffith sends forth is that when two people have enough love for each other, the fact that they have each other makes life worth living, in spite of the hardships they might endure. This movie is also a powerful indictment of how war, and the hate breeded by such, results in horrible atrocities to innocent, hard working people.

400. Janice Meredith [a.k.a. *The Beautiful Rebel*]

Rating: ☆☆

Cosmopolitan/Metro-Goldwyn; ***Directed by*** E. Mason Hopper; ***Running Time:*** 140 minutes; ***Cast:*** JANICE MEREDITH, Marion Davies (1897–1961); CHARLES FOWNES, Harrison Ford (1884–1957); LORD JOHN CLOWES, Holbrook Blinn (1872–1928); SQUIRE MEREDITH, Maclyn Arbuckle (1863–1931); MRS. MEREDITH, Hattie Delaro (1861–1941); PHILEMON HENNION, Olin Howland (1886–1959); SQUIRE HENNION, Spencer Charters (1875–1943); SUSIE (THE MAID), Mae Vokes (1882–1957); TABITHA LARKIN, Mildred Arden; GEORGE WASHINGTON, Joseph Kilgour (1863–1933); SIR FREDERICK MOBRAY, Douglas Stevenson (1885–1934); LORD HOWE, George Nash (1873–1944); A BRITISH SERGEANT, W.C. Fields (1879–1946); COLONEL RAHL, George Siegmann (1882–1928); MRS. LORING, Helen Lee Worthing (1905–1948); GENERAL CORNWALLIS, Tyrone Power, Sr. (1869–1931); MARIE ANTOINETTE, Princess Marie de Bourbon; PAUL REVERE, Ken Maynard (1895–1973)

Here we have a historical epic drama set during the American Revolution. It is obvious that it cost a fortune to make. It has all of the qualities that a fine historic epic should have—casts of thousands, lavish costumes and sets, impressive battle sequences, and most of all, a topnotch cast headed by Marion Davies. Harrison Ford, an underrated actor, turns in a very competent performance as Charles Fownes, Janice Meredith's love interest who happens to be an indentured servant to her father, Squire Meredith.

As Janice Meredith, Ms. Davies gives a fine dramatic performance. Her character, Janice, is the daughter of wealthy aristocratic loyalists. Her father is outraged that she likes a "common bond servant," and disapproves immediately.

As the story progresses, Janice gives her father still more to disapprove of—by supporting the cause of the colonists over the loyalists. This really makes her father mad, and he ships her off to a cousin's house in Boston. While here, Janice learns of British plans to invade Concord, and gets the word to Paul Revere, prompting his legendary warning to the colonists.

One of the best sequences in this film is the one depicting the crossing of the frozen Delaware River. This is such a realistic sequence that one really is left in awe that our forefathers braved such hardship for the cause of independence. This sequence looks like it was actually filmed in the winter time, with an actual frozen river. The sequence in which Charles Fownes is awaiting execution precedes a great battle sequence as well.

Another interesting sequence features W.C. Fields in a comedy cameo as a British sergeant who flirts with Janice.

With as many great elements as this film has, it is a shame that director E. Mason Hopper did not seem to be able to pull it together as effectively as he should have. *Janice Meredith* is a ploddingly directed film that crawls at a snail's pace. In addition, Marion Davies simply does not exhibit the pizzazz and enthusiasm in it as she does in *Little Old New York* and in her later comedies in the final years of the silent era. She was a good dramatic actress, but her true talent was as a comedienne.

401. Kriemhild's Revenge

Rating: ☆☆☆½

UFA Studios/Germany; ***Directed by*** Fritz Lang; ***Screenplay by*** Thea von Harbou; ***Based on the Ancient Poem,*** *Die Nibelungenlied*; ***Photography by*** Carl Hoffman, Gunther Rittau; ***Art Direction:*** Otto Hunte, Karl Vollbrecht, Erich Kettelhut; ***Running Time:*** 90 minutes; ***Cast:*** KRIEMHILD, Margaretta Schoen (1895–1985); GUNTHER, Theodor Loos (1883–1954); ***Supporting Cast:*** Rudolf Klein-Rogge (1888–1955); Georg August Koch

This is the second part of the *Die Nibelungenlied* saga. In the first half, Princess Kriemhild was portrayed as a fair princess with a heart of gold. In this second half, she is a bitter woman set out to avenge her husband Siegfried's death at any cost.

This intense follow-up to *Siegfried* allows Margaretta Schoen to live up to the full potential of her acting ability. Like Lillian Gish (1893–1993), she could convey more emotion with one movement of her eye than most people could with a thousand or more words.

Kriemhild's Revenge has Kriemhild married to the notorious Atilla the Hun in her scheme to wreak vengeance upon her brother Gunter's kingdom and her uncle Hagen Tronge, who carried out the murder of Siegfried. All that Gunther has to do to stop the terror of Kriemhild's wrath is to turn Tronge over to her, but in keeping with the conspiracy pact, he refuses to do so. The steadfast stubbornness on the part of both parties results in a fiery finale in which Kriemhild has Gunther, Hagen Tronge, and his entire entourage trapped in a burning building.

Although this second half of the *Die Nibelungenlied* saga is not as elaborate and well put-together as its predecessor, it is still an exhilarating film filled with suspense. Margaretta Schoen gives a superb performance in the title role that is unforgettable. Seeing her in *Kriemhild's Revenge* whets one's appetite to see more of her. Unfortunately, *Siegfried* and *Kriemhild's Revenge* are her only films that are available on video in the United States. Schoen makes such an impression in these two films that even if she had never done any other film work, these accomplishments on their own merit alone give her an indelible place in motion picture history. Ms. Schoen remained active in her later years, and made appearances at a number of European film festivals in the 1970s. She died at age 90 in 1985.

402. Manhandled

Rating: ☆½

Paramount; ***Directed by*** Allan Dwan; ***Story by*** Arthur Stringer; ***Screenplay by*** Frank Tuttle; ***Film Editor:*** William Le Baron; ***Photography by*** Hal Rosson; ***Titles by*** Julian Johnson; ***Running Time:*** 53 minutes; ***Cast:*** TESSIE MCGUIRE, Gloria Swanson (1897–1983); JIMMY HOGAN, Tom Moore (1883–1955); PINKIE DORAN, Lilyan Tashman (1899–1934); ROBERT

BRANDT, Ian Keith (1899–1960); CHIP THORNDIKE, Arthur Housman (1889–1942); PAUL GARRETTSON, Paul McAllister (1875–1955); ARNO RICCARDI, Frank Morgan (1890–1949); A MODEL, Marie Shelton (died 1949); LANDLADY, Mrs. Carrie Scott (1879–1928); A BOARDER, Frank Allsworth (1900–1935)

Manhandled was one of the sophisticated social comedies of the 1920s. It is said that Gloria Swanson's slick, bobbed hair style in it was partly responsible for starting the fashion trend toward bobbed hair.

This film depicts a day in the life of a department store salesgirl, with Swanson playing Tessie McGuire. It opens with Swanson caught up in the hustle and bustle of New York City, with the pushing and shoving on a crowded subway car, etc.

She is happily dating plumber Jimmy Hogan, who is also working on an invention. Co-worker Pinkie invites Tessie to a party—where they can mingle among the high society crowd. She goes to work as a fashion model, enduring sexual harassment on the part of Riccardi, her new boss. Once she has had a taste of high society life, she is content to stay home with fiancé Jimmy, figuring out that she had it right the first time. Unfortunately, he feels that she has been "manhandled," and is no longer interested. Tessie faces the challenge of trying to win him back.

While this is an interesting record of the fashion world of New York, giving us an idea of social attitudes of the time, *Manhandled* is a rather bland film overall. It did well at the box office mostly due to Gloria Swanson's drawing power, and the fact that she was setting a trend for the new, liberated women of the 1920s, who were beginning to come into their own after having won the right to vote four years earlier.

Most silent film fans will find that *Manhandled* is disappointing, especially in light of how highly the film is touted in most movie history books. It has its moments, but otherwise falls short of expectations. Clara Bow did a far better job with the same type of film in *It* (1927) three years later.

Look out for a young Frank Morgan, who plays Riccardi. Morgan is best remembered for the title role in *The Wizard of Oz* (1939). Supporting player Frank Allsworth dropped dead on stage in 1935 during a performance in *Portuguese Gal*.

403. Monsieur Beaucaire

Rating: ☆☆½

Paramount; ***Directed by*** Sidney Olcott; ***Based on the Story by*** Booth Tarkington; ***Screenplay by*** Forrest Halsey; ***Art Direction by*** Natacha Rambova; ***Edited by*** E. Lloyd Sheldon; ***Photography by*** Harry Fischbeck; ***Running Time:*** 100 minutes; ***Cast:*** LOUIS PHILIPPE, Rudolph Valentino (1895–1926); PRINCESS HENRIETTE, Bebe Daniels (1901–1971); MARIE LECZINSKA, Lois Wilson (1894–1988); LADY MARY CARLISLE, Doris Kenyon (1897–1979); KING LOUIS XV, Lowell Sherman (1888–1934); MARQUISE OF POMPADOUR, Paulette Duval; ARMAND [DUKE OF RICHELIEU], John Davidson (1886–1968)

This costume drama set during the French Revolution was Rudolph Valentino's comeback film after a two-year absence from the screen resulting from a contractual dispute with Paramount. It did relatively well with the critics and with urban audiences, but with a damp reception in rural areas, *Monsieur Beaucaire* lost money, as the lavish production costs insisted upon by Natacha Rambova exceeded the less than expected box-office receipts.

In this film, Valentino plays a French prince who defies a royal command to marry a woman he does not love, and escapes to Bath, England disguised as a barber, where he falls for Lady Mary Carlisle. Since he is disguised as a commoner, this works as an obstacle to his winning the heart of the aristocrat that he sets his sights on.

Monsieur Beaucaire is mediocre in comparison to some of Valentino's other films. On the positive side, the wit of Tarkington's play is preserved with sharp quips in the titles. Natacha Rambova did a gorgeous job with the costumes and sets—despite the criticism that she made Valentino look too effeminate.

This film's main weakness is that it is a bit overlong and slow moving in parts. This really has more to do with deficiencies in Sidney Olcott's (1872–1949) directorial style than with anything that Natacha Rambova did.

While this film does fall short of the 1946 remake directed by George Marshall, it is not a bad adaptation of Tarkington's classic, and is still worth watching.

Grapevine Video has released a video version of this film which features Valentino's only surviving audio, with his rendition of the *Kashimiri Love Song* during a sequence in which he is singing to a group of ladies at the beginning of the film.

404. The Navigator *Rating:* ☆☆☆

Buster Keaton Productions/MGM; ***Directed by*** Buster Keaton and Donald Crisp; ***Story by*** Clyde Bruckman, Joseph Mitchell, Jean Havez; ***Photography by*** Elgin Lessley, Byron Houck; ***Technical Director:*** Fred Gabourie; ***Running Time:*** 59 minutes; ***Cast:*** ROLLO TREADWAY, Buster Keaton (1895–1966); SHIP OWNER, Frederic Vroom (1857–1942); HIS DAUGHTER, Kathryn McGuire (1903–1978); ***Supporting Cast:*** Noble Johnson (1881–1978); Clarence Burton (1881–1933)

This comedy classic features Buster Keaton as a wealthy heir whose girlfriend has just refused his marriage proposal. Feeling dejected, he goes aboard a ship to forget his sorrows. What he does not know is that the ship captain has been kidnapped, with the vessel turned loose. Keaton's character of Treadway also discovers that the girl who spurned him is also aboard, as her father owns the ship. A number of misadventures occur as Keaton, knowing nothing about boat navigation, tries to figure out a way to steer the Navigator in the right direction.

Among the famous sequences in *The Navigator* are the kitchen sequence, during which Keaton tries to prepare dinner, and everything that can go wrong does. Another sequence shows Keaton in an altercation with a folding chair that refuses to cooperate. In addition, there is a sequence showing Keaton holding himself up in an almost horizontal position, with one hand on the ship's rope, and another holding binoculars. The highlight of the film is a brilliantly staged underwater sequence.

The leading lady is Kathryn McGuire, who had also costarred with Keaton in *Sherlock, Jr.* (1924). She starred in a few other films in the late 1920s, including a supporting role in *Lilac Time* (1928).

For many years, *The Navigator* was among the scarcest of the Keaton films. Fortunately, Kino Video brought it out of obscurity with their "Art of Buster Keaton" series in 1995.

This film has the distinction of being Buster Keaton's biggest box-office hit.

405. Near Dublin *Rating:* ☆☆½

Hal Roach/Pathé Exchange; ***Running Time:*** 8 minutes, 34 seconds; ***Cast:*** MR. PATRICK, James Finlayson (1887–1953); RICHARD O'MONROY, Stan Laurel (1890–1965)

This slapstick short features James Finlayson as a brick magnate and slumlord who is competing with Laurel's Richard O'Monroy for the affections of a pretty blonde. O'Monroy and Patrick have an altercation, and to teach the slumlord a lesson, O'Monroy schemes with the girl to make Patrick think he has killed him.

This was among the early shorts that James Finlayson appeared in with Stan Laurel before Laurel & Hardy became a team. He would later costar in a number of Laurel & Hardy shorts of the late silent and early talkie eras.

406. Our Congressman

Rating: ☆☆☆

Hal Roach/Pathé Exchange; ***Director*** Unidentified; ***Running Time:*** 18 minutes; ***Cast:*** ALFALFA DOOLITTLE, Will Rogers (1879–1935); "MA" DOOLITTLE, Madge Hunt (1875–1935); MARY DOOLITTLE, Beth Darlington; HEMINGWAY ABBOTT IV, Frank Butler (1890–1967); LADY HEMINGWAY-ABBOTT, Helen Gilmore (1862–1936)

This was the sequel to Will Rogers' *Going to Congress*, which shows Doolittle after he has arrived in Congress and taken office. He poses for his first publicity portrait, which shows him milking a cow, as "a good milker goes a long way in Congress." The next sequence has him opening his mail—which is quoted as being more than Fairbanks gets. One piece is a box with a note reminding him that the farmers need help, with crickets in it, which swarm all over Doolittle's office.

The rest of the film follows Doolittle as he becomes accustomed to the workings of Congress, providing excellent parodies on "high society."

Our Congressman is not quite as funny as its predecessor, *Going to Congress*, but is still a good, enjoyable parody on the politicians of the time.

The Helen Gilmore who appeared in this film should not be confused with a younger actress of the same name, who was born circa 1900 and died in 1947.

It has been stated that the name of "Alfalfa" in the later "Our Gang" talkies came from Rogers' character of Alfalfa Doolittle.

407. Peter Pan

Rating: ☆☆☆½

Paramount; ***Directed by*** Herbert Brenon; ***Assistant Director:*** Roy Pomeroy; ***Based on the Play by*** J.M. Barrie; ***Screenplay by*** Willis Goldbeck; ***Photographed by*** James Howe; ***Settings by*** Edward Smith; ***Running Time:*** 100 minutes; ***Cast:*** PETER PAN, Betty Bronson (1906–1971); CAPTAIN HOOK, Ernest Torrence (1878–1933); MRS. DARLING, Esther Ralston (1902–1994); WENDY DARLING, Mary Brian (born 1908); MR. DARLING, Cyril Chadwick; TINKER BELL, Virginia Brown Faire (1904–1980); TIGER LILY, Anna May Wong (1905–1961); NANA THE DOG, George Ali (1866–1947); MICHAEL DARLING, Philippe De Lacy (1917–1995); JOHN DARLING, Jack Murphy

This was the first of several screen adaptations of *Peter Pan*, and is by far the best. Lillian Gish stated in her memoirs that she very much wanted the part, but contractual disputes with Charles Duell prevented her from being able to audition for it. Madge Bellamy was considered, but Barrie felt that her features were too delicate and feminine, and offered her the part of Wendy, which she turned down. May McAvoy was also considered for the role. The moment that Barrie saw the face of newcomer Betty Bronson, he knew immediately that he wanted her to play the part. She was absolutely delightful in this role—by far the best of all of the actresses and actors who played Peter Pan on stage and on screen. Paramount realized Bronson's magical quality, and with the demise of Mary Miles Minter, had intentions of building Bronson's reputation as "Paramount's answer to Mary Pickford."

In addition to Bronson's flawless characterization in the lead role, the film featured an all-star supporting cast as well. Ernest Torrence was the ultimate villain as Captain Hook, and stole the show in every sequence he appeared in. It was obvious in Steven Spielberg's adaptation of *Hook* (1992) that he had seen this original film and modeled Dustin Hoffman's appearance after Torrence's. Madge Bellamy's rejection of the part of Wendy resulted in the film debut of a 16-year-old newcomer named Louise Dantzler, whom Herbert Brenon renamed Mary Brian. Esther Ralston, Anna May Wong, and Virginia Brown Faire were among the other notables who rounded out the supporting cast.

The great director Herbert Brenon deserves much credit for having been the only director thus far who has succeeded in translating the magic of *Peter Pan* to the screen. As Joe Franklin stated in *Classics of the Silent Screen*, "not even Disney could pull off the trick." The scene in which Peter appeals for audience participation for the people to clap their hands to show their belief in fairies to save Tinkerbell is the most notable audience participation sequence of the silent era. Only fifty years later did *The Rocky Horror Picture Show* (1974) appeal to audience participation as well.

A 35 mm tinted and toned print of *Peter Pan* is currently in the George Eastman House. The Disney Company bought the rights to this film when they did their version in the 1950s, apparently to keep from having to compete with possible reissues of this, the first and best film version of the classic. They have not released a high quality copy on video from the 35 mm tinted and toned print in the George Eastman House, and the only way the general public can see it is in the form of rare, inferior quality bootleg copies. It is high time that this film receives the revival that it deserves.

408. Riders of the Range *Rating:* ☆☆

Clifford S. Elfelt Productions; ***Directed by*** Otis B. Thayer; ***Photography by*** W.E. Smith; ***Story by*** Courtney Riley Cooper; ***Produced by*** Roy M. Langdon; ***Running Time:*** 61 minutes; ***Cast:*** MARTIN LETHBRIDGE, Edmund F. Cobb (1892–1974); ALICE RANDALL, Dolly Dale; BLUNT VANIER, Frank Gallagher (1901–1929); GREGG RANDALL, Clare Hatton (1869–1943); BOB RANDALL, Roy Langdon; INEZ CORTEZ (BIT PART), Helen Hayes (1900–1993)

This rare western would have ordinarily gone down in history as just another "B" western. What differentiates it and gives it a prominent place in motion picture history is the presence of the great stage actress Helen Hayes, who went on to win two motion picture Oscars [Best Actress in 1931–32 for *The Sin of Madelon Claudet* (1931) and Best Supporting Actress in 1970 for *Airport*]. Hayes would occasionally do bit parts in silent films while on one of her breaks from stage work. As far as can be determined, this is the only one of these early Hayes silent film appearances that has survived. She received second billing, although she actually plays only a walk-on cameo of about 90 seconds' duration.

The star of the film is Edmund F. Cobb, who was quite a popular western actor during the silent era. He plays the lead as Martin Lethbridge, president of the local Cattle Rancher's Association. The leading lady is played by Dolly Dale, for whom no further

Helen Hayes, who received second billing for her cameo in *Riders of the Range* (1924), in the late 1920s.

information could be found. The villain role is played by Frank Gallagher, who was only 28 years old when he died in 1929, five years after his appearance in this film.

There is little to this movie or the story. Sheep herders move into cattle herders' territory. Good guys on both sides are trying to keep peace. Bad guys on the cattle herders' side, led by villain Blunt Vanier, conspire to kill cattle and blame it on the sheep herders as an excuse to drive them out of the area. Martin Lethbridge, the leader of the cattle herders, falls in love with Alice Randall, the daughter of the leader of the sheep herders. In the end, the bad guys are caught, and Lethbridge and Randall get married and live happily ever after.

This is a rather predictable western, and not among the best of the genre. Nonetheless, the rare chance to see one of the few surviving films of western star Edmund F. Cobb, as well as the earliest surviving film appearance of Helen Hayes, make it worth having a copy. The title is widely available on video, but unfortunately all available prints are of only fair quality. Some of the title cards are so faded that they are often difficult to read.

409. Romola

Rating: ☆☆½

Inspiration Pictures/Metro-Goldwyn; ***Directed by*** Henry King; ***Scenario by*** Will M. Ritchey; ***From the Novel by*** George Eliot; ***Art Direction by*** Robert M. Haas; ***Production Manager:*** Joseph C. Boyle; ***Running Time:*** 120 minutes; ***Cast:*** ROMOLA, Lillian Gish (1893–1993); TESSA, Dorothy Gish (1898–1968); TITO MALEMA, William Powell (1892–1984); CARLO SUCELLINI, Ronald Colman (1891–1958); BELDASSARRE CALVO, Charles Lane (1869–1945); SAVONAROLA, Herbert Grimwood (1875–1929); ADOLFO SPINI, Frank Puglia (1892–1975); BRIGIDA, Amelia Summerville (1862–1934); MONNA CHITA, Tina Ciccacci Renaldi; NELLO, Eduilio Mucca; BRATTI, Angelo Scatigna; PIERE DE MEDICI, Alfredo Bertone (died 1927)

This was the second of two films that Lillian Gish starred in for the independent Inspiration Pictures, produced by Charles H. Duell under the direction of Henry King. It would also be the last film that both of the Gish sisters would star in together.

Filmed on location in Italy, this is the story of a young woman named Romola who is coerced into marrying the corrupt politician Tito Malema. She falls in love with an architect, and must wait until her husband's misdeeds result in his downfall before she can marry the man she truly loves. Dorothy Gish plays a young peasant girl who is tricked by villain Tito into believing that she, too, is married to him. In this role as in the other two features that the Gish sisters starred in together, Dorothy steals the show. She demonstrates true ability as a dramatic actress, although she specialized in comedy.

Romola was highly acclaimed worldwide, and did well at the box office. Unfortunately, the immense cost of filming in Italy, reconstructing sets modeled after actual structures, and the massive mob scenes caused it to lose money.

In appraising this film today, it is a good film with a good story, but moves very slowly in some parts. What saves the film is the magnificent cast. William Powell is excellent as villain Tito, the corrupt politician who not only leads two women on, but who deserted his own father during a pirate attack for personal gain. This is the earliest William Powell film available on video for evaluation. He went on to significant success in the talkie era, winning three Academy Award nominations.

Ronald Colman also went on to receive recognition from the Academy of Motion Picture Arts and Sciences, having received three Academy Award nominations as well as one Academy Award in the talkie era.

Among the supporting players, Frank Puglia makes a distinctive impression as Adolfo Spini. He had been a supporting player with the Gish sisters in *Orphans of the Storm* (1921) as well. Amelia Summerville was a widely renowned stage comedienne. She worked as a voice coach for various actors during the early talkie era. Her death was caused by an accidental fall in January, 1934.

For years, this film was unavailable for evaluation. The only known print was in the hands of a private collector. Finally, another print was discovered elsewhere, and fortunately the collectors who gained possession of this print made *Romola* widely available on video in the mid–1980s. Film preservationist Robert Gitt recently restored *Romola* in 35 mm format for UCLA.

410. The Sea Hawk

Rating: ☆☆☆☆

Frank Lloyd Productions/Associated-First National; ***Directed by*** Frank Lloyd; ***Based on the Novel by*** Rafael Sabatini; ***Screen Adaptation by*** J.G. Hawks; ***Photographed by*** Norbert F. Brodin; ***Edited by*** Edward M. Roskam; ***Art Direction by*** Stephen Goosson; ***Titles by*** Walter Anthony; ***Ships Designed by*** Fred Gabourie; ***Research by*** William J. Reiter; ***Costumes by*** Walter J. Israel; ***Running Time:*** 123 minutes; ***Cast:*** Sir Oliver Tressilian, Milton Sills (1882–1930); Lady Rosamund Godolphin, Enid Bennett (1893–1969); Lionel Tressilian, Lloyd Hughes (1897–1958); Captain Jasper Leigh, Wallace Beery (1885–1949); Sir John Killigrew, Marc MacDermott (1881–1929); Peter Godolphin, Wallace MacDonald (1891–1978); Nick, Bert Woodruff (1856–1934); Siren, Claire DuBrey (1892–1993); Justice Anthony Baine, Lionel Belmore (1868–1953); The Infanta of Spain, Christine Montt (1897–1969); Yusuf-Ben-Moktar, Albert Prisco; Basha of Algiers, Frank Currier (1857–1928); Marsak, William Collier, Jr. (1902–1987); Frenzilch, Medea Radzina; Ali, Fred De Silva (1885–1929); Andalusian slave girl, Kathleen Key (1907–1954); Tsmanni, Hector V. Sarno (1880–1953); Ayoub, Robert Bolder (1859–1937); Boatswain, Fred Spencer (1901–1952)

This is the first screen version of the highly popular sea epic, *The Sea Hawk.* Milton Sills plays the title role in what is considered his greatest role and performance. It is a classic tale of jealousy, betrayal, and revenge, set during the early part of the Spanish Inquisition.

Sills plays Sir Oliver Tressilian, a prominent Englishman whose half-brother, Lionel, kills obnoxious nemesis Peter Godolphin in a fair duel. Unfortunately, there were no witnesses to the fact that it was a fair duel, and he fears being charged with murder. He betrays Oliver, who has had past altercations with Godolphin, and arranges to have Oliver kidnapped by Captain Jasper Leigh and sold into slavery in the Moors. The disappearance of Oliver would imply that he ran because he was guilty of murdering Godolphin.

The plan goes awry when the ship that Oliver is shanghaied on is attacked by Spanish pirates, who make galley slaves of the entire crew. After years of torturous slavery, Oliver finally manages to escape, and sets his heart on revenge and retribution. He becomes "the sea hawk"—the leader of a band of pirates much feared by the Spanish Armada.

Milton Sills, debonair and charismatic star of *The Sea Hawk* (1924).

The Sea Hawk was remade in 1940, directed by Michael Curtiz and starring Errol Flynn. The remake was highly acclaimed, and nominated for three Academy Awards. As outstanding as the remake was, it is inferior to this original version. The remake changed the story line a great deal, and does not even really parallel with the original until the sequence in which the main character (whose name is different in the two versions) escapes from the galleys. The action in the remake was good, but the plot was rather thin. This original version has an engrossing plot throughout which constantly holds the attention. There is a much more detailed story line in this original, emphasizing the personal reasons that the sea hawk goes on his rampage. And, the action sequences in this original are superior to the downplayed battles in the remake.

The 1940 version features the novelty of gold tinting for about 20 minutes of its duration, which was rare in the talkie era. But, this original has multiple tints throughout. It even sports a hand colored sequence as well, showing the flames of light torches colored orange against a blue tinted background!

Much of the success of this original version can be attributed to the direction of Frank Lloyd (1888–1960), who would go on to win two Academy Awards for Best Director (1929 and 1933), in addition to his *Mutiny on the Bounty* (1935) winning the Best Picture Oscar.

As to the cast, this is Milton Sills' film all the way, although he is capably supported by a fine supporting cast as well. Wallace Beery, who plays the crooked sea captain who later turns into one of the good guys, is especially impressive. He steals many of the scenes in which he appears.

We are fortunate that this, the definitive screen version of *The Sea Hawk*, is finally available for evaluation again. The film was meticulously restored by the UCLA Film and Television Archives with an excellent organ score composed and performed by Robert Israel. Although this version of *The Sea Hawk* is not yet released on video, it has been aired on Turner Classic Movies a few times. It is Frank Lloyd's masterpiece—far superior to his three Academy Award winning films previously mentioned in this review. It is unlikely that this version of *The Sea Hawk* could possibly be improved upon.

411. Siegfried

Rating: ☆☆☆☆

UFA Studios/Germany; ***Directed by*** Fritz Lang; ***Screenplay by*** Thea von Harbou; ***Based on the Poem*** *Die Nibelungenlied*; ***Photography by*** Carl Hoffman and Gunther Rittau; ***Art Direction:*** Otto Hunte, Karl Vollbrecht, Erich Kettelhut; ***Edited and Titled by*** Katharine Hilliker and H.H. Caldwell; ***Running time:*** 96 minutes; ***Cast:*** SIEGFRIED, Paul Richter (1895–1961); KRIEMHILD, Margaretta Schoen (1895–1985); KING GUNTHER, Theodor Loos (1883–1954)

This is the first half of Fritz Lang's (1890–1976) two-part adaptation of the ancient German mythological poem, *Die Nibelungenlied.* This part of the film portrays how Siegfried travels through the Woden Wood, which only the gods can allegedly get through alive, on his way to win the hand of the princess Kriemhild. By slaying a formidable fire-breathing dragon, he acquires the ability to understand the birds' language, and is told by them that if he bathes in the dragon's blood, his body will be invulnerable to injury. A leaf falls during his bath, and leaves one spot on his back uncovered by the blood.

Upon conquering several more obstacles, Siegfried finally makes it to Gunther's castle to propose to Kriemhild. There is one problem that must be solved first before they can marry. As the sister of King Gunther, it is customary that the king must be married before his sister can take marriage vows. The woman Gunther has his sights set on is Brunhilde, the queen of Iceland who requires her suitors to either defeat her in three athletic feats or die. In order to win Brunhilde for Gunther so that he can marry Kriemhild, Siegfried does the stunts for Gunther, using a magic cap acquired on his travel through the Woden Wood which gives him the ability to become invisible or take any form he desires.

All is well in Siegfried and Kriemhild's marriage until Kriemhild lets out the secret that it was actually Siegfried that won Brunhilde for Gunther. This results in a murder conspiracy against Siegfried, who is killed by a spear thrown through the one vulnerable spot on his back.

This film features some impressive special effects, the most notable being the sequence in which the dwarfs are conquered by Siegfried and are shown turning into stone from their feet upwards.

In many ways, *Siegfried* and *Kriemhild's Revenge* were the exact opposite of Fritz Lang's follow-up, *Metropolis* (1927). While *Metropolis* was a visionary interpretation of the future, the *Siegfried/Kriemhild's Revenge* epic was a fantasy interpretation of the ancient past.

This first part of the *Die Nibelungenlied* saga was clearly dominated by Paul Richter in the title role, whereas the second part, *Kriemhild's Revenge,* belongs to Margaretta Schoen. The woman who plays Brunhilde is also extremely impressive, but unfortunately no further information is known about her.

Thea von Harbou (1888–1954), who wrote the screenplay for both parts of this epic, was the wife of director Fritz Lang, having married him in 1924 after her divorce from Rudolf Klein-Rogge (1888–1955). Her support and affiliation with the Nazi party caused Lang to divorce his wife in 1934, and he emigrated to the United States while she stayed on in Germany. Ms. von Harbou became an official screenwriter for the Nazi regime, and directed two unsuccessful films as well.

In referring to the Nazi Party, *Siegfried* is said to have the dubious distinction of being Adolf Hitler's (1889–1945) favorite film.

412. Terror

Rating: ☆½

Epinay Film Company/France; ***Directed by*** Edward José; ***Running Time:*** 37 minutes; ***Cast:*** HELENE LORFEUIL, Pearl White (1889–1938); ROGER DURANT, Robert Lee; MADAME GAUTHIER, Arlette Marchal (1902–1984); ***Supporting Cast:*** Henry Baudin; Martin Mitchell; Paul Vermoyel (died 1925)

Terror is historically significant as Pearl White's last starring film, produced in France. It was directed by Edward José (died 1930), whom many will remember as one of the stars of *A Fool There Was* (1914).

This is a rather trite and silly film in which Pearl plays the daughter of a scientist who has discovered "Radiominium" and is experimenting with a device that can turn the substance into energy. Her leading man is Roger Durant, assistant to her father. Helene and Roger fall in love, much to her father's disapproval. There are villains who steal her father's secrets, and Helene and Roger eventually foil the villains and win her father's respect and approval to live happily ever after. It turns out that although there was a plot to steal her father's invention, he actually stole it himself out of fear that it might not be as successful as he hopes.

Terror is probably Pearl White's worst film. It is a film to be appreciated for its historic importance rather than for entertainment.

413. The Thief of Bagdad

Rating: ☆☆☆☆

United Artists; ***Directed by*** Raoul Walsh; ***Art Director:*** William Cameron Menzies; ***Photography by*** Arthur Edeson; ***Scenario by*** Elton Thomas; ***Running Time:*** 139 minutes; ***Cast:*** THE THIEF OF BAGDAD, Douglas Fairbanks, Sr.(1883–1939); THE PRINCESS, Julanne Johnston (1900–1988); THE PRINCESS' SLAVE, Anna May Wong (1905–1961); THE MONGOL PRINCE, So-Jin Kamiyama (1891–1954); THIEF'S COMPANION, Snitz Edwards (1862–1937); THE HOLY MAN, Charles Belcher (1872–1943); THE CALIPH, Brandon Hurst (1866–1947); THE INDIAN PRINCE, Noble Johnson (1881–1978); THE PERSIAN PRINCE, M. Comont (1886–1938)

Filmed on a budget of over $2 million, *The Thief of Bagdad* was Douglas Fairbanks' most elaborate spectacle, as well as one of the most expensive films of the silent era. It was a great success at the box office, too, turning a comfortable although not gigantic profit.

Here we have Fairbanks as a cunning and clever thief in this "Arabian Nights" fantasy. As the thief, he is incorrigible—until he falls in love with the princess, which gives him the incentive to mend his ways and turn himself into a prince. Although he wins the princess' heart, her father disapproves of him, and forces his daughter to make another choice before he makes it for her. To buy time, the princess sends the competing suitors on a quest for a rare treasure, with the stipulation that the suitor who brings the rarest treasure will win her hand in marriage.

It is at this part of the film that the real fantasy elements come in. Of the three suitors, Fairbanks is the fourth. The other three suitors manage to find a rare crystal which can tell the future, a golden apple that can raise the dead, and a magic carpet that one can use to fly to any destination. The thief's quest is for a silver chest on the moon that can grant any wish at will. But, to get to the chest on the moon, he must brave a series of obstacles that nobody has ever before survived to tell about.

The Thief of Bagdad has it all—gorgeous color tinting, magnificent special effects, over 10,000 extras in the final sequence, and finally the elaborate and breathtaking sets which represent what is art director William Cameron Menzies' best work in his Academy Award winning career. The intriguing fantasy story was written by Fairbanks under his pseudonym of Elton Thomas.

Although Fairbanks does over-exaggerate his gestures in parts of the film, he gives a good overall performance, and has a fine supporting cast to back him up. As far as can be determined, the "M. Comont" who plays the plump Persian prince in this film is actually a female player by the name of Mathilde Comont dressed as a man. Anna May Wong, the famous Oriental actress, is superb as the servant who conspires against her princess. So-Jin Kamiyama is just as impressive, if not more, as the evil Mongol prince whose real attraction to the princess results from his diabolical plans to invade and conquer Bagdad. Julanne Johnston, who was not well known until this film, gives a competent performance as the princess, but her role did not give her much to do except stand around and look pretty.

The only real disappointment is the crude portrayal of the winged horse. The horse does not actually fly to the moon by flapping its wings, but is merely shown in a superimposed shot galloping against the sky, which isn't very convincing.

With this film's imposing size, grandeur, and excellent action direction, it ranks as one of the best fantasy films produced in the United States during the silent era. Widely available on the video market, *The Thief of Bagdad* is in many ways Douglas Fairbanks, Sr.'s, finest production, as well as an excellent showcase for the talents of director Raoul Walsh (1887–1980), being among his better films as well.

414. A Truthful Liar

Rating: ☆☆

Hal Roach/Pathé Exchange; ***Director*** Unidentified; ***Running Time:*** 18 minutes; ***Cast:*** ALFALFA DOOLITTLE, Will Rogers (1879–1935); "MA" DOOLITTLE, Madge Hunt (1875–1935); MARY DOOLITTLE, Beth Darlington

This was the third and final entry in the "Alfalfa Doolittle" trilogy, which has the politician coming back to his home town to report to his constituents. He tells a tall tale about his ambassadorship in Europe, and the chimney falls in.

This is the weakest entry in the Doolittle trilogy, which doesn't live up to its potential. Instead of inventing a tale about Europe, Rogers could have instead satired about the wonderful things Congress had done for America, and had a much more appealing film.

415. Venus of the South Seas

Rating: ☆☆

Lee-Bradford Corporation/Davis Distributing Company; ***Directed by*** James R. Sullivan; ***Running Time:*** 54 minutes; ***Cast:*** SHONA ROYAL, Annette Kellerman (1887–1975); JOHN ROYAL, Roland Purdie; JOHN DRAKE, Normand French; ROBERT QUANE, JR., Robert Ramsey

For over seventy years, none of the films of the famed Olympic swimmer and silent screen actress Annette Kellerman [also spelled Kellermann in some sources] were widely available for evaluation. It was thought that all prints of *Venus of the South Seas* (1924) were held hostage in the George Eastman House. Fortunately, in 1997, another print that nobody knew existed turned up in a private collection in a Boston basement. Mr. Jack Hardy of Grapevine Video acquired the contents of this private collection, and it is Mr. Hardy that we have to thank for getting Ms. Kellerman represented in the video market.

Venus of the South Seas was Annette Kellerman's last film, produced by an independent company, and directed by Kellerman's husband, James R. Sullivan. Ms. Kellerman was 37 years old when she starred in this film. She plays the daughter of the owner of a South Seas island pearl business. She falls in love with a wealthy traveler named Robert Quane. Her father dies, and she leaves the island, taking her pearls with her. The villainous captain of the boat, John Drake, is after the pearls, and will stop at nothing to get them. Drake goes as far as setting Shona's love interest, Robert, adrift.

While *Venus of the South Seas* is not among Kellerman's best, done after she had been in her prime, it is the only one of her features known to verifiably exist in complete form. The film contains a beautifully done underwater fantasy sequence, luciously tinted with a brief, hand-colored two-tone segment. The film is worth seeing for this sequence alone.

It has been alleged that a complete 16 mm print of one of Kellerman's most highly acclaimed films, *Neptune's Daughter* (1914), exists in a European archive. In addition, one reel of Kellerman's second collaboration and masterpiece with Herbert Brenon, *A Daughter of the Gods* (1916), was said to be in Russia's Gosfilmofond archive. This reviewer was unable to verify the existence of a complete print of *Neptune's Daughter*. An inquiry regarding the reel of *A Daughter of the Gods* (1916) at Gosfilmofond resulted in a response from Vladimir Malyshev, who stated that the Kellerman footage held by their archive was actually about 150 meters (approximately 5 minutes) of *Neptune's Daughter*, and that no material on *A Daughter of the Gods* was in their archives.

While Kellerman's better work is probably lost forever, at least something of hers has survived in complete form, which is better than nothing. Since this extra print of *Venus of the South Seas* turned up, perhaps a complete print of *Neptune's Daughter* or *A Daughter of the Gods* might follow.

1925

416. Are Parents People?

Rating: ☆☆☆

Paramount; ***Directed by*** Malcolm St. Clair; ***Running Time:*** 63 minutes; ***Cast:*** LITA HAZLITT, Betty Bronson (1906–1971); ALITA HAZLITT, Florence Vidor (1895–1977); DR. JOHN DACER,

Lawrence Gray (1898–1970); JAMES HAZLITT, Adolphe Menjou (1890–1963); DEAN OF THE SCHOOL, Emily Fitzroy (1860–1954); THE SERVANT, Cesare Gravina (1858–1954?)

One of the most grossly overlooked of the delightful silent era actresses would have to be Betty Bronson. *Are Parents People?* is the most accessible of Bronson's few surviving films, and was also one of her best comedies. The movie starts out showing the characters of Mr. and Mrs. James Hazlitt cleaning out their dresser drawers, closets, and other items. The audience is made aware—without the use of any title cards until five minutes into the film—that the couple are feuding and preparing to separate. Florence Vidor, who plays the wife, was in actuality married to Hollywood director King Vidor (1894–1982) from 1915 to 1924. Adolphe Menjou, who plays the husband, would later gain notoriety for his extreme right wing politics in the 1940s and 1950s.

Betty Bronson plays the daughter of the feuding parents who, of course, wants to save their marriage. Bronson demonstrates her unique brand of pantomimic talent during a scene at her boarding school after being told of the impending divorce. She is reading a book called *Divorce and Its Cure.* The camera cuts to a close-up of her feet, and one can tell from simple, subtle movements of her toes that she is excited about what she is reading. She reads in the book that if parents believe that their children are in danger, they often reunite. So, Bronson's character of Lita concocts a plan.

Lita's first plan of action is to get herself into trouble at school. The plan seems to work, as her parents both have to come to the boarding school for a conference. But, the parents end up fighting and arguing again.

Along the way, Lita meets up with Dr. Dacer, a young doctor. She visits his office while he is out, and falls asleep in his chair. Meanwhile, she leaves one of his business cards at her parents' house with a note stating how heartbroken she is that they quarreled over her. It is interesting to see how everything plays out in the end.

Are Parents People? is a truly delightful romantic comedy, and is acclaimed as one of the best of the comedies that Betty Bronson played in after her roles in *Peter Pan* and *A Kiss for Cinderella.* It is fortunate that this is among the few extant Bronson silents, and has been made accessible to modern day Betty Bronson fans.

417. Battleship Potemkin

Rating: ☆☆☆☆

[a.k.a. *Potemkin*]

Produced in Russia; ***Directed by*** Sergei Eisenstein; ***Photographed by*** Edward Tisse; ***Running Time:*** 62 minutes

This is the second in a series of Communist propaganda films that Sergei Eisenstein (1898–1948) was commissioned by Joseph Stalin to produce. It remains the most highly acclaimed of all of the Russian films, and is considered one of the great masterpieces of cinema.

This series of films depicts the events leading up to the Russian Revolution of 1917. The first in the series, *Strike* (1925) was good, but not nearly as impressive as *Battleship Potemkin. Battleship Potemkin* deals specifically with an incident of 1905, during which the sailors of one of the battleships are pushed over the edge by the spoiled, maggot-infested meat that is served to them. The sailors refuse to eat it.

The commander of the ship gathers all of the ship's crew on deck. He separates those who state displeasure with the food served, and orders that they be shot. The

Original Russian promotional material for *Battleship Potemkin* (1925).

sailors refuse to shoot their comrades, and instead turn on the Czar's officers and take over the ship. As this battle ensues, Eisenstein expertly edited the footage to show the facial expressions of many of the characters as they fought. Once the ship reaches Odessa, many sympathizers gather to meet the ship and to provide supplies to the victorious crew. It is at this point that the "Odessa Steps" massacre occurs, in which the Czar's troops randomly shoot every sympathizer in their path—regardless of age, sex, or disability. Two of the most intense portrayals of these mindless troops are when they shoot a woman and her injured child dead when she is trying to peacefully appeal to them, and when the woman with a baby carriage is killed, showing the baby in the carriage rolling down the steps. The vivid murders of two who attempt to save the baby are also shown. The sailors on the battleship answer this military brutality by blowing up the Odessa Theater.

The original negative of this film was destroyed by the Nazis during World War II, and there is no way of determining how close the versions available today are to the original director's cut. Nonetheless, the images depicted in what is left of this film are unforgettable. This is the openly gay director Sergei Eisenstein's crowning achievement, as well as the greatest cinematic achievement to come out of Russia. Clips of this film routinely appear in many cinema documentaries, and Eisenstein's directorial style has been studied by many of the most accomplished directors of cinema. It has stood the test of time well, and is an absolute "must" for classic film enthusiasts and historians.

418. Chess Fever *Rating:* ☆

Produced in the U.S.S.R.; ***Directed by*** Vsevolod Pudovkin and Nicolai Shpikovsky; ***Pho-***

A scene from *Chess Fever* (1925).

tographed by Anatoly Golovny; ***Running Time:*** 28 minutes; ***Cast:*** THE HERO, Vladimir Fogel (died 1929); THE HEROINE, A. Zemtsova; World Chess Champion José Capablanca as himself

Chess Fever was V.I. Pudovkin's (1893–1953) first directorial project released. In actuality, it was his second film, but was released before his actual directorial debut *Mechanics of the Brain* (1926).

This film is a romantic comedy which finds the hero becoming so preoccupied with the game of chess that it is threatening his marriage. Much of the movie was filmed at the International Chess Tournament held in Moscow in 1925. José Capablanca, who was the world chess champion, appears in the film. Pudovkin's cameraman posed as a news reel photographer, and Capablanca had no idea that this footage was actually going to be used in a movie.

This comedy is a departure for Pudovkin, who is best known for his powerful dramatic classics. Unfortunately, this reviewer found nothing amusing or entertaining at all in this production.

419. Cobra

Rating: ☆☆½

Rudolph Valentino/Paramount; ***Directed by*** Joseph Henabery; ***Settings by*** William Cameron Menzies; ***Costumes by*** Adrian and Natacha Rambova; ***Photography by*** J.D. Jennings, Harry Fischbeck; ***Edited by*** John H. Bonn; ***Running Time:*** 70 minutes; ***Cast:*** COUNT TORRIANI,

Rudolph Valentino (1895–1926); JACK DORNING, Casson Ferguson (1891–1929); DORNING'S SECRETARY, Gertrude Olmstead (1904–1975); ELISE VAN ZILE, Nita Naldi (1897–1961)

Cobra was one of the worst received films of Rudolph Valentino's career. It was a box-office flop, as well as a critical failure when it was originally released. It is still panned by modern day critics today, although this author, upon evaluating the film, believes that the film isn't as bad as most other critics think.

Much of the blame for this film's failure is generally attributed to Natacha Rambova (1897–1966), who was married to Valentino. She was a domineering force in her husband's career. To her credit, she did a beautiful job on the costume designs. But, she reportedly insisted on so many changes in the story line to match her ideas of art that much of the action and plot was watered down by the time she got through amending it.

The story line features Valentino as a playboy count who has incurred significant debts with his extravagant lifestyle. He takes a job with an antique dealer to pay off some of the debts. Complications abound as the count has affairs with Dorning's secretary and is vamped by Nita Naldi's character of Elize Van Zile, Dorning's new wife, who has herself around Valentino as a cobra.

Director Joseph Henabery (1888–1976) directed some good films with Douglas Fairbanks, Sr., in the late 1910s, and these as well as *Cobra* are his most notable directorial projects. He is perhaps best remembered for having played Abraham Lincoln in *The Birth of a Nation* (1915).

420. Cyrano de Bergerac

Rating: ☆☆☆☆

Unione Cinematographica Italia/Pathé; ***Produced in*** France and Italy; ***Directed by*** Augusto Genina; ***Running Time:*** 114 minutes; ***Cast:*** CYRANO DE BERGERAC, Pierre Magnier; ROXANE, Linda Moglia; COUNT DE GUICHE, Angelo Ferrari

One of the major new video releases of 1996 was this 1925 version of *Cyrano de Bergerac*, based on the classic tragedy by Edmond Rostand. Long believed to have been lost, this film is a rare surviving example of Pathecolor, a process in which each frame of the film was colored by hand. The hand colored pastel images are, in themselves, a thing of beauty, and the film would be worth watching for the color alone.

In addition to the gorgeous pictorial quality, the movie itself is one of great substance, based on one of the most highly acclaimed romantic tragedies in literary history.

For those unfamiliar with the story, the plot centers around Cyrano de Bergerac, a Gascon guard during the reign of Louis XIII. He falls in love with a woman named Roxane, but feels insecure about himself because of his unusually large nose. He feels that nobody would ever have him because of his appearance. Although troubled by his appearance, de Bergerac is a man of quick wit, as well as one of the most highly acclaimed swordsmen in the country. Through another man, de Bergerac writes poetic prose to see what kind of reaction his eloquent writing would bring. Unfortunately, de Bergerac is wounded in a duel, and Roxane does not find out that he is the actual author of the cherished love letters until he is near death.

This tragedy has been adapted for the screen many times. The 1950 version starred Jose Ferrer in the leading role, for which he won an Oscar for Best Actor. A recent 1990 French version was also very good.

The director of this silent adaptation was the highly acclaimed Italian director, Augusto Genina. He is perhaps best remembered for having directed Louise Brooks in the 1930 French talkie, *Prix de Beauté*. While *Prix de Beauté* left quite a bit to be desired as a film, it is this film which shows us Genina's true directorial talent.

421. Felix the Cat Trips Thru Toyland *Rating:* ☆☆☆☆

E.W. Hammons/Educational; ***Directed by*** Pat Sullivan; ***Running Time:*** 8 minutes, 30 seconds; ***Cast:*** Felix the Cat (born 1914)

Before Walt Disney brought Mickey Mouse onto the scene in 1928, Felix the Cat was the reigning popular cartoon character. Creator Pat Sullivan (1887–1933) was 27 years old when he first introduced Felix in comic strips in 1914, and later in the year brought the character to the screen for the first time. This character's popularity has continued to endure, and "Felix the Cat" souvenirs are abundant on the market in the late 1990s. Although Pat Sullivan died in 1933 at age 45, his son has carried his father's creation into the television era.

In this fun episode, Felix rescues a girl from a dog that is trying to steal her doll. He chases the dog, who has taken the doll and ran away with it. Felix gets the doll away from the dog, and the doll comes to life and takes Felix on a trip to Toyland in gratitude for the rescue. In Toyland, Felix finds a rival suitor for the doll's affections in a clown who looks much like Koko the Klown, and this is where the fun really begins.

This *Felix* cartoon is just as much fun as it was in 1925, having stood the test of time well. This reviewer finds the early *Felix* cartoons to be far superior and more appealing than most of the earliest Disney cartoons.

422. The Freshman *Rating:* ☆☆☆☆

Harold Lloyd Corporation/Pathé; ***Directed by*** Sam Taylor and Fred Newmeyer; ***Assistant Director:*** Robert A. Golden; ***Story by*** Sam Taylor, John Grey, Ted Wilde, Tim Whelan, Clyde Bruckman, Lex Neal, Jean Havez, and Brooks B. Harding; ***Titles by*** Thomas J. Grey; ***Photography by*** Walter Lundin and Henry N. Kohler; ***Editor:*** Allen McNeil; ***Production Manager:*** John L. Murphy; ***Technical Director:*** William MacDonald; ***Art Direction by*** Liell K. Vedder; ***Cast:*** HAROLD "SPEEDY" LAMB, Harold Lloyd (1893–1971); PEGGY, Jobyna Ralston (1900–1967); THE COLLEGE CAD, Brooks Benedict (died 1968); CHET TRASK, James Anderson; THE COLLEGE BELLE, Hazel Keener (1904–1979); THE COLLEGE TAILOR, Joseph Harrington; THE COLLEGE COACH, Pat Harmon (1886–1958)

The Freshman was the last of the Lloyd features distributed through Pathé. It turned out to be his biggest silent money maker, and its success resulted in a number of other college comedies being produced, including *The Plastic Age* (1925), *College* (1927), *The Fair Co-Ed* (1927), and Universal's popular "Collegians" series of the late 1920s. Many historians consider this to be the greatest of all of Lloyd's films. With its box office success, it is obvious that much of the public agreed with this appraisal as well. Harold Lloyd's own personal favorites of his films were *The Freshman* (1925), *Grandma's Boy* (1922), *Safety Last* (1923), and *The Kid Brother* (1927).

In this film, Harold plays a freshman weakling who desperately tries to fit in, but is the brunt of everyone's jokes. Peggy, the girl that Harold is trying to win over, realizes that people are making fun of him, but doesn't have the heart to tell him so. He tries out for the football team and, as a joke, the coach makes him the water boy, with Harold being naive enough to believe that he has made the team. The finale comes with Harold on the sidelines during a make or break game. Several of the team members are injured, and the coach has no choice but to put Harold in the game. He saves the day by making a crucial, last-second touchdown, and is the hero of the team.

This is a classic comedy of the underdog who comes from being the brunt of everyone's jokes to a prominent position of respect, which was a recurring theme in many of Lloyd's films.

Unfortunately, *The Freshman*, among Lloyd's best films, is also one of the hardest to come across. It was not chosen as one of the Lloyd titles that Photoplay Productions restored for TV presentation and video in the early 1990s. A couple of companies that were selling the Time-Life version on video were forced to withdraw the title from the market by the Harold Lloyd Trust. The only way this reviewer was able to screen a copy of this film was by recording the Time-Life reissue when it was aired on a local television station in the early 1980s.

423. Go West

Rating: ☆☆☆½

Buster Keaton Productions/MGM; ***Written and Directed by*** Buster Keaton; ***Scenario by*** Raymond Cannon; ***Photography by*** Elgin Lessley, Bert Haines; ***Art Direction by*** Fred Gabourie; ***Running Time:*** 69 minutes; ***Cast:*** OWNER OF THE DIAMOND BAR RANCH, Howard Truesdale (1861–1941); HIS DAUGHTER, Kathleen Myers; THE FOREMAN, Ray Thompson (1898–1927); FRIENDLESS, Buster Keaton (1895–1966)

This is a Keaton classic that animal lovers will especially enjoy. Keaton plays the character of Friendless, a drifter who is down on his luck, and happens to befriend Brown Eyes, a cow that rescues him from being attacked by another cow while Friendless is working as a farm hand.

When the time comes for Brown Eyes to be sent to the slaughter house, Friendless determines to save her. He follows the train and unwittingly turns all of the cattle loose into the busy city streets. This is a classic sequence in which thousands of cows are used. In the end, the farmer decides to let Friendless keep Brown Eyes.

Much of *Go West* was filmed on location in the deserts of Arizona. When some of the crew suggested going back to Hollywood and finishing the desert sequences on the MGM lot, Keaton refused. His attitude was much like Erich von Stroheim's—"If it looks real, that is not good enough. It has to be real." Thus, the crew dealt with the problems of working in the extreme heat. Many retakes were required, as the film stock actually melted. Finally, the cameras were submerged in ice to preserve the film stock and to keep the cameras operable. The production delays during the Arizona location footage, as well as the big cow stampede sequence, resulted in *Go West* being among Keaton's most expensive films, and it did not do as well at the box office as was hoped.

This was not among Keaton's personal favorite films, but when evaluated today, it stands the test of time. It is one of this reviewer's favorite Keaton classics. Fortunately, this title was made available on video by Kino in 1995.

Ray Thompson, who played the foreman in this film, was one of three people who drowned during the filming of *Trail of '98* (1929) in Alaska in 1927, when he was only 29 years old.

424. The Gold Rush

Rating: ☆☆

Charles Chaplin/United Artists; ***Directed and Written by*** Charles Chaplin; ***Running Time of Complete Version:*** 82 minutes; ***Running Time of Re Edited Version:*** 71 minutes; ***Cast:*** THE LONE PROSPECTOR, Charles Chaplin (1889–1977); GEORGIA, Georgia Hale (1900–1985); BIG JIM MCKAY, Mack Swain (1876–1935); BLACK LARSEN, Tom Murray (1874–1935); HANK CURTIS, Henry Bergman (1868–1946)

The Gold Rush is Chaplin's most highly acclaimed feature comedy. At the time of its release, it was also the longest—at nine reels, and one of the most expensive as well. In 1942, Chaplin re-edited *The Gold Rush*, shortening it, putting an orchestra score on it, and narrating it. Of all of the films that have been reissued and re-edited in this manner, this is the one case in which the re-editing actually improved the film, rather than ruined it such as in the cases of the reissues of *Noah's Ark* (1929), *The Passion of Joan of Arc* (1928), and others. Perhaps the reason that it worked in this case is because Chaplin, the original creator of the film, was personally in charge of the re-editing process. There are many aspects of *The Gold Rush* that are admirable. The trick photography in the sequence with the cabin rocking back and forth on the edge of a mountain cliff is especially impressive. Chaplin's pantomimic facial expressions demonstrate true acting talent on his part.

While *The Gold Rush* does have the aforementioned attributes, it is difficult to comprehend why this film is ranked by so many critics as highly as it is. Part of this high acclaim stems from two sequences in the film—the one in which Chaplin eats a shoe, and the "dance of the dinner rolls." These two sequences are supposed to pass for humor, but what is humorous about somebody starving to death and eating a nasty shoe? The same thing goes for the sequence in which Big Jim sees Chaplin's character as a chicken. It is idiotic to see Chaplin running around in a not-very-convincing chicken suit. The dance of the dinner rolls was not bad, but certainly not a great sequence that deserves a reputation as being among the best in comedy history.

The best attribute in *The Gold Rush* is the presence of actress Georgia Hale as the leading lady. Unfortunately, her role is limited and downplayed. This was due in part to the fact that Lita Grey (1908–1995) was originally slated for the part, but was plagued with problems that caused many delays in the introduction of the female lead. It was when it was confirmed that there was no way that Lita Grey was going to be able to play the part that Ms. Hale was brought in. Ms. Hale was a wonderful actress. Her performances in *The Gold Rush* and *The Salvation Hunters* (1925) make one long to see more of her.

While *The Gold Rush* is not a bad film, it certainly pales in comparison to other Chaplin feature comedies like *The Kid* (1921) and *Modern Times* (1936). Furthermore, it does not hold a candle to many of the Lloyd and Keaton feature comedies. As assessed for this book, *The Gold Rush* is far overrated, and only a mediocre Chaplin vehicle at best. Nonetheless, the rocking cabin sequence and Georgia Hale's appearance make it one that is worth watching at least once and worthy of preservation.

425. The Joyless Street

Rating: ☆☆☆½

Produced in Germany; ***Directed by*** G.W. Pabst; ***Running Time:*** 96 minutes; ***Cast:*** GRETA, Greta Garbo (1905–1990); Asta Nielsen (1881–1972); Werner Krauss (1884–1959)

The delightful and talented Georgia Hale in a scene with Charlie Chaplin in *The Gold Rush* (1925).

The Joyless Street was the last German film that Greta Garbo starred in, made during a lull in projects with her mentor, Mauritz Stiller (1882–1928). After she completed work in this film, she and Stiller went to MGM, where Garbo took the world by storm.

This collaboration with the great director G.W. Pabst (1885–1967) is among the best of all of Garbo's silent era performances. *The Joyless Street* appears to have possibly been inspired by D.W. Griffith's *Isn't Life Wonderful?* (1924). It is set in war torn Austria, a country in the middle of an economic crisis. Greta Garbo plays the daughter of a veteran who has cashed in his pension for a lump sum out of desperation, and loses most of it on the stock market. Money gets tight, and Garbo is sexually harassed by her greedy, profiteering boss who fires her when she won't respond to his advances.

For extra money, Greta's family rents a room to an American soldier. She takes the money received for the room rent to pay off her father's stock brokers. Out of desperation, she takes a job in a nightclub, which causes a rift in her and the American soldier's budding romance.

Much like Griffith's *Isn't Life Wonderful?* (1924), this film tells a sympathetic story of what the European countries went through after the war. It contrasts how the average middle class people suffer, whereas greedy and licentious profiteers take advantage of the hard economic times and find a way to get richer at the expense of others.

Greta Garbo turns in a first class performance as the girl who sacrifices her self respect and happiness to help her family to survive the hard times brought upon them. Some prints of this film are tinted and have beautiful art titles.

This was director Pabst's third directorial project, and the first of his films that was a significant success.

Greta Garbo had just been shot to stardom the previous year with her performance in *The Saga of Gosta Berling* (1924), and this follow-up appearance helped to solidify her reputation worldwide.

Contrary to what has previously been printed, Marlene Dietrich (1901–1992) did not appear as an extra in this film.

426. A Kiss for Cinderella *Rating: ☆☆☆☆*

Paramount; ***Directed by*** Herbert Brenon; ***Screenplay by*** Willis Goldbeck, Townsend Martin; ***Based on the Play by*** J.M. Barrie; ***Supervising Editor:*** William Le Baron; ***Photographed by*** J. Roy Hunt; ***Running Time:*** 108 minutes; ***Cast:*** CINDERELLA, Betty Bronson (1906–1971); POLICEMAN, Tom Moore (1883–1955); FAIRY GODMOTHER, Esther Ralston (1902–1994); RICHARD BODIE, Henry Vibart (1863–1939); QUEEN, Dorothy Cumming (1899–1983); MR. CUTAWAY, Ivan Simpson (1875–1951); MRS. MALONEY, Dorothy Walters (1877–1934); SECOND CUSTOMER, Flora Finch (1869–1940); THIRD CUSTOMER, Juliet Brenon (1885–1979); GLADYS, Marilyn McLaine; MARIE-THERESE, Patty Coakley; SALLY, Mary Christian (1900–1951?); GRETCHEN, Edna Hagen; LORD MAYOR, Sidney Paxton (1860–1930); MRS. LANDLADY, Florence Ashbrook

A Kiss for Cinderella is a prime example of a masterpiece held "hostage." Since Paramount Pictures did not include this title among the nine silents that they released on video in 1987, it is inaccessible to the general public. Paramount holds the copyright on the film, which will not expire until 2001. Even when the film enters the public domain, there is no guarantee that it will be released on video.

While a reviewer should ultimately see a film at least twice before writing about it, *A Kiss for Cinderella* is the one exception to the rule in this book. It is such a magnificent film that the book would not have been complete without it. This author was lucky enough to be able to see this magical film at a film festival many years ago at age 14. The film made such an indelible impression on this then-teenager that most of the details are still in memory over 17 years after the fact.

Esther Ralston and Betty Bronson never looked better than they did in *A Kiss For Cinderella* (1925), a masterpiece directed by Herbert Brenon.

Upon comparing this film to J.M. Barrie's play, one can see that it is as close to perfect as any film adaptation of a play ever was. Brenon followed the play almost to the letter. The only major difference was that in the play, one of Cinderella's wishes was to be accepted as a nurse so that she could do her part in the war effort, which Brenon mentioned earlier in the film, but did not include as among the three wishes.

Brenon is able to improve somewhat on the play with fascinating special effects that simply could not be done on stage. The transformation of the pumpkin and mice into a coach and horses is absolutely breathtaking. The most beautiful title card ever to appear in a silent film is included in this film. It shows Esther Ralston as the fairy godmother to the left of the titles as she is seeing Cinderella off in the coach, which is on its way to the ball. Ralston never looked better in any film than she looked as the fairy godmother in *A Kiss for Cinderella*. The same goes for the adorable and beautiful Betty Bronson in her role as Cinderella. This was by far her greatest role.

Unfortunately, *A Kiss for Cinderella* was a box-office bomb. It was really too complex a story for younger children to be able to follow, and the adults were more interested in the jazz age than they were in innocence, beauty, and charm. After the failure of this high budget masterpiece, Paramount chose not to do anymore similar follow-ups. Brenon started turning out what the public would respond to, and Betty Bronson was relegated to flapper roles, which were not her specialty.

The story of the preservation history of this film is a sad one. William K. Everson's *American Silent Film* relays it as follows:

> A major tragedy connected with *A Kiss for Cinderella* is that the last surviving 35 mm print—a richly toned, crystal clear print that was in itself a thing of beauty...was allowed to deteriorate badly before a preservation copy was made. The only viewing print available today, in black and white and with splotchy hypo deterioration disfiguring and obscuring much of the highlight sequence of the ball, is only a shadow of the original. Failure to preserve the original while there was still time was virtually a cultural crime.

Friends of this author who saw this film when it was originally released reported that when they saw it, the bowing lamp posts had their light fixtures hand-colored yellow as if to glow in the dark, as did the lanterns on the coach that transported Cinderella to the ball. This hand coloring of yellow against a dark blue tinted background had to really be something to see.

Although it is highly unlikely that anybody will ever restore *A Kiss For Cinderella* to look close to the way it once did, at least the film is not totally lost. If there is ever the opportunity to catch a rare public screening of this film, it is a film worth dropping everything to see.

427. The Last Laugh

Rating: ☆☆☆½

Produced in Germany; ***Directed by*** F.W. Murnau; ***Scenario by*** Karl Meyer; ***Settings by*** Herlth and Roehrig; ***Photography by*** Karl Freund; ***Running Time:*** 73 minutes; ***Cast:*** HOTEL DOORMAN, Emil Jannings (1886–1950); HIS DAUGHTER, Maly Delschaft; HER FIANCÉE, Max Hiller; HIS AUNT, Emilie Kurz; HOTEL MANAGER, Hans Unterkirchen (1895–1971?)

Emil Jannings, star of *The Last Laugh* (1925).

This is one of F.W. Murnau's most highly acclaimed films; some critics believe it to be Murnau's masterpiece.

One of the things this psychological portrayal of a hotel doorman is known for is the fact that it told its story without the use of titles successfully. Other efforts to produce title-less silents, such as Charles Ray's *The Old Swimmin' Hole* (1921), did not come off as well.

Karl Freund's cinematography is masterful. The film opens with a point of view shot from a hotel elevator as it descends to the lobby, zeroing in on the doorman, played by Emil Jannings. He is proud and robust as he helps the guests find their way to their cars on the busy, crowded streets in the pouring-down rain.

What is unique about this film is that the story is set in the changes of the character, rather than the character simply following the story line. This proud doorman who takes pride in his job and uniform makes a total transformation when he receives notice that he is being demoted to laundry room attendant. It is absolutely mind boggling to see Emil Jannings age at least 10 or 15 years right in front of our eyes in the course of a couple of minutes.

One especially striking sequence shows Jannings drowning his sorrows in alcohol, and the camera shows the blurry images as he sees them around the room. He opens his eyes and sees double images of his aunt as she is pouring his morning coffee.

As Jannings progresses on his downward spiral, we see things through his eyes—neighbors laughing at him, looks of contempt, etc. In keeping with the title of the film, Jannings' character has "the last laugh" when one of his wealthy customers dies and leaves his entire fortune to him.

The Last Laugh is a masterpiece of psychological study, perhaps the best ever portrayal of what goes through one man's mind under varying situations. While this reviewer does not agree that it is Murnau's greatest film, it is certainly a striking artistic accomplishment worthy of respect.

428. Little Annie Rooney

Rating: ☆☆☆½

United Artists; ***Directed by*** William Beaudine; ***Written by*** Catherine Hennessy; ***Collaborator:*** Tom McNamara; ***Adaptation by*** Hope Loring, Louis Lighton; ***Photography by*** Charles Rosher, Hal Mohr; ***Art Direction by*** John D. Schulze; ***Film Editor:*** Harold

Mary Pickford in *Little Annie Rooney* (1925).

McLernon; ***Running Time:*** 93 minutes; ***Cast:*** LITTLE ANNIE ROONEY, Mary Pickford (1892–1979); JOE KELLEY, William Haines (1900–1973); OFFICER ROONEY, Walter James (1882–1946); TIM ROONEY, Gordon Griffith (1907–1958); TONY, Carlo Schipa (1900–1988); ABIE, Spec O'Donnell (1911–1986); SPIDER, Hugh Faye (died 1926); MAMIE, Vola Vale; MICKEY, Joe Butterworth; ATHOS, Oscar Rudolph (1911–1991)

After the great success of her remake of *Tess of the Storm Country* (1922), Mary Pickford starred in *Rosita* (1923) and *Dorothy Vernon of Haddon Hall* (1924), neither of which was as successful as hoped. Having run out of ideas for existing stories that would suit her public image, Mary Pickford wrote her own story of *Little Annie Rooney* using the alias of Catherine Hennessy, which was actually her maternal grandmother's name. The film turned out to be a big success—her first in three years.

In this film, 33-year-old Mary Pickford plays 12-year-old *Little Annie Rooney*, whose father is a police officer, living in the poor district of the city. The film starts off with Annie Rooney taking over a dozen boys to task for drawing an unflattering picture of her, holding her own quite nicely considering the odds against her. The kids get into trouble when they knock down a fruit vendor's goods, and have to raise $5 to pay for the damage. This leads to a funny benefit show that they put on, which is supposed to be a western. This is hilarious as Annie is playing the sheriff, but can't get the horse to cooperate so that she can make the rescue she's supposed to make.

Tragedy strikes when the notorious Kelley family organizes a fund raiser to raise bail money for a family member. The ball is raided for bootleg liquor, and Annie's father is shot during the raid. The real culprit, Spider, spreads the word that Joe Kelley did the murder, and when Annie's brother Tim hears this, he sets out to kill his father's murderer. It is later found out who the real murderer is, thanks to one of the neighborhood kids who overhears a confession in Russian, but it is too late. Tim Rooney has already shot Joe Kelley, and it is up to Annie to donate blood to keep him alive so that her brother won't go to prison for murder.

While this film is among Ms. Pickford's more dramatic films that wrenches tears in many parts, it has great touches of comedy relief to keep it from being too heavy and overwhelming.

Little Annie Rooney, in addition to being among the most loved of the Pickford films, is also historically significant as William Haines' first really big role as well. Annie's brother, Tim Rooney, is played by none other than Gordon Griffith, whom readers may remember was the first actor to play Tarzan, having played Tarzan as an adolescent child in the first part of the original *Tarzan of the Apes* (1918). Another interesting cast member is Hugh Faye, who plays "Spider." This is the only film this reviewer has seen with him in it, and it was among his last films, as he died in 1926. It is alleged that an actor named Hughie Faye was among the big drug dealers on the movie lots of the time, and possibly the dealer who got Mabel Normand (1892–1930) hooked on cocaine and other drugs. This would lead one to speculate that possibly the Hugh Faye who appeared in this film was also Hollywood drug dealer Hughie Faye.

Mary Pickford, even at age 33, still looked believable in child roles as evidenced in this film.

429. The Lost World

Rating: ☆☆☆

First National; ***Directed by*** Harry Hoyt; ***Running Time on Edited Kodascope Version:*** 62 minutes; ***Running Time on Complete Version:*** Approximately 120 minutes; ***Cast:*** PROFESSOR CHALLENGER, Wallace Beery (1885–1949); SIR JOHN ROXTON, Lewis Stone (1879–1953); PAULA WHITE, Bessie Love (1898–1986); EDWARD MALONE, Lloyd Hughes (1897–1958); PROFESSOR SUMMERLEE, Arthur Hoyt (1874–1953); GLADYS HUNGERFORD, Alma Bennett (1904–1958); MRS. CHALLENGER, Margaret McWade (1872–1956); THE APE MAN, Bull Montana (1887–1950); COLIN MCARDLE, George Bunny (1867–1952); MAJOR HIBBARD, Charles Wellesley (1873–1946)

The Lost World was the first of the big dinosaur extravaganzas, and was far ahead of its time, holding up very well seven decades after its release. The 1993 release of Steven Spielberg's *Jurassic Park* resulted in significantly renewed interest in this film.

Work began on this film's production in 1918, taking seven years to complete from the beginning of its production to its release in 1925. The dinosaur photography was filmed by using clay models, which had to be shot frame by frame. The meticulous work was accomplished by Willis O'Brien (1886–1962), who had begun doing animation in the late 1900s, and started experimenting with Thomas Edison's studios in stop-motion clay model animation in the 1910s.

This film was directed by Harry Hoyt (1891–1961), but the credit for its success is attributed to the genius of Willis O'Brien, as well as the fabulous cast it featured. Three of the main cast members would later win recognition by the Academy of Motion Picture Arts and Sciences in the form of nominations or awards in the acting category. Wallace Beery won a Best Actor Oscar in the 1931–32 season for his performance in *The Champ* (1931), having tied for the award with Fredric March for the only time a tie was declared in the entire history of the awards for this category. Bessie Love received a nomination for Best Actress of the 1928–29 season for her performance in *The Broadway Melody* (1929). Lewis Stone received a Best Actor nomination in the 1928–29 season as well for his performance in *The Patriot* (1928), one of the most sought of the lost films of the silent era. George Bunny was the brother of the famed 1910s comedian John Bunny (1863–1915).

The original running time of *The Lost World* when it was released was approximately two hours. An edited, Kodascope print, which had only half the running time of the original, was all that was believed for years to have survived of this film. In 1996, a relatively complete original print was discovered in a Czechoslovakian film archive, and acquired by the George Eastman House for restoration. Hopefully, the complete film will once again be made available to the general public on video once it is restored.

430. Madame Behave!

Rating: ☆☆☆

Christie/P.D.C.; ***Directed by*** Scott Sidney; ***Screen Adaptation by*** F. McGrew Willis; ***Photography by*** Gus Peterson, Alex Phillips; ***Running Time:*** 54 minutes; ***Cast:*** JACK MITCHELL/MADAM BROWN, Julian Eltinge (1882–1941); GWEN TOWNLEY, Ann Pennington (1892–1971); SETH MORGAN, Lionel Belmore (1868–1953); HENRY JASPER, Jack Duffy (1882–1939); "HENRY", Tom Wilson (1880–1965); PERCY FAIRWEATHER, Stanhope Wheatcroft (1888–1966); DICK MORGAN, David James; LAURA BARNES, Evelyn Francisco

Julian Eltinge was the premier female impersonator of the 1910s and 1920s. He

Top Left: **Julian Eltinge, star of** ***Madame Behave!*** **(1925) in drag.** *Top Right:* **Julian Eltinge, star of** ***Madame Behave!*** **(1925) in men's attire.**

starred in at least 11 silents, and did a last film in sound in 1940 just before he died. His real name was William Dalton. Of the silents he starred in, *Madame Behave!* is the only one known to survive, and is planned for video release in the future.

In this comedy, Eltinge plays a struggling architect who is the roommate of one Dick Morgan, who has squandered his significant inheritance and is broke. The rent on their luxury apartment is due, and they don't have it. Jack Duffy plays the crusty landlord who not only demands his rent, but has his uncle in court over an accident in which his new Rolls-Royce was wrecked. There was one female witness to the accident who cannot be found. The race is on between the uncle and landlord to find and marry the witness. If the uncle marries her first, the law states that a wife cannot testify against her husband. But, if the landlord marries her, then he can make her testify against Seth Morgan.

Through a variety of incidents Julian Eltinge as Jack Mitchell ends up posing as the missing witness, and as Madam Brown has both Seth Morgan and Henry Jasper fighting over him. Meanwhile, he is trying to get an engagement ring for Gwen Townley, the girl he loves, who has a richer rival suitor.

This is a delightful situation comedy, which shows that female impersonation has been around in the movies from their very beginnings. Even the burly, masculine actor Tom Wilson dons a dress during a chase sequence, although his appearance in drag is more comedic than convincing.

Jack Duffy is hilarious as the old landlord. Duffy was the brother of comedienne Kate Price (1872–1943), and looks over 80 in this film, although he was actually only

42. His older appearance is so convincing that this author checked several sources to verify that 1882 was indeed his correct birth year.

Leading lady Ann Pennington is highly appealing. She made her film debut in 1916, and the year after *Madame Behave!* was released, she popularized the "Black Bottom" dance craze. As far as can be determined, this is Pennington's only surviving silent era work, although the last 18 minutes of an early talkie, *Gold Diggers of Broadway* (1929) survives.

This is a sidesplitting situation comedy that will keep viewers laughing for its entire duration. Its historic value as Julian Eltinge's only known surviving silent makes it well worth watching, in addition to the rare chance to see Ann Pennington.

The only flaw with this film is its weak ending. If the ending had been stronger and not so abrupt, the film would have easily rated 3½ stars. Even with the weak ending as it is, the film is still good, solid comedy entertainment.

431. The Merry Widow *Rating:* ☆☆☆½

MGM; ***Directed by*** Erich von Stroheim; ***Screen Adaptation by*** Erich von Stroheim, Benjamin Glazer; ***Based on the Musical Comedy by*** Victor Leon, Leo Stein; ***Titles by*** Marion Ainslee; ***Settings by*** Cedric Gibbons, Richard Day; ***Photography by*** Oliver Marsh; ***Film Editor:*** Frank E. Hull; ***Running Time:*** 113 minutes; ***Cast:*** SALLY O'HARA [THE MERRY WIDOW], Mae Murray (1889–1965); PRINCE DANILO, John Gilbert (1899–1936); CROWN PRINCE MIRKO, Roy D'Arcy (1894–1969); QUEEN MILENA, Josephine Crowell (died 1934); KING NIKITA, George Fawcett (1860–1939); BARON SODOJA, Tully Marshall (1864–1943); AMBASSADOR, Edward Connelly (1855–1928); BIT PART, Clark Gable (1901–1960)

This was the second of four screen adaptations of *The Merry Widow*, and is widely acclaimed as the best of the four. The first film adaptation came out in 1912, and is not known to survive. The 1934 and 1952 talkie remakes both won Academy Awards, as this one probably would have if the Awards had been given out in 1925.

This film has historic significance for many reasons. The most significant of these is the fact that it was Erich von Stroheim's greatest box-office success, and it was the only film of von Stroheim's that was released essentially as he had meant for it to be seen. It also has significance as being one of the legendary Mae Murray's few surviving films, and is widely acclaimed as the best film of her entire career. In addition then up-and-coming romantic lead John Gilbert attained super stardom overnight as a result of his performance in this film.

The Merry Widow was plagued with problems, as were many of von Stroheim's productions. The big clash in this film that caused production delays were the fights between director von Stroheim and the temperamental Mae Murray. Murray objected to the risqué character that von Stroheim was turning the part of Sally into. She refused to do as von Stroheim instructed, which led to a standoff between the two, with production being halted for two days until Murray and von Stroheim came to terms. There were also clashes between von Stroheim and Irving Thalberg, whose job as a producer it was to curb von Stroheim's excessive spending. While a few elaborate bordello sequences were edited, the film turned out essentially as the director had planned.

Mae Murray is stunningly beautiful with her trademark "bee stung lips" as Sally, a commoner who is in love with Prince Danilo, but marries a crippled old baron, Sodoja, for his vast wealth and social position. Roy D'Arcy plays the evil crown prince who tries

Mae Murray and John Gilbert in *The Merry Widow* (1925).

to win Sally for himself, over his cousin Danilo who is next in line after him to ascend to the throne. It is only when the Baron dies and the Crown Prince is assassinated that Sally and Danilo can marry and live happily ever after.

In this satire of European aristocracy, von Stroheim managed to present an unconventional foot fetish on the part of the crown prince—over the strong objections of Irving Thalberg. This and other elements gave *The Merry Widow* an unprecedented eroticism.

The Merry Widow is also notable as the first film in which Clark Gable, as an extra, had a close-up. He can be seen shortly after a ball sequence for a few seconds on the right side of the screen.

While Mae Murray hated working with director von Stroheim, she later admitted that *The Merry Widow* was her best screen performance. After her appearance in this film, she married one Prince David Mdivani, who took control of her life as well as her bank accounts. At his insistence, she walked out on her MGM contract, and faded into obscurity by 1933, when the prince had spent most of Murray's fortune and divorced her. Murray lost custody of her son and declared bankruptcy, living most of the rest of her life on the kindness and generosity of friends in the profession.

While *The Merry Widow* does circulate on video in the form of poor quality copies among a few private collectors, it has not been officially released by Turner Entertainment. This is a film that is worthy of a legitimate, high quality video release.

432. The Monster

Rating: ☆☆☆

MGM; ***Directed by*** Roland West; ***Based on the Play by*** Crane Wilbur; ***Scenario by*** Willard Mack and Albert G. Kenyon; ***Film Editor:*** A. Carle Palm; ***Photography by*** Hal Mohr; ***Titles by*** C. Gardner Sullivan; ***Running Time:*** 86 minutes; ***Cast:*** DR. ZISKA, Lon Chaney, Sr. (1883–1930); BETTY WATSON, Gertrude Olmstead (1904–1975); WATSON'S HEAD CLERK, Hallam Cooley (1895–1971); THE UNDER CLERK, Johnny Arthur (1883–1951); THE CONSTABLE, Charles A. Sellon (1870–1937); CALIBAN, Walter James (1882–1946); DAFFY DAN, Knute Erickson (1870–1945); RIGO, George Watson; LUKE WATSON, Edward McWade (1865–1943); MRS. WATSON, Ethel Wales (1878–1952)

The Monster was not among Lon Chaney's more highly acclaimed films. Many modern day Chaney fans describe it as among the least liked of all of his films. Contemporary reviews from the time of its release have a variety of complaints ranging from too much comedy to the comment that Chaney could have made the character of Dr. Ziska more frightening.

In this film, Chaney plays a lunatic inmate who takes over an asylum and poses as its director. He lures unsuspecting motorists into his clutches by causing them to have accidents, and then uses them as "guinea pigs" for his diabolical experiments. Johnny Arthur, who is best remembered for his low budget comedies for the Christie Company, plays an amateur detective who sets out to prove himself, and ultimately succeeds in solving the mystery of the disappearances at the asylum. Arthur had previously starred in *Mademoiselle Midnight* (1924), directed by Robert Z. Leonard, the husband of leading lady Gertrude Olmstead. Olmstead is highly appealing in this film, especially in the shots with her hair down.

Silent screen star Crane Wilbur (1886–1973), best remembered for playing the hero in Pearl White's *The Perils of Pauline* (1914), wrote the play upon which this film was based, and later wrote the script for *House of Wax* (1953).

This was one of director Roland West's (1887–1952) few films. West is best remembered for *The Bat* (1926) and *The Bat Whispers* (1931). His directing style was rather uneven and erratic—as was his life. West was married to actresses Jewel Carmen and Lola Lane. It was when West was married to Carmen that he had an affair and was a business partner with Thelma Todd as a co-owner of a restaurant/night club. When Ms. Todd mysteriously died in 1935, West and Carmen were both questioned by investigators, and although it has never been proven whether her death was a result of murder, suicide, or an accident, it has been widely speculated that she was murdered, and that West was the prime suspect. After this scandal, West and Ms. Carmen became estranged, and West's film career was finished.

Some historians assert that *The Monster* was the first of the diabolical mad doctor films. However, it was predated by at least two other films of the same genre—*Frankenstein* (1910) and *The Cabinet of Dr. Caligari* (1919).

Despite *The Monster*'s mixed past reviews, when reviewed today, it stands as a highly enjoyable horror comedy, even if it isn't among Chaney's best. Turner Classic Movies aired a restored, orchestra scored version of the film in early 1997.

433. The Phantom of the Opera

Rating: ☆☆☆☆

Universal; ***Directed by*** Rupert Julian; ***Assistant Director:*** Edward Sedgwick; ***Screenplay by*** Raymond Schrock, Elliott J. Clawson; ***From the 1911 Novel by*** Gaston Leroux; ***Titles by*** Tom Reed; ***Photography by*** Virgil Miller, Milton Bridenbecker, Charles J. Van Enger; ***Art Direction by*** Charles D. Hall; ***Film Editor:*** Maurice Pivar; ***Running Time of Complete 1925 Road Show Edit:*** 89 minutes; ***Running Time of 1929 Re-Edit:*** 79 minutes; ***Cast:*** THE PHANTOM OF THE OPERA, Lon Chaney, Sr. (1883–1930); CHRISTINE DAAE, Mary Philbin (1903–1993); RAOUL DE CHAGNEY, Norman Kerry (1889–1956); SIMON BUQUET, Gibson Gowland (1887–1951); CARLOTTA, Mary Fabian; CARLOTTA'S MOTHER, Virginia Pearson (1888–1958); PHILIPPE DE CHAGNEY, John Sainpolis (1873–1946); LEDOUX OF THE SECRET POLICE, Arthur Edmund Carewe (1884–1937); JOSEPH BUQUET, Bernard Siegel (1868–1940); FLORINE PAPILLON, Snitz Edwards (1862–1937); MAMA VALERIUS, Edith Yorke (1867–1934); PROMPTER, Anton Vaverka (died 1937); LA SORELLI, Olive Ann Alcorn; MANAGER, Cesare Gravina (1858–1954?); M. RICARD, George B. Williams (1866–1931); M. MONCHARMIN, Bruce Covington; FAUST, Edward Cecil (1878–1940); VALENTIN, John Miljan (1892–1960); MEPHISTOPHELES, Alexander Bevani (1871–1938); MARTHA, Grace Marvin; COUNT RUBOFF, Ward Crane (1890–1928); ORDERLY, Chester Conklin (1886–1971); DIRECTOR OF OPERA ORCHESTRA, William Tryoler; PRIMA BALLERINA, Carla Laemmle

This is quite possibly the most popular film to come out of the silent era. Theatrical screenings are a yearly Halloween tradition in many larger cities to this day. Many people who are not generally familiar with silent films are familiar with *The Phantom of the Opera*. It is revived on cable TV on a regular basis, and is possibly one of the best selling silents on the video market.

This version of *The Phantom of the Opera*, billed as "Universal's million dollar super jewel production" has frequently been regarded as one of the greatest American horror films of all time, and the very best of the many adaptations of Gaston Leroux's 1911 literary work. It should be, as the star, Lon Chaney, Sr., went through more physical pain and torture than any other actor in history to pull off his gruesome illusions, notably as the phantom. What other "phantom" actor endured the pain and agony of having fishhooks jabbed into his cheeks and metal discs shoved up his nostrils?

In addition to no pain being spared, no expense was spared, as is evident with the lavish reconstruction of the interior of the Paris Opera House. Some of the sets for this sequence were also used in the 1943 remake with Claude Rains as well. Furthermore, filming many of the sequences in 2-strip Technicolor was outrageously expensive at the time. To this very day, the unmasking sequence has never been outdone or even come close to being equaled by any of the many Phantom remakes. This fact would blow a hole in the allegations propagated by some historians and critics that Mary Philbin was an incompetent actress. She was just as big a part in the success of this sequence as was Chaney and director Rupert Julian.

Three major restoration efforts have been done on this film, each one trying to outdo the other. David Shepard of Film Preservation Associates did the first restoration for video, which was black and white with the Technicolor Bal Masque sequence, and which featured an excellent organ score by Gaylord Carter which is one of the best organ scores this reviewer has ever heard on a silent film. Shepard did a second restoration distributed by Kino in 1995, this time with color tinting, an orchestral score, as well as an operetta chorus in the opera sequences. Kevin Brownlow of England also did a restora-

Lon Chaney, Sr., in an unforgettable pose from *The Phantom of the Opera* (1925).

tion which featured an orchestral score by the great musician Carl Davis, and featured Chaney's cape hand colored in red during the sequence in which he is on top of the Paris Opera House eavesdropping on Christine's conversation with Raoul. Currently, film preservationist Robert Gitt is working on a high quality 35mm restoration of the complete silent version, too. All previous restorations have used material from the sound reissue that was made from alternate takes, so Gitt's restoration will definitely be something to see. This Gitt restoration will be hopefully made available on video so that people can see it.

A "modernized" version of this film was done in 1990, with a rock score recorded by Rick Wakeman of the acclaimed musical group Yes. It was actually this version that was the first video version to be presented with color tinting. The visual quality of this restoration was nice. It even had an introduction by 1950s horror star Christopher Lee, which was very good. But, the rock track simply was not appropriate for this film, and the music fought the action rather than enhanced it. Some of the non-vocal parts of the track were very well done. The first few minutes of the film are fine—until the vocals and the electric guitar are introduced into the music score, which totally ruins the film. It seems that once one gets into the film, Wakeman insists on constantly interrupting the enjoyment. This "modernized" rock score version is worth seeing just to see why it is ill-advised to try to "modernize" the silents with contemporary and hard rock scores.

The history of *The Phantom of the Opera* is quite complicated. The original 1925 road show version was approximately 89 minutes in length. Virginia Pearson played the part of Carlotta in all segments of the 1925 version. In addition, each player is introduced by his/her own title card in this version. There are a few minutes of footage at the beginning showing more of the crowds arriving at the opera house, and a few other snippets of footage here and there which are not used in other versions of the film. In addition, the ending shows Raoul and Christine on their honeymoon, which is not shown in subsequent versions. This original 1925 version does still exist, and is available on video and laser disc, but the master prints are of poor quality. A company called the Niles Company acquired the last surviving 35 mm print of the complete, original version in the 1960s. The print was starting to decompose, and they hastily struck several 16 mm prints from the original nitrate print. The resulting prints were of poor quality, but at least this original version was preserved in some form and available for evaluation to satisfy one's curiosity.

In 1929, Universal Pictures re-released *The Phantom of the Opera* as a part-talking picture. Since Virginia Pearson was not an opera singer, her opera sequences were re-shot with a singer named Mary Fabian. Fabian became Carlotta, and Virginia Pearson became Carlotta's mother. When doing the 1929 re-edit, the producers forgot to make the appropriate change in the final cast list, which still lists Pearson as Carlotta, and omits Mary Fabian's name. The print was also slightly re-edited, and, in this author's opinion, some of the sequences were actually improved and made more exciting with this re-editing job. In 1929, this re-edited version was released in both silent and sound versions. No prints of the talking version are currently known to exist. However, the 1929 silent version is what has survived in superior quality prints, and it is this 1929 silent version that is primarily shown today. In the original version of the film, there were apparently several Technicolor sequences, which were not preserved in subsequent prints struck from it. None of the Technicolor sequences were known to have survived, until David Shepard rediscovered Technicolor footage on the one Bal Masque sequence, finally restoring at least some of the Technicolor footage.

This is a great film to use when introducing friends to silents and trying to get them hooked. It is a classic that every silent film collection—whether a personal collection, library collection, or video rental store collection—should have at least one copy of.

434. The Plastic Age

Rating: ☆☆☆

B.P. Schulberg Productions; ***Directed by*** Wesley Ruggles; ***Screen Adaptation by*** Eve Unsell and Frederica Sagor; ***Continuity by*** Wesley Ruggles and Eve Unsell; ***Photography by*** Al Siegler and Gilbert Warrenton; ***Running Time:*** 66 minutes; ***Cast:*** CYNTHIA DAY, Clara Bow (1905–1965); CARL PETERS, Gilbert Roland (1905–1994); HUGH CARVER, Donald Keith (1903–1969); HENRY CARVER, Henry B. Walthall (1878–1936); MRS. HENRY CARVER, Mary Alden (1883–1946); COACH JAMES HENLEY, David Butler (1895–1979); A FOOTBALL PLAYER [CAMEO], Clark Gable (1901–1960)

The Plastic Age was the second of the college co-ed films which became so popular in the mid and late 1920s, following a few months after Harold Lloyd's *The Freshman*, which originally started the college comedy trend.

Henry B. Walthall and Mary Alden, who played in D.W. Griffith's *The Birth of a Nation,* are reunited in this film, playing the parents of one Hugh Carver, our leading man. Carver starts as a freshman at the prestigious Prescott College as a track star. His roommate at college is Carl Peters. They get along very well at first—until Cynthia Day comes into the picture, and they both are attracted to her. Here, the rivalry begins and gets vicious. In the beginning, Cynthia and Hugh are dating. The first big confrontation occurs at a dance at the Log Cabin Club, a speakeasy frequented by the college crowd. The two college athletes get into a brawl just as the speakeasy is being raided. The day after the big showdown, Cynthia dumps the mild mannered Hugh, reasoning that she prefers the fast life of a flapper, and does not wish to corrupt him by dragging him into her lifestyle.

Two years pass, and our leading man is now a Junior, and still has Cynthia Day on his mind. The rivalry between Hugh and Carl flares up again at football trials. Both men are vying for the prestigious quarterback position. Since Hugh Carver has been training hard, he is the coach's first choice for the position. At the trials, Carl Peters deliberately sprains Hugh's ankle. The big game comes, and the injury causes Hugh to miss a crucial goal point. The coach reluctantly sends Peters in as his replacement. The team is still losing with minutes to play, and the coach sends Hugh back into the game. This leads into the film's final minutes, in which we see the outcome of the game and how Cynthia Day deals with the situation.

This is a film of significant historical importance in that it is Gilbert Roland's only silent film that is widely available to the general public on video. In addition, it features an early glimpse of none other than Clark Gable, who can be seen briefly in the locker room sequence. This is, if not his earliest appearance on film, one of his earliest screen appearances.

435. The Rainbow Trail

Rating: ☆☆☆

Fox; ***Written and Directed by*** Lynn Reynolds; ***Photography by*** Daniel Clark; ***Based on the Novel by*** Zane Grey; ***Titles by*** Tom Miranda; ***Original Running Time:*** 70 minutes; ***Running Time of Currently Available Version:*** 57 minutes; ***Cast:*** JOHN SHEFFORD, Tom Mix (1880–

1940); FAY LARKIN, Anne Cornwall (1897–1980); ANNIE, Diana Miller (1902–1927); VENTERS, Thomas Delmar; VENTERS' WIFE BESS, Vivien Oakland (1895–1958); JAKE WILLETS, George Bancroft (1882–1956); JOE LAKE, Lucien Littlefield (1895–1960); SHADD, Fred De Silva (1885–1929); ***Supporting Cast:*** Mark Hamilton; Steve Clements (1885–1950); Doc Roberts; Carol Halloway

For many years, this sequel to *Riders of the Purple Sage* (1925) was believed lost. In 1997, a reissue print turned up, and the film was made available to the public on video through Grapevine.

While this sequel is not as strong as its predecessor, it is still an interesting film to see, with good stunt work by Tom Mix as well as an excellent supporting cast.

This sequel starts off with a bang—literally—as Tom Mix's character John Shefford arrives at a point in the terrain during his travels in which a family traveling in a horse and buggy is being attacked by Indians. Shefford has been for years looking for his uncle, Jim Carson, a.k.a. Lassiter. Shefford disguises himself as an Indian, and then opens fire, driving off the attackers and saving the travelers. It turns out that his good deed pays off, as Venters was a friend of Lassiter. Venters then flashes back to scenes from *Riders of the Purple Sage*, telling the story about how Lassiter saved Jane Withersteen and her adopted daughter Fay Larkin from outlaws, but was trapped in Surprise Valley alone after an avalanche. Further investigation leads Shefford to the outlaw town of Stoneridge, where his new adventure really begins.

George Bancroft, in one of his early western roles, plays saloon owner Jake Willets. *The Rainbow Trail* is also interesting in that it features Diana Miller as Annie, the manager of the saloon. Ms. Miller was the wife of director George Melford (1877–1961). She was only 25 years old when she died in 1927 from a lung hemorrhage. It is sad also to note that Lynn Reynolds (1891–1927), the director of this film, died the same year at age 35 from suicide. His suicide was a major news event, as he had first threatened his wife and guests in a drunken rage before turning the gun on himself. Fred DeSilva's death of unspecified causes at age 44 followed two years later in 1929.

436. The Red Kimono

Rating: ☆☆☆

Mrs. Wallace Reid Productions; ***Directed by*** Walter Lang; ***Screenplay Adaptation by*** Dorothy Arzner; ***Based on a Story by*** Adela Rogers St. Johns; ***Running Time:*** 70 minutes; ***Cast:*** NARRATOR, Dorothy Davenport [Mrs. Wallace] Reid (1895–1977); GABRIELLE DARLEY, Priscilla Bonner (1899–1996); CLARA, Nellie Bly Baker (1894–1985?); HOWARD BLAINE, Carl Miller (1893–1979); THE JAIL MATRON, Mrs. Mary Carr (1874–1973); MRS. FONTAINE, Virginia Pearson (1888–1958); GABRIELLE'S FATHER, Tyrone Power, Sr. (1869–1931); DISTRICT ATTORNEY, Sheldon Lewis (1868–1958); FREDDY THE CHAUFFER, Theodore Von Eltz (1893–1964); MRS. FONTAINE'S HOUSEKEEPER, Emily Fitzroy (1860–1954); DR. MACK, George Siegmann (1882–1928); THE INQUISITIVE ONE, Pat Farley

This is a narrative based on real-life events, depicting a 1917 incident of a woman unjustly exploited. Priscilla Bonner gives a convincing performance as Gabrielle, a woman who falls for en empty promise of marriage by con artist Howard Blaine, in a desperate effort to escape her tyrannical father. Instead of marrying Gabrielle as promised, Blaine puts her to work in a New Orleans whorehouse. Having no place else to go and desperate for money, Gabrielle endures years of bondage in the house of ill fame.

Upon learning that Blaine is traveling to Los Angeles to marry another woman, Gabrielle follows him there, and, on impulse, shoots and kills him. A sympathetic jury acquits her. After the trial, she is taken in by one Mrs. Fontaine, a "notoriety seeking old biddy" who exploits her for the publicity value to further her reputation as a philanthropist—only to throw her back out in the streets to fend for herself after the publicity value is gone. Unable to find legitimate employment, Gabrielle returns to New Orleans with the intent of going back into prostitution. An unexpected chain of events prevents this from happening, and she eventually finds happiness. At the end of the movie is a personal plea from Dorothy Davenport Reid for society to give fallen women a chance to make good as opposed to shunning and condemning, and thereby forcing them to remain in seedy lifestyles.

Unfortunately, Dorothy Reid used Gabrielle Darley's real name in this story, prompting a lawsuit from the real Gabrielle Darley. Darley sued Reid for $50,000, as she had married and become a respected figure of the society scene. Once her new circle of friends found out about her past, she was shunned by many of them. Darley claimed that her privacy was violated. Eventually, the California courts ruled in Darley's favor in 1931. They rejected the claim that an ex-convict had a right to privacy, but did rule that Reid had violated the California Constitution by denigrating Darley's right to pursue happiness. Reid could have prevented this suit by simply using a different name for Darley, but did not do so in the interest of preserving authenticity.

The reviews for *The Red Kimono* were mixed, but mostly negative. Positive reviews did come in for Priscilla Bonner's acting performance. The negative reviews were not deserved, as *The Red Kimono* delivers a very powerful message, and was years ahead of its time. It is the only known surviving movie of the series of three that Ms. Reid produced in the immediate aftermath of husband Wallace Reid's death from drug addiction. The first two in the series were the famous lost film, *Human Wreckage* (1923), which dealt with drug trafficking, and *Broken Laws*, which addressed juvenile delinquency. Judging from *The Red Kimono*, Reid appears to have been a good woman coping with the pain of having lost her husband to drug addiction in the best way that she could. Her efforts seem to have been sincerely motivated by the desire to educate the public about some of society's dangers, hopefully saving a few people from going through the heartache that she went through. *The Red Kimono* is very well-produced, and Reid deserves far more credit than what past critics have given her.

It is ironic to note that this movie, with its message against judgment, condemnation, and exploitation, was based on a story written by none other than the infamous Adela Rogers St. Johns. St. Johns was the queen of exploitation during the 1920s, having been the predecessor of notorious columnists Louella Parsons and Hedda Hopper. The exaggeration and distortion of facts in St. John's articles helped to ruin the careers of Roscoe Arbuckle and Mary Miles Minter.

437. Riders of the Purple Sage

Rating: ★★★½

Fox; ***Directed by*** Lynn Reynolds; ***Based on the Novel by*** Zane Grey; ***Scenario by*** Edfrid Bingham; ***Photography by*** Daniel Clark; ***Running Time:*** 54 minutes; ***Cast:*** JIM CARSON [LASSITER], Tom Mix (1880–1940); JANE WITHERSTEEN, Mabel Ballin (1885–1958); LEW WALTERS, Warner Oland (1880–1938); MILLIE ERNE, Beatrice Burnham (1897 or 1902–??);

Tom Mix and horse Tony, stars of *Riders of the Purple Sage* (1925).

FRANK ERNE, Arthur Morrison (1877–1950); METZGER, Fred Kohler (1888–1938); HERD, Charles Newton (1874–1926); SLACK, Joe Rickson (1880–1958); BESSIE ERNE [AS A CHILD], Sessel Johnson; RICHARD TULL, Charles LeMoyne (1880–1956); VENTERS, Harold Goodwin (1902–1987); BESS ERNE, Marion Nixon (1904–1983); FAY LARKIN, Dawn O'Day (1918–1993) [a.k.a. "Anne Shirley"]; OLDRING, Wilfred Lucas (1871–1940)

This was the first film adaptation of Zane Grey's 1912 western classic, and is acclaimed as one of Tom Mix's best films. This author would go further to classify it as one of the best westerns of the silent era, earning a place beside such classics as *Tumbleweeds* (1925).

Legendary western star Tom Mix plays Texas Ranger Jim Carson, known as Lassiter, whose sister Millie Erne and her daughter Bess have been kidnapped by lecherous attorney Lew Walters, who has been forced to leave town. Lassiter spends the film in search of the two, and finds out that Walters is now passing himself off as "Judge Dyer" in a remote town, having had Bess kidnapped and leaving Millie to die.

Lassiter gets a job on the ranch of Jane Withersteen while he searches for Walters. One Richard Tull is determined to marry Withersteen for her money and ranch, and conspires with Judge Dyer to force her to marry him, as she wants nothing to do with him. Meanwhile, Withersteen has become the target of a gang of cattle rustlers put up by Tull and leader Oldring to break her financially and force her to submit to Tull. It is up to Lassiter to bring the conspirators and Judge Dyer to justice, and to free his young niece from the Oldring gang that she has been forced into and been a part of since childhood.

In addition to this film's excellent story and non-stop action, it also features a number of interesting players. Warner Oland is excellent as villain Judge Dyer, formerly Lew Walters, as the man you love to hate. Marion Nixon is appealing as Lassiter's kidnapped niece in one of her best films. Leading lady Mabel Ballin was the wife of film director Hugo Ballin (1880–1956), whose career from 1917–1927 including directing *Jane Eyre* (1921) and *East Lynne* (1921), as well as serving as art director on Gloria Swanson's *The Love of Sunya* (1927), his final project before retiring. Child actress Dawn O'Day, who would later change her name to Anne Shirley for her famous title role as *Anne of Green Gables* (1934), is charming as little Fay Larkin, the orphaned girl that Jane Withersteen has adopted, and who is taken away from Jane by the contemptible judge. She is especially charming in the sequence in which she asks Lassiter to act like "a big wooly dog" and plays piggy-back with him.

Riders of the Purple Sage is a fine film that lets us see Tom Mix at his best. It is a title that every western buff should have in his or her collection. Critic's Choice in 1997 released a beautiful, tinted video version with an excellent piano score, which is highly recommended.

At least two remakes of *Riders of the Purple Sage* were done in the talkie era. George O'Brien starred in a 1931 version, and a made-for-television version was done in the 1980s.

438. Sally of the Sawdust

Rating: ☆☆☆

D.W. Griffith/Paramount; ***Directed by*** D.W. Griffith; ***From the Play Poppy by*** Dorothy Donnelly; ***Screen Adaptation by*** Forrest Halsey; ***Running Time:*** 113 minutes; ***Cast:*** SALLY, Carol Dempster (1901–1991); PROFESSOR EUSTACE MCGARGLE, W.C. Fields (1879–1946); PEYTON LENNOX, Alfred Lunt (1892–1977); MRS. FOSTER, Effie Shannon (1867–1954); JUDGE FOSTER, Erville Anderson; LEON (THE ACROBAT), Glenn Anders; MR. LENNOX, Charles Hammond (1878–1941); THE DETECTIVE, Roy Applegate

Sally of the Sawdust was the second of three films that D.W. Griffith directed under contract with Paramount Pictures, after he was forced to close his independent Mamaroneck Studios due to financial problems. The first of the three Griffith-Paramount features was *That Royle Girl* (1925), which is one of the few Griffith features that is considered lost. In addition to being one of three Griffith-Paramount films, *Sally of the Sawdust* has many other attributes that make it historically significant. It is the only one of Alfred Lunt's very few silents which is available on video. Lunt was an accomplished stage actor, who, with his wife, Lynn Fontanne, won wide critical acclaim. He was nominated for the Best Actor Oscar for 1931–32 based on his performance in *The Guardsman* (1931). In addition, this film has historic importance as being the first major role of W.C. Fields in a silent feature. Previously, Fields had done a couple of shorts and had a cameo in *Janice Meredith* (1924).

In addition to its historic importance, this film has a charming story which blends comedy and drama most effectively. It opens with a young adult woman named Mary Foster being ordered out of the home of her wealthy parents, who disapprove of her marriage to a traveling circus performer. Her husband dies, and she finds her only friend in the lovable shyster and card shark Professor Eustace McGargle. Foster has a young daughter, and dies shortly after giving birth. Before she dies, she hands a slip of paper to McGargle, with the name and address of the baby's grandparents. McGargle takes Sally under his wing, and raises her as his own. The years pass, and Sally becomes an attractive dancer, still traveling in road shows. The time comes when a fellow performer tries to force himself onto Sally, but is prevented from doing so as McGargle bursts a bottle over his head. It is at this point that McGargle realizes the parental responsibilities he has taken on, and tries to find Sally's grandparents. The road show takes them to Green Meadows, where McGargle discovers that the grandparents, the Aldersons, are very wealthy. The grandfather, Judge Alderson, is a powerful judge, who absolutely despises "show people."

While playing the carnival in Green Meadows, Sally meets a wealthy young man by the name of Peyton Lennox. Peyton's father disapproves immediately, and the rest of the plot deals with his efforts to work with higher-ups, including Judge Alderson (who does not realize that Sally is his own granddaughter) to have Sally and her adopted father arrested to thwart the marriage plans.

Although Carol Dempster has not been highly acclaimed, she demonstrates her competence as a versatile actress in this film, playing both comedic and dramatic scenes effectively. W.C. Fields adds just the right touch of comedy, while Alfred Lunt is good as the romantic male lead. Although this does not compare to Griffith's earlier epics, it is still quite enjoyable, and a fun film to watch.

439. The Salvation Hunters

Rating: ☆☆½

Academy Photoplays/United Artists; ***Written and Directed by*** Josef Von Sternberg; ***Assistant Directors:*** George Ruric, Robert Chapman; ***Photography by*** Edward Gheller; ***Running Time:*** 74 minutes; ***Cast:*** THE BOY, George K. Arthur (1899–1985); THE GIRL, Georgia Hale (1896–1985); THE CHILD, Bruce Guerin; THE MAN, Otto Matieson (1893–1932); THE WOMAN, Nellie Bly Baker (1894–1985?); THE BRUTE, Olaf Hytton (1888–1955)

In the mid–1910s, Joe Stern was a young film cutter for the World Film Company. By 1924, he reemerged under the name of Josef Von Sternberg, and directed his first film at age 29. This first effort was independently produced by Von Sternberg and was financed on a shoestring budget by British actor George K. Arthur, who just came to the U.S. from London.

This was an experimental film, and reportedly the first deliberately "artsy" film produced in the United States. Charlie Chaplin and Douglas Fairbanks, Sr., were impressed with it, and saw that *The Salvation Hunters* got a theatrical release through United Artists.

The Salvation Hunters got mixed critical reviews on its release. Some critics praised it as an artistic accomplishment, and others called it out as a depressing bore. In evaluating the film today, both summations have some validity. The film is an artistic representation of the sordid side of life—with the three main characters introduced in their grim, muddy surroundings. A dredging machine on the docks is shown repeatedly picking up mud and moving it to another spot. The boy, played by the film's financier George K. Arthur, encounters the girl. They witness a child being beaten, and the girl pushes the boy forward to help the child and put a stop to the beating.

The couple take the child in, and the boy and girl make a determination to escape the grim, dirty, depressing surroundings that they feel trapped in. Together, the "children of the mud" struggle against their own weaknesses and adversities that life has handed them, and in the end become "children of the sun."

This film does have plenty of flaws. It is slow moving in many parts, and is certainly not a film that most people would find entertaining. But, its artistic value makes an impression even today, and made a good enough impression on the Hollywood moguls of the time that doors of opportunity were opened for Von Sternberg, who would turn out some of the finest films of the late silent era.

The Salvation Hunters was the film debut of then-unknown actress Georgia Hale, who so impressed Charlie Chaplin that he replaced wife Lita Grey (1908–1995) in *The Gold Rush* with Ms. Hale. Ms. Hale's performance is impressive when seen today, and one longs to see more of her work. She starred in a few more silents in the late 1920s, but her career did not survive the transition to talkies. Still spry when she was in her 80s, she was an actress who actually looked better as she got older. She could have easily passed for a woman in her late 30s or early 40s when she was interviewed in 1982 at the age of 86.

Supporting actress Nellie Bly Baker plays a fallen prostitute in this film. Ms. Baker was Charlie Chaplin's secretary, and had bit parts in a few of his early features. A film scholar got in touch with her in 1984, but she was in such deteriorated health by this time that she was not mentally coherent. It is assumed that Ms. Baker died shortly after 1984. She all but disappeared from the film world after the late 1920s, and no further information is known on her except that she was financially stable in her later years.

The Salvation Hunters, despite its limited entertainment appeal, is worth seeing for Georgia Hale's performance, as well as its historic value.

440. Secrets of the Night

Rating: ★½

Universal; ***Directed by*** Herbert Blaché; ***Scenario and Adaptation by*** Edward J. Montagne; ***Based on The Nightcap by*** Guy Bolton, Max Marcin; ***Photography by*** Gilbert Warrenton; ***Titles by*** Marion Ainslee; ***Film Editor:*** Harold McLernon; ***Art Direction by*** E.E. Sheeley;

Running Time: 72 minutes; ***Cast:*** ROBERT ANDREWS, James Kirkwood (1875–1963); ANNE MAYNARD, Madge Bellamy (1899–1990); CELIA STEBBINS, Zasu Pitts (1898–1963); JERRY HAMMOND, Tom Ricketts (1853–1939); COLONEL JAMES CONSTANCE, Tom S. Guise (died 1930); LESTER KNOWLES, Arthur Stuart Hull (1878–1951); ALFRED AUSTIN, Edward Cecil (1878–1940); FREDDY HAMMOND, Frederick Cole (1901–1964); MRS. LESTER KNOWLES, Rosemary Theby (1885-??); THOMAS JEFFERSON WHITE, Tom Wilson (1880–1965); CHARLES, Joe Singleton (1881-??); CORONER, Otto Hoffman (1879–1944); JOSHUA BROWN, Anton Vaverka (died 1937); ***Supporting Cast:*** Bull Montana (1887–1950); Tyrone Brereton (1894–1939); Arthur Thalasso (1883–1954)

This was a routine Universal programmer. James Kirkwood plays a bank officer who sits on the board of trustees that made a bad loan, and are facing prison unless they can come up with $500,000 before the Federal Bank Examiner audits them. Kirkwood as Andrews throws a party at his home where he stages his own death so that his life insurance can be collected to replace the money.

The night of the party has some "old house" horror elements with hands appearing, the wind blowing at strategic times, etc. *Secrets of the Night* in many ways reminds one of *The Cat and the Canary* (1927), but it is not nearly as good as the latter film.

This might have been a better film if it had been directed by Alice Guy-Blaché instead of her husband, as Guy-Blaché's surviving work indicates that she was a good comedy director.

Zasu Pitts has a good comedy part as a bespectacled guest at the party who reads murder mysteries and gets hysterical from time to time.

441. Seven Chances

Rating: ☆☆☆☆

Buster Keaton Productions/MGM; ***Directed by*** Buster Keaton; ***Adapted from David Belasco's Play by*** Roi Cooper Megrue; ***Adaptation by*** Clyde Bruckman, Jean Havez, Joseph Mitchell; ***Photography by*** Elgin Lessley, Byron Houck; ***Art Director:*** Fred Gabourie; ***Running Time:*** 56 minutes; ***Cast:*** JAMES SHANNON, Buster Keaton (1895–1966); HIS PARTNER, T. Roy Barnes (1880–1937); HIS LAWYER, Snitz Edwards (1862–1937); HIS GIRL, Ruth Dwyer (1897–1978); HER MOTHER, Frankie Raymond (1869–1961); THE CLERGYMAN, Edwin Connelly (1879–1931); THE HIRED MAN, Jules Cowles (1877–1943)

This Keaton masterpiece is among the best of all romantic comedies. In *Seven Chances*, Keaton plays James Shannon, a lawyer whose firm has been tricked into a shady financial scam, and must raise a lot of money to avoid possible disgrace and legal prosecution. Shannon gets good news when it is revealed that he stands to inherit millions—provided that he is married by a certain time. The girl he has been meaning to marry for a long time, but was unable to work up the courage to propose to, refuses his proposal—thinking that he does not really love her, and is simply interested in his inheritance. So, Shannon tries desperately to find a woman to marry, not having any success. One sequence has him passing by a billboard advertising a show by Julian Eltinge (1882–1941), the nation's premiere female impersonator of the time.

Out of desperation, Keaton's advisers tell him to run an ad explaining his situation as a most eligible bachelor. Women come out of the woodwork to marry this soon-to-be millionaire, and the rest of the film comprises one huge chase sequence as Shannon flees from the mobs of women who are after him.

Keaton did some dangerous stunts for this film. One of these was when he was lifted high into the air, dangling from a mechanical fork lift as he is let down on the other side of the fence. But, the big sequence that helped to make this film really famous has Keaton running down a mountainside, being chased by huge boulders. Although the boulders were specially made, they were still heavy enough to cause significant injury. One can see Keaton actually being hit by a few of the boulders, and taking hard falls in frantic efforts to avoid them. It was reported that Keaton's body was covered with bruises for weeks after filming this sequence.

Seven Chances is a timeless film whose plot is as entertaining and appealing today as it was 70 years ago. It was reported that a new, young writer recently sold a screenplay for a remake of this film to New Line Cinema for over $1 million. It will be interesting to see how the remake holds up against Keaton's original. Keaton's version is an enduring masterpiece that is going to be very difficult to equal.

This was the one film that leading lady Ruth Dwyer starred in with Keaton. She made most of her other film appearances in westerns. *Seven Chances* also has a Technicolor sequence at the beginning, having been the only color footage of Keaton from the silent era. Unfortunately, the color has faded to the point that it simply looks tinted when watching it today.

442. She

Rating: ☆☆½

A.G.B. Samuelson Productions/Great Britain; ***Directed by*** Leander DeCordova; ***Running Time:*** 63 minutes; ***Cast:*** SHE-WHO-MUST-BE-OBEYED, Betty Blythe (1893–1972); KALLIKRATES/LEO VINCEY, Carlyle Blackwell (1884–1955); USLANE, Mary Odette; AMENARLAS,

Betty Blythe, star of *She* (1925).

Marjorie Statler; HORACE HOLLEY, Henry George; JOB, Tom Reynolds (1866–1942); BILLALI, Jerrold Robertshaw (1866–1941); MAHOMEL, Alexander Butler

This 1925 production of *She* was filmed in Great Britain, and is acclaimed as the best of all of the silent versions. Since only the 1911 version survives of the other silent adaptations for comparison, it is hard to tell for sure. But, based on what we have, this 1925 version is by far superior to the 1911. H. Rider Haggard, the author of the original 1902 fantasy novel, wrote the titles for this adaptation just before he died.

The story in this version has all of the elements presented in the novel, and is among the more elaborate surviving British films of the silent era. This version features an encounter with cannibals, mass mob scenes, and some interesting, though simple special effects. The scenes in which "She" bathes in fire to maintain her youth are accomplished with simple double exposure. But, the final sequence in which "She" shrivels up and disappears is quite impressive.

This version of *She* has historic significance as one of only two of Betty Blythe's silent films that is widely available on video for evaluation. Ms. Blythe began her film career in 1918. She scored her greatest success in the title role of Fox Film Company's *The Queen of Sheba* (1921), which is one of the most sought of the lost films, as Theda Bara's successor at Fox. She survived the transition to the talkie era, but by this time was playing character and supporting roles. Her last film appearance was a cameo in *My Fair Lady* (1964).

Leander DeCordova (1878–1969), who originally started directing films in America, made *She* three years after leaving the U.S. for Great Britain. He went on to be a production executive for Gainsborough Pictures.

Carlyle Blackwell had started out as one of the early American matinee idols of the 1910s, having starred opposite such notable leading ladies as Mary Pickford, Mae Marsh, and Mary Miles Minter. He was 41 when he played the 25-year-old Leo Vincey in *She*, which was one of his last films. It is difficult to imagine why he was chosen for this role, as he certainly looked his true age and did not come close to being able to pass for 25. Mary Odette, who plays Uslane, was relatively well known in the British silent film industry, but little other information is known on her.

While the ultimate and best movie adaptation of *She* was the 1935 talkie produced by Merian C. Cooper (of *Chang* and *King Kong* fame) and starring Randolph Scott, this silent version is not bad, and definitely worth watching if only to see Betty Blythe's performance.

443. The Sporting Venus

Rating: ☆☆½

MGM; ***Directed by*** Marshall Neilan; ***Assistant Director:*** Thomas Held; ***Based on the Story by*** Gerald Beaumont; ***Scenario by*** Thomas Geraghty; ***Art Direction by*** Cedric Gibbons; ***Wardrobe by*** Ethel P. Chaffin; ***Photography by*** David Kesson; ***Running Time:*** 65 minutes; ***Cast:*** LADY GWENDOLYN, Blanche Sweet (1896–1986); DONALD MACALLEN, Ronald Colman (1891–1958); PRINCE MARNO, Lew Cody (1888–1934); COUNTESS VAN ALSTYNE, Josephine Crowell (died 1934); SIR ALFRED GRAYLE, Edward Martindel (1873–1955); HOUSEKEEPER, Kate Price (1872–1943); MARNO'S VALET, Hank Mann (1887–1971); DETECTIVE, Arthur Hoyt (1874–1953); FATHER, George Fawcett (1860–1939)

The Sporting Venus was the Neilan/Sweet follow-up to their lost masterpiece, *Tess*

of the D'Urbervilles (1924). To get Ronald Colman for the male lead, Sweet agreed to do a film with him for Goldwyn Pictures in exchange for their loaning him out for this film. Of the 25 films that Ms. Sweet made during the 1920s, this is one of only three known to survive. The other two are reviewed elsewhere in this book.

In this film, Sweet plays a royal figure who falls in love with a commoner, played by Colman. Discouraged from marrying outside "her station," Gwen starts dating Prince Marno, a playboy who is deeply in debt, and marries her for her money. Once he goes through her fortune, Gwen is left broke and alone. Meanwhile, commoner Donald MacAllen has risen to a position of prominence.

Blanche Sweet in *The Sporting Venus* (1925), directed by husband Marshall Neilan.

In addition to being one of Blanche Sweet's few later silents to survive, this film is also a rarity in that it is one of about a half dozen known surviving films of the nearly 50 that Lew Cody starred in.

Aside from the starring vehicles that director Neilan did with Mary Pickford, of which almost all, if not all, survive, *The Sporting Venus* is one of only two non-Pickford silents that Neilan directed which still survives. The rest of his silent era work is lost.

Blanche Sweet's role in *The Sporting Venus* marks a significant departure from the types of roles with which she was typically associated. When she was with Griffith, she played innocent heroine types. *That Girl Montana* and *Anna Christie* had her playing roles of women who were victimized by their surroundings and upbringings, but who triumphed in the end. *The Sporting Venus* does have this same element to some extent, but has her becoming a flapper type character in keeping with the "jazz age" types of films which were so popular at the time. Lady Gwendolyn is a woman whose mother died when she was born, whose father was distant, and who was brought up by servants. Yet, her royal family heritage requires her to marry within an aristocratic social class, which proves to be counteractive to her true happiness.

The Sporting Venus was one of the films that was done at the time when Marshall Neilan's (1891–1958) alcoholism was just starting to escalate. Director Neilan and star Blanche Sweet had been married in 1922, but Neilan's drinking caused Sweet to divorce him in 1929.

444. The Swan *Rating:* ☆☆½

Paramount; ***Scenario and Direction by*** Dmitri Buchowetzki; ***Based on the Play by*** Ferenc Molnar; ***Titles by*** Julian Johnson; ***Photography by*** Alvin Wyckoff; ***Running Time:*** 63 minutes; ***Cast:*** PRINCE ALBERT, Adolphe Menjou (1890–1963); PRINCESS ALEXANDRA, Frances

Howard (1903–1976); DR. WALTER, Ricardo Cortez (1899–1977); COUNTESS WANDA, Helen Lee Worthing (1905–1948); DUCHESS DOMINICA, Claire Eames (1896–1930); COLONEL WUNDERLICH, Michael Vavitch (1885–1930); LUTZOW, W. Soussanin; PRINCESS BEATRICE, Ida Waterman (1852–1941); AMPHIROSA, Helen Lindroth (1874–1956); FATHER HYACINTH, Michael Visaroff (1892–1951)

This is the only one of the seven silent films directed by Dmitri Buchowetzki (1885–1932) in America known to survive. He started directing films in Russia prior to the Bolshevik Revolution, and emigrated to Germany in 1917. His most notable German productions were *The Brothers Karamazov* (1919) and *Othello* (1922). Buchowetzki was imported to America in 1924. After limited success in the silent era, he was assigned to direct the German versions of early talkies like *The Letter* (1929) and a French talkie version of *Manslaughter* (1930) before his death in 1932 at 46.

This was the first of three film adaptations of Ferenc Molnar's classic romantic comedy, *The Swan*, which debuted on stage in 1921. Elsie Ferguson, who had played the role of Princess Alexandra on stage, was the first choice for this first film version, but she turned down the role, and it went to Frances Howard. This was Ms. Howard's one big film role of the few that she played.

As Princess Alexandra, Ms. Howard's character is that of an aristocratic woman whose family has arranged a marriage between her and the indifferent Prince Albert. Complications arise as his roving eye is noticed, and the princess' family suggests that she start going out with Dr. Walter, her fencing instructor and tutor of the royal children, to make Albert jealous and more attentive. Alexandra actually falls in love with Dr. Walter, who is poor and outside her aristocratic social class.

Adolphe Menjou gives the best performance in the film as the indifferent Prince Albert who really has his eyes on Countess Wanda. He brings charisma to the role, and it is his performance that really saves the film. Ricardo Cortez is appealing and looks great as the fencing instructor/tutor, but unfortunately his performance itself was rather lackluster, and not among his best.

Frances Howard was competent as Princess Alexandra, and probably could have continued in her acting career if she had chosen to do so. Instead, she married film producer Sam Goldwyn shortly after finishing her work in this film, and retired from the screen, working with her husband more on the business end of filmmaking. Ms. Howard, while a competent actress, wasn't a particularly pretty woman, and really didn't have the personality to bring to this role the life and color that it needed. Her performance pales in comparison to the later performances that Lillian Gish gave as her talkie debut in a 1930 version of *The Swan* [a.k.a. *One Romantic Night*], as well as Grace Kelly's colorful and acclaimed performance in her 1956 remake.

Helen Lee Worthing was appealing and attractive as Countess Wanda. She made only a few films before dropping out of sight at the beginning of the talkie era. She married a doctor in 1927, but the marriage was annulled in 1933. The former Ziegfeld Follies beauty died in abject poverty in 1948 at age 43. Her friends had to raise money to give her a proper burial.

This film was well directed and beautifully produced by director Buchowetzki. The lavish costumes and sets are impressive, and the pace of the film is snappy and witty. It was highly acclaimed and relatively successful at the time of its release and certainly not a bad film at all. But, this first version of *The Swan* pales in comparison to the two remakes of the talkie era, which were both improvements over the original.

445. Tumbleweeds

Rating: ☆☆☆☆

United Artists; ***Directed by*** King Baggot and William S. Hart; ***Original Running Time:*** 73 minutes; ***Running Time with 1939 Prologue:*** 81 minutes; ***Cast:*** DON CARVER, William S. Hart (1864?-1946); MOLLY LASSITER, Barbara Bedford (1903–1981); KENTUCKY ROSE, Lucien Littlefield (1895–1960); NOLL LASSITER, J. Gordon Russell (1883–1935); BILL FREEL, Richard R. Neill (1875–1970); BART LASSITER, Jack Murphy; JOE HINMAN, James Gordon (1871–1941); A WIDOW, Lillianne Leighton (1874–1956); AN OLD COUPLE, George Marion, Sr. (1860–1945) and Gertrude Claire (1852–1928)

William S. Hart's last western, *Tumbleweeds*, is a historic epic of the opening of the Cherokee Strip in 1889. To provide the reader some historical background of the incident which inspired this film, the Cherokee Strip was a body of land consisting of 1,200 square miles on a front 200 miles long. It was the last major area that the U.S. government opened for American citizens to claim on a first-come, first-served basis. This story takes place in Caldwell, Kansas, which was on the edge of the strip.

Hart plays the role of Don Carver, the ultimate western cowboy of the highest moral and ethical standing. In the beginning of the film, Carver starts off by making a rather bad enemy of the town bully, Bill Freel. Carver sees Freel harassing a young boy and his dog. Freel refuses to apologize, so Carver pushes him into a water trough, and then makes him apologize to both the boy and the dog, taking off his hat to both of them.

The plot thickens when Carver encounters Molly Lassiter, the boy's older sister. They take a liking to each other, and he pledges to help her stake a claim to a prime piece of land once the Cherokee strip is officially opened. Unfortunately, her half-brother, Noll Lassiter, is in the same league as Bill Freel, and they conspire to stake their own claim to the Box K ranch—using any means necessary. To carry out their devious plan, Freel and the elder Lassiter have Carver falsely arrested as a "sooner," and then turn Molly against him by telling her that he had been planning to cheat her out of her claim. They then sneak into the strip as real "sooners," and illegally try to stake the claim for themselves, murdering a law officer in the process. It is thrilling to see how Carver escapes from the makeshift jail that sooners were held in at the beginning of the land rush, and brings the villains to justice.

The land rush sequence is among the most spectacular sequences in the entire history of Hollywood westerns. Thousands of extras, and hundreds of horse and buggy carriages, were employed. A melee of people travel at what seems the speed of lightning on horseback, by carriage, and even bicycle. The sequence comes complete with carriage accidents. According to western historians, stock footage from this sequence was used in several later westerns of the 1930s and 1940s.

Although James Cruze's *The Covered Wagon* (1923) is widely acclaimed as the foremost of the silent westerns, that assessment is not unanimous. *Tumbleweeds* was filmed on just as grand a scale as *The Covered Wagon* was, and was just as historically authentic, with a much more entertaining storyline.

For western enthusiasts, this film is an absolute "must" and is highly recommended.

Theda Bara, star of *The Unchastened Woman* (1925).

446. The Unchastened Woman

Rating: ☆☆☆

Chadwick; ***Directed by*** James Young; ***Screen Adaptation by*** Douglas Z. Doty; ***Based on the 1915 Play by*** Louis K. Anspacher; ***Photography by*** L. William O'Connell; ***Edited by*** Sam Zimbalist; ***Art Direction:*** Clifford P. Saum, Earl Sibley; ***Running Time:*** 54 minutes; ***Cast:*** CAROLYN KNOLLYS, Theda Bara (1885–1955); HUBERT KNOLLYS, Wyndham Standing

(1881–1963); EMILY MADDEN, Eileen Percy (1900–1973); AUNT SUSAN, Mayme Kelso (1867–1946); LAWRENCE SANBURY, John Miljan (1892–1960); HILDEGARDE SANBURY, Dale Fuller; MICHAEL KRELLIN, Harry Northrup (1875–1936); A DANCER, Frederick KoVert; ***Supporting Cast:*** Kate Price (1872–1943); Eric Mayne (1865–1947)

This is one of the two films that Theda Bara made in the mid–1920s as part of a comeback attempt after a six-year hiatus. The other film, *Madame Mystery* (1926), does exist, but the one surviving complete print is held by the UCLA Film and Television Archive, inaccessible to the public.

The Unchastened Woman has Bara playing a woman who is the perfect, loving wife. She discovers that her husband is having an affair and, tired of being heartbroken, devises a hilarious scheme to put both him and his girlfriend in their proper place.

This film, unfortunately, was not successful, and this reviewer cannot understand why. It is a delightfully funny film, and Theda Bara looked magnificent in it. She was 40 years old at the time, and looked better than she had at the height of her fame.

Eve Golden, author of the highly acclaimed Bara biography *Vamp: The Rise and Fall of Theda Bara,* and who has seen all four of Bara's surviving films, has stated that *The Unchastened Woman* is the best of Bara's known surviving work.

Although not a great masterpiece, *The Unchastened Woman* features better production values than most of the other Chadwick releases of the same period, with more lavish settings. This was really the perfect type of comeback vehicle for Theda Bara—a lighthearted satire on her former "vamp" characters as she goes back into the role to teach her husband the error of his ways. Even if Bara wasn't a great actress (based on her surviving work), she was competent, and deserved far better treatment from Hollywood than she got.

447. The Unholy Three *Rating: ☆☆☆½*

MGM; ***Directed by*** Tod Browning; ***Scenario by*** Waldemar Young; ***Story by*** Tod Robbins; ***Settings by*** Cedric Gibbons, Joseph Wright; ***Photography by*** David Kesson; ***Edited by*** Daniel Gray; ***Running Time:*** 86 minutes; ***Cast:*** ECHO THE VENTRILOQUIST, Lon Chaney, Sr. (1883–1930); ROSIE O'GRADY, Mae Busch (1901–1946); HECTOR MCDONALD, Matt Moore (1888–1960); HERCULES, Victor McLaglen (1886–1959); TWEEDLEDEE, Harry Earles (1902–1985); REGAN, Matthew Betz (1881–1938); JUDGE, Edward Connelly (1855–1928); DEFENSE ATTORNEY, William Humphrey (1874–1942); PROSECUTING ATTORNEY, E.A. Warren (1874–1940)

Named by the *New York Times* as one of the ten best films of 1925, *The Unholy Three* was director Tod Browning's (1880–1962) first film for MGM. While Browning was initially hired by MGM for a one-picture deal only, the critical and box-office success of this film resulted in an extended MGM contract for Browning.

The Unholy Three is the story of three circus sideshow performers who form a criminal ring. Lon Chaney plays a ventriloquist who masquerades as an old lady under the alias of Mrs. O'Grady. Victor McLaglen had one of his first big roles as Hercules, a strong man. Midget Harry Earles was 23 when he played Tweedledee, a midget disguised as a baby. Leading lady Mae Busch plays Rosie O'Grady, whom Echo the ventriloquist is dating while posing as her grandmother.

The plot begins with the unholy three planning a robbery of a wealthy residence.

While Echo intends only to rob, things go awry when Hercules murders the owner of the house. Rosie's friend, Hector, who is a clerk at O'Grady's pet shop—the blind for the unholy three's real operations—is accused of the murder, and Echo is the only one who can save him from execution. Will Echo's ventriloquist abilities work in the courtroom? That is what is revealed in the courtroom finale.

Chaney remade *The Unholy Three* as his one and only talkie in 1930, just before his death from throat cancer. For this sound version, Chaney should have received at least a posthumous Academy Award nomination for Best Actor. The talkie version came off just as well, if not better than, this original silent version. In the talkie, Chaney is dressed as the grandmother, and he is exposed when his voice inadvertently drops back to his normal male tone. The silent version has him using his ventriloquism ability to testify on Hector's behalf. Both versions are excellent and intriguing.

Turner Classic Movies presented a beautifully restored, orchestra score and color tinted print of this film in early 1997.

448. Variety

Rating: ☆☆☆

Produced in Germany; ***Directed by*** E.A. Dupont; ***Screenplay by*** E.A. Dupont and Leo Birinski; ***Photography by*** Karl Freund; ***Running Time of Complete Version:*** 100 minutes; ***Running Time of Most Edited Versions:*** 62-79 minutes; ***Cast:*** BOB, Emil Jannings (1886–1950); HIS WIFE, Maly Delschaft; THE GIRL, Lya de Putti (1899–1931); ARTINELLI, Warwick Ward (1891–1967); SEAMANN, George John (died 1934); RUMMELPLATZBESUCHER, Kurt Gerron (1897–1944)

For nearly 70 years, this film was available in the United States only in a heavily edited, censored version. It was not until 1995, when video dealer Peter Kavel found a complete print from Germany, that it was possible to see the complete version in the U.S. Kavel had the original German titles translated in order to present the complete version with English titles.

Most of the edited prints start the film with the circus show at Wintergarten. In the complete version, there is 28 minutes of footage leading up to this event. The formerly missing prologue starts with Emil Jannings as "prisoner #28," who is being considered for parole after having served ten years for murder. He relays how he started working for a traveling circus, met one of the beauty contest winners (played by Lya de Putti, who specialized in "vamp" roles), and allowed her to stay with him and his wife. He then abandons his wife and child and runs away with the younger woman, thus leading into the Wintergarten sequence. The United States censors found this introductory footage too racy for American audiences, and it was deleted from all American prints of the film.

In Wintergarten, the star of the show is Artinelli, a trapeze artist, who is unable to perform due to the death of his partner. The show goes on with Artinelli in the audience instead of as a performer, and we are treated to a number of entertaining circus acts in this part of the film. A few weeks pass, and Bob and his new partner reappear with the show. They become the star attractions of the show with their trapeze act, and eventually team up with Artinelli. Bob gets caught in the fast lane, which gives Artinelli the opportunity to make his move on the girl. This is where the trouble starts, as the girl takes advantage of both men, causing them to destroy each other over her.

E.A. Dupont (1893–1956) did an excellent job of directing this, his most highly acclaimed film. Emil Jannings provides a magnificent performance as Bob. Lya de Putti also gives a remarkable performance in this film as the female lead—probably the best of her career. She would make only one part-talking film, *The Informer* (1929), in England. She died at age 32 in 1931, after developing pneumonia following an operation to remove a chicken bone from her throat.

This film in its edited versions is incoherent and difficult to follow. One must see the complete version of the film to fully enjoy and understand it.

449. Wizard of Oz

Rating: ☆

Chadwick; ***Directed by*** Larry Semon; ***Screenplay Adaptation by*** L. Frank Baum, Jr., Larry Semon, and Leon Lee; ***Running Time:*** 79 minutes; ***Cast:*** A FARMHAND/THE SCARECROW, Larry Semon (1889–1928); DOROTHY, Dorothy Dwan (1907–1981); PRINCE KYND, Bryant Washburn (1889–1963); THE WIZARD, Charles Murray (1872–1941); PRIME MINISTER KRUEL, Joseph Swickard (1866–1940); "PRINCE CHARMING" OF THE FARM/THE TIN MAN, Oliver N. Hardy (1892–1957); AUNT EM, Mrs. Mary Carr (1874–1973); AMBASSADOR WIKKED, Otto Lederer (1886–1965); THE PHANTOM OF THE BASKET, Frederick KoVert; SNOWBALL/THE LION, G. Howe Black; ***Supporting Cast:*** William Hauber (1891–1929); William Dinus; Frank "Fatty" Alexander (1879–1937)

This abysmal film may be the worst screen adaptation of a novel in Hollywood history, and one of the worst films ever created. Ed Wood's *Plan 9 from Outer Space* (1959) may win the overall "Golden Turkey" Award, but if an award for "Golden Turkey of the Silent Era" were ever given out, *Wizard of Oz* would be this reviewer's prime nominee. Larry Semon was either so cheap or so lazy that he did not even bother to put the word "The" in front of "*Wizard of Oz*" in his main title card.

This adaptation was co-written by Larry Semon, who quite obviously revamped the story to make himself the star of the show as the scarecrow, no matter how badly he had to bastardize the original story to facilitate such. Dorothy is played by Semon's wife, Dorothy Dwan. One can see potential in Dwan, who rises above the material she was working with under her egotistical husband. She is really a bit too tall for the role of Dorothy, so the story was revamped to make her 18 years old. The Aunt Em character is well-played by character actress Mrs. Mary Carr, a petite woman in her 50s who was known in the silent era for her portrayal of older women.

The film starts out with an older man reading *The Wizard of Oz* to his granddaughter while showing figurines of Dorothy, the Tin Man, and the Scarecrow on a table next to him. The audience is then taken to Oz, a kingdom in which the ruler-to-be has vanished without a trace. Prime Minister Kruel is the self-proclaimed dictator, aided by Lady Vishuss and Ambassador Wikked. When coronation day draws near, Prince Kynd leads the townspeople to revolt against Kruel and demand the return of the rightful ruler of Oz. Kruel, in a precarious situation, summons the Wizard to perform some amazing feat to distract the crowd. The wizard does so by appearing to produce the "phantom of the basket" from an empty box. This "phantom" is actually a drag queen, wearing a head dress that must span three feet and weigh in excess of 20 pounds.

The movie then proceeds to the farm in Kansas. With Dorothy's 18th birthday fast approaching, Aunt Em decides to tell her about how she arrived at the farm shortly after her birth, in a basket with a note telling about secret papers inside which cannot be opened until her 18th birthday. In the meantime, we are introduced to a farm hand played by Larry Semon, and the "Prince Charming" of the farm played by Oliver Hardy, who are both vying for Dorothy's affections. Also introduced is Snowball, a black character portrayed by a man billed as "G. Howe Black" in a stereotypical "Stepin Fetchit" fashion.

After some idiotic slapstick routines, Dorothy's 18th birthday arrives, upon which she finds out that she is the rightful ruler of the Kingdom of Oz. Villains arrive in Kansas by airplane, having been sent by Kruel and Lady Vishuss to retrieve and destroy the papers. During the fight for the papers, a cyclone strikes the farm, picking up the shack in which all our characters (except Aunt Em, who suddenly disappears from the story and is unaccounted for) are whisked away to Oz. The next scenes of consequence are those in which the scarecrow, the tin man, and the lion materialize. The rest is relatively easy to figure out, if one can make sense of the incoherent script.

This *Wizard of Oz* adaptation has many inconsistencies in the plot. Dorothy and Prince Kynd had to have been moronic beyond belief, sadomasochistically submissive, or a combination of the two to have fallen for some of the lines from Kruel and associates as long as they did. The titles are loaded with idiotic puns and corny plays on words. One example is in the introduction of black character Snowball, described as "a promising case of meloncholic," while shown eating watermelons. This stereotypical portrayal of blacks as ignoramuses who lie around eating watermelon and who are too dumb to notice lightning striking their heads is especially appalling. This portrayal of blacks is far more offensive than anything that D.W. Griffith's *The Birth of a Nation* (1915) presented. At least *The Birth of a Nation* presents the faithful black servants as intelligent and kind enough to devise a scheme by which to save Dr. Cameron from the lynch mobs.

The director and star of this film, Larry Semon, reportedly had an inflated ego, and suffered from chronic alcoholism. He died in 1928 at the age of 38. Causes of death listed in reference sources are tuberculosis and/or alcoholism. His wife at the time, Dorothy Dwan, showed much promise as an actress. Historians have for years been trying to track Dwan down to find out what became of her. So far, it has been determined that in 1962, she was living in Van Nuys, California, working for a factory and living under the name of Molly Mills. What happened to Dwan after that point remains a mystery. It is possible that she is still alive at this writing at age 90. Bryant Washburn was a major matinee idol of the 1910s. This is one of only three of his silent era appearances that is widely available on video [he also had a cameo in the 1927 version of *The King of Kings*].

As poor as this film is, it is good that it survived and is available for evaluation on video, if for no other reason than to satisfy viewer curiosity.

450. Zander the Great *Rating:* ☆☆☆½

Cosmopolitan/Metro-Goldwyn; ***Directed by*** George Hill; ***Assistant Director:*** Frank O'Neil; ***Based on a Story by*** Salisbury Field; ***Photography by*** George Barnes and Harold Wenstrom; ***Film Editor:*** James McKay; ***Costumes by*** Gretl Urban; ***Settings by*** Joseph Urban; ***Screen Adaptation by*** Lillie Hayward and Frances Marion; ***Running Time:*** 80 minutes; ***Cast:*** MAMIE SMITH, Marion Davies (1897–1961); JUAN FERNANDEZ, Holbrook Blinn (1872–1928); DAN

MURCHISON, Harrison Ford (1884–1957); GOOD NEWS, Harry Watson (1876–1930); TEXAS, Harry Myers (1882–1938); BLACK BART, George Siegmann (1882–1928); THE MATRON, Emily Fitzroy (1860–1954); THE SHERIFF, Hobart Bosworth (1867–1943); MR. PEPPER, Richard Carle (1871–1941); MRS. CALDWELL, Hedda Hopper (1890–1966); ELMER LOVEJOY, Olin Howland (1886–1959); ZANDER, Master John Huff

Zander the Great is among the finest of the Marion Davies silents available for evaluation. In this film, Davies plays Mamie Smith, an orphaned girl who is brutally treated by a member of the orphan asylum staff. She is taken in by Mrs. Caldwell, a kindhearted woman with a baby son named Alexander. Mrs. Caldwell has been abandoned by her husband, and after a few years of happiness, dies, leaving the son (whom Mamie nicknames Zander) orphaned. The town officials determine that since Zander's father cannot be found, he is to be placed in an orphanage. Mamie, horrified at the thought of Zander being placed in the same institution that had so mistreated her, determines to find the boy's father. In many ways, this film is similar to the type of film one would expect to see Mary Pickford (1892–1979) in. The beginning reminds one of Pickford's *Suds* (1920) and *Pollyanna* (1920). The last part of the film in some ways reminds one of Pickford's final starring film, *Secrets* (1933).

Marion Davies, star of *Zander the Great* (1925), in later years.

While many of the Marion Davies silents [*Little Old New York* (1923), *Janice Meredith* (1924), and *Quality Street* (1927)] start off very slowly and gradually get better, this is a vehicle that grips the interest from beginning to end. Ms. Davies brings a certain charm to the role of Mamie, and plays the part extremely well. Her makeup in the orphanage sequences is so good that it is hard to recognize her at first.

In addition to Ms. Davies, *Zander the Great* features a fine supporting cast as well. Emily Fitzroy, one of this reviewer's favorite character actresses, looks meaner than ever as the matron of the orphanage. Harrison Ford does well in the male lead role as one of the outlaws that Mamie encounters in her search for Zander's father. Hedda Hopper as Mrs. Caldwell turns in a fine performance. Although the role is a small one, Hopper is most impressive. In addition, George Siegmann and the great character actor Hobart Bosworth are featured in the film.

Marion Davies wrote in her autobiography, *The Times We Had*, of a sequence in this film which found her in a cage with a lion. She wrote that Charlie Chaplin put on her dress and did these scenes for her, and the close-ups were done with Marion in the cage by herself. This sequence that Davies writes about obviously did not make it into the final cut of the film.

This is the earliest example of director George Hill's work to become widely available for evaluation. Hill (1895–1934) was the husband of scenario writer Frances Marion (1887–1973) from 1930–31. He committed suicide in 1934 at the age of 39. His most highly acclaimed directorial achievement was *The Big House* (1930).

Zander the Great is a fine piece of entertainment, featuring good melodrama supplemented by amusing comedy relief.

1926

451. April Fool

Rating: ☆☆☆

Chadwick; ***Directed by*** Nat Ross; ***Screenplay by*** Zion Myer; ***Photography by*** L. William O'Connell; ***From the Story An April Shower***; ***by*** Edgar Allen Wolfe, Alexander Carr; ***Running Time:*** 63 minutes; ***Cast:*** JACOB GOODMAN, Alexander Carr (1878–1946); AMELIA ROSEN, Mary Alden (1883–1946); IRMA GOODMAN [AS A CHILD], Baby Peggy Montgomery (born 1918); MR. APPELBAUM, Snitz Edwards (1862–1937); LEON STEINFELD [ADULT], Raymond Keane (1906–1973); JOE APPELBAUM [ADULT], Eddie Phillips (1899–1965); JOE APPELBAUM [CHILD], Pat Moore; LEON STEINFELD [ADOLESCENT], Leon Holmes; MOISHA GINSBURG, Nat Carr (1886–1944)

This film is historically significant as the last silent film that child star Baby Peggy appeared in. She came down from making $1 million a film to $150 a week in this Poverty Row production, as it was the only film work she could get. Her father, western stunt man Jack Montgomery (1891–1962), got on the bad side of Carl Laemmle (1867–1939) and a few other film producers, which resulted in Peggy and himself being virtually blacklisted at all of the major studios.

Despite this film's low budget production values, it is a well done screen adaptation of an old Jewish play that was co-written by Alexander Carr, who also plays the lead role in the film. Carr plays Jacob Goodman, a poor man who strikes it rich through ingenuity, determination, and hard work. His daughter, Irma Goodman, falls in love with Leon Steinfeld, the adopted son of Mr. Appelbaum, nemesis and competitor of her father. Appelbaum has repeatedly tried to buy Goodman's business, who keeps turning his offers down.

Trouble starts when Appelbaum's son, an alcoholic gambler who is lazy and spoiled, steals $30,000 in bonds from the business. The elder Appelbaum automatically blames adopted son Leon for the theft, assuming he has stolen the money to marry Irma. Jacob Goodman, for the sake of his daughter's and Leon's happiness, gives up everything he owns to Appelbaum so that he won't prosecute. This means also that he must give up his own plans to marry Amelia Rosen, a cafe owner he has loved for years.

In the end, everything works out as Joe Appelbaum is caught trying to cash in the bonds he stole thus getting Leon off the hook. Goodman and Rosen get married and live happily ever after.

This light romantic story was the first of the Baby Peggy films to come out on video in 1994. Baby Peggy's part is portraying Irma Goodman as a child in the first part of the film. Although this reviewer had really hoped that the film would have more footage of Baby Peggy than it does, she is charming and delightful, and has a hilarious slapstick sequence at the lunch table during which the boy sitting next to her ends up wearing his lunch.

The director of this film, Nat Ross, was only 22 when he did *April Fool.* Ross met a tragic end in 1941, when he was only 36 years old. He was murdered when a disgruntled employee shot him in the heart at point blank range with a double barrel shotgun.

452. The Bat

Rating: ☆☆☆

United Artists; ***Written and Directed by*** Roland West; ***Based on the Play by*** Mary Roberts Rinehart; ***Titles by*** George Marion, Jr.; ***Photography by*** Arthur Edeson; ***Art Direction by*** William Cameron Menzies, Ned Mann; ***Running Time:*** 85 minutes; ***Cast:*** BROOKS BAILEY, Jack Pickford (1896–1933); DALE OGDEN, Jewel Carmen (1897–??); LIZZIE ALLEN, Louise Fazenda (1889–1962); GIDEON BELL, André de Beranger (1895–1973); COURTLEIGH FLEMING, Charles Herzinger (1864–1953); CORNELIA VAN GARDNER, Emily Fitzroy (1860–1954); RICHARD FLEMING, Arthur Housman (1889–1942); DR. WELLS, Robert McKim (1886–1927); BILLY [JAPANESE BUTLER], So-jin Kamiyama (1891–1954); MOLETTI, Tulio Carminati (1894–1971); DETECTIVE ANDERSON, Eddie Gribbon (1890–1965)

For years, *The Bat* was among the most coveted of "lost" films. A print turned up in the early 1980s, and was restored by Robert Gitt for UCLA. This was the first of three film adaptations of Mary Roberts Rinehart's popular stage play set in a haunted house—the first of a string of "old house" movies to come. Roland West remade his most successful silent film in 1930 under the title, *The Bat Whispers* (1930), and Vincent Price starred in the 1959 remake.

This adaptation starts out with the title that asks, "Can you keep a secret? Don't reveal the identify of 'the bat'. Future audiences will fully enjoy the mystery play if left to find out for themselves." And the mystery begins with what appears at first to be a shot of two car headlights, revealed upon closer examination to be the eyes of a bat.

Jack Pickford plays Brooks Bailey, a bank cashier who has been fingered in a bank robbery. He takes a job as a gardener in a wealthy residence haunted by the bat—a villain dressed in a bat suit who has sent threatening letters.

As guests arrive at the "haunted" mansion, the image of a bat is projected on the wall—which turns out to be merely the shadow of a moth on a car's headlight.

Once everybody is congregated at the house, the film challenges the audience to see if they can figure out which of the guests is the bat.

It is obvious upon seeing this original version of *The Bat* that Bob Kane, who created the popular *Batman* comic strip, probably saw this film. The "bat signal" looks just like the moth projected on the wall in the very beginning of the film.

Jack Pickford makes a weak leading man. The real standouts in the cast are Louise Fazenda, the hysterical maid who provides many comedic elements, and Emily Fitzroy, who plays Cornelius. While she spends much of her time knitting, nothing can pass by her unnoticed; it seems she knows everything that is going on around her and then some.

In keeping with this film's request, you will have to see it yourself to find out who "the bat" is. Fortunately, this title is one that is widely available on the video market.

453. The Better 'Ole

Rating: ☆☆☆

Warner Brothers; ***Directed by*** Charles Riesner; ***Assistant Director:*** Sandy Roth; ***Screenplay*** *by* Darryl F. Zanuck and Charles Riesner; ***Edited by*** Ray Enright; ***Titles by*** Robert Hopkins; ***Photography by*** Ed P. Dunbar; ***Art Director:*** Ben Carré; ***Running Time:*** 95 minutes; ***Cast:*** WILLIAM "OLD BILL" BUSBY, Sydney Chaplin (1885–1965); BERT CHESTER, Harold Goodwin (1902–1987); LITTLE ALF, Jack Ackroyd; CORPORAL AUSTIN, Ed Kennedy (1890–1948); MAJOR RUSSETT, Charles Gerard (1887–??)

The film career of Sydney Chaplin has been overshadowed by his younger half-brother Charlie. It was Sydney who got Charlie his first stage job with the famous Fred Karno Company. In the late 1910s, Sydney served as his brother's business manager as well. Despite Syd Chaplin's being overshadowed by his younger brother, he was just as talented. Unfortunately, only three of Syd's few solo efforts are widely available for evaluation.

The Better 'Ole was one of the last, as well as one of the best, Syd Chaplin vehicles. In this war comedy, Syd plays "Old Bill" Busby, who gets into a number of misadventures on the front, and can't seem to stay out of trouble. In the end, "Old Bill" triumphs as he exposes a spy within the ranks. Turnabout is fair play as those who bullied him get their just desserts in the end.

For years, *The Better 'Ole* was known to survive only in fragmented form. As one of the first films to have a synchronized Vitaphone score and sound effects, some of the discs were missing, as well as one or two reels of footage. Fortunately, the missing footage and discs were recovered, the UCLA Film and Television Archive restored it, and Turner Classic Movies aired the complete restored version with color tinting in the mid–1990s. It was released on laser disc for the rich, but not on video for the average person. *The Better 'Ole* is a delightfully funny film, almost as good as Charlie Chaplin's *Shoulder Arms* (1918), which Syd had also played in.

Director Charles Riesner had his first full directorial credits with the Sydney Chaplin films, this being the third. His successful career lasted through 1962.

Unfortunately, this was among Sydney Chaplin's last films. In 1927, he got into trouble with the Internal Revenue Service, and moved back to England where he made one more film before his retirement from the screen in 1928.

454. The Black Pirate

Rating: ☆☆☆½

United Artists; ***Directed by*** Albert Parker; ***Screenplay by*** Jack Cunningham; ***Based on a Story by*** Elton Thomas; ***Photographed by*** Henry Sharp; ***Art Direction by*** Carl Oscar Borg; ***General Manager:*** Robert Fairbanks; ***Production Manager:*** Theodore Reed; ***Technicolor Staff:*** Arthur Ball, George Cave; ***Scenario Editor:*** Lotta Woods; ***Research Director:*** Arthur Woods; ***Film Editor:*** William Nolan; ***Running Time:*** 90 minutes; ***Cast:*** THE BLACK PIRATE, Douglas Fairbanks, Sr. (1883–1939); THE PRINCESS, Billie Dove (1900–1997) and Mary Pickford (1892–1979) [uncredited]; ***Supporting Cast:*** Donald Crisp (1882–1974); Sam DeGrasse (1875–1953); Tempe Piggott (1884–1962); Anders Randolph (1870–1930); Charles Stevens (1893–1964); John Wallace (1869–1946); Fred Becker (1882–1966); Charles Belcher (1872–1943); E.J. Ratcliffe (1863–1948)

The Black Pirate film was the second feature film to be filmed entirely in 2-strip Technicolor, and the first such feature that was over an hour in length. In this film, Douglas Fairbanks plays an aristocrat who is the sole survivor of a pirate attack in which his father was killed. To seek justice, Fairbanks' character joins the band of pirates responsible for the fatal attack. To convince the pirates that he is worthy of being accepted into

Billie Dove, leading lady of *The Black Pirate* (1926).

their clan, he first bests their ringleader in a sword fight and then proceeds to capture a ship singlehandedly. The ship he takes happens to be the one on which a princess, played by Billie Dove, is traveling. "The black pirate" convinces the gang to refrain from blowing up the ship, and instead hold it and the princess for ransom. All the while, he works out his scheme to bring the band of pirates to justice, and to save the princess.

Fairbanks wrote the story for this film under the pseudonym of Elton Thomas.

He also, as lead actor, performs a number of impressive stunts. The most impressive of these is the famous sequence in which Fairbanks slides down a sail with a knife, splitting the sail as he goes along. One sequence in which Fairbanks swings up on a sail is actually footage of him swinging down, run backwards to create the illusion of swinging up.

In one of the final sequences, where the black pirate kisses the princess, Mary Pickford refused to let Billie Dove do the kissing scene with her husband. Pickford donned Dove's wig and costume, and played this scene herself. *The Black Pirate* is one of only two Billie Dove silents known to survive outside the archives, and possibly at all. Ms. Dove died on December 31, 1997, at age 97 in the Motion Picture Country Home.

For many years, the only copies of *The Black Pirate* that were widely available were black and white versions and color versions of extremely poor quality. Upon seeing one of the poor quality color versions with a tacky score, this reviewer found the film only mediocre. Fortunately, in 1996, Kino Video released the restored version that Harold Brown did for the National Film Archive of London in the late 1950s. With an orchestra score by renowned musician Robert Israel based on the original 1926 score by Mortimer Wilson, as well as an excellent picture and color restoration, *The Black Pirate* seems like a totally different film, and is highly enjoyable and highly recommended. This early Technicolor classic is a film not to be missed.

455. The Blackbird

Rating: ☆☆☆½

MGM; ***Directed by*** Tod Browning; ***Story by*** Tod Browning; ***Screenplay by*** Waldemar Young; ***Titles by*** Joe Farnham; ***Settings by*** Cedric Gibbons and Arnold Gillespie; ***Photography by*** Percy Hilburn; ***Film Editor:*** Errol Taggart; ***Wardrobe by*** Kathleen Kay, Maude Marsh, Andre Ani; ***Running Time:*** 85 minutes; ***Cast:*** THE BLACKBIRD/THE BISHOP, Lon Chaney, Sr. (1883–1930); WEST END BERTIE, Owen Moore (1886–1939); FIFI, Renée Adorée (1898–1933); LIMEHOUSE POLLY, Doris Lloyd (1896–1968); THE SHADOW, Andy MacLennan; RED, William Weston

The Blackbird is yet another of the Chaney/Browning collaborations, with this one set in the London Limehouse district—as were D.W. Griffith's *Broken Blossoms* (1919) and *Dream Street* (1921).

In this collaboration, Chaney plays a double role as an able bodied crime boss who poses as a kindly, crippled minister. To create this illusion of the "bishop," Chaney contorts his legs and arms in a gruesome fashion. He ends up having one close call too many, falling and really becoming crippled in his haste to change his appearance.

Chaney's contortion work in his role as the cripple reminds one much of his appearance in the stills and four minutes extant footage from *The Miracle Man* (1919). The Browning touch is evident in the puppet show sequence during which a large head appears to be supported by a small, hand-sized body.

Renée Adorée gives a good performance as the blackbird's girlfriend, and Doris Lloyd is appealing as Limehouse Polly. Owen Moore, who is discussed at length elsewhere in this book, plays West End Bertie. Moore died in his early 50s from alcoholism, which was also the cause of Pickford's divorcing him. No further information could be found on supporting players Andy MacLennon or William Weston.

456. The Blue Eagle

Rating: ☆☆☆

Fox; ***Directed by*** John Ford; ***Based on*** *The Lord's Referee* ***by*** John Beaumont; ***Scenario by*** L. Grigby; ***Photography by*** George Schneiderman; ***Titles by*** Malcolm Stuart Boylan; ***Approximate Running Time of Original Release:*** 84 minutes; ***Running Time of Surviving Footage:*** 49 minutes; ***Cast:*** GEORGE DARCY, George O'Brien (1900–1985); BIG TIM RYAN, William Russell (1886–1929); KELLY, Janet Gaynor (1906–1984); CHAPLAIN O'REGAN, Robert Edeson (1868–1931); ***Supporting Cast:*** Margaret Livingston (1895–1984); David Butler (1895–1979); Ralph Sipperly (1890–1928); Phillip Ford (1900–1976); Lew Short (1875–1958); Jerry Madden

The Blue Eagle is an obscure John Ford (1894–1973) title that is not known to survive in complete form. A partial print that included four reels of the film was held in a private collection and was deteriorating fast when it was transferred to video. The nitrate film print has reportedly decomposed entirely, and the only elements of this film known to survive are the two or three video copies of the partial print in the hands of private collectors.

In this film, George O'Brien and William Russell are the male leads as archenemies who served in World War I together, and who both fall in love with Kelly, played by Janet Gaynor in one of her earliest film roles. Robert Edeson plays a priest who has been trying to get the two rivals to work together to break up a drug smuggling gang that has infested their neighborhood. At first, they refuse to work together—until mutual friends of theirs who are police officers are killed by the smugglers. The two agree to come together to break up the drug ring, and the priest then allows them to settle their old score in a private boxing ring. George wins after a protracted battle and gets the girl, but the priest introduces Tim to the widow of one of his close comrades in the war, and he marries her, with everyone living happily ever after.

This fine film is one that appears from the surviving footage to have been well done, and would possibly receive a rating higher than three stars if it could be evaluated in complete form. George O'Brien was an actor whose muscular upper body earned him a nickname as "the chest," and in the final boxing sequence, he is shown wearing boxing shorts, showing off his physique perhaps more than in any of his other surviving films.

Not only is *The Blue Eagle* historically significant as one of Janet Gaynor's earliest roles but it is also the latest footage of William Russell known to survive. Russell died just three years after this film was released, in 1929.

George O'Brien, star of *The Blue Eagle* (1926), in an appealing pose from one of his early western talkies.

One of the supporting players, Ralph Sipperly, also died relatively young at age 38, just two years after starring in this film, in 1928. Sipperly reportedly grieved himself to death after his wife, Grace, died.

It is highly unlikely at this late date that another more complete print of *The Blue Eagle* will turn up, but at least something has survived on the film, which is better than nothing.

457. Brown of Harvard

Rating: ☆☆☆

MGM; ***Directed by*** Jack Conway; ***Adapted by*** Donald Ogden Stewart; ***From the Stage Play by*** Rida Johnson Young; ***Screenplay by*** A.P. Younger; ***Titles by*** Joe Farnham; ***Settings by*** Cedric Gibbons and Arnold Gillespie; ***Wardrobe by*** Kathleen Kay and Maude Marsh; ***Photography by*** Ira Morgan; ***Film Editor:*** Frank Davis; ***Running Time:*** 85 minutes; ***Cast:*** TOM BROWN, William Haines (1900–1973); MARY ABBOTT, Mary Brian (born 1908); JED DOOLITTLE, Jack Pickford (1896–1933); BOB MCANDREWS, Francis X. Bushman, Jr. (1903–1978); MRS. BROWN, Mary Alden (1883–1946); MR. BROWN, David Torrence (1864–1951); PROFESSOR ABBOTT, Edward Connelly (1855–1928); HAL WALTERS, Guinn Williams (1899–1962)

Brown of Harvard is one of the popular college comedies of the late 1920s, and the first such comedy to be produced by MGM. William Haines plays Tom Brown, a college freshman at Harvard, who aspires to be an athlete. One of his other aspirations is to win the heart of Mary Abbott, the daughter of the Harvard professor Dr. Abbott. Upon his arrival at the dormitory, Brown encounters some trouble with the upper classmen, and ends up rooming with one Jed Doolittle, a bookworm type of guy with small stature. Unfortunately, another man by the name of Bob McAndrews is also hoping to win Mary's hart, as well as choice positions on the Harvard rowing team. The rivalry gets vicious and hilarious throughout, culminating in a Harvard-Yale football game.

Mary Brian, female lead in *Brown of Harvard* (1926).

Brown, thinking he has been dropped from the team, fails to show up for the game preparations. It is the roommate, Jed Doolittle, who contracts pneumonia in his efforts to get Brown to the game on time. Included in the football sequence is footage from an actual football game at Harvard University. In addition, we are treated to a cameo by John Wayne. This cameo is widely regarded as Wayne's first-ever appearance on film, in the part of a football player. The game, of course, is much in the tradition of the football sequence in Harold Lloyd's *The Freshman* (1925), and keeps the audience in suspense to the last minute.

This film is well directed by Jack Conway (1887–1952), who is also famous for films such as *Our Modern Maidens* (1929), the sound version of *The Unholy Three* (1930), as well as for Jean Harlow's last starring role in *Saratoga* (1937). William Haines heads up the excellent cast, and was one of MGM's most popular leading men of the late 1920s and early 1930s. After his last film, *Here Come the Marines* (1934) was released, Haines' homosexuality was leaked to the public, which resulted in his abandonment of the motion picture profession, after which he became one of the most prominent interior decorators in Hollywood at the time. Mary Brian is among the major silent screen players who is still with us at this writing. She is 89 years old, and played in many significant silents as well as talkies. She is perhaps best remembered by modern audiences as the mother in the 1953 television series, *Meet Corliss Archer.* Jack Pickford, the brother of Mary Pickford, had his greatest success in the lead role in William Desmond Taylor's 1920 version of *Huckleberry Finn.* Sadly, he was plagued with alcoholism, and died at age 36 in 1933 from multiple neuritis. Francis X. Bushman, Jr., was best known for the roles he played in action films in the late silent era. His father was Francis X. Bushman, Sr., who gained immortal fame by playing "Messala" in the 1927 version of *Ben-Hur.*

Brown of Harvard is a delightful film, and one which has fortunately been made widely available to the public by Critic's Choice Video in conjunction with the Killiam Collection for the first time since its original release.

458. By the Law

Rating: ☆☆☆

Goskimo Productions U.S.S.R.; ***Directed by*** Lev Kuleshov; ***Scenario by*** Victor Shklovsky; ***Based on*** "The Unexpected" ***by*** Jack London; ***Photographed by*** Konstantin Kuznetsov; ***Running Time:*** 80 minutes; ***Cast:*** MICHAEL DENNIN, Vladimir Fogel (died 1929); HANS NELSON, Sergei Komarov; EDITH NELSON, Alexandra Khokhlova; DUTCHY, Porlirl Podobed; HARKY, Pyotr Galadzhev

This was the first film directed by Lev Kuleshov after the Soviet government cut off his studio funding due to objections over political content in *The Death Ray* (1925). Due to lack of funding, Kuleshov filmed *By the Law* on an extremely low budget. The film remains the least expensive of all Soviet features to date, as well as one of the best. Kuleshov demonstrates that a lot of money is not always necessary to turn out a quality production. It did very well at the box office, and was highly profitable.

Based on a Jack London story called "The Unexpected," *By the Law* is set during the Alaskan Klondike gold rush. Five partners initiate an independent gold expedition. After a long period of lean times, Michael Dennin, the leading character, strikes gold. Feeling that he is being undermined by his partners, he flies into a rage and kills two of them. The other two partners intend to turn Michael over to the law, but their way into a court jurisdiction is barred by the winter blizzards and spring floods. Being cut off from society, the surviving expedition members are forced to take the law into their own hands.

Especially notable are the performances by Vladimir Fogel and Alexandra Khokhlova. Vladimir Fogel was very attractive, providing an intense performance as the prospector-turned-murderer. This film brought out the best in his talent, as opposed to

***By the Law* (1926), featuring popular Russian actor Vladimir Fogel as the condemned man.**

Chess Fever (1925), which provided little if any opportunity for Fogel to demonstrate true acting talent. His early death in 1929 cut short the career of this actor who had so much potential based on his performance in this film. Alexandra Khokhlova was not a particularly attractive actress, but extremely talented, providing some of the most thrilling sequences in this film.

By the Law is a faithful adaptation of Jack London's classic story, and stands as one of the great classics of Russian cinema.

459. The Chess Player

Rating: ☆½

Produced by La Societé des Films Historiques; ***Directed by*** Raymond Bernard and Jean-José Frappé; ***From the novel by*** Henri Dupuy-Masuel; ***Photographed by*** Joseph-Louis Mundviller and Marc Bujard; ***Assistant Director:*** Jean Hemard; ***Production Assistant:*** Lily Jumel; ***Art Direction:*** Jean Perrier; ***Costume design by*** Eugene Lourié; ***Costumes by*** La Maison Granier; ***Special Effects by*** W. Percy Day; ***Running Time:*** 133 minutes; ***Cast:*** BOLESUS VOROWSKI, Pierre Blanchar (1892–1963); BARON VON KEMPELIN, Charles Dullin (1885–1949); SOPHIE NOVINSKA, Edith Jehanne; MAJOR NICOLAIEFF, Camille Bert; PRINCE SERGEI OBLOMOFF, Pierre Batcheff (1901–1932); CATHERINE II, Marcelle Charles-Dullin; WANDA, Jacky Monnier; ROUBENKO, Armand Bernard; OLGA, Alexiane; KING STANISLAS, Pierre Hot; KING ORLOFF, James Devesa; POLA, Fridette Fraton

This story takes place starting in 1776, the time of the Russian takeover of Poland during the reign of Catherine II. Bosesus Vorowski is the leader of the Polish resistance. Baron Von Kempelin specializes in building robots. This film deals mostly with the Polish struggle for independence from Russia, and includes some impressively staged battle sequences.

The most impressive sequence in the film occurs toward the end, in which a room full of robots come alive and attack their creator. In addition, the leading lady of the film, Edith Jehanne is especially appealing.

While this film is technically marvelous and innovative, it is too long. It drags in a lot of areas, and only the technical innovation keeps it from being a solid bore.

The director of this film, Raymond Bernard (1891–1977), was the son of novelist Tristan Bernard. He started out as an actor making his debut opposite Sarah Bernhardt in *Jeanne Doré* (1915), followed by comedies. His first major directorial effort was *Le Petit Café* (1919), which starred the highly acclaimed comedian Max Linder (1883–1925).

The leading man, Pierre Blanchar, was a popular French actor who began his film career in 1920. He attained the height of his career in the 1930s, notably in a French version of *Crime and Punishment* (1935).

The Chess Player has been widely acclaimed by many notable historians, and may be perfectly fine for some tastes. But, a reviewer's job is to call a film as he or she sees it. *The Chess Player* is a bore that almost put this reviewer to sleep, and will prove a disappointment to many others as well. This negative impression cannot be attributed to print quality, because the print accessed for this review was a beautifully restored and color tinted print with orchestra score by the great musician Carl Davis.

460. The Clinging Vine *Rating:* ☆☆½

DeMille Pictures/P.D.C.; ***Directed by*** Paul Sloane; ***Screenplay by*** C. Gardner Sullivan; ***Adaptation by*** Jack Jevne, Rex Taylor; ***From the Play by*** Zelda Sears; ***Titles by*** John Krafft; ***Photography by*** Arthur Miller; ***Settings by*** Max Parker; ***Running Time:*** 72 minutes; ***Cast:*** A.B., Leatrice Joy (1893–1965); T.M. BANCROFT, Robert Edeson (1868–1931); DOC TUTWEILER, Snitz Edwards (1862–1937); GRANDMA BANCROFT, Toby Claude; JIMMIE BANCROFT, Tom Moore (1883–1955); B. HARVEY DOOLITTLE, Dell Henderson (1877–1956)

When *The Clinging Vine* was first provided for review, this author took one look at director Paul Sloane's name in the credits, and thought it would be another dud like *Made for Love* (1926). It was a pleasant surprise to find that *The Clinging Vine* wasn't as bad as expected. While it is no great masterpiece, it is not a total waste of time, either.

In this film, Leatrice Joy gives a nice performance as A.B.—a corporate genius whose official title is assistant to the vice president of a paint company, but who actually runs the show, with the president doing as she dictates, and pretending that her actions are his ideas.

At the beginning of the film, A.B. has a mannish appearance. Ms. Joy actually looks like a man, and this reviewer backed up the tape to make sure the credits had been read right. She is a no-nonsense business woman who promptly fires the president's grandson from the company. She gets to the point that she is tired of being looked at as an

Leatrice Joy, star of *The Clinging Vine* (1926).

asexual prude, and goes to spend some time with Grandma Bancroft, wife of the vice president she works for. Needless to say, the wise grandmother teaches A.B. how to dress pretty and talk dumb. It turns out that she becomes romantically interested in the very grandson, Jimmie Bancroft, that she fired by telegram. Without telling Jimmie who she really is, they begin dating.

Jimmie comes up with an invention of an egg beater that he hopes to sell to his grandfather and make a lot of money from. The demonstration bombs, but A.B. secretly buys the invention as a vote of confidence for the man she loves. All is going well until Jimmie invests the entire $25,000 with a swindler, and A.B. must use her business knowledge to figure a way to salvage the investment money.

The Clinging Vine is interesting in its social portrayal of the new, liberated woman who throws down her apron and rises up within the corporate ranks. In Ms. Joy's character, one sees how men who were just being exposed to strong women for the first time were at first taken aback and repulsed until they got to know the other traditional side of the woman.

Leatrice Joy carries this film well, although she should have grown her hair back a little bit longer for the scenes in which she dresses more feminine. The hair is way too short for these scenes, to the extent that she still looks like a man in a dress.

Overall, *The Clinging Vine* is a light, enjoyable programmer—not bad but not great, and worth taking a look at.

461. The Devil's Circus *Rating:* ☆☆½

MGM; ***Written and Directed by*** Benjamin Christensen; ***Titles by*** Katharine Hilliker and H.H. Caldwell; ***Settings by*** Cedric Gibbons and James Basevi; ***Photography by*** Benjamin Reynolds; ***Film Editor:*** Ben Lewis; ***Wardrobe by*** Kathleen Kay, Maude Marsh, Andre Ani; ***Running Time:*** 71 minutes; ***Cast:*** MARY, Norma Shearer (1900–1983); CARL, Charles Emmett Mack (1900–1927); VENNA, Carmel Myers (1901–1980); HUGO, John Miljan (1892–1960); MRS. PETERS, Claire McDowell (1878–1966); LITTLE ELSA, Joyce Coad (1917–1987)

This was director Benjamin Christensen's directorial debut in the United States. For years, none of Christensen's work in America, other than *Seven Footprints to Satan* (1929), was known to survive. *The Devil's Circus* and *Mockery* (1927) have both turned up in the last 15 to 20 years. Upon evaluation, neither of these two Christensen rediscoveries holds up as well as one would expect from his reputation.

The Devil's Circus opens with the devil looking down at the world, manipulating people on earth as if his hands, by their movements, were some form of remote control. Charles Emmett Mack plays Carl, who is just being released from prison. He decides to go straight for Mary, a country girl played by Norma Shearer who has just started work at the circus. In hopes of getting the pure and innocent Mary out of the circus to avoid her being corrupted by the negative influences of her coworkers, he decides to commit one more robbery to get enough money for him and Mary to start a new life on. He is caught and goes to prison, and while he is there, Mary becomes the target of Hugo, a womanizing lecher.

Just as it looks like Mary and Carl are going to be reunited, the devil, from up above, works his spell, and Carl is drafted into World War I upon getting out of prison, and Mary is injured and hospitalized, leaving them with no way of contacting each other. Love conquers even the devil's power, and everything works out in the end.

Although not a film totally without interest, *The Devil's Circus* falls short of what one would expect from Benjamin Christensen. The only real Christensen touches that are prevalent in this film are the sequence in which the robbery is shown in shadows, without actually showing Carl himself doing it, and the sequences showing the devil exercising his evil influence.

462. Don Juan

Rating: ☆☆☆½

Warner Brothers; ***Directed by*** Alan Crosland; ***Screenplay by*** Bess Meredyth; ***Score Performed by*** the New York Philharmonic Orchestra; ***Synchronized Sound by*** Vitaphone; ***Running Time:*** 113 minutes; ***Cast:*** DON JOSÉ DE MARANA/DON JUAN DE MARANA, John Barrymore (1882–1942); DON JUAN (AGE 10), Philippe De Lacy (1917–1995); DON JUAN (AGE 5), Yvonne Day; ADRIANE DELLA VARNESE, Mary Astor (1903–1987); CESARE BORGIA, Warner Oland (1880–1938); LUCREZIA BORGIA, Estelle Taylor (1894–1958); COUNT GIANO DONATI, Montague Love (1877–1943); MAI, LADY IN WAITING, Myrna Loy (1905–1993); TRUSIA, June Marlowe (1903–1984); DONNA ISOBEL, Jane Winton (1905–1959); LEANDRO, John Roche (1893–1952); DUKE DELLA VARNESE, Joseph Swickard (1866–1940); PEDRILLO, Willard Lewis; MARCHIS RINALDO, Nigel De Brulier (1877–1948); MARCHISE RINALDO, Hedda Hopper (1890–1966); HUNCHBACK, John George (1898–1968); A MURDERESS, Helene Costello (1903–1957); DUKE MARGONI, Lionel Braham (1879–1947); IMPERIA, Phyllis Haver (1899–1960)

This was the first feature length movie to feature its own synchronized sound effect/orchestra score, using the then-revolutionary sound-on-disc system from the Vitaphone Company. It is also one of the legendary John Barrymore's better-known movie performances.

This is a highly fictionalized biopic of the life of the historic great lover, Don Juan. Despite the fictionalization of many of the facts, the fictionalization is a good one, and quite interesting.

Barrymore is excellent in this film, playing a double role as Don José, father of Don Juan in the prologue, as well as the adult role of Don Juan. In the title role, Barrymore certainly makes use of not only his athletic ability, but his extraordinary acting talent. He even manages to throw in a "Jekyll-Hyde" sequence toward the end of the picture, contorting his face into an evil grin to resemble Neri, the torture and poison expert employed by the contemptible Borgias. Barrymore convincingly alters his appearance without the use of makeup.

Mary Astor at the height of her career in *Don Juan* (1926).

Don Juan is a lighthearted, combative adventure-romance without an idle moment. In addition to the lavish production values, it features two of the most outstanding swashbuckling sequences from the silent era. It is difficult to choose between the one-on-one, double sworded dual between Don Juan and villain Count Donati, or the sequence in which Barrymore's character takes on a dozen men—on horseback.

In addition to Barrymore, *Don Juan* features an all-star supporting cast. Mary Astor, who would become one of the prominent character actresses from the 1930s through the 1960s, plays the leading role in this film, being one of the most prominent roles she ever had. The great Myrna Loy has a bit part in one of her earliest screen appearances. In addition, it is interesting to see June Marlowe in a small part as a brunette. Marlowe is perhaps best remembered for her delightful performances as the platinum blonde school teacher "Miss Crabtree" in some of the early "Our Gang" talkies.

Considering all that *Don Juan* has going for it—technical innovation, superior cast, and excellent screenplay by Bess Meredyth based on one of the most infamous characters of all time—there was no way it could miss. This title was widely released on video by MGM/UA Home Video in 1990, and is highly recommended.

463. Faust

Rating: ☆☆☆☆

Produced in Germany; ***Directed by*** F.W. Murnau; ***Running Time:*** 116 minutes; ***Cast:*** FAUST, Gosta Ekmann (1890–1938); MEPHISTO, Emil Jannings (1886–1950); GRETCHEN, Camilla Horn (1903–1996); MUTTER, Freida Richard (1873–1946); VALENTIN, Wilhelm (William) Dieterle (1893–1972); MARTHA, Yvette Guilber (1865–1944); HERZOG, Eric Barcleq; HERZOGIN, Hanna Ralph (1885–1978); ERZENGEL, Werner Fuetterer

Johann Wolfgang von Goethe's (1749–1832) *Faust* legend was filmed a minimum of 15 times during the silent era—in 1902, 1904, 1907, 1909, three times in 1910; 1911, 1921, 1922, 1923, 1926, and 1927. The legend was filmed under the title of *Faust and Marguerite* in 1900, 1904, and 1911. It appeared under the title of *Faust and Mephistopheles* in 1898. *Faust and the Lily* was filmed in 1913. *Faust in Hell* was filmed in 1903. This 1926 silent version, which is an adaptation of *Faust Part I*, remains the definitive motion picture version of the legendary tale.

It opens with a wager between Satan and an angel. Satan bets that he can wrest the soul of Faust, a righteous and elderly man. The angel states that if Satan can win Faust over, he can have complete control of the earth. Satan immediately gets to work, by cursing the world with the bubonic plague. Faust, an alchemist searching for a cure, becomes frustrated that his prayers to God have not been fulfilled. As a last resort, he summons the aid of Satan in the form of Mephisto. They make a one-day pact which allows Faust to cure victims of the plague. Just before the pact runs out, Satan offers Faust a deal he can't refuse—eternal youth in exchange for an eternal pact. Faust becomes infatuated with a young, virginal girl named Gretchen. Although Satan insists that she is too pure and innocent, Faust insists on having her. Under the curse of Satan, Faust and Gretchen engage in adultery, and Gretchen becomes pregnant. Shunned by the community, she is forced onto the streets with her baby. The baby becomes ill, and despite Gretchen's pleas for help, the door is slammed in her face. The baby freezes to death, and Gretchen is charged with murder and burned at the stake. Faust's love for Gretchen results in his renunciation of eternal youth and Satan, and he turns old again, joining Gretchen at the stake. Is their love enough to save his soul and the earth from the devil?

This adaptation accomplishes what simply could not be accomplished in the operatic stage versions of the *Faust* legend. It contains the massive mob scenes during the plague panic, as well as stunning camerawork—especially during the sequences in which Faust and Mephisto travel over the earth which is at their feet. The special effects during which Faust initially summons the devil are truly astounding.

In addition to F.W. Murnau's magnificent direction and fabulous cinematography, this movie features an outstanding cast. Emil Jannings is truly unforgettable as Mephisto. When he first appears before Faust and nods his head, he looks so evil that it sends chills up one's spine. The makeup work on Jannings is astonishingly effective, and it is hard to recognize him at first. Camilla Horn's impressive debut as Gretchen resulted in her being signed to play the female lead in two John Barrymore films in the United States—*Tempest* (1927) and *Eternal Love* (1929). A relatively young William Dieterle plays the role of Valentin. Dieterle gained prominence as a director of such classics as *The Hunchback of Notre Dame* (1939), *The Story of Louis Pasteur* (1936), and *The Life of Emile Zola* (1937). The director, Murnau, was also lured by the Fox Film Company to direct films in the United States and, as a result, *Faust* was the last film that he directed in Germany before emigrating.

F.W. Murnau's *Faust* is truly masterful cinematic expression on the highest level, as well as his greatest achievement. Without hesitation, it can be ranked among the greatest of silent masterpieces—in the same league as *Intolerance* (1916), *Greed* (1924), *Ben-Hur: A Tale of the Christ* (1927), and *Napoléon* (1927).

464. Fig Leaves

Rating: ☆☆☆

Fox; ***Written and Directed by*** Howard Hawks; ***Photography by*** Joseph August; ***Titles by*** Malcolm Stuart Boylan; ***Settings by*** William Cameron Menzies and William Darling; ***Costumes by*** Adrian; ***Edited by*** Rose Smith; ***Scenario by*** Louis D. Lighton; ***Running Time:*** 69 minutes; ***Cast:*** EVE/EVE SMITH, Olive Borden (1906–1947); ADAM/ADAM SMITH, George O'Brien (1900–1985); ALICE ATKINS, Phyllis Haver (1899–1960); EDDIE MCSWIGGEN, Heinik Conklin; JOSEPH ANDRÉ, André de Beranger; ANDRÉ'S ASSISTANT, William Austin (1884–1975)

This is a film of historic interest because it is the only silent film starring Olive Borden that is widely available for evaluation. Borden started her career in 1925 at age 19 as one of Mack Sennett's bathing beauties. Soon, she was starring in films directed by John Ford, Allan Dwan, and Howard Hawks, who directed *Fig Leaves* as his second major film. When talkies came in, Borden's career went downhill, and she turned to alcohol. Destitute and broke, she died at age 41 from pneumonia in a charity shelter.

Fig Leaves gives us an opportunity to see Borden at the height of her career during better days, which reveals her to be a beautiful and delightful comedienne. In this film, Borden plays Eve in a hilarious battle of the sexes type of romantic comedy. George O'Brien plays Adam.

The movie starts out in the stone age, with the couple portraying the first documented man and wife team on earth, Adam and Eve. In this part of the film, we see the various aspects of their lives. Their newspaper is delivered on a slab of stone, and the film also depicts their exercise regime, as well as their "alarm clock" in a hilarious fashion, among other things. Adam even gets angry with a dinosaur, and chastises him for eating the trees. In this first part of the film, the audience is told that each of the three biggest problems faced by women are "I haven't a thing to wear."

Fig Leaves then cuts to the modern story, in which George O'Brien plays Adam Smith, a plumber, and Olive Borden plays his wife. Since Eve wants more fashionable clothes, she takes a job modeling—much to the chagrin of her husband.

The fashion show sequences are elaborate, and were originally filmed in 2-strip Technicolor, although all prints currently available today are black and white or color tinted all the way through.

465. Fine Manners

Rating: ☆☆½

Paramount; ***Directed by*** Richard Rosson; ***Adaptation by*** James Ashmore Creelman; ***Story by*** James Ashmore Creelman and Frank Vreeland; ***Screenplay by*** J. Clarkson Miller; ***Photography by*** George Webber; ***Running Time:*** 69 minutes; ***Cast:*** ORCHID MURPHY, Gloria Swanson (1897–1983); BRIAN ALDREN, Eugene O'Brien (1880–1966); BUDDY MURPHY, Walter Goss; AUNT AGATHA, Helen Dunbar (1863–1933); COURTNEY ADAMS, John Miltern (1870–1937)

Fine Manners was the last silent film that Gloria Swanson made for Paramount Pictures, before going into independent production with United Artists.

It starts out with a New Year's Eve party, where Orchid Murphy meets Brian Alden and they hit it off. Orchid's brother, Buddy, is the typical overprotective brother, who is skeptical of the relationship.

When Brian introduces Orchid to his Aunt Agatha, it is decided that in order for Orchid to fit in better with their wealthy "jet set," she must spend time with Aunt Agatha to be coached in "fine manners." By the time Agatha gets through with Orchid, she is much more refined in her mannerisms, but so much that her warm, vibrant personality grows cold, and Brian falls out of love with her. She was not good enough as she was, and the "new" Orchid is not acceptable, either. A confrontation takes place, and Orchid and Brian have words. The grand finale is hilarious.

Director Richard Rosson (1894–1953) was the brother of silent screen actress Helen Rosson, and director Hal Rosson, who was Jean Harlow's third and last husband. Hal Rosson received a special Academy Award for his pioneering Technicolor work in the 1936 version of *The Garden of Allah*.

Fine Manners is probably among the better films that Gloria Swanson made for Paramount after the Cecil B. DeMille collaborations of the late 1910s and early 1920s. It is a light and fun romantic story that blends comedy and drama. In comparing this film with *Manhandled* (1924), another Swanson film with Paramount, as well as the one other post–DeMille Swanson-Paramount picture not held hostage in the archives or lost, they both offer Swanson the same types of roles, with not much potential for the quality dramatic parts that Swanson played in her independent productions with United Artists. One can definitely understand why she left Paramount when she did.

466. For Heaven's Sake

Rating: ☆☆☆

Harold Lloyd Corporation/Paramount; ***Directed by*** Sam Taylor; ***Assistant Director:*** Robert A. Golden; ***Story by*** John Grey, Ted Wilde, and Clyde Bruckman; ***Titles by*** Ralph Spence; ***Photography by*** Walter Lundin and Henry N. Kohler; ***Editor:*** Allen McNeil; ***Production Manager:*** John L. Murphy; ***Technical Director:*** William MacDonald; ***Art Director:*** Liell K. Vedder; ***Cast:*** J. HAROLD MANNERS, Harold Lloyd (1893–1971); HOPE, Jobyna Ralston (1900–1967); THE ROUGHNECK, Noah Young (1887–1958); THE GANGSTER, James Mason (1889–1959); BROTHER PAUL, Paul Weigel (1867–1951)

This was the first of the Lloyd features to be distributed through Paramount Pictures. In it, Lloyd plays a spoiled millionaire who is so rich that when he wrecks his car, he just trots down to the car dealer and writes a check for the full amount of their top-of-the-line model, and drives off. He gives $1,000 to a man just because he asks for it, and before he knows it, he had made headlines as the founder of a homeless mission with his name on it. This upsets him, and he demands that his name be disassociated with the mission.

Harold later takes an interest in the mission, having a change of heart influenced by the fact that the founder of the mission has an attractive daughter, nicely portrayed by Jobyna Ralston. Love makes him end up doing more than he had originally intended. Ralph Spence's wit is in full form in one of the titles in which he describes the couple as "a man with a mansion and the miss with a mission."

One especially funny sequence has Harold being chased by thugs, and he gets out of it by aggravating people on the way as he is running, and getting them after the thugs who are chasing him.

The finale has Harold kidnapped on his wedding day, and facing a number of obstacles to get to the ceremony on time.

467. The Great K & A Train Robbery *Rating:* ☆☆☆½

Fox; ***Directed by*** Lewis Seiler; ***Story by*** Paul Leicester Ford; ***Scenario by*** John Stone; ***Photography by*** Daniel Clark; ***Titles by*** Malcolm Stuart Boylan; ***Running Time:*** 53 minutes; ***Cast:*** TOM GORDON, Tom Mix (1880–1940); MADGE CULLEN, Dorothy Dwan (1907–1981); EUGENE CULLEN, William Walling (1874–1932); DELUXE HARRY, Harry Grippe (1885–??); BURTON, Carl Miller (1893–1979); BANDIT LEADER, Edward Peil (1883–1958); CULLEN'S BUTLER, Curtis McHenry; Tony the horse as Himself

This is one of the best of the Tom Mix silent westerns, and the first of his films directed by Lewis Seiler (1891–1964), who was a former comedy gag writer, and became known for his adeptness at action pictures and westerns in a directorial career that lasted through 1958.

In this action packed western, the K & A Railroad Company owned by Eugene Cullen is subjected to a series of train robberies. Tom Mix plays Tom Gordon, the detective hired to solve the crimes and bring the perpetrators to justice. In order to carry out his mission, he poses as an outlaw.

Tom Mix, known for his elaborate stunts, does some impressive ones. He makes his grand entrance into the picture by sliding down a rope from the top of a mountain onto his horse. Other sequences have him riding underneath a train, riding his horse out a window and into a swimming pool, and jumping on top of a moving train.

It is alleged that western star John Wayne (1907–1979) appeared as an extra in this film, but this reviewer could not spot him, and his participation cannot be confirmed.

The Great K & A Train Robbery is a true western classic in which there is not a single dull moment. It is a title that every western buff should have in their video collection.

468. Her Man o' War *Rating:* ☆☆☆

DeMille/P.D.C.; ***Directed by*** Frank Urson; ***Running Time:*** 50 minutes; ***Cast:*** MARIETTE,

Jetta Goudal (1891–1985); Big Bertha, Kay Deslas; Ludwig Krantz, Frank Reicher (1875–1965); Colonel Franz Marwitz, Michael Vavitch (1885–1930); Countess Von Lebedour, Grace Darmond (1898–1963); Jim Sanderson, William Boyd (1895–1972); Shorty Flynn, Jimmie Adams (1888–1933); Peterle, Junior Coghlan (born 1916)

This is a World War I story set in Germany. William Boyd plays an Allied spy who gets across the German lines by posing as a "deserter" who wants to join the Kaiser's side. As leading lady, Jetta Goudal plays Mariette, a poor German orphan who is trying to raise enough food to support herself and her younger brother, Peterle, who is crippled. Jim is put to work on Mariette's farm by the German commander. He and Mariette become romantically involved, which puts Mariette in the position of having to choose between loyalty to her country and her love for Jim.

This was the first film for which Frank Urson (1887–1928), an assistant to Cecil B. DeMille, received full directorial credit. Just as Urson's career looked promising, he drowned in Lake Michigan, dying in August of 1928 at the age of 41.

Frank Reicher started his entertainment career on stage in 1899, starting in films in 1915. Most of his work in the early silent era was as a director. In the talkie era, he acted in such notable films as *Mata Hari* (1931), *King Kong* (1933), *The Story of Louis Pasteur* (1936), *The Song of Bernadette* (1943), and *Samson and Delilah* (1949). His performance in *Her Man o' War* was among his first film work after having left Hollywood for a five year stint to work on the stage again.

Her Man o' War is among the earliest of William Boyd's leading roles, and one in which his appearance is at its best. Jetta Goudal had starred in this film just before making *White Gold* (1927), which is widely regarded as her greatest success.

469. Irene

Rating: ☆☆☆

First National; ***Directed by*** Alfred E. Green; ***From the Play by*** James Montgomery; ***Scenario Editing by*** June Mathis; ***Continuity by*** Rex Taylor; ***Titles by*** George Marion, Jr.; ***Art Director:*** John D. Schulze; ***Film Editor:*** Edwin Robbins; ***Costumes by*** Cora MacGeachy; ***Fashion Show by*** Ernest Belcher; ***Color Sequences by*** Technicolor; ***Running Time:*** 91 minutes; ***Cast:*** Irene O'Dare, Colleen Moore (1900–1988); Mrs. O'Dare, Kate Price (1872–1943); Denis O'Dare, Charlie Murray (1872–1941); Cordella Smith, Betty Francisco (1900–1950); Harry Hadley, Edward Earle (1882–1972); Donald Marshall, Lloyd Hughes (1897–1958); Bob Harrison, Lawrence Wheat (1876–1963); Madame Lucy, George K. Arthur (1899–1985); Eleanor Hadley, Eva Novak (1898–1988); Jane Gilmour, Bess Flowers (1898–1984)

In this light comedy, Colleen Moore plays Irene, a girl from a poor but honest family, with Kate Price playing the mother who keeps husband Charlie Murray in line with a rolling pin. Irene is told by her mother to leave, and ends up in New York with a friend of hers, where she becomes a fashion model. She falls in love with Donald Marshall, a wealthy businessman. A confrontation arises when Marshall's and Irene's parents meet at the big fashion show. Mrs. Marshall calls Irene a common gold digger, and her family vulgarians, and Irene tells her that just because they are poor, it does not make them "common," and leaves, disillusioned with the high society crowd that she was once fascinated by. She really loves Donald, wishing that he was from a more modest background so that they could be together. Eventually, all is worked out, and they live happily ever after.

This delightful film is among the rarest of the surviving Colleen Moore films, and

Colleen Moore, star of *Irene* (1926), models a swimsuit.

was originally filmed with Technicolor sequences. Unfortunately, all available screening prints today are in black and white only. In an interview, Ms. Moore stated that the big fashion show sequence was put in for her grandmother, who had a fascination with high fashion clothing.

The credits listing with George K. Arthur as Madame Lucy is not a typographical error. He plays the owner of a fashion design business inherited from his aunt, and the characters still use her namesake in referring to him.

470. It's the Old Army Game

Rating: ☆☆

Paramount; ***Directed by*** Edward Sutherland; ***Screenplay by*** Tom J. Geraghty; ***Story by*** Joseph P. McEvoy; ***Edited by*** Tom Geraghty; ***Photographed by*** Alvyn Syckoff; ***Titles by*** Ralph Spence; ***Running Time:*** 70 minutes; ***Cast:*** ELMER PRETTYWILLIE, W.C. Fields (1879–1946); MARILYN SHERIDAN, Louise Brooks (1906–1985); ELMER'S SISTER, Mary Foy (died 1987); HIS NEPHEW, Mickey Bennett (1915–1950); TESSIE GILCH, Blanche Ring (1877–1961); WILLIAM PARKER, William Gaxton (1893–1963); A SUCKER, Eugene Pallette (1889–1954)

This was W.C. Fields' first film after having completed *Sally of the Sawdust* (1925) and *That Royle Girl* (1926) under the direction of D.W. Griffith (1875–1948).

With the witty talents of Ralph Spence as title writer, as well as the acting talent of Fields and Louise Brooks, one expects much more from this comedy than it delivers.

This film finds Fields as a pharmacist for whom everything seems to go wrong. As he is trying to get motivated to start his day, his nephew hits him in the head with a hammer. Then, a false alarm goes off in his drug store, bringing the firemen who want sodas on the house when they get there. After Elmer gets rid of them with another false alarm, a real fire breaks out, and it seems every time Fields tries to put it out, he trips or drops the water containers before he can get to the fire. The sequence showing him filling a small wine glass with water and taking a sip of it as he goes to put out the fire is a repeat performance of a gag that Roscoe Arbuckle did 11 years earlier in *Fatty's Plucky Pup* (1915).

The title of the film comes from a sequence in which Eugene Pallette plays a man outwitted by Fields while playing a "slide of hand" game. Fields exposes him saying "it's the old army game" as well as the quotation, "never give a sucker an even break." The film goes into a "family picnic" sequence in which Elmer, his pushy niece, and bratty nephew get into chaos.

Louise Brooks plays Elmer's pharmacy assistant, who falls for a man selling plots of land in Florida. Rumor goes around that his operation is a scam, but the conclusion reveals that the operation was legitimate, and everyone gets rich and is happy.

Ms. Brooks' role in this film does not really give her much to do but act as a display ornament. While Fields does have some classic, hilarious moments, the script is generally banal and without much substance. The only factors keeping the film out of the abyss are Fields' antics and Ralph Spence's witty titles.

At this point in Louise Brooks' career, she was married to director Edward Sutherland (1895–1973). Although Brooks reported in her book, *Lulu in Hollywood*, that Sutherland was a heavy drinker, the drinking obviously did not adversely affect his career, as he continued directing successfully through the 1950s.

Eugene Pallette, most remembered as the attractive male lead in the French story of D.W. Griffith's *Intolerance* (1916), had by this stage in his career ballooned up to over 300 pounds, and settled into character roles. Child star Mickey Bennett, who plays Fields' bratty nephew, was only 35 when he died from a heart attack in 1950.

471. Kid Boots

Rating: ☆☆☆

Paramount; ***Directed by*** Frank Tuttle; ***Adaptation by*** Luther Reed; ***Screenplay by*** Tom Gibson; ***Titles by*** George Marion, Jr.; ***Editor:*** F. Lloyd Sheldon; ***Photographed by*** Victor Milner; ***Running Time:*** 59 minutes; ***Cast:*** SAMUEL "KID" BOOTS, Eddie Cantor (1892–1964); BIG

BOYLE, Malcolm Waite (1892–1949); CLARA MCCOY, Clara Bow (1905–1965); TOM STERLING, Lawrence Gray (1898–1970); CARMEN MENDOZA, Natalie Kingston (1905–1991); ELEANOR, Billie Dove (1900–1997)

Eddie Cantor, star of *Kid Boots* (1926) in later years.

This romantic situation comedy marked the film debut of the highly renowned stage comedian Eddie Cantor, based on a Broadway play he starred in. Cantor plays Kid Boots, a bumbling men's clothing salesman who has made a bad enemy of heavy muscleman "Big Boyle," whose girlfriend is the petite Clara, played by Clara Bow. Lawrence Gray plays a wealthy heir whose conniving wife, played by Natalie Kingston, is doing everything she can to prevent husband Tom Sterling from getting his final divorce decree. Sterling helps Kid Boots to escape from Big Boyle, and in return, Kid Boots helps him to overcome the obstacles that his wife has put in the way of the divorce hearing. Screen beauty Billie Dove has a part as a pretty girl at a hotel resort, who is paid by one of Carmen's henchmen to "vamp" Kid Boots, the star witness at the divorce hearing, from Clara, with whom Boots is just starting to make some progress.

This is a light, funny comedy, and an excellent example of Cantor's hilarious pantomimic talent. One sequence has him trying to create the appearance that a pretty woman is sitting next to him. Situated next to a door, Cantor uses his own hand decorated to look like the hand of a woman accompanying him. Another highlight sequence occurs when Kid Boots arrives for his massage, with the masseuse being none other than Big Boyle, the angry heavy that Cantor's character had a run-in with at the beginning of the film. He bends Cantor's legs back around behind his neck in a position that would be impossible for most people to do.

Director Frank Tuttle (1892–1963) began his directorial career in 1922, specializing in light comedies such as this one. He branched out later into various genres of films in a career which lasted into the 1950s. He, as a former Communist, was forced to testify against other Hollywood figures, which effectively ended his career.

472. La Bohème

Rating: ☆☆☆½

MGM; ***Directed by*** King Vidor; ***Screenplay by*** Fred De Gresac; ***Based on Henry Murgers' Life in the Latin Quarter***; ***Continuity by*** Ray Doyle and Harry Behn; ***Titles by*** William Conselman and Ruth Cummings; ***Film Editor:*** Hugh Wynn; ***Photography by*** Henrik Sartov; ***Running Time:*** 93 minutes; ***Cast:*** MIMI, Lillian Gish (1893–1993); RODOLPHE, John Gilbert (1899–1936); MUSETTE, Renée Adorée (1898–1933); VICOMTE PAUL, Roy D'Arcy (1894–1969); BENOIT (JANITOR), Karl Dane (1886–1934); SCHAUNARD, George Hassell (1881–1937); COLINE, Edward Everett Horton (1887–1970); THEATRE MANAGER, Frank Currier (1857–

1928); MADAME BENOIT, Mathilde Comont (1886–1938); MARCEL, Gino Corrado (1893–1982); BERNARD, Gene Pouyet (1883–1950); ALEXIS, David Mir; LOUISE, Catherine Vidor; PHEMIE, Valentina Zimina (1899–1928)

La Bohème was the first of the five films that Lillian Gish starred in for MGM, following two productions that she did for Inspiration Pictures. For this film, Gish selected King Vidor as her director, on the basis of the impression that *The Big Parade* (1924) made on her. This film also has historic significance as the first MGM film to be shot with panchromatic film.

This is a classic love story based on the popular opera of the same name, of which a stage production is touring at this writing. Lillian Gish plays Mimi, a poor seamstress who sacrifices everything—including her health—for the writing career of her lover, Rodolphe. When he is fired from his job as a magazine staff writer, she starts working day and night to earn money for both of them—never telling Rodolphe of his dismissal. Once he finds out the truth, he falsely believes that Mimi has been accepting money from a wealthy playboy, and is enraged. Mimi leaves and goes to work in the slums of Paris in a factory. Eventually, overwork results in her terminal illness of tuberculosis. By the time Rodolphe's play succeeds and a reconciliation occurs, it is too late.

La Bohème is an excellent film featuring the best in directorial talent as well as acting talent. The settings of the artist community in Paris are realistic and well photographed. Lillian Gish's death scene is most highly acclaimed. Director King Vidor stated that the death scene was among the best acted he had ever seen in his career. Greta Garbo, who had just started to work at MGM studios at the time this movie was filmed, studied Gish's death scene to learn her technique. In order to make these scenes of illness and death as vivid as possible, Gish stuffed cotton balls in her cheeks and did not drink liquids for the three days prior to the filming of these scenes, thus achieving the gaunt appearance.

It is ironic to note that in this film about Mimi, who dies from tuberculosis, the lead supporting actress, Renée Adorée, would in reality die from the disease seven years later. Roy D'Arcy played a number of villain roles in several significant films until his retirement in the late 1930s. Valentina Zimina died at age 29 from influenza just two years after making this film. No further data could be found on Catherine Vidor or David Mir.

La Bohème would turn out to be the only screen pairing of Lillian Gish and John Gilbert, who made a wonderful team. Lillian Gish had originally been slated to play the female lead in *Love* (1927), but the part ended up going to Greta Garbo.

For years, this film was available only in the form of a poor quality bootleg version. In the early 1990s, Turner Classic Movies presented a restored version taken from beautiful 35 mm print material and enhanced with a nice piano and orchestral score specifically composed for the film. Although this restored version has not been officially released on video, TCM continues to air it from time to time.

473. Lightning Hutch

Rating: ☆☆☆

Hurricane/Arrow; ***Directed by*** Charles Hutchison; ***Scenario by*** J.F. Natteford; ***Photographed by*** Leon Shamroy; ***Edited by*** Bernard B. Ray; ***Lighting by*** Louis Myers; ***Total Running Time:*** 230 minutes; ***Cast:*** LARRY HUTCHDALE/"LIGHTNING HUTCH," Charles Hutchison (1879–

1949); DIANE WINTERS, Edith Thornton (1896–1984); BORIS KOSLOFF, Sheldon Lewis (1868–1958); CLIFFORD PRICE, Eddie Phillips (1899–1965); JANET THORNWALL, Virginia Pearson (1888–1958); HENRY [THE VALET], Ben Walker (1859–1924?); MARIE BRUSEFF, Violet Schram (1898–??); HUGH THORNWALL, Gordon Sackville (1880–1926); FRANK PROCTOR, LeRoy Mason (1903–1947)

For many years, it was believed that none of Charles Hutchison's serial work survived in complete form. It was in early 1997 that a complete print of this Hutchison serial was rediscovered in a Boston basement with a number of other films that were acquired by Jack Hardy of Grapevine Video and released on videocassette to the public.

Lightning Hutch finds Sheldon Lewis as the villain. He seeks the secret formula for a deadly poisonous gas invented by Hugh Thornwall, and is willing to do whatever it takes to get his hands on it. Eddie Phillips plays Clifford Price, a friend of the Thornwalls who is bribed by Boris Kosloff to help him steal the formula for "Thornite." They plan to use incriminating letters stolen from Mrs. Thornwall to get her to give up the formula. Mrs. Thornwall's sister is Diane Winter, who is the fiancée of "Lightning Hutch."

Hutch, a former secret service agent, performs a number of impressive stunts throughout the serial in his attempts to recover the letters and the deadly chemical formula. Among the most spectacular stunts that Hutchison performs are crashing a car down an embankment, jumping over a river on a motorcycle, crashing into trees on a motorcycle, falling over a balcony, and crashing his motorcycle into the ocean. He also makes one escape by swinging from a chandelier out a window.

Of the silent serials from the 1920s available for evaluation, *Lightning Hutch* is among the finest of them all. If Charles Hutchison was doing work of this high quality during the latter part of his career when he was past his prime, one can imagine how good his earlier work must have been.

474. The Lodger *Rating: ☆☆☆☆*

Produced in Great Britain; ***Directed by*** Alfred Hitchcock; ***Assistant Director:*** Alma Reville; ***From the Novel by*** Mrs. Belloc Lowndes; ***Photography by*** Baron Ventimiglia; ***Art Direction by*** C. Wilfrid Arnold, Bertram Evans; ***Edited and Titled by*** Ivor Montague; ***Title Designs:*** E. McKnight Kauffer; ***Running Time:*** 99 minutes; ***Cast:*** THE LODGER, Ivor Novello (1893–1951); THE LANDLADY, Marie Ault (1870–1951); HER HUSBAND, Arthur Chesney (1882–1949); JOE [POLICE DETECTIVE], Malcolm Keen (1887–1970)

This was the ninth film that director Alfred Hitchcock (1899–1980) was involved in the production of, and the first real suspense film that he directed on his own, which would popularize the film genre that he specialized in. *The Lodger* was a sensational box office hit both in Europe and America, making Hitchcock's first major film project the most successful of his silent era films.

Lead actor Ivor Novello, who had just finished work in the highly acclaimed film, *The Rat* (1925) with Mae Marsh (1895–1968), plays Jonathan Drew, a mysterious man whose arrival at a boarding house in London happens to coincide with a string of strange murders committed by someone who leaves notes on the murder victims signed as "the avenger."

Alfred Hitchcock's skillful direction keeps the audience in suspense for the entire

A scene from *The Lodger* (1926) with Ivor Novello.

film. As in most of his suspense films, *The Lodger* has the usual surprise twist near the end. This was also the first of the Hitchcock films in which he makes his trademark cameo appearance. This one features a view of Hitchcock from the back, which shows him sitting at a desk in the newspaper office. He had black hair in this early effort.

Leading man Ivor Novello not only was a popular actor, but a talented playwright as well. Among the later films he starred in was a 1932 remake of *The Lodger*, which was released as *The Phantom Fiend* in America. The film was remade two more times in the talkie era, but all of the remakes are practically forgotten, whereas this original version is one of the most widely circulated of all silent films.

475. Made for Love *Rating:* ☆

DeMille/PDC; ***Directed by*** Paul Sloane; ***Story by*** Garrett Fort; ***Photographed by*** Arthur Miller; ***Titles by*** George Marion, Jr.; ***Production Editor:*** Elmer Harris; ***Running Time:*** 67 minutes; ***Cast:*** NICHOLAS AINSWORTH, Edmund Burns (1892–1980); LADY DIANA TRENT, Ethel Wales (1878–1952); JOAN WHIPPLE, Leatrice Joy (1893–1985); PRINCE MAHMOUD, Bertram Grassby (1880–1953); SELIM, Snitz Edwards (1862–1937); ANGEL BURTON, Lincoln Stedman (1906–1948); GEORGE WADDAMS, Frank Butler (1890–1967); ALPHONSE VICHY, Neely Edwards (1883–1965)

This is a film that was obviously inspired by the 1922 excavation of King Tut's tomb. Nicholas Ainsworth is leader of the expedition to explore the tomb of two ancient Egyptian lovers. Lady Diana Trent is his attractive assistant, and Joan Whipple is his fiancée. There is a flashback sequence, complete with dancing girls, which tells the story of the lovers whose tomb is being excavated. It was obviously thought up by Cecil B. DeMille, but is inferior to DeMille's typical flashbacks as directed by Paul Sloane.

Joan feels neglected, as if she is being ignored by her fiancé for his work. An evil prince, who would like to have Joan as his girl, plots to kill Ainsworth, and make the death look like an ancient curse on desecrators of the tomb. When Joan learns of the prince's plans, it is up to her to rescue fiancé Nicholas from the fate planned for him.

This was a programmer directed by Paul Sloane (1893–1963), who was at best a mediocre director, and at worst an atrocious director on the level of Harry Hoyt or Lloyd Ingraham. The story of *Made for Love* had potential to be an interesting film, especially considering that Edmund Burns and Leatrice Joy were cast in the lead roles, but its potential is stultified by Sloane's sorry directorial techniques. The film's star, Leatrice Joy, obviously did not think much of the film, as she makes no mention of it in any of her accessible interviews.

476. The Magician

Rating: ☆☆☆½

Metro-Goldwyn; ***Written and Directed by*** Rex Ingram; ***Assistant Director:*** Michael Powell; ***Based on a Play by*** Somerset Maugham; ***Photography by*** John Seitz; ***Settings by*** Henri Menessier; ***Film Editor:*** Grant Whytock; ***Running Time:*** 71 minutes; ***Cast:*** DR. OLIVER HADDO, Paul Wegener (1874–1948); MARGARET DAUNCEY, Alice Terry (1899–1987); DR. ARTHUR BURDON, Ivan Petrovich (1897–1962); DR. POHOET, Firmin Geier; SUSIE BOND, Gladys Haner; HADDO'S SERVANT, Henry Wilson

This was Rex Ingram's follow-up to *Mare Nostrum* (1925), filmed in Nice, France, where Ingram and wife Alice Terry were living in the late 1920s. (While *The Magician* was technically released by MGM, director Ingram hated Louis B. Mayer, and refused to allow his name to appear on any of his films, so the credits on all of the Ingram MGM films appear as Metro-Goldwyn.) German actors Paul Wegener and Ivan Petrovich were recruited to costar with Alice Terry in this macabre drama about a mad scientist who has discovered how to create a living being. One of the ingredients he needs for his experiment is the heart of a virgin woman. Alice Terry as Margaret Dauncey becomes his target. Her love interest is played by Petrovich, the doctor who falls in love with her after he performs the operation that saves her life following an accident. It is he who rescues her at the last minute just as the diabolical Oliver Haddo has her in his lab and is ready to remove her heart for his intended creation.

Paul Wegener gives what is one of the best performances of his career as the magician who turns up at every corner in his pursuit of Margaret. He first targets her when she picks a rose, and the couple sees him again at a carnival show where he renders a poisonous snake harmless. He later shows up at her studio, and when she won't go with him willingly, he hypnotizes her to submit to his will.

One of the most artistic sequences in the film is one in which Ingram portrays hell. The macabre laboratory headquarters of Haddo inspired much of the decor used in James Whale's *Frankenstein* (1931) as well as *The Old Dark House* (1932). The final showdown is especially impressive as Arthur Burdon comes to rescue his sweetheart from Haddo, and the villain tries to throw Burdon into a blazing fire.

477. Mantrap

Rating: ★★★

Paramount; ***Directed by*** Victor Fleming; ***Photographed by*** James Howe; ***Inspired by*** Sinclair Lewis' story; ***Adaptation and Titles by*** George Marion, Jr.; ***Running Time:*** 65 minutes; ***Cast:*** ALVERNA, Clara Bow (1905–1965); JOE EASTER, Ernest Torrence (1878–1933); RALPH PRESCOTT, Percy Marmont (1883–1977); WESSON WOODBURY, Eugene Pallette (1889–1954); CURLY EVANS, Tom Kennedy (1885–1965); MRS. MCGAVITY, Josephine Crowell (died 1934); MR. MCGAVITY, William Orlamond (1867–1957); INDIAN GUIDE, Charles Stevens (1893–1964); MRS. BARKER, Patricia "Miss" DuPont (1894–1973)

This is a spoof on Sinclair Lewis' originally somber tale of backwoods adultery in the southern Canada sticks. Clara Bow stars in her first big Paramount hit as a New York manicurist who gives up her carefree life to marry hick Joe Easter, proprietor of the Mantrap River Trading Company, doing business in a tiny, obscure riverside settlement. Percy Marmont plays Ralph Prescott, a New York attorney who comes to Mantrap in hopes of escaping the fast life of New York, as well as the jazz age flappers. When he gets to Mantrap, he runs into none other than Alverna. Although he tries to resist the charm at first, he and Alverna end up hitting it off, and he defies convention and caves in. Alverna and Ralph initially elope, but Ralph goes back to New York, deciding that it is less complicated than Mantrap, and Alverna goes back to her husband.

It is interesting to see Ernest Torrence in a departure from his typical heavy villain roles, as the husband who is being cheated on. British actor Percy Marmont, whose acting career began on stage in 1900, is appealing as Ralph Prescott, the attractive lawyer that Alverna tries to elope with. He made only two more films in the U.S. after *Mantrap* before returning to England in 1928, where his career continued through the talkie era, with his last film appearance being in 1968.

It was during the filming of *Mantrap* that Clara Bow and director Fleming began a romantic affair which led to their brief engagement. Bow broke the engagement after a few weeks for Gary Cooper.

Mantrap was a smashing success both critically and financially, and was responsible for starting Clara Bow on her way to international stardom—just before starring in *It* (1927), which catapulted her to her status as a legendary sex symbol. It is a delightful romantic comedy that has aged well—far better than the earlier fidelity comedies that Cecil B. DeMille starred Gloria Swanson in during the late 1910s and early 1920s.

478. Mare Nostrum

Rating: ★★★½

Metro-Goldwyn; ***Directed by*** Rex Ingram; ***Scenario by*** Willis Goldbeck; ***Photography by*** John F. Seitz; ***Edited by*** Grant Whytock; ***Running Time:*** 101 minutes; ***Cast:*** FREYA TALBERG, Alice Terry (1899–1987); ULYSSES FERRAGUT, Antonio Moreno (1887–1967); THE TRITON, Uni Apollon; DON ESTEBAN FERRAGUT, Alex Nova; CARAGOL, Hughie Mack (1884–1927); DON CINTA, Mlle. Kithrou; ESTEBAN, Michael Brantford; PEPITA, Rosita Ramirez; TONI, Frederick Mariotti; DR. FEDELMANN, Mlle. Paquerette; COUNT KALEDINE, Fernand Mailly; SUBMARINE COMMANDER, Andre von Engelman

This World War I story takes place in the area surrounding the Mediterranean Sea. The film's title is Latin for "our seas." The film was shot on location in France and Spain. *Mare Nostrum* was for many years believed lost. A beautiful, pristine print of the film was in the MGM archives in the mid–1990s.

Antonio Moreno plays the male lead as Ulysses, captain of the merchant ship called the "Mare Nostrum." While touring the ancient ruins of Italy, he meets Freya Talberg, an attractive Austrian spy, with her cohort Dr. Fedelmann, a large, rotund, bespectacled woman. Freya "vamps" the captain, who ignores his ship missions under her spell. Eventually, she truly falls in love with him, and vice versa.

Tragedy strikes when Ulysses agrees to help the spy on a mission with his ship. While at sea, one of the spies breaks his promise not to shoot at civilian passenger ships. Ulysses finds out first that this passenger ship was carrying his own son, who had traveled from Spain to Italy to find him. Freya regrets this occurrence, and sends a letter of condolences and apology to Ulysses. Unfortunately, the letter is intercepted by Dr. Fedelmann, who interprets the letter as a possibility that Freya might be willing to betray her country for the sake of love. She sets Freya up to be caught by the French for espionage.

Rex Ingram (1893–1950) was such a perfectionist that the final underwater sequence was reportedly shot 185 times before he got the effect he wanted. We are fortunate that this fine example of Ingram's work has been rediscovered. Of all of the films starring Antonio Moreno that have been evaluated, his performance in *Mare Nostrum* is by far the best of the lot, and is also Alice Terry's best film as well.

Although *Mare Nostrum* has not officially been made available on video, it is shown on Turner Classic Movies from time to time, and is highly recommended.

479. Mistaken Orders

Rating: ☆☆½

Directed by J. P. McGowan; ***Running Time of Abridged Version:*** 25 minutes; ***Cast:*** HELEN BARTON, Helen Holmes (1893–1950); VINCENT BARTON, Hal Waters; GENERAL BARTON, Henry Barrows (1875–1945); THE AGENT, Mack V. Wright (1895–1965); GEORGE SHELBY, Cecil Kellogg; TOM LAWSON, Jack Perrin (1896–1967); TONY SHARKEY, Harry Tenbrook (1887–1960)

This was one of Helen Holmes' last railroad dramas before her retirement from the screen. In *Mistaken Orders*, she plays the daughter of a railroad entrepreneur. Jack Perrin is the leading man as Tom Lawson, the new railroad operator that her father has just hired.

Trouble begins when Helen's wayward brother, Vincent, is given a chance to make good, and gets a job at another railroad station. The operator he is replacing, George Shelby, is disgruntled and knocks Vincent out, giving the wrong information to another station and causing a barely averted collision. The equipment is sabotaged at the station, and it is up to Helen to save the day.

This film features a number of impressive stunts, including one in which Helen is seen climbing a rope to get to the top of a raised drawbridge so that she can get to the controls to lower the bridge before a train engine crosses it. Another has her jumping down from a roof and into the driver's seat of her car.

While this is not among Helen Holmes' best films, it is not bad, and is still entertaining.

480. Officer 444 (1926 serial)

Rating: ☆☆

Goodwill Pictures; ***Directed by*** Francis Ford; ***Running Time:*** 200 minutes; ***Cast:*** ROBERT PRESTON [OFFICER "444"], Ben Wilson (1876–1930); NURSE GLORIA GREY, Neva Gerber (1892–??); CHIEF OF POLICE, August Vollmer; THE VULTURE, Ruth Royce (1893–1971); DAGO

FRANK, Frank Baker (1892–1980); JAMES J. BAVERLEY, Arthur Bickel; OFFICER PATRICK MICHAEL CASEY, Jack Mower (1890–1965); JERRY DUGAN, Lafe McKee (1872–1959); SNOOPY (REPORTER), Harry McDonald; FRANK HAVERLY, Phil Ford (1900–1976); DR. BLAKLEY, Al Ferguson (1888–1971)

Ben Wilson and Neva Gerber were among the most popular serial players of the late 1910s. Unfortunately, none of their earlier work is available for evaluation. *Officer 444* was made in the late 1920s, toward the end of each player's career. Wilson, who also starred in westerns, produced this serial, which was distributed by Goodwill. He died in 1930 at age 54. Neva Gerber started with Kalem in the early 1910s, and was featured in some of William Desmond's earliest directorial efforts in 1914. She seems to have vanished in the late 1920s. There is no record of how and when she died. It is highly unlikely that she is still alive, as she would have to be 105 years old at this writing.

The plot of *Officer 444* centers around a chemist who has invented a wonder solution called Haverlyite. The chemist is murdered, and the one existing vial of solution is taken. The chemist's son is the only person who knows the secret formula, and he is kidnapped by the gang. Ben Wilson plays "Officer 444," who gets into a variety of scrapes trying to break the case. Neva Gerber plays Gloria Grey, who becomes involved trying to deliver a vital message. The story takes us through ten chapters of action-packed episodes without a dull moment.

This serial features good acting, a simple and easy to follow plot, and very capable direction by Francis Ford (1881–1953), the older brother of John Ford. It features great chase sequences, but lacks one main ingredient found in some of the better silent serials—the death defying stunt work. Without the good stunt work, this serial simply does not measure up to what silent serials were supposed to be, and is a major disappointment.

481. Old Ironsides

Rating: ☆☆☆

Paramount; ***Directed by*** James Cruze; ***Adapted for Screen by*** Harry Carr and Walter Woods; ***Story by*** Laurence Stallings; ***Based on the 1830 Poem*** "Constitution" ***by*** Oliver Wendell Holmes; ***Titles by*** Rupert Hughes; ***Photography by*** Alfred Gilks; ***Running Time:*** 111 minutes; ***Cast:*** THE BOY, Charles Farrell (1901–1990); THE GIRL, Esther Ralston (1902–1994); THE BOSS, Wallace Beery (1885–1949); THE GUNNER, George Bancroft (1882–1956); COMMODORE PREBLE, Charles Hill Mailes (1870–1937); STEPHEN DECATUR, Johnnie Walker (1894–1949); RICHARD SOMERS, Eddie Fetherston (1896–1965); THE COOK, George Godfrey (1897–1947); A GUARD (BIT PART), Boris Karloff (1887–1969)

This epic was based on an 1830 poem by Oliver Wendell Holmes, which in turn was based on actual events in early American history. The story is set in 1798, a time when pirates ruled the seas, and forced countries to pay them bribes to leave their ships alone. The U.S. government, which has no money to pay bribes, opts to fight the pirates rather than borrow money to pay them off. The main plot centers around the U.S.S. *Constitution*, one of the ships dispatched. Because of the ship's construction with solid oak that was thick enough to resist being penetrated with a cannonball, it was nicknamed "Old Ironsides." The film goes on to portray the voyage of the ships, the battles, and ultimate triumph of the Americans who took on the pirates and freed the seas for the entire world.

A subplot has Charles Farrell as a young man determined to prove his masculinity and ability as a seaman on the voyage. Esther Ralston plays the girl who is his love interest.

At one point, the Esther, the ship on which the characters of Wallace Beery, Charles Farrell, and George Godfrey are sailing, is captured by pirates, and the crew are sold into slavery. This is a big sequence, with many extras and excellent costumes and settings. On Paramount's video packaging, Boris Karloff is erroneously identified as being among the three crew members held captive instead of the noted professional boxer George Godfrey, who actually played the role of the burly black cook. Boris Karloff appears in a small role as a guard. His part was unbilled when *Old Ironsides* was originally released, and this reviewer had to watch the film several times to spot him.

Old Ironsides is the best of all of director James Cruze's silent era projects. It is far better than *The Covered Wagon*, for which Cruze is best known. Unfortunately, *Old Ironsides* was not successful at the box office, and Cruze relegated himself to routine films for the rest of his career. He died in poverty in 1942, having suffered from chronic alcoholism.

Esther Ralston and Charles Farrell give nice performances, but the performance that really stands out is Wallace Beery's, as the shipmate who treats Farrell's character as a patsy. Johnnie Walker also shines as the captain of the ship that rescues the other American ships in the Mediterranean.

The U.S.S. *Constitution*, the ship which serves as this film's namesake, is preserved to this day. On July 8, 1997, the newly restored ship sailed on a brief voyage under its own power for the first time since 1881.

482. On the Beach

Rating: ☆

Running Time: 10 minutes

This is another example of pornography produced during the silent era. The main character is a man called Anthony Browning. He is reading a book behind a fence on the beach, when three girls on the other side who think they are alone decide to go for a swim in the nude. Browning peeks through a hole in the fence as the three women take off their clothes. He then confronts them, picking up the clothes and telling them they have to "come through" to get them back. The women refuse until he offers $50 plus their clothes. They agree, but stipulate that all sex must be conducted through the hole in the fence. Browning gropes each woman through the fence. When it comes time for the sex, the women find a goat and put it up next to the fence, making Browning think he is having sex with one of them.

Every month afterward, Browning returns to the same spot in search of his "Cleopatra." There is a dream sequence in which he is shown actually having sexual contact with one of the women through the fence. He wakes up and the women are headed in his direction. One of the women sees him before he sees them, and stuffs a pillow under her shirt to make it look like she is pregnant. After she makes Browning give up all of his money for child support, the three women walk away, throwing the pillow at Browning in the process, and then moon him before they depart. The film ends with the title which states, "Moral—watch your step because there's one born every second."

Although this porno film does not show actual penetration, the fact that it depicts bestiality makes it far more vulgar than most of the current hard-core pornography on the market today. The titles are filled with satiric and sexual innuendo. The three women in the film are attractive and well-endowed. The male character is bespectacled, but relatively good-looking underneath the glasses.

483. The Road to Mandalay *Rating:* N/A

MGM; ***Directed by*** Tod Browning; ***Story by*** Tod Browning and Herman Mankiewicz; ***Continuity by*** Elliott Clawson; ***Titles by*** Joe Farnham; ***Settings by*** Cedric Gibbons and Arnold Gillespie; ***Running Time of Available Fragmented Version:*** 36 minutes; ***Cast:*** SINGAPORE JOE, Lon Chaney, Sr. (1883–1930); ROSEMARY, Lois Moran (1908–1990); "THE ADMIRAL," Owen Moore (1886–1939); FATHER JAMES, Henry B. Walthall (1878–1936); ENGLISH CHARLIE WING, Sojin [Kamiyami] (1891–1954); PANSY, Rose Langdon; YAKIMO, John George (1898–1968)

The Road to Mandalay is a film of which no complete print is known to survive in any one location. The print in the MGM library is missing some footage. In the early 1980s, private collectors came across a copy of what appears to be a condensed version, which is the footage that has been available for evaluation. The private collectors' print contains footage that is missing from the MGM archive print, and vice versa. When collectors tried to strike a deal with MGM to swap footage, MGM refused. MGM was willing to take the collectors' footage, but refused to provide their footage in return. As a result, the collectors' film footage was donated to the American Film Institute with the restriction that MGM was never to have access to it.

In the footage available for evaluation, Chaney plays "Singapore Joe," the head of an illegal smuggling operation. He falls in love with Rosemary, and decides to go straight to win her—after two more years of crime during which he hopes to make enough money for them to retire on, as well as to have surgery to repair his missing eye. It turns out that Rosemary intends to marry someone else. The climax of the film features a showdown with the feuding suitors.

In this film, Chaney's disguise is that of a one-eyed thug. To create the illusion of the missing eye, it appears that an improvised opaque white version of the modern day contact lens was used. Lois Moran, who made her impressive American film debut in *Stella Dallas* (1926) at age 18, gives a good performance in this film as well.

It would be historically and academically irresponsible to critique this film on the basis of the fragmented and inferior quality print that was accessible for evaluation. With Turner Entertainment's acquisition of the MGM silents in the late 1980s, there is a glimmer of hope that a restored version of this film might eventually be made available.

484. The Sacred Mountain [a.k.a. *The Holy Mountain*] *Rating:* ☆☆

UFA Studios/Germany; ***Written and Directed by*** Arnold Fanck; ***Running Time:*** 28 minutes; ***Cast:*** DIOTIMA, Leni Riefenstahl (born 1902); FRANTZ VIGO, Luis Trenker (1893–1990)

This was the second film of renowned ballet dancer Leni Riefenstahl, which followed her film debut in *Mountain of Destiny* (1926). World renowned athlete Luis Trenker was the leading man, and, like Riefenstahl, took up directing in the 1930s, with his last film in 1962. Paired in three films together, they were one of Germany's hottest screen couples, until Trenker had a quarrel with Riefenstahl and director Fanck, causing strained relations among the three.

In *The Sacred Mountain*, Riefenstahl at 24 plays Diotima, a dancer with a passion for the sea. She is shown dancing in a silhouette, with her body in flowing motion following much the motion of the ocean waves, scenes of which are paralleled with Riefenstahl's dance rhythm. Several more dancing scenes in various settings follow, with Luis Trenker playing her male admirer. Their romance blossoms, and the film shows Trenker in a ski competition.

Later, as Diotima is giving a dance recital to a packed house, it is announced that her lover has gone up on a mountain climb, and not returned. Diotima goes up to the mountain to search for Frantz.

This is a film that has a rather thin plot, but some gorgeous mountain scenery, which was director Fanck's specialty as a nature photographer.

Mountain dramas were a highly popular genre of film in Germany during the 1920s.

485. The Scar of Shame *Rating:* ☆☆½

Colored Players Film Company; ***Directed by*** Frank Perugini; ***Story by*** David Starkman; ***Photography by*** Al Liguori; ***Running Time:*** 75 minutes; ***Cast:*** ALVIN HILLYARD, Harry Henderson; LOUISE HOWARD, Lucia Lynn Moses; "SPIKE" HOWARD [LOUISE'S STEP-FATHER], William E. Pettus; EDDIE BLAKE, Norman Johnstone; RALPH HATHAWAY, Lawrence Chenault; ALICE HATHAWAY, Pearl McCormack; LUCRETIA GREEN, Ann Kennedy

This is one of four features produced by the Colored Players Film Company in Philadelphia, Pennsylvania, during its brief existence from 1926–1928. It is one of only about a half dozen or so all-black films from the silent era known to survive.

Lucia Lynn Moses, in her one and only screen performance, plays the lead role as Louise, a young black woman desperately trying to escape the brutality of her alcoholic step-father. Harry Henderson plays Alvin Hillyard, a black man from a well-off family who married Louise out of sympathy. Her step-father and a local bar owner scheme to get Louise away from her new husband so that they can exploit her good looks in a new uptown cabaret that the bar owner wants to open. To carry out the scheme, they send a fake telegram to Hillyard saying that his mother is ill and needs him immediately. Once he is out of the way, they make their move. Alvin arrives just as Louise has been enticed to leave for 50% of the new cabaret profits, and in a scuffle, the bar proprietor draws his gun on Alvin, and accidentally shoots Louise in the neck. Alvin is blamed for the shooting and goes to prison, while Louise goes to work in the new cabaret, always wearing a scarf to cover the "scar of shame" where she was shot. Alvin eventually escapes from jail and runs into Louise in the upscale club where she is now working. At this point, she must make the decision to either clear Alvin's name and put her own luxurious life in jeopardy, or turn him over to the police as an escaped fugitive.

Although a depressing film shot on a low budget, *The Scar of Shame* is well produced, and holds the viewer's interest throughout.

This was Frank Perugini's one and only film directing project. Harry Henderson starred in two more of the four films that the short-lived Colored Players Film Company produced, which were the only films he made. Lawrence Chenault appeared in a number of Oscar Micheaux's films of the same time period.

Unfortunately, little else is known about any of the players in this film, except that Lucia Lynn Moses was a chorus girl in Harlem's famous Cotton Club. Efforts to contact the Institute for the Advanced Study of Black Family Life and Culture for leads on some of the black actors of the silent era went unanswered by that organization.

486. The Scarlet Letter

Rating: ☆☆☆☆

MGM; ***Directed by*** Victor Seastrom; ***Assistant Director:*** Harold Bucquet; ***Adaptation, Scenario, and Titles by*** Frances Marion; ***Settings by*** Cedric Gibbons and Sidney Ullman; ***Costumes by*** Max Rée; ***Photography by*** Henrik Sartov; ***Film Editor:*** Hugh Wynn; ***Original Running Time:*** 86 minutes; ***Running Time of Present Restoration:*** 79 minutes; ***Cast:*** HESTER PRYNNE, Lillian Gish (1893–1993); ARTHUR DIMMESDALE, Lars Hanson (1887–1965); ROGER CHILLINGWORTH, Henry B. Walthall (1878–1936); GILES, Karl Dane (1887–1934); THE GOVERNOR, William D. Tocker; MISTRESS HIBBINS, Marcelle Corday; THE JAILER, Fred Herzog (1868–1928); THE BEADLE, Jules Cowles (1877–1943); PATIENCE, Mary Hawes; PEARL, Joyce Coad (1917–1987); THE SEA CAPTAIN, James A. Marcus (1867–1937)

The Scarlet Letter was the second film that Lillian Gish starred in under the MGM banner. According to Gish's autobiography, she had to fight to be able to film this adaptation of Hawthorne's novel. It was on the "blacklist" of church and civic organizations in light of the morals codes brought about in the wake of the Arbuckle scandal. Ms. Gish went to the organizations herself and obtained their approval to lift the ban on the film, and the result was this beautifully acted, directed, and photographed production.

The film was directed by Victor Seastrom (1879–1960). Lars Hanson was chosen as Gish's leading man, on the basis of his performance opposite Greta Garbo in *The Saga of Gosta Berling* (1924), which Gish had seen and admired.

One of the more striking aspects about this version of *The Scarlet Letter* is the way in which the symbolism of the letter "A" was presented. From the time that Hester is first sentenced to wear the scarlet letter, we see it appear as a symbol of adultery. Then there are sequences in which Pearl, her daughter, draws the letter "A" in the sand, as a symbolic gesture. In the sequence during which Prynne and Dimmesdale meet and resolve to start over in another area, Hester takes the "A" off of her dress, only to have it replaced by her daughter. One of the most haunting sequences in the film is when Arthur Dimmesdale finally confesses to being the father of Prynne's daughter on the scaffold, and reveals a horrible scar on his chest in the form of a letter "A," which he had branded onto himself as punishment.

The cinematography in this adaptation is especially striking. The sequences by the lakeside are beautifully photographed, with the reflections in the lake showing up well.

In addition to Lillian Gish and Lars Hanson, the fine supporting cast included Henry B. Walthall and Karl Dane. Walthall, who appeared opposite Lillian Gish in *The Birth of a Nation*, was reunited with her in this film, playing Prynne's estranged husband. Karl Dane, a fine character actor, achieved success in *My Four Years in Germany* (1918), but got his first really big break in *The Big Parade* (1924). He is absolutely hilarious as Giles Cory in some scenes of comic relief. One favorite part is when he is in church and mocks Mistress Hibbins, the town gossip who got Hester Prynne into trouble for running and playing on the Sabbath. Tragically, Karl Dane's thick Swedish accent precluded him from carrying his career into the talkie era, and he committed suicide in 1934 at age 48.

A restored version of this film was featured on Turner Classic Movies in early 1997. Half of the 35 mm print in the MGM archives had been lost, so the remaining part of the film had to be blown up from a bootleg 16 mm print to provide the missing footage. An excellent orchestra score was added, making the watching of this restored version a wonderful experience. The only footage missing from this version is an amusing sequence in which Giles Cory dresses himself up to look like Mistress Hibbins, makes derogatory remarks about the governor to passersby, thus getting revenge on Hibbins when she is sentenced to be dunked. The dunking incident is also cut from the final restored version.

Since this 1926 adaptation of *The Scarlet Letter*, the Hawthorne story has been remade several times in the talkie era. A 1934 version starring Colleen Moore was not bad, but Ms. Moore herself stated in interviews that she preferred Gish's version over her own. The awful reviews that the 1995 Demi Moore version received have spoken for themselves. More than 70 years after its release, this 1926 version is widely regarded as the definitive film adaptation of *The Scarlet Letter*.

487. The Sea Beast

Rating: ☆☆☆½

Warner Brothers; ***Directed by*** Millard Webb; ***Screenplay by*** Bess Meredyth; ***Based on Herman Melville's Moby Dick***; ***Running Time:*** 100 minutes; ***Cast:*** AHAB CEELEY, John Barrymore (1882–1942); ESTHER HARPER, Dolores Costello (1905–1979); DEREK CEELEY, George O'Hara (1899–1966); ORIENTAL SHIP NAVIGATOR, So-Jin Kamiyama (1891–1954)

This was the first of two screen adaptations of Herman Melville's 1851 classic, *Moby Dick*, in which John Barrymore starred. He remade this film as a talkie under the original book title in 1930. This was part of a three-film deal that Barrymore signed with Warner Brothers. The company had wanted *Don Juan* (1926) to be the first film in the series, but Barrymore insisted on doing *The Sea Beast* first, and so it was.

The screenplay by Bess Meredyth does deviate somewhat from Melville's story as written. In this adaptation, Meredyth created a love triangle consisting of two half-brothers who are vying for the affections of one Esther Harper. While on a whaling mission, Derek Ceeley decides to eliminate Ahab from competition by pushing him overboard, where his lower leg is bitten off by the elusive, mammoth whale "Moby Dick."

Barrymore wanted to play this role to prove his versatility as an actor, by playing a character similar to the deformed types that Lon Chaney, Sr., played. Barrymore's performance is excellent as he progresses from a proper gentleman with his classic profile to a bitter, one-legged man hobbling around on a wooden leg, obsessed with gaining vengeance on the great whale, being unaware that his brother pushed him into the water on purpose.

The romantic chemistry between Barrymore and Dolores Costello shows, and they were married in 1928, two years after this film came out. This film, as one of Warner Bros.' top grossing films of 1926, proved to be Dolores Costello's big break, and she was Warner's top box-office attraction, taking the distinction previously held by the dog star Rin-Tin-Tin.

As the first and best screen adaptation of Melville's classic, it is a pity that no company has released *The Sea Beast* on video. Currently, the only copies of this film available are a few extremely contrasty and poor quality copies among private collectors. It is high time that somebody gave this cinematic classic the legitimate, high quality video release that it deserves.

488. So This Is Paris

Rating: ☆☆☆

Warner Brothers; ***Directed by*** Ernst Lubitsch; ***Assistant Directors:*** George Hippard; Ernst Laemmle; ***Based on the French Play by*** Meilhac and Halevy; ***Screen Adaptation by*** Hans Kraly; ***Photography by*** John J. Mescall; ***Art Direction by*** Harold Grieve; ***Titles by*** Robert Wagner, Robert Hopkins; ***Running Time:*** 66 minutes; ***Cast:*** DR. PAUL GIRAUD, Monte Blue (1890–1963); SUSANNE GIRAUD, Patsy Ruth Miller (1904–1995); MAURICE LALLE, André de Beranger (1895–1973); GEORGETTE LALLE, Lilyan Tashman (1899–1934); BIT PART, Myrna Loy (1905–1993)

After having made his United States directorial debut with Mary Pickford's *Rosita* (1923), Ernst Lubitsch went to Warner Brothers, where he directed six marital/society satires, including *The Marriage Circle* (1924) and *Lady Windemere's Fan* (1925). *So This Is Paris* was the last of his silents for Warner Brothers, after which he went to MGM to do *The Student Prince in Old Heidelberg* (1927). This light bedroom comedy starts off with a hilarious sequence featuring the Lalles enacting their sexual fantasy as Rudolph Valentino and his conquest in *The Sheik*. André de Beranger and Lilyan Tashman are shown dressed in "sheik" regalia, until he picks her up, and complains that she is too heavy.

Monte Blue, star of *So This Is Paris* (1926).

The "Lubitsch touch" of making fun of American culture against a foreign background continues to the home of the Girauds, with Patsy Ruth Miller as Susanne reading a steamy Arabian romance novel. She sees her next door neighbors through the window, with Maurice Lalle shirtless, and tells husband Paul to put a stop to it. It turns out that Paul becomes infatuated with Georgette Lalle, and her husband Maurice becomes infatuated with Susanne. The partner switching leads into a number of hilarious situations as the story progresses. Disaster occurs, and the moral of the story is "when you appear at your window, put on your shirt."

The Ernst Lubitsch (1892–1947) fidelity comedies in many ways remind one of the early DeMille/Swanson marriage comedies, except that Lubitsch had a far wittier and funnier style in presenting his comedies, as DeMille was more suited to direction dramatic epics.

So This Is Paris is a delightfully funny comedy that provides a good example of the "Lubitsch touch" from the silent era.

489. Son of the Sheik

Rating: ☆☆☆½

United Artists; ***Directed by*** George Fitzmaurice; ***Screen Adaptation by*** Frances Marion and Fred DeGresac; ***Titles by*** George Marion, Jr.; ***Photography by*** George Barnes; ***Settings by*** William Cameron Menzies; ***Running Time:*** 68 minutes; ***Cast:*** AHMED, SON OF THE SHEIK/ AHMED BEN HASSAN,THE SHEIK, Rudolph Valentino (1895–1926); YASMIN, Vilma Banky (1898–1991); ANDRÉ, George Fawcett (1860–1939); GHABA, Montague Love (1877–1943); RAMADAN, Karl Dane (1886–1934); S'RIR, William Donovan; DIANE, WIFE OF THE SHEIK, Agnes Ayres (1896–1940); ALBI, Bull Montana (1887–1950); THE PINCHER, Bynunski Hyman

Rudolph Valentino had originally planned this tongue-in-cheek sequel to *The Sheik* (1921) as a much needed career boost, just after having rid himself of the burden of wife Natacha Rambova, who had caused him to make some poor career decisions. The combination of bad business decisions and bad press had put Valentino's career into a slump. *Son of the Sheik* was everything Valentino had hoped it would be, but he unfortunately did not live to see it theatrically released. He died of peritonitis during a prerelease publicity tour promoting it.

The plot of the film is a story of the son of the sheik, who falls for an impoverished gypsy dancer Yasmin. When he goes to meet Yasmin in a secluded area in the desert, he is kidnapped and held for ransom by some of Yasmin's fellow gypsies. They do this without Yasmin's knowledge, but lead Ahmed to think that he was deliberately set up by Yasmin. He vows revenge, and kidnaps Yasmin once he is freed, and takes her back to his lodgings. Then, complications arise when Ahmed's father disapproves of his choice in women. Yasmin at another point in the film falls into the clutches of the evil gypsies again, and the finale of the film is Ahmed's valiant effort to rescue her.

This last appearance was by far Valentino's best post–1921 performance. He demonstrated his athletic prowess as well as versatility in a challenging double role, playing both the sheik and his son. With the use of split-screen photography, he even played the roles side by side, appearing both as father and son simultaneously. Had the Oscars been around one year earlier, he would surely have deserved a nomination for Best Actor of 1926–27. [In light of the fact that Madonna (born 1958) was not nominated for the 1996 Best Actress Oscar for her performance in *Evita* (1996), and that the great Lillian Gish (1893–1993) never won a competitive Oscar, "deserved" a nomination is the appropriate wording.] Valentino's performance in *Son of the Sheik* demonstrates that when he was given decent material to work with, he indeed lived up to his image as the great lover of the screen.

With all of the necessary ingredients for an exciting, action-packed movie—fast-paced swashbuckling scenes, last-minute rescues, excellent stunt work, etc.—and its important contribution to cinematic history as the last and possibly best performance from one of the greatest male legends ever known to Hollywood—*Son of the Sheik* is essential to any silent film repertoire.

490. The Sorrows of Satan

Rating: ☆☆☆

Paramount; ***Directed by*** D.W. Griffith; ***Based on the Novel by*** Marie Corelli; ***Screen Adapta-***

tion by Forrest Halsey, John Russell, George Hull; ***Titles by*** Julian Johnson; ***Photography by*** Harry Fishbeck; ***Film Editor:*** Julian Johnson; ***Art Direction by*** Charles Kirk; ***Running Time:*** 111 minutes; ***Cast:*** GEOFFREY TEMPEST, Ricardo Cortez (1899–1977); MAVIS CLAIRE, Carol Dempster (1901–1991); PRINCE LUCIO DE RIMANEZ/SATAN, Adolphe Menjou (1890–1963); PRINCESS OLGA, Lya de Putti (1896–1931); AMIEL, Ivan Lebedoff (1894–1953); LANDLADY, Marcia Harris (1880–??); LORD ELTON, Lawrence D'Orsay (1853–1931); DANCING GIRL, Nellie Savage

This Paramount project had originally been planned to be directed by Cecil B. DeMille who, after a dispute with studio executives, left and went into independent production.

The Sorrows of Satan was written as a novel in 1895 by Marie Corelli (died 1924), and was one of Europe's best selling novels of its era. A 1918 British film adaptation starred Gladys Cooper (1888–1971) and was reportedly unremarkable.

Filmed on a budget of $650,000, Griffith's screen adaptation of the novel proved to be a box-office bomb, thus making it his last picture for Paramount. Part of this failure was due to the Victorian era tone of the story. It might have succeeded if released a few years earlier, but didn't go over well at the height of the jazz age. Also, the competition at the time of this film's release was stiff. Among those films Griffith was competing with was Paramount's own *Beau Geste* (1926), which studio executives saw more potential in, and therefore promoted to a greater extent than Griffith's film. Most of the critical reviews for *The Sorrows of Satan* were positive, but without strong studio support, the film had little chance at success.

In reviewing *The Sorrows of Satan* today, it is an intriguing film which in some ways could be considered a modernization of *Faust*.

The film starts with artistic shots of Lucifer at the gates of heaven, with God's shadow coming down the steps in a magnificently photographed sequence. Lucifer is kicked out of heaven, and his name changed to Satan. God tells him that for every person who turns from him on earth, he will be entitled to an hour of paradise in heaven, but cannot come back to heaven until all evil is vanquished from the earth.

Ricardo Cortez plays the male lead as a struggling and impoverished writer who falls in love with Mavis Claire, another aspiring writer in the same economic position. The two plan to marry, and even scrape up enough money for a marriage license. Just as the couple are making wedding plans, Satan comes to Geoffrey in the form of Prince Lucio, who offers him an inheritance of millions of dollars provided that he marry Princess Olga, a vampish character who is marrying Geoffrey only to be near Satan/Prince Lucio, whom she really loves. Geoffrey lives an unhappy life of luxury while Mavis is left behind, broken hearted, to get along as best she can. Satan as Prince Lucio tries to tempt her by guaranteeing her literary fame and fortune provided she become mistress to a publishing magnate, and she refuses. Finally, Satan shows his true colors to Geoffrey after wife Princess Olga has died, and haunts him in the form of a shadowy bat-like creature. Eventually, the sincerity of Geoffrey's and Mavis' love prevails, and the shadow of Satan retreats.

This is a good film that should have enjoyed greater success than it did. Ricardo Cortez gives the best of his performances evaluated by this reviewer in this film—especially in the finale during which he is pursued by Satan. Carol Dempster gives a moving, emotional, sensitive, and excellent performance as well. Adolphe Menjou's performance was highly acclaimed, and he is found to be appropriate in his role of Satan posing as the slimy prince.

Shades of the old Griffith are evident in the bordello scenes which show dancing girls reminiscent of the Babylonian orgy sequences in *Intolerance* (1916).

If Cecil B. DeMille had directed this film as planned, it is likely that he would have used more elaborate special effects in the sequence in which the prince shows his true form as Satan. Double exposure photography would likely have been used to show the transformation itself, rather than just showing Satan's shadow appearing on the wall behind Geoffrey.

While this film, like many of Griffith's, takes a while in the beginning to develop, it generally is a good film even if it is not one of his masterpieces.

The Sorrows of Satan could benefit significantly by being presented in a high quality format from 35 mm print material with a good orchestra score specifically composed for it.

491. Sparrows

Rating: ☆☆☆☆

United Artists; ***Directed by*** William Beaudine; ***Story by*** Winifred Dunn; ***Adaptation by*** C. Gardner Sullivan; ***Titles by*** George Marion, Jr.; ***Photography by*** Charles Rosher, Karl Struss, Hal Mohr; ***Settings by*** Harry Oliver; ***Film Editor:*** Harold McLernon; ***Running Time:*** 81 minutes; ***Cast:*** MOLLY, Mary Pickford (1892–1979); DENNIS WAYNE, Roy Stewart (1884–1933); DORIS WAYNE, Mary Louise Miller; MR. GRIMES, Gustav von Seyffertitz (1863–1943); MRS. GRIMES, Charlotte Mineau; AMBROSE, Spec O'Donnell (1911–1986); BAILEY, Lloyd Whitlock (1891–1966)

If this reviewer were giving an award for Best Actress of 1926, Mary Pickford would be the top choice for her role in *Sparrows*. Pickford's performance in this film was even better than Lillian Gish's performance in *The Scarlet Letter* (1926). *Sparrows* is one of the finest of all of the Pickford films, and contains the finest of all of Pickford's performances with the possible exception of her role in *Stella Maris*. Fortunately, *Sparrows* is also one of the most widely accessible of all silent films, having been among the first silents to come out on video. This reviewer purchased his first video copy of this film in 1981, when the video revolution was in its earliest years.

In *Sparrows*, Pickford plays a teenager named Molly, who, with other orphaned children, is held prisoner on a baby farm by the evil Mr. Grimes. Grimes deals with "unruly" children by simply chucking them into an alligator infested swamp. It isn't long before Grimes is party to a group of kidnappers who kidnap a baby from a wealthy family, and hold it hostage at Grimes' farm, with Grimes of course getting a cut of the ransom. Finally, Molly reaches the breaking point, and leads herself and the other children to freedom, braving the alligator-infested swamps and risking her life in dangerous peril to do so.

On the escape scene, director William Beaudine (1892–1970) made Pickford do this sequence authentically—with real alligators! Ms. Pickford was justifiably frightened, and the terror she emotes is real. This stunt was as dangerous as any of Buster Keaton's or Harold Lloyd's most dangerous stunts, and Pickford certainly demonstrates courage. Douglas Fairbanks, Sr., voiced objection to Beaudine making Mary do these stunts her-

Sparrows (1926).

self without trick photography, and this was probably one of the reasons that Pickford did not work with Beaudine again.

Another person whose best performance is found in *Sparrows* is Gustav von Seyffertitz as the diabolical and cruel Mr. Grimes. This is the greatest performance of the 1926 films evaluated by a supporting player. Mr. von Seyffertitz looks truly evil, and certainly had to have had the audience booing and jeering him every time he appeared on the screen.

Sparrows is an enduring classic that will be enjoyed for many generations to come, and is a title that no silent film collector should be without.

492. Stella Dallas

Rating: ☆☆☆☆

Samuel Goldwyn/United Artists; ***Directed by*** Henry King; ***Based on the Novel by*** Olive Higgins Prouty; ***Adaptation by*** Frances Marion; ***Photography by*** Arthur Edeson; ***Edited by*** Stuart Heisler; ***Art Director:*** Arthur Stibolt; ***Costumes by*** Sophie Wachner; ***Running Time:*** 107 minutes; ***Cast:*** STEPHEN DALLAS, Ronald Colman (1891–1958); HELEN DANE/MRS. MORRISON, Alice Joyce (1890–1955); STELLA MARTIN/STELLA DALLAS, Belle Bennett (1891–1932); LAUREL DALLAS, Lois Moran (1909–1990); ED MUNN, Jean Hersholt (1886–1956); RICHARD GROVSENOR, Douglas Fairbanks, Jr. (born 1909); STEPHEN DALLAS, SR., Charles Lane (1869–1945); MISS PHILIBURN, Vera Lewis (1873–1956); MRS. GROVSENOR, Beatrix Prior

Douglas Fairbanks, Jr., and Lois Moran in a scene from the original *Stella Dallas* (1926). Belle Bennett is the girl's mother peering in, who gives her daughter up so that she will have the advantages she needs to fit into society.

This is the first and original adaptation of Olive Higgins Prouty's classic novel. Ronald Colman plays Stephen Dallas, whose father was exposed as an embezzler, committing suicide in disgrace. The younger Dallas gives up his childhood sweetheart Helen Dane to go to a smaller area where his name is not known. Belle Bennett plays the title role as Stella Martin, a poorly educated, unrefined woman whom Stephen marries. As Stella is embarrassing herself in high society, Stephen is promoted to a position which requires him to move to New York. Stella chooses to stay behind with their daughter, and has an affair with Jean Hersholt's character of Ed Munn, an alcoholic. As daughter Laurel Dallas grows up, trying to fit into a more refined lifestyle, Stella realizes that she is an embarrassment, and gives up her daughter for her own sake, knowing that father Stephen can give her the opportunities she needs.

Stella Dallas has historic significance as the biggest or most pivotal role of three of the players who appear in it. Belle Bennett, whose career began in 1916, was excellent in the title role, which was her best and most significant performance. Bennett was only 41 years old when she died of an unspecified long illness in 1932. Lois Moran won her first big role as Laurel Dallas after having had parts in two prior films in France. At age 15, she did an excellent job playing the heartbroken 10-year-old whose birthday party nobody attends on account of her mother's reputation. Only two of her silents are known to survive in complete form. The other silent is *Just Suppose* (1926), in which she played opposite Richard Barthelmess. *The Road to Mandalay* (1926) survives only in fragmented form. Ms. Moran retired from films in 1931, and went to Broadway until 1935, when she married business executive Clarence M. Young. In the 1950s, she taught at Stanford University, and from 1953 to 1956 starred in the television series *Waterfront.* This is also the film that really helped to bring then-16-year-old Douglas Fairbanks, Jr., into the limelight, as Richard, the adolescent male that Laurel falls in love with. Fairbanks's three previous films had bombed, but he made an excellent impression in *Stella Dallas.*

Sam Goldwyn, who produced this film, had a hard time convincing Henry King to direct it, as they had had an unpleasant confrontation some years before. But, Goldwyn was persistent, having recognized King's talent and success, and their lawyer drew up a contract with terms that they could agree on. They ended up collaborating on three more films after this one, including *The Winning of Barbara Worth* (1926), which was the last of King's really impressive silents after *Stella Dallas.*

Stella Dallas was remade twice in the talkie era. The 1937 version holds up very well, and Barbara Stanwyck won a nomination for a Best Supporting Actress Oscar in the title role, and Anne Shirley was also nominated in her reprisal of Lois Moran's role. If the Oscars had been around in 1926, Belle Bennett and Moran would have also been worthy of nominations. In 1989, a third adaptation called *Stella* starred Bette Midler in the leading role. While the 1989 version won no high acclaim, this reviewer does not feel that it was as bad as the critics said it was. Nonetheless, it is hard to beat a cast including Ronald Colman, Alice Joyce, Jean Hersholt, Douglas Fairbanks, Jr., Lois Moran, and Belle Bennett. While the 1937 version may be considered by most to be the definitive version of Prouty's classic, this original version could stand its ground if made as widely accessible for people to watch. Currently, the film circulates in the form of 16 mm prints, but not on video. United Artists should really consider giving this film a legitimate video release with a good music score. If they don't, perhaps someone else will when *Stella Dallas* enters the public domain in 2002.

493. The Strong Man

Rating: ☆☆☆½

Harry Langdon Corporation/First National; ***Directed by*** Frank Capra; ***Assistant Director:*** J. Frank Holiday; ***Written by*** Arthur Ripley; ***Adapted by*** Hal Conklin and Robert Eddy; ***Production Manager:*** William H. Jenner; ***Art Direction by*** Lloyd Brierly; ***Film Editor:*** Harold Young; ***Electrician:*** Denver Harmon; ***Photography by*** Elgin Lessley, Glenn Kershner; ***Running Time:*** 76 minutes; ***Cast:*** PAUL BERGOT, Harry Langdon (1884–1944); MARY BROWN, Priscilla Bonner (1899–1996); "HOLY JOE" BROWN, William V. Mong (1875–1940); LILY, Gertrude Astor (1887–1977); ZANDOW, Arthur Thalasso (1883–1954); MIKE MCDEVITT, Robert McKim (1886–1927)

This film is highly acclaimed as Harry Langdon's best work, as well as one of the best comedy features of the silent era.

The Strong Man begins with Langdon's character, Paul, on a World War I battlefield. This sequence appears to have been inspired partially by Charles Chaplin's *Shoulder Arms* (1918) or possibly Sydney Chaplin's *The Better 'Ole* (1926). When the armistice is signed, Paul returns home in hopes of finding the girl, Mary Lou, with whom he has been corresponding. During his search, he unwittingly becomes involved with a disreputable woman named Lily. Lily puts a large cash stash in Paul's pocket when the police start coming her way. She then poses as Mary Lou in an attempt to recover the money. Throughout a number of hilarious sight gags, as well as a sequence in which an apartment is totally torn apart, Lily finally recovers her money, and Paul resumes his search for Mary.

Paul makes his way to Cloverdale with a touring stage act. The leading lady, Mary Brown, is from Cloverdale, and it is at this point about 38 minutes into the film that she and Paul meet for the first time. She is the preacher's daughter and is also blind, which she hadn't told Paul in their correspondence. This sequence is heart-rending and moving. Paul's love for Mary is undaunted by her blindness, and they laugh together and are compatible.

Paul's touring stage act finds him working in "The Palace," a new speakeasy with gambling, bootleg liquor, and dancing girls among its attractions. The owner of the speakeasy, Mike McDevitt, tries unsuccessfully to bribe the last person who fights his establishment—preacher "Holy Joe" Brown, who is the father of Mary Brown.

The real fun starts when the star of the show, Zandow the strong man [name obviously parodied on famous strong man Eugene Sandow, mentioned elsewhere in this book] is too drunk to perform, and Paul ends up having to take his place.

Robert McKim, who plays the speakeasy owner, died at 39 from a cerebral hemorrhage just a year after this film came out.

This is perhaps the most prominent role that Priscilla Bonner ever played. Although she was featured in a bigger role in *The Red Kimono* (1925), this is the only real blockbuster in which she had a leading performance, and she is very convincing in her portrayal of Paul's blind sweetheart.

Harry Langdon and director Frank Capra did a lot of infighting and arguing during their collaboration on this film. Contemporary sources mostly state that Langdon's egotistical attitude was to blame, and also led to his downfall. However, Harry Langdon fans vehemently deny that this was the case.

Regardless of which version one believes of the Langdon/Capra story, *The Strong Man* is a marvelous and delightful comedy classic not to be missed, and reflects positively on both Capra and Langdon. This reviewer agrees that it is one of the outstanding comedy features of the silent era.

494. Tarzan and the Golden Lion *Rating:* ☆☆☆

Joseph P. Kennedy/F.B.O. Studios; ***Running Time:*** 57 minutes; ***Cast:*** TARZAN/LORD GREYSTOKE, James Pierce (1900–1983); JANE/LADY GREYSTOKE, Dorothy Dunbar (1902–1992); BETTY GREYSTOKE, Edna Murphy (1899–1974); JACK BRADLEY, Harold Goodwin (1902–1987); ESTEBAN MIRANDA, Frederick Peters (1884–1963); AWAZA, Boris Karloff (1887–1969)

This was the fourth of the silent Tarzan films, which followed *Tarzan of the Apes* (1918), *The Son of Tarzan* (1921), and *The Adventures of Tarzan* (1921). In this Tarzan film, the ape man was played by James Pierce, a former college football hero. Pierce was reportedly the first of the Tarzan actors who really fit the image that author Edgar Rice Burroughs had in mind. He was by far the best looking of all of the actors to play the role in the silent era.

The print of this film that was available for evaluation was a restored version that had been done for German television. It had French titles, and German subtitles and narration. Thus, the plot was a bit difficult to follow. This Tarzan episode features a number of good stunts by James Pierce, shown swinging from tree to tree in some sequences. It also features an impressive set for the headquarters of the villains as well.

In addition to James Pierce, *Tarzan and the Golden Lion* features a good supporting cast as well. We are treated to an early look at Boris Karloff, who plays a tribe leader. Dorothy Dunbar, best remembered for her roles as leading lady in a number of westerns, gives a competent but not necessarily dynamic performance as Jane. Edna Murphy, who plays a relative of the Greystokes, was the first wife of director-producer Mervyn LeRoy (1900–1987), who was Paramount co-founder Jesse Lasky's cousin.

It was during the making of this film that leading star James Pierce met and courted Joan Burroughs, daughter of author Edgar Rice Burroughs. They married, and later played the roles of Tarzan and Jane in the Tarzan radio series of the 1930s.

This adaptation of *Tarzan and the Golden Lion* was highly faithful to the Burroughs novel. It is a film which deserves to be made available with English titles for viewers in the English-speaking countries to enjoy.

495. The Temptress

Rating: ☆☆

MGM; ***Directed by*** Fred Niblo; ***Assistant Director:*** H. Bruce Humberstone; ***Based on a Novel by*** Vicente Blasco Ibañez; ***Scenario by*** Dorothy Farnum; ***Titles by*** Marion Ainslee; ***Settings by*** Cedric Gibbons/James Basevi; ***Wardrobe by*** André Ani; ***Photography by*** Gaetano Gaudio and William Daniels; ***Film Editor:*** Lloyd Nosler; ***Running Time:*** 115 minutes; ***Cast:*** ELENA, Greta Garbo (1905–1990); MANUEL ROBLEDO, Antonio Moreno (1887–1967); M. FONTENOY, Marc MacDermott (1881–1929); CANTERAC, Lionel Barrymore (1878–1954); MARQUIS DE TORRE BIANCA, Armand Kaliz (1887–1941); MANOS DURAS, Roy D'Arcy (1894–1969); PIROVANI, Robert Anderson (1890–??); TIMOTEO, Francis McDonald (1889–1968); ROJAS, Hector V. Sarno (1880–1953); CELINDA, Virginia Brown Faire (1904–1980)

The direction of this film was originally begun by Mauritz Stiller (1882–1928). Louis B. Mayer had offered contracts to both Stiller and Garbo. Due to the fact that Mayer and Stiller clashed, he was only assistant director on the first Garbo/MGM film, *The Torrent* (1926). Garbo convinced Mayer to give Stiller a chance with *The Temptress* (1926), but upon clashing again, Stiller was replaced by Fred Niblo shortly after he began work on the film.

Upon completion of *The Temptress*, even Garbo herself did not think much of the work that MGM was putting her in. She was quoted: "I do not want to be a silly temptress. I cannot see any sense in getting dressed up and doing nothing but tempting men in pictures."

In this film, it is Antonio Moreno as Manuel Robledo who comes under Garbo's vampish spell. This is after she has driven one husband to ruin, and another man to suicide.

Robledo takes the drastic step of moving to another continent to escape Elena's seductive spell, and she follows him there. The rivalry she causes between the men on Robledo's construction site results in Robledo being severely injured and temporarily blinded in a duel with whips.

While *The Temptress* does have its good scenes and moments, as well as a good cast, it is not among Garbo's better films, although it is better than some of the substandard garbage that MGM later put her in—like *Flesh and the Devil* (1927), *A Woman of Affairs* (1928), and *Wild Orchids* (1929).

496. Tramp, Tramp, Tramp

Rating: ☆☆☆

Promotional material for Harry Langdon's *Tramp, Tramp, Tramp* (1926).

Warner Brothers/First National; ***Directed by*** Harry Edwards; ***Written by*** Frank Capra; ***Photographed by*** Elgin Lessley; ***Running Time:*** 61 minutes; ***Cast:*** HARRY LOGAN, Harry Langdon (1884–1944); BETTY BURTON, Joan Crawford (1904–1977); JOHN BURTON, Edwards Davis (1867–1936); NICK KARGUS, Tom Murray (1874–1935); AMOS LOGAN, Alec B. Francis (1867–1934); TAXI DRIVER, Brooks Benedict (died 1968)

This classic comedy was responsible for having launched the success of three major motion picture personalities—Frank Capra, Joan Crawford, and Harry Langdon. Frank Capra wrote this film, which is the first feature film that he worked on. He had previously directed an independent short in 1922, and is said to have been a co-director on *Tramp, Tramp, Tramp* although credited only as a writer. Although Harry Langdon and Joan Crawford had both starred in films before this one, it was this film that was their first major success that really got them noticed by the public.

Harry Langdon plays the son of Amos Logan, owner of a small time family-owned shoe store which has fallen on hard times due to inability to compete with Burton's, a large shoe store chain that has moved into town. The salvation of the business is put into the hands of naive son Harry, who promises to raise the required money within three months "if it takes a year."

Joan Crawford plays the daughter of the owner of the competing shoe store, whom Harry is smitten with by seeing her pictures on the company billboards.

Harry decides to enter a walking marathon for which grand prize is $25,000 —oblivious to the fact that the race is a promotion for the competing Burton's shoe stores. Among the hilarious misadventures that Harry gets into along the way is his ending up in a chain gang. Among the competitors Harry must defeat is World Walking Champion Nick Kargus, the landlord that Harry's father owes so much money.

As if being put in a chain gang wasn't enough of an obstacle, Harry must also battle a destructive cyclone on his way to the finish line. This cyclone sequence has Harry and his leading competitor Nick Kargus trapped in a building being rocked back and forth by the cyclone and being ripped apart in the process. It remains one of the famous and spectacular sequences of silent comedy, and was said to have inspired the cyclone sequence in Buster Keaton's *Steamboat Bill, Jr.* (1928).

Tramp, Tramp, Tramp is a superb comedy which Langdon would top in quality only with *The Strong Man.*

497. Twinkletoes

Rating: ☆☆½

First National; ***Directed by*** Charles Brabin; ***Photography by*** James Von Treef; ***Scenario by*** Winifred Dunn; ***Based on the Limehouse Stories of*** Thomas Burke; ***Running Time:*** 76 minutes; ***Cast:*** TWINKLETOES, Colleen Moore (1900–1988); CHUCK, Kenneth Harlan (1895–1967); TWINKLETOES' FATHER, Tully Marshall (1864–1943); CISSIE, Gladys Brockwell (1894–1929); TWINKLETOES' MANAGER, Warner Oland (1880–1938); ***Supporting Cast:*** Lucien Littlefield (1895–1960); John Philip Kolb; Julanne Johnston (1900–1988); William MacDonald; Dorothy Vernon (1875–1970); Ned Sparks (1883–1957); Dick Sutherland (1881–1934); Carl Stockdale (1874–1953); Aggie Herring (1876–1939); Harold Lockwood, Jr.; Nola Luxford (1895–1994)

This is yet another screen adaptation of the popular stories by Thomas Burke, set in the London Limehouse district. *Twinkletoes* was lost for years before a print turned up sometime in the late 1970s or early 1980s.

In this film, Colleen Moore plays Twinkletoes, a poor girl who is trying to rise above her rough surroundings. She aspires to become a great ballet dancer. A subplot centers around Chuck, a Limehouse brute whom Twinkletoes despises because of his coarse nature, but who eventually changes his ways. Gladys Brockwell is excellent playing his jealous and possessive girlfriend.

Twinkletoes features a great performance by Colleen Moore, and has some beautifully choreographed ballet sequences. Character actor Tully Marshall stands out well as Moore's father.

While *Twinkletoes* is not a bad film, its weak story line leaves a bit to be desired. On the whole, it proved to be mildly disappointing. Nonetheless, it is a good film to have for its cast performances and ballet sequences.

498. The Unknown Soldier

Rating: ☆☆

Charles R. Rogers Productions; ***Directed by*** Renaud Hoffman; ***Running Time:*** 71 minutes; ***Cast:*** MARY PHILLIPS, Marguerite de la Motte (1902–1950); JOHN PHILLIPS, Henry B. Walthall (1878–1937); FRED WILLIAMS, Charles Emmett Mack (1900–1927); FRED WILLIAMS' MOTHER, Ethel Wales (1878–1952); JOHN PHILLIPS' SISTER, Claire McDowell (1878–1966); CORPORAL FOGARTY, George Cooper (1892–1943); "PEACEFUL" PERKINS, Sid Crossley (1885–1960); MIKE GINSBERT, Jess Devorska

This is a film that had been totally forgotten until Unknown Video released it in 1996. It is set during World War I, and is basically a war movie with a subplot consisting of the romance of Fred Williams and Mary Phillips, the leading roles played by Charles Emmett Mack and Marguerite de la Motte. Fred goes off to war, leaving wife Mary behind with their baby. He takes on a dangerous assignment and disappears. His identification tag is found, and he is presumed dead and classified as missing in action. Sid Crossley was known primarily for his comedy work. No further information on Jess Devorska could be found.

The Unknown Soldier is rather standard fare, but for those who like war films, it will be an addition to the collection of those silents available to the general public.

499. Up in Mabel's Room

Rating: ☆☆½

Christie; ***Directed by*** E. Mason Hopper; ***Screenplay by*** F. Andrew Willia; ***Photography by*** Hal Rosson, Alex Phillips; ***Settings by*** Charles Cadwallader; ***Titles by*** Walter Graham; ***Running Time:*** 65 minutes; ***Cast:*** MRS. GARRY AINSWORTH, Marie Prevost (1898–1937); GARRY AINSWORTH, Harrison Ford (1884–1957); PHYLLIS WELLS, Phyllis Haver (1899–1960); LEONARD MASON, Paul Nicholson (1877–1935); HENRIETTE [MASON'S SISTER], Maud Truax (1884–1939); JIMMY LARCHMONT, Harry Myers (1882–1938); ARTHUR WALKERS, Carl Gerard (1885–1966)

This was one of a series of low budget bedroom farces from when Marie Prevost was at the height of her career, receiving top billing in her films. *Up in Mabel's Room* is the best in the series.

In this film, Prevost plays a wife who has divorced her husband, and realizes she made a mistake. To win her husband back, she wreaks havoc when he tries to pass himself off as a bachelor in front of his friends. Phyllis Haver plays Phyllis Welles, who is madly in love with Ainsworth, and refuses a marriage proposal from another suitor. It is interesting to see how this complicated situation is finally resolved.

Phyllis Haver and Marie Prevost, while vibrant and happy in this light comedy, would sadly meet tragic deaths. Ms. Prevost was constantly battling with her weight, and in despair over her career which started going downhill in the mid–1930s, became an alcoholic. She died broke and alone in 1937 at age 38. Some sources give her cause of death as chronic alcoholism, and others give malnutrition resulting from anorexia nervosa as the cause.

Phyllis Haver got her start as one of Mack Sennett's bathing beauties in the 1910s. She retired from films in 1929 to marry a millionaire businessman. They lived happily, but when Mack Sennett died in 1960, she was reportedly distraught over his death, and committed suicide at 61 by taking an overdose of barbiturates.

500. The Volga Boatman

Rating: ☆☆☆

DeMille/Producer's Distributing Company; ***Directed by*** Cecil B. DeMille; ***Assistant Director:*** Frank Urson; ***Scenario by*** Lenore Coffee; ***From the Novel by*** Konrad Bercovici; ***Art Direction by*** Anton Grot; ***Assistant Art Directors:*** Max Parker, Michell Leisen; ***Costumes by*** Adrian; ***Film Editor:*** Anne Bauchens; ***Running Time:*** 120 minutes; ***Cast:*** FEODOR (THE VOLGA BOATMAN), William Boyd (1895–1972); VERA (PRINCESS OF RUSSIA), Elinor Fair (1903–1957); PRINCE NIKITA, Robert Edeson (1868–1931); PRINCE DIMITRI, Victor Varconi (1891–

The Volga Boatman (1926) starring William Boyd in one of his earliest roles.

1976); MARIUSHA, Julia Faye (1893–1966); STEPHEN, Theodore Kosloff (1882–1956); VASILI, Arthur Rankin (1900–1947)

This small-scale epic on the Russian Revolution was the first of Cecil B. DeMille's independently produced films of the 1920s. The "Volga boatmen" are specifically defined as "the human mules of Russia." William Boyd plays the title role as one of the leaders of the revolution movement against the Russian aristocracy. Elinor Fair turns in her best performance of those evaluated as Princess Vera, who is engaged to Prince Dimitri. Dimitri is played by Victor Varconi, who made his film debut in the German epic *Sodom and Gomorrah* (1922), and also played in the famous Italian epic, *The Last Days of Pompeii* (1926). When he came to the United States, he starred in a number of DeMille films of the 1920s, including the role as Pontius Pilate in *The King of Kings* (1927). Varconi's role in this film is the most prominent of his films available for evaluation, and he is excellent playing the arrogant, snobbish aristocrat who looks upon the common people as mere "animals." On the contrary, his fiancée Princess Vera is a more compassionate character. DeMille expertly practiced the art of diplomacy in this film, having good and evil characters on both sides. Once the revolution movement begins to take hold in Russia, Feodor becomes a high ranking Red Army officer. He is ordered to execute Princess Vera, but is so intrigued by her bravery in facing execution that he spares her life, risking his own and sacrificing his high standing to do so. There are a number of intriguing twists of fate as the couple run for their lives—unable to seek safety with either the Czarist White Army or Communist Red Army territories.

Although *The Volga Boatman* moves a bit slowly in some parts, it is generally well put-together, and gets better as it goes along. DeMille was inspired to do this film partly because of the high critical acclaim for Sergei Eisenstein's films on the Russian Revolution. The great box-office success of this film helped to compensate for financial losses on other DeMille films. It also inspired a number of other American films on the Revolution—including the Academy Award winning film, *The Last Command* (1928). William Boyd fans will especially enjoy this movie, as he gives an excellent performance in a role that deviated from the western roles that he is so famous for.

501. What Price Glory? *Rating:* ☆½

Fox; ***Directed by*** Raoul Walsh; ***Screenplay by*** J.J. Donahue; ***Photographed by*** J.B. McGill; ***Titles by*** Malcolm Stuart Boylan; ***Sets by*** William S. Darling; ***Running Time:*** 122 minutes; ***Cast:*** CAPTAIN FLAGG, Victor McLaglen (1886–1959); SERGEANT QUIRT, Edmund Lowe (1890–1971); CHARMAINE, Dolores Del Rio (1905–1983); COGNAC PETE, William V. Mong (1875–1940); SHANHAI MABEL, Phyllis Haver (1899–1960); CARMEN, Elena Jurado; LIEUTENANT MOORE, Leslie Fenton (1902–1978); PRIVATE LEWISOHN, Barry Norton (1909–1956); PRIVATE PIPINSKY, Sammy Cohen (1902–1981); PRIVATE KIPER, Ted McNamara (1891?-1928); FRENCH MAYOR, August Tollaire (1866–1959); A PRIVATE, Jack Pennick

What Price Glory? was Fox's answer to MGM's *The Big Parade*.

Victor McLaglen and Edmund Lowe won notoriety in their leading roles as two military officers who are constantly at each other's throats trying to win the affection of Charmaine, an attractive girl played by Dolores Del Rio. When the time comes for their first big combat battle, the rivals are shocked back into reality, knowing that their duty is to cover each other in unity against the enemy forces.

Despite *What Price Glory?*'s added attraction of color tinting, as well as some good battle sequences, it pales in comparison to *The Big Parade* and *Wings*. The film is loaded with idle footage and sequences that are just plain hokey and silly. A little bit of the silly hokum, which dominates the first two-thirds of the film, goes a long way and becomes trifle fast.

While the film did provide a good showcase for the talents of Victor McLaglen and Edmund Lowe, the only real opportunity to see Dolores Del Rio's acting talent comes close to the end of the film, when she is fretting whether her friends will return from the front again. Two of the supporting players in this film died relatively young. Barry Norton died at 47 from a heart attack. Ted McNamara died just two years after *What Price Glory?* was made at age 36 from pneumonia.

Why this film has been so highly acclaimed as one of director Raoul Walsh's finest achievements is beyond this reviewer. Despite its great success and popularity, this reviewer finds *What Price Glory?* to be the absolute worst of Walsh's evaluated silents.

1927

502. The Adventures of Prince Achmed *Rating:* ☆☆☆☆

Produced in Germany by Lotte Reiniger; ***Directed by*** Karl Koch; ***Running Time:*** 64 minutes

For many years, it has been repeatedly and erroneously stated that Walt Disney's *Snow White and the Seven Dwarfs* (1937) was the first feature length animated motion picture. In actuality, Disney was beaten to the punch ten years earlier by the renowned German female producer Lotte Reiniger (1899–1981). Reiniger was the inventor of the technique known as silhouette animation—a process using silhouette cutouts as moving picture images to tell a story. She first experimented with this technique in 1916, having done intertitles for other films, as well as some short subjects. She and husband Karl Koch began work on *The Adventures of Prince Achmed* in 1923, and after three years' work released it in 1927.

This artistic masterpiece portrays a number of the "Arabian Nights" tales using the silhouette process. Among the tales incorporated is that of Aladdin and the magic lamp. With its marvelous tints and tones and superb animation, *The Adventures of Prince Achmed* proved to be an international success both critically and at the box office. Many of the special effects were devised with the help of Walter Ruttman (1887–1941), who is best remembered for his *Berlin: Symphony of a Great City* (1927). Ms. Reiniger continued her career until just before her death, with *The Rose and the Ring* (1979) being her last project. *The Adventures of Prince Achmed* remains the most famous of all of the films from Reniger's 53-year career, and is truly a rare gem that everyone should see at least once.

503. Anything Once *Rating:* ☆☆☆½

Hal Roach/Pathé Exchange; ***Directed by*** Hal Yates; ***Running Time:*** 18 minutes; ***Cast:*** THE

GIRL, Mabel Normand (1892–1930); THE SUITOR, Theodore Von Eltz (1893–1964); ***Supporting Cast:*** James Finlayson (1887–1953); Gustav Von Seyffertitz (1863–1943); Max Davidson (1875–1950); Leo White (1882–1948)

Anything Once was among the last six films that Mabel Normand made during a comeback attempt with the Hal Roach Company. In this film, Mabel plays a laundress in a ritzy dress shop. She wears a fancy dress belonging to one of the wealthy clients, and impersonates her at a costume ball. She is eventually exposed as a fraud, but the rich suitor ends up liking Mabel better than the woman she is impersonating, and marries her instead.

This film demonstrates that Mabel was doing quality work for Hal Roach, who simply could not afford to keep Ms. Normand on the payroll when he let her go. Shortly after her films for this company were completed, she came down with tuberculosis, from which she died in 1930.

504. Beau Geste

Rating: ☆☆☆½

Paramount; ***Directed by*** Herbert Brenon; ***Based on the Novel by*** Percival Christopher Wren; ***Screenplay by*** Paul Schofield; ***Adapted by*** John Russell; ***Edited by*** Julian Johnson; ***Photography by*** J. Roy Hunt; ***Running Time:*** 101 minutes; ***Cast:*** MICHAEL "BEAU" GESTE, Ronald Colman (1891–1958); DIGBY GESTE, Neil Hamilton (1897–1984); JOHN GESTE, Ralph Forbes (1905–1951); ISOBEL, Mary Brian (born 1908); LADY PATRICIA BRANDON, Alice Joyce (1890–1955); SERGEANT LEJAUNE, Noah Beery, Sr. (1882–1946); BOLDINI, William Powell (1892–1984); MAJOR HENRI DE BEAUJOLAIS, Norman Trevor (1877–1929); HANK, Victor McLaglen (1886–1959); BUDDY, Donald Stuart (1898–1944)

In the 1920s, the French foreign legion was known as an establishment that one could literally disappear into. Basically, one left one's old identity behind, with all corroborating documentation destroyed. Members were given brand new identities. This resulted in the foreign legion becoming a haven for people who wanted to disappear—including fugitives and those who simply wanted to start a new life.

This popular classic novel's familiar story has the three Geste brothers taking the blame for stealing the valuable "Blue Water" diamond from their guardian Isobel's home. Their solidarity and code of honor is followed rigorously. To keep from having any one of them suspected over the other, the brothers all join the foreign legion, where they not only fight the enemy, but become victims of a sadistic and cruel sergeant. Only one brother comes back home alive, and there is an intriguing twist to the plot when it is revealed who actually stole the diamond and why.

Director Herbert Brenon (1880–1958) assembled one of the finest casts of any silent film since D.W. Griffith's *Intolerance* (1916). Eight of the ten main cast members were top name stars. Three of these eight cast members—Victor McLaglen and William Powell as supporting cast members, and Ronald Colman in the title role—would go on to either win Academy Awards or gain nominations in later years.

Under Herbert Brenon's skillful direction as the creator of several of the greatest films of the silent era, *Beau Geste* was a magnificent critical and box-office success. Ronald Colman and Noah Beery, Sr., give the standout performances respectively as the protagonist and the sadistic, despicable sergeant. Excellent performances are also provided by Neil Hamilton, Ralph Forbes, William Powell, and Victor McLaglen. Mary Brian and Alice Joyce have a nice presence in the film, although their small roles didn't really give them a chance to do much.

Beau Geste was remade as a talkie in 1939 by director William Wellman, and starred Gary Cooper in the title role. The film was a tremendous hit, presented almost exactly as this Brenon original, but did not have anything like the stellar cast of the silent version.

This was Herbert Brenon's last really great epic. Although he had a couple of subsequent silent films that were noteworthy, including Lon Chaney's *Laugh, Clown, Laugh,* he found the talkies hard to adapt to, and gave up in 1935 after a string of unremarkable sound films.

Supporting players Norman Trevor and Donald Stuart met tragic ends. Stuart was only 45 when he died of a heart attack in 1944. Norman Trevor had the misfortune of having what is described as a "brain malady" shortly after having starred in *Beau Geste.* His good friend H.B. Warner had him declared insane, and Trevor died in an insane asylum in 1929.

505. Ben-Hur: A Tale of the Christ

Rating: ☆☆☆☆

MGM; ***Directed by*** Fred Niblo; ***Assistant Directors:*** B. Reeves Eason, Charles Stallings, Alfred Raboch; ***Screen Adaptatation by*** June Mathis; ***Based on the Novel by*** General Lew Wallace; ***Scenario by*** Carey Wilson; ***Continuity by*** Carey Wilson and Bess Meredyth; ***Photography by*** René Guissart, Percy Hilburn, Karl Struss, Clyde DeVinna; ***Art Effects by*** Ferdinand P. Earle; ***Settings by*** Cedric Gibbons and Horace Jackson; ***Titles by*** Katharine Hilliker and H.H. Caldwell; ***Film Editor:*** Lloyd Nosler; ***Costumes by*** Theaterkunst, Hermann J. Kaufmann, Berlin; ***Running Time of Original, Complete Version:*** 148 minutes; ***Running Time of 1930 Re-Issue:*** 128 minutes; ***Cast:*** JUDAH, BEN-HUR, Ramon Novarro (1899–1968); MESSALA, Francis X. Bushman, Sr. (1883–1966); ESTHER, May McAvoy (1901–1984); PRINCESS OF HUR [BEN-HUR'S MOTHER], Claire McDowell (1878–1966); MARY [MOTHER OF JESUS], Betty Bronson (1906–1971); TIRZAH, Kathleen Key (1907–1954); SIMONIDES, Nigel De Brulier (1877–1948); SHEIK ILDERIM, Mitchell Lewis (1880–1956); SANBALLAT, Leo White (1882–1948); ARRIUS, Frank Currier (1857–1928); BALTHASAR THE EGYPTIAN, Charles Belcher (1872–1943); JOSEPH, Winter Hall (1872–1947); IRAS THE EGYPTIAN, Carmel Myers (1901–1980); ***Notable Cameos in the Chariot Sequence:*** Myrna Loy (1905–1993); Clark Gable (1901–1960)

This second silent adaptation of *Ben-Hur* is by far superior to the 1959 remake. The executives at MGM knew this, thus explaining why they did everything in their power to make sure that all known existing prints of the 1927 version were destroyed when the 1959 version came out. They did not want people to compare the two and see how inferior the 1959 version was. William K. Everson had a print of the 1930 reissue of the 1927 version, and held a screening which coincided close to the release of the 1959 version. MGM's attorneys immediately sent the FBI out to confiscate the print. Fortunately, MGM did preserve the negative of the 1927 version. A beautiful, original print with the Technicolor sequences in tact was preserved in Czechoslovakia, and these Technicolor sequences in the Czechoslovakian print were used for the film's restoration in the 1980s. Kevin Brownlow produced a magnificent presentation of the restoration, using a full orchestral score by Carl Davis. The 1930 reissue version, which is completely in black and white, containing a Vitaphone track with music and sound effects, exists among pri-

A promotional poster for *Ben-Hur: A Tale of the Christ* (1927).

vate collectors. In being able to evaluate all of the various screen versions of *Ben-Hur*, one can go as far as to say that the 1959 sound version is quite boring and drawn-out in spots, and cannot even compare to the original action-packed silent version. Many others who have seen both versions agree. William K. Everson, in his fine 1978 book, *American Silent Film*, went so far as to say, "By any standards, [the 1927 *Ben-Hur*] is far superior to the abysmal 1959 remake...The granting of a dozen Academy Awards to the remake was the final insult!"

This is not to say that the 1959 version was a bad film. It obviously had something going for it to have won 11 of its 12 Academy Award nominations, including Best Picture of 1959. However, it is difficult to improve on an original that was so splendidly and magnificently filmed. William Wyler tried by expanding and adding a few minor details not contained in this original, but the process of making the movie more detailed and historically accurate left it with some very boring sequences.

This story combines the life of Christ with an account of how Messala, a Roman soldier, falsely accused his friend, Judas, Prince of Hur, of deliberately assaulting Gratus, the conqueror of Rome with a ceiling tile, which in actuality accidentally fell from the Hur Palace. Portrayed further in the film are Judas' experiences as a galley slave, his redemption from his sentence, and his ultimate revenge against Messala. The birth and crucifixion of Jesus Christ are also portrayed. The scene with the birth of Jesus Christ is filmed in Technicolor. The portrayal of the Star of Bethlehem over Jesus' manger site is especially well done in this version of the film. Betty Bronson is fabulous in her portrayal of Mary. Some critics criticize the fact that a halo was shown over the Virgin Mary's head, but this is simply a visual interpretation of what the producers imagined might have happened during Jesus' birth. This portrayal of the birth of Christ was magnificently filmed—among the best portrayals of the event in motion picture history. The crucifixion sequence does legitimately leave itself open to a bit of criticism. As Cecil B. DeMille had done in his 1927 adaptation of *The King of Kings*, the producers of *Ben-Hur* made the mistake of showing the nails in the middle of Jesus' palms, rather than just below the hands through the wrist.

Among the other highlights of this film are the spectacularly staged pirate attack sequence, the sequence in the betting ring during which Messala and Ben-Hur come face to face for the first time in years, and, of course, the unforgettable chariot race.

This 1927 *Ben-Hur* was the most expensive film to date at the time it was produced, costing more than $4 million. The producers, directors, and staff overcame many obstacles to complete the film. For starters, the production was begun on location by Samuel Goldwyn's company in Italy. Some of the Italian crew were making so much more money than they were used to that they did not want production, and, ultimately, their jobs, to end. Therefore, they did everything in their power to slow down production progress. Some of their shenanigans included burning down dressing rooms, sabotaging the sets, and even threatening to kidnap May McAvoy. After overcoming these setbacks and returning to Hollywood (where Goldwyn's company merged with Metro and Louis B. Mayer to form MGM), it became apparent that the distractions had marred the Italian location footage to the extent that it was unfit to use, and the whole picture was re-shot at MGM studios. Production work began in late 1923 or early 1924. The film did not premiere until December 30, 1925, at the George M.

Cohan Theatre. Most people who saw it upon its original release saw it in 1926, and the film was copyrighted in 1927.

The sea battle against the pirates was directed by B. Reeves Eason, who was renowned as an excellent director of action sequences based on his westerns. Grotesquely realistic, this is one of the better battle sequences in history, giving even the great battle sequences in *Intolerance* (1916) and *Joan the Woman* (1916) stiff competition. The pirate attack sequence in the 1959 remake is short, limited, inept with obviously miniature models, and absolutely abysmal and unimpressive compared to the 1927 version.

The betting ring sequence is another prime example of this version's superiority over the remake. In this version, one sees Sanballat teasing and chiding the Romans into betting against Ben-Hur, racing as "the unknown Jew." Sanballat urges Messala to bet 10,000 pieces of gold, with 6 to 1 odds—"the difference between a Roman and a Jew." Messala practically strangles Sanballat, calling him a braying fool and asking sarcastically who has 10,000 pieces of gold to wager. At this point, the tension comes to a climax as Ben-Hur pushes his way through the crowd, pulls Messala off of Sanballat, and comes face to face with Messala for the first time since being shipped off to the galleys. Ben-Hur gives Messala the ultimate challenge—betting 50,000 pieces of gold, with no odds. This all takes place within the span of about two minutes of footage, and is an exhilarating part of this movie. On the contrary, the betting sequence in the remake is dragged out into a nearly 10-minute uneventful session of dialogue, without any of the zeal of this original.

The chariot race was filmed using 42 cameras in a setting of over 100 acres. Extras were hired by the thousands for the crowd scenes. Among the extras who can be glimpsed in cameos at an early point in their careers are Clark Gable and Myrna Loy. Myrna Loy has a prominent, brief close-up as part of Messala's entourage of fans, and is readily identifiable. Clark Gable cannot be spotted easily in video versions of the film, although one book features an enlarged still photo in which Gable can be spotted in the crowd. This chariot race holds up just as well as the race in the remake. The only major difference is that the spiked wheels on Messala's chariot which were in the remake do not appear in this original. This is really the only sequence in which the remake was comparable in quality to the one in the 1927 silent.

This classic MGM masterpiece ranks among the few pictures in history that can come close to being worthy of comparison to *Intolerance*, and was certainly far more successful at the box office, having almost broken even on its enormous costs.

506. Berlin: Symphony of a Great City

Rating: ★★★½

Produced in Germany; ***Directed by*** Walter Ruttman; ***Photography by*** Reimar Kuntze, Robert Baberske, Laszlo Schaffe; ***Running Time:*** 62 minutes

This is the highly acclaimed documentary on Berlin, Germany, considered by many to be Walter Ruttman's (1887–1941) finest achievement. The film portrays events in Berlin on a typical day, starting at dawn and ending at midnight. What makes this film so unique is that the montage images are paced in accordance with the rhythm of accompanying symphony music. Despite Ruttman's controversial right wing politics, *Berlin: Symphony of a Great City* demonstrates that he was a brilliant and talented man. Watching it is a fascinating experience.

Walter Ruttman was killed during World War II, while photographing newsreel footage of the war. A stray bullet from the battlefield mortally wounded him.

507. Bringing Up Father

Rating: ☆☆☆

MGM; ***Directed by*** Jack Conway; ***Based on the Newspaper Comic Strip by*** George McManus; ***Continuity by*** Frances Marion; ***Titles by*** Ralph Spence; ***Settings by*** Cedric Gibbons and Merrill Pye; ***Photographed by*** William Daniels; ***Wardrobe by*** Gilbert Clark; ***Film Editor:*** Margaret Booth; ***Running Time:*** 67 minutes; ***Cast:*** JIGGS, J. Farrell MacDonald (1875–1952); DINTY MOORE, Jules Cowles (1877–1943); MAGGIE, Polly Moran (1883–1952); ANNIE MOORE, Marie Dressler (1869–1934); ELLEN, Gertrude Olmstead (1904–1975); DENNIS, Grant Withers (1904–1959); OSWALD, David Mir; GINSBERG, Tenen Holtz (1887–1971)

This is a hilarious marital comedy, filled with witty quips and one-liners by title writer Ralph Spence. One example is a line spoken by the character of Jiggs, who comments on people singing in the bar he frequents: "With that singin'—no wonder Lindbergh stays in the air."

Another great attribute to the film is the irresistible comedy team of Polly Moran and Marie Dressler. This was one of the first films to feature the two together, resulting in unprecedented popularity for both actresses. Dressler plays the wife of Dinty Moore, owner of a bar, as well as the sister of Jiggs, who is married to Maggie, played by Polly Moran. Dressler's and Moran's antics in whipping their husbands into shape (in Moran's case, with Maggie's ever-famous rolling pin) provide riotously funny situations which will provoke laughter for the film's entire duration. The fun really begins when Ellen, the daughter of Dinty and Maggie, meets a man from a wealthy background and invites him to dinner. The role of Ellen's beau, Dennis, is played by Grant Withers, in one of the few "A" pictures that he starred in before being relegated mostly to poverty row productions.

Bringing Up Father is a delightful comedy, based on the popular comic strip of the same name that ran in the Sunday newspapers for several decades. It has never been shown on Turner Classic Movies or released on video by Turner Entertainment or MGM/UA Home Video. It is a shame that this comedy classic circulates only among a few private collectors in copies of poor quality. It deserves better exposure than what it currently has, and is highly worthy of restoration and revival.

Gertrude Olmstead, who plays the daughter in *Bringing Up Father* (1927).

508. Casanova

Rating: ☆☆☆☆

[a.k.a. *The Loves of Casanova*]

Produced in France; ***Directed by*** Alexandre Volkoff; ***Art Direction by*** Noe Bloch; ***Scenario by*** Norbert Falk, Ivan Mosjoukine, and Alexandre Volkoff; ***Running Time:*** 132 minutes; ***Cast:*** CASANOVA, Ivan Mosjoukine (1889–1939); MARIA MARI, Diana Karenne; CATHERINE II, Suzanne Bianchetti (1894–1936); THERESE, Jenny Jugo; CORTICELLI, Rina de Liguoro (1892–1966); LA COMTESSE VERENTZELL, Nina Kochitz; LADY STANHOPE, Olga Day; ORLOFF, Paul Guide; MENUCCI, Carlo Tedeschi; LENEGRILLON, Bouamerane; PIERRE III, Rudolf Klein-Rogge (1888–1955)

This elaborate biopic is the finest achievement of director Alexandre (also spelled "Alexander" in some sources) Volkoff, who had also acted and been a screenwriter in France during the silent era.

Ivan Mosjoukine, who played the title role in addition to having collaborated on the script, was one of France's most popular leading male actors of the 1920s. *Casanova* helped to solidify his reputation, and was the film that Mosjoukine made just before coming to the United States to star in his one and only film in Hollywood, *Surrender* (1927), directed by Edward Sloman and costarring Mary Philbin. Mosjoukine remained a prominent actor throughout the silent era, but his career faltered with the coming of sound. One of his last projects was an unsuccessful 1933 sound remake of *Casanova* called *Les Amours de Casanova*. He retired from the screen in 1936, and died in poverty in 1939.

Casanova starts with an amusing sequence in which Casanova wards off notorious moneylender Menucci, the villain of the film. Menucci, threatening to confiscate everything Casanova owns, is shocked when he practices "sorcery" before his eyes with the help of a book. With a pump handled by unseen friends, Casanova has himself blown up to gigantic proportions, fooling Menucci into thinking that he used something from the book to perform the feat. Menucci demands the book, and Casanova lets him have it on condition that his debt be canceled.

The rest of the film takes us through some of Casanova's various exploits with women, as well as through an account of his second triumph over villain Menucci, who has Casanova arrested and brought before the "Council of Ten" on a variety of trumped-up charges.

This biography on Giacomo Casanova is not only well told and convincingly played, but the film is a thing of beauty in itself. In addition to impressive special effects, the film is richly tinted, and contains an impressive hand colored masked ball sequence as well.

UCLA and the Cinématheque Française collaborated on a beautiful restoration of *Casanova*, adding an excellent orchestral score in 1986. This restoration has recently been shown on European television, from which the evaluated copy was obtained. There has, unfortunately, been no effort to make the film widely available in the United States on video or television.

Casanova is among the finest achievements of French silent cinema, surpassed only by some of the works of Abel Gance. It helps both director Alexandre Volkoff (1885–??) and actor Ivan Mosjoukine assume an indelible place in motion picture history.

509. The Cat and the Canary

Rating: ☆☆☆½

Universal; ***Directed by*** Paul Leni; ***Screenplay by*** Robert F. Hill, Alfred A. Cohn; ***Based on the Stage Play by*** John Willard; ***Titles by*** Walter Anthony; ***Photography by*** Gilbert Warrenton; ***Settings by*** Charles D. Hall; ***Running Time:*** 93 minutes; ***Cast:*** ANNABELLE WEST, Laura LaPlante (1904–1996); PAUL JONES, Creighton Hale (1882–1965); CHARLES WILDER, Forrest Stanley (1889–1969); ROGER CROSBY, Tully Marshall (1864–1943); CECILY YOUNG, Gertrude Astor (1887–1977); HARRY BLYTHE, Arthur Edmund Carewe (1884–1937); SUSAN SILSBY, Flora Finch (1869–1940); "MAMMY" PLEASANT, Martha Mattox (1879–1933); DR. PATTERSON, Lucien Littlefield (1895–1960); HENDRIKS, George Siegmann (1882–1928); MILKMAN, Joe Murphy (1877–1961); TAXI DRIVER, Billy Engle (1889–1960)

For director Paul Leni's American directorial debut, he chose *The Cat and the Canary*, which had been a major success on stage. So popular this story proved to be that three talkie remakes were done in 1930, 1939, and 1978. None had the excellent atmospheric quality of this original silent version.

The story opens with a shot of cats meowing and hovering around the house of Cyrus West, an eccentric millionaire whose family states that he is insane. Like cats around a canary, they hover waiting for him to die so that they can collect his millions.

The day of the will reading comes, and Cyrus West has prepared two envelopes—one with the will, and another with the name of the alternate person that his fortune will go to if the original beneficiary does not meet the conditions of the original will. As his family has gotten on his nerves, the estate is left to his most distant relative with the last name of West—on the condition that said beneficiary is proven by a doctor to be sane.

The beneficiary is Annabelle West. Attorney Roger Crosby, the executor of the will, is just about to tell her the name of the alternate beneficiary when a hand comes from behind a book case and drags him behind it, where Crosby is murdered. Over the rest of the night, strange incidents abound as the unknown alternate beneficiary is trying to drive Annabelle insane so that he or she can collect the inheritance instead.

Laura LaPlante, star of *The Cat and the Canary* (1927), her most famous role.

The Cat and the Canary was widely acclaimed on its original release. The *New York Times* praised it as "one of the finest examples of motion picture art."

Fortunately, this is a film that is in the public domain and widely accessible. Coming out on the heels of the success of Lon Chaney's *The Phantom of the Opera*, this film convinced Universal executives that horror films were big business, and the company is most famous today for its horror films of the early talkie era, a trend originating with *The Cat and the Canary.*

Most video versions of *The Cat and the Canary* are in black and white, but a color tinted version has been released on laser disc.

This was also one of the best roles of silent screen actress Laura LaPlante, and the one, for which she is most readily identified. Other standouts in the cast are Tully Marshall as executor of the estate, and Martha Mattox as the mysterious housekeeper.

510. Crazy to Act

Rating: ☆☆☆

Mack Sennett Comedies; ***Directed by*** Mack Sennett; ***Running Time:*** 21 minutes; ***Cast:*** ETHEL ST. JOHN, Mildred June (1906–1940); ARTHUR YOUNG, Matty Kemp (born 1907); MRS. ST. JOHN, Sunshine Hart (1886–1930); GORDON BAGLEY, Oliver Hardy (1892–1957)

This Sennett comedy features Oliver Hardy as a millionaire who has been chosen by Ethel St. John's mother to be her daughter's future husband. Ethel, who is movie struck, is really in love with Arthur Young, an attractive man who happens to be poor. She agrees to marry Gordon Bagley on the condition that he makes her a movie star. With a whole crew of people who know absolutely nothing about movie making, pandemonium occurs as every conceivable type of mishap occurs.

Mildred June is appealing as the attractive leading lady of *Crazy to Act.* She was 21 years old when it was made. Sadly, she died at age 34 in 1940. No cause of her premature death could be found in the reference sources available.

Of the Sennett comedies from the late 1920s evaluated, this is among the best.

511. The End of St. Petersburg

Rating: ☆☆☆☆

Mezhrabpom-Rus Studio/U.S.S.R.; ***Directed by*** Vselovod Pudovkin and Mikhail Doller; ***Scenario by*** Natan Zarkhi; ***Director of Photography:*** Anatoli Golovnia; ***Art Direction by*** Sergei Kozlovsky; ***Camera Work by*** K. Vents; ***Running Time:*** 87 minutes; ***Cast:*** COMMUNIST WORKING MAN, Alexander Chistiakov; HIS WIFE, Vera Baranovskaia; VILLAGE LAD, Ivan Chuvelev; LEBEDER, V. Obelenski; BALD REVOLUTIONARY, A. Gromov; DISTRICT POLICE CHIEF, Sergei Komarov; REPORTER, M. Tereshkovich; VILLAGE LAD'S FRIEND, V. Chuvelov; ANTI-GERMAN PATRIOT, V. Tsoppi; STOCK BROKER, Nikolai Khmelev; STOCK BROKER, M. Tsibulski; GERMAN OFFICER, Vsevolod Pudovkin (1893–1953); GERMAN OFFICER, Vladimir Fogel (died 1929)

This film was commissioned by the government of the U.S.S.R., in commemoration of the 10-year anniversary of the overthrow of the Czarist regime by the Bolsheviks. It is a classic and powerful film presented in three segments. One plot has a peasant boy in the middle of a labor uprising. The second plot portrays rebellion against the social order of the U.S.S.R. under Czarist rule, and the third shows the storming of St. Petersburg by the Bolshevik revolutionists.

Director Pudovkin, who was greatly inspired by D.W. Griffith's *Intolerance* (1916), presents the strike sequence in a similar fashion to the strike sequence in *Intolerance.* The strikers are shown filing out as the replacement workers file in who, like the scab workers in Griffith's film, do so out of desperation. Pudovkin puts a more personal element on the replacement workers, zeroing in on the boy who is in need of a job and glad for any work that he can get—until he sees the horrible abuses that the workers suffer at the hands of the Czarist soldiers. Griffith's film shows the masses of scab workers from a distance, and concentrates on the personal stories of the strikers who have been replaced.

Pudovkin also followed Griffith fashion in his portrayal of war. Pudovkin deliberately shows the soldiers marching with their heads out of camera range, to symbolize the mindless glory as they are marching off to war, with blasting trumpets, confetti, waving flags and arms, etc. Pudovkin directly leads from this sequence into the contrasting, horrific realities of war, including the nasty, muddy trenches, falling corpses, and even a "point of view" shot showing from a fallen soldier's viewpoint the enemy beating him about the head with a bayonet. Many of the battle sequences on the war front are paralleled with sequences of marching mobs in St. Petersburg.

Of all of Vsevolod Pudovkin's silent era work, this is by far his crowning achievement, ranking with Sergei Eisenstein's *Battleship Potemkin* (1925) and *October* (1927) as among the finest of all Russian silents. It captures one's attention from the outset, and there is not a single idle moment in the entire film.

The End of St. Petersburg was beautifully restored at Mosfilm in 1969 with a magnificent orchestra score and sound effects, and is available on video in the United States from Kino.

512. Eve's Love Letters *Rating:* ☆☆☆

Hal Roach/Pathé; Director Unidentified; ***Running Time:*** 20 minutes; ***Cast:*** THE WIFE [EVE], Agnes Ayres (1896–1940); THE HUSBAND [ADAM], Forrest Stanley (1889–1969); THE BUTLER, Stan Laurel (1890–1965)

Here we have a romantic comedy of historic interest not only because it starred Stan Laurel before he was teamed with Oliver Hardy, but because it was among the last films in which Agnes Ayres would receive top billing. This film, for some reason, does not appear in Ayres' filmographies either in *The Film Encyclopedia* by Ephraim Katz, or in John T. Weaver's *Twenty Years of Silents*.

Eve's Love Letters has Ayres playing a wife who is being blackmailed with steamy love letters she has written to one "Sir Oliver Hardy," who appears in the film in name only. The ransom demanded is $10,000, and she seeks help retrieving the letters from her butler, played by Laurel. They go to Hardy's house in search of the letters, and the husband comes looking for his wife. Wife and butler disguise themselves as female fashion models to get back home before the husband does. Stan Laurel, in drag, makes the husband, who flirted with him/her, think he's got to get rid of the extra woman before his wife returns.

Agnes Ayres demonstrates a good penchant for comedy in this delightful and rare situation farce. Unfortunately, she was among the actresses who did not make the transition to sound successfully. In 1940, she died of a cerebral hemorrhage in a sanitarium where she was seeking treatment for extreme depression. She was only 44 when she died on Christmas Day.

Of three filmographies of Stan Laurel, only one listed *Eve's Love Letters*. It is a shame that this highly entertaining and funny title remains such an obscure rarity that is hardly ever mentioned. It is one that deserves to be brought back into the limelight.

513. Exit Smiling

Rating: ☆☆½

Beatrice Lillie, star of *Exit Smiling* (1927) in later years. She actually looked better as she got older.

MGM; ***Directed by*** Sam Taylor; ***Story by*** Marc Connelly; ***Scenario by*** Sam Taylor and Tim Whelan; ***Titles by*** Joe Farnham; ***Settings by*** Cedric Gibbons, Frederic Hope; ***Wardrobe by*** Andre Ani; ***Photography by*** Andre Barlatier; ***Film Editor:*** Denise J. Gray; ***Running Time:*** 69 minutes; ***Cast:*** VIOLET, Beatrice Lillie (1894–1989); JIMMY MARSH, Jack Pickford (1896–1933); OLGA, Doris Lloyd (1896–1968); ORLANDO WAINWRIGHT, DeWitt Jennings (1872–1937); JESSE WATSON, Harry Myers (1882–1938); TOD POWELL, Tenen Holtz (1887–1971); PHYLLIS, Louise Lorraine (1902–1981); CECIL LOVELACE, Franklin Pangborne (1889–1958)

This was the one and only silent film to star the great stage comedienne Beatrice Lillie. In this film, she plays Violet, the "patsy" with a second string touring stage show. She gets stuck with the behind the scenes jobs and parts that nobody else wants. The leading man is Jack Pickford, who plays Jimmy Marsh, a banker who has been falsely accused of stealing money. Violet takes a liking to Marsh, and helps him to get hired with her company until he can find another job. While Marsh is with the company, Violet single-handedly foils the thieves who really took the bank's money, and manages to get evidence that will clear Marsh in the process. Unfortunately, Marsh is never made aware of what Violet did for him, and goes back to his regular life and sweetheart.

Exit Smiling is a delightful film with a good blend of drama and comedy sequences. The bittersweet ending is disappointing, but conveys a significant message. It gets across the point that often the people who make things happen behind the scenes do not get the credit and recognition that they deserve.

While Beatrice Lillie is excellent in this film, one can see why she stopped at one silent. Much of her appeal rested in her voice and manner of speaking. If one does not hear the golden voice, one misses out on a significant part of the Beatrice Lillie experience. Jack Pickford is a competent actor, but a rather weak leading man who leaves a bit to be desired in this film. Doris Lloyd has a nice presence as the wisecracking and sarcastic Olga, the star of the stage production.

514. The Fair Co-Ed

Rating: ☆☆☆½

MGM; ***Directed by*** Sam Wood; ***Adaptation and Continuity by*** Byron Morgan; ***Titles by*** Joe Farnham; ***Settings by*** Cedric Gibbons and Arnold Gillespie; ***Photography by*** John Seitz; ***Running Time:*** 69 minutes; ***Cast:*** MARION BRIGHT, Marion Davies (1897–1961); BOB DIXON,

Johnny Mack Brown (1904–1974); BETTY, Jane Winton (1905–1959); ROSIE COOK, Thelma Hill (1906–1938); HOUSEKEEPER, Lillianne Leighton (1874–1956); HERBERT, Gene Stone
Cast Member Deleted from Final Cut: BIT COMEDY PART, Pepi Lederer (1910–1935)

Starting with the success of Harold Lloyd's *The Freshman* (1925), a number of popular college comedies were released by various artists of the late 1920s. Clara Bow and Gilbert Roland got into the act with *The Plastic Age*, released in late 1925. MGM followed in 1926, starring William Haines and Mary Brian in *Brown of Harvard.* As good as the other college comedies were, Marion Davies topped them all in *The Fair Co-Ed.*

The story starts out with Ms. Davies as Marion Bright arguing with her father about Bingham College. She refuses to attend because of the college's ban of automobiles on campus. But, she changes her mind when a handsome salesman from Bingham knocks on the door—selling books to pay his tuition. Marion declares to her father, "I'll go to Bingham, but you'll never know the reason why."

Once Marion gets to Bingham, she discovers her talent for basketball, and makes the team. She falls for Bob Dixon, the coach of the women's team. Her arrogant wit and sarcasm get her into hot water with both her teammates and the coach. Her one big shot at redemption is to lead the team to victory in the big game against Claxton, which provides an entertaining finale to the film.

Among the highlights of *The Fair Co-Ed* are the sequence of the students protesting against the campus ban on automobiles, and the big basketball game at the end. But, what really puts this film over is the wit of Marion Bright.

This film was directed by Sam Wood (1883–1949), whose other silent era credits include *Peck's Bad Boy* (1921) with Jackie Coogan and *Beyond the Rocks* (1922) with Rudolph Valentino and Gloria Swanson. In the talkie era, he directed such classics as *Goodbye, Mr. Chips* (1939), *Kitty Foyle* (1940), *The Pride of the Yankees* (1942), and *For Whom the Bell Tolls* (1943). His role in the blacklisting of many Hollywood performers during the McCarthy hysteria of the 1950s gave him an infamous distinction as a man who ruined many lives and destroyed many promising careers.

The Fair Co-Ed is also historically important as the first major role that Johnny Mack Brown played during his career of nearly 40 years. He started out in roles featuring boy-next-door types in such films as *Our Dancing Daughters* (1928), *Annapolis* (1928), and *Coquette* (1929). With his success in the title role of *Billy the Kid* (1930), the rest of his movie career was in westerns and serials, the last being *Apache Uprising* (1966).

Lillianne (also spelled "Lillian" in some sources) Leighton's career began in 1911 in *The Two Orphans* when she was 37 years old. She played character roles in a number of films which included *Cinderella* (1914), *Joan the Woman* (1916), *The Jack-Knife Man* (1920), *The Girl from God's Country* (1921), *Peck's Bad Boy* (1921), and *Abraham Lincoln* (1924). Thelma Hill's career began as one of Mack Sennett's bathing beauties. She died at the young age of 32 in 1938. No further data on Gene Stone is known.

In Louise Brooks' book, *Lulu in Hollywood*, there is a chapter on Marion Davies' niece, whose name was Pepi Lederer. Lederer was a lesbian who suffered from chronic alcoholism which eventually led to cocaine addiction. She had a witty personality, and was given a small comedy role by Sam Wood in this film. Unfortunately, for some reason or another, despite praise from those who saw her perform, her part was deleted from the final cut. When Ms. Lederer was only 25 years old, Marion Davies and William

Randolph Hearst realized that she desperately needed help for her cocaine addiction, and had her committed to a drug rehabilitation sanitarium. Lederer committed suicide by jumping out her window, and was killed instantly upon impact. *The Fair Co-Ed* is a film that is, unfortunately, inaccessible to the general public. The copy reviewed here was a poor quality copy from a private collection. This is yet another Marion Davies silent that deserves to be seen by a wider audience. A pristine print does exist in Turner Entertainment's archives, but it has not been aired on Turner Classic Movies or released on video.

515. The First Auto

Rating: ☆☆½

Warner Brothers; ***Directed by*** Roy Del Ruth; ***Assistant Director:*** D. Ross Lederman; ***Written by*** Darryl F. Zanuck; ***Screenplay by*** Anthony Colewey; ***Photography by*** David Abel; ***Edited by*** Martin Bolger; ***Titles by*** Jack Jarmuth; ***Art Direction by*** Lewis Geib, Esdras Hartley; ***Electric Effects:*** F.N. Murphy; ***Costumes by*** Alpharetta; ***Music Score by*** Herman Heller; ***Synchronization by*** Vitaphone; ***Running Time:*** 77 minutes; ***Cast:*** ROSE ROBBINS, Patsy Ruth Miller (1904–1995); BOB ARMSTRONG, Charles Emmett Mack (1900–1927); HANK ARMSTRONG, Russell Simpson (1880–1959); MAYOR ROBBINS, Frank Campeau (1864–1943); THE BLACKSMITH, Gibson Gowland (1877–1951); THE AUCTIONEER, Anders Randolph (1870–1930); THE VILLAGE CUT-UP, William Demarest (1892–1983); STEVE, Paul Kruger (1895–1960); SQUIRE STEBBINS, Douglas Gerrard (1891–1950); THE MASTER DRIVER, Barney Oldfield (1878–1946)

This film was one of the silents with synchronized music and sound effects that was featured as part of the "Dawn of Sound" restoration project completed by Robert Gitt of UCLA in conjunction with AT & T, the Packard Foundation, and various archives. It could technically be considered a part-talkie, as three words are spoken in it—one at a time on three different occasions. Hank Armstrong calls his son Bob's name twice in different intervals in the film, and the word "go" is heard at the beginning of a race pitting a horseless carriage against a horse and carriage.

The First Auto uses a nice blend of comedy and drama to portray the story of the coming of age of the automobile, also known as "the horseless carriage." Charles Emmett Mack plays Bob Armstrong, the son of Hank Armstrong, a prominent horse dealer who is resistant to the coming of the automobile, as such would endanger the horse business. Patsy Ruth Miller plays Bob's girlfriend. Friction is created between father and son when Bob realizes and accepts the inevitability of the automobile taking over, going against his father's resistance to the change.

Roy Del Ruth (1895–1961), the director of this film, started his film career in 1915 as a writer and gag man for Mack Sennett. In the late 1910s and early 1920s, he directed a number of two-reel comedies starring such comedians as Ben Turpin, Billy Bevan, and Harry Langdon. He graduated to features in the mid–1920s, and maintained his career until his death in 1961. Some of his significant talkie era credits include the 1931 version of *The Maltese Falcon* and *The Broadway Melody of 1936*.

The First Auto was the last film that Charles Emmett Mack was to star in. When filming in Los Angeles was almost completed, Mack went to Riverside to film the sequences for the car race finale at the end of the film. On his way to the Riverside race track from his hotel, he was speeding down the highway, hit another vehicle, and was killed in the accident. A double was used for the long shots in the race sequence, and the ending had to be modified to compensate for Mack's absence. Instead of showing Bob and Rose married and living happily ever after, the film instead shows Bob and his father's new automobile business. The absence of Bob and Rose is explained in the titles as their having attended the horse show instead of the car race.

Those who remember William Demarest as "Uncle Charlie" in the *My Three Sons* television series will be delighted to see him in a bit part in this film, which was one of his earliest screen appearances. Also making a cameo is the famous race car driver Barney Oldfield.

The First Auto would be considered standard fare by most standards, but it is an interesting and entertaining film, with some interesting history behind it. It has not been released on video, but is aired on Turner Classic Movies every now and then, and worth watching.

516. Flesh and the Devil

Rating: ☆½

MGM; ***Directed by*** Clarence Brown; ***Assistant Director:*** Charles Dorian; ***Based on Hermann Sudermann's*** *The Undying Past*; ***Titles by*** Marion Ainslee; ***Settings by*** Cedric Gibbons and Frederic Hope; ***Wardrobe by*** Andre Ani; ***Photography by*** William Daniels; ***Film Editor:*** Lloyd Nosler; ***Running Time:*** 103 minutes; ***Cast:*** LEO VON HARDEN, John Gilbert (1899–1936); FELICITAS, Greta Garbo (1905–1990); ULRICH VON ELTZ, Lars Hanson (1887–1965); HERTHA, Barbara Kent (born 1906); UNCLE KUTOWSKI, William Orlamond (1867–1957); PASTOR VOSS, George Fawcett (1860–1939); LEO'S MOTHER, Eugenie Besserer (1868–1934); COUNT VON RHADEN, Marc McDermott (1881–1929); MINNA, Marcelle Corday

This is a trite and tiresome romantic drama that used the box-office drawing power of Greta Garbo, Lars Hanson, and John Gilbert to give it appeal to the public.

Set in Austria, Gilbert and Hanson play officers in the military who fall in love with Garbo's character, Felicitas. Their fascination with her causes a rift in their long term friendship, culminating in the two suitors challenging each other to a duel. The men reflect on their friendship and good times of the past, and neither can draw on the other, and they embrace. Meanwhile, Felicitas, having had Hertha, the sister of Leo, appeal to her conscience, is on her way to stop the duel when she falls through thin ice in a frozen lake and drowns.

The only factor that brings any life to *Flesh and the Devil* at all is the excellent performance of Barbara Kent as Hertha. Ms. Kent steals the show from all three of the leading players, and the film is worth watching for her performance and her performance only.

Director Clarence Brown (1890–1987) did the best he could with the material he was working with, but as the old cliché goes: "garbage in, garbage out."

This film is typical of much of the substandard material that Louis B. Mayer and Irving Thalberg were putting Garbo into, and it is a miracle that her career survived long enough for her to display the full potential of her marvelous talent in *Queen Christina* (1933).

517. Frate Francesco

Rating: ☆☆½

Produced in Italy; ***Directed by*** Guilio Antamaro; ***Titles by*** Franklin Murray; ***Edited by*** Pierre

Arnaud; ***Synchronized Music and Effects by*** Powers Cinephone; ***Running Time:*** 75 minutes; ***Cast:*** SAINT FRANCIS, Alberto Pasquali; PIETRO DE BERNARDONE (FATHER OF FRANCIS), Alfredo Robert; DONALDO SASSOROSSO, Romuald Joube (1876–1949); COUNT DE SCIFI, Franz Sala; LANDO DEGLI ONESTI, Ugo Biandi; MONA PICA (MOTHER OF FRANCIS), Elene Baranowich; MINIA DI LEROS, Donatella Gimo; CLARE, Bice Jani; AGNES, Enna De Rasi

This is a rare Italian biopic on the life of the Roman Catholic Saint Francis. The movie begins showing the young adult Francis, the son of a wealthy merchant, at a party for the nobility. A leper shows up at the party, wreaking havoc and panic among the crowd. It is at this point that Francis has pity for the leper, and resolves to devote his life to helping the poor and less fortunate. We are then shown to the battle of Assisi, a city fighting to maintain its independence from Perugia. The battle sequences are brief, but the crowd scenes of the aftermath of the battle are impressive. Assisi is conquered. At this point, Francis becomes a warrior knight for Pope Innocent III. Shortly after accepting the post, he becomes ill, and the vision of an angel comes to him pleading against war and for peace, resulting in his return to Assisi amidst jeers from his fellow colleagues. The rest of the film details the trials and tribulations of Francis and his followers, which included Saint Clare, through to his eventual death.

While this film falls short of masterpiece status, it is well put-together and interesting. It features impressive settings and good costumes, and has a number of good scenes.

518. The Gaucho

Rating: ☆☆☆½

United Artists; ***Directed by*** F. Richard Jones; ***Story by*** Elton Thomas; ***Photographed by*** Tony Gaudio; ***Production Manager:*** Theodore Reed; ***Scenario Editor:*** Lotta Woods; ***Research Director:*** Arthur Woods; ***Art Direction by*** Carl Oscar Borg; ***Costumes by*** Paul Burns; ***Film Editor:*** William Nolan; ***Running Time:*** 95 minutes; ***Cast:*** THE GAUCHO, Douglas Fairbanks, Sr. (1883–1939); MOUNTAIN GIRL, Lupe Velez (1908–1944); GIRLS OF THE SHRINE, Geraine Greear and Eve Southern; RUIZ [THE USURPER], Gustav von Seyffertitz (1863–1943); USURPER'S FIRST LIEUTENANT, Michael Vavitch (1885–1930); GAUCHO'S FIRST LIEUTENANT, Charles Stevens (1893–1964); PADRE, Nigel de Brulier (1877–1948); VICTIM OF BLACK DOOM, Albert McQuarrie (1882–1950); THE VIRGIN MARY [UNBILLED], Mary Pickford (1892–1979)

The Gaucho was one of Douglas Fairbanks' more serious efforts. Fairbanks' biographer Gary Carey states in his book, *Doug and Mary*, that "[Lupe Velez] is...one of the few good things about *The Gaucho*, which is...arguably [Fairbanks'] worst film." This reviewer fails to see the basis for such an opinion. It is true that *The Gaucho* pales in comparison to *The Mark of Zorro* (1920), *The Thief of Bagdad* (1924), and *The Iron Mask* (1929), but it is better than *Mr. Robinson Crusoe* (1932), *Robin Hood* (1922), or *The Nut* (1921).

The Gaucho opens up with a miracle being performed at a small pond which has healing powers that cure the sick and bring the dead back to life. Fairbanks is "the gaucho," an Argentine bandit determined to protect the shrine of the miracle from being taken over by greedy officials wanting to cash in. He takes over the city, and ends government abuse. But, karma comes to roost when a leper appeals to him for help, and he banishes him from the township, telling him that he should go kill himself. The gaucho contracts "the black doom" himself, and his only hope of being saved is by the miracle shrine and prayer.

Lupe Velez and Douglas Fairbanks, Sr., in *The Gaucho* (1927).

This plot follows the same formula as some of Fairbanks' previous efforts in which he frees people from tyranny and terrorism, but puts a new twist with himself also being saved from the doom of leprosy. He also demonstrates the fact that smoking is glamorous, with his frequent cigarette smoking adding an aura of sophistication. Lupe Velez, as leading lady, spices up the film with her presence as the mountain girl who helps the gaucho. This was Ms. Velez's second film appearance, following her debut in Laurel and Hardy's *Sailors Beware* (1927). She is as hot blooded in this film as she reportedly was in real life. Gustav von Seyffertitz is good as the villain, but not as strikingly evil and repulsive as he was in other films—namely Mary Pickford's *Sparrows* (1926). Speaking of Pickford, she makes an unbilled appearance as the image of the Virgin Mary, and appears in the miracle scenes. Among the other supporting players is Eve Southern, who is the first girl to be healed at the miracle shrine after a fall. Although she was 29 when she appeared in *The Gaucho*, she had a youthful enough appearance to have passed for 14 or 15. Ms. Southern made her debut as an extra in *Intolerance* (1916), and did close to 20 films from 1921 to 1929. As far as can be determined, *The Gaucho* is her only other surviving work besides *Souls for Sale* (1923).

Among the many impressive sequences is the cattle stampede at the end of the film, featuring thousands of bulls running together for as far as one can see in the camera range.

The Gaucho was originally released with a Technicolor sequence. Unfortunately, all currently available prints of the film have this sequence in black and white only.

519. The General

Rating: ☆☆☆☆

United Artists; ***Directed by*** Buster Keaton and Clyde Bruckman; ***Running Time:*** 107 minutes; ***Cast:*** JOHNNIE GRAY, Buster Keaton (1895–1966); ANNABELLE LEE, Marion Mack (1902–1989); HER FATHER, Charles Smith (1865–1942); HER BROTHER, Frank Barnes (1875–1940); CAPTAIN ANDERSON, Glenn Cavender (1883–1962); GENERAL THATCHER, Jim Farley (1882–1947); RECRUITING OFFICER, Frank Hagney (1884–1973); CONFEDERATE OFFICER, Joe Keaton (1867–1946)

The General is widely acclaimed as Buster Keaton's masterpiece, as well as one of the top ten comedies of all time.

The story starts out in Atlanta, Georgia, with Keaton as Johnnie Gray, a railroad engineer who has two loves in his life—his engine, which is his train called the General Lee—and his girl, Annabelle Lee. All is well until Fort Sumter is fired upon—the short heard 'round the world, which started the Civil War. Of course, the first thing Annabelle asks Johnnie is if he plans to enlist in the Confederate Armed Forces.

Gray, wanting to enlist, runs to the recruiting office to be first in line. Despite his repeated efforts, his important occupation as railroad engineer precludes him from being accepted into the forces—the reason being that he is more valuable to the South as an engineer than he would be on the war front. When Gray tries to explain this to Annabelle, she does not believe him and thinks he is a coward, refusing to see him again.

The story cuts to a year later, where the Union Army is plotting to steal Keaton's train and rob it for the use of the Northern troops. Among the passengers on the train is Annabelle, who is kidnapped as a hostage. When Gray sees that his train has been stolen, the great railroad chase begins. Throughout the chase, a number of amazing, death-defying stunts are performed. The cleverness of these sequences is unparalleled, and only a genius like Keaton could have contrived such situations and pulled off the routines.

Following the chase, Keaton ends up in Yankee territory, hidden under the table of the Union soldiers. It is here that he sees that Annabelle is being held hostage, and also overhears plans for a surprise attack on the Confederates. Gray must now find a way to rescue Annabelle and get back to his home territory to warn of the impending attack.

A most spectacular sequence which occurs in this film is when Keaton's character sets a bridge on fire, partially burning it behind him to keep the Union Army from being able to cross. The Union general determines that the bridge is not burned enough to be unsafe, and gives orders to proceed. The train gets halfway across the bridge before it collapses. This clip is used in many retrospective documentaries on silent comedy. Knowing that this is a real train going down with the collapse of the bridge makes it that much more exciting to watch.

In addition to being one of Buster Keaton's best films, *The General* is also the one film of Marion Mack's known to survive. Ms. Mack made only four films during her career in the movies. The first, *Mary of the Movies* (1923) was among the first films produced by Columbia Pictures, and was one of the all-star silent extravaganzas—much in the style of *Souls for Sale* (1923), *Hollywood* (1923), and *Show People* (1928). She also starred in *One of the Bravest* (1925) and *The Carnival Girl* (1926) before making *The General*, which was her last film. Despite the brevity of Ms. Mack's career, her role in *The General* gives her an immortal place in motion picture history.

When *The General* was released, it lost money. This was in part due to the high production costs. Due to Keaton's unwillingness to compromise and economize on his independent productions, he would independently produce only one film after *The General*, which was *Steamboat Bill, Jr.*, before going to work for MGM as a contract player.

520. Hotel Imperial

Rating: ☆☆☆

Paramount; ***Directed by*** Mauritz Stiller; ***Screenplay by*** Jules Forthmann; ***Titles by*** Edwin Justus Mayer; ***Photography by*** Bert Glennon; ***Edited by*** F. Lloyd Sheldon; ***Running Time:*** 78 minutes; ***Cast:*** ANNA, Pola Negri (1897–1987); LIEUTENANT ALMASY, James Hall (1900–1940); RUSSIAN GENERAL, George Siegmann (1882–1928); PETROFF, Michael Vavitch (1885–1930); ELIAS, Max Davidson (1875–1950); ANTON, Otto Fries (1887–1938); AUSTRIAN GENERAL, Joseph Swickard (1866–1940); ADJUTANT, Nicholas Soussanin (1889–1975)

This is the last of director Mauritz Stiller's surviving work, and is also among the best of Pola Negri's surviving silents available for evaluation. The success of this film led to a follow-up collaboration between Stiller and Negri called *The Woman on Trial* (1927), which is classified as a lost film. Stiller died the following year from a respiratory ailment.

Set in World War I Austria, *Hotel Imperial* has Pola Negri playing Anna, a hotel maid in whose place of employment a Russian army invades. A handsome Austrian spy, Lieutenant Almasy, is wounded and seeking refuge, and Anne takes him in and hides him, disguising him as a waiter. The Russian general is keen on Anna, showering her with gifts and wanting her to be his mistress. She plays the game as long as she can out of fear, but the time comes when the lieutenant assassinates one of Russia's top spies in the hotel, and Anna puts her life on the line to provide him with an alibi.

Pola Negri, star of *Hotel Imperial* (1927).

This was the fourth film appearance of James Hall, and was his first major role that shot him to stardom. He went on to another good role in John Ford's *Four Sons* (1928), but is best remembered for his starring role in *Hell's Angels* (1930) opposite Jean Harlow. Unfortunately, chronic alcoholism led to the demise of Hall's career after 1932, and he went from being a top paid star making $2,500 a week to being unemployed and broke. The alcohol eventually led to his death at 39 in 1940 from cirrhosis of the liver.

Another supporting player, Michael Vavitch, also died just three years after starring in this film. His death at age 53 in 1930 was caused by a heart attack that he suffered while driving.

521. Hula

Rating: ☆☆☆

Clara Bow, star of *Hula* (1927).

Paramount; ***Directed by*** Victor Fleming; ***Photography by*** William Marshall; ***Editor:*** F. Lloyd Sheldon; ***Adapted by*** Doris Anderson; ***From the Novel by*** Armine Von Tempski; ***Titles by*** George Marion, Jr.; ***Screenplay by*** Ethel Doherty; ***Running Time:*** 62 minutes; ***Cast:*** HULA CALHOUN, Clara Bow (1905–1965); ANTHONY HALDANE, Clive Brook (1887–1974); MARGARET HALDANE, Patricia DuPont (1894–1973); HARRY DEHAN, Arnold Ken; KAHANA, Agostino Borgato (1871–1939); BILL CALHOUN, Albert Gray; MRS. BANE, Arlette Marchal (1902–1984)

Another Victor Fleming/Clara Bow collaboration, following their success with *Mantrap* (1926), *Hula* is set in the Hawaiian islands. Clara Bow plays the title role as the girl who falls in love with engineer Anthony. There is one obstacle standing in the way of their being able to marry—Anthony's estranged wife. Margaret Haldane, who has left her husband because he is poor, suddenly reappears when she finds out that he is about to become wealthy. It is up to Hula to hatch a plot to expose her for the gold digging leech that she really is.

This film, while highly enjoyable, was not quite the success that *Mantrap* was. This is in part due to the fact that leading man Clive Brook came off as very bland. While Brook was a highly accomplished and capable actor, silent comedies just weren't his thing. He came across much better in silent dramas like *Underworld* (1927) and later in comedies like *On Approval* (1943) in the talkie era. Clara Bow's spunk is what really puts this film over, and makes it well worth watching.

Unfortunately, all circulating copies of *Hula* are of only mediocre print quality, and a lot of the beauty of the island scenery is lost in these inferior prints. But, with as many of the Paramount silents that were lost, it is fortunate that *Hula* has survived at all and is available for viewing today.

522. It!

Rating: ☆☆☆½

Paramount; ***Directed by*** Clarence Badger and Josef Von Sternberg; ***Photography by*** H. Kinley Martin; ***Story and Adaptation by*** Elinor Glyn; ***Screenplay by*** Hope Loring and Louis D. Lighton; ***Titles by*** George F. Marion, Jr.; ***Editor:*** F. Lloyd Sheldon; ***Running Time:*** 69 minutes; ***Cast:*** BETTY LOU SPENCE, Clara Bow (1905–1965); CYRUS T. WALTHAM, Antonio Moreno (1887–1967); MOLLY, Priscilla Bonner (1899–1996); MONTY, William Austin (1884–1975); MRS. VAN NORMAN, Julia Swayne Gordon (1878–1933); NEWSPAPER REPORTER, Gary Cooper (1901–1961); Elinor Glyn (1864–1943) as herself

Of all of the flapper movies of the 1920s, this is "it"—the definitive flapper movie of the period. Based on the book by Elinor Glyn, the film opens with a title card which gives the specific definition of "it" as written by Glyn herself, as follows:

> "It" is that quality possessed by some which draws all others with its magnetic force. With "it," you can draw all men if you are a woman, and all women if you are a man. "It" can be a quality of the mind as well as a physical attraction.

The only thing that Elinor Glyn forgot to think about was the gay segment of the population in her wording of the definition of "it."

In this film, Clara Bow plays a department store clerk named Betty Lou Spence at Waltham's. Antonio Moreno plays Cyrus T. Waltham, the young heir and owner of the store, to whom Spence is attracted. When he does not pay attention to her, and her coworkers needle her about it, she tells her coworkers, "Just you wait—I'll take the snap out of your garters yet!"

Betty Spence overhears Waltham's plans to dine at the Ritz that night, and makes up her mind to conveniently show up at the same time. Since she does not have an evening gown, and no money to buy one, she and her roommate, Molly, take a pair of scissors to one of her work outfits and improvise.

When Betty arrives at the Ritz with her date, Waltham sees her and is obviously attracted, but does not recognize her from the store. They hit it off immediately. It is in this restaurant sequence that Elinor Glyn makes a cameo appearance.

Although this is essentially a light romantic comedy, there is a sequence reminiscent of D.W. Griffith's *Intolerance*. It is discovered by meddling "uplifters" that Betty's roommate, Molly, has a baby, but due to health complications cannot return to work at Waltham's for some time. The uplifters, upon hearing of this single mother with no job, investigate and try to take the baby away from her. Betty comes onto the scene and claims that the baby is hers, telling the uplifters where to go. Clara Bow has a certain, inimitable way of portraying this sequence, and can pull it off like no one else can. The claim that the baby is hers is overheard, gets all over town as "fact," and causes problems in Spence's relationship with Waltham.

This is a really delightful film, and gives us a historic glimpse of what life in the urban areas of the carefree late 1920s was like—from clothing styles, word expressions, society fads, morals, attitudes, etc. Clara Bow is the quintessential flapper with "it," and for viewers who are attracted to men, Antonio Moreno possesses "it" to the same degree as Bow. In addition, Gary Cooper can be seen in an early cameo appearance.

This is a good movie to watch for those days when one wants to see something that is light, funny, and does not require a lot of thought to comprehend.

523. The Italian Straw Hat

Rating: ☆

Albatros Pictures/France; ***Directed by*** René Clair; ***Running Time:*** 84 minutes; ***Cast:*** MARC MICHEL, Eugene Labiche; COUSINS, Alice Tissot (1890–1971), Alexis Bondi; LA MARIEE, Maryse Maia; NANANCOURT, M. Yvonneck; ROBIN, M. Prefils; FADINARD, Albert Prejean (1893–1979); LIEUTENANT TAVERNIER, Vital Geymand; ANAIS DE BEAUPERTHUIS, Olga Tschekova; L'ONCLE VESINET, Paul Olivier; FELIX, Alex Allin; LE MAIRE, M. Volbert; BEAUPERTHUIS, Jim Gerald (1889–1958)

This is a situation comedy that revolves around a wedding. A certain Italian straw hat has been eaten by a horse, and the quest to get another hat like it before the wedding starts is complicated. This film is considered by many historians to be René Clair's (1898–1981) most outstanding achievement.

While *The Italian Straw Hat* does have its hilarious satirical moments, the narrative is rather haphazardly put together. The story is illogical and makes little sense. If this is Clair's best work, he has obviously been overrated as a director.

524. The Jazz Singer

Rating: ☆☆☆

Warner Brothers; ***Directed by*** Alan Crosland; ***Assistant Director:*** Gordon Hollingshead; ***Based on the Play by*** Samson Raphaelson; ***Screen Adaptation by*** Alfred A. Cohn; ***Photography by*** Hal Mohr; ***Edited by*** Harold McCord; ***Titles by*** Jack Jarmuth; ***Sound Synchronization by*** Vitaphone; ***Vitaphone Score Conducted by*** Louis Silvers; ***Running Time:*** 89 minutes; ***Cast:*** JAKIE RABONOWITZ [JACK ROBIN], Al Jolson (1886–1950); MARY DALE, May McAvoy (1901–1984); THE CANTOR, Warner Oland (1880–1938); SARA RABINOWITZ, Eugenie Besserer (1868–1934); MOISHA YADELSEN, Otto Lederer (1886–1965); JAKIE RABINOWITZ [AGE 13], Bobby Gordon; HARRY LEE, Richard Tucker (1883–1942); CONCERT RECITAL CANTOR, Cantor Joseff Rosenblatt (1882–1933)

Here we have what is widely and erroneously credited as the first talkie. It was awarded a Special Academy Award in 1927–28 for its technical innovation. It was neither the first talkie nor the first film with talking sequences. The first all-talking picture was *Lights of New York* (1928). Films with talking sequences had been experimented with in the early 1900s. A performance by musician Eubie Blake was recorded in sound in 1923. Alice Guy-Blaché was experimenting with sound films in the early 1900s. *The Jazz Singer*'s legitimate claim to fame was that it was the first feature with talking sequences to really become a box-office hit, causing the public to clamor for and demand more talking pictures. It was the film that sounded the death knell for the silent era—setting the progress of motion picture photography back many decades. The art of silent film which was really starting to become perfected with masterpieces such as *The Wind* was stopped in its tracks when sound came in, returning the movies once again to a somewhat primitive state.

The Jazz Singer was cleverly produced, and was probably the most appropriate type of story to open the talkie era with. Al Jolson demonstrates an aura of great charisma, and one can see why he was so successful on the vaudeville circuit, and why it was he who was able to put over a transformation in motion pictures which had previously met with great resistance. He gives an excellent performance in this film, in which he plays the adult role of Jack Robin, who is a successful Broadway and vaudeville entertainer disowned by his father, who had his heart set on his son following in his footsteps as a Jewish cantor. When Jack gets his big break, his father becomes terminally ill, and he must decide whether to postpone the show, possibly giving up his chance at super stardom, or whether to go to his dying father, who wants him to sing for the church.

The leading lady of this film is May McAvoy. Ms. McAvoy, as the leading actress, was surprisingly not among the characters chosen to speak in this film. It was revealed in interviews that the reason McAvoy was not chosen to speak was because she resisted the sexual advances of Darryl F. Zanuck, then a powerful figure at Warner Brothers. To

Al Jolson as *The Jazz Singer* (1927).

retaliate against McAvoy's rejection, Zanuck refused to let McAvoy do a speaking role in this film, and instead made sure that the publicity papers erroneously stated that McAvoy's voice was not suited to the new medium because of a "lisp" which indeed was nonexistent. In fact, McAvoy was very well received in *The Terror* (1928). Shortly after this talkie was completed, McAvoy married Maurice Cleary, who was at the time treasurer of United Artists. She made the decision to retire from film work to devote her time to her family. She later worked for MGM in bit parts in the 1940s and 1950s.

Although *The Jazz Singer* is a rather mediocre film compared to the many silent masterpieces, it remains the best version of the three motion picture adaptations (1927, 1953, and 1980) of the story. Its place as one of the five most historically important films in all of movie history makes it a "must" for all movie enthusiasts and historians.

525. The Kid Brother *Rating:* ☆☆☆☆

Harold Lloyd Corporation/Paramount; ***Directed by*** Ted Wilde, J.A. Howe, and Lewis Milestone; ***Assistant Director:*** Gaylord Lloyd; ***Story by*** John Grey, Ted Wilde, and Tom Crizer; ***Scenario by*** John Grey, Lex Neal, and Howard Green; ***Photography by*** Walter Lundin and Henry N. Kohler; ***Production Manager:*** John L. Murphy; ***Editor:*** Allen McNeil; ***Art Direction by*** Liell K. Vedder; ***Technical Director:*** William MacDonald; ***Cast:*** HAROLD HICKORY, Harold Lloyd (1893–1971); MARY POWERS, Jobyna Ralston (1900–1967); JIM HICKORY, Walter James (1882–1946); LEO HICKORY, Leo Willis (1890–1952); OLIN HICKORY, Olin Francis (1892–1952); SANDONI, Constantine Romanoff (1873–??); "FLASH" FARRELL, Eddie Boland (1885–1935); SAM HOOPER, Frank Lanning (1872–1945); HANK HOOPER, Ralph Yearsley (1896–1928)

This Lloyd classic was the first silent film that this reviewer ever saw, which sparked a lifelong fascination with and addiction to silent films. One aspect about the film that made an impression was the underlying theme with Lloyd playing the underdog who comes back in a big way. But, what really hooked the reviewer was Lloyd's stunt work, which turned silent cinema into an obsession.

In *The Kid Brother*, Lloyd plays Harold Hickory, the youngest of three sons of the burly county sheriff. He is treated like the family "patsy"—given all of the household chores and cleaning to do, while the older brothers treat him like a male Cinderella.

Trouble starts when a traveling medicine show comes into town. Jobyna Ralston as leading lady plays the daughter of the deceased medicine show proprietor, who is talked into carrying on the show by two dishonest thugs. Ralston's partners in the show steal a sum of money that is left in Sheriff Jim Hickory's custody. Despite valiant efforts by Sheriff Hickory and the two oldest sons, they are unable to recover the money, and the townspeople prepare to lynch the sheriff, thinking that he stole the money himself.

In the end, it is Harold who takes on the murderous thief—single-handedly capturing both the thug and the money just in time to save his father at the last minute. The "weakling" succeeds where his two egotistical brothers failed, and gets the girl, too. The final sequence also has Harold getting the last laugh on nemesis Hank Hooper as well.

In addition to an engrossing story line, *The Kid Brother* also is packed with good sight gags. One such gag has Harold putting a dress on a sheep, to make it look from a distance like the girl bending over picking flowers. Another good gag shows Harold being mercilessly and repeatedly beaten over the head with a steel rod by Constantine Romanoff. The rod bends as Romanoff keeps striking blows, and it is fun to see how Harold gets out of that situation. In addition, Harold makes friends with a monkey, and puts his shoes on the monkey's feet, so that when the monkey walks on the ship, the villain thinks it is Harold. Yet another famous sequence has Harold pretending to be the girl, and having his brothers waiting on him hand and foot—until they open the curtain and see Harold.

Constantine Romanoff is unforgettable as the evil villain that Lloyd captures. Romanoff had appeared in a few Lloyd films, and then seems to have disappeared without a trace. It is not known what became of him, or when he died.

In 1970, just a year before his death, Lloyd took *The Kid Brother* on tour to various universities and film societies where it was very well received, and demonstrated without a doubt that it was a masterpiece that has stood the test of time.

The Kid Brother most definitely ranks as one of Lloyd's greatest films, and will likely remain a perfect introduction into the fine art of silent cinema.

526. The King of Kings *Rating: ☆☆☆☆*

DeMille/Pathé; ***Directed by*** Cecil B. DeMille; ***Scenario by*** Jeanie MacPherson; ***Music Score by*** Hugo Reisenfeld; ***General Music Director:*** Josiah Zuro; ***Synchronization by*** R.C.A. Photophone; ***Running Time:*** 115 minutes; ***Cast:*** JESUS OF NAZARETH, H.B. Warner (1875–1958); MARY (MOTHER OF JESUS), Dorothy Cumming (1899–1983); MARY MAGDALENE, Jacqueline Logan (1902–1983); CAIAPHUS, Rudolph Schildkraut (1862–1930); THE PHARISEE, Sam DeGrasse (1875–1953); THE SCRIBE, Casson Ferguson (1891–1929); PONTIUS PILATE, Victor Varconi (1891–1976); PROCULLA (WIFE OF PILATE), Majel Coleman; ROMAN CENTURION, Montague Love (1877–1943); SIMON OF CYRENE, William Boyd (1895–1972); MALCHUS (CAPTAIN OF HIGH PRIEST'S GUARD), Theodore Kosloff (1882–1956); BARRABUS, George Siegmann (1882–1928); MARTHA, Julia Faye (1893–1966); MARY OF BETHANY, Josephine Norman (1904–1951); LAZARUS, Kenneth Thomson (1899–1967); SATAN, Alan Brooks, (1888–1936); WOMAN TAKEN IN ADULTERY, Viola Louie; THE BLIND GIRL, Muriel McCormack; DYSMAS (REPENTANT THIEF), Clarence Burton (1881–1933); GESTAS (UNREPENTANT THIEF), James Mason (1889–1959); MOTHER OF GESTAS, May Robson (1858–1942); MAID SERVANT OF CAIAPHUS, Dot Farley (1881–1971); CAPTAIN OF THE ROMAN GUARD, Jack Padjan (1887–1960); AN EXECUTIONER, James Farley (1882–1947); ***The Twelve Disciples:*** PETER, Ernest Torrence (1878–1933); JUDAS ISCARIOT, Joseph Schildkraut (1895–1964); JAMES, James Neill (1860–1931); JOHN, Joseph Striker (1899–1974); MATTHEW, Robert Edeson (1868–1931); SIMON, Robert Ellsworth; JAMES (THE LESS), Charles Requa (1892–1967); THADDEUS, John T. Prince (1871–1937); ***Guests of Mary Magdalene:*** EBER (A PHARISEE), Otto Lederer (1886–1965); A YOUNG ROMAN, Bryant Washburn (1889–1963); A ROMAN NOBLE, Lionel Belmore (1868–1953); A RICH JUDEAN, Monte Collins (1856–1929); A PRINCE OF PERSIA, So-jin Kamiyama (1891–1954); A WEALTHY MERCHANT, Andre Cherron (1880–1952); A BABYLONIAN NOBLE, William Costello (1898–1971); A GALLANT OF GALILEE, Lucia Flamma; SLAVE TO MARY MAGDALENE, Sally Rand (1904–1979); CHARIOTEER, Noble Johnson (1881–1978); ***Soldiers of Rome:*** Robert St. Angelo; Redman Finley; James Dime (1897–1981); Richard Alexander (1902–1989); Budd Fine (1894–1966); William DeBoar; Robert McKee; Tom London (1889–1963); Edward Schaeffer; Peter Norris; Dick Richards

The King of Kings was Cecil B. DeMille's second major biblical epic, following four years after the 1923 version of *The Ten Commandments*. This original version of *The King of Kings* features an impressive cast, and was filmed on a lavish scale. It is truly one of the great masterpieces of the silent era. James Card states in his 1994 book, *Seductive Cinema*, that "the 1927 *King of Kings* was, in many ways, DeMille's most successful biblical epic." It is still compelling to watch.

The story starts in Judea at the home of Mary Magdalene, played by Jacqueline Logan. These sequences are portrayed in typical DeMille fashion, with exotic costumes and sets—complete with feather fans. When Magdalene hears about how Judas has left her to follow the famous carpenter from Nazareth, she is skeptical, even when one of her own people tells of how he saw Jesus heal a blind man. Shortly afterward, the film depicts a lame boy regaining his ability to walk—courtesy of Jesus Christ. After this miracle, the formerly lame boy leads a blind friend to Jesus to regain his sight. This sequence is beautifully photographed, with the boy being gradually covered with a beam of light, and then seeing the face of Jesus fading in as his sight is restored. Further along in the story, the once-skeptical Mary Magdalene is cleansed of the seven deadly sins, and resolving to mend her ways.

The rest of the movie shows how Caiaphus [fabulously portrayed by the great actor Rudolph Schildkraut in his best surviving silent era role] conspired with the higher-ups of Israel to get Jesus Christ out of the way, as he was starting to become too much of a threat to their power. They try everything, but nothing works until Judas [well played by Rudolph Schildkraut's son, Joseph], one of Jesus' own followers, betrays him for 30 pieces of silver. The crucifixion scene is very well done, with the exception of the error of placing the nails in Jesus' palms on the cross rather than in his wrist. In actuality,

NATIONAL THEATRE

DIRECTION, W. H. RAPLEY — BUSINESS MANAGEMENT, S. E. COCHRAN

BEGINNING SUNDAY, DECEMBER 18, 1927

Twice Daily Thereafter at 2:30 and 8:30

PATHE PRESENTS

For the First Time in Washington Cecil B. DeMille's
"Picture of Pictures"

"The King of Kings"

Story Adapted by Jeanie Macpherson
Musical Score by Dr. Hugo Riesenfeld

Jesus, the Christ		H. B. Warner
Mary, the Mother		Dorothy Cumming
The Twelve Disciples	Peter	Ernest Torrence
	Judas	Joseph Schildkraut
	James	James Neill
	John	Joseph Striker
	Matthew	Robert Edeson
	Thomas	Sidney D'Albrook
	Andrew	David Imboden
	Philip	Charles Belcher
	Bartholomew	Clayton Packard
	Simon	Robert Ellsworth
	James, the Less	Charles Requa
	Thaddeus	John T. Prince
Mary Magdalene		Jacqueline Logan
Caiaphas, High Priest of Israel		Rudolph Schildkraut
The Pharisee		Sam De Grasse
The Scribe		Casson Ferguson
Pontius Pilate, Governor of Judea		Victor Varconi
Proculla, wife of Pilate		Majel Coleman
The Roman Centurion		Montagu Love
Simon of Cyrene		William Boyd
Mark		M. Moore
Malchus, Captain of the High Priest's Guard		Theodore Kosloff
Barabbas		George Siegmann
Martha		Julia Faye
Mary of Bethany		Josephine Norman
Lazarus		Kenneth Thomson
Satan		Alan Brooks
The Woman Taken In Adultery		Viola Louie
The Blind Girl		Muriel MacCormac

Above and facing: An original theater program for *The King of Kings* (1927).

PROGRAM

Dysmas, the Repentant Thief	Clarence Burton
Gestas, the Unrepentant Thief	James Mason
The Mother of Gestas	May Robson
A Maid Servant of Caiaphas	Dot Farley
Captain of the Roman Guard	Jack Padjan
Soldiers of Rome	Robert St. Angelo, Redman Finley, James Dime, Richard Alexander, Budd Fine, William de Boar, Robert McKee, Tom London, Edward Schaeffer, Peter Norris, Dick Richards
An Executioner	James Farley
Guests of Mary Magdalene	Eber, a Pharisee — Otto Lederer; A Young Roman — Bryant Washburn; A Roman Noble — Lionel Belmore; A Rich Judaean — Monte Collins; A Prince of Persia — Sojin; A Wealthy Merchant — Andre Cherron; A Babylonian Noble — William Costello; A Gallant of Galilee — Lucia Flamma
Slave to Mary Magdalene	Sally Rand
Charioteer	Noble Johnson

when people were crucified, the nails went through the wrists just below the hands. If the nails had gone through the palms of the hands, the body weight of the person would rip the hand apart from the middle. Another minor problem with the film is the casting of H.B. Warner as Jesus Christ. Although Warner gave a very good performance, he was too old for the part.

After the crucifixion sequence comes the phenomenal earthquake sequence. This sequence at least equals the Red Sea sequence in *The Ten Commandments* (1923). Shortly after the earthquake sequence comes the Resurrection sequence, which is gorgeously filmed in 2-strip Technicolor.

In addition to its stunning visual quality, this film is enhanced with the original R.C.A. Photophone track, which contains an orchestral score and sound effects. The sound effects especially enhance the sequence in which Judas is accepting the bribe from Caiaphus—one piece of silver at a time, with the audience hearing each piece of silver hitting the table one by one. Furthermore, the Palm Sunday sequence is backed by a vocal choir.

This fabulous masterpiece is an experience not to be missed.

527. Laugh, Clown, Laugh

Rating: ☆☆☆

MGM; ***Directed by*** Herbert Brenon; ***Running Time:*** 61 minutes; ***Cast:*** TITO, Lon Chaney, Sr. (1883–1930); SIMON, Bernard Siegel (1868–1940); SIMONETTA, Loretta Young (born 1913); GIACINTA, Cissy Fitzgerald (1873–1941); LUIGI, Nils Asther (1897–1981); LUCRETIA, Gwen Lee (1904–1961)

Laugh, Clown, Laugh has the distinction of having been Lon Chaney, Sr.'s personal favorite of his MGM films. It was also the first major role played by actress Loretta Young, who had previously had bit parts in three prior films. Chaney and Nils Asther play the male leads who are both in love with Simonetta, an orphaned girl that Chaney found when she was very young. Tito, a circus clown who has spells of crying, is advised that he can overcome his crying affliction when he finds the right woman. Luigi, played by Nils Asther, is a wealthy count who laughs uncontrollably, and believes that love with the right woman will cure him of his laughing fits. Loretta Young's character is caught in the middle of the triangle. When Simonetta chooses Luigi over Tito, he becomes unhinged, providing the climactic sequence to the film.

Although not among the masterpieces of either director Herbert Brenon (1880–1958) or Chaney, *Laugh, Clown, Laugh* is an intriguing film that keeps one waiting to see what happens next. Chaney does a remarkable stunt in one of his circus act scenes, sliding down a rope on his head! The film also provides the opportunity to see Loretta Young as she was at age 14. Ms. Young would go on to even greater stardom in talkies, having won an Oscar in 1947 for *The Farmer's Daughters* and another nomination in 1949 for *Come to the Stable*. In the 1950s, she had her own television show, for which she won three Emmy Awards. Ms. Young's sister was silent screen actress Sally Blane, who died in August, 1997.

528. Love

Rating: ☆☆☆½

MGM; ***Directed by*** Edmund Goulding; ***From Leo Tolstoy's Novel,*** *Anna Karenina*; ***Continuity by*** Frances Marion; ***Titles by*** Marion Ainslee and Ruth Cummings; ***Settings by*** Cedric

Gibbons and Alexander Toluboff; ***Wardrobe by*** Gilbert Clark; ***Photography by*** William Daniels; ***Film Editor:*** Hugh Wynn; ***Running Time with Original Ending:*** 76 minutes; ***Running Time with Happy Ending:*** 81 minutes; ***Cast:*** ANNA KARENINA, Greta Garbo (1905–1990); VRONSKY, John Gilbert (1899–1936); GRAND DUKE, George Fawcett (1860–1939); GRAND DUCHESS, Emily Fitzroy (1860–1954); KARENIN, Brandon Hurst (1866–1947); SEREZHA [ANNA'S SON], Philippe De Lacy (1917–1995)

This was the first of four film adaptations of Leo Tolstoy's classic tale of forbidden love, betrayal, and revenge. Originally planned to go into production with Lillian Gish (1893–1993) playing opposite John Gilbert, the public's demand for more Garbo and Gilbert pairings resulted in Garbo getting Gish's role, and Gish starring in *Annie Laurie* (1927), the only one of her MGM films that was not accessible for evaluation.

Several different titles were proposed for this second Garbo/Gilbert pairing. Greta Garbo and John Gilbert in *Heat* was laughed off the proposal table for obvious reasons, and finally ended up as Garbo and Gilbert in *Love*.

In this classic romantic tragedy, Garbo plays Anna, a woman unhappily married to a high ranking Russian official who becomes infatuated with John Gilbert's character of Vronsky. Anna is willing to give up all to be near the man she truly loves, suffering through ostracization from her own son, whom she loves dearly. It reaches the point that Vronsky faces dismissal from his high military post because of the adulterous affair, which would put the family name in total disgrace. Two different endings were used for this film. The sad ending in which Anna commits suicide by jumping in front of a train was released in the prints that circulated abroad. For American audiences, a hokey happy ending was tacked on, in which Garbo's husband dies, and she and Vronsky are able to get married and live happily ever after.

Love is by far the best of the Garbo/Gilbert pairings during the silent era. It was such a great success that Garbo remade the film as a talkie in 1935 starring opposite Fredric March. For the remake, she was awarded the New York Film Critic's Best Actress designation for 1935.

While Garbo ultimately did a fine job with this excellent vehicle, Lillian Gish would have transformed it into a masterpiece.

529. The Love of Jeanne Ney

Rating: ☆☆☆

Produced in Germany; ***Directed by*** G.W. Pabst; ***Assistant Director:*** Marc Sorkin; ***Screenplay by*** Ladislas Vadja, Rudolf Leonhardt; ***Based on Novel by*** Ilya Ehrenburg; ***Photographed by*** Fritz Arno Wagner and Robert Lach; ***Production Design:*** Otto Hunte, Viktor Trivas; ***Running Time:*** 105 minutes; ***Cast:*** JEANNE NEY, Edith Jehanne; ANDREA LABOV, Uno Henning (1895–1970); KHALIBIEV, Fritz Rasp (1891–1976); GABRIELLE, Brigitte Helm (1906–1996); RAYMOND NEY, Adolph Edgar Licho (1876–1944); ANDRE NEY, Eugen Jensen

This is a chilling and powerful melodrama of love, betrayal, deceit, greed, and murder. Edith Jehanne gives an impressive performance as Jeanne Ney, a girl from a wealthy family who is in love with a Bolshevik. Her love transcends the fact that lover Andrea killed her aristocratic father over a list of spies he had obtained. Jeanne, with the aid of her lover, escapes from Russia to France and goes to live with her uncle Raymond Ney.

The uncle has a blind daughter named Gabrielle. Khalibiev, a scoundrel, tries to marry Gabrielle, with the intention of killing her once he has her money. This attempt is foiled. The uncle Raymond is in on a diamond theft, and Khalibiev murders Raymond, framing Jeanne's lover Andrea for the murder.

This intriguing film features excellent direction by G.W. Pabst. Edith Jehanne and Uno Henning turn in fabulous performances in the protagonist roles. Fritz Rasp does very well in his role as the villain. Brigitte Helm makes a good impression in her second film performance as Jeanne's blind cousin. The only flaw with Helm's performance is that in some scenes, she gives too much of a zombie-like expression with her eyes, which does not realistically represent somebody who is blind. But, she makes up for this with her unforgettable performance in the scene in which she finds her father has been murdered.

The Love of Jeanne Ney is a film that this reviewer appreciated more and more with each respective viewing. It is fortunately widely available on video, and recommended.

530. The Love of Sunya

Rating: ☆☆☆

Gloria Swanson Productions/United Artists; ***Directed by*** Albert Parker; ***Assistant Director:*** Paul Madeux; ***Adaptation by*** Earle Brown; ***Titles by*** Cosmo Hamilton; ***Art Direction by*** Hugo Ballin; ***Camerawork by*** Robert Martin; ***Special Cameraman:*** Dudley Murphy; ***Costumes by*** René Hubert; ***Running Time:*** 80 minutes; ***Cast:*** SUNYA ASHLING, Gloria Swanson (1897–1983); PAUL JUDSON, John Boles (1895–1969); ANNA HAGAN, Pauline Garon (1901–1965); LOUIS ANTHONY, Ian Keith (1899–1960); PAOLO DE SALVO, Andre de Segurola (1875–1953); ROBERT GORING, Anders Randolph (1870–1930); THE OUTCAST, Hugh Miller (1889–1956); HENRI PICARD, Robert Schable (1873–1947); TED MORGAN, Ivan Lebedoff (1894–1953); ASA ASHLING, John Miltern (1870–1937); KENNETH ASHLING, Raymond Hackett (1902–1958)

For many years, it had been known that the Killiam Collection held the only existing print of *The Love of Sunya*. This was a film that silent film enthusiasts never expected to be able to see, but when Critic's Choice Video got interested in the silent films, they worked out an arrangement with the Killiam Collection to release the title on video, making it widely available to the general public for the first time since its original release. This title also has historic significance as the first film that was shown at New York City's famous Roxy Theater Movie Palace.

The Love of Sunya is a remake of the 1919 film, *Eyes of Youth*, which is reviewed elsewhere in this book. The story lines are very similar, but *The Love of Sunya* features more stylized costumes and sets.

The story is about a Hindu spiritualist who believes that he has wronged Sunya in a past life. To make amends, he determines to help her in the present life. At this point, Sunya is going through one of the toughest decisions she has ever faced. The man she truly loves is being transferred with his job to South America. She wants to marry and join him, but some difficult circumstances come up. Her father's business is being called on its loans. The only way out, her father says, is to marry Mr. Goring, the proprietor of the financial institution that his business owes so much money to. Then, she has an opera coach who wants to represent her in Paris, and make a major opera singer out of her. Not knowing which of the three paths to take, she is being pressured from all sides. Enter the Hindu spiritualist. He finally finds Sunya, and, as part of amends for what he believes he did to her in a past life, gives her the opportunity to look into the future and see the outcome which would happen in each option she has. This insight helps her to make the right decision.

The only major difference in the plot between *Eyes of Youth* and *The Love of Sunya* is that *Eyes of Youth* has a fourth situation to explore, which is not used in the Swanson version.

In addition to Gloria Swanson, other important cast members of this film included Pauline Garon, Anders Randolph, and John Boles. *The Love of Sunya* was John Boles' third film, and his first major role. Because he had a good voice to match his good looks, he made a smooth transition into the talkie era. Other important films he appeared in include Paul Leni's *The Last Warning* (1929), *Rio Rita* (1929), *The King of Jazz* (1930), *Frankenstein* (1931), and *Stella Dallas* (1937). Anders Randolph was a prolific character actor in many silents, including *The Black Pirate* (1926), *The Viking* (1928), and *Noah's Ark* (1929). Pauline Garon starred in a number of silent era romantic comedies, including *The Average Woman* (1924) with Harrison Ford. She was married to Lowell Sherman. One can see why *The Love of Sunya* was among Gloria Swanson's personal favorites of her career.

531. The Loves of Carmen

Rating: ☆☆☆

Fox; ***Directed by*** Raoul Walsh; ***Screenplay by*** Gertrude Orr; ***Based on Carmen by*** Prosper Merimée; ***Photography by*** Lucien Andriot; ***Running Time:*** 83 minutes; ***Cast:*** CARMEN, Dolores Del Rio (1905–1983); JOSÉ, Don Alvarado (1904–1967); ESCAMILLO, Victor McLaglen (1886–1959); MICHAELA, Nancy Nash; MIGUEL, Rafael Valverda; EMILIA, Mathilde Comont (1886–1938); MORALES, Jack Baston (1892–1970); TERESA, Carmen Costello; GYPSY CHIEF, Fred Kohler (1888–1938)

This is a rare and obscure version of *Carmen* about which little has been previously written. When one thinks of "Carmen" in the silent era, the first version that comes to mind is the Pola Negri–Ernst Lubitsch adaptation, known under the title of *Gypsy Blood* (1919). When this Negri-Lubitsch version was reviewed, it was extremely disappointing.

This adaptation of the "Carmen" story is far superior to the more famous Negri version. Unfortunately, it has rarely been seen. This is partially because it was considered for many years to have been lost. It was screened one time on PBS as part of a "Lost and Found" series that was featured in the late 1970s, which is how it became accessible for evaluation in this book. It has never been widely released on video, but hopefully that will change once it enters the public domain in 2003.

What puts this adaptation over is Dolores Del Rio. Ms. Del Rio puts a somewhat mischievous and conniving spin on the "Carmen" character. She gives Carmen a definitive personality, showing both the likable and vampish sides of her. Of the three silent era performances of Ms. Del Rio's that have been evaluated, this role is the best of the three. When one sees her version of *Carmen*, one wonders why hers isn't the name that immediately comes to mind when the subject of silent era *Carmen*s are brought up. In addition to fitting the role better, she was among the most beautiful stars in Hollywood history. She retained her beauty into old age, and looked the same when she was in her 70s as she did in this film. From 1930 to 1941, Del Rio was married to MGM art director Cedric Gibbons. She enjoyed a smooth and successful transition to talkies, and was appearing in Mexican films as late as the 1960s.

In addition to Ms. Del Rio, Don Alvarado and Victor McLaglen turn in good performances in the leading male roles. Alvarado plays Don Jose, the man whose life Carmen ruins by charming him into breaking her out of jail, and then allowing smugglers to cross the border with illegal goods, costing him his prestigious position. Victor McLaglen is at his best as Escamillo, the prize bullfighter who at first spurns Carmen, but is eventually lured into her web.

In addition to the contributions of the leading cast members, much of the credit for this film is attributable to director Raoul Walsh. He added a number of good artistic touches—the first example which occurs at the very beginning of the film. In the first shot after the credits, the camera focuses on a paper fan, which is slowly folded in to reveal more of the scenery behind it. This sequence reminds one of the opening sequence Abel Gance shot in the first part of the second epoch of *Napoléon*, which showed a close-up of a fan being removed to reveal that Charlotte Corday was hiding a knife in her breast area with which to murder Marat.

Hopefully, as this adaptation of *Carmen* is seen by a wider audience, people will see for themselves that it puts the erroneously and highly acclaimed Lubitsch-Negri version to shame.

532. Man, Woman, and Sin *Rating:* ☆

MGM; ***Directed by*** Monta Bell; ***Assistant Director:*** Nick Grinde; ***Scenario by*** Alice D.G. Miller; ***Titles by*** John Colton; ***Settings by*** Cedric Gibbons and Merrill Pye; ***Wardrobe by*** Gilbert Clark; ***Photography by*** Percy Hilburn; ***Film Editor:*** Blanche Sewell; ***Running Time:*** 65 minutes; ***Cast:*** VERA WORTH, Jeanne Eagels (1890–1929); AL WHITCOMB, John Gilbert (1899–1936); MRS. WHITCOMB, Gladys Brockwell (1894–1929); ***Supporting Cast:*** Marc McDermott (1881–1929); Phillip Anderson; Hayden Stevenson; Charles K. French (1860–1952)

Man, Woman, and Sin was Jeanne Eagels' first film after a ten year hiatus during which she was one of the most highly renowned stage stars in the country. Her co-star was John Gilbert, one of the most popular leading men of the era.

The story begins with a prologue featuring a boy who lives in poverty with his mother, and who determines to bring himself and his mother out of poverty through hard work. The film then cuts to a period of a few years later, with John Gilbert playing Al Whitcomb as a young adult. He is just beginning to make his dreams for himself and his mother a reality, through hard work in the press room of the local newspaper, *The Morning Review*. In total dedication and loyalty to his mother, Whitcomb focuses totally on work—resisting the temptation to date any of the women who have asked him out.

Whitcomb's aspirations to work his way up from the press room to reporter are finally realized. All is going well with his writing for the society page when he is asked to escort Vera, the "Society Page" editor, to a local press party. Jeanne Eagels plays the part of Vera Worth, a woman who is "kept" by newspaper publisher Mr. Bancroft, who already has a wife and kids of his own. During his debut into high society, Whitcomb becomes smitten with the Camille-like Vera. He finally gets up the courage to ask her out, and she accepts when her sugar daddy Bancroft is called away for business over the weekend. A torrid affair begins, and Al starts spending the money he had painstakingly been saving for himself and his mother on Vera. Finally, the time comes when Bancroft finally finds out about the affair. A confrontation occurs, and Bancroft is accidentally killed in the struggle. Al Whitcomb is put on trial for murder, and the only way he can be saved is if Vera comes clean and tells the truth.

Man, Woman, and Sin was a potboiler that MGM headed up with Jeanne Eagels and John Gilbert to give an otherwise dull film some sort of appeal. In some ways, this film reminds one of *The Misfits* (1960), which starred Marilyn Monroe, Clark Gable, and Montgomery Clift. Both films had impressive casts and directors which would lead one to think that a film with such names associated with it would be one of high quality. In both cases, the stories had so little substance that there was simply nothing for anybody to work with—no matter how talented.

Jeanne Eagels' performance in *Man, Woman, and Sin* is unremarkable, not because she was not the great actress she was acclaimed as, but because the part itself provided little opportunity to demonstrate acting ability. John Gilbert fared a little better. The part of Al Whitcomb provided him the opportunity to play a naive young adult male, which shows a different, unique type of Gilbert performance. Gladys Brockwell, one of the great character actresses of the period, gives a nice performance as Mrs. Whitcomb, the loving mother who stands by her son through good and bad. Just two years after her appearance in this film, she was killed in a tragic car accident at the age of 34 on July 2, 1929. Jeanne Eagels' death from drug addiction followed on October 3, 1929. Also in 1929, Marc McDermott was murdered.

While *Man, Woman, and Sin* has a lot of appeal to this day as one of the rare surviving films of Jeanne Eagels, it is probably the worst of the eight films she made. It is one that is appealing for its significant historic value only.

533. Metropolis

Rating: ☆☆☆☆

UFA/Germany; ***Directed by*** Fritz Lang; ***Scenario by*** Thea von Harbou; ***Photography by*** Karl Freund, Gunther Rittau; ***Special Effects by*** Eugene Schufftan; ***Set Design by*** Otto Hunte, Erich Kettelhut, Karl Vollbrecht; ***Sculptures by*** Walter Schulze-Mittendorf; ***Costumes by*** Aenne Willkomm; ***Running Time of Kino Restoration:*** 89 minutes; ***Cast:*** MARIA/ROBOT, Brigitte Helm (1906–1996); FREDER, Gustav Frohlich (1902–1987); ROTWANG, Rudolf Klein-Rogge (1888–1955); JOHN FREDERSON, Alfred Abel (1865–1937); JOSEPH, Theodor Loos (1883–1954); GROTH, Heinrich George (1883–1946); SLIM, Fritz Rasp (1891–1976); GEORG [#11811], Erwin Biswanger; JAN, Olaf Storm; MARINUS, Hans Leo Reich; MASTER OF CEREMONIES, Heinrich Gotho; ROBOT, Fritz Alberti (1877–1954?)

Metropolis was the first and foremost of the great science fiction features. It is one of the most popular and widely seen films of the silent era. It was two years in the making, and was Germany's most expensive production at the time. Over 40,000 extras were reportedly used. As a futuristic science fiction film, it was far ahead of its time, thus possibly explaining why it was a total box-office failure which nearly bankrupted the UFA Studios.

Metropolis is the story of a 21st century city in which the rich live in paradise, while the workers live many levels below ground—slaves to the machines. Alfred Abel plays John Frederson, one of the aristocratic lords of Metropolis. His son begins to question his father's treatment of the workers as he meets Maria. Maria is arbitrator for the workers, who meet in secret. She pleads for a peaceful resolution to the problems between the aristocrats and the workers. These meetings are brought to the attention of Frederson, whose associate Rotwang has just invented a robot with the ability to give it a human likeness. In order to have an excuse to use violence against the workers, Frederson orders Rotwang to make the robot into Maria's likeness. Maria is kidnapped, and the robot likeness is sent to incite the workers to riot. Because of this film's prolabor stance, the Nazis heavily censored *Metropolis* upon their rise to power in 1933.

Metropolis was the film debut of Brigitte Helm, who achieved international fame despite the film's poor box-office performance. The sequence of her transformation into the robot was especially well done, remaining one of the most memorable sequences in the history of the cinema. [At the 1997 Academy Awards ceremony during which those actors who died in 1996 were memorialized, it was this clip that was shown in memory of Ms. Helm.] As the robot, Helm dances in a ritzy nightclub, performing a dance that was quite risqué for the time. Ms. Helm's career continued successfully into the mid–1930s before she retired from the screen. She later married the president of BMW Motors, and lived in wealthy retirement in Switzerland until her recent death at 89.

In 1989, Kino Video released what is regarded as the definitive restoration of *Metropolis*, featuring a futuristic sounding score which complements the film well. Some of the previously censored footage was also recovered and restored to the film as well.

In 1981, a "modernized" version of *Metropolis* received a theatrical release in the United States, with color tints and a rock music score. The color tints are nice, and this modernized edition is available on video, but is not recommended. The hard rock music score, comprised of songs by several hard rock musicians, does not complement the film at all, and only serves to detract from the enjoyment. Because of this inappropriate score, a fabulous tinting job was totally ruined and made useless. As in the case with the modernization of *The Phantom of the Opera* (1925), the author repeats in no uncertain terms that rock music is incompatible with silent films, as every silent film released with such a score has proven to be a bastardization. Such "modernization" has been tried twice, and has resulted in failure both times.

Shown in its proper format with appropriate music, *Metropolis* has held up well, and is just as fascinating to watch today as it was when it was released over seven decades ago. This one film alone gives both director Fritz Lang (1890–1976) and lead actress Brigitte Helm immortal places in motion picture history.

534. Mockery

Rating: ☆

MGM; ***Written and Directed by*** Benjamin Christensen; ***Continuity by*** Bradley King; ***Titles by*** Joe Farnham; ***Edited by*** John W. English; ***Settings by*** Cedric Gibbons and Alexander Toluboff; ***Photography by*** Merritt B. Gerstad; ***Wardrobe by*** Gilbert Clark; ***Running Time:*** 67 minutes; ***Cast:*** SERGEI, Lon Chaney, Sr. (1883–1930); DMITRI, Ricardo Cortez (1899–1977); TATIANA, Barbara Bedford (1903–1981); MR. GAIDAROFF, Mack Swain (1876–1935); MRS. GAIDAROFF, Emily Fitzroy (1860–1954); IVAN, Charles Puffy (1884–1942); THE BUTLER, Kai Schmidt

This was Benjamin Christensen's follow-up to *The Devil's Circus* (1926). For many years, *Mockery* was believed to have been lost. Private collectors turned up a print sometime in the 1970s. Considering the horrific nature of the films that Lon Chaney and director Christensen were known for, one would have normally expected *Mockery* to be a horror genre film. It is nothing like one would expect.

In *Mockery*, Chaney plays Sergei, a Russian peasant who saves the life of a fleeing aristocrat, by lying and pretending to be her husband. In return, Tatiana provides him with employment as a servant in her family's mansion. Sergei reads this as a sign of love on her part, and feels betrayed when he sees that she is engaged to Dmitri, a high ranking aristocratic military officer. Sergei attacks her when Dmitri is gone during a revolution by the servants of the house, but she pleads that his life be spared when the troops return to punish those involved in the uprising. Sergei in turn saves Tatiana when another attack on the mansion occurs.

This film is more of a costume romantic melodrama, and the story line is rather bland. *Mockery* is the least remarkable film of all of the Chaney films evaluated, and is Benjamin Christensen's worst surviving film as well. Nonetheless, it is good that this "lost" film was rediscovered so that we of the current generation could see it and judge it for ourselves.

This is a prime example of a lost film that proved a big disappointment once it was finally recovered.

535. My Best Girl

Rating: ☆☆☆

United Artists; ***Directed by*** Sam Taylor; ***From the Story by*** Kathleen Norris; ***Screenplay by*** Allen McNeil and Tim Whelan; ***Adaptation by*** Hope Loring; ***Photography by*** Charles Rosher; ***Art Direction by*** Jack Schulze; ***Running Time:*** 78 minutes; ***Cast:*** MAGGIE JOHNSON, Mary Pickford (1892–1979); JOE GRANT, Charles "Buddy" Rogers (born 1904); MA JOHNSON, Sunshine [a.k.a. Lucia] Hart (1886–1930); PA JOHNSON, Lucien Littlefield (1895–1960); LIZ JOHNSON, Carmelita Geraghty (1901–1966); ROBERT MERRILL, Hobart Bosworth (1867–1943); ESTHER MERRILL, Evelyn Hall; MILLICENT ROGERS, Avonne Taylor (1899–1992); JUDGE, Mack Swain (1876–1935), NICK POWELL, John Junior (1890–??)

Although this is sometimes referred to as Mary Pickford's last silent, it technically wasn't, as *The Taming of the Shrew* (1929) was released in both silent and sound versions. However, *My Best Girl* could be considered Pickford's last film released exclusively as a silent. It is Pickford's last silent that is widely available for evaluation, as only the talkie version of *The Taming of the Shrew* is available outside of the archives; the silent version exists, but is inaccessible to the public.

In this highly regarded and delightful romantic story, Pickford plays a shop girl from a poor family who falls in love with Joe Grant, the son of the department store magnate she works for, with the impression that he is a mere stock boy. As their friendship progresses, he finally lets her know who he really is. When his father finds out that his son wants to marry Maggie instead of the rich society girl he has hand picked, it doesn't set well with him. To further complicate matters, there is a scandal when Maggie goes to night court to bail her sister out of a scrape she has gotten into resulting from seeing a disreputable scoundrel that she was warned against. The scoundrel makes a derogatory comment questioning Maggie's purity, and Joe defends her honor, landing in jail after the brawl, and ending up on the front page of the newspaper the next day. The climactic sequence showing the resolution of the story is especially good.

Leading actor Charles Rogers makes a charming leading man. As is well known,

Buddy Rogers and Mary Pickford in *My Best Girl* (1927).

Rogers became Pickford's third husband in 1937, ten years after they starred in this film together. The marriage lasted until Pickford's death in 1979. Rogers became a successful band leader in the 1930s and 1940s. Until the last couple of years, Rogers maintained an active life, and made many personal appearances at various film festivals around the world. He is reportedly in failing health at age 93, and has been for about a year. Those people who know Rogers say that he has just as charming a personality off screen as he does on screen.

My Best Girl is also interesting in that it provides the opportunity to see Mack Swain in a serious role without his mustache.

Director Sam Taylor (1895–1958) went on to direct Pickford in all of her talkies except for *Secrets* (1933), having risen to fame as the director of Harold Lloyd's best silent features. He retired in the mid–1930s to work as a publicist, and came back in 1945 to direct Laurel and Hardy in *Nothing But Trouble*, his final directorial project.

536. Napoléon

Rating: ☆☆☆☆

Billancourte Studios France; ***Foreign Distributor:*** UFA; ***American Distributors:*** Gaumont-Metro-Goldwyn, MGM; ***Directed by*** Abel Gance; ***Assistant Directors:*** Henri Andreani, Pierre Danis, Henry Krauss, Anatole Litvak, Mario Nalpas, Viacheslav Tourjansky, Alexandre Volkoff; ***Photographers:*** Joseph-Louis Mundwiller, Jules Kruger, Paul Briquet, Leonce-Henry Burel, Marcel Eywinger, Roger Hubert, Georges Lucas, Emile Monnoit, Emile Pierre, Lee Planskoy; ***Edited by*** Marguerite Beauge; ***Art Direction by*** Alexandrew Benois, Pierre Schildknecht, Alexandrew Lochakoff, Georges Jacouty, Meinhardt, Pimenoff; ***Chief Technical Director:*** Simon Feldman; ***Casting Director:*** Louis Osmont; ***Production Manager:*** William Delafontaine; ***Special Effects by*** W. Percy Day, Edward Scholl, Eugene Schufftan, Nicolas Wilcke, Minime, Segundo de Chomon; ***Make-up by*** Wladimir Kwaning, Boris de Fast; ***Josephine's Costumes by*** Jeanne Lanvin; ***Original Running Time:*** Approximately 380-420 minutes; ***Running Time of Current Restored Version:*** 313 minutes; ***Running Time of MCA/Universal Video Version:*** 235 minutes; ***Cast:*** NAPOLÉON AS AN ADULT, Albert Dieudonne (1892–1976); NAPOLÉON AS A BOY, Vladimir Roudenko; JOSEPHINE DE BEAUHARNAIS, Gina Manes (1893–1989); TRISTAN FLEURI, Nicolas Koline; VIOLINE FLEURI, Annabella (1909–1996); BARRAS, Maxudian; CAROLINE BONAPARTE, Pierette Lugan; ELISA BONAPARTE, Yvette Dieudonne; JEROME BONAPARTE, Roger Chantal; JOSEPH BONAPARTE, Georges Lampin (1901–1979); LAETITIA BONAPARTE, Eugenie Buffet; LOUIS BONAPARTE, Fernand Rauzena; LUCIEN BONAPARTE, Sylvio Caviccia; PAULINE BONAPARTE, Simone Genevois; THERESA CABARRUS, Andree Standard; CARTEAUX, Leon Courtois; ANDRE CHENIER, Vonelly; CHARLOTTE CORDAY, Marguerite Gance; COUTHON, Vigier; DANTON, Koubitzky; EUGENE DE BEAUHARNAIS, Georges Henin; HORSENSE DE BEAUHARNAIS, Janine Pen; VICOMTE DE BEAUHARNAIS, G. Cahuzac; ROUGET DE LISLE, Harry Krimer (1896–1991); CAMILE DESMOULINS, Robert Vidalin; LUCILE DESMOULINS, Francine Mussey (died 1933); POZZO DI BORGO, Acho Chakatouny; DUGOMMIER, Alexandre Bernard; DU TEIL, Dacheux; MARCELLIN FLEURI, Serge Freddy-Karll; FOUCHE, Guy Faviere; FRERON, Daniel Mendaille; GREEN EYE, Boris Fastovich-Kovansko; HOCHE, Pierre Batcheff (1901–1932); JUNOT, Jean Dalbe; LA BUSSIERE, Jean D'yd (1880–1964); LA MARSELLAISE, Maryse Damia (1889–1978); MLLE. LENORMAND, Carrie Carvalho; LOUIS XVI, Louis Sance; MARAT, Antonin Artaud (1896–1948); MASSENA, Philippe Rolla, MOUSTACHE, Henry Krauss; MUIRON, Pierre Danis; MURAT, Genica Missirio; PECCADUC, Roblin; PHELIPEAUX, Vidal; MME. RECAMIER, Suzy Vernon; ROBESPIERRE, Edmond van Daele; SAINT-JUST, Abel Gance (1889–1981); SALICETTI, Philippe Heriat (1898–1971); SANTO-RICCI, Henri Baudin; SCHERER, Mathillon; TALLIEN, Jean Gaudray; MME. TALLIEN, Andree Standard; TALMA, Roger Blum

This French bio-epic by Abel Gance was, for many years, believed to have been lost. Respected cinema scholar Kevin Brownlow took on the 30-plus-years task of painstakingly acquiring bits and pieces of the original film from around the world. With the cooperation of Gance himself, he presented a restored version for theatrical rerelease in 1981. The film did so well on its American rerelease premiere in New York that it was number 11 at the box office for that particular week. To this day, bits and pieces of the film continue to surface, and the complete restoration of the original production

Above and opposite page: **Annabella, who was the last surviving star of Abel Gance's *Napoléon* (1927) before her death in 1996.**

remains an ongoing process. Currently, the restoration of what survives consists of 5 hours, 13 minutes of footage. The version distributed in America is a version that runs 3 hours, 55 minutes. This new American version was produced and edited by Francis Ford Coppola, under the authority of Robert A. Harris and Zoetrope Studios. It features an orchestra score composed and conducted by Carmine Coppola, who was Francis Ford Coppola's father.

Napoléon is a unique example of extraordinarily advanced technical cinematographic innovation, placing it in a category of its own, incomparable to any other film in history. Some examples of cinematographic innovation featured are rapid cutting, cross-cutting between images of a rough sea and the crowds present at the first guillotine executions of the French Revolution, and Polyvision, the three-screen process invented by Gance.

The biography starts in 1781 with one of Napoléon's first battles—a snowball fight at Brienne College. The movie also depicts how Napoléon was laughed at and ridiculed in his early years, and how he gradually gained respect and worked himself into a position of power. Also detailed are the rise and demise of revolution leaders St. Just and Robespierre, as well as Napoléon's courtship of and marriage to Josephine. The last scene covers Bonaparte's invasion of Italy as newly appointed general-in-command, and is presented in Polyvision. The tricolor finale—presented in blue, white, and red—representative of France's flag—must be seen to be believed. Abel Gance had originally planned to cover more of Napoléon's life clear through to his being exiled in his older age, but he ran out of money and backers and was unable to complete the film as he had intended.

Napoléon was a smashing success at its French premiere. The original ran somewhere between six and seven hours in length. There were several Polyvision sequences in the original film version. Unfortunately, the American distributors truncated the film for a variety of reasons. One was that they saw the superiority of this film over anything done in America, and did not want to have to compete with a film of this grandeur.

Therefore, they distributed only a heavily edited version of *Napoléon* in the United States. The Polyvision sequences were simply shrunken down to fit into the space of a regular screen, shown in a miniaturized version on one screen instead of the three that they were designed to be shown on. This is partially because the talkies had already invaded by the time *Napoléon* was distributed in 1928 in the United States. Many theater owners were already going into debt to rewire for sound pictures, and it was felt that asking theaters to remodel for Polyvision would be too much to ask at the time. Many years later, Abel Gance, in despair over not feeling that there was a place for him in motion pictures because he was too far ahead of his time, burned all of the Polyvision segments of the film that he had. This is why only the finale survives in Polyvision today. In short, the majority of the Polyvision sequences were lost because the public was simply too ignorant to appreciate an epic of *Napoléon*'s stature at the time, just as they did not appreciate *Intolerance* when it came out.

In the early 1930s, Gance reedited *Napoléon* and added dialogue on a soundtrack, presenting an abridged and truncated talking version of *Napoléon* in 1934. It was in this tampering that the vast majority of the silent version of *Napoléon* became lost. Then, in the 1950s, Kevin Brownlow took an interest in the film, and it is Brownlow who should be thanked for restoring *Napoléon* to an approximation of how it was originally meant to be seen.

In the United States, only a truncated version of *Napoléon* is available. The version that is now out is a fabulous improvement over the joke of a release that MGM did domestically in 1928, but it is still missing over an hour of available footage. The version in the United States gives one only a glimpse of the footage of Annabella as Violine Fleuri, yet her part is far more significant in the complete version of the restoration as produced by Kevin Brownlow. Nonetheless, until Kevin Brownlow's complete restoration with score by Carl Davis is made available to us in the United States, the footage that is widely available in the Coppola version is better than nothing, and still quite interesting and enjoyable.

537. October

Rating: ☆☆☆☆

[a.k.a. *Ten Days That Shook the World*]

October Revolution Jubilee Committee/U.S.S.R.; ***Directed by*** Sergei Eisenstein and Grigori Alexandrov; ***Photography by*** Edward Tisse; ***Running Time:*** 100 minutes

After Sergei Eisenstein's (1898–1948) phenomenal success with *Battleship Potemkin* (1925), he started work on *The General Line* (1929). After working a month on this project, he was commissioned by Nikolai Podvolsky to do a film to commemorate the 10th anniversary of the Bolshevik Revolution of 1917, and thus dropped what he was doing on *The General Line*, and went to work with Grigori Alexandrov (1903–1983) to produce this film, inspired by John Reed's book, *Ten Days That Shook the World*.

For this project, Eisenstein and Alexandrov got the full cooperation of the Soviet government, being granted access to the Kremlin, as well as thousands of members of the Armed Forces for the mob sequences. Although the filming ran behind schedule and wasn't quite ready for release in time for the 10th anniversary celebration as planned, *October* turned out to be a masterpiece that equaled the quality of *Battleship Potemkin*.

The film starts out powerfully enough with a mob of thousands destroying a statue of Alexander III, former Czar of Russia. What follows are powerful reenactments of the battles of the Red Army against the provisional government that was in control in February of 1917. One sees how the people suffer as a result of empty promises broken by the provisional government, and how starvation and war prevail in continued suffering of the working class. One exceptional sequence shows a night time incident with a spotlight shining on the crowds of people awaiting the arrival of Vladimir Lenin on April 3, who rallies supporters to fight the provisional Bourgeise government in favor of Communism.

With thousands of extras lining the streets of Leningrad, as well as the fact that the location had not changed much in appearance since 1917, *October* presents a realistic re-enactment of the revolution activities much as they actually were when the revolution was in progress.

Another powerful sequence shows a car load of aristocrats taunting and attacking a Bolshevik, who is killed. The drawbridge leading into Leningrad is raised, with the dead Bolshevik and a horse falling into the river beneath. This sequence with the horse is almost as powerful as the Odessa Steps sequence in *Battleship Potemkin*.

When General Kornilov of the provisional army begins to advance on Leningrad, the Bolsheviks know that they can compromise no longer, and it is determined that if they don't seize total power then and there, the cause of the people is lost, and the counter-revolutionaries will claim victory, leading into the powerful finale of the film.

Just as Eisenstein was putting the final touches on *October*, Leon Trostsky was expelled from the Communist Party, and Joseph Stalin had taken complete control. Under the watchful eye of Stalin, Eisenstein had to make last minute changes in the film, doing some retakes and cutting about 1,000 feet of footage.

October was not nearly as successful as *Battleship Potemkin* had been. Nonetheless, it is just as powerful and compelling as its predecessor, and probably more artistic, as Eisenstein experimented with a lot of techniques not used in *Potemkin*.

538. Old San Francisco

Rating: ☆☆☆

Warner Brothers; ***Directed by*** Alan Crosland; ***Assistant Director:*** Gordon Hollingshead; ***Written by*** Darryl F. Zanuck; ***Screenplay by*** Anthony Coldeway; ***Photography by*** Hal Mohr; ***Edited by*** Harold McCord; ***Titles by*** Jack Jarmuth; ***Art Direction by*** Ben Carré; ***Electrical Effects by*** P.N. Murphy; ***Costumes by*** Alpharetta; ***Art Titles by*** Victor Vance; ***Music Score by*** Hugo Riesenfeld; ***Running Time:*** 87 minutes; ***Cast:*** **Prologue:** CAPTAIN VASQUEZ, Lawson Butt (1883–1956); VASQUEZ GRANDSONS, Walter McGrail (1888–1970) and Otto Matiesen (1893–1932); MOTHER, Martha Mattox (1879–1933); CAPTAIN STONE, Tom Santschi (1880–1931); ***Story:*** HERNANDEZ VASQUEZ, Joseph Swickard (1866–1940); DOLORES

Dolores Costello, star of *Old San Francisco* (1927).

VASQUEZ, Dolores Costello (1905–1979); MICHAEL BRANDON, Anders Randolph (1870–1930); TERRENCE O'SHAUGHNESSY, Charles Emmett Mack (1900–1927); CHRIS BUCKWELL, Warner Oland (1880–1938); CHINESE BUSINESSMAN, So-Jin Kamiyama (1891–1954); CHANG LOO, Angelo Rossita (1908–1991); BUCKWELL'S MISTRESS, Anna May Wong (1905–1961)

This is an intriguing story in which Dolores Costello plays a young woman whose grandfather is heir to an estate started by her ancestors, who were among the original pioneering settlers in San Francisco. The estate is the target of one of the lord of the Chinese underworld. Dolores' father refuses to sell his estate to Chris Buckwell, who determines instead to take the estate using intimidation and other unethical means.

Dolores falls in love with Terrence O'Shaughnessy, the son of Michael Brandon, who negotiates Buckwell's deals and does much of his dirty work. Dolores is kidnapped and sold into white slavery, and Terrence, with the help of the San Francisco earthquake of 1906, affects a rescue.

Warner Oland gives an impressive performance as the lord of Chinatown's underground world, who has risen to great heights by selling out his own people. His undoing comes when it is discovered and proven that he is not full-blooded Chinese as he represents himself. Charles Emmett Mack does a nice job in his leading role. *Old San Francisco* was the last film that he completed before his untimely death during the filming of *The First Auto* (1927), a film for which the ending had to be changed due to his death. Since this film was being heavily promoted in the Asian market, Anna May Wong played a significant role as Buckwell's mistress. During the 1920s, any American film that hoped to succeed in the Asian market had to feature Ms. Wong in order to do so. She was the pre-eminent Oriental actress of the time. Dolores Costello, who was by this time Warner Brothers' top box-office draw, is appealing, but her role did not provide her the opportunity to do much but stand and model.

Director Alan Crosland (1894–1936) directed this film just before doing *The Jazz Singer* (1927). He does an excellent job, and the phenomenal earthquake sequence especially showcases his talent at its best.

For many years, *Old San Francisco* languished in studio vaults. In the late 1980s, Robert Gitt of UCLA restored this film as part of the "Dawn of Sound" series. Although the film has not been released on video, a beautiful, color tinted restoration with the original Vitaphone score is aired occasionally on Turner Classic Movies.

539. The Patsy

Rating: ☆☆☆☆

MGM; ***Directed by*** King Vidor; ***Based on the Play by*** Barry Connors; ***Continuity by*** Agnes Christine Johnson; ***Titles by*** Ralph Spence; ***Settings by*** Cedric Gibbons; ***Wardrobe by*** Gilbert Clark; ***Photography by*** John Seitz; ***Film Editor:*** Hugh Wynn; ***Running Time:*** 76 minutes; ***Cast:*** PAT HARRINGTON, Marion Davies (1897–1961); TONY ANDERSON, Orville Caldwell (1896–1967); MA HARRINGTON, Marie Dressler (1869–1934); PA HARRINGTON, Dell Henderson (1877–1956); BILLY CALDWELL, Lawrence Gray (1898–1970); GRACE HARRINGTON, Jane Winton (1905–1959)

The Patsy was among the best of the light social comedies of the 1920s. Although most people today know Marion Davies primarily for her drama films of the 1930s, her true talent was in comedy. It is a shame that William Randolph Hearst insisted on Ms. Davies playing melodrama. If he had allowed her to continue in light comedy, she would

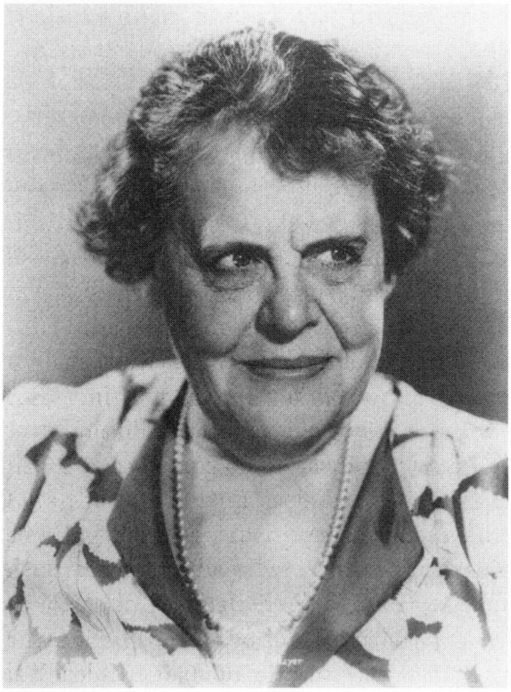

Marie Dressler, the domineering mother in *The Patsy* (1927).

have surely been ranked with comediennes like Lucille Ball and Gracie Allen.

In this film, Davies plays the younger sister in a family of four, which includes spoiled sister Grace, a domineering mother who always gets her way, and a loving father who despises how Pat is treated by her sister and mother. Pat is "the patsy"—the one who gets stuck doing the household chores, the one who gets stuck with the second-hand clothes while her sister dresses in high fashion, the one who gets dumped on in a fashion similar to Cinderella.

Pat falls in love with one Tony Anderson, whom sister Grace dates off and on at her own convenience. Since Pat is always kept under Grace's thumb, it seems impossible to catch Tony's eye. So, she develops a distinctive personality in the hopes of catching his eye, as well as to play mind games with her sister and mother to make them think that she is losing her sanity.

To get Tony to notice her, Pat leads him on to think that another man is in love with her. When sister Graces notices that Pat is making some progress, she decides to date Tony again, and threatens Pat with exposure of the non-existent "other man" to Tony if she interferes. So, Pat and her father concoct a plan to produce another man. This leads into one of the funniest sequences in the film. She arrives at Billy Caldwell's house to get him to take notice of her, but he is really too hung over (during prohibition) to express much interest. So, Pat takes note of a variety of various movie star portraits on the walls. The first she sees is a portrait of Mae Murray. So, Pat "becomes" Mae Murray—imitating the bee-stung lips, walk, and mannerisms to a tea. This personality fails to arouse interest, so she takes a look at Lillian Gish's portrait from *The Scarlet Letter* (1926). This parody of Lillian Gish is absolutely hilarious. Davies purses her lips much like Gish did, and it is surprising to see the resemblance that Davies is able to create with a simple bed sheet and some facial expressions. The next star parody is on Pola Negri in *Gypsy Blood*, an adaptation of *Carmen*. Pat chases Billy with a knife around the living room in yet another humorous parody. After the ploy with Billy Caldwell has failed, there is a major confrontation in the Harrington home which provides an entertaining climax.

The Patsy shows Marion Davies at her comedic best. It was among Ms. Davies' personal favorites of all of her films. Her ability to mimic three other stars as convincingly as she did demonstrates her versatility as an actress. In Danny Peary's book, *Alternate Oscars*, he gave his 1927–28 Best Actress Award to Mary Pickford for *My Best Girl*

(1927). If the book had been written by this reviewer, the award would have gone without hesitation to Marion Davies for *The Patsy*.

While Marion Davies is the star attraction of this film, other significant people contributed their talents to the success of *The Patsy* as well. Title writer Ralph Spence was so witty and satirical in his writing that he was among the few title authors to have his name featured on the marquees of the theaters where his films were shown. His titles are half of what makes *The Patsy* such a fun film to watch. Director King Vidor, best known for his dramatic masterpieces, demonstrated his versatility as a director with the two Marion Davies comedies he directed—*The Patsy* (1927) and *Show People* (1928).

Orville Caldwell is an appealing leading man in *The Patsy*, but never attained a high stature in Hollywood. His career had started in 1919 in an experimental color film produced by J. Searle Dawley, after which he had roles in just under a dozen films from 1920 to 1928. Lawrence Gray appeared in a number of light comedies in the mid to late 1920s. He played opposite Betty Bronson in *Are Parents People?* (1925); Gloria Swanson in *Stage Struck* (1925); Louise Brooks in *The American Venus* (1926); Clara Bow in *Kid Boots* (1926); and was teamed with Marion Davies a second time in *Marianne* (1929). In the 1930s, he abandoned acting for production work. He moved to Mexico as a liaison between the American and Mexican film industries. Dell Henderson began his distinguished film career in 1909. From 1914, he also directed a number of films. Among these directorial credits are westerns such as *Pursued* (1925) and *The Rambling Ranger* (1927). Other significant credits as a character actor include *The Crowd* (1928), *The Laurel and Hardy Murder Case* (1930), *The Champ* (1931), *It's a Gift* (1934), *The Ruggles of Red Gap* (1935), *Poppy* (1936), and *Wilson* (1945).

Although all of Marion Davies' MGM silent comedies are known to survive, only *Show People* (1928) has been made widely available on video. *The Patsy* was being offered by one of the independent video companies at one time, but Turner Entertainment forced this company to halt distribution—without making it available themselves.

540. Quality Street

Rating: ☆☆½

MGM; ***Directed by*** Sidney Franklin; ***From the Play by*** James M. Barrie; ***Adaptation by*** Hans Kraly, Albert Lewin; ***Scenario by*** Albert Lewin, Hans Kraly; ***Titles by*** Marion Ainslee, Ruth Cummings; ***Settings by*** Cedric Gibbons, Allen Ruoff; ***Photography by*** Henry Sartov; ***Wardrobe by*** René Hubert; ***Film Editor:*** Ben Lewis; ***Running Time:*** 77 minutes; ***Cast:*** PHOEBE THROSSEL, Marion Davies (1897–1961); DR. VALENTINE BROWN, Conrad Nagel (1897–1970); SUSAN THROSSEL, Helen Jerome Eddy (1897–1990); MARY WILLOUGHBY, Flora Finch (1869–1940); NANCY WILLOUGHBY, Margaret Seddon (1872–1968); HENRIETTE TURNBULL, Marcelle Corday; PATTY, Kate Price (1872–1943)

This is yet another J.M. Barrie play to be adapted for the silent screen, following *Peter Pan* (1924) and *A Kiss for Cinderella* (1925), which were produced at Paramount. Barrie's *Quality Street*, a romantic comedy, departs from the fairy tale genre of his previously filmed plays and is much weaker, based on an absurd and rather unbelievable premise.

Marion Davies plays Phoebe Throssel, whose former love interest, Dr. Valentine, has returned from the Napoleonic wars. When they meet again for the first time in several years, Phoebe has an older appearance in her role as a school teacher, and Valentine is hesitant to continue their relationship in his shock over how much older she looks.

Phoebe sheds the clothes and glasses that give her the older appearance, and takes on a double role as Miss Livvy, her young niece, to see if looks are all that he is interested in.

With Marion Davies' extraordinary ability to change her appearance, she makes the Phoebe/Livvy transition believable, and comes as close as anybody could to pulling it off. She gives her usual delightful performance. Conrad Nagel as her leading man is a bit on the bland side, but the supporting cast helps to make up for his deficiency as the male lead. Comediennes Flora Finch and Kate Price especially stand out as Phoebe's companions who are always looking out for her.

Marion Davies, at around the time she appeared in *Quality Street* (1927).

Quality Street was one of the more expensive of the Marion Davies silents with its elaborate costumes and sets, and unfortunately lost $188,000 at the box office. Katherine Hepburn starred in a 1937 talkie remake, which, although more faithful to Barrie's play, does not hold up well in comparison to Davies' original.

Unfortunately, the surviving print material on this extremely rare film has suffered from significant nitrate decomposition. It is a film that deserves to be restored and made more widely available, and Turner Entertainment would do the public a tremendous service to take on this film as a preservation project. While they're at it, they should do something for the other Davies silents that they own the rights to—*The Red Mill* (1927), *Tillie the Toiler* (1927), and *Her Cardboard Lover* (1928). Marion Davies was one of the great comediennes of the silent era, and her silent comedies deserve to be brought out of obscurity and before the public where they belong.

541. The Relay *Rating: ☆☆*

(an episode from the comedy series "The Collegians")

Universal; ***Directed by*** Wesley Ruggles; ***Story by*** Carl Laemmle, Jr.; ***Continuity by*** George H. Plympton; ***Photography by*** Ben H. Kline; ***Titles by*** Gardner Bradford; ***Film Editor:*** Thomas Malloy; ***Cartoons by*** Merryman; ***Running Time:*** 22 minutes; ***Cast:*** COACH JONES, Hayden Stevenson; JUNE MAXWELL, Dorothy Gulliver (born 1906-1997); ED BENSON, George Lewis (1901–1955); DOC WEBSTER, Churchill Ross (1901–1962); DON TRENT, Eddie Phillips (1899–1965)

This is an episode from Universal's highly popular comedy series "The Collegians." This episode features a college athletic competition decided by a final women's relay event. This relay sequence features Dorothy Gulliver, a highly popular comedy actress

of the time, who went on later to star in a vast number of westerns.

After the victory, the college co-eds celebrate with a party at which bootleg liquor is served. This sequence features a number of antics which are supposed to pass for humor.

It is surprising that such a silly, meaningless story would have been written by Carl Laemmle, Jr., the son of Universal Pictures founder Carl Laemmle, Sr. It was Laemmle, Jr., who later guided Universal's transition from minor, lower budget films into an era of more prestigious productions such as *Lonesome* (1928), *All Quiet on the Western Front* (1930), *Dracula* (1931), *Frankenstein* (1931), *The Invisible Man* (1933), and *Show Boat* (1936).

Dorothy Gulliver, star of *The Relay* (1927), an episode from the popular "Collegians" comedy series.

542. Rubber Tires

Rating: ☆☆☆

DeMille/P.D.C.; ***Directed by*** Alan Hale, Sr.; ***Running Time:*** 52 minutes; ***Cast:*** MARY ELLEN STACK, Bessie Love (1898–1986); BILL JAMES, Harrison Ford (1884–1957); MRS. STACK, May Robson (1858–1942); PA STACK, Erwin Connelly (1879–1931); "JUNIOR" STACK, Junior Coghlan (born 1916); ***Supporting Cast:*** John Patrick; Clarence Burton (1881–1933)

Rubber Tires was the directorial debut of Alan Hale, Sr. (1892–1950). Hale had been an actor in several silent films. His son, Alan Hale, Jr., played the role of "The Skipper" in the popular *Gilligan's Island* television series of the 1960s.

This is a light romantic comedy starring Harrison Ford as the boyfriend of Mary Ellen Stack. It seems that the Stack family has fallen on hard times on the East Coast. So, they sell their furniture to pay for a car and the back taxes on a home in California. Bill James, not wanting to see Mary Ellen leave without him, buys an old wreck of a car to follow them in. Pandemonium arises when the "wreck" he bought turns out to be the very first car produced by the Tourist Car Factory, for which the company has posted a $10,000 reward.

Bessie Love, the leading lady, had a long and distinguished acting career. One of her first big parts was in William S. Hart's controversial 1916 film, *The Aryan*. She also achieved immortality in D.W. Griffith's *Intolerance*, as the Bride of Cana in the Judean story. One of her most highly acclaimed performances was as a drug addicted mother in Dorothy Davenport Reid's *Human Wreckage* (1923), which is, unfortunately, a lost film. She also appeared in Warren Beatty's highly acclaimed film *Reds* (1981) just before her last film appearance in *The Hunger* (1983).

May Robson was also a highly acclaimed actress, who received an Academy Award nomination for her performance in *Lady for a Day* (1933). She made a few silent films,

Bessie Love, leading lady in *Rubber Tires* (1927).

but is best remembered for her films of the 1930s. She played the "Queen of Hearts" in *Alice in Wonderland* (1933), and was also in such classics as *Dinner at Eight* (1933), *Anna Karenina* (1935), *A Star Is Born* (1937), and *The Adventures of Tom Sawyer* (1938).

Junior Coghlan was one of the foremost child actors of the silent screen. After *Rubber Tires*, his popularity was so great that he began receiving top billing in all of his films.

543. Running Wild

Rating: ☆☆☆☆

Paramount; ***Directed by*** Gregory LaCava; ***Story by*** Gregory LaCava; ***Screen Adaptation by*** Roy Briant; ***Editor-in-chief:*** Ralph Block; ***Photographed by*** Paul Vogel; ***Running Time:*** 68 minutes; ***Cast:*** ELMER FINCH, W.C. Fields (1879–1946); MRS. FINCH, Marie Shotwell (1886–1934); MARY FINCH, Mary Brian (born 1908); DAVE HARVEY, Claude Buchanan; MR. HARVEY, Frederick Burton (1871–1957); JUNIOR, Barnett Raskin; AMOS BARKER, Frank Evans; HYPNOTIST, Edward Roseman

For a number of years, *Running Wild* was on the American Film Institute's "rescue list" of endangered films. Fortunately, this comedy classic was saved, and was also one of nine silents that Paramount released on video in 1987.

In this comedy classic, W.C. Fields plays family man Elmer Finch, who is timid and takes constant abuse from his employers, his second wife, and his stepson. If it wasn't for bad luck, he would have no luck at all. When he has the chance to land a much coveted account for the small toy factory where he works, everything that can possibly go wrong does. He manages to accidentally set off several boxes of firecrackers, thus souring the prospective new client on the business.

Elmer's luck changes when he throws a horse shoe over his shoulder, and accidentally breaks a display window. When he is chased by the irate store owner, he ducks into a theater where a hypnotist is performing. Elmer is hypnotized into thinking that he is a lion, and begins to act like one—collecting an overdue debt from Amos Barker which nobody else has succeeded in doing, and telling his bosses off while presented a new company contract he has procured which means over $1,000,000 for them. After cleaning up at work, he goes home to lay down the law.

The famous Fields quote "You can't keep a good man down" comes from this film, in the finale during which Fields stomps the portrait of his wife's first husband, to whom he is always compared, and puts his own portrait in its place.

Running Wild is riotously funny, and is this reviewer's favorite of all of Fields' comedies made in either the silent or talkie eras. It is his masterpiece and is second only to Harold Lloyd's *Safety Last* (1923) and possibly Buster Keaton's *The General* (1927).

544. 7th Heaven
[*Seventh Heaven*]

Rating: ☆☆☆☆

Fox; ***Directed by*** Frank Borzage; ***Assistant Directors:*** Lew Borzage, Park Frane; ***From the Play by*** Austin Strong; ***Scenario by*** Benjamin Glazer; ***Edited/Titled by*** Katharine Hilliker, H.H. Caldwell; ***Photography by*** Ernest Palmer, J.A. Valentine; ***Settings by*** Harry Oliver; ***Costumes by*** Kathleen Kay; ***Film Editor:*** Barney Wolf; ***Running Time:*** 120 minutes; ***Cast:*** DIANE, Janet Gaynor (1900?–1984); CHICO, Charles Farrell (1901–1990); BOUL, Albert Gran (1862–1932); GOBIN, David Butler (1895–1979); MADAM GOBIN, Marie Mosquini (1902–1983); NANA, Gladys Brockwell (1894–1929); PERE CHEVILLON, Emile Chartaud; SEWER RAT, George Stone (1903–1967); AUNT VALENTINE, Jessie Haslett; ARLETTE, Lillian West (1890–??)

This is the film for which Frank Borzage (1893–1962) won the first Best Director Academy Award. Janet Gaynor won the first Best Actress Academy award based on her performance in this and two other films. Joe Franklin, author of *Classics of the Silent Screen*, said "There's no doubt that *Seventh Heaven* was the screen's most popular love story … the original *Seventh Heaven* is still the yardstick for all movie love stories."

Janet Gaynor and Charles Farrell in a classic pose from *7th Heaven* (1927).

7th Heaven is indeed a classic love story. Charles Farrell plays Chico, a sewer cleaner who works beneath the slums of Paris, desperately hoping to be moved up to street washer. Janet Gaynor plays Diane, a waif who is mercilessly beaten and whipped by her cruel sister. After yet another such beating, she collapses. Chico as sewer maintenance worker rises up through the street drain, finds Diane, and takes pity on her. Pity turns into resentment as Chico fights his feelings of love for Diane, but he finally relents, and together they determine to build a better life for themselves. Then comes World War I, which puts a damper on their plans just before they are to get married.

Janet Gaynor as Diane is told that Chico has been killed in action, but she refuses to believe it. Finally, after many months, she accepts that Chico probably is dead, and loses all hope and faith in humankind.

This is a classic love story that is really going to have you alternately crying and yelling at the screen. One especially great scene has Nana, Diane's older and abusive sister, taking an opportune time during Chico's absence to take back control over Diane just as she has really freed herself from bondage. By this time, Diane's love for Chico has given her confidence in herself, and it is exhilarating to see Nana finally being put in her place by Diane.

Director Frank Borzage well deserved the Best Director Academy Award that he won for this film. The man took what would have ordinarily been simply an average romance story and transformed it into a masterpiece. Janet Gaynor's heart rending performance as Diane was by far the best of the three performances that won her the 1927–28 Best Actress designation. If Gaynor had not been up against Gloria Swanson's performance in *Sadie Thompson* (1928) and Marion Davies' performance in *The Patsy* (1927), she would have definitely been worthy of the Academy Award she received. It was a most award-worthy performance; this reviewer simply felt that she had tough competition in a year that was chock full of great performances. But, Janet Gaynor prevailed, and it certainly was no travesty that she won the first Best Actress award. In addition to the Academy Awards that *7th Heaven* won, it was also nominated for Best Picture.

7th Heaven is a film that has finally been released in a high quality video format as of late 1997, and is well worth having in your collection. The credit for this good deed goes to Critic's Choice Video, which released the film in conjunction with the Killiam Collection.

The blockbuster success of this film had the public clamoring for more Gaynor/Farrell pairings, and they would ultimately be teamed in four silent films together, as well as about a half dozen talkies. Their popularity surpassed even MGM's Garbo/Gilbert films.

In 1937, a talkie remake of *7th Heaven* was made with James Stewart (1908–1997) and Simone Simon (born 1911). Without the chemistry of Borzage, Farrell, and Gaynor, it was a total bomb which miserably failed in attempting to recapture the flavor of this classic original production.

545. The Show

Rating: ☆☆☆½

MGM; ***Directed by*** Tod Browning; ***Screenplay by*** Waldemar Young; ***Based on The Day of Souls by*** Charles Tenny Jackson; ***Titles by*** Joe Farnham; ***Settings by*** Cedric Gibbons, Richard Day; ***Wardrobe by*** Lucia Coulter; ***Photography by*** John Arnold; ***Film Editor:*** Errol Taggart; ***Running Time:*** 67 minutes; ***Cast:*** ROBIN, John Gilbert (1899–1936); SALOME, Renée Adorée (1898–1933); THE GREEK, Lionel Barrymore (1878–1954); SOLDIER, Edward Connelly (1855–1928); LENA, Gertrude Short (1900–1968); FERRET, Andy MacLennan

This Tod Browning effort received mixed reviews when it was originally released. *Variety* praised Browning's direction. The *New York Times* cited weakness on Browning's part, but praised the performances of Renée Adorée and Lionel Barrymore.

The Show, in the tradition of Tod Browning, is a bizarre film centered around a circus freak show. It starts off with the freak show exhibit, followed by the dance of Salome, in which Renée Adorée plays Salome, and Lionel Barrymore plays the Greek who appears to behead John the Baptist, played by John Gilbert.

What follows this intriguing opening sequence is a love triangle, as per the familiar Browning formula, in which Gilbert and Adorée's characters are in love, and Barrymore as the Greek is insanely jealous. The Greek walks in on Robin and Salome and tells her, "If it's his heart you want, I'll cut it out and give it to you!" With Robin's ex-girlfriend Lena being jealous of Salome, Robin is caught in the middle on both sides.

The complications really arise when one of the workers has a large sum of money that her father gave to her from sales of his sheep, and Robin steals it—the same night that the girl's father is found murdered. Salome harbors Robin and tries to get him to give back the money. It so happens that Salome's brother is being executed for murder across the street, and this parallel element foreshadowing Robin's own fate if he is arrested for the murder of the co-worker's father convinces him to return the stolen money. There is a twist, as when he is getting the money out of the hiding place he has put it in, the Greek has booby-trapped the hiding place with a reptile whose bite is fatal.

In re-evaluating *The Show* today, the conclusion is that both Browning and the cast deserved praise for their work. Browning's directorial style keeps the viewer in suspense—especially in the sequence during which the Greek is about to really behead Robin during the *Salome* show, by using the real sword instead of the fake sword.

Lionel Barrymore's and Renée Adorée's performances are very good, but John Gilbert is the real standout. The performance he gives in *The Show* ranks with his performance in *The Big Parade* as among his best.

546. Slide, Kelly, Slide

Rating: ☆☆☆

MGM; ***Directed by*** Edward Sedgwick; ***Titles by*** Joe Farnham; ***Settings by*** Cedric Gibbons and David Townsend; ***Wardrobe by*** Andre Ani; ***Technical Adviser:*** Mike Donlin; ***Photography by*** Henry Sharp; ***Film Editor:*** Frank Sullivan; ***Running Time:*** 82 minutes; ***Cast:*** JIM KELLY, William Haines (1900–1973); MARY MUNSON, Sally O'Neil (1908–1968); TOM MUNSON, Harry Carey, Sr. (1878–1947); MICKEY MARTIN, Junior Coghlan (born 1916); SWEDE HANSEN, Karl Dane (1886–1934); DILLON, Paul Kelly (1899–1956); MCLEAN, Guinn "Big Boy" Williams (1899–1962); CLIFF MACKLIN, Warner Richmond (1886–1948); ***Cameo Roles:*** Johnny Mack Brown (1904–1974); George Herman "Babe" Ruth (1895–1948); Lou Gehrig; Tony Lazzare (1903–1946)

Slide, Kelly, Slide was the first major baseball film to be produced by MGM, with the story centering around the New York Yankees. William Haines plays Jim Kelly, a breezy, egotistical baseball player who insists that he is a better player than any of the New York Yankees. He starts out for the Yankees' training camp to prove his point, along the way picking up a homeless waif by the name of Mickey Martin, played by Junior Coghlan, who was loaned out to MGM for this film.

Kelly proves himself by striking out one of the Yankees' best hitters, and by knocking a ball out of the park. He is accepted on the team, and sidekick Mickey becomes a water boy. Kelly achieves wide acclaim as a pitcher, becoming known as "no hit Kelly." The praise goes to his head, enlarging his hat band by yet another couple of sizes, and he becomes convinced that it is he and he alone who is winning the games. This arrogant attitude alienates the other team members. The straw that breaks the camel's back is when Kelly gets drunk (yet another stab at prohibition—very common in 1920s films) and calls Tom Munson, the aging team catcher and father of his love interest, Mary, a has-been who keeps his job only because of Kelly's own pitching. This results in Kelly's suspension from the team. Even Mickey, who is Kelly's biggest fan, becomes disenchanted with him and tells him so. Hearing things from Mickey's viewpoint makes Kelly wake up and try to redeem himself. He drops off of the team, which manages to get to the World Series without him. By the end of the sixth game, it is a draw between New York and St. Louis, with the seventh game to decide the world championship. Kelly returns to the team for game seven with a new attitude, providing his opportunity to redeem himself.

Edward Sedgwick (1892–1953) started his directorial career with westerns in the early 1920s, and reached the pinnacle of his career at MGM directing comedies, which included Buster Keaton's *Spite Marriage* (1929) and *The Cameraman* (1928), as well as this film.

Sally O'Neil, the leading lady, achieved popularity in late silents and early talkies, having had her first significant success at age 17 in *Sally, Irene, and Mary* in 1925. She also starred in *The Battle of the Sexes* (1928), which was one of D.W. Griffith's last silent films. Her sister is screen actress Molly O'Day (born 1911). Warner Richmond's significant silent era career began in 1916, and *Eyes of Youth* (1919), *Tol'able David* (1921), *Trail of the Lonesome Pine* (1923), and *The Crowd* (1928) were among the other silents he appeared in.

Paul Kelly began his entertainment career on stage at age 8, and appeared in a number of silents including *Anne of Green Gables* (1919) with Mary Miles Minter. Three weeks after the release of *Slide, Kelly, Slide*, Kelly had a drunken brawl with a friend of his, Ray Raymond. Raymond died two days after the fight from complications caused by alcoholism. Unfortunately, Kelly was blamed for having caused Raymond's death during their fight, and was convicted of manslaughter. He was released for good behavior after having served 25 months in San Quentin prison. Despite the scandal, Kelly made a successful comeback upon his release, and worked steadily in films until his death in 1956.

Slide, Kelly, Slide, according to Junior Coghlan's 1993 autobiography, was the film debut of Johnny Mack Brown in a cameo appearance—just a few months before his first major role in Marion Davies' *The Fair Co-Ed.* In addition, a number of important baseball stars of the time made cameo appearances.

This is a light, entertaining film which features a good blend of drama and comedy. In addition, it has historic importance as a nostalgic look at the New York Yankees of 1927. This is a film which has appeal for silent film fans as well as baseball buffs. The copy reviewed here was from Junior Coghlan's private collection. It is a shame that *Slide, Kelly, Slide* is among hundreds of silents in the vaults of Turner Entertainment that have neither been aired on television nor released on video.

547. Special Delivery

Rating: ☆☆☆½

Paramount; ***Directed by*** William Goodrich [Roscoe Arbuckle's alias]; ***Photographed by*** Harry

Roscoe Arbuckle standing outside his nightclub, The Plantation, around the time he was directing *Special Delivery* (1927) under the alias of William Goodrich.

Hallenberger; ***Screenplay by*** John Goodrich; ***Titles by*** George Marion, Jr.; ***Edited by*** Louis D. Lighton; ***Running Time:*** 58 minutes; ***Cast:*** EDDIE BEAGLE, Eddie Cantor (1892–1964); MADGE WARREN, Jobyna Ralston (1900–1967); HAROLD JONES, William Powell (1892–1984); FLANNIGAN, Jack Dougherty (1895–1938); HARRIGAN, Donald Keith (1903–1969); JOHN BEAGLE, Louis Stern (1860–1941)

This is Eddie Cantor's follow-up to *Kid Boots* (1926), as well as his second, last, and best silent film.

In *Special Delivery*, Cantor plays Eddie Beagle, who comes from a long line of employees of the postal secret service. Their biggest secret was how Eddie ever managed to get in. He is given an ultimatum by his father that he is disowned until he makes good. So, Eddie sets his sights high to prove himself—by capturing Blackie Morgan, a notorious criminal that no secret service man has succeeded in nabbing. Eddie gets into a variety of misadventures, and everything that could possibly go wrong does. Through several unexpected mishaps and good luck, he finally gets his man, and proves himself worthy of the Beagle name, getting a $20,000 reward in the process.

This is one of the extremely few extant silents that were directed by Roscoe Arbuckle (1887–1933) under the alias of William Goodrich. Jobyna Ralston, best remembered as Harold Lloyd's leading lady in the mid–1920s, is the leading lady to Eddie Cantor in this film as well. William Powell plays the villain, who is masquerading under the name of Harold Jones. Jack Dougherty, who plays Flannigan, one of Eddie's roommates and rivals for the affections of Madge Warren, was at one point married to Barbara LaMarr (1896–1926). He was only 32 in this film, but appeared fortyish, thus showing that life had not been easy for him. In 1938, he committed suicide at age 43 by inhaling carbon monoxide fumes.

This delightful comedy is by far the better of Eddie Cantor's two silent comedies—accomplished without the all-star cast of *Kid Boots*. This is due in part to the expert comedy direction of Roscoe Arbuckle as William Goodrich.

548. Stark Love

Rating: ☆☆☆½

Paramount; ***Written and Directed by*** Karl Brown; ***Adaptation by*** Walter Woods; ***Photography by*** James Murray; ***Running Time:*** 72 minutes; ***Cast:*** ROB WARWICK, Forrest James; JASON WARWICK, Slios Miracle; BARBARA ALLEN, Helen Munday; QUILL ALLEN, Rob Grahon

This film was the directorial debut of Karl Brown (1897–1990), who is best known for his excellent cinematography work in many of D.W. Griffith's films, which include *The Birth of a Nation* (1915), *Intolerance* (1916), *Hearts of the World* (1918), and *A Romance of Happy Valley* (1918). He also photographed the widely acclaimed James Cruze westerns, *The Covered Wagon* (1923) and *The Pony Express* (1925). After his directorial debut with this film, Brown went on to direct and co-script a number of films in the talkie era into the 1940s.

Stark Love was filmed on location in the mountains of North Carolina. No big name stars were used; all parts were played by local North Carolina residents. The story centers around a young man named Rob Warwick, who has risen above his cultural heritage and learned how to read—becoming the only person among his neighbors and family to do so. He takes a liking to Barbara Allen, a young woman from a neighboring family. He treats her with tenderness and respect—an act which is unprecedented in their surroundings.

Encouraged by his mother, he determines to take his horse to the city and sell it to pay for schooling. Once he gets the horse sold, he sacrifices his own education aspirations, and decides to use the money to put Barbara through school instead. While he is in the city, his mother dies from overwork and stress—inevitable in the atmosphere in which they live, in which men are the rulers and women are slaves whose sole purpose is to either work themselves to death or to die during one of many childbirths. In light of his wife's death, Jason Warwick decides that Barbara would be a perfect replacement slave. So, he gets permission from Quill Allen, Barbara's father, to marry her—although she herself was never asked what she thought. Once Rob finds out what his father's intentions are for Barbara, the big confrontation occurs between father and son.

Of the love stories adapted for silent cinema which have been evaluated for this book, *Stark Love* is among the most compelling. Karl Brown did a wonderful job with this directorial debut, and one wonders why he never moved beyond "B" pictures with his later directorial efforts. Forrest James and Helen Munday give fine performances. If one did not know that they were local residents with no previous acting experience, one would think that they were prominent, established actors. Helen Munday is especially good in the sequence toward the end, in which she stands up to Jason Warwick and determines to rescue the younger Warwick, who has just been thrown into a flooding river current by his father.

Very little has been written about this obscure film. William K. Everson's *American Silent Film* makes only passing reference to it, mentioning it as a film that sought out the primitive and sordid. *Stark Love* and *Greed* were cited as two examples of such films. In *Greed*, the characters revert to primitive and sordid lifestyles as a result of Trina McTeague's obsession with money. *Stark Love* portrays exactly the opposite situation. In this film, it is Rob Warwick's selflessness and sacrifice that helps him and Barbara Allen to rise above their primitive surroundings and into the pursuit of a better life for themselves.

Stark Love was previously classified as a lost film, but was rediscovered in a Czechoslovakian archive. It was restored and shown one time on television, as part of a series called "Lost and Found" presented by PBS in the 1970s. It is because of this screening that this film was accessible for evaluation. Hopefully, more screenings and programs of this type will be done on television in the future.

549. The Student Prince in Old Heidelberg [a.k.a. *Old Heidelberg*] *Rating:* ☆☆☆

MGM; ***Directed by*** Ernst Lubitsch; ***Continuity by*** Hans Kraly; ***From the Book by*** Karl Heinrich; ***Titles by*** Marion Ainslee and Ruth Cummings; ***Settings by*** Cedric Gibbons, Richard Day; ***Wardrobe by*** Ali Hubert; ***Photography by*** John Mescall; ***Film Editor:*** Andrew Marton; ***Running Time:*** 104 minutes; ***Cast:*** PRINCE KARL HEINRICH, Ramon Novarro (1899–1968); KATHI, Norma Shearer (1900–1983); DR. JUTTNER, Jean Hersholt (1886–1956); KING KARL VII, Gustav von Seyffertitz (1863–1943); HEIR APPARENT, Philippe De Lacy (1917–1995); KELLERMAN, Bobby Mack; COURT MARSHAL, Edward Connelly (1855–1928); OLD RUDER, Otis Harlan (1865–1940); STUDENT, John S. Peters (1894–1963)

This is the second of three screen adaptations of *Old Heidelberg*. The first was done in 1915, and reviewed elsewhere in this book. The third version was a highly successful 1954 musical.

The story is familiar to most movie buffs. Prince Karl falls in love with Kathi, a waitress whom he meets while in school. He is forbidden to marry outside his social class. Lubitsch did a good job with contrasting how wonderful many people thought it would be to be a prince, and the reality of the unhappiness that a royal title brings. It features lavish production values, and is a significant improvement over the 1915 version.

Of all of Ernst Lubitsch's surviving silent era work, this film is the only one that really comes across well. His other silent era work left a lot to be desired. For some reason, Lubitsch came across better in the talkie era. (*The Patriot* [1928], which was more highly acclaimed than *The Student Prince in Old Heidelberg*, remains one of the most coveted of the lost silent films. The stills from *The Patriot* are remarkable and cause for lament over the loss of what would probably be considered Lubitsch's masterpiece.) Among Lubitsch's highly acclaimed talkies are *The Love Parade* (1929), *Trouble in Paradise* (1932), *To Be or Not to Be* (1942), and *Heaven Can Wait* (1943). He received an honorary Academy Award in 1937.

Before seeing this film, this reviewer could not picture Ramon Novarro in the role of the prince. But, he carries it off surprisingly well, although it is opined that Wallace Reid (1891–1923) was the ultimate actor for the role based on his performance in the 1915 version. Norma Shearer is competent in the lead female role of Kathi.

550. Sunrise: A Song of Two Humans

Rating: ☆☆☆

Fox; ***Directed by*** F.W. Murnau; ***Scenario by*** Carl Meyer; ***Photography by*** Charles Rosher and Karl Struss; ***Titles by*** Katherine Hillicker and H.H. Caldwell; ***Running Time:*** 110 minutes; ***Cast:*** THE FARMER, George O'Brien (1900–1985); HIS WIFE, Janet Gaynor (1906–1984); THE VAMP, Margaret Livingston (1895–1984); THE MAID, Bodil Rosing (1877–1941); THE PHOTOGRAPHER, J. Farrell MacDonald (1875–1952); THE BARBER, Ralph Sipperly (1890–1928); THE MANICURE GIRL, Jane Winton (1905–1959); THE OBTRUSIVE GENTLEMAN, Arthur Housman (1889–1942); THE OBLIGING GENTLEMAN, Eddie Boland (1885–1935)

This film was the biggest Academy Award winner of the 1927–28 season, the first year of the Academy Awards. It won a total of three, one of which for Best Cinematography. In addition, it was the "other" Best Picture award winner in the only year that two awards were given out—for best production, and best artistic quality of production. *Sunrise* won for the latter, and *Wings* for the former. The third Academy Award went to Janet Gaynor, who was nominated on the basis of her performances in *Sunrise* (1927), *7th Heaven* (1927), and *Street Angel* (1928). The critical acclaim for this film has stood the test of time. In a recent poll conducted by *Classic Images*, *Sunrise* ranked in the "Top Ten" list of favorites.

The story is a relatively simple one. A farmer, who is happily married to his wife falls for a vamp from the nearby city. The vamp tries to convince the farmer to sell his farm and move to the city with her. When the farmer asks what is to be done with his wife, the vamp suggests that she be conveniently drowned. The farmer's lust takes over his instincts of decency, and he decides to give it a try. The next day, he takes his wife on a "boating trip," starts to commit the murder, but comes to his senses and cannot carry it out. The wife, absolutely horrified, boards a street car bound for the city. The farmer follows her, eventually regaining her trust again, and they experience a renewal of their love for one another. On their way back to the farm, a violent storm hits, capsizing their boat. The husband gets away, but the wife is nowhere to be found, as was originally intended. Murnau keeps the audience in suspense throughout the rest of the film wondering if she will be alive, or if her corpse will be found.

Despite the film's magnificent and well-deserved critical acclaim, it lost a great deal of money. This was due mostly to extraordinary production costs. The sets of the city were specifically built for this movie. In addition, the railroad tracks for the street car going from the country to the city were specifically built. Another factor that hurt this film was that the talkie revolution was well underway by the time *Sunrise* was released in late 1927.

The only thing that really mars this film are the attempts by F.W. Murnau to include sequences of comic relief. Some examples of the attempts at humor are the sequence of the drunk pig running around the ball room; the man and wife knocking over a statue and thinking they have broken the head off, trying to improvise with a rubber ball; and other acts of silliness during their night on the town. Murnau did not originally want to include these sequences, but the Fox executives insisted that comic relief be included in order to "play to the audience." In this case, the public was wrong, and Murnau was right, as these attempts at humor are the only weak parts of an otherwise perfect film.

The cinematography in this film is magnificent, and definitely worthy of the first Cinematography Academy Award awarded to it. The tracking shots of the man crossing the swamp to meet the vamp of the story are atmospheric and well executed. In addition, one of the most artistic uses of a title card appears in this film. In the sequence in which the temptress vamp asks, "Couldn't she get—drowned?" the final word appears after all of the others are on the screen, elongates downward, and gives the illusion of melting and dissolving.

With this film's historic importance as the film receiving the most Academy Awards in the first year of the ceremonies, it is one that nobody should miss. It is encouraging to see that this film has finally been revived on video, laser disc, and American Movie Classics as it should be.

551. Tell It to the Marines

Rating: ☆☆☆

MGM; ***Directed by*** George W. Hill; ***Screenplay by*** Richard Schayer; ***Titles by*** Joe Farnham; ***Settings by*** Cedric Gibbons and Arnold Gillespie; ***Wardrobe by*** Kathleen Kay and Maude Marsh; ***Film Editor:*** Blanche Sewell; ***Photography by*** Ira Morgan; ***Running Time:*** 93 minutes; ***Cast:*** SERGEANT O'HARA, Lon Chaney, Sr. (1883–1930); PRIVATE "SKEET" BURNS, William Haines (1900–1973); NORMA DALE, Eleanor Boardman (1898–1991); CORPORAL MADDEN, Eddie Gribbon (1890–1965); ZAYA, Carmel Myers (1901–1980); CHINESE BANDIT CHIEF, Warner Oland (1880–1938); NATIVE, Mitchell Lewis (1880–1956); GENERAL WILCOX, Frank Currier (1857–1928); HARRY, Maurice Kains

While Lon Chaney was most famous for his gruesome disguises, it is ironic that this film, in which he played a "straight" role as a marine sergeant, was among the highest grossing of his MGM silents.

Tell It to the Marines is a light military comedy, with some drama mixed in. Actor William Haines stars as a new recruit in the Marine Corps who is constantly at odds with Sergeant O'Hara, a drill sergeant who appears to have a heart of stone on the outside, but actually has a heart of gold beneath his tough exterior. The two really become at odds with each other when they both want to date the Navy nurse played by Eleanor Boardman. It seems that everything that can possibly go wrong for Private Burns does, but all works out in the end when Burns proves himself in a real combat situation, and he and O'Hara become friends.

With the pairing of Lon Chaney and William Haines, two of MGM's most bankable stars of the time, there was no way this film could miss at the box office. Leading lady Eleanor Boardman was on her way up the ladder of significant success as well. *Tell It to the Marines* is a fun film, holding up well 70 years after its release. Unfortunately, the only copies of this film that are available are taken from mediocre prints on which some of the titles are dim and barely readable. It is a film that deserves a quality, legitimate release by Turner Entertainment.

This film was produced with the full cooperation of the United States Marine Corps. It is rather ironic that the armed services would cooperate, as William Haines, lead star of this film, and Ramon Novarro (1899–1968), star of *The Flying Fleet* (1928), which the Navy cooperated on, were both openly gay.

552. Underworld

Rating: ☆☆☆☆

Paramount; ***Directed by*** Josef Von Sternberg; ***Photography by*** Bert Glennon; ***Edited by*** F. Lloyd Sheldon; ***Story by*** Ben Hecht; ***Adaptation by*** Charles Furthmann; ***Screenplay by*** Robert N. Lee;

Titles by George Marion, Jr.; ***Running Time:*** 80 minutes; ***Cast:*** BULL WEED, George Bancroft (1882–1956); FEATHERS, Evelyn Brent (1899–1975); ROLLS ROYCE, Clive Brook (1887–1974); BUCK MULLIGAN, Fred Kohler (1888–1938); HIS GIRL, Helen Lynch (1900–1965); SLIPPY LEWIS, Larry Semon (1889–1928); PALOMA, Jerry Mandy (1892–1945)

Underworld was Josef Von Sternberg's first really great hit, and it was a box office as well as a critical success. It was the preeminent gangster picture of the late 1920s, and several of the scenes were copied in the later gangster films that were so popular in the 1930s and 1940s.

This film also sent stars George Bancroft and Evelyn Brent to stardom. Bancroft, who had starred mostly in westerns, had his first hit with *Pony Express* (1925), as the villain in James Cruze's follow up to *The Covered Wagon* (1923). Before Von Sternberg turned Marlene Dietrich into a glamour queen in 1930, he did the same with Evelyn Brent, using his unique sense of lighting and camera angles to bring out Brent's best features to their fullest luminescent beauty. *Underworld* is also Clive Brook's best silent era performance, and provided the opportunity for Larry Semon to make a departure from slapstick comedy into a serious character role just before his death a year later.

In this film, the shady underworld of New York is portrayed, with Bancroft playing the likable Bull Weed, a prominent mob leader. Evelyn Brent plays Feathers, Bull Weed's mistress. Rolls Royce is a new member of the gang whom Feathers becomes attracted to. Bull Weed is framed for a murder he actually didn't commit by a rival mobster, and is sentenced to hang. Feathers and Rolls Royce are torn between carrying out an escape plan to free the mob boss, or simply making a run for happiness, leaving Bull Weed behind. Loyalty wins out, but the plans go awry, and they aren't at the appointed place and time, which leads into the thrilling, fast paced climax of the film.

Kevin Brownlow's magnificent 1968 book, *The Parade's Gone By*, acclaims *Underworld* as: "the film that began the gangster cycle, and it remains the masterpiece of the genre." While *Underworld* was certainly not the first gangster picture, having been predated by such early films as *The Musketeers of Pig Alley* (1912), *Regeneration* (1915), and *Alias Jimmy Valentine* (1915), among others, it was the film that popularized the gangster genre. The subsequent gangster classics that followed were mostly slick variations, containing many of the atmospheric elements that originated in *Underworld*.

For years, this film was available only in extremely poor quality, barely watchable bootleg copies. In 1995, Grapevine Video released an excellent copy of the film, making it once again widely available as it was meant to be seen for the first time since its original release. With its first rate direction and photography, as well as a top notch cast, *Underworld* is highly recommended, and is a must-see especially for fans of the gangster film genre.

553. The Unknown

Rating: ☆☆☆½

MGM; ***Directed by*** Tod Browning; ***Scenario by*** Waldemar Young; ***Story by*** Tod Browning; ***Titles by*** Joe Farnham; ***Settings by*** Cedric Gibbons and Richard Day; ***Wardrobe by*** Lucia Coulter; ***Photography by*** M. Gerstad; ***Film Editors:*** Harry Reynolds and Errol Taggart; ***Running Time:*** 49 minutes; ***Cast:*** ALONZO, Lon Chaney, Sr. (1883–1930); MALABA, Norman Kerry (1889–1956); NANON, Joan Crawford (1904–1977); ZANZI, Nick De Ruiz; COJO, John George (1898–1968); COSTRA, Frank Lanning (1872–1945)

The Unknown is widely regarded as Lon Chaney's weirdest and most bizarre film. Director Tod Browning (1882–1962), like Chaney, specialized in the bizarre and unusual, and they made an excellent team. Browning, who had been a circus performer and contortionist in his younger days, reportedly based the story of this film loosely on some of his own actual experiences.

The story has Lon Chaney as Alonzo, a fugitive who uses a strait jacket to disguise himself as an armless, knife-throwing circus performer. Chaney actually throws knives around Joan Crawford with his feet and toes! Alonzo falls in love with Nanon, who feels secure with him because she has a phobia of men putting their arms around her.

To please the object of his affections, Alonzo actually has his arms surgically removed. When he returns to Nanon, she has gotten over her phobia and married Malabar, a strong man portrayed by Norman Kerry. One of Malabar's circus feats is to tie each arm to running horses going in opposite directions, appearing to hold them back with his vast strength. Alonzo, in a rage, plots to rig the show so that Malabar's arms will be torn off.

This was Joan Crawford's first really big part under her new contract with MGM. *The Unknown* is a favorite among Chaney buffs, and is just as bizarre and strange as any film that could be released today. Turner Classic Movies aired a restored version of this macabre classic in early 1997, with a full orchestral score performed by the Alloy Orchestra.

554. Wings

Rating: ☆☆☆½

Paramount; ***Directed by*** William Wellman; ***Story by*** John Monk Saunders; ***Screenplay by*** Hope Loring and Louis D. Lighton; ***Editor-in-chief:*** F. Lloyd Sheldon; ***Photographed by*** Harry Perry; ***Titles by*** Julian Johnson; ***Running Time:*** 139 minutes; ***Cast:*** MARY PRESTON, Clara Bow (1905–1965); JOHN "JACK" POWELL, Charles (Buddy) Rogers (born 1904); DAVID ARMSTRONG, Richard Arlen (1899–1976); AUGUST SCHMIDT, El Brendel (1891–1964); SYLVIA LEWIS, Jobyna Ralston (1900–1967); AIR COMMANDER, Richard Tucker (1883–1942); CADET WHITE, Gary Cooper (1901–1961); SERGEANT, Edward "Gunboat" Smith (1887–1974); MR. ARMSTRONG, Henry B. Walthall (1878–1936); MRS. ARMSTRONG, Julia Swayne Gordon (1878–1933); CELESTE, Arlette Marchal (1902–1984); MR. POWELL, George Irving (1874–1961); MRS. POWELL, Hedda Hopper (1890–1966); PEASANT, Nigel de Brulier (1877–1948)

Wings was Paramount's answer to Fox's *What Price Glory?* (1926) and MGM's *The Big Parade* (1924). It featured a stellar, multi-star cast, and was the first big success of director William Wellman (1896–1975), who would go on to win three Academy Award nominations for Best Director in 1937, 1949, and 1954. Among his finest achievements were *A Star Is Born* (1937), *The Public Enemy* (1931), and *Beau Geste* (1939). It features a familiar story of two neighborhood chums who leave their admiring sweethearts behind to go off to battle in World War I. Stationed together in France, they both fall for their neighborhood friend Mary Preston, who is doing her part in the war effort as an ambulance driver. In an exhilarating air combat sequence, David is shot down and held captive by the Germans. He manages to escape in a German plane, and in the course of returning to his home base, is spotted by best friend Jack, who recognizes only the German plane. Unaware that David is the pilot, Jack shoots the plane down.

Buddy Rogers, Clara Bow, and Richard Arlen in a scene from *Wings* (1927).

Wings features some of the best combat footage of any war film ever made. It successfully meets the challenge of MGM's *The Big Parade* (1924) [even if not equaling or surpassing it] and is far superior to Fox's atrocious and overrated *What Price Glory?* (1926).

Richard Arlen and Buddy Rogers give pleasing performances in the male lead roles. Rogers is especially delightful in a comedy sequence during which he is drunk. Gay viewers will especially enjoy the male to male kiss between Rogers and Arlen. Clara Bow gives an energetic performance as the bubbly Mary Preston. Gary Cooper gives a distinctive appearance in his cameo as an aviator who is killed during a flight training accident.

As good a film as *Wings* is, this reviewer does not feel that it deserved to win the first "Best Production" Academy Award. There were too many far more worthy masterpieces competing in the same year, including *Sadie Thompson* (1928) and *The Crowd* (1928), among others.

555. The Yankee Clipper *Rating:* ☆☆☆

DeMille Productions; ***Directed by*** Rupert Julian; ***Assistant Director:*** Leigh R. Smith; ***Story by*** Dennison Clift; ***Adaptation by*** Garnett Weston; ***Titles by*** John W. Krafft; ***Photography by*** John Mescall; ***Film Editor:*** Harold McLernon; ***Running Time:*** 69 minutes; ***Cast:*** HAL WINSLOW, William Boyd (1895–1972); MICKEY, Junior Coghlan (born 1916); LADY JOCELYN, Elinor Fair (1902–1957); QUEEN VICTORIA, Julia Faye (1893–1966); LORD ANTHONY HUNTINGTON, Louis Payne (1873–1953); IRONHEAD JOE, Walter Long (1879–1952); PAUL DE VIGNEY, John Miljan (1892–1960)

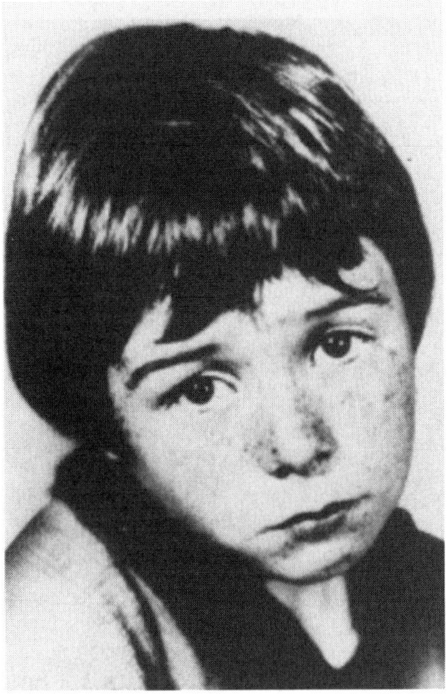

Junior Coghlan, child star of *The Yankee Clipper* (1927).

The Yankee Clipper was the first film project taken on by director Rupert Julian upon completion of *The Phantom of the Opera* (1925). The story is concerned with the rivalry between America and England during the mid–1800s for the world tea trade. To settle the score, a race is on to see which ship can travel from China to Boston Harbor in the least amount of time. The loser gives up both the tea trade and his ship to the winner.

Heading up the cast as captain of the "Yankee Clipper" is William Boyd, who starred in a number of important silents, but who is best remembered for the "Hopalong Cassidy" films of the 1930s and 1940s. Elinor Fair plays Lady Jocelyn, a member of the British aristocracy who is stranded on the Yankee Clipper by accident, along with her fiancee, Paul de Vigney, who is portrayed by John Miljan. Miljan was known for villain roles throughout his career, which lasted from 1924 to 1958. Junior Coghlan plays a young stowaway named Mickey who is accepted among the crew when he demonstrates unusual bravery for a child of age 10.

During the race, Captain Winslow falls in love with Lady Jocelyn, who is engaged to scoundrel de Vigney, who has another woman on the side, and is interested in Jocelyn only for her money. Mickey, the stowaway, hates women due to the cruel treatment he suffered at the hands of his two aunts, which prompted him to run away. An amusing incident occurs in which the clipper is ashore, and Mickey thinks he is getting a ship tattooed on his back. When he sees in the mirror that the "ship" is actually a mermaid, he hits the tattooer over the head with the mirror, and trashes his entire shop.

The first major obstacle faced by the Yankee Clipper's crew is a typhoon in which four crew members are lost, and during which one of the main water tanks is destroyed. This leads to a shortage of water for the rest of the trip. De Vigney, of course, demonstrates his cowardice during the storm, and also hoards some of the emergency kegs of water for his own use. A mutiny occurs among the thirsty crew. It is during this mutiny that "Ironhead Joe" takes advantage of the situation and tries to have his way with Lady Jocelyn. Mickey, who decides that women are not so bad after all, foils the attempt by hitting Ironhead over the skull with a belaying pin, and he helps Jocelyn to escape to safety. A chase occurs when Ironhead regroups his wits, which is an exhilarating part of the film. This film keeps the audience in suspense as the final outcome of the voyage unfolds.

The Yankee Clipper is entertaining fare, and considered to be among the better sea adventures of the silent era. Rupert Julian does a fine job of directing, and the cast is equally as good. Junior Coghlan refers to this film as his favorite memory of his entire film career.

1928

556. Across to Singapore

Rating: ☆☆☆☆

MGM; ***Directed by*** William Nigh; ***Based on*** Ben Ames Williams' book *All the Brothers Were Valiant*; ***Adaptation by*** Ted Shane; ***Continuity by*** Richard Schayer; ***Titles by*** Joe Farnham; ***Settings by*** Cedric Gibbons; ***Wardrobe by*** David Cox; ***Photography by*** John Seitz; ***Film Editor:*** Ben Lewis; ***Running Time:*** 85 minutes; ***Cast:*** JOEL SHORE, Ramon Novarro (1899–1968); PRISCILLA CROWNINSHIELD, Joan Crawford (1904–1977); CAPTAIN MARK SHORE, Ernest Torrence (1878–1933); JEREMIAH SHORE, Frank Currier (1857–1928); NOAH SHORE, Dan Wolhelm; MATTHEW SHORE, Duke Martin; JOSHUA CROWNINSHIELD, Edward Connelly (1855–1928); FINCH, James Mason (1889–1959)

This is a film that was saved just in time. By the time it was accessed from the vaults, it was discovered that the negative had begun to decompose. So, there are sequences in which decomposition is evident, but fortunately the film is still very watchable, and in complete form.

Director William Nigh (1881–1955) began his career with Mack Sennett in 1915, and worked steadily through 1948, when he retired. His earliest drama work that is widely available is *My Four Years in Germany* (1918), which was highly acclaimed. A clip from his film, *The Fire Brigade* (1927) appeared in Kevin Brownlow's *Hollywood* (1980) documentary series, and has whetted many a collector's appetite to see the entire film, but so far Turner Entertainment has not made any effort to make it available. One of Nigh's other rare surviving silents is *Mr. Wu* (1927), which starred Lon Chaney, Sr.

Across to Singapore was made at a time before Joan Crawford was receiving top billing. She and Ernest Torrence shared second billing below Ramon Novarro, who was one of MGM's hottest properties at the time.

In this film, Novarro plays Joel Shore, the youngest son in a ship captain's family with three older brothers who treat him like a child who isn't worthy of responsibility as they are. Ernest Torrence plays his older brother Mark. Both Mark and Joel are in love with Ms. Crawford's character of Priscilla. Older brother Mark has Mr. Crowninshield's permission to marry Priscilla after his next trip, but Priscilla actually prefers Joel.

On the next trip, Joel is making his debut as a ship mate, and works hard to prove himself as a man who has come of age. While the rivalry at home has been lighthearted, with each brother playing pranks on the other, the intensity of the rivalry escalates once the brothers are out to sea.

Once aboard the ship, one of the middle brothers, who is first mate, dies in a storm, and Captain Mark moves brother Joel into the position, for the second time bypassing Priscilla's brother, Finch. Finch is set on revenge, and determines to take over the ship himself. He gets Mark drunk, and thinks he has succeeded in getting him killed in a drunken brawl. Then, he lies and says that Joel deserted his brother, and is to blame for getting him killed. To keep from spoiling the film for those who have not yet seen it, the reviewer will simply state that this is the point where *Across to Singapore* really starts getting good. You won't be able to take your eyes off the screen until the very end.

Across to Singapore is a fabulous drama of love, rivalry, and betrayal. William Nigh demonstrates his excellence as a director with this film. It features a great story, with a top notch cast giving top notch performances. Ramon Novarro gives one of his best performances—second only to his performance in *Ben-Hur* (1927)—as Joel. Joan Crawford will be almost unrecognizable as the beautiful heroine with an aura of charm and innocence which belied her later reputation as more of a sultry, sophisticated figure. Ernest Torrence as older brother Mark gives his usual expected exceptional performance as the captain betrayed by a disgruntled subordinate. James Mason as Finch gives what is the best performance of his career. This James Mason (1889–1959) is not to be confused with the British actor James Mason (1909–1984) who started his career in British talkies in 1935, and was most famous for *A Star Is Born* (1954). The silent era James Mason began his career in 1914, and appeared mostly in westerns and action films like this one.

Ramon Novarro, star of *Across to Singapore* (1928).

It is interesting also to note that both of the actors who played the father figures in this film died the year it was completed.

Turner Classic Movies did the world a fabulous service by making *Across to Singapore* accessible for viewing on television, with an excellent new piano score. It is good to see that this film has finally been brought out of obscurity, and is starting to get the wide audience that it deserves. If you haven't seen it yet, you should make a point to catch it the next time it is aired on TCM, or borrow a copy if you can find somebody who taped it. It is an action sea thriller on a par with *Mutiny on the Bounty* (1935), not to be missed.

557. Alraune

Rating: ☆☆☆½

AMA Film/Germany; ***Directed by*** Henryk Galeen; ***Based on the Novel by*** Hanns Heinz Ewers; ***Screenplay by*** Henryk Galeen, Hanns Heinz Ewers; ***Photography by*** Franz Planer; ***Settings by*** Walter Reiman, Max Hellbronner; ***Running Time:*** 97 minutes; ***Cast:*** ALRAUNE, Brigitte Helm (1906–1996); PROFESSOR BRINKEN, Paul Wegener (1874–1948); FRANZ BRAUN, Ivan Petrovich (1896–1962); DIE DIME, Mia Pankau; VON DER GASSE, Valeska Gert (1896–1978); SOLFCHEN, Wolfgang Zilzer; ZAUBERKUNSTLER, Louis Ralph; DOMPTEUR, Hans Trautner; VICOMTE, John Loder (1898–1988); MAN IN BAR, Heinrich Schroth; MAN IN CAR, Alexander Sascha

This was the third of at least four screen adaptations of Hanns Heinz Ewer's famous 1913 novel. The first two adaptations came out in 1918, and were in direct competition with each other. One was produced in Germany, and the other was produced in Austria and Hungary. The Austrian version was co-directed by none other than Michael Curtiz, when he was using the name Mihaly Kertesz. This third adaptation was the first of two versions to star Brigitte Helm, and is acclaimed as the definitive film version.

Brigitte Helm, star of *Alraune* (1928), in the late 1930s.

The 1931 sound version starring Ms. Helm is widely regarded as inferior to her original version.

Paul Wegener, who is best remembered for his roles in *The Student of Prague* (1913) and *The Golem* (1920), plays a mad professor who impregnates a prostitute with the semen of a convicted murderer hanged at the gallows. Brigitte Helm plays Alraune, the product of this diabolical experiment. She gives an excellent performance as the woman who finds out how she was conceived, and determines to destroy her creator.

The difference between this and prior adaptations was that Alraune is given a more human portrayal in Galeen's version. In prior versions, she became a vamp who lured men into her web only to destroy them. This time around, she actually falls in love with another man, showing that she is not evil at heart, but simply the product of evil intentions which backfire on her creator. She goes on to a happy, fulfilling life after she puts her evil roots behind her.

Ivan Petrovich plays Franz Braun, the man whose love redeems Alraune. He had previously co-starred with Paul Wegener in Rex Ingram's *The Magician* (1926) before returning to Germany to make this film.

Director Henryk Galeen (1882–1949) had a long professional relationship with Paul Wegener which began in 1914 with the original version of *The Golem* that they co-directed. In 1920, Galeen directed Wegener in the title role in his remake of *The Golem.* He had just finished a 1926 remake of *The Student in Prague* with Conrad Veidt prior to starting work on *Alraune.*

558. The Battle of the Century

Rating: ☆☆☆

Hal Roach/MGM; ***Directed by*** Clyde Bruckman; ***Supervised by*** Leo McCarey; ***Photographed by*** George Stevens; ***Edited by*** Richard Currier; ***Titles by*** H.M. Walker; ***Running Time of Surviving Footage:*** 11 minutes; ***Running Time with Still and Script Restoration:*** 17 minutes; ***Cast:*** Canvasback Clump a.k.a. "the human mop," Stan Laurel (1890–1965); His manager, Oliver Hardy (1892–1957); Thunderclap Callahan, Noah Young (1887–1958); Insurance salesman, Eugene Pallette (1889–1954) [footage lost]; Spectator at boxing match, Lou Costello (1906–1959); Man who slips on banana peel, Charlie Hall (1899–1959); Woman who slips on pie, Anita Garvin (1906–1994)

For many years, this rare Laurel and Hardy classic was believed lost. The original negative decomposed in the late 1950s, shortly after the famous pie sequence had been copied for a documentary. It was thought that this pie sequence was all that remained of the film. In 1979, all of the first reel of the film turned up. The beginning of reel 2 is

Laurel and Hardy, stars of *Battle of the Century* (1928).

still lost, but has been restored with the use of stills and the original continuity script. This lost footage featured Eugene Pallette (best remembered for his role in the French story of *Intolerance*) as a salesperson who sells Ollie an insurance policy which pays off in the event that Stan is injured.

The first reel starts out with Stan in a boxing match with prizefighter Thunderclap Callahan. By a stroke of luck, Stan knocks Callahan down for a long enough period of time to have won the fight. But, with the delays in the count that Stan unwittingly causes, Callahan recovers before the ten-count is reached, and wins the match. This is the end of the extant first reel. In this first reel, one can catch a glimpse of Lou Costello as a ringside spectator in the only silent film footage he appeared in, years before he teamed with Bud Abbott to form Abbott and Costello.

The missing footage at the beginning of reel 2 contained the sequence of Ollie buying the insurance policy on Stan. Stan and Ollie walk down the street, with Stan doing a lot of falling in order to try to collect on the policy. The extant footage of reel 2 begins with a pie delivery man slipping on a banana peel that he thinks Stan dropped. This marks the start of one of the greatest pie fights in the history of slapstick comedy. Anita Garvin appears at the very end as a woman who slips on a pie.

Noah Young is perhaps best remembered as Harold Lloyd's sidekick in *Safety Last* (1923). Charlie Hall began his career in comedies in Charlie Chaplin's *The Gold Rush* (1925). In the late silent era, he made a transition to horror films. Among the numerous notable films he appeared in were *The Cohens and the Kellys* (1926), *The Cat and the Canary* (1927), *The Man Who Laughs* (1928), *The Circus* (1928), *The Last Warning* (1929), *Dracula* (1931), *Frankenstein* (1931), *The Old Dark House* (1932), *The Invisible Man* (1933), *Magnificent Obsession* (1935), and *Show Boat* (1936).

559. Buried Treasure

Rating: ☆

Climax Fables; ***Running Time:*** 4½ minutes; ***Cast:*** "Eveready" Horton

This is a hard core pornographic animated film. The character, Eveready Horton, is cast on a desert island. He has an unusually large sex organ that literally has a mind of its own. The film takes us through the many sexual adventures of Horton and his organ. Every type of sex act imaginable and unimaginable is depicted in an unusually vulgar fashion.

If a live action version of this film were ever made, it would likely be banned in even the most liberal parts of the United States and the world.

560. The Cameraman

Rating: ☆☆☆☆

MGM; ***Directed by*** Edward Sedgwick; ***Story by*** Clyde Bruckman, Lew Lipton; ***Continuity by*** Richard Schayer; ***Titles by*** Joe Farnham; ***Settings by*** Fred Gabourie; ***Wardrobe by*** David Cox; ***Photography by*** Elgin Lessley, Reggie Lanning; ***Film Editor:*** Hugh Wynn; ***Running Time:*** 69 minutes; ***Cast:*** BUSTER, Buster Keaton (1895–1966); SALLY, Marceline Day (born 1907); STAGG, Harold Goodwin (1902–1987); EDITOR, Sidney Bracy (1877–1942); COP, Harry Gribbon (1885–1961)

This is yet another American classic that was almost lost, and saved when a print was discovered in France. It was Buster Keaton's first film as a contract player for MGM. Although Keaton was very unhappy having to give up his artistic autonomy, this film shows that MGM was giving Keaton good material to work with at first, and for this film, the quality of Keaton's productions was maintained while he had his own crew working with him.

The Cameraman is a parody of the newsreel photographers—namely the William Randolph Hearst newsreels and publications. One of the reasons that Keaton reportedly chose to do a subtle parody on Hearst is because he was still seething over how the Hearst papers smeared his good friend, Roscoe Arbuckle, in 1921 and 1922.

In this film, Keaton plays a tin type photographer who has fallen for a pretty secretary at the MGM newsreel headquarters, played by Marceline Day. To impress her, he purchases a movie camera and endeavors to become a newsreel photographer.

As usual in the Keaton comedies, everything that can possibly go wrong does. One sequence has Keaton with his camera right in the middle of a violent Chinese gang war, only to find out that there was no film in the camera. Just as Buster has given up hope, he is filming on a lake when Sally and rival suitor Stagg have a boating accident. Buster pulls Sally to safety, but Stagg takes the credit. It turns out that Buster's monkey filmed the entire incident, thus exposing Stagg for the liar he is, and Buster as the real hero.

Keaton has some good sight gags in this picture. In one sequence, he is shown walking down the sidewalk with Sally, and slipping on a banana peel. Then, he is shown approaching yet another banana peel that the audience expects him to do a repeat slip on, but he walks right over it. Another good scene shows a bunch of muscle men admir-

Promotional poster for *The Cameraman* (1928).

ing Sally at a swimming pool, with Keaton coming out of the locker room and taking her hand, dumbfounding all of the other men.

The Cameraman stands the test of time as one of Keaton's finest achievements. Such was not the case with the follow-up, *Spite Marriage*, and the absence of Keaton's original production crew shows in that film.

At this writing, leading lady Marceline Day is 90 years old and believed to be living in California, although she lives a reclusive and very private life. Ms. Day was at the height of her fame when she starred in *The Cameraman*, and is also well remembered as the female lead in the highly coveted lost Lon Chaney film, *London After Midnight* (1927). Her career spanned from 1925 to 1933. Her only other silent available on video is *The Beloved Rogue* (1927), in which she co-starred with John Barrymore. An early talkie, *The Wild Party* (1929), also can be had on video.

In 1948, MGM did a remake of *The Cameraman* called *Watch the Birdie* with Red Skelton (1910–1997). Keaton was an uncredited gag consultant on the remake.

561. The Campus Vamp

Rating: ☆☆

Mack Sennett Productions/Pathé Exchange; ***Directed by*** Harry Edwards; ***Running Time:*** 19 minutes; ***Cast:*** CAROLE, Carole Lombard (1908–1942); MATTY, Matty Kemp (born 1907); DORA, Daphne Pollard (1894–1978); BARNEY BENSON, Johnny Burke; SALLY, Sally Eilers (1908–1978); Mack Sennett's Bathing Beauties

This is a romantic comedy set on the Beverly College campus. Sally is a plain girl (who could be attractive), whom Matty, the typical "All American" frat boy, studies with. Every time Sally makes progress and starts to get Matty's attention, the pretty socialite Carole always manages to divert his attention away from Sally. Dora and Barney, a homely couple, conspire to help Sally get her man.

The story line of this subject contains little substance. But, *The Campus Vamp* is interesting for its cast, and the fact that some of the sequences were filmed in 2-strip Technicolor. This is among the few early silent film appearances of Carole Lombard available for evaluation on video. She was highly popular in classic comedy talkies such as *My Man Godfrey* (1936) before her 1939 marriage to Clark Gable (1901–1960). Just after having completed filming of Ernst Lubitsch's *To Be or Not to Be* (1942), she was killed in an airplane crash at the height of her fame.

Carole Lombard, star of *The Campus Vamp* (1928), in the 1930s.

Matty Kemp, the male lead in this film, is appealing with his good looks and charm. He starred mostly in 2-reel comedies, never graduating to features. As a close friend of Charles "Buddy" Rogers (born 1904), husband of Mary Pickford at the time of her death, he was put in charge of the Mary Pickford Film

Company for many years until his retirement a few years ago. He is currently 90 years old and living in Beverly Hills.

Sally Eilers had just graduated from bit parts at the time she starred in this film. Her most highly acclaimed performance was in Frank Borzage's *Bad Girls* (1931). She was highly popular in the 1930s, but was playing only occasional parts in low budget films in the 1940s, until her retirement from the screen in 1951. Her first marriage was to western star Hoot Gibson from 1930–1933. She died of a heart attack at age 69.

Mack Sennett's famous "bathing beauties" are featured in a couple of beach shots in Technicolor.

562. The Circus

Rating: ☆☆☆

United Artists; ***Written, Produced, and Directed by*** Charles Chaplin; ***Photography by*** Rollie Totheroh; ***Running Time:*** 71 minutes; ***Cast:*** A TRAMP, Charlie Chaplin (1889–1977); CIRCUS PROPRIETOR/RING MASTER, Allan Garcia (1887–1938); HIS STEP-DAUGHTER, Merna Kennedy (1908–1944); REX [A TIGHTROPE WALKER], Harry Crocker (1893–1958); A MAGICIAN, George Davis (1889–1965); AN OLD CLOWN, Henry Bergman (1868–1946); HEAD PROPERTY MAN, Stanley Sanford (1894–1961); ASSISTANT PROPERTY MAN, John Rand (1878–1940); A PICKPOCKET, Steve Murphy

The Circus came out in the first season of the Academy Awards in January, 1928. Charlie Chaplin received two nominations—for Best Comedy Direction and for Best Actor. He did not win in these categories, but was given a Special Academy Award for "versatility and genius in writing, acting, directing, and producing *The Circus*." Chaplin's only other nominations came in 1940 when *The Great Dictator* was nominated for Best Original Screenplay and Best Actor. He was also nominated for Best Original Screenplay in 1947 for *Monsieur Verdoux* (1947). It was not until 1972 that Chaplin would receive a second Honorary Academy Award.

In *The Circus*, Chaplin plays a tramp who gets a job as a prop man. Everything seems to go wrong for him, and he bungles so badly that he becomes the hit of the circus—without even trying. He falls in love with Merna, the step-daughter of the cruel and abusive circus proprietor. When she falls in love with Rex, the tightrope walker, the tramp finds that he can't be funny anymore. He acts as a sort of "guardian angel" for Merna, and arranges for her to marry the man she loves. He realizes that there is no place for him within the circus, and stays behind, having completed the mission of putting Merna on the road to a better life.

Two favorite sequences of this author's are the lion sequence and the celebrated tightrope sequence. In the lion sequence, Chaplin is unwittingly locked in a cage with a "ferocious" lion, who couldn't really care less who was in the cage with him. The attack Chaplin suffers in the cage comes from a dog that is outside the cage, who attacks Chaplin's foot. The tightrope sequence is the most famous, and it is clips of this sequence that are most often shown in retrospective documentaries. It has the tramp taking the place of Rex, who can't be located, and all goes well until the safety harness attached to him breaks, causing pandemonium. The house of mirrors sequence at the beginning is also amusing.

Production on *The Circus* was laden with complications. The first calamity occurred when the circus tent that was constructed for the film was damaged by severe weather.

As if that wasn't enough, a film lab error ruined all of the footage that was shot in the first weeks of production, thus causing Chaplin and crew to have to start over from scratch. Another blow came when a fire caused severe damage to the studio. With the complications in Chaplin's messy divorce proceedings with Lita Grey, as well as problems with the Internal Revenue Service, it is a miracle that this movie was ever completed.

It is sad to note that leading lady Merna Kennedy, who was only 19 when she appeared in *The Circus*, died at age 35 from a heart attack in 1944. She had been married briefly to the great choreographer Busby Berkeley in the 1930s. She was a childhood friend of Lita Grey, and it was through this connection that she was recommended for the part in this film.

In 1970, Chaplin reissued *The Circus* with his own original musical score and the title song *Swing, Little Girl* which he sang himself at age 80.

563. The Crowd

Rating: ☆☆☆☆

MGM; ***Directed by*** King Vidor; ***Screenplay by*** King Vidor and John V.A. Weaver; ***Titles by*** Joe Farnham; ***Settings by*** Cedric Gibbons and Arnold Gillespie; ***Wardrobe by*** André-Ani; ***Photographed by*** Henry Sharp; ***Film Editor:*** Hugh Wynn; ***Running Time:*** 104 minutes; ***Cast:*** JOHN SIMS, James Murray (1901–1936); MARY, Eleanor Boardman (1898–1991); BERT, Bert Roach (1891–1971); JIM, Daniel G. Tomlinson; DICK, Dell Henderson (1877–1956); MOTHER, Lucy Beaumont (1873–1937); JUNIOR, Freddie Burke Frederick (1921–1986); DAUGHTER, Alice Mildred Puter

In the first year of the Academy Awards, *The Crowd* won a nomination for Best Artistic Quality of Production, losing to F.W. Murnau's *Sunrise* (1927). King Vidor was nominated for the Best Director Oscar, losing to Frank Borzage, who won for *7th Heaven.*

The Crowd is a masterpiece of artistic imagery. Vidor starts out many shots showing masses of people in the typical New York City crowds, and then zeroing in on the specific characters of the story, providing identities for some of these "faces in the crowd." The audience is introduced to the characters, and the important events and tragic circumstances in their lives. Vidor makes the point that despite how important many of us think our lives are to us, we are, in reality, just faces in the crowd.

The story is about a man named John Sims, who has a good bookkeeping job, and marries his sweetheart, Mary. On one of their trips to town, they see a man dressed as a clown, juggling balls to advertise a company product. They laugh at him, referring to him as a poor sap. All is well in their marriage until Mary gets disgusted with John for his lack of ambition to further his career, despite the fact that he is highly talented in advertising. The couple have children, and are struggling to make ends meet in a small apartment. John finally, after much nagging by his wife, enters his slogan into a contest, and wins $500. Unfortunately, tragedy strikes when their girl is hit by a car. John seems unable to concentrate on anything but the accident, and is totally nonproductive, and eventually dismissed from his job. He tries a number of jobs with no success, while Mary is working as a seamstress to try to make the bills. He is finally offered a job—as a clown juggling balls—the very same position he laughed at in ridicule when times were better.

For this film, Vidor cast the unknown actor James Murray and the moderately known star Eleanor Boardman (who was also his wife) into the lead roles. This is among Eleanor Boardman's best performances, and James Murray is quite impressive as well as the erring husband. They play ordinary people with ordinary lives. It shows them in circumstances that the average family goes through—from their disappointments, triumphs, tragedies, birth, and death. It is not an epic or masterpiece in the colossal fashion as were films such as *Intolerance* (1916), *Napoléon* (1927), and *Ben-Hur* (1927), but a masterpiece in its simplicity of showing two average people and their families. The film shows how its main character sticks out like a sore thumb when he has fallen on hard times and out of favor with the crowd, and how he blends in with the rest once he gets things together again. This reviewer would venture to say that *Sadie Thompson* (1928) should have won the Academy Award for Best Production that went to *Wings* (1927), and *The Crowd* (1928) should have won the Oscar for Best Artistic Quality of Production. Both *Sadie Thompson* and *The Crowd* were far superior to *Wings* and *Sunrise.*

It is unfortunate to note that James Murray, whose performance in *The Crowd* gives him a permanent place in Hollywood history, never had another major starring role. He suffered from chronic alcoholism, and was relegated to minor bit parts because of it. King Vidor saw Murray in the early 1930s panhandling for money to buy liquor. Vidor, knowing Murray's potential, asked him if he could sober up long enough to play the lead role in *Our Daily Bread* (1933), Vidor's talkie sequel to *The Crowd.* Murray was too far gone, and simply was unable and or unwilling to pull himself together. In 1936, Murray's body was found floating in a New York River, cause of death unknown.

564. The Docks of New York

Rating: ☆☆☆½

Paramount; ***Directed by*** Josef Von Sternberg; ***Story/Screenplay by*** Jules Furthman; ***Suggested by*** *The Dock Walloper* ***by*** John Monk Saunders; ***Photography by*** Harold Rosson; ***Titles by*** Julian Johnson; ***Running Time:*** 59 minutes; ***Cast:*** THE STOKER [BILL ROBERTS], George Bancroft (1882–1956); HIS PAL, Clyde Cook (1891–1984); THE GIRL, Betty Compson (1897–1974); THE THIRD ENGINEER, Mitchell Lewis (1880–1956); HIS WIFE, Olga Baclanova (1899–1974); HYMN-BOOK HARRY, Gustav von Seyffertitz (1863–1943)

For this early masterpiece of cinematography, director Josef Von Sternberg (1894–1969) presents the grim story of two people largely forgotten by contemporary society—a stoker on a ship who, on one of his shore periods, meets a poor, unrefined, but very attractive girl at a waterfront bar. The girl tries to commit suicide by jumping into the ocean, and is saved by the stoker. Finding out that the raggedy dress the girl wore was the only clothing she possessed, Bancroft's rough and tough character sets off to a store to buy her some clothes. The store is closed, and in his drunken state, he simply breaks into the store and takes the clothes.

The following night, while engaged in heavy drinking, the stoker and girl are married in a shotgun wedding ceremony in the bar. There is no wedding ring, so the girl's friend gives the couple her ring—which her husband whom she had not seen in three years until now had given to her before having deserted her.

Betty Compson's character, although not holding her breath, genuinely hopes that stoker Bill Roberts will be ready to settle down to a domestic life and take the marriage seriously. She is arrested for possession of the stolen clothes, and is in court at the time when Bill has to make the decision to either go back to his stoking job on the ship, or to stay on shore and build a life with his wife.

This film is highly acclaimed as a masterpiece of cinematography, owing mostly to director Von Sternberg's unique way of lighting sets. He knew how to use light to emphasize every shadow, every cloud of smoke, and also to bring out the very best in his stars' facial features.

In addition to masterful cinematography, the film features stirring performances by the excellent cast. Although Betty Compson was nominated for a Best Actress Oscar for 1928–29, it was for another film, *The Barker*, that she won her nomination. George Bancroft was nominated the same year for *Thunderbolt* (1929), but not for this film. Danny Peary gives nominations to both Bancroft and Compson for this film in his book, *Alternate Oscars*. Olga Baclanova also is impressive as Betty Compson's best friend. If an award for supporting actress had been given out in 1928–29, she would have given Seena Owen a good run for her money for her performance in *Queen Kelly* (1929).

As highly acclaimed as *The Docks of New York* was, it was completely snubbed by the Academy Awards, not garnering a single nomination. This could possibly have been due to the fact that *The Last Command* (1928), also directed by Von Sternberg, was so prominently recognized the previous year, having won nominations for Best Original Screenplay and Best Picture, as well as the Best Actor Award for Emil Jannings' performance. It is also possible that the grim, unpleasant setting for *The Docks of New York* presented a side of life that people did not want to acknowledge existed, and was snubbed for that reason.

565. Eagle of the Night *Rating:* N/A

H.V. Productions/Pathé Exchange; ***Directed by*** Jimmie Fulton; ***Written by*** Paul Cruger; ***Running Time of Surviving Footage:*** 99 minutes; ***Cast:*** TED PETERS, Jack Richardson (1883–1957); PROFESSOR PAYSON, Joseph Swickard (1866–1940); JUNE PAYSON, Shirley Palmer; PAUL MURDOCK, Earle Metcalf (1890–1928); "STUPE" WILLIAMS, Max Hawley; COLONEL ELLIOTT, Maurice Costello (1877–1950); LIEUTENANT FRANK BOYD, Frank Clarke (1898–1948); IVAN CARLSON [THE SMUGGLER], Roy Wilson (1902–1932)

This serial was the last of the Pathé silent serials. Only a fragmented copy survives today, rescued from the last surviving 35 mm print material. The first two chapters are complete. On the third chapter, only the first half is extant. Chapter 4 is complete, and the last halves of Chapters 5 and 6 are extant. The 7th, 8th, and 9th chapters are lost, as is the first half of Chapter 10, although the ending of the serial is complete.

Eagle of the Night is an action serial whose plot revolves around a professor who has invented an airplane engine that runs silently, thus being a good potential asset for the military and other purposes. Paul Murdock is the head of a gang of villains trying to steal the plans for the engine. Frank Clarke, who was a professional stunt pilot, plays the male lead as Lieutenant Frank Boyd, who helps to rescue the professor, who has been kidnapped by the villains.

What is left of this film is impressive. The first chapter ends in a thrilling cliffhanger in which June Payson unknowingly gets into a plane with one of the villains, thinking that friend Frank Boyd is piloting the plane. When she discovers that the pilot is one of the villains, she tries to take over control of the plane, but is knocked down and falling rapidly to the ground thousands of feet below. Chapter 4 shows the protagonists being rescued from a burning house. The last half of Chapter 6 ends with the hero and heroine in a car headed straight for a valley over which the bridge is out. The car is shown crashing into the embankment, but unfortunately the footage showing the resolution of this perilous catastrophe is missing, and the surviving footage does not pick back up again until the last half of the final chapter.

Based on what survives of this serial, it appears to have been an excellent, action packed piece of entertainment—among the better silent serials of the 1920s. This film is also historically significant as one of Maurice Costello's last silent films. He did one more silent called *Black Feather* (1928) before his retirement from the screen, and reemerged in 1936 in *Hollywood Boulevard*, with his final two talkies produced in 1940 and 1941.

Unfortunately, no further information could be found on Shirley Palmer. Earle Metcalf, who played the leading villain role, was killed shortly after completion of this serial at age 38 when he fell from a plane. Roy Wilson, who played his partner in the smuggling operation, also suffered an early demise in 1932 at age 30. No cause of death for Wilson could be found in any of the available reference books.

566. The Enemy *Rating:* ☆

MGM; ***Directed by*** Fred Niblo; ***Assistant Director:*** Harold S. Bucquet; ***Based on the Play by*** Channing Pollock; ***Adaptation by*** Willis Goldbeck; ***Continuity by*** Willis Goldbeck and Agnes Christine Johnston; ***Titles by*** John Colton; ***Settings by*** Cedric Gibbons and Richard Day; ***Film Editor:*** Margaret Booth; ***Photography by*** Oliver Marsh; ***Wardrobe by*** Gilbert Clark; ***Original Running Time:*** approximately 94 minutes; ***Running Time of Surviving Footage:*** 82 minutes; ***Cast:*** PAULI ARNDT, Lillian Gish (1893–1993); CARL BEHREND, Ralph Forbes (1905–1951); BRUCE GORDON, Ralph Emerson (1899–1984); PROFESSOR ARNDT, Frank Currier (1857–1928); AUGUST BEHREND, George Fawcett (1860–1939); MITZI WINKELMANN, Fritzi Ridgeway (1898–1961); FRITZ, John S. Peters (1894–1963); JAN, Karl Dane (1886–1934); BARUSKA, Polly Moran (1883–1952); KURT, Billy Kent Schaefer

In order to fully understand *The Enemy*'s place in Lillian Gish's career, one must have some background information. When Lillian Gish was hired into MGM, she was lured by a lucrative contract which gave her $800,000 per year, as well as authority to choose her own stories, directors, and leading men. From what has survived in the historic record, Irving Thalberg and Louis B. Mayer lured Gish over to MGM so that they could destroy her. She was an actress of such stature and power that she was the only obstacle which kept the studios from having complete control over their stars. If they could break Lillian Gish, no other star would dare to stand up to them.

Thalberg and Mayer tried everything they could think of to bring Gish down—from negative press campaigns to sabotaging *The Wind*. Even these efforts did not daunt Gish, so Thalberg tried to trick her into allowing him to arrange a fake scandal for her, which she refused. The next operation was to find a way to get Gish to make a bad film. Mayer called Gish into his office, demanding that she sign a statement allowing MGM to take her off salary until a proper story could be found for her. She refused, but was conned into doing *The Enemy*.

The story takes place in Austria, just before the beginning of World War I in 1914.

Lillian Gish still looking great 20 years after Mayer and Thalberg tried to sabotage her career with *The Enemy* (1928).

Lillian Gish plays Pauli, the granddaughter of a college professor. She is the toast of the graduates, with two suitors—Carl, whom she mutually loves, and Bruce, his best friend, who is hopelessly in love with her. Carl's grandfather, August Behrend, is best friends with Pauli's grandfather.

Political tensions arise when Bruce comes over for dinner before returning to England, and it is announced that England has declared war on Austria. Needless to say, he departs his best friend's home on a sour note. After Carl and Pauli marry, he is called away to go to war.

Pauli's grandfather, an outspoken pacifist, loses his job as professor due to his "unpatriotic" viewpoints. August Behrend, a wealthy merchant who is holding back wheat to drive the price up and profit off of the war, offers help to the professor's family, which the professor refuses. When Carl returns home on leave, he finds that the Arndt's have been evicted from their home as "traitors." He is enraged with his father and "the enemy" of war turns father and son against each other. Eventually, the birth of Pauli's and Carl's baby brings the two families together again. The last sequence extant in the surviving footage shows the two families preparing for Carl's homecoming, after which the final reel is missing from the unique print that currently exists.

This film features some good camera work, as well as a good cast. The shots of Lillian Gish swinging on the swing set with Ralph Forbes are well done, as the camera follows the couple with each up swing and each down swing. In addition, the footage showing the newspaper presses announcing World War I happening as each country declares war on the other is effective. But, the story itself simply has little substance or action to it. No matter what caliber of talent is brought in, the best actors cannot do anything if there is nothing to work with. It seems that 20 percent of the film's footage is of soldiers marching off to war—a way of "padding" the film so that the lack of substance in the script is not quite as noticeable. It is ploddingly directed, and moves at a snail's pace.

After this film was released, Lillian Gish left MGM and went back to Broadway. In the talkie era of the movies, she came back to do films occasionally, with her last film being *The Whales of August* (1987), which she starred in at the age of 92. She died at age 99 on February 27, 1993.

Ralph Forbes, the leading man, made his U.S. film debut in Herbert Brenon's *Beau Geste* (1926), and worked in films well into the 1940s. He was the son of the British actress Mary Forbes (1883–1974), who played in such classics as *A Farewell to Arms* (1932), *Cavalcade* (1933), and *Jane Eyre* (1944).

The Enemy was the last film of Frank Currier, who died shortly after its completion.

567. The Flying Fleet

Rating: ☆☆☆

MGM; ***Directed by*** George Hill; ***Story by*** Lt. Cmdr. Frank Wead, Byron Morgan; ***Screen Adaptation by*** Richard Schayer; ***Titles by*** Joe Farnham; ***Art Direction by*** Cedric Gibbons; ***Wardrobe by*** David Cox; ***Photography by*** Ira Morgan; ***Air Photography by*** Charles A. Marshall; ***Film Editor:*** Blanche Sewell; ***Running Time:*** 87 minutes; ***Cast:*** Tommy Winslow, Ramon Novarro (1899–1968); Anita Hastings, Anita Page (born 1910); Steve Randall, Ralph Graves (1900–1977)

This is yet another film that Turner Entertainment has rescued from obscurity. A print of this film was rediscovered and presented as a "Preservation Showcase" in 1995 on Turner Classic Movies.

The Flying Fleet is a light romantic comedy centered around a class of flight training students in the U.S. Navy. It follows their graduation from their first round of schooling, and follows as the students apply for actual flight school, in which they train to earn their wings by hands-on experience in Pensacola, Florida. The sad cases of those in flight school are shown, with one student crashing his plane, as are the triumphs and mischievous happenings at the school. Tommy and Steve, two of the students who make it through, both fall for the same girl, played by Anita Page, and compete for her affection.

The film features footage of what appears to be an actual graduation from the Annapolis Military Academy. Furthermore, there was some footage taken on location at N.A.S. Pensacola, as well as over the famous white sands of Pensacola Beach. The most recognizable landmark is the old lighthouse built in 1830, which still stands today as a tourist attraction.

Not only is this film historically important as one of the rare early films with footage of Pensacola, the birthplace of naval aviation, but it is a delightful and entertaining film as well. Ramon Novarro looks great with his more closely cropped than usual hair, and Anita Page is a beauty as well.

As a local resident of Pensacola, this author was surprised to see that the general appearance of N.A.S. Pensacola has not changed as radically as one would have expected it to over 50 years. Unfortunately, the last two standing hangars from World War I which were featured in this film were torn down in late 1997.

Director George Hill demonstrates that he had a great talent for producing films with a good, unique blend of comedy and drama. Prior to *The Flying Fleet*, he similarly demonstrated this talent with *Zander the Great* (1925) and *Tell It to the Marines* (1927).

The print of this film aired on Turner Classic Movies features the original soundtrack with music and sound effects that accompanied the film when it was originally released.

568. The Gallopin' Gaucho *Rating: ☆☆☆½*

Disney Cartoons; ***Produced by*** Walt Disney; ***Music Score/Sound Effects by*** Cinephone; ***Running Time:*** 6 minutes, 30 seconds; ***Cast:*** THE GAUCHO, Mickey Mouse (born 1928); THE GIRL, Minnie Mouse (born 1928)

The Gallopin' Gaucho is one of the many parodies that Walt Disney (1901–1966) produced in the late 1920s. This is a parody of Douglas Fairbanks, Sr.'s 1927 film, *The Gaucho*. Mickey Mouse, in one of his earliest film appearances, plays the gaucho, riding his horse and then blowing smoke rings as Minnie Mouse dances erotically. Minnie is then kidnapped, and it is up to Mickey as the "gallopin' gaucho" to rescue her.

This cartoon is hilarious in itself, but is really a lot of fun when one has seen *The Gaucho* (1927) and knows the extent of the parody that Disney did. While *The Gallopin' Gaucho* is technically a sound film with music and sound effects, the story is told visually, without dialogue except for a couple of words. Incidentally, Disney released the first all-talking cartoon later in 1928. This debut talking cartoon was *Steamboat Willie* (1928), a parody of Buster Keaton's *Steamboat Bill, Jr.* (1928).

569. The Garden of Eden *Rating: ☆☆½*

United Artists; ***Directed by*** Lewis Milestone; ***Adaptation by*** Avery Hopwood; ***From a Story by*** Adolf Bernnauer, Rudolph Gesterreiche; ***Titles by*** George Marion, Jr.; ***Photography by*** John Arnold; ***Art Direction by*** William Cameron Menzies; ***Interior Decorator:*** Casey Roberts;

Running Time: 115 minutes; ***Cast:*** TONI LEBRUM, Corinne Griffith (1894–1979); ROSA, Louise Dresser (1878–1965); HENRI D'AVRIL, Lowell Sherman (1888–1934); MADAME BAUER, Maude George (1888–1963); RICHARD DUPONT, Charles Ray (1891–1943); COLONEL DUPONT, Edward Martindel (1873–1955)

This is the romantic comedy that Lewis Milestone (1875–1980) did right after winning the one and only Best Comedy Direction Oscar for *Two Arabian Knights* (1927). He would win Best Director again in 1930 for *All Quiet on the Western Front* (1930), which also won the Best Picture Oscar for 1929–30. Another actress who appeared in this film and won Academy recognition was Louise Dresser, who was nominated for the 1927–28 Best Actress Oscar for her role in *A Ship Comes In* (1927). It is also historically significant as Charles Ray's last silent film, and one of only two films from Corinne Griffith's 16-year screen career known to survive.

In this film, the stunningly beautiful Corinne Griffith stars as a girl whose ambition is to become an opera star. She ends up working in a cabaret instead, but quits when she finds that one of the requirements of the job is to dress provocatively. Louise Dresser plays Rosa, a co-worker of Toni's who is a baroness, and saves her money to have one big, grand blowout each year, while living frugally the rest of the year. She takes Toni with her to a high priced, luxury resort in the hopes that she can meet influential people who can make her dream a reality. Charles Ray plays Richard DuPont, the wealthy musician who Toni meets at the resort. A number of obstacles come up which prevent DuPont from being able to propose marriage to Toni before hers and Rosa's money runs out and they have to leave the resort. First, DuPont must rouse Toni from a deep sleep. Then, there is a slight problem with Richard's own father competing for Toni's affection.

This is a relatively good romantic comedy, and it has the distinction of being the only Corinne Griffith film available on videocassette, and is worth having for the rare chance to see her perform.

570. Hangman's House

Rating: ☆☆☆☆

Fox; ***Directed by*** John Ford; ***From the Story by*** Donn Byrne; ***Adapted by*** Philip Klein; ***Film Editor:*** Margaret V. Clancey; ***Scenario by*** Marion Orth; ***Photography by*** George Schneiderman; ***Titles by*** Malcolm Stuart Boylan; ***Running Time:*** 72 minutes; ***Cast:*** CONNAUGHT O'BRIEN, June Collyer (1907–1968); DERMOT MCDERMOTT, Larry Kent (1900–1967); BARON O'BRIEN, Hobart Bosworth (1867–1943); JOHN D'ARCY, Earle Fox (1891–1973); CITIZEN HOGAN, Victor McLaglen (1886–1959); A CHEERING SPECTATOR, John Wayne (1907–1979)

In reviewing some of John Ford's (1894–1973) other silent films like *The Iron Horse* (1924), the impression of his work was not that great. But, upon viewing *Hangman's House*, the acclaim that he has received was justified. *Hangman's House* demonstrated that John Ford was truly a great directorial genius. The viewing of other John Ford films since has reaffirmed this.

The story takes place in Ireland, and centers around the home of a man named Baron O'Brien, also known as "Hangin' Jimmy," a retired judge who rose to power by sending many people to their deaths at the gallows. The judge finds out from his doctors that he is near death. He has a daughter named Connaught, who is very much in love with a man named Dermot McDermott. The daughter, knowing that her father is near death,

June Collyer, leading lady of *Hangman's House* (1928).

goes against her true desire and marries one John D'Arcy, a man of aristocracy that her father wants her to marry for the sake of status. Connaught is up front from the very beginning that she does not love D'Arcy, and is going through the marriage only to satisfy the wishes of her dying father.

Unfortunately, what the baron did not know about D'Arcy is that he is an alcoholic, gambler, and swindler. Through the course of the film, Connaught has to wait until D'Arcy's bad karma comes back to destroy him before she can marry the man she truly loves.

Victor McLaglen plays a man who has an ax to grind with John D'Arcy. John Wayne can be spotted in a cameo role as a cheering spectator during the steeplechase sequence.

This movie is classic silent melodrama at its best. John Ford's artistry in presenting the imagery makes this an exhilarating and powerful film. The sequences showing the mirage that the dying Baron O'Brien sees of the people he sent to the gallows are unforgettable. Of the silent films viewed, this has become among the reviewer's top ten favorites. It comes very highly recommended.

571. The Last Command

Rating: ☆☆☆☆

Paramount; ***Directed by*** Josef Von Sternberg; ***Story by*** Lajos Biro; ***Photographed by*** Bert Glennon; ***Screenplay by*** John F. Goodrich; ***Titles by*** Herman J. Mankiewicz; ***Running Time:*** 88 minutes; ***Cast:*** GRAND DUKE SERGIUS ALEXANDER, Emil Jannings (1886–1950); THE DIRECTOR [LEO ANDREYEV], William Powell (1892–1984); NATALIE, Evelyn Brent (1899–1975); THE ASSISTANT, Jack Raymond (1886–1953); THE ADJUTANT, Nicholas Soussanin (1889–1975); THE BODYGUARD, Michael Visaroff (1892–1951); REVOLUTIONIST, Fritz Feld (1900–1993)

This is director Josef Von Sternberg's most highly acclaimed silent. Emil Jannings won the first Best Actor Oscar on the basis of his performances in this film and *Way of All Flesh* (1927), a lost film. *The Last Command* also received Academy Award nominations for Best Production of 1927–28, and Best Original Screenplay.

Emil Jannings is magnificent in this role. In the first segment of the film, he portrays a very nervous, humble, frightened man whose head shakes uncontrollably as the result of some past trauma. He is a nobody—one of thousands of extras in the costume lines, glad to put up with the pushing and shoving to make that $7.50 per day as a Hollywood extra that he so desperately needs. However, when the movie cuts from 1928 Hollywood to 1917 Russia, Jannings' portrayal of Grand Duke Alexander, powerful Army general and cousin to the Czar, contrasts sharply.

This movie is a haunting portrayal of just how far the high and mighty can fall in a short period of time. It is a classic tale of karma—"what goes around comes around." William Powell plays the director of the Hollywood movie studio at which the former Grand Duke applies for work. When Director Andreyev spots Alexander's photo in the pile of applicants, he remembers him as the general who whipped him and had him arrested as a revolutionist in Russia eleven years before. He hires Alexander, and is now in the position of having the upper hand.

With the use of crosscutting, the movie goes back and forth between the two time periods starting with 1928 Hollywood, then back to 1917 Russia where the two main characters arrived at their present-day positions. It is especially interesting to see the director and former Russian aristocrat meet for the first time since Alexander barely escaped from Russia alive as a result of the revolution.

This was the last film that Emil Jannings made in America. When he won the Best Actor Oscar, he immediately went back to Germany, and eventually worked on films for Nazi Cinema. He died in 1950, and was considered no great loss by the group of contemporaries who had once given him their highest honor. It was when Evelyn Brent started working under Josef Von Sternberg (1894–1969) that she had her greatest opportunities to demonstrate her full acting potential. She was wonderful in this film, with beauty as well as demonstrated acting talent. Von Sternberg did for Brent what he would later do for Marlene Dietrich.

This film was one of the nine silent titles that Paramount Home Video released in the late 1980s, and is highly recommended.

572. Let 'Er Go, Gallegher

Rating: ☆☆☆½

Pathé; ***Directed by*** Elmer Clifton; ***Associate Producer:*** Ralph Block; ***Adaptation by*** Elliott Clawson; ***From the Story*** *Gallegher* ***by*** Richard Harding Davis; ***Running Time:*** 55 minutes; ***Cast:*** JOHN "SHERLOCK HOLMES" GALLEGHER, Junior Coghlan (born 1916); HENRY CALLAHAN, Harrison Ford (1884–1957); CLARISSA MAHAFFEY, Elinor Fair (1903–1957); FOUR FINGERED DAN, Ivan Lebedoff (1894–1953); MCGINTY, Wade Boteler (1888–1943); CITY EDITOR, E.H. Calvert (1863–1941)

This mystery-adventure features Junior Coghlan in the starring role of "Sherlock Holmes" Gallegher, a 10-year-old "wanna be" detective. "Watson" is Gallegher's companion—his dog. It turns out that he witnesses a murder committed by the notorious outlaw, "Four Fingered Dan." He goes to his friend, newspaper reporter Henry Callahan, with the story. Callahan receives so much praise that he becomes hot headed and quits his job. He even manages to alienate his fiancee, Clarissa Mahaffey, as well as his young friend John Gallegher, who gave him the story to begin with.

John, disillusioned, goes to the train station with intentions of leaving when he sees none other than the villain, "Four Fingered Dan" in line ahead of him. Gallegher immediately gets a ticket to the same destination and follows him. Once Gallegher gets to the hideout, he is discovered by the villain, whom tries to intimidate him over dinner.

Fortunately, Callahan and another newspaper reporter are on the way as Gallegher had previously alerted them to the fact that he was on the gangster's trail. Some twists and turns occur, leading into a chase sequence as the grand finale of the film.

This is a wonderfully entertaining film, directed by Elmer Clifton (1890–1949). Junior Coghlan's performance in the lead role is delightful. It is also good to see Harrison Ford in a role other than the marital farces that he was generally cast in. Ivan Lebedoff is the ultimate villain as "Four Fingered Dan." He had made his Hollywood debut in D.W. Griffith's *The Sorrows of Satan* (1926), and also had a part in Gloria Swanson's *The Love of Sunya* (1927). His film career lasted until his death in 1953. Elisha Helm Calvert was married to actress Lillian Drew (1883–1924). Lillian Drew made headlines when she mysteriously died from poisoning at age 41.

Of Junior Coghlan's starring films, this is his personal favorite, an opinion shared by this reviewer as well.

573. Lilac Time

Rating: ☆☆☆½

First National; ***Directed by*** George Fitzmaurice; ***Assistant Director:*** Cullen Tate; ***Art Direction by*** Horace Jackson, III; ***Adaptation by*** Willis Goldbeck; ***Based on the Book by*** Guy Fowler ***and the Play by*** Jane Murfin and Jane Cowl; ***Cinematography by*** Sidney Hickox; ***Film Editing by*** Alexander Hall; ***Running Time:*** 90 minutes; ***Cast:*** JEANNE, Colleen Moore (1900–

1988); CAPTAIN PHILLIP BLYTHE, Gary Cooper (1901–1961); AUNT MARIE, Eugenie Besserer (1868–1934); THE MAYOR, Emile Chautard (1864–1934); THE ENEMY ACE, Eddie Clayton; MECHANIC'S HELPER, George Cooper (1891–1943); MIKE THE MECHANIC, Edward Dillon (1879–1933); AVIATORS: Dan Dowling, Dick Grace (1898–1965), Harlan Hilton (1900–1930), Richard Jarvis, Stuart Knox, Jack Ponder (1903–1970; THE UNLUCKY ONE, Arthur Lake (1905–1987); GERMAN OFFICER, Philo McCullough (1893–1981); FRENCH DRUMMER, Nelson McDowell (1870–1947); LADY IRIS RANKIN, Kathryn McGuire (1903–1978); GENERAL BLYTHE, Burr McIntosh (1862–1942); CAPTAIN RUSSELL, Cleve Moore (1904–1954); THE KID, Jack Stoney; ***Supporting Cast:*** Kathryn McGuire (1903–1978)

Lilac Time is yet another war film of the 1920s that was a box-office sensation, but has been overshadowed by *Wings* (1927). In this film, Colleen Moore plays a housekeeper at the barracks of a World War I air squadron. While at first she has the best of intentions, she often gets in the way. But, the troops begin to become attached to her, and she becomes important to them. Gary Cooper plays in one of his earliest leading roles as Captain Blythe, a new squadron captain who meets Jeanne when she runs out in front of his airplane while he is trying to land, and wrecks in avoiding her. The two don't get along at first, but eventually grow to love each other.

Colleen Moore's antics provide some great comedy relief. A favorite scene is when she is curious and tries to pilot an airplane, with the whole squadron scrambling to rescue her. In trying to get control of the plane, she unknowingly fires the machine gun, chasing the entire squadron around the field. When she has wrecked the plane, Gary Cooper takes her into his arms for the first time to see if she is injured, and the romance blossoms from there. The first real love scene between them is poignant and moving. There was an excellent chemistry between the two of them that, in this reviewer's opinion, was far greater than the Garbo-Gilbert pairings, or even the Gaynor-Farrell pairings.

The time comes when the squadron, including Phillip, has to go on a combat mission, and Jeanne desperately prays that Phillip will be among those who return. Like *Wings, Lilac Time* has some excellent air combat sequences well.

Colleen Moore got top billing for this film, with Gary Cooper's name as second. This is most definitely Moore's film all the way. Of her evaluated silents, this is her greatest performance. Gary Cooper as leading man is also impressive, and it was his performance in this film that really shot him to stardom.

Critic's Choice Video, in conjunction with the Killiam Collection, released this long coveted film on video in late 1996.

574. Linda *Rating:* ☆☆☆½

Mrs. Wallace Reid Productions; ***Directed by*** Mrs. Wallace (Dorothy Davenport) Reid; ***Assistant Director:*** Walter Sheridan; ***Based on the Story by*** Margaret Prescott Montague; ***Adaptation by*** Frank O'Connor and Maxine Alton; ***Titles by*** Ruth Todd; ***Screenplay by*** Wilfred Noy; ***Production Manager:*** Cliff Broughton; ***Film Editor:*** Edith Wakeling; ***Photography by*** Henry Cronjager, Bert Baldridge, and Ernest Laszlo; ***Running Time:*** 75 minutes; ***Cast:*** LINDA STILLWATER, Helen Foster (1906–1982); HER FATHER, Mitchell Lewis (1880–1956); HER MOTHER, Lillian Brockwell; DR. PAUL RANDALL, Warner Baxter (1889–1951); ARMSTRONG DECKER, Noah Beery, Sr. (1882–1946); ANNETTE WHITTEMORE, Bess Flowers (1898–1984); KENNETH WHITTEMORE, Allen Connor; NAN, Kate Price (1873–1943)

This film has historic importance as the last film produced by Mrs. Wallace Reid Productions, and the first on which Dorothy Davenport Reid (1895–1977) received full directorial credit.

Helen Foster gives a nice performance as Linda, a girl who lives in the back woods and is forced by her sleazy father to marry a man she does not love. She at first refuses, and her mother backs her, telling her husband that she will not let him ruin Linda's life as he ruined hers. Her father beats her mother almost to death. Warner Baxter plays the young and handsome doctor who informs Linda that another incident of this sort could be fatal to her mother. So, she relents and marries Armstrong Decker.

Although Linda does not love Decker as he loves her, his kindness towards her earns her respect and gratitude. Then comes the day when Decker's wife and child that he had allegedly abandoned six years earlier show up on his doorstep.

This is the earliest performance of Warner Baxter that is widely available. Having started in films in 1914, he went on to win the 1929–30 Academy Award for Best Actor for his performance in his talkie debut, *In Old Arizona* (1929). He remained a popular leading man through the early 1940s, and continued in low budget productions up until a year before his death in 1951.

Helen Foster was a very attractive and talented actress, but for some reason never managed to graduate above "B" westerns and poverty row features. This is her best performance, as well as her most prominent role.

Noah Beery, Sr., also gives a good performance in a role that deviates from the villainous "heavy" roles he was generally associated with. In his death bed scene in this picture, one really feels a great deal of sympathy for him.

Bess Flowers, who plays the part of Linda's mentor and teacher, started out in low budget westerns, and graduated to supporting roles in prestigious productions such as *It Happened One Night* (1934), *The Awful Truth* (1937), *Ninotchka* (1939), *All About Eve* (1950), and *The Greatest Show on Earth* (1953). She also made hundreds of bit part appearances through 1964.

Dorothy Davenport Reid continued working as a scriptwriter, producer, and director for a number of poverty row studios from the 1930s through the 1950s. Her last significant work was in writing the scripts for the popular *Frances the Talking Mule* films from 1950–1956. Of all of the major female directors/producers of the silent era, Ms. Reid's career was the longest.

Unfortunately, the original Vitaphone track for this late silent is lost, but Jack Hardy of Grapevine Video reconstructed a nice orchestra score for his release of the film. With this film's historic value as well as good story, good cast, and competent direction by Dorothy Davenport Reid, it will be worth having in your collection.

575. Lonesome

Rating: ☆☆☆☆

Universal; ***Directed by*** Paul Fejos; ***Adaptation by*** Andre Rigaud; ***Running Time:*** 69 minutes; ***Cast:*** MARY, Barbara Kent (born 1906); JIM, Glenn Tryon (1899–1970)

Lonesome is one of those rare, generally inaccessible films that is available for viewing only by a "privileged few." The only surviving print features French title cards, with English dialogue sequences.

The film opens with a shot of New York skyscrapers, which reminds one to some extent of the futuristic sets in *Metropolis* (1927). It proceeds to a tracking shot of the busy New York subway system and streets, zeroing in on the modest apartment of Mary. We see her getting up in the morning to face the New York crowds, and then we are taken to the apartment of Jim, who is rushing in a frantic frenzy to get ready. These are the two main stars of the film, supported by largely unknown extras in the crowd sequences.

The story is a simple one, but yet surprisingly touching as a romantic film. We see Mary at her busy job as a telephone operator, and Jim at his job in a factory. They meet at the beach on their day off, and fall in love. It is on the beach that the first talking sequence comes in. Basically, Jim and Mary misrepresent themselves to make the other think that they are more affluent than they really are. Eventually, they reveal their true social status to each other, and go out on a date to what is presumably Coney Island. Here, they have a fabulous time, and Jim resolves to propose marriage. Before he can, Mary is lost in the crowd, and Jim is detained by a police officer before he can catch up to her.

What really makes this film is the fabulous cinematography. When the work day of each character is presented, we see double exposure images of their surroundings superimposed over our characters as they work. With rapid cutting, we see Mary with images of various troublesome customers gabbing away as she tries to handle them politely. With Jim, we see him attending to his post at the factory, with images of the churning machines superimposed. We also see a clock image indicating the time going by from 9 to 5. This is some of the most impressive cinematography caught on film, in some ways comparable to the techniques used by French director Abel Gance. This type of double and triple exposure appears throughout the film. In addition, the visual quality is further enhanced in some sequences with Technicolor.

Lonesome is a fast paced film with nonstop action. The only periods in which the film slows down are in the two brief talking sequences. In these sequences, the dialogue is a bit corny, which was typical in most of the early talkies due to the primitive sound technology of the time.

Of the available Barbara Kent silents, her performance in *Lonesome* is among her best. Glenn Tryon's talent shines as well.

With as simple a story as *Lonesome* contains, it is amazing how director Paul Fejos (1897–1963) was able to turn it into a cinematic masterpiece. If the opportunity ever presents itself for the reader to see *Lonesome*, it is an opportunity that should not be missed. This is definitely a film that deserves to be made widely accessible on the video market.

576. The Man Who Laughs *Rating:* ☆☆☆½

Universal; ***Directed by*** Paul Leni; ***Based on Victor Hugo's Classic, L'Homme Qui Rit*; *Adaptation/Continuity by*** J. Grubb Alexander; ***Art Direction:*** Charles D. Hall, Joseph Wright, Thomas O'Neil; ***Technical Research:*** Professor R.H. Newlands; ***Costumes by*** Dave Cox, Vera West; ***Titles by*** Walter Anthony; ***Film Editor:*** Edward Carr; ***Photography by*** Gilbert Warrenton; ***Running Time:*** 108 minutes; ***Cast:*** DEA, Mary Philbin (1903–1993); GWYNPLAINE, Conrad Veidt (1893–1943); GWYNPLAINE [CHILD], Julius Molnar, Jr.; DUCHESS JOSIANA, Olga Baclanova (1899–1974); BARKILPHEDRO, Brandon Hurst (1866–1947); URSUS, Cesare

Gravina (1858–1954?); LORD DIRRY-MOIR, Stuart Holmes (1884–1971); KING JAMES, Sam DeGrasse (1875–1953); DR. HARDQUANONNE, George Siegmann (1882–1928); QUEEN ANNE, Josephine Crowell (died 1934); INN KEEPER, Charles Puffy (1884–1942); CLOWNS, Frank Puglia and Jack Goodrich; DEA'S MOTHER, Carmen Costello

This was the last and most highly acclaimed of three screen adaptations of *L'Homme Qui Rit*. Previous adaptations were made in 1909 in France and in 1921 in Austria.

Set in England in the 1600, *The Man Who Laughs* is the story of a nobleman who has incurred the wrath of King James II, who has him executed in the cruel device, the iron lady, which causes a lingering death. The nobleman's son, Gwynplaine, is surgically deformed at the order of King James, with his mouth carved permanently into a grin, giving the illusion that he is, as James puts it, "laughing eternally at his fool of a father." He is then sold to gypsies. When the gypsies are banished from England, Gwynplaine is abandoned to fend for himself. He is taken in by Father Ursus, who has a traveling road show in which Gwynplaine becomes famous as "the laughing man."

Mary Philbin plays Dea, a blind girl who is also traveling with the show, who cannot see Gwynplaine's deformed grin, and sees only the good in him. When it is found out that Gwynplaine has noble blood, the two are separated when he is lured away by Duchess Josiana, who has an ulterior motive for wanting to marry Gwynplaine.

Mary Philbin never looked better than she appears in this film as a blonde. Conrad Veidt was excellent as Gwynplaine, and his makeup work with the permanent grin is flawless. Olga Baclanova likewise turns in a good performance as the vampish Duchess. Cesare Gravina has one of his best roles as Ursus, who heads up the freak show. Additionally, Josephine Crowell has an excellent character role as the domineering Queen Anne, as does Sam DeGrasse as the diabolical King James II.

Director Paul Leni did a first class job on this film, one of only four he made in the United States before he died at age 44 in 1929. The snowstorm sequence is especially visually stimulating. The sets and costumes are meticulous in historical authenticity of the time portrayed. Of all of Leni's films in Germany and the U.S., this is widely acclaimed as his crowning achievement.

577. Marked Money

Rating: ☆☆☆

Pathé; ***Directed by*** Spencer Gordon Bennet; A Hector Turnbull Production; ***Titles by*** John Krafft; ***Story and Adaptation by*** Howard J. Green; ***Continuity by*** George Dromgold and Sanford Hewitt; ***Photography by*** Edward Snyder; ***Film Editor:*** Fred Maguire; ***Art Direction by*** Edward Jewell; ***Production Manager:*** Richard A. Blaydon; ***Music Director:*** Josiah Zuro; ***Synchronization by*** R.C.A. Photophone; ***Running Time:*** 60 minutes; ***Cast:*** THE KID, Junior Coghlan (born 1916); THE AVIATOR, George Duryea (1898–1963); THE GIRL, Virginia Bradford; THE COOK, Tom Kennedy (1885–1965); THE CAPTAIN, Bert Woodruff (1856–1934); A CROOK, Maurice Black (1891–1938); ANOTHER CROOK, Jack Richardson (1883–1957)

Marked Money is an adventure film that was adapted especially for Junior Coghlan. By 1928, Cecil B. DeMille gave up independent production to go to MGM. Joseph P. Kennedy bought his studios, which would then be known as Pathé.

In this film, Junior Coghlan plays a boy whose father has died and sent him to a former ship captain's home to be looked after. Along with the son, he sends a box containing $25,000 cash for expenses and education. Hoodlums are after the money.

Captain Fairchild has a niece, the girl of the story, who is in love with an aviator, of whom the uncle disapproves. As she sneaks out the window to elope, she is kidnapped by the crooks, who hold her ransom for the boy's money. The climax of this film is an airplane chase sequence, which is well staged and fun to watch.

In addition to being a fine adventure film, *Marked Money* has some sequences of comic relief—well played by Junior Coghlan. The funniest of these is when Captain Fairchild's niece has her aviator friend over for dinner, trying to pass him off as a sailor that her uncle would approve of. When Junior tells too much, the boyfriend kicks him under the table, and Junior mentions what happened where everybody at the table can hear it.

This film was George Duryea's first movie role. Cecil B. DeMille had hired him for *The Godless Girl* (1929), and used him in this film to give him some initial experience in front of a movie camera. In 1931, he changed his name to Tom Keene, and starred in a number of westerns under that name. In 1944, he changed his name again to Richard Powers, and played character roles. His last film was the science fiction cult classic, *Plan 9 from Outer Space* (1959). The leading lady was Virginia Bradford, who moved to England sometime in the 1930s, but on whom no other information is known.

578. The Marvelous Life of Joan of Arc

Rating: ☆☆½

Produced in France; Aubert-Franco-Film/Pathécinema; ***Directed by*** Marco de Gastyne; ***Scenario by*** Jean-José Frappé; ***Historical Research by*** M. Camille Vergniol; ***Running Time:*** 124 minutes; ***Cast:*** JEANNE D'ARC, Simone Ginedois; JEABEAU DE PAULE, Cboura Milena; GILLES DE RAIS, Philippe Heriat (1898–1971); LA TREMOILLE, Jean Toulout (1887–1962); CHARLES VII, Jean Debucourt; GLASDALL, Gaston Modot (1887–1970); LORD TALBOT, Daniel Mandaille; LA CAPITAIN LA HIRE, Fernand Mailly; PIERRE CAUEBON, Pierre Douvan; LOYSELEUR, Georges Paulais; FRERE PASQUEREL, Francois Viguier; REMI LOISEAU, Louis Allibert; JEAN DE METZ, Jean Manoir; LE PAGE POITOU, Jean Stock; LA SORCIERE, Dorab Starny

This is one of two European biopics of Joan of Arc from 1928. The other was Carl-Theodore Dreyer's Swedish masterpiece, *The Passion of Joan of Arc* (1928). This French version is, unfortunately, not available with English titles yet. A version with French titles is available from video dealer Peter Kavel, which was the source material accessed for this review.

The Marvelous Life of Joan of Arc starts out with Joan on her modest farm hearing of the latest attack on France at the hands of the British. Double exposure images depict her visions of the various saints and the Virgin Mary indicating that she is the person chosen to save France from Britain. The film then progresses to her journey to Paris to obtain the necessary blessing from Charles VII to carry out her mission. The battle of d'Orleans is competently staged, using hundreds of extras, but does not come close to comparing to the excellent and impressive staging of this battle in Cecil B. DeMille's *Joan the Woman* (1916). Simone Ginedois' presence is not nearly as commanding as Geraldine Farrar's was in the DeMille version, either.

The interrogation and trial sequences are well done, capturing the facial expressions of the mocking tribunal that decides her fate. The burning is decently staged, but not particularly remarkable.

The Marvelous Life of Joan of Arc is generally a good film overall, but falls far short of the outstanding status of DeMille's *Joan the Woman* (1916), and does not have a unique quality that sets it apart as does Dreyer's *The Passion of Joan of Arc* (1928).

579. Matchmaking Mamma

Rating: ☆☆☆

Sennett/Pathé; ***Directed by*** Harry Edwards; ***Costumes by*** Madame Violette; ***Running Time:*** 20 minutes; ***Cast:*** SALLY MCNITT [THE STEP-DAUGHTER], Sally Eilers (1908–1978); MR. CORNELIUS MCNITT [SALLY'S FATHER], Johnny Burke; MRS. MCNITT [SALLY'S STEP-MOTHER], Daphne Pollard (1894–1978); LARRY LODGE, Matty Kemp (born 1907); PHYLLIS MCNITT, Carole Lombard (1908–1942); Mack Sennett's Bathing Beauties

This Sennett vehicle finds Sally Eilers playing Carole's step-sister, a Cinderella-type character who has returned home. Daphne Pollard plays Sally's step-mother [the matchmaking mother], who plans to hook daughter Carole up with Larry Lodge, the rich and handsome "preppy" type. These plans are dealt a blow when Sally arrives onto the scene unexpectedly. Mrs. McNitt lies to Sally, telling her that Larry and Phyllis are already engaged, and that he is just flirting with her for fun. The father, as well as Carole's own love interest, rectify the situation, much to the chagrin of the matchmaking mother.

A play rehearsal is filmed in 2-strip Technicolor, featuring Mack Sennett's bathing beauties, as well as the lead players in the film. This is a fun romantic comedy, and is among the better 1920s Sennett films evaluated.

Harry Edwards (1889–1952), the director, directed a number of Sennett comedy shorts with such stars as Billy Bevan, Ben Turpin, and Harry Langdon. He is perhaps best remembered for having directed Langdon's highly acclaimed feature, *Tramp, Tramp, Tramp* (1927), reviewed elsewhere in this book.

For more details on the stars of this film, see the review herein of *The Campus Vamp* (1928).

580. The Matinée Idol

Rating: ☆☆☆

Columbia; ***Directed by*** Frank Capra; ***From the Story*** *Come Back to Aaron* ***by*** Robert Lord and Ernest S. Pagano; ***Screen Adaptation by*** Elmer Harris; ***Continuity by*** Peter Milne; ***Photography by*** Phillip Tannura; ***Editing by*** Arthur Roberts; ***Running Time:*** 55 minutes; ***Cast:*** DON WILSON/HARRY MANN, Johnnie Walker (1894–1949); GINGER BOLIVAR, Bessie Love (1898–1986); BOLIVAR, Lionel Belmore (1868–1953); ARNOLD WINGATE, Ernest Hilliard (1890–1947); ERIC BARRYMAINE, David Mir

This delightful "quickie" was completed by director Frank Capra in six weeks time—two weeks to write it, another two to shoot it, and the final two weeks for editing. It features a perfect blend of comedy and romance.

Bessie Love, female lead in *The Matinée Idol* (1928).

Johnnie Walker plays Don Wilson, a highly successful Broadway actor who is on a much-needed vacation. He and his directors and producers are in a small town where their car breaks down. Right across the street from the garage is a touring tent show featuring the Bolivar Players. Bessie Love plays the daughter of the man who founded the show. The leading actor quits, and auditions are held for a replacement. As a lark, Broadway star Don auditions for and gets the role under the name of "Harry Mann." The show is so poorly done, it is hilarious although it is not intended to be so. It would make *Plan 9 from Outer Space* look like *Intolerance*. Wilson is fired for being a "terrible" actor. His producers decide to book the Bolivar Players onto Broadway as a joke. While Don goes along with the joke at first, complications arise when he discovers that he loves Ginger Bolivar, and doesn't want to break her heart.

Of the performances that this author has seen of Johnnie Walker's, this is the most favorite. Walker does a wonderful job in this film and is appealing as leading man. Bessie Love is delightful as the actress-director who thinks she is doing a quality drama, but is missing the mark. She is especially funny when conducting the audition for a new actor. One of the auditioners squirts her in the face using a "gag" lapel, and she takes his handkerchief out of his front pocket, wipes her face, and replaces it. This is among the last silents that Bessie Love starred in, just before her talkie debut in *The Broadway Melody* (1929), for which she was nominated for the 1928–29 Best Actress Oscar.

For many years, this Capra classic was believed lost. Once again, the European archives have saved a film that the Americans did not bother with. A print was rediscovered at the Cinématheque Française in 1996. The film was restored with a new orchestra score and shown on Turner Classic Movies in May 1997 for the first time in nearly 70 years.

581. Monsters of the Past Pathé Review *Rating:* ☆☆☆

Pathé; Director Uncredited; ***Running Time:*** 4 minutes, 45 seconds; ***Cast:*** THE SCULPTOR, Virginia May

This is an interesting dinosaur documentary released by Pathé in the late 1920s.

It shows the image of a dinosaur's fossils being assembled, and shows how artist Virginia May could reconstruct accurate images of the dinosaurs from the remaining bones. She is shown constructing, shaping and moving a clay dinosaur model, which provides good documentation of how the early stop-motion photography was done. The film proceeds to show two different dinosaurs preparing to do battle.

No further information could be found on sculpture artist Virginia May, who appeared to be in her late 20s when this film was made.

582. The Mysterious Lady *Rating:* ☆☆☆½

MGM; ***Directed by*** Fred Niblo; ***Assistant Director:*** Harold Bucquet; ***Based on Ludwig Wolff's War in the Dark***; ***Treatment/Continuity by*** Bess Meredyth; ***Titles by*** Marion Ainslee and Ruth Cummings; ***Wardrobe by*** Gilbert Clark; ***Settings by*** Cedric Gibbons; ***Photography by*** William Daniels; ***Film Editor:*** Margaret Booth; ***Running Time:*** 96 minutes; ***Cast:*** TANIA, Greta Garbo (1905–1990); KARL, Conrad Nagel (1897–1970); GENERAL ALEXANDROFF, Gustav von Seyffertitz (1863–1943); MAX, Albert Pollet; COUNT VON RODEN, Edward Connelly (1855–1928); GENERAL'S AIDE, Richard Alexander (1902–1989)

Greta Garbo, the alluring star of *The Mysterious Lady* (1928), in one of her most glamourous poses.

This is a spy thriller that was likely done at a time when the MGM executives decided that they needed to protect their investment in Greta Garbo, and give her some decent material to work with. An added attraction to this film is that it is the one and only MGM/Garbo silent that is available with color tinting today.

This beautifully portrayed romantic drama is set in Vienna, Austria, during World War I. Garbo plays Tania, a Russian spy whose husband is a high officer in the Russian army. She falls in love with Karl, an Austrian military officer whom she meets by chance at an opera performance. The love scenes on this introductory night provide Garbo with some of the most beautiful close-ups she ever had in any film. Her luminescent beauty is at its peak.

Tania is finally put into the position of having to betray either her country or the man she truly loves.

Conrad Nagel, who was rather bland a year before this film in *Quality Street* (1927), matured significantly by 1928, and came across very well as Garbo's leading man in this film. Greta Garbo was simply breathtaking. It is this film that was the first of the MGM vehicles that really gave her the opportunity to demonstrate the full potential of her glamour, sophistication, beauty, and talent. Cameraman William Daniels (1895–1970) deserves great praise for having so flawlessly photographed Garbo's close-ups.

With its outstanding photography, great acting, and interesting storyline that keeps the audience in suspense, *The Mysterious Lady* is among the best of Garbo's American silents, and is highly recommended.

583. Our Dancing Daughters

Rating: ☆☆☆½

MGM; ***Directed by*** Harry Beaumont; ***Assistant Director:*** Harold Bucquet; ***Story/Scenario by*** Josephine Lovett; ***Titles by*** Marion Ainslee and Ruth Cummings; ***Settings by*** Cedric Gibbons; ***Wardrobe by*** David Cox; ***Photography by*** George S. Barnes; ***Film Editor:*** William Hamilton; ***Running Time:*** 83 minutes; ***Cast:*** DIANA MEDFORD, Joan Crawford (1904–1977); BEN BLAINE, John Mack Brown (1904–1974); NORMAN, Nils Asther (1897–1981); BEATRICE, Dorothy Sebastian (1905–1957); ANN, Anita Page (born 1910); ANN'S MOTHER, Kathlyn Williams (1888–1960); FREDDIE, Edward Nugent; DIANA'S MOTHER, Dorothy Cumming (1899–1983); DIANA'S FATHER, Huntly Gordon (1887–1956); FREDDIE'S MOTHER, Evelyn Hall; FREDDIE'S FATHER, Sam DeGrasse (1875–1953)

This was among the first films in which Joan Crawford received top billing. It is a romantic drama centered around the yacht club, "jet set" crowd, at the height of the free wheeling, free spending late 1920s before the Great Depression brought the era to a screeching halt. *Our Dancing Daughters* portrays a rare period in time during which wealth among the jet set was so great that the adolescents portrayed were not concerned with career goals, and were only worried about finding that special someone to share their lives with in blissful luxury.

Anita Page, who gives an unforgettable performance in *Our Dancing Daughters* (1928).

Joan Crawford plays the lead role as Diane Medford, a fun loving, good hearted flapper who enjoys sowing her wild oats, and makes no secret of it. She is genuinely attracted to Ben Blaine, a college football star who has just inherited millions. Anita Page plays an excellent role as Ann, a conniving gold digger who is interested in Blaine mainly for his money, and plays "little Miss innocent" long enough to get her man. Once she is married to Blaine, she breaks out—having affairs, drinking heavily, and becoming an all-around bad girl.

When Medford finally does decide to slow down, she is heartbroken that her friends have married, and she remains alone. She experiences deep remorse for not having played the game earlier when she had the chance, as her friends had done.

Turnabout is the order of the day as Ann's true colors come to light, and eventually destroy her in a powerful drunken finale at the end of the film.

Our Dancing Daughters is perhaps best remembered for its art deco sets, which capture the jazz age era in its full glory. Joan Crawford does the Charleston, giving a good idea of what that dance craze was all about.

Although this film is mostly silent, it has a synchronized score and sound effects, and a couple of brief lines of dialogue technically classify it as a part talkie. Director Harry Beaumont (1888–1966) was at the height of his career when he made this film, which he would follow up with *The Broadway Melody* (1929), which won the second Best Picture Oscar. *Our Dancing Daughters* did not fare badly at the first Academy Awards, either, garnering two nominations for Best Writing and Best Cinematography. If awards had been given out for Supporting Actress at the time, Anita Page would have likely been in the running for a nomination in that category as well.

Anita Page, at the time of this writing, is 87 years old and living happily in Los Angeles, California. She has made herself widely accessible to film historians and fans, having granted a number of interviews.

It is fortunate that *Our Dancing Daughters* is one of the MGM silents that is widely accessible for viewing. Not only has it been frequently shown on Turner Classic Movies, but it was also among the silents released by MGM/UA Home Video.

584. The Pace That Kills

Rating: ☆☆☆

True-Life Photoplays; ***Directed by*** Norton S. Parker and William A. O'Connor; ***Produced by*** Willis Kent; ***Photographed by*** Ernest Laszlo; ***Titles by*** Ruth Todd; ***Edited by*** Edith Wakeling; ***Running Time:*** 64 minutes; ***Cast:*** THE BOY [EDDIE BRADLEY], Owen Gorin; HIS SWEETHEART, Thelma Daniels; HIS MOTHER [MRS. BRADLEY], Florence Turner (1887–1946); HIS SISTER [GRACE], Florence Dudley; UNCLE CALEB, Harry Todd (1863–1935); HANDSOME NICK, Arnold Dallas; THE GIRL [FANNY O'REILLY], Virginia Roye

This is an early exploitation film on the evils of cocaine—the predecessor of the 1936 sound film, *Cocaine Fiends*, which has become a cult classic.

The boy of the story starts out living happily on the family farm in the country. A friend of the family offers him a job at a large department store in the big city. He goes to the city with the intention of making good, as well as to find his sister Grace, who has not been heard from since she left the farm.

Once he arrives in the city, he at first writes letters faithfully to his parents and his sweetheart, and all seems well, except for the fact that he has not succeeded in finding his sister. Then, one of his coworkers, Fannie O'Reilly, gives him some white powder to cure a headache, starting the boy on to "the pace that kills."

The addiction cycle is realistically portrayed in this film, despite its obviously low budget. First comes the stealing to finance the habit, then the job loss, and finally the miserable withdrawal symptoms which drive the addict to the lowest level of degeneracy to obtain drug money. When the boy does find his sister, it is in a sleazy opium/heroin den, when both of them are in the depths of despair and beyond hope.

Owen Gorin and Virginia Roye give especially fine performances as the drug addicted couple portrayed in this film. *The Pace That Kills* delivers a message that is just as relevant today as it was when it was originally produced.

585. Pandora's Box

Rating: ☆☆☆☆

Nero Film/Germany; ***Directed by*** G.W. Pabst; ***Adapted from Two Frank Wedekind Plays*** *Erdgeist* and *Die Bueschse der Pandora*; ***Running Time:*** 108 minutes; ***Cast:*** LULU, Louise Brooks (1906–1985); LUDWIG SCHOEN, Fritz Kortner (1892–1970); ALWA SCHOEN, Francis Lederer (born 1906); JACK THE RIPPER, Gustav Diessl (1899–1948); SCHIGOLCH, Carl Goetz; COUNTESS GESCHWITZ [THE SCREEN'S FIRST LESBIAN], Alice Roberts; RODRIGO QUAST, Carl Raschig

This was the first of two masterpieces on which director G.W. Pabst (1885–1961) and Louise Brooks collaborated. It is one of the most famous of all of the German silents. Considered very risqué for its time, *Pandora's Box* is a film that has it all—incest, prostitution, blackmail, lesbianism, gambling, murder, and so on.

The film starts with Lulu, accompanied by a drunk, disreputable old man who poses as her father, but is actually a pimp. Ludwig Schoen, a wealthy newspaper magnate whose reputation has been tarnished after coming under Lulu's hypnotizing spell, breaks off their illicit affair. Undaunted, Lulu simply starts an affair with his younger and attractive son, Alwa, an aspiring musician and playwright. At Alwa's and Lulu's wedding reception, Louise Brooks shocked the world by dancing with the wealthy Countess Geschwitz, a lesbian played by Alice Roberts. This dance is one of the earliest screen portrayals of lesbianism. Alwa's father, who sees the road of destruction his son is headed for under Lulu's spell, pulls a gun on her, demanding that she leave his son alone. A struggle ensues, and the elder Schoen is killed. Lulu is convicted of manslaughter, and she and Alwa escape together on a cruise ship. As a fugitive, Lulu is blackmailed, and the blackmailer drains all of Lulu's and Alwa's money. Alwa is caught cheating at poker to win money to pay off the blackmailer. Once again, the couple escapes to London—totally penniless and living in an attic with broken windows. Lulu turns to prostitution to support herself, Alwa, and Schigolch, and is killed by Jack the Ripper on Christmas Eve. Alwa ends up in the Salvation Army, broke, ruined, and having to start all over again.

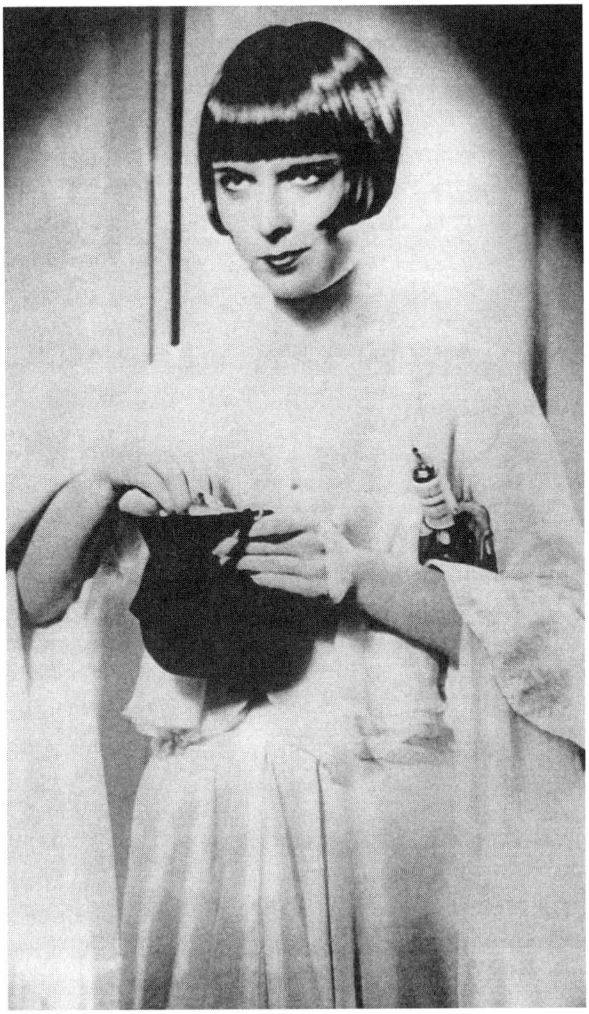

Louise Brooks in a scene from *Pandora's Box* (1928).

This film role of Louise Brooks' character, Lulu, was so notorious that the word "Lulu" became a household term, and "lulu of a storm" a common expression. Louise Brooks stated in her book, *Lulu in Hollywood*, that the sequence in which Fritz Kortner shakes her was acted with such passion that she had bruise marks on her arm from the scene.

Ms. Brooks gave an electrifying and alluring performance. Although *Pandora's Box* was completed in 1928, it did not play in the United States until mid–1929. Since the talkie era was already in full swing here, the film had a limited run, although it was a sensation in Europe. In Danny Peary's book, *Alternate Oscars*, he gives his 1929–30 Best Actress award to Louise Brooks for her performance in *Pandora's Box*: "[Louise Brooks'] spellbinding portrayal of Lulu ... was one of the great portraits of silent films and one of the most erotic in film history."

Francis Lederer had his most famous role as Alwa in this film, giving the best performance of his career. At age 91, he lives in Los Angeles and remains active, although somewhat reclusive, refusing to answer fan mail.

Louise Brooks chose to stay in Germany to do *Pandora's Box*, refusing to go back to America to dub her voice for *The Canary Murder Case* (1929). As a result, she had the opportunity to demonstrate the full potential of her acting ability under the direction of G.W. Pabst, for whom Greta Garbo did her best silent work as well. When one sees the stodgy direction of *Canary Murder Case*, one can hardly blame Brooks for leaving Margaret Livingston to the task of dubbing the voice for her character's part.

James Card, formerly of the George Eastman House, was largely responsible for the belated resurrection of the Pabst-Brooks collaborations, reviving the films at the Dryden Theatre in the 1950s. Ms. Brooks, who by that time was working at Macy's Department Store, was brought to the Eastman House as a visiting scholar in her final years. Her published, insightful essays are fascinating and informative. With her last two silent films, those two Brooks performances alone guarantee her a permanent status as one of the most legendary female sex symbols ever to grace the silver screen.

Thanks to James Card (for preserving the film) and Janus Films, the company that released *Pandora's Box* on video in the 1980s, future generations will have the pleasure of seeing Louise Brooks on screen.

586. The Patent Leather Kid *Rating:* ☆½

First National; ***Directed by*** Alfred Santell; ***Written by*** Rupert Hughes; ***Adaptation by*** Adela Rogers St. Johns; ***Scenario by*** Winifred Dunn; ***Titles by*** Gerald C. Duffy; ***Photography by*** Arthur Edeson; ***Art Direction by*** Stephen Godsson, Jack Okey; ***Film Editor:*** Hugh Bennett; ***Running Time:*** 127 minutes; ***Cast:*** THE PATENT LEATHER KID, Richard Barthelmess (1895–1963); CURLEY CALLAHAN, Molly O'Day (born 1911); HUGO BREEN, Lawford Davidson; JAKE STUKE, Matthew Betz (1881–1938); PUFFY KINCH, Arthur Stone; MOLASSES, Raymond Turner (1895–1981)

The Patent Leather Kid is historically significant as one of the films for which Richard Barthelmess received a 1927–28 Academy Award nomination for Best Actor. Upon seeing it, one concludes that he had to have been nominated more on the basis of *The Noose* (1928) than for this film, in which Barthelmess gives no better than a competent performance. To have given a nomination to Barthelmess and not to Lionel Barrymore's performance in *Sadie Thompson* (1928) is downright ludicrous. If anyone in this film deserved an Academy Award nomination, it would be Molly O'Day for Best Actress; she gives an excellent performance that Barthelmess doesn't come close to matching in quality.

The Patent Leather Kid has many similarities to *The Big Parade*, but simply isn't nearly as well done as the preceding film. In this film, Barthelmess plays a poor kid from the slums who rises to fame as a champion boxer. He gets a swelled head, but is gradually brought somewhat back down to earth by girlfriend Curley Callahan. World War I comes, and Barthelmess' character faces pressure from Curley and others to enlist. The decision is made for him when he gets a draft notice, and he finds out that fighting is not all fun and games.

While this film starts off pretty well, it really starts to drag after the first hour. The last half of the film seems to take forever with its needless padding.

587. Return of the Rat *Rating:* ☆☆

Gainsborough Pictures/England; ***Directed by*** Graham Cutts; ***Running Time:*** 83 minutes; ***Cast:*** PIERRE, Ivor Novello (1893–1951); ZELLE, Isabel Jeans (1891–1985); LISETTE, Mabel

Poulton (1901–1994); MOREL, Gordon Harker (1885–1967); HENRI, Bernard Nedell (1893–1972); MERE COLLINE, Marie Ault (1870–1951); ALF, Scotch Kelly [a.k.a. James Steele] (1889–1967); YVONNE, Gladys Frazier (1901–1939)

This was one of the lackluster sequels to *The Rat* (1925), which is not accessible for review, but has wide acclaim as an excellent film with nonstop action. Mae Marsh costarred with Ivor Novello in the first picture, but did not come back for any of the sequels. This was the third entry in this series of films.

In *Return of the Rat*, the title character played by Novello is married to Zelle de Chaumet, who is having an affair with Henri de Verral. Pierre and Henri have a duel, and Pierre is believed dead.

At a costume ball, Zelle announces her engagement to Henri. Pierre has attended the ball in costume and becomes involved in an altercation as the lights go out. Zelle is found stabbed to death, and Pierre is the prime suspect.

While the story makes this film sound good, *Return of the Rat* is disappointing and slow paced, becoming downright boring at times. Mabel Poulton is appealing as is Ivor Novello, and they are what saves the film from the abyss.

It is sad to note that Gladys Frazier, who had a supporting role in this film, committed suicide 11 years after she starred in *Return of the Rat* by jumping out a window. She had been married to film comedian and director Monty Banks (1897–1950).

588. The Road to Ruin *Rating:* ☆

Cliff Broughton Productions; ***Directed by*** Norton S. Parker; ***Assistant Director:*** David Hampton; ***Photography by*** Henry Cronjager; ***Film Editor:*** Edith Wakeling; ***Running Time:*** 41 minutes; ***Cast:*** SALLY CANFIELD, Helen Foster (1906–1982); DON HUGHES, Grant Withers (1904–1959); EVE TERRELL, Virginia Roye; MRS. CANFIELD, Florence Turner (1887–1946); JIMMY, Tom Carr; AL, Don Rader; MR. CANFIELD, Charles Miller; Los Angeles Police Department Captain Leo W. Marden as himself

"Don't let your children stay at another friend's house away from home overnight! Such misguided and blind trust will put them on the 'road to ruin!'" This is the general gist of this low budget, juvenile crime and prostitution exploitation drama. It contains a personal introduction by Captain Leo W. Marden of the Los Angeles Police Department. This movie is so bad, it is funny—earning a place in the same category as *Reefer Madness* (1937).

Sally Canfield is a juvenile girl who innocently asks her mother for permission to stay overnight at her friend Eve's house. The mother grants permission. Sally starts on the road to ruin with reading steamy novels with Eve that night, and going to a party by the lake with Eve and two boys the next. For some reason, Eve starts crying on her male partner's shoulder, although the reason is never explained.

Within a short time, the first major catastrophe of the road to ruin occurs when Sally and Eve are arrested by the authorities at a "strip poker" party. The girls are subjected to a medical examination at juvenile hall, which reveals Eve's positive test for a venereal disease. With no explanation, this is the last we see of the Eve character, who unaccountably disappears from the film at this point. Weeks later, Sally discovers that she is pregnant with Don Hughes' child. He promises to finance a back alley abortion in return for allowing herself to be pimped out to a friend of his. The first customer who shows up for Sally turns out to be her own father. She is deathly ill from the botched abortion, and he takes her home to die.

The role as Sally's mother was one of the last roles played by Florence Turner, who from 1906–1913 was known as "The Vitagraph Girl," and one of the most popular actresses of the time. She was 41 when she appeared in this film, but looked much older than she really was. Those who wish to see Ms. Turner at the height of her career can watch her as Lucie Manette in *A Tale of Two Cities* (1911), which is available on video.

Grant Withers had a few parts in "A" pictures like *College* (1927) and *Bringing Up Father* (1927), but ended up doing mostly low budget serials and action pictures. He played supporting parts in a number of TV westerns of the 1950s before committing suicide in 1959.

This film is not quite as bad as Larry Semon's *Wizard of Oz* (1925) or *Plan 9 from Outer Space* (1959), but very close.

589. Sadie Thompson

Rating: ☆☆☆☆

Gloria Swanson Productions/United Artists; ***Directed by*** Raoul Walsh; ***Scenario by*** Raoul Walsh; ***Based on*** *Miss Thompson* ***by*** Somerset Maugham; ***Photographed by*** George Barnes, Robert Kurrle, Oliver Marsh; ***Art Direction by*** William Cameron Menzies; ***Editing and Titles by*** C. Gardner Sullivan; ***Running Time of Current Restoration:*** 97 minutes; ***Cast:*** SADIE THOMPSON, Gloria Swanson (1897–1983); SERGEANT TIMOTHY O'HARA, Raoul Walsh (1887–1980); ALFRED DAVIDSON, Lionel Barrymore (1878–1954); MRS. ALFRED DAVIDSON, Blanche Frideric; DR. ANGUS MCPHAIL, Charles Lane (1869–1945); MRS. ANGUS MCPHAIL, Florence Midgley (1890–1949); JOE HORN, James A. Marcus (1867–1937); AMEENA, Sophia Artego; QUARTERMASTER BATES, Will Stanton (1885–1969)

This was the first and finest of three screen adaptations of Somerset Maugham's short story called *Miss Thompson*. Before this movie adaptation, the story had been adapted as the stage play called *Rain*, which made actress Jeanne Eagels a stage sensation. This original film adaptation won two Oscar nominations for 1927–28. Gloria Swanson was nominated as Best Actress, and George Barnes received a nomination for Cinematography.

Ms. Swanson had to fight hard with the Hays office to make this film, as the play *Rain* was declared strictly off limits. This is part of the reason why it was filmed under the title of *Sadie Thompson*. Its plot has Swanson in the lead role of Sadie Thompson, a San Francisco prostitute who is seeking to start a new life, but is temporarily detained on an island which happens to be the current target of "reformer" Alfred Davidson, who seeks to rid the island of sin. Davidson and Thompson clash when she befriends a group of Army men, and she is accused of immorality with the men, one of whom she falls in love with—Sergeant Tim O'Hara. Davidson makes it a point to have O'Hara confined to quarters, and he threatens to have Thompson deported back to San Francisco, a city that he finds out Thompson has fled from because she was framed for a crime she did not commit. Faced with the prospect of going back to prison instead of to Australia to start a new life with O'Hara, Thompson must find a way to keep Davidson from sending her back to San Francisco.

Sadie Thompson is highly acclaimed as the greatest performance of Gloria Swanson's career, and this reviewer supports that acclaim. The author goes further to say that

Swanson's performance in this film should was better than the three performances that Janet Gaynor was given the first Best Actress Oscar for. Gaynor's performances were definitely Oscar-worthy, but still fall short of Swanson's performance in this film and Marion Davies' performance in *The Patsy* (1927).

In praising Swanson's performance, we cannot overlook the terrific performance given by Lionel Barrymore as the evil reformer. His performance should have been at least nominated for the Best Actor Oscar. Film critic Danny Peary's *Alternate Oscars* lists Barrymore as among those he felt deserved Oscar nominations for 1927–28.

Lip readers had fun with this film, as there are a number of sequences in which Swanson uses profanity. No profanity appears in the titles except for one in which Thompson tells Davidson "Hang me and be damned!" Swanson's answer to the Hays office was that one could not censor what one could not hear.

For many years, this film remained unseen because the one and only surviving print of *Sadie Thompson* was missing the final reel. In 1987 Dennis Doros reconstructed the last reel using titles, stills, and film footage from other parts of the film where appropriate. At last, this masterpiece is back before the public where it belongs, and this restored version is available from Kino Video.

Sadie Thompson is among the finest dramatic achievements of the 1920s, and is a film that every classic or silent film enthusiast should own. It should have won the first Academy Award for Best Production.

590. Show People

Rating: ☆☆☆☆

MGM; ***Directed by*** King Vidor; ***Adaptation by*** Agnes Christine Johnson, Laurence Stallings; ***Continuity by*** Wanda Tuchock; ***Titles by*** Ralph Spence; ***Settings by*** Cedric Gibbons; ***Wardrobe by*** Henriette Frazier; ***Film Editor:*** Hugh Wynn; ***Photographed by*** John Arnold; ***Running Time:*** 78 minutes; ***Cast:*** PEGGY PEPPER, Marion Davies (1897–1961); BILLY BOONE, William Haines (1900–1973); COLONEL PEPPER, Dell Henderson (1877–1956); ANDRE, Paul Rolli; CASTING DIRECTOR, Tenen Holtz (1887–1971); COMEDY DIRECTOR, Harry Gribbon (1885–1961); DRAMATIC DIRECTOR, Sidney Bracy (1877–1942); THE MAID, Polly Moran (1883–1952); PRODUCER, Albert Conti (1887–1967); ***As Themselves:*** King Vidor (1894–1982); Louella Parsons (1893–1972); Leatrice Joy (1893–1965); John Gilbert (1899–1936); Douglas Fairbanks, Sr. (1883–1939); Charlie Chaplin (1889–1977); William S. Hart (1864?–1946); Rod LaRocque (1896–1969); Mae Murray (1889–1965); Norma Talmadge (1897–1957); Elinor Glyn (1864–1943); Lew Cody (1883–1934); Eleanor Boardman (1898–1991)

This was the last of the really big all-star silent extravaganzas, as well as the best of those available for evaluation. It is widely acclaimed as Marion Davies' best film, although this reviewer is torn between *The Patsy* (1927) and *Show People* (1928), liking them both so well that it is difficult to put one over the other. Danny Peary's book, *Alternate Oscars*, gives a Best Actress nomination to Ms. Davies for 1928–29.

In *Show People*, Ms. Davies plays Peggy Pepper, a naive girl from Savannah, Georgia, whose father brings her to Hollywood to break into movies. She is as green as green can be, but under the fostering hand of Billy Boone, becomes a big success in slapstick comedies and moves to the big time dramas. Once she makes it, she gets a swelled head, changing her name to Patricia Pepoire, becoming involved with Andre, a fellow dramatic actor formerly known as Andy, who has bestowed upon himself the fake royal title of "count." She forgets all about her mentor, Billy Boone, in her snob-

William Haines, leading man in *Show People* (1928), circa 1930.

bishness, and is just about to marry "Count Andre" when she is finally brought back down to earth.

Davies' pantomimic comedy really comes through in this film. In one especially funny scene, she does hilariously wicked parodies of both Gloria Swanson and Mae Murray. When she is introducing herself as Peggy Pepper to the casting office, her father uses a handkerchief as a theater curtain as she demonstrates expressions of the various moods —joy, sorrow, passion, etc. in a delightfully hokey and exaggerated manner. Another good sequence occurs when she is demonstrating her "drama" acting to her new comedy director, who compliments her on what great hokum she's performing.

Show People is a comedy that also has an underlying message in that Peggy Pepper's ascension to stardom was much like Gloria Swanson's—starting out in comedy, working up to drama, and then marrying a count (as did Mae Murray) for status, who takes her for a ride and nearly ruins her career. It emphasizes a moral to all aspiring stars not to let success go to their head. *Show People* provides a fascinating behind the scenes look at Hollywood as it was in the late 1920s.

This was the top grossing film of all of Marion Davies' silents, as well as the second most profitable, coming in $4,000 behind *Beverly of Graustark* (1925), currently held in Turner Entertainment's archives.

William Haines has the best role of his career as Billy Boone. Another interesting aspect about *Show People* is that it contains the only surviving footage of the lost film, *Bardelys the Magnificent* (1928), which starred John Gilbert and Eleanor Boardman. The main title and a few seconds of the opening scenes are shown in the theater sequence.

Show People was released originally with a synchronized score and sound effects, and it is this original score that appears with the film on its laser disc release, as well as on Turner Classic Movies. Kevin Brownlow produced a version with a new score by Carl

Davis, and it is the Davis score that comes with the videotape release from MGM/UA Home Video.

This film is great fun, and it is fortunate that it is as widely available as it is. What is unfortunate is that this is the only Marion Davies silent that Turner Entertainment has released, despite pleas from thousands of Marion Davies fans for them to air or release her other silents.

591. The Singing Fool

Rating: ☆☆½

Warner Brothers; ***Directed by*** Lloyd Bacon; ***Assistant Director:*** Frank Shaw; ***Based on a Story by*** Leslie Burrows; ***Music Score Performed by*** Vitaphone Symphony Orchestra; ***Adaptation by*** G. Graham Baker; ***Photography by*** Byron Haskins; ***Edited by*** Ralph Dawson; ***Dialogue/Titles by*** Joseph Jackson; ***Running Time:*** 103 minutes; ***Cast:*** AL STONE, Al Jolson (1886–1950); GRACE, Betty Bronson (1906–1971); MOLLY WINTON, Josephine Dunn (1906–1983); BLACKIE JOE, Arthur Housman (1889–1942); LOUIS MARCUS, Edward Martindel (1873–1955); MAID, Helen Lynch (1900–1965); JOHN PERRY, Reed Howes (1900–1964); SONNY, David Lee; CAFE OWNER, Robert O'Connor (1885–1962)

In this follow-up to *The Jazz Singer* (1927), Al Jolson plays a waiter in a speakeasy cabaret who aspires to be a song writer. He is in love with Molly Winton, the cabaret's star singer, who refuses to even look at some of the songs that he has composed. He finally convinces cabaret owner Blackie Joe to let him sing the song himself. He does, and goes over big. He and Molly get married, but she is unfaithful to him and breaks his heart, sending him into an alcoholic depression. It is Grace, a true friend who has always remained loyal, who helps Al to bounce back.

This was the first important directorial project of Lloyd Bacon (1890–1955). Bacon started out as supporting villain in comedy shorts with Lloyd Hamilton in 1913. He moved into directing Sennett-Hamilton comedies from 1921 to 1926. He went on to direct such films as *Moby Dick* (1930), *Gold Diggers of 1937* (1936), and many others in the talkie era. He was among Hollywood's most prolific directors until his death. The camera work in this film is unusually mobile—especially in the introductory cabaret sequences.

According to William K. Everson's *American Silent Film*, *The Singing Fool* was the top grosser of the silent era, having taken in $5 million at the box office. [This status is open to argument, as D.W. Griffith's *The Birth of a Nation* (1915) is believed to have grossed as much as $50,000,000, but inadequate documentation makes it difficult to provide concrete verification of exactly how much Griffith's film actually grossed.]

Al Jolson gives a good performance in this film, but it follows much the same formula as *The Jazz Singer*. This film gives one the impression that if you have seen one Jolson movie, you have seen them all.

The primary factor that interested this reviewer in *The Singing Fool* is the fact that it is one of the few extant features of Betty Bronson from the silent era. With the disappointing box-office performance of the fairy tale films that Bronson did with Herbert Brenon, Paramount did not know what to do with their new discovery. She had been tried in flapper films such as *The Cat's Pajamas* (1927), and went to Warner Brothers when her Paramount contract expired. *The Singing Fool* provided Bronson with her first speaking role, although she does not speak until the second half of the film. As small as Bronson's role was, it is her performance that makes *The Singing Fool* worth preserving and having on video. MGM/UA Home Video released this title in 1996—the first silent/part-talkie that they have released in a few years.

592. Speedy

Rating: ☆☆☆☆

Harold Lloyd Corporation/Paramount; ***Directed by*** Ted Wilde; ***Story and Scenario by*** John Grey, Lex Neal, Howard Rogers, Jay Howe; ***Titles by*** Albert DeMond; ***Photography by*** Walter Lundin; ***Production Manager:*** John L. Murphy; ***Dog Trainer:*** Ebenezer Henry; ***Running Time:*** 85 minutes; ***Cast:*** HAROLD "SPEEDY" SWIFT, Harold Lloyd (1893–1971); JANE DILLON, Ann Christy (1905–1987); POP DILLON, Bert Woodruff (1856–1934); STEVE CARTER, Brooks Benedict (died 1968); THE DOG, King Tut; George Herman "Babe" Ruth (1895–1948) as himself

This final Lloyd silent has him portraying the fiancé of the granddaughter of the operator of New York's last horse driven trolley system. A crooked railroad entrepreneur won't pay the price that Pop Dillon [the grandfather of Jane Dillon] wants, and resolves to force him out of business. It is up to Harold Swift, an avid baseball fan, to save Pop Dillon's business, and force the competing entrepreneurs to pay Dillon's asking price.

Speedy is not only a highly entertaining comedy, but is one of significant historic interest as well. The beginning has some excellent location footage of New York City as it was in 1928. In addition, footage from an actual professional baseball game is shown, and Babe Ruth has a cameo as one of Harold's taxi customers.

Ann Christy, Lloyd's leading lady in this film, had a brief career, having made her debut in William Nigh's *The Fire Brigade* (1927). Six films for the years 1927 and 1928 are listed in her filmography in John T. Weaver's *Twenty Years of Silents*. According to the historic record, her last film was made in 1932. Director Ted Wilde (1893–1929) received a posthumous Academy Award nomination as Best Director for his work on this film, which was the last he completed. He died of a stroke at age 36 when he was in the middle of another project.

As Lloyd's last silent, *Speedy* was also his last really great film. Although his follow-up, *Welcome Danger* (1929), was originally filmed as a silent, it was re-shot as a talkie. According to various sources, adding dialogue to *Welcome Danger* ruined it, and although it was Lloyd's biggest box-office success, this was mainly because the public was curious to hear his voice. Today, *Welcome Danger* is regarded as one of Lloyd's worst films. Over the next 18 years, Lloyd made seven talkies, and none of them managed to come close to the success of any of his silents.

593. Steamboat Bill, Jr.

Rating: ☆☆☆½

United Artists; ***Directed by*** Charles Riesner; ***Assistant Director:*** Sandy Roth; ***Story by*** Carl Harbaugh; ***Running Time:*** 75 minutes; ***Cast:*** STEAMBOAT BILL, JR., Buster Keaton (1895–1966); STEAMBOAT BILL, SR. [WILLIAM CANFIELD], Ernest Torrence (1878–1933); STEAMBOAT CAPTAIN, Tom Lewis (1867–1927); J.J. KING'S DAUGHTER, Marion Byron (1911–1985); J.J. KING, Tom McGuire (1869–1954)

This was Buster Keaton's last independently produced silent feature. It is also considered by many film historians to be his last really great classic, although this reviewer thoroughly enjoyed his two MGM-produced silents as much or more than this film.

In this vehicle, Keaton plays a young man who is just returning from college in the big city to his river front hometown. His father is the owner of a steamboat that has fallen on hard times due to the arrival of a nicer and bigger "floating palace"—owned by the father of the girl that Keaton's character falls for. It is up to Steamboat Bill, Jr. to prove himself by saving the floundering family business from the new competition, while at the same time getting the girl.

Steamboat Bill, Jr. contains what is one of the most famous sequences in comedy history—the cyclone segment. This sequence is spectacular as Bill, Jr. is blown from his house into a horse stable as the house falls down all around him. At one point, the entire side of a house falls right where Keaton is standing, although he comes out unscathed because an open window happens to be the part of the house that falls on Keaton. Clips from this sequence have been used in modern day television commercials over the past few years.

Marion Byron was only 16 years old when she starred in this film. She was reportedly hired on the basis of her looks, and could not swim, thereby disqualifying her from playing the underwater sequences. For these sequences that Byron could not play, Keaton used his sister, Louise Keaton, as a double for Byron.

Tom Lewis, who played the steamboat captain, died shortly after his part in this film was completed. The veteran stage actor succumbed after an operation.

Due to the perfectionism of Buster Keaton, many retakes were done on this film, which made production costs soar. *Steamboat Bill, Jr.*, like *The General* (1927), did not do as well as expected at the box office. Keaton was forced at this point to sacrifice his independence and go into contract work for MGM. This brought on the depression which escalated his alcoholism and by the early 1930s, his career and life were in a slump.

594. Storm Over Asia

Rating: ☆½

Produced in the U.S.S.R.; ***Directed by*** Vsevolod Pudovkin; ***Scenario by*** Osip Brik; ***From a Story by*** I. Novokshonov; ***Photographed by*** Anatoli Golovnia; ***Running Time:*** 125 minutes; ***Cast:*** BAIR [THE MONGOL], Valeri Inkizhinov

Storm Over Asia was the final silent film directed by Vsevolod Pudovkin (1893–1953), who was inspired to enter the motion picture industry upon seeing D.W. Griffith's *Intolerance* (1916).

This film is the story of a Mongolian Civil War incident of 1920. It is historically important as the first film to have been shot on location in Mongolia, and is important documentation of what this area of the world was like in the 1920s. If not for this film, there would be no

Storm Over Asia **(1928).**

documentation at all of this period in Mongolia's history. The gist of the plot has a poor Mongolian's ill father give him a rare and valuable silver fox skin to sell at the market—stipulating that he is not to accept less than the sum of 500 silvers for it. [The man who played Bair's father was his father in real life, and the sequences featuring him were filmed in the actual residence that he lived in.] A British fur trader, who is under the protection of the occupying British army, cheats Bair, the Mongol, out of the rare skin. When Bair takes the trader to task, he escapes and avoids capture, becoming a fugitive.

The time comes when the British Forces demand that the Mongols relinquish their cattle to them, and Bair is on this occasion captured and ordered executed. As he is being shot, it is discovered by the British forces that Bair is the direct descendant of Jenghis Khan, the ancient Mongolian ruler. Thinking that they can use Bair for their own purposes, the British recover Bair, who is barely alive, and nurse him to recovery. He goes along with the diabolical plan at first, until he sees a fellow Mongolian wantonly hunted down and killed by the British forces. This act inspires Bair to lead a revolt against the occupation forces, and this incident is the symbolic "storm over Asia."

Of interest only to scholars and professors of Russian/Asian history, this film will be a waste of time for most others. It is over an hour into the film before the real action starts, and these periods are sporadic. The print evaluated took over 2 hours to tell a story which could have been more effectively told in half that time. While some of these sequences served a valid purpose, the big flaw is that Pudovkin lingered too long on these sequences. He took several minutes to document an old Mongolian religious ceremony, and he could have served his purpose by showing the highlights of the ceremony in 90 seconds to 2 minutes, or 3 minutes tops. Also, this is the type of film which really requires a good background on Asian/Russian history to be able to fully appreciate and comprehend. One would have to do a lot of research to be able to garner enough knowledge to properly comprehend what is going on. Introductory titles providing historical background in simple, concise terminology could have really helped this film in presenting it to the American market. The average American silent film buff is not going to go through the trouble to do hours of research before viewing this film, and they shouldn't be required to. The film should be able to stand on its own two feet, and this one, unfortunately, doesn't, whereas Pudovkin's prior effort, *The End of St. Petersburg* (1927), does. Upon *Storm Over Asia*'s original release, it was necessary for the titles in all prints circulating in Europe and Asia outside of the U.S.S.R. to be changed from referring to the British Army to refer instead to a "White Russian Army."

Storm Over Asia was a box-office hit abroad, but due to the exceptional anti–Communist feeling in the United States, it was not successful in this country.

595. Street Angel

Rating: ☆☆☆☆

Fox; ***Directed by*** Frank Borzage; ***Assistant Directors:*** Lew Borzage, Ralph Kaufman; ***From the Play by*** Monckton Hoffe; ***Continuity by*** Marion Orth; ***Production Editors:*** Katharine Hilliker, H.H. Caldwell; ***Photographed by*** Ernest Palmer, Paul Ivano; ***Adaptation by*** Philip Klein, Henry Roberts Symonds; ***Settings by*** Harry Oliver; ***Costumes by*** Kathleen Kay; ***Running Time:*** 100 minutes; ***Cast:*** ANGELA, Janet Gaynor (1906–1984); GINO, Charles Farrell (1901–1990); LISETTA, Natalie Kingston (1905–1991); SERGEANT OF POLICE, Guido Trento (1892–1957)

Janet Gaynor, star of *Street Angel* (1928), in the 1930s.

This strong Borzage/Farrell/Gaynor follow-up to *7th Heaven* is set in Naples, Italy. Janet Gaynor plays Angela, a poor girl from the slums whose mother is ill, and needs a prescription to save her life. With no money to buy the needed prescription, Angela resorts to trying to prostitute herself to get the money. She is caught, but escapes and travels with a small vaudeville show, during which she meets Gino, an aspiring artist. They fall in love, and when they both have high hopes of a life together, she cannot explain to Gino why she can't go back to Naples, where she is still wanted by the law.

The couple move to Naples, and all is well until the police sergeant recognizes Angela, and on the eve of hers and Gino's wedding, sends her back to prison. Although she tries to keep Gino from finding out where she is, a prostitute named Rosetta tells him, and he is totally turned off, knowing that Angela was arrested for solicitation, but not knowing the circumstances. Once Angela gets out of prison, the challenge is to see if Gino's love can overcome his anger and repulsion in favor of forgiveness.

This is a beautiful portrayal of triumph over adversity, poverty, desperation, and other cruel obstacles, and Janet Gaynor plays Angela, the "street angel" most effectively. Charles Farrell gives a fine performance as Gino. Among the impressive supporting cast members is Natalie Kingston, the prostitute who refuses to let Angela live down her past, but a force that the power of love overcomes.

Street Angel is one of the few films that maintains the quality of its predecessor.

Unfortunately, the only prints that circulate on video are extremely poor quality copies among a few private collectors. *Street Angel* is deserving of a legitimate, high quality video release.

596. That Certain Thing

Rating: ☆☆☆

Columbia; ***Directed by*** Frank Capra; ***Story by*** Elmer Harris; ***Photography by*** Joseph Walker; ***Titles by*** Al Boasberg; ***Edited by*** Arthur Roberts; ***Art Director:*** Robert E. Lee; ***Running Time:*** 65 minutes; ***Cast:*** MOLLY KELLY, Viola Dana (1897–1987); A.B. CHARLES JR., Ralph Graves (1900–1977); MAGGIE KELLY, Aggie Herring (1876–1939); A.B. CHARLES SR., Burr McIntosh (1862–1942)

This romantic comedy bears historic significance not only as one of the early works of Oscar-winning director Frank Capra, but as one of just a couple of the films of Viola Dana that is widely available to the public.

In *That Certain Thing*, Ms. Dana plays Molly, a poor girl who works as a hotel cigar girl to support her mother and two siblings. She has aspirations of meeting and marrying a millionaire.

The leading male character is A.B. Charles Jr., the son of a wealthy owner of a chain of A.B.C. Restaurants. He literally bumps into Molly as she is leaving work. She has met her millionaire—or so she thinks. When she marries the wealthy restaurant heir, his father is outraged and cuts his son off. Charles Jr. gets a job digging ditches—the first work he has done in his privileged life. It is while on the job that he comes up with the idea for him and Molly to go into the lunch box business. He and wife Molly soon have an enterprise which threatens the very existence of his father's chain of restaurants, using the "sandwich with a secret." It is fun to follow the progression of this film as A.B. Charles Sr. is finally forced to admit that he was wrong about Molly.

Viola Dana, popular female star of the early Capra comedy, *That Certain Thing* (1928).

This is a highly entertaining comedy, and one that we are fortunate to have access to on video. Ralph Graves has thinner hair on top, and aged a great deal between the early 1920s and 1928, when he played this role. However, Viola Dana looks as young and radiant as ever. Viewers will remember Burr McIntosh, who plays the father, from his role as the squire in *Way Down East* (1920).

While Viola Dana plays a comedy role in this film, it was drama that really made her reputation in the late 1910s. It was during this period of her life that she was starring in melodramas under the direction of her first husband, John Collins (1889–1918). Collins met an early death during the Spanish influenza epidemic, which killed 20 million worldwide—a death toll greater than the casualties of World War I. At least three of the Collins-Dana films are known to survive [*Blue Jeans* (1918), *The Cossack Whip* (1917), and *Children of Eve* (1915)], but are held in archives and are inaccessible to the public.

597. The Viking

Rating: ☆☆☆

MGM; ***Directed by*** Roy William Neill; ***Produced by*** Herbert T. Kalmus; ***Color Art Direction by*** Natalie Kalmus; ***Screenplay by*** Jack Cunningham; ***Based on the Novel*** *The Thrill of Leif the Lucky* ***by*** Ottilie A. Liljencrantz; ***Manager of Production:*** J.T. Reed; ***Photography by*** George Cave; ***Film Editor:*** Aubrey Scotto; ***Settings by*** Tec-Art; ***Supervising Art Director:*** Carl Oscar Borg; ***Running Time:*** 89 minutes; ***Cast:*** HELGA NILSSON, Pauline Starke (1900–1977); ALWIN, LeRoy Mason (1903–1947); LEIF ERICSSON, Donald Crisp (1882–1974); ERIC THE RED, Anders Randolph (1870–1930); SIGURD, Richard Alexander; EGIL, Harry Lewis Woods (1889–1968); KARK, Albert McQuarrie (1882–1950); KING OLAF, Roy Stewart (1884–1933); LADY EDITHA, Claire McDowell (1878–1966)

This is the first silent feature film which MGM produced entirely in Technicolor, and one which has been largely forgotten. The color art director listed in the credits was Natalie Kalmus, the wife of Herbert T. Kalmus, the pioneer and inventor of the 2-strip Technicolor process. It was part of the couple's divorce settlement that Natalie's name was to be credited on all Technicolor productions.

Considering the rarity of Technicolor silent features, *The Viking* is a film of historic importance. Yet, in nineteen years of research, only a few of hundreds of books on motion picture history made so much as a scant mention of the film. This reviewer featured a complete review of *The Viking* in the 1996 book *Silent Films on Video*, which, as far as can be determined, was the first time since the 1920s that any in-depth material had been written on the film.

Although not a film of epic or masterpiece status, this is an interesting movie based on a novel detailing the lives of Eric the Red and his crew of Viking voyagers. Typical of many films in the era of the Hays office, this one dabbles into religion—portraying the conversion from paganism to Judeo-Christianity of Eric the Red, much to the distaste of his father, Leif Ericsson. It also portrays how the Vikings invaded territories and took people captive, and the fear that the mere mention of the name "Viking" instilled into the people. In the final sequence, the arrival of the Vikings in Newport, Rhode Island, is portrayed, and a watchtower built by them in the 1000s which still stands is shown.

Donald Crisp is given top billing in the introductory title of this film. In actuality, his role as Leif Ericsson is a minor one, and Crisp does not even come into the film until the second half.

For many years, the only copies one could see of this film were poor quality bootlegs in which the color was so deteriorated that it was difficult to tell that the film was ever shot in color. In 1995, Turner Classic Movies at last presented a pristine print of the film. One can finally see it in the vibrant color that it was meant to be seen with. Produced at the cusp of the silent and talkie eras, the film features a synchronized soundtrack with music, sound effects, and singing using the Vitaphone sound-on-disc process.

598. The Wedding March

Rating: ☆☆☆

Paramount; ***Directed by*** Erich von Stroheim; ***Written by*** Erich von Stroheim and Harry Carr; ***Original Score by*** J.S. Zamecnile; ***Synchronization by*** Victor Talking Machine Company; ***Running Time of Original Version:*** 116 minutes; ***Running Time of Paramount Video Version:*** 113 minutes; ***Cast:*** PRINCE NIKKI, Erich von Stroheim (1885–1957); MITZI, Fay Wray (born 1907); CECELIA, Zasu Pitts (1898–1963); SCHANI, Matthew Betz (1881–1938); PRINCE VON WILDELIEBE-RAUFFENBURG, George Fawcett (1860–1939); PRINCESS VON WILDELIEBE-RAUFFENBURG, Maude George (1888–1963); SCHWEISSER, George Nichols (1864–1927); MITZI'S MOTHER, Dale Fuller; MITZI'S FATHER, Cesare Gravina (1858–1954); SCHANI'S FATHER, Hughie Mack (1884–1927)

The Wedding March was Erich von Stroheim's last completed silent film, and the one film that he did for Paramount, with the financial support of independent film producer Pat Powers. In actuality, it was filmed in two parts. The first part is *The Wedding March* as we know it today. The film had a second half, which was released as a totally different film that played in Europe, but was never shown in the United States. Part two of *The Wedding March* was known under the names of *The Honeymoon* and *Wedding of the Prince*. The last known extant print of *The Honeymoon* was lost by the Cinémathèque Française while Henri Langlois was the archive's director. No other print has been found since, and therefore the second half of *The Wedding March* is probably lost forever.

In this first half of *The Wedding March*, Erich von Stroheim directed himself in the part of Nikki, an Austrian prince. He is a free-spending playboy whose parents finally tell him that if he wants to keep up his reckless spending, he must marry a rich woman. Nikki agrees to let his mother choose his bride—with the only requirement being that she have "mountains of money."

Shortly after this agreement, Nikki leads a parade, and just before it begins, his horse is frightened, causing injury to a poor, beautiful spectator named Mitzi. He falls in love with her when he goes to the hospital to visit her. Unfortunately, the symbolic "iron man" determines to keep them apart. Nikki is forced to marry Cecelia, who comes from an exceedingly wealthy family, but is slightly deformed and walks with a limp. Mitzi is forced to marry a revolting butcher named Schani, who is the epitome of "white trash." The wedding between Nikki and Cecelia is where the first part ends.

In *The Honeymoon*, Nikki and Mitzi were to be reunited, but both would die tragically in the end. It is a pity that *The Honeymoon* is lost, as the ending of the first half of *The Wedding March* leaves one hanging and wanting to know what happened after the wedding.

The Wedding March was the film that gave Fay Wray her first really big break. She gives a good performance and is appealing in the role. Ms. Wray is currently 90 years old and divides her time between her homes in New York City and Los Angeles.

Two of the players in this film died before it was released. Hughie Mack was 43 when he died from a heart attack. His immense weight, at over 400 pounds, likely contributed to his early death. In addition, character actor George Nichols, Sr., died at 62 in 1927.

The Wedding March was released with a synchronized music score and sound effects, which complemented the film well. In addition, there was a Technicolor sequence used

Promotional poster for *The Wedding March* (1928).

for the parade at which Mitzi is injured. When Paramount released this film for video in 1987, the restored Technicolor sequence was included, but the synchronized soundtrack was replaced with an organ score by Gaylord Carter. While Carter did a nice job with the score, the film is far more enjoyable with its original synchronized sound track. Why Paramount spent thousands of dollars to commission a new score when the perfectly good original score still existed is beyond this reviewer's ability to comprehend.

While this reviewer still regards *Greed* as Erich von Stroheim's undisputed masterpiece, the late, great film historian William K. Everson had a different opinion, cited from his book *American Silent Film*: "*The Wedding March* is arguably Stroheim's finest film. In purely film making terms, it is his most sophisticated work."

Perhaps if this film could ever be seen in its entirety as Stroheim meant for it to be seen, this reviewer would be more in agreement with Everson's appraisal. Unfortunately, the chances of a print of *The Honeymoon* being found at this late date are very slim.

599. West of Zanzibar

Rating: ☆☆☆½

MGM; ***Directed by*** Tod Browning; ***Based on a Story by*** Chester DeVonde, Kilbourne Gordon; ***Screenplay by*** Elliott Clawson, Waldemar Young; ***Titles by*** Joe Farnham; ***Photographed by*** Percy Hilburn; ***Settings by*** Cedric Gibbons; ***Running Time:*** 64 minutes; ***Cast:*** PHROSO/FLINT, Lon Chaney, Sr. (1883–1930); CRANE, Lionel Barrymore (1878–1954); DOC, Warner Baxter (1889–1951); MAIZIE, Mary Nolan (1905–1948); ANNA, Jacqueline Gadsden [a.k.a. Jane Daly]; TINY, Roscoe Ward (1893–1956); BABE, Kalla Pasha (1879–1933); BUMBO, Curtis Nero (1906–1942)

This intriguing Chaney/Browning collaboration features Chaney as a former vaudeville performer who is paralyzed from his waist down as a result of a confrontation with Crane, a former friend who has taken his fiancée from him. The fiancée dies after about a year, and Flint resurfaces as an embittered ivory merchant, bent on revenge against Crane and his daughter. He lures the daughter to his settlement, and degrades her in every way imaginable. Flint's final revenge is a plot to have Crane's daughter sacrificed in an African ritual. Just as it is too late to stop the sacrifice, he finds out that Maizie is actually his own daughter—conceived before his fiancée ran off with nemesis Crane.

This is by far Chaney's most intense performance in any of the films he did for MGM. Mary Nolan stars as his daughter, Maizie. Ms. Nolan at age 23 was a highly attractive blonde, and just on the verge of real stardom when she made this film. Her biggest role was in *Desert Nights* (1929), in which she played opposite John Gilbert in his last silent. Ms. Nolan was found dead in 1948 at age 42, and it was rumored that she died under mysterious circumstances. Lionel Barrymore gives a competent performance as Crane, but is overshadowed by Chaney. Warner Baxter plays Doc, the man that Maizie falls in love with, in the last silent he starred in, just before his talkie debut, *In Old Arizona* (1929). Jane Daly, who played the female lead in *The Mysterious Island* (1929), was billed under the name of Jacqueline Gadsden in her role as Anna, Flint's fiancée, in the first part of this film.

With two Academy Award winning players, as well as Lon Chaney, *West of Zanzibar* sports an impressive cast. It ranks as one of the best of the Browning/Chaney collaborations for MGM.

West of Zanzibar has been released on laser disc, and shown on Turner Classic

Movies, but has not yet been officially released by Turner Entertainment on video cassette.

600. White Shadows in the South Seas *Rating:* ☆☆☆☆

MGM; ***Directed by*** W.S. Van Dyke; From Frederick O'Brien's book; ***Photography by*** Clyde DeVinna, George Nogle, Bob Roberts; ***Titles by*** John Colton; ***Edited by*** Ben Lewis; ***Running Time:*** 84 minutes; ***Cast:*** DR. MATTHEW LLOYD, Monte Blue (1890–1963); FAYAWAY, Racquel Torres (1908–1987); SEBASTIAN, Robert Anderson (1890–??); LUCY, Renee Bush

This was the first film that MGM promoted as a part talkie, which was technically true, but stretching the truth a bit. The one word of dialogue, the word "hello," shouted by Monte Blue less than a half dozen times, is the only dialogue that appears in the film. Originally, W.S. Van Dyke (1889–1943) was hired as an assistant to Robert Flaherty (1884–1951), whom the directorial job was initially given to. Flaherty walked off the project shortly after starting it, refusing to meet the studio schedules and requirements. So, W.S. Van Dyke took over the project, and did a magnificent job of it. Van Dyke was a director popular with studio heads because he was consistently dependable, on schedule, and rarely if ever went over budget. Joe Franklin is absolutely right in *Classics of the Silent Screen*, in which he states that Van Dyke produced a film that was far better than Flaherty's own *Moana of the South Seas* (1926) [or *Nanook of the North* (1922) in this author's opinion], and puts the high intellectuals in their place who lament about what a greater film *White Shadows in the South Seas* would have been if Flaherty had directed it. Franklin even goes as far to say that if any lamenting was to be done, people should be wondering how much better Flaherty's *Man of Aran* (1934) would have been if Van Dyke had directed it instead.

Racquel Torres, leading lady of *White Shadows in the South Seas* (1928).

White Shadows in the South Seas is a pictorially beautiful, magnificent work of art that should rate right up with Murnau's *Tabu* (1931). Filmed on location in the South Seas islands, Monte Blue gives the best performance of his career as a doctor who finds a beautiful island yet untouched by commercialism and civilization. He falls in love with Fayaway, a native played by the alluring actress Racquel Torres. They marry, and live in heavenly bliss until Lloyd in a weak moment, thinks of the money he could make off of the abundant supply of pearls. He starts a fire hoping to signal to passing boats, but comes to his senses and puts it out—realizing how modern civilization would corrupt the island. Unfortunately, it is too late, and the rest of the film is a powerful tale of how modern "civilization" brought greed, murder, death, rivalry, and suffering to yet another of the last unspoiled islands of paradise left on the planet.

The location photography of the islands is absolutely magnificent, and the beauty of the film is greatly enhanced with rich, vibrant color tinting. There is gorgeous underwater photography as the natives are shown diving for pearls. There is a great blue tinted storm sequence with good wind effects from the disc track that accompanies the film. A really nice touch is the closing shot, which shows Torres in tears next to a native statue, with a black shadow coming over the image in increments of darker shades, symbolizing the corruption that white civilization had on the lives of the natives who had at first welcomed them with open arms.

W.S. Van Dyke's Journal: White Shadows in the South Seas and Other Van Dyke on Van Dyke (1996) contains the diaries of director Woody Van Dyke from the period during which he was making this film. Turner Classic Movies shows a gorgeous, pristine restoration of this masterpiece from time to time, and it is highly recommended. D.W. Griffith himself attended this film's premiere, and praised it as a great work of art.

This was the film debut of leading lady Racquel Torres, who made only ten films in her short career that spanned from 1928 to 1934. She retired from the screen to marry a wealthy businessman, whom she survived. Her second marriage in 1959 was to actor Jon Hall (1913–1979), who is best remembered for his role in John Ford's classic epic, *The Hurricane* (1937). This was Ms. Torres' only silent. Her most famous talkie role was in the Marx Brothers' *Duck Soup* (1933).

601. The Wind

Rating: ☆☆☆☆

MGM; ***Directed by*** Victor Seastrom; ***Assistant Director:*** Harold S. Bucquet; ***Scenario by*** Frances Marion; ***From the Novel by*** Dorothy Scarborough; ***Titles by*** John Colton; ***Settings by*** Cedric Gibbons and Edward Withers; ***Wardrobe by*** André-Ani; ***Photographed by*** John Arnold; ***Film Editor:*** Conrad A. Nervig; ***Running Time:*** 82 minutes; ***Cast:*** LETTY, Lillian Gish (1893–1993); LIGE, Lars Hanson (1887–1965); RODDY, Montague Love (1877–1943); CORA, Dorothy Cumming (1899–1983); BEVERLY, Edward Earle (1882–1972); SOURDOUGH, William Orlamond (1867–1957); CORA'S CHILDREN, Carmencita Johnson; Laom Ramon; Billy Kent Schaefer

This was the last great silent masterpiece that Lillian Gish starred in. Louise Brooks relayed the story behind this film in her fascinating and revealing book, *Lulu in Hollywood.* She states, "Of all the detestable stars who stood between the movie moguls and the full realization of their greed and self aggrandizement, it was Lillian Gish who most painfully imposed her picture knowledge and business acumen upon the producers." MGM had hired Gish at the salary of $800,000 per year for the sole purpose of manipulating and destroying her. The only problem they had was that on the pictures that Lillian Gish supervised the production of, she was turning out quality work despite the concerted propaganda that MGM was using in their efforts to destroy her. *La Bohème* and *The Scarlet Letter* both did well under Gish's fostering hand. *Annie Laurie* (1927), the only one of the Gish MGM silents that was unavailable for evaluation, was set up for production while Gish was abroad with her mother, who was ill. Gish, in her autobiography, disclaimed any responsibility for this film, which she was apparently unsatisfied with. With Gish once again taking control of *The Wind*, she again had a superior picture. Irving Thalberg and Louis B. Mayer claimed that the exhibitors refused to release the film with the original unhappy ending that depicts Letty Mason running out into the desert to die. As Gish related in an introduction she did for the 1988 video release of the film, she was told "One unhappy ending could ruin your career." Gish had previously had seven unhappy endings, and was still on top. Despite this fact, the film's ending was re-shot with a hokey happy ending tacked on, which Gish and Seastrom found to be morally unjust, but reluctantly went along with.

In this film, Gish plays Letty Mason, a sheltered girl who, at the urging of her cousins, leaves her comfortable home in Virginia to stay with them at their ranch in the Mojave Desert area. Once she gets there, she finds the living conditions extremely primitive, and is constantly tormented by the high winds and uncomfortable atmosphere. Her cousin, Cora, soon becomes afraid that Letty is after her husband, and demands that she move out of their house. She is told that two men want to marry her, and that she should make up her mind which one she wants to accept. She marries Lige, who is the leading man of this film, not because she loves him, but because he is the lesser of two evils. When he is out trying to round up cattle being driven out of the mountains with the north winds, she is tormented while alone in the house, and driven to the brink of insanity. The villain of the story, a two-timing scoundrel named Roddy, takes advantage of Lige's absence and tries to rape Letty while he is gone. Gish demonstrates especially superior acting ability in her attempts to maintain her sanity, as well as to fight off her attacker, leading into the highly charged climax of the film.

In an interview, Gish recalled the horrendous filming conditions during which the temperature was rarely below 120°F. In order to do the wind effects, eight airplane propellers were used, which blew burning cinders all over the set. Gish refers to *The Wind* as her most uncomfortable movie making experience ever. To endure what she did obviously took a lot of guts, determination, and sheer grit.

In Danny Peary's book, *Alternate Oscars*, he gave the 1928–29 Best Picture and Best Actress "Alternate Oscars" to *The Wind* and Gish's magnificent performance in it. Louis B. Mayer once again sabotaged this film's chances of winning an Oscar for 1928–29 when it was finally released. Instead, he pushed for *The Broadway Melody* (1929) to win the second "Best Picture" Oscar, and *The Wind* was not even nominated in the category. Neither was Lillian Gish nominated for Best Actress. Mary Pickford sat on the Academy Board, and, according to Danny Peary's *Alternate Oscars*, decided to campaign for the Oscar herself for her performance in *Coquette* (1929). Pickford won the Oscar that year. Although Pickford's performance in *Coquette* was, in this reviewer's opinion, Oscar-worthy, Lillian Gish's performance in *The Wind* was still the more Oscar-worthy of the two competitors.

In 1988, sixty years after this film was originally released, Kevin Brownlow produced a presentation of *The Wind* with a magnificent orchestral score by musician Carl Davis. MGM/UA Home Video released this Brownlow restoration on video in 1989.

In comparing this film to Gish's other silent era performances, this reviewer would rank this role as Letty Mason a close third behind her performances in *Broken Blossoms* (1919) and *Way Down East* (1920). It is one of the last masterpieces to come out of the silent era, and is an enthralling melodrama.

602. A Woman of Affairs

Rating: ☆½

Douglas Fairbanks, Jr., who gave *A Woman of Affairs* (1928) its only redeeming factor, in a pose from the 1980s.

MGM; ***Directed by*** Clarence Brown; ***Based on Michael Arlen's*** *The Green Hat*; ***Continuity by*** Bess Meredyth; ***Titles by*** Marion Ainslee and Ruth Cummings; ***Art Direction by*** Cedric Gibbons; ***Gowns by*** Adrian; ***Photography by*** William Daniels; ***Film Editor:*** Hugh Wynn; ***Running Time:*** 98 minutes; ***Cast:*** DIANA, Greta Garbo (1905–1990); NEVILLE, John Gilbert (1899–1936); HUGH, Lewis Stone (1879–1953); DAVID, John Mack Brown (1904–1974); JEFFRY, Douglas Fairbanks, Jr. (born 1909); SIR MORTON, Hobart Bosworth (1867–1943); CONSTANCE, Dorothy Sebastian (1905–1957)

This is a much sanitized version of Michael Arlen's steamy novel *The Green Hat*, which was considered risqué at the time. Greta Garbo plays Diana, who is very much in love with Neville, whom her father does not approve of. She gives up her true love to marry a man her father does approve of. When her husband commits suicide shortly after their marriage, there is gossip all over the place about how her "fast life" and affairs contributed to it. So, she decides that if she is going to have a reputation, she is going to live up to it. She tours the world having affairs with any man she takes a fancy to at the time.

In the book on which this film was based, the husband killed himself because he had syphilis. This heavily censored adaptation makes no mention of this, saying only that he "died for decency." Because of the sanitation job done on this story, a lot of the intriguing aspects are left out. Furthermore, this is a film in which one constantly waits for something to happen, and nothing ever does. It is a solid bore all the way across the board.

The only redeeming factor in this film at all is Douglas Fairbanks, Jr.'s fabulous performance as Diana's alcoholic brother. The film is worth seeing for this performance alone.

With the excellent cast that *A Woman of Affairs* has, as well as the directorial talents of Clarence Brown, this film had a lot of potential, but is unfortunately a big disappointment.

1929

603. The Andalusian Dog
[a.k.a. *Un Chien Andalou*]

Rating: ☆☆☆

Produced in France; ***Directed by*** Luis Buñuel and Salvador Dali; ***Running Time:*** 15 minutes

This film was the debut production of cinematographer Luis Buñuel (1900–1983), on which the world renowned artist Salvador Dali (1904–1989) also collaborated.

The Andalusian Dog, more familiarly known as *Un Chien Andalou*, is the most famous of all of the surrealistic avant garde films. The sequences seem unrelated and erratic, but the film's consistent theme centers around a man's dream of sexual desire and the consequences of acting on it. The opening sequence is a gruesome one, showing an eye being slit with a razor blade in close-up, also featuring a point-of-view shot as the blade is making contact with the eye. Other optical illusions show a competing male suitor's hand falling off, and collected in a box, only to show him being hit head on by a car. The man is shown fondling the woman's breast, and then a sequence is shown to symbolize how social attitudes toward sex provide a burden with the weight of a piano being dragged. This sequence of the man pulling the piano with ropes fades into an image of two Puritans being hanged with ropes. The man then appears to wake up from his dream to be shot by another man, and the final image shows the man and woman buried in the sand on the beach.

The Andalusian Dog is an artistic achievement designed to encourage the viewer to look at things in a different light, and also exploits the unusual and strange as a form of shock to keep the viewer's attention. It is a highly artistic accomplishment, even if some of the images are repulsive.

Luis Buñuel had been an assistant to Jean Epstein (1879–1953) on the famous French film *The Fall of the House of Usher* (1928) before he and Salvador Dali collaborated on this project. Buñuel followed *The Andalusian Dog* with a 1930 surrealistic masterpiece, *The Golden Age*. While Salvador Dali did some limited work on the script for the follow-up, he dropped out of the production process after a quarrel.

Buñuel remained in the motion picture industry into the 1970s. Dali abandoned films until 1945, when he designed the dream sequence in Alfred Hitchcock's *Spellbound* (1945). He also designed the sets and costumes for the 1951 Spanish film *Don Juan Tenorio*.

604. Cat, Dog, and Company *Rating:* ☆☆☆☆

Hal Roach/MGM; ***Directed by*** Anthony Mack; ***Photography by*** Art Lloyd; ***Edited by*** Richard Currier; ***Titles by*** H.M. Walker; ***Story by*** Robert McGowan; ***Running Time:*** 20 minutes; ***Cast:* "Our Gang":** Bobby "Wheezer" Hutchins (1925–1945); Joe Cobb (born 1917); Farina Hoskins (1920–1980); Harry Spear (1921–1969); Jean Darling (born 1922); Mary Ann Jackson (1923–1991); Donnie "Beezer" Smith; Pete the pup (1923–1930); ***Supporting Cast:*** PRESIDENT OF BE KIND TO ANIMALS SOCIETY, Hedda Hopper (1890–1966); CAB DRIVER, Chet Brandenberg; PEDESTRIANS, Jack Hill; Clara Guiol; Dorothy Vernon (1875–1970); Don Sandstrom; POLICE OFFICER, Silas D. Wilcox

This was the 87th of 88 "Our Gang" silents produced although some of the early talkies were released before the last of the silents. As one of the last "Our Gang" silents, it is also among the best of all of the "Our Gang" films of the silent or talkie eras—a true masterpiece of kiddie comedy.

Cat, Dog, and Company starts off with Joe Cobb, Farina, and another of the "little rascals" riding down the street in dog powered vehicles. The kids are turned in to Mrs. President of the Be Kind to Animals Society, played by none other than Hedda Hopper.

"Our Gang" members around the time that *Cat, Dog, and Company* (1929) was filmed.

She gives them a nice talk about being kind to animals, who will return their love, and has Farina and Joe Cobb in tears, promising to look after animals and insects from now on. The society president gives them badges, making them "officers" in the society.

The kids keep their promise—all too well. They end up freeing animals from the dog catcher's truck, all of the mice and rabbits at a medical laboratory, and end up wreaking havoc with wild animals running all over town.

The hardest of the gang to convert to the animal society is "Wheezer the Slayer" who "slews everything"—throwing rocks at owls, chasing chickens and pulling their tails, etc. In a classic dream sequence, Wheezer finds himself on trial for cruelty to animals. The arresting officer of the court is a bulldog dressed up in a police uniform. The prosecuting attorney is a monkey with a briefcase. The dressed-up jury consists of chickens, ducks, geese, dogs, cats, etc. The judge is the very owl that Wheezer threw rocks at. The jury convicts Wheezer of first degree tail pulling, among other charges, and the sentence is that he be devoured by the jury. Wheezer is shown in a box, being terrorized by larger than life animals carrying out the sentence. The beginning of the dream sequence is technically sophisticated, showing Wheezer full sized falling asleep, side by side with a miniature image of him in the box that serves as his jail cell.

This "Our Gang" episode also has some animated sequences, showing a flea that has attached herself to the reformed Joe Cobb, who won't hurt the flea. These sequences of the flea thumbing its nose at Cobb are hilarious.

Among the female members of the gang are Jean Darling and Mary Ann Jackson. Mary Ann Jackson happens to be this reviewer's favorite of all of the "Our Gang" kids, and there are some good shots of both Jean and Mary Ann in this film. While Mary

Ann Jackson died of cancer at age 68 in 1991, Jean Darling is among the surviving "Our Gang" members, currently living in Ireland at age 75. Joe Cobb, another favorite who turned 80 this year, lives in Culver City, California. Wheezer Hutchins was killed at age 20 during a training exercise in World War II.

Another tragedy surrounds Pete the pup, the extraordinary dog star of this and many other "Our Gang" silents and early talkies. The dog lived to make only a few talkies before he was murdered by arsenic poisoning at age 7 in 1930.

Cat, Dog, and Company is a "must" for all *Our Gang/Little Rascals* fans. Fortunately, it is readily available on video as part of *The Little Rascals* video compilations put out by Cabin Fever Entertainment. It appears as the last subject on compilation tape #15 of the series.

605. Diary of a Lost Girl

Rating: ☆☆☆☆

Produced in Germany; Hom-Film; ***Directed by*** G.W. Pabst; ***Scenario by*** Rudolph Leon; ***Based on the Novel by*** Margarethe Boehme; ***Photography by*** Sepp Algeier; ***Set Decoration by*** Erno Metzner; ***Running Time:*** 100 minutes; ***Cast:*** THYMIANE, Louise Brooks (1906–1985); ***Supporting Cast:*** Joseph Rovensky; Fritz Rasp (1891–1976); Andre Roann (1896–1959?); Edith Meinhard; Valeska Gert (1896–1978); Andrews Engelmann

This was the second of two controversial films that Louise Brooks made under the direction of G.W. Pabst in Germany. The films Brooks made with Pabst are highly regarded and universally acclaimed as masterpieces of cinema. While part of the acclaim can be attributed to the fine direction of G.W. Pabst, the other part goes to the outstanding acting talents of Louise Brooks. Ms. Brooks had worked for Paramount in the mid–1920s, in films such as *The American Venus* (1926), *Love 'Em and Leave 'Em* (1926), and *A Girl in Every Port* (1928). The last film she completed for Paramount was *The Canary Murder Case* (1929). Paramount had decided at the last minute to re-film *The Canary Murder Case* as a talkie. When Brooks was asked to return from Germany to the United States to do the retakes, she refused. As a result, she was blacklisted upon her return to the United States, and the Hollywood moguls made sure that she never got a decent film role again. But, the film roles Brooks played in Germany won her revenge, as all have stood the test of time and provided Ms. Brooks with an indelible place in motion picture history.

Diary of a Lost Girl starts out with a housekeeper named Elizabeth pleading with her wealthy employers not to throw her out—for the sake of her unborn child. The employers, being the prudish type, turn her out in spite of the pleas. It turns out that the husband's business partner in the pharmacy was the one who got the housekeeper pregnant, thus portraying the double standard that unmarried women who get pregnant are looked down upon as sluts, whereas the single and/or married men who get them pregnant suffer no consequences at all. Having no means of support, Elizabeth commits suicide, and Meinert the pharmacist goes back to business as usual.

Louise Brooks enters the film as Thymiane, the daughter of the employers. She asks why the housekeeper has been fired, and they provide no explanation. So, she asks the pharmacy manager what happened. He leads her on and gets her pregnant, too—just after she receives a diary for her birthday. When the parents find out that Thymiane is pregnant, they demand to know who the father is. They find out in her diary that the father is Meinert. Nothing is done to him, but Thymiane's baby is adopted out, and she is in turn sent to a girls' reformatory known as the "Young Women's Re-Education Society."

Soon, we find out what a "loving" home the Young Women's Re-Education Society is. Thymiane eventually escapes from the home, and is driven to prostitution as a means to support herself.

The subject matter of *Diary of a Lost Girl* would be controversial even in today's society. It was certainly way ahead of its time in 1929 when it was originally released.

Critics all over the world have given Ms. Brooks well-deserved praise. Danny Peary's book, *Alternate Oscars*, gives Ms. Brooks the 1929–30 Best Actress award for *Pandora's Box* (1928), using *Diary of a Lost Girl* as an award-worthy runner-up. French critic Ado Kyrou stated that "Louise Brooks is the only woman who had the ability to transfigure no matter what film into a masterpiece." Henri Langlois, former director of the Cinématheque in Paris, France once stated "There is no Dietrich! There is no Garbo! There is only Louise Brooks!"

606. The Divine Lady

Rating: ☆☆☆½

First National; ***Directed by*** Frank Lloyd; ***Story by*** E. Barrington; ***Adaptation by*** Forrest Halsey; ***Continuity by*** Agnes Christine Johnson; ***Photography by*** John Seitz; ***Film Editor:*** Hugh Bennett; ***Art Director:*** Horace Jackson; ***Costumes by*** Max Rée; ***Titles by*** Harry Carr, Edwin Justus Mayer; ***Running Time:*** 107 minutes; ***Cast:*** EMMA HART, Corinne Griffith (1894–1979); HORATIO NELSON, Victor Varconi (1891–1976); SIR WILLIAM HAMILTON, H.B. Warner (1875–1958); CHARLES GREVILLE, Ian Keith (1899–1960); MRS. HART, Marie Dressler (1869–1934); CAPTAIN HARDY, Montague Love (1877–1943); ROMNEY, William Conklin (1872–1935); QUEEN MARIA CAROLINA, Dorothy Cumming (1899–1983); KING FERDINAND, Michael Vavitch (1885–1930); DUCHESS OF DEVONSHIRE, Evelyn Hall; LADY NELSON, Helen Jerome Eddy (1897–1990)

This is an extremely rare First National film that was believed lost until a print turned up and was restored with its original score by Robert Gitt for UCLA and the Museum of Modern Art in the 1990s. Gitt had to get some elements from the film from Czechoslovakia to do the restoration. Director Frank Lloyd won the Best Director Oscar for 1928–29, the second season of the Academy Awards. When Turner Classic Movies ran the film, they stated that Corinne Griffith won a nomination for Best Actress, but that was an erroneous statement. Ms. Griffith was never nominated for an Oscar of any type. Whether the Academy liked her or not, Griffith laughed all the way to the bank. She was an astute business woman who saved her money while she was on top, and retired shortly after the talkie invasion as one of the wealthiest women in the motion picture industry. She reportedly did not have a good voice for talkies, but she was too rich to care if people liked her voice or not.

The Divine Lady is set in England in 1782. Griffith plays Emma, the daughter of a cook who is working for wealthy aristocrat Horatio Nelson. Horatio takes his "unpolished gem" and helps her to conform to high society. He intends to marry her—until he finds out that if he marries before his uncle, he will be disinherited. So, Horatio tricks Emma into going away to Italy with his uncle, on the premise that he will join her later. When she finds out that Horatio will not be joining her in Italy, she marries Sir William

Hamilton, and rises to a position of influence as an ambassador. Sir William, the brother of Marie Antoinette, finds himself in a difficult situation when England declares war on France. Italy's position of neutrality between the two countries is questioned when a British ship, much in need of supplies to ward off starvation for their crew, arrives and it is up to Emma to convince the Italian officials to come to their aid. She ends up finding a way around the neutrality order, and effectively saves England.

The Divine Lady is an excellent historical costume epic, with lucious photography, magnificent battle scenes, and a great performance by the beautiful and talented Corinne Griffith. The film also provides a rare chance to see H.B. Warner in a silent era performance other than *The King of Kings* (1927).

It is fortunate that *The Divine Lady* is one of the two surviving Corinne Griffith silents. This film really shows the beauty and grace that inspired Griffith's nickname as "the orchid lady."

Marie Dressler makes only a brief appearance at the beginning of the film, which is little more than a cameo.

607. Double Whoopee

Rating: ☆☆½

Hal Roach/MGM; ***Directed by*** Lewis Foster; ***Photographed by*** George Stevens; ***Edited by*** Richard Currier; ***Titles by*** H.M. Walker; ***Running Time:*** 19 minutes; ***Cast:*** STAN, Stan Laurel (1890–1965); OLLIE, Oliver Hardy (1892–1957); A HIGH SOCIETY BLONDE, Jean Harlow (1911–1937)

This slapstick short features Laurel and Hardy as the doormen in a high class hotel. This hotel is expecting a noted Prussian Prince's arrival. At first, the comedy duo are mistakenly believed to be the prince and an associate. When the real prince does arrive (played by an Erich von Stroheim look-alike), the bumbling duo manages to cause anything that possibly can to go wrong.

This film would have gone down in history as simply a standard Laurel and Hardy comedy, but the fact that it was among the first films to prominently feature Jean Harlow makes it one of the duo's most famous. The 18-year-old Harlow is stunningly attractive as a girl of high society whose dress is ripped after Stan unknowingly shuts the cab door on it.

Double Whoopee is the only silent of Jean Harlow's that is widely available on video. Harlow's first really big break came in Howard Hughes' *Hell's Angels* (1930), which features the only color footage of her in existence. In 1932, Harlow was married to producer Paul Bern (1889–1932), who allegedly committed suicide a few months later. A 1933 marriage to Hal Rosson ended in divorce in 1934. She then dated actor William Powell (1892–1984). In 1937, during the filming of *Saratoga*, Harlow became ill and was hospitalized for uremic poisoning. While hospitalized, she developed cerebral edema, from which she died at age 26.

608. Drifters

Rating: ☆☆½

New Era Films/Great Britain; ***Directed and Edited by*** John Grierson; ***Photographed by*** Basil Emmott; ***Running Time:*** 48 minutes

Drifters was the directorial debut of John Grierson (1898–1972). Grierson was reportedly the first person to use the term "documentary" when describing such films,

Jean Harlow, who plays a cameo in *Double Whoopee* (1929) at the height of her career in the 1930s.

having coined the phrase in his review of Robert Flaherty's *Moana* (1926) for the *New York Sun*.

This is Grierson's highly acclaimed documentary on the lives of the North Sea fishermen. The film portrays a day in the life of these fishermen—showing how they set up their nets, capture and preserve their herring, and prepare their product for the marketplace. There are some excellent underwater shots of the vast schools of fish swimming by the camera.

Drifters was exceptionally well received in Great Britain, although rather obscure in the United States. Grierson directed only one more film, *The Fishing Banks of Skye* (1934), and worked mostly as a production executive through 1954. *Drifters* is a film to be appreciated for its cinematography, documentary value, and historic value. In some ways, it reminds one of Josef Von Sternberg's directorial debut, *The Salvation Hunters* (1925), reviewed elsewhere in this book. It was offered on laser disc in the early 1990s.

609. Eternal Love

Rating: ☆

United Artists; ***Directed by*** Ernst Lubitsch; ***Assistant Directors:*** Thornton Freeland, George Hippard; ***Adaptation by*** Hans Kraly; ***Titles by*** Katharine Hilliker, H.H. Caldwell; ***Photography by*** Oliver Marsh; ***Film Editor:*** Andrew Marton; ***Sets by*** Walter Reimann; ***Running Time:*** 71 minutes; ***Cast:*** MARCUS PAITRAN, John Barrymore (1882–1942); GIGLIO, Camilla Horn (1903–1996); LORENZ GRUBER, Victor Varconi (1891–1976); PIA, Mona Ribon; REVEREND TASS, Hobart Bosworth (1867–1943); PIA'S MOTHER, Evelyn Selbietz (1871–1950); HOUSEKEEPER, Bodil Rosing (1877–1941)

This film takes about 70 minutes to tell a story with enough material for about 15 or 20 minutes. It is set in Europe in 1806. John Barrymore plays Marcus, a man who leads a revolution against the mandatory forfeiture of the weapons belonging to citizens of the village. He and Giglia, played by Camilla Horn, are in love, escape to a remote area, and freeze to death.

Eternal Love is pretty standard fare for director Ernst Lubitsch, whose output, with the exception of a handful of titles, during the silent era was mediocre at best, and abysmal in this film's case. Even the magnificent acting talents of John Barrymore, Camilla Horn, and Hobart Bosworth couldn't do anything for this awful film. Horn went back to Germany after starring in this and one talkie.

Eternal Love is a waste of great acting talent. It has never been released officially on video, although some copies do exist in private collections. When one sees it, one can understand why it has never been widely released; the film simply is not worthy of the time and effort that would be required. It ranks as John Barrymore's very worst film as well as one of the worst films of the entire silent era.

610. The Four Feathers

Rating: ☆☆☆☆

Paramount; A Cooper-Schoedsack Production; ***Directed by*** Ernest B. Schoedsack, Merian C. Cooper, Lothar Mendes; ***Photographed by*** Robert Kurrle; ***From the Novel by*** A.E.W. Mason; ***Adapted by*** Hope Loring; ***Screenplay by*** Howard Estabrook; ***Titles by*** Julian Johnson; ***Musical Score by*** William F. Peters; ***Running Time:*** 81 minutes; ***Cast:*** HARRY FEVERSHAM, Richard Arlen (1899–1976); ETHNE, Fay Wray (born 1907); CASTLETON, Clive Brook (1887–1974); TRENCH, William Powell (1892–1984); DURRANCE, Theodore Von Eltz (1893–1964); GENERAL FEVERSHAM, George Fawcett (1860–1939); AN ARMY COMMANDER, Noah Beery (1882–1946); AFRICAN TRIBE LEADER, Noble Johnson (1881–1978); HARRY FEVERSHAM AS A CHILD, Philippe De Lacy (1917–1995)

This was the fifth screen adaptation of the classic novel of cowardice and valor in the British Army, set in the late 1890s. It had previously been filmed in 1915, 1918, 1921, and 1925. None of these earlier versions are available for evaluation. This is the final silent version that was filmed. Two talkie remakes were made in 1939 and 1978. Of all of the versions, the 1939 version is the most highly acclaimed. This 1929 version also holds up well upon evaluation.

Richard Arlen plays the lead role as Harry Feversham, the son of a decorated war general. In childhood, he is brought up with a career as an Army officer chosen for him. When he does become an Army Lieutenant, it is just before the British wage war in South Africa. Fearing that he cannot live up to the courage and valor that his father expects from him, he drops out of the army. Three of his army buddies, as well as his fiancée, give him a white feather—widely known as a symbol of cowardice. The news of Harry's cowardice gives his father a heart attack, which kills him. Feversham goes on a mission to redeem himself. In doing so, he proves more effective and helpful outside the Army than he would have been if he had stayed in. He saves each of his army buddy's lives, and personally gives each of them their feathers back.

This version of *The Four Feathers* is significant as the first fiction film of the great production team comprised of Merian C. Cooper (1893–1973) and Ernest B. Schoedsack (1893–1979). Before doing this film, they collaborated on two documentaries—*Grass* (1925) and *Chang* (1927). Their most famous collaboration was the monster classic *King Kong* (1933).

Richard Arlen gives a first-class performance in the lead role of this film. He is even better here than he was in *Wings* (1927). Unfortunately, Arlen has not received the credit due him. It is this reviewer's opinion that Arlen's performance in *The Four Feathers* was far superior to George Arliss' Oscar-winning performance in *Disraeli* (1929), and was far more worthy of the award.

Fay Wray is appealing as leading lady Ethne. However, her role is a rather minor one, and did not present real opportunity for her to demonstrate acting talent. However, her next collaboration with Cooper-Schoedsack in *King Kong* gave her an immortal place in film history.

Part of the reason that this version of *The Four Feathers* has not been as highly acclaimed as the 1939 version is because few people have seen it in recent years. The film circulates on video among a few private collectors, and only in fair quality prints. This is a film that most definitely deserves a modern-day revival on cable television and or the video market. If more people could see it, it would receive the appreciation that it deserves. The original synchronized music and effects track still exists, which means it would not even be necessary to commission a new score for it.

611. Habeas Corpus

Rating: ☆☆☆

Hal Roach/MGM; ***Directed by*** James Parrot; ***Photographed by*** Len Powers; ***Edited by*** Richard Currier; ***Titles by*** H.M. Walker; ***Running Time:*** 19 minutes; ***Cast:*** STAN, Stan Laurel (1890–1965); OLLIE, Oliver Hardy (1892–1957); PROFESSOR PADILLA, Richard Carle (1871–1941); PADILLA'S "ASSISTANT," Charlie Rogers

This dark comedy finds Laurel and Hardy applying for a job with Professor Padilla, who has presumably escaped from a mental institution. Their first assignment in their new job is to dig up a body from the local cemetery, for Padilla's use to conduct scientific experiments on. The professor's "assistant" happens to be an undercover cop, who immediately notifies the police to come get the "professor" and take him back to the looney bin. Meanwhile, Laurel and Hardy embark on their mission to the cemetery, not knowing that a detective has been assigned to follow them to scare them off. In the cemetery, they get into a variety of spooky misadventures. The sound effects on the original Vitaphone track that accompanies this film really add a lot to the atmospheric mood.

One of the funniest parts of the film occurs when Ollie is climbing a street pole to get into the cemetery. The pole happens to have just been freshly painted. Ollie spends the rest of the night with a white stripe down the middle of his clothes.

For many years, the excellent Vitaphone track for *Habeas Corpus* was believed to be lost. In the early 1990s, it was finally rediscovered in an unmarked box.

The director was James Parrot (1892–1939), the brother of silent film comedian Charlie Chase. He died of a heart attack at age 46.

612. The Kiss

Rating: ☆☆☆½

MGM; ***Directed by*** Jacques Feyder; ***From the Story by*** George M. Saville; ***Scenario by*** Hans Kraly; ***Titles by*** Marion Ainslee; ***Photographed by*** William Daniels; ***Art Director:*** Cedric Gibbons; ***Gowns by*** Adrian; ***Film Editor:***Ben Lewis; ***Running Time:*** 60 minutes; ***Cast:*** IRENE, Greta Garbo (1905–1990); ANDRÉ, Conrad Nagel (1897–1970); GUARRY, Anders Randolph (1870–1930); LASSALLE, Holmes Herbert (1878–1956); PIERRE, Lew Ayres (1908–1996); DURANT, George Davis (1889–1965)

As far as the American Garbo silents are concerned, MGM saved the best for last.*The Kiss* was also the film debut of Lew Ayres, who would go on to play his greatest role in *All Quiet on the Western Front* (1930) and to an Academy Award nomination for *Johnny Belinda* (1948).

In *The Kiss*, Garbo plays Irene, a woman unhappily married to a raving, jealous lunatic of a husband. While married, she has a side affair with André, a lawyer played by Conrad Nagel—whom she would marry if she was able to divorce her husband. Irene and André break off the affair, but her life becomes complicated when Pierre, the naive, young son of a family friend, falls head over heels in love with her. Irene likes Pierre as a friend, but he is really too young for her tastes. On his final night in town before going to school, Pierre gives Irene an innocent goodbye kiss, and her husband walks in, misinterprets what is going on, and flies into a violent tirade. He beats Pierre, and Garbo intercedes to keep her husband from killing him. The husband is accidentally shot and killed in the process, and Irene is tried for murder—with her lover André as her attorney.

Director Jacques Feyder (1885–1948) started his directorial career in France in 1916. After his highly acclaimed film, *Shadows of Fear* (1928), he did a satirical comedy, *The New Gentlemen* (1928), which was banned in Europe for undermining Parliament. This is when he came to America, and *The Kiss* was his American film debut. After *The Kiss*, Feyder directed the foreign versions of *The Unholy Night* (1929) and John Gilbert's *His Glorious Night* (1929). He went back to France in 1931. His greatest success of the talkie era came in 1935, when his *Carnival in Flanders* won the New York Film Critics Award for Best Foreign Film, and Best Direction at the Venice Film Festival.

Lew Ayres makes an impressive debut as Pierre, and this is also one of the last films that Anders Randolph played in before his death in 1930.

For Greta Garbo fans, *The Kiss* is a film that should not be overlooked. It is widely available on video, and is also frequently shown on Turner Classic Movies.

613. Lucky Star *Rating:* ☆☆☆

Fox; ***Directed by*** Frank Borzage; ***Based on*** *Three Episodes in the Life of Timothy Osborn* ***by*** Tristram Tupper; ***Scenario by*** Sonya Levien; ***Photography by*** Chester Lyons, William Cooper Smith; ***Edited by*** Katharine Hilliker, H.H. Caldwell; ***Art Direction by*** Harry Oliver; ***Running Time:*** 83 minutes; ***Cast:*** MARY TUCKER, Janet Gaynor (1906–1984); TIM OSBORNE, Charles Farrell (1901–1990); MARTIN WRENN, Guinn Williams (1899–1962); MRS. TUCKER, Hedwig Reicher (1884–1971); JOE, Paul Fix (1901–1983)

For years, it was believed that this other follow-up featuring the team of director Frank Borzage and players Janet Gaynor and Charles Farrell was lost. *Lucky Star* just turned up again in the 1990s after being discovered in The Nederlands Filmmuseum.

This film pretty much duplicates the same formula as *7th Heaven* (1927) and *Street Angel* (1928). It is set in a rural area, with Janet Gaynor as a worker on the family farm. As she is delivering milk, she has an encounter with Charles Farrell's character, Tim Osborne, who catches her stealing. World War I is declared, and Tim goes to war to help France, and returns a year later paralyzed from waist down. Gaynor's character of Mary Tucker comes back to visit, and they fall in love, eventually overcoming obstacles that stand between them and happiness.

While this is a poignant, entertaining, and well done movie with gorgeous photography, a successful formula can only be reused so many times before it starts to get stale. *Lucky Star* borders on the point of being an overworked combination that has lost its punch.

614. The Man with a Movie Camera *Rating:* ☆☆☆½

Vuvka/Russia; ***Directed by*** Dziga Vertov; ***Photographed by*** Mikhail Kaufman; ***Assistant Editor:*** Elizaveta Svilova; ***Running Time:*** 67 minutes

This is an avant garde film produced in Russia. It is filmed without the use of subtitles, actors, or studio sets. It traces a typical day in 1929 Russia, starting with dawn, when everyone is asleep, and the city looks like a ghost town. The desolate streets of Leningrad are shown, as well as the idle factory machines in the buildings. As the city wakes up, the camera captures montage images of everything coming to life. The film progresses at a faster and faster rate of speed throughout. Many innovative techniques were used, including split screen photography, multiple exposure, rapid cutting, and variable running speeds.

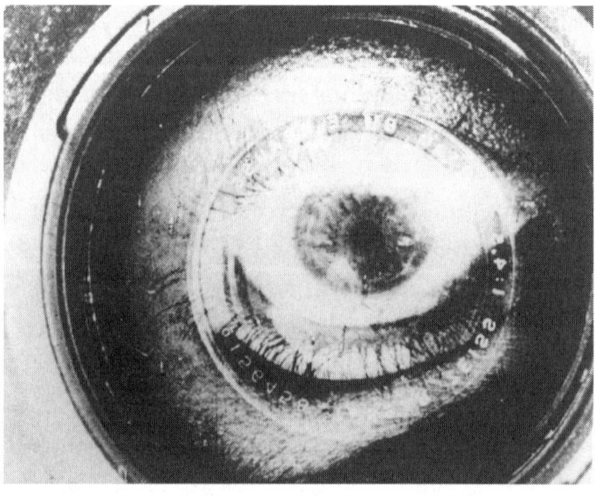

A shot from the Russian avant garde effort, *The Man with a Movie Camera* (1929).

The Man with a Movie Camera

was a family project, as the photographer was Vertov's younger brother, and the film editor was Vertov's wife. It is an artistic masterpiece, among the most fascinating avant garde films of all time. It is the most famous of all of the works of Dziga Vertov (1896–1954), whose first film was *Anniversary of the Revolution* (1919), produced when he was only 25 years old. Vertov also received wide acclaim for his *Three Songs of Lenin* (1934), which is widely available on video as *The Man with a Movie Camera* is.

615. The Mysterious Island

Rating: ☆☆☆☆

MGM; ***Directed by*** Lucien Hubbard; ***Screenplay by*** Lucien Hubbard; ***From the Book by*** Jules Verne; ***Music Score by*** Martin Broones and Arthur Lange; Recorded on Western Electric System; ***Recording Engineer:*** Douglas Shearer; ***Art Direction by*** Cedric Gibbons; ***Photography by*** Percy Hilburn; ***Film Editor:*** Carl L. Pierson; ***Running Time:*** 93 minutes; ***Cast:*** ANDRE DAKKAR, Lionel Barrymore (1878–1954); SONIA DAKKAR, Jane Daly; FALON, Montague Love (1877–1943); MIKHAIL, Harry Gribbon (1890–1965); ANTON, Snitz Edwards (1862–1937); DMITRY, Gibson Gowland (1877–1951); TERESA, Dolores Brinkman

This was MGM's first major science fiction spectacle, and also the second MGM feature produced entirely in 2-strip Technicolor.

Three directors worked on this film. Benjamin Christensen started work on the production, and walked out after just a few scenes due to differences with Irving Thalberg. Judging from Christensen's other MGM work prior to this, and how good this film turned out, it was probably for the best that he did quit before he could do too much damage. Director Maurice Tourneur was brought in as Christensen's replacement, and he, too, walked out in the middle of production due to differences with Thalberg. Lucien Hubbard, who wrote the screenplay, ended up finishing *The Mysterious Island* and being given directorial credit.

The delays caused by having to replace directors twice, as well as the lavish and ambitious special effects, brought production costs to a little over $1 million. Talking sequences were added to the film so that it could be promoted as part-talking, but for some reason the film did not do as well as it should have at the box office, and reportedly ended up losing over $800,000.

Unfortunately, this film no longer exists with its original 2-strip Technicolor, and is available today only in black and white prints. Turner Classic Movies has aired *The Mysterious Island* a few times, and it has stood the test of time well. It remains, in this reviewer's opinion, the cream of the crop as far as film adaptations of Jules Verne novels are concerned.

Included among the intriguing elements are the underwater civilization at the bottom of the sea, including sea creatures which look similar to the modern depictions of aliens today. Among the other perils faced by the underwater explorers are what appears to be a giant sea spider, and a creature that looks like a cross between a dragon and a fish.

In addition to the unprecedented special effects, *The Mysterious Island* features a top notch cast to boot. Lionel Barrymore plays Count Dakkar, who has invented the underwater ship that can go to depths beneath what humankind has ever been able to previously explore. Montague Love, in another of his renowned villain roles, plays Falon, who will do anything he has to in order to get Dakkar's secrets. Lloyd Hughes turns in a good performance as Nikolai, assistant to Dakkar, in what was among his last big roles. Jane Daly (a.k.a. Jacqueline Gadsden) is highly appealing as the female lead who is kidnapped and held hostage by Falon. Unfortunately, no further information on this actress could be found under either of the two names she used. Gibson Gowland, who is best remembered for his role as McTeague in *Greed* (1924), plays a supporting role, as does former slapstick comedian Snitz Edwards.

The Mysterious Island is an early science fiction classic not to be missed. Unfortunately, it is no longer available on the video market, but it is still aired on Turner Classic Movies occasionally.

616. Noah's Ark

Rating: ☆☆☆☆

Warner Bros.; ***Directed by*** Michael Curtiz; ***Story by*** Darryl Frances Zanuck; ***Photography by*** Hal Mohr and Barney McGill; ***Adaptation by*** Anthony Coldeway; ***Titles by*** De Leon Anthony; ***Edited by*** Harold McCord; ***Vitaphone Symphony Orchestra Conducted by*** Louis Silvers; ***Running Time:*** 99 minutes; ***Cast:*** MIRIAM/MARLENE, Dolores Costello (1905–1979); JAPHETH/TRAVIS, George O'Brien (1900–1985); KING NEPHILUM/NICKOLOFF, Noah Beery, Sr. (1882–1946); HAM/AL, Guinn Williams (1899–1962); NOAH/THE MINISTER, Paul McAllister (1879–1955); SLAVE GIRL/A DANCER, Myrna Loy (1905–1993); SHEM/BULKAH, Malcolm Waite (1892–1949); ***Supporting Cast:*** William V. Mong (1875–1940); Louise Fazenda (1889–1962); Anders Randolph (1870–1930); Nigel De Brulier (1877–1948)

Noah's Ark is one of the most grossly underrated films in motion picture history. When it was released at the cusp of the silent/talkie eras, the reviews were terrible. *The New Yorker* called it "An idiotic super spectacle ... widely conceded to be the worst picture ever made." *The New York Post* said it was "a solid bore." The *New York Times* stated "[*Noah's Ark*] frequently borders on the ridiculous ... this cumbersome production ... is a great test of patience."

Part of the reason that this production failed critically was that Warner Bros. had advertised it as a talking picture, when it was actually mostly silent with a few dialogue sequences. In addition, the word got out that between one and three people were killed in the flood sequences. People boycotted this film because they felt that no picture was worth sacrificing human lives for. Another reason that *Noah's Ark* has a negative reputation is due to the fact that for years, the complete version has not been seen. In 1957, Warner Bros. reissued it in a reedited, truncated version. All of the titles were cut out, and narration was added. In addition, the reediting job cut a lot of vital footage out, and jumbled much of the rest of the footage around. The picture was ruined with this reediting process.

In the 1980s, Turner Entertainment acquired the rights to all of the pre-1948 Warner Brothers pictures, and in 1989, Robert Gitt finally restored *Noah's Ark* to its intended format from the original nitrate negative at UCLA. For the first time since its original release, it is possible to evaluate *Noah's Ark* as it was meant to be seen. The only thing missing from the restoration is the 2-strip Technicolor sequences, which are now in black and white.

This epic interweaves two stories—a modern story dealing with World War I, and the biblical story of Noah's ark and the great flood. The action gets started immediately with a then-current portrayal of the stock exchange being compared to the biblical story of the worship of the golden calf. William V. Mong plays a man who has lost everything in the market, confronts his broker (played by Anders Randolph), and shoots him dead. The film then moves into the World War I story, with passengers on a train that wrecks in France. In this modern story, the lead star, Dolores Costello (at the time the wife of John Barrymore, and the grandmother of Drew Barrymore) plays Marlene, a German show girl. She meets with two chums from America—Travis and Al. She marries Travis, who is eventually persuaded by Al to join the Allied cause in the war. Noah Beery, Sr., plays Nickoloff, a Russian agent for the Allied Forces, who falsely accuses Marlene of being a spy when she resists his advances. Paul McAllister plays a minister who is at first laughed at, similar to the way Noah, whom he plays in the biblical segment, was also scorned. It is in the war story that the talking sequences take place. These talking sequences are the only parts of the movie for which criticism is justified. Owing to the primitive state of sound technology at the time, the talking sequences are stagy, and slow down an otherwise rapidly paced film. In the first talking sequence, when Dolores Costello and George O'Brien are sitting on a park bench, it is obvious that Costello is reading from a cue card. The dialogue in these sequences is so ludicrous as to be funny. If the film had been released completely as a silent, it would have been free of these major flaws. The idiocy of the dialogue in these talking sequences is partially what killed Ms. Costello's chances of making a good transition into the talkie era. Her reputation as an actress suffered a great deal, which is sad, because she was truly talented as was demonstrated in some of her other films like *Old San Francisco* (1927), *The Sea Beast* (1925), and the silent sequences in *Noah's Ark*.

The biblical story is filmed on a colossal scale. Some of the sequences were originally filmed in 2-strip Technicolor. Over 7,500 extras were used in the flood sequences. A concrete lake was built, which contained over 1 million gallons of water. Full-sized, breakaway sets were used in the sequences of the flood destruction. In addition to the human extras, thousands of animals of all types were used—tigers, lions, zebras, bears, monkeys, elephants, deer, oxen, geese, etc. In addition a real floating ark was constructed which could actually hold hundreds of these animals. Another asset to this story is the impressive special effects used. When Noah is receiving his instructions from God, they are written in fire on a mountainside, which has large stone pages turning as the pages of a book would.

Noah's Ark is truly a fabulous, entertaining epic of colossal proportions. It was the last film that made a concerted effort to try to outdo D.W. Griffith's *Intolerance* (1916). No epic of this scale has been attempted since, nor will such a future effort likely be attempted. It is extremely fortunate that this original, monumental motion picture has been restored to a state close to its original glory. As more of today's critics see this film in its restored format, it will hopefully start to receive the high praise that it truly deserves—as a biblical epic which deserves a place beside *Intolerance* (1916), *The Ten Commandments* (1923), *Ben-Hur: A Tale of the Christ* (1927); and *The King of Kings* (1927)—an epic of mammoth stature unsurpassed by any film made since. Although neither MGM or Warner Bros. have officially released this restored version of *Noah's Ark* on video, it is shown from time to time on Turner Classic Movies. Turner Entertainment did release the film on laser disc in late 1997.

617. Our Modern Maidens

Rating: ☆☆☆

MGM; ***Directed by*** Jack Conway; ***Story/Continuity by*** Josephine Lovett; ***Music Score by*** Arthur Lance; ***Synchronization by*** Western Electric; ***Titles by*** Marion Ainslee, Ruth Cummings; ***Art Director:*** Cedric Gibbons; ***Photography by*** Oliver Marsh; ***Gowns by*** Adrian; ***Film Editor:*** Sam Zimbalist; ***Running Time:*** 75 minutes; ***Cast:*** BILLIE BROWN, Joan Crawford (1904–1977); ABBOTT, Rod LaRocque (1896–1969); GIL, Douglas Fairbanks, Jr. (born 1909); KENTUCKY, Anita Page (born 1910); REG, Edward Nugent; GINGER, Josephine Dunn (1906–1983); B. BICKERING BROWN, Albert Gran (1862–1932)

Actress Joan Crawford received top billing again in this snappy follow-up to *Our Dancing Daughters* (1928). This film was directed by Jack Conway (1887–1952), who started directing films in 1917, and really began to come into his own with MGM in the mid–1920s.

Our Modern Maidens was filmed at a time when studios were rebelling against the puritanical standards of the Hays office, and started dealing with subjects that were previously considered taboo. So, a lot of movies dealing with sex issues came out in the period from 1929 until 1934, when the new motion picture production code went into effect and again clamped down on the industry with rigid standards.

In this film, Douglas Fairbanks, Jr., plays Gil, a man who is engaged to Crawford's character of Billie Brown, who is the daughter of a wealthy radio station owner. Billie falls in love with another man, which Gil doesn't know about, and Gil falls in love with Anita Page's character, Kentucky. Gil is in a bind trying to decide whether to marry his fiancée, or to marry Kentucky, who is pregnant with his baby.

Although this sequel to *Our Dancing Daughters* is not quite as good as its predecessor, it is still solid, entertaining fare. It is historically important as Douglas Fairbanks, Jr.'s first really big leading role in a major production. His imitations of John Barrymore and John Gilbert are especially amusing. The film's subject matter which was scandalous for the time adds interest to the film as well.

Like its predecessor, *Our Modern Maidens* is mostly silent, but deals with the competing radio market by having the radio broadcast filmed with sound in a way that the radio announcer's voice is heard.

618. The Pagan

Rating: ☆☆☆

MGM; ***Directed by*** W.S. Van Dyke; ***From the Story by*** John Russell; ***Scenario by*** Dorothy Farnum; ***Titles by*** John Howard Lawson; ***Art Direction by*** Cedric Gibbons; ***Photography by*** Clyde DeVinna; ***Film Editor:*** Ben Lewis; ***Running Time:*** 77 minutes; ***Cast:*** THE PAGAN [HENRY SHOESMITH], Ramon Novarro (1899–1968); HIS FRIEND, Renée Adorée (1898–1933); HIS GIRL, Dorothy Janis (born 1912); MR. SLATER, Donald Crisp (1882–1974)

Director Woody Van Dyke (1889–1943) followed up his successful masterpiece, *White Shadows in the South Seas* (1928) with *The Pagan*, another melodrama set in the South Sea islands as well. Using most of the same technical crew as he had with the previous film, *The Pagan* is similarly engraced with flawless photography of the lush tropics of the Paumotu islands. The only thing missing is that this film was not color tinted as its predecessor was.

The Pagan could be considered a semi-sequel to *White Shadows in the South Seas*, as it seems to pick up where the prior film left off. This film starts in the islands that are

Promotional poster for *Our Modern Maidens* (1929).

already developed. Ramon Novarro plays the laid-back Henry Shoesmith, owner of the largest plantation on the island. His heavenly paradise is dealt a blow with the arrival of a greedy profiteer, Mr. Slater. Slater uses slick methods to swindle Shoesmith out of the deed to his plantation, as well as his wealth, and Shoesmith doesn't bat an eyelash at this deception.

Dorothy Janis plays the female lead as a woman whom Slater has as his traveling companion, supposedly having taken her in as a part of his "Christian duty." He treats her like a slave and is physically and mentally abusive. Henry and she fall in love, and it is when Slater tries to force Janis' character to leave with him on the boat that Shoemaker abandons his usually laid-back personality, and fights for his girl. Unlike *White Shadows in the South Seas*, the evil force loses out in *The Pagan*, and justice prevails for the pagan couple, whose ethics are far superior to those of scoundrel Slater who hides behind the Judeo-Christian Bible to justify his despicable deeds. The climactic sequence is thrilling.

Donald Crisp is magnificent as the villainous Slater, and this was probably his best villain role since his role as Battling Burroughs in *Broken Blossoms* (1919) ten years earlier.

Leading lady Dorothy Janis stated in an interview with historian Michael G. Ankerich that *The Pagan* was her favorite of the five films she starred in during her brief career that spanned from 1928 to 1930. She started out with three westerns, and *The Pagan* was her final silent film. She made one talkie, *Lummox* (1930) under the direction of Herbert Brenon. Another film project for Universal Studios, *The White Captive*, was started under the direction of Harry Garson on location in the Orient. This film was never released, as Garson was fired for incompetence. After this fiasco, Ms. Janis married band leader Wayne King in a marriage that lasted 53 years until his death in 1985. Ms. Janis is currently 85 years old, and divides her time between her homes in Arizona and Colorado.

Renée Adorée has a good supporting role as a friend of Henry's who would love to have a closer relationship with him, but is a good enough friend not to interfere when she sees that he is in love with Janis' character, and is helpful in defeating Slater.

This was the last of Ramon Novarro's silents. Although he enjoyed moderate success in the talkie era, mostly because of his good singing voice, his star faded in the mid–1930s, after which he played only a few sporadic character roles, his last being in *Heller in Pink Tights* (1960). Openly gay, he was quite well off, and reportedly drank heavily and indulged in a number of vices in his later years. Tragically, on Halloween night of 1968, he was brutally beaten to death by two brothers, Paul and Tom Ferguson, who had reputations as gay hustlers. They had reportedly heard from another hustler that Novarro kept large amounts of cash around his house, and the primary motive for the murder was robbery. Kenneth Anger wrote in *Hollywood Babylon* that a lead dildo, supposedly given to Novarro by Rudolph Valentino, was the murder weapon—shoved down Novarro's throat. Historian Michael Morris, in his book *Madam Valentino*, discredits this story, reporting that one of the officers who actually worked on the crime scene stated that no such object was present. Morris' account is far more believable than Anger's account, which has been soundly discredited along with some of his other allegations.

For years, the accompanying synchronized music discs for *The Pagan* were lost. In response to numerous requests by viewers, Turner Classic Movies ran *The Pagan* without sound in 1994. After this airing, a complete set of discs for the film was recovered, and the film was aired with music in 1995. At last, *The Pagan* can once again be seen as it was originally meant to be presented—for the first time in over 65 years. It sounds like Ramon Novarro's own voice was used in some of the vocal musical segments in the film, which would thus make this the first film in which his voice was heard.

619. Pursued

Rating: ☆

J. Charles Davis Productions; ***Written and Directed by*** Horace B. Carpenter; ***Running Time:*** 50 minutes; ***Cast:*** BILL STRONG, Art Acord (1890–1931); RED HANK, Cliff Lyons (1901–1974);

Art Acord's appearance around the time he starred in *Pursued* (1929), showing the ravages of years of severe alcoholism.

BUD JENKINS, Lynn Sanderson; SHERIFF MORTON, Bill Conant; POSTMASTER STEVVINS, James Tromp; MARY GRANT, Carol Lane; JAKE GRANT, H.B. Carpenter (1875–1945)

In early photos and film clips of Art Acord from the early 1910s, one sees a robust, muscular, attractive man who could turn heads anywhere he went. The 1910s had Acord in impressive films like Cecil B. DeMille's *The Squaw Man* (1913) and Theda Bara's *Cleopatra* (1917). From 1919 to 1927, Acord had a lucrative contract with Universal Pictures. Unfortunately, Acord had a severe alcohol problem, which ruined three marriages, and caused him to be fired from Universal as unreliable.

By the time he ended up working for small independent companies in the late 1920s, Acord was a shadow of his former self, as seen in the accompanying illustration. He was haggard and tired looking, with none of the charisma and charm present in his earlier work. These independent companies hired him only to cash in on his name to give the poor pictures they produced some box-office appeal.

Pursued has got to be one of the worst films ever made—even worse, if one can believe it, than the 1925 version of *Wizard of Oz*. In this film, Acord plays a detective who disguises himself as a sissified cowboy to infiltrate an outlaw gang. Acord's performance is the worst this reviewer has ever seen. The only scene reminiscent of the old Art Acord that led to his popularity is a scene in which he demonstrates some rope tricks. Even these aren't too impressive, as they are nothing compared to what Will Rogers did in *The Ropin' Fool* (1922).

As bad as this film is, it is good that something of Acord's later work did survive for posterity's sake. When the talkie era came about, Acord knew that his career in films was over, as he reportedly had the voice of a child. After doing some touring with his horse in Mexico, he committed suicide on January 4, 1931, by taking cyanide tablets.

620. Queen Kelly

Rating: ☆☆½

Gloria Swanson Pictures/United Artists; ***Produced by*** Gloria Swanson and Joseph P. Kennedy; ***Directed by*** Erich von Stroheim; ***Screenplay by*** Erich von Stroheim; ***Art Direction by*** Harold Miles; ***Titles by*** Marion Ainslee; ***Photography by*** Gordon Pollock, Paul Ivano; ***Film Editor:*** Viola Lawrence; ***Originally Planned Running Time:*** Approx. 300 minutes; ***Running Time of Restored Version:*** 97 minutes; ***Running Time of European Release:*** 93 minutes; ***Cast:*** PATRICIA KELLY, Gloria Swanson (1897–1983); PRINCE WOLFRAM, Walter Byron (1899–1972); QUEEN REGINA V, Seena Owen (1894–1966)

This film has notoriety as "the unfinished masterpiece." Erich von Stroheim had been hired by Gloria Swanson and Joseph P. Kennedy to do the film, and had been given free reign and an open checkbook. It was originally supposed to have run approximately 5 hours. Von Stroheim had intended for it to be his greatest achievement, but it would instead turn out to be his last film. Swanson, who lost patience with von Stroheim's extravagance and excessive spending, fired him from the production after 11 of the planned 30 reels had been completed. She then assigned a variety of editors and directors the job of trying to piece together a coherent film from the footage that was shot. *Queen Kelly* was cut to 8 reels, a new ending was shot, and this version was released in Europe, and is widely available on the public domain video market. By "completion" time, the talkies had already overtaken the American market, thus prompting Swanson's decision against a theatrical release in the United States.

The photography for the footage of *Queen Kelly* that was completed is first-class. The interior settings and decorum in the palace sets are especially lavish.

Swanson portrays an orphan by the name of Patricia Kelly. Raised in a convent, Kelly happens on an outing to cross paths with Prince Wolfram, the fiancé of Queen Regina V—a selfish, vicious, tyrannical woman. Seena Owen does a wonderful job in this role, and certainly would have deserved a Best Supporting Actress Oscar if one had been given out in 1929, and if *Queen Kelly* had been released in the United States.

Although Wolfram is scheduled to marry Regina (actually, it is the other way around) the next day, he is infatuated with Kelly, and determines to see her that night at all costs. He takes extraordinary measures—going so far as to create a fake fire in the convent to set off the alarm, allowing him to take Kelly under the guise of rescuing her. Wolfram gets Kelly to the palace, and they have a wonderful time—until Regina comes onto the scene and catches them together. Kelly is chased out of the house by Regina, wearing nothing but her nightgown. She jumps into the river. This is where the main differences between the restored version and European release version occur. In the European release, Wolfram, who truly loves Kelly, goes to the convent to find her. Upon getting to the convent, he finds Kelly dead, and commits suicide. This was not the way that Erich von Stroheim intended the film to end. The restored version shows us that after Kelly escapes into the river, she finds that she has been left a chain of brothels by her wealthy aunt. She gets caught up into a white slavery racket, and after overcoming these perils, finally marries the prince. The restored version put out by Kino has some of the footage of Kelly's forced marriage to the sleazy proprietor of the white slavery racket. Tully Marshall plays the scoundrel, and Madame Sul-Te-Wan also appears in this segment. The rest of the story is restored through stills and titles, all based on Erich von Stroheim's original script. The restoration is not much longer than the European release, as some of the footage of Kelly's and Wolfram's night together is redundant and unimportant to the film, and edited from the restoration.

Queen Kelly is an interesting curiosity piece, and well worth watching for its historic value alone.

621. The River

Rating: ☆☆☆½

Fox; ***Directed by*** Frank Borzage; ***Assistant Director:*** Lew Borzage; ***Adaptation by*** Phillip Klein, Dwight Cummings; ***From a Novel by*** Tristram Tupper; ***Photography by*** Ernest Palmer; ***Settings by*** Harry Oliver; ***Film Editor:*** Barney Wolf; ***Running Time of Current Reconstruction:*** 48 minutes; ***Cast:*** ALLEN JOHN PENDER, Charles Farrell (1901–1990); ROSALEE, Mary Duncan (1895–1993); SAM THOMPSON, Ivan Linow (1888–??); WIDOW THOMPSON, Margaret Mann (1868–1941); MARSDON, Alfredo Sabato (1894–1956); THE MILLER, Bert Woodruff (1856–1934)

This is a Borzage classic that was believed to be completely lost until 1974, when film historian William K. Everson (1929–1996) discovered an incomplete print in the vaults of 20th Century-Fox. A reduction 16mm print of the material was made for William K. Everson before the 35 mm nitrate was discarded, and it was from this 16mm material that Anthony Slide preserved it in 1974 at the Library of Congress. *The River* is still not complete, but a reconstruction has been assembled. This reconstructed version has aired on television in Europe, but so far has not been made available to the public in the United States. The surviving footage and stills indicate that the film in its complete form was among the finest directed by Frank Borzage (1893–1962).

The lost footage of *The River* includes the first reel, last reel, and two reels in the middle. Charles Farrell plays Allen Pender, who has constructed a houseboat so that he can travel and live on the river. He is delayed in his progression by the construction of a dam, of which the construction camp's foreman has murdered an employee he caught with his mistress, Rosalee. Complications cause Pender to have to stay longer than expected, and he and Rosalee fall in love. In constantly trying to prove himself a better man than Rosalee's imprisoned lover, he goes into a dangerous blizzard to cut fire wood, and suffers hypothermia and frostbite. With the help of Rosalee's fostering hand, he survives and all is well—until Rosalee's ex-lover Marsdon breaks out of prison and comes back.

The photography in this film is lucious and flawless, featuring gorgeous scenery against a mountain river. Charles Farrell looked better in this film than he ever did in any other, and Mary Duncan is excellent as well. It is really a pity that Duncan's career, as short as it was, is hardly ever mentioned even in passing in movie history books. She is every bit as impressive as Janet Gaynor was in the Farrell/Gaynor movies.

While it is good that we have this reconstructed version of *The River*, the stills indicate that much of the best footage is among that which is lost. Perhaps a complete print of *The River* might turn up in the future, but until then, Anthony Slide and William K. Everson can be thanked for rescuing a partial copy.

622. Seven Footprints to Satan *Rating:* ★★★½

First National; ***Directed by*** Benjamin Christensen; ***Based on a Story by*** Abraham Merritt; ***Screenplay by*** Richard Bee; ***Titles by*** William Irish; ***Photography by*** Sol Polito; ***Film Editor:*** Frank Ware; ***Running Time:*** 77 minutes; ***Cast:*** EVE MARTIN, Thelma Todd (1905–1935); JIM KIRKHAM, Creighton Hale (1882–1965); THE PROFESSOR, William V. Mong (1875–1940); THE SPIDER, Sheldon Lewis (1868–1958); SATAN'S MISTRESS, Laska Winters; JIM'S VALET, Ivan Christy (1887–1949); UNCLE JOE, DeWitt Jennings (1872–1937); OLD WITCH, Nora Cecil (1879–??); PROFESSOR VON VIEDE, Kalla Pasha (1879–1933); EVE'S CHAUFFER, Harry Tenbrook (1887–1960); OLD LADY, Cissy Fitzgerald (1873–1941)

When director Benjamin Christensen (1879–1959) left MGM during mid-production of *The Mysterious Island* (1929), he went to First National Pictures, where he directed *The Haunted House* (1928) and its sequel, *Seven Footprints to Satan* (1929) prior to returning to Europe. *The Haunted House* is lost, but *Seven Footprints to Satan* was saved by the Danish Film Museum. This rare film has been among the most coveted of the existing silent rarities, partially because it was Thelma Todd's last silent, and partially because it is one of the few Christensen films that survives. In late 1995, Turner Classic Movies scheduled the film for a 5 A.M. showing, but it never did air. Fortunately, the film was aired on Italian television which was accessible in the United States via satellite. So, copies of *Seven Footprints* with Italian titles circulate in private collections. It is rumored that plans are underway for a video release with English titles in the future.

In this film, Thelma Todd plays Eve, the girlfriend of Creighton Hale's character of Jim. They attend a party at a castle, where they are lured to look for a rare and valuable missing gem. Throughout the course of the party, strange happenings begin to

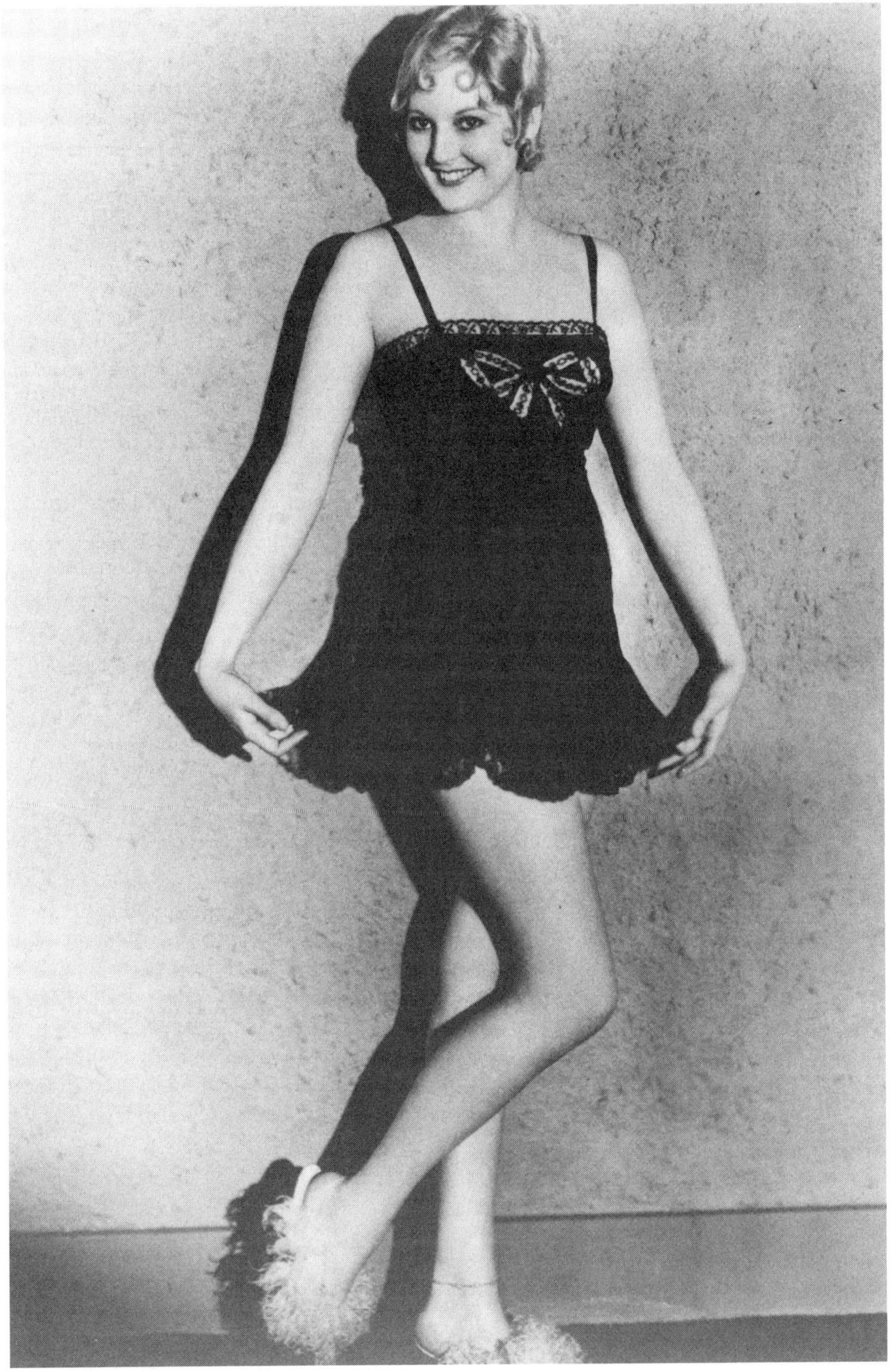

Thelma Todd, who starred in *Seven Footprints to Satan* (1929), at her prime in the early 1930s before her mysterious death.

occur with witches, dwarfs, and other unusual and macabre creatures making appearances and terrorizing the couple. At the end, the whole affair turns out to be an elaborately played joke.

While Christensen's other surviving American films are disappointing, *Seven Footprints to Satan* lives up to the expectations that one would have from the man who directed the visually stunning *Witchcraft Through the Ages* (1922). The visual style is evident in the very first shot of the film, which first shows a close-up of Creighton Hale loading his gun, and then another close-up of a hand ringing his doorbell, giving the film an aura of suspense right from the start. When Eve and Jim first get to the party, Sheldon Lewis peers through a door in his gruesome and scary spider outfit, and the camera backs away to show Eve and Jim, with the spider's shadow coming toward them. It seems that there is a different, unique, horrific creature lurking at every corner one turns when going through the castle. The steps leading up to "Satan's lair" with illuminated numbers on each step are also visually striking.

Benjamin Christensen's talent as a director is evident in this film, which does not disappoint. It is his best surviving American work. He took his inspiration from the formula evident in Roland West's *The Bat* (1926) and Paul Leni's *The Cat and the Canary* (1927) and turned out a far more intriguing, artistic, atmospheric, and macabre film than either of his predecessors. It is by far the best of the horror comedy genre produced during the silent era.

While *Seven Footprints to Satan* was originally released with a Vitaphone synchronized track with music and sound effects, no copies of the discs are known to exist. This is a shame, as the original track with atmospheric sound effects probably complemented the film greatly. Perhaps a reconstructed score can eventually be added to the film.

623. She Goes to War

Rating: N/A

Inspiration Pictures/United Artists; ***Directed by*** Henry King; ***Associate Producers:*** Victor Halperin and Edward Halperin; ***Photography by*** Tony Gaudio and John Fulton; ***Art Direction by*** Al D'Agostino and Robert M. Haas; ***Editor:*** Lloyd Nosler; ***Based on a Story by*** Rupert Hughes; ***Screenplay by*** Howard Estabrook and Fred DeGresac; ***Music Score by*** Modest Altschuler; ***Synchronization by*** R.C.A. Photophone; ***Running Time of Surviving Footage:*** 42 minutes; ***Cast:*** MARY, Eleanor Boardman (1898–1991); MARY'S BOYFRIEND, Edmund Burns (1892–1980); THE MAN MARY FALLS IN LOVE WITH ON THE FRONT, John Holland; CANTEEN SINGER, Alma Rubens (1897–1931); ***Supporting Cast:*** Al St. John (1892–1963); Yola D'Avril (1907–1984); Glen Waters; Margaret Seddon (1872–1968); Evelyn Hall; Augusto Borgato (1871–1939); Dina Smirnova (1889–1947)

This was a part-talking war film in which Eleanor Boardman played Mary, a wealthy, shallow, and arrogant socialite who is called to combat duty in World War I. Once on the front, she sees the horror of war's reality and sees life in a totally different light. Her boyfriend, at one time as shallow thinking as she is, is killed in the war, and she takes his place on the front lines. With her new attitude, she earns the love and respect of one of her fellow comrades in war.

There are a number of impressively staged battle sequences in this film—the most notable being a huge fire on the battlefield. One can tell that this was a good film in its complete form. Unfortunately, all that survives of *She Goes to War* is a truncated version of 42 minutes. For this reissue, all of the titles were cut out, and other important footage was eliminated as well. The surviving film begins on the war front, and does not even include the introductory footage of Mary's life before the war. The only reason we know what she was like before the war is due to the synopses that have made it into the historical record. It is fortunate that we at least have the synopsis of the original film, as the surviving footage is incoherent and difficult to follow and comprehend.

Eleanor Boardman gives a good performance, but does not speak in the surviving footage. The only time her voice is heard is when she screams upon seeing her severely injured comrade.

This film has historic significance as the last film that Alma Rubens appeared in, and also contains the only extant audio of her voice. She had a pleasant speaking voice, and also sings two songs—one at the beginning of the film and another toward the end. While she was not a great singer, she was competent, and had a decent voice range. Unfortunately, she is painfully thin appearance-wise, as by this time she was at the height of her addiction to hard drugs. Her drug addiction led to her early death at age 33 in January 1931—about a year and a half after she made this final appearance.

Although *She Goes to War* was effectively ruined when it was reedited, it is fortunate that at least some footage survives and is widely available on video. It is hoped that the complete version might eventually turn up.

624. Ship of Lost Men *Rating:* ☆

Produced in Germany; ***Directed by*** Maurice Tourneur; ***Photography by*** Nikolaus Farkas; ***Running Time:*** 97 minutes; ***Cast:*** MISS ETHEL [AN AVIATRIX], Marlene Dietrich (1901–1992); T.W. CHEYNE, Robin Irvine (1901–1933); GRISCHA, Vladimir Sokoloff (1889–1962); FERNANDO VELA, Fritz Kortner (1892–1970); MORIAN, Gaston Modot (1887–1970)

For the first time since the late 1920s, it is now possible to view a Marlene Dietrich silent in the United States with English subtitles. Before now, the only Dietrich silent available for evaluation to us was *The Woman Men Yearn For* (1928), with German titles only.

Ship of Lost Men is a grim portrayal of sailor life in Germany. We see various crews getting into drunken barroom brawls and the like. The grim working conditions that they work under at sea are also shown. Approximately 40 minutes into the film, Marlene Dietrich, playing an aviatrix, crashes into the ocean. She is rescued by the ship's crew, and sees a different side of life.

The story line of this film leaves a great deal to be desired. It is one of those films very much like Greta Garbo's 1928 film, *A Woman of Affairs*, in which one waits for something to happen, but nothing significant ever does happen.

Although *Ship of Lost Men* features no entertainment value whatsoever, it is a movie of significant historic importance. Maurice Tourneur (1873–1961), the director, is universally acclaimed as one of the outstanding directors of silent cinema, based on such classics as *The Wishing Ring* (1914), *The Poor Little Rich Girl* (1917), *The Last of the Mohicans* (1920), and *Lorna Doone* (1922). In 1928, he was working for MGM studios, and had started work on *The Mysterious Island* (1929). He walked off the set due to artistic differences with Louis B. Mayer and Irving Thalberg, and was replaced by Lucien Hubbard. Upon leaving MGM, Tourneur went back to Germany. *Ship of Lost Men* is the second film he directed upon his departure from the United States. In addition, it allows viewers to see what Marlene Dietrich was like before Josef Von Sternberg started working with her.

625. Show Boat

Rating: ☆☆☆½

Universal; ***Directed by*** Harry A. Pollard; ***Assistant Director:*** Robert Ross; ***Continuity by*** Charles Kenyon; ***Story Supervision by*** Edward J. Montagne; ***Dialogue Arranged by*** Harry

Pollard and Tom Reed; ***Titles by*** Tom Reed; ***Film Editor:*** Daniel Mandell; ***Cinematographer:*** Gilbert Warrenton; ***Art Director:*** Charles D. Hall; ***Costumes by*** Johanna Mathieson; ***Supervising Film Editor:*** Maurice Pivar; ***Synchronization/Score by*** Joseph Cherniavsky; ***Recording Supervisor:*** C. Roy Hunter/Western Electric; ***Running Time:*** 106 minutes; ***Cast:*** MAGNOLIA, Laura LaPlante (1904–1996); GAYLORD RAVENAL, Joseph Schildkraut (1895–1964); PARTHENIA ANN HAWKS, Emily Fitzroy (1860–1954); CAPTAIN ANDY HAWKS, Otis Harlan (1865–1940); JULIE, Alma Rubens (1897–1931); WINDY, Jack McDonald (1880–??); MAGNOLIA AS A CHILD/KIM, Jane LaVerne; SCHULTZY, Neely Edwards (1883–1965); LILY, Elise Bartlett (died 1944); JOE, Stepin Fetchit (1902–1985)

This first film adaptation of *Show Boat* for many years sat dormant in the MGM vaults. Released as a part-talkie, the music and soundtrack were recorded on Vitaphone discs, which for years were believed lost. In the early 1990s, Turner Entertainment came across an incomplete set of discs for this film, and restored what was available. Some of the sound discs are still missing. Where the discs were missing in dialogue sequences, lip readers were brought in to translate what was being said, and the restoration has small subtitles with the dialogue printed at the bottom of the screen. In 1995, this film was shown on Turner Classic Movies for the first time since its original release, and was also released on laser disc with the 1936 and 1951 versions of *Show Boat* as part of a set.

Laura LaPlante plays the lead role of Magnolia, a show girl whose parents own a prestigious river boat. She falls in love with a traveling actor and gambler, and marries him despite her parents' objections. She finds out through the course of a few years that her stern mother was right. Gaylord gambles away everything they have, and Magnolia is fed up and leaves, becoming a highly successful singer.

Most of the discs for the parts of the film in which LaPlante sings are lost. Another person's singing was reportedly dubbed in for these sequences. This was also one of two part-talkies that Alma Rubens starred in before her heroin addiction ruined her career and eventually killed her. She had a speaking role, but the discs for this part of the film are among those still lost. Joseph Schildkraut gives a good performance as leading man Gaylord Ravenal. Unfortunately, he was reported to have had an inflated ego. Both Laura LaPlante and Frank "Junior" Coghlan reported in interviews that Schildkraut was very snobbish and arrogant. Junior Coghlan reported that Joseph's father, Rudolph, whose reputation on stage made the Schildkraut name famous in the first place, was far more down to earth and pleasant than his son. Despite Joseph Schildkraut's unpleasant off-screen personality, he demonstrated great talent as an actor as evidenced by his 1937 Academy Award for his performance in *The Life of Emile Zola*.

This was the first film that Harry Pollard directed after his highly acclaimed 1927 version of *Uncle Tom's Cabin*, which unfortunately bombed at the box office despite good reviews. Although Pollard felt that he was not a successful director after the failure of *Uncle Tom's Cabin*, seeing this version of *Show Boat* demonstrates that he was highly competent and underrated.

While many critics would disagree, this reviewer considers this first version of *Show Boat* as the best of the three versions filmed. The sets and costumes in this original version were just as good as those in the lavish remakes. What really distinguishes this

Opposite page: **Laura LaPlante as Magnolia in *Show Boat* (1929).**

version is that it features more of a storyline than the subsequent remakes, which primarily focused on singing and dancing. This version also features one of the best performances of Laura LaPlante. She never looked more attractive than she did in this film with her long, brunette wig. She was one of the last surviving big stars of the silent era when she died in 1996.

626. Spite Marriage

Rating: ☆☆☆

MGM; ***Directed by*** Edward Sedgwick; ***Story by*** Lew Lipton; ***Adaptation by*** Ernest S. Pagano; ***Continuity by*** Richard Schayer; ***Titles by*** Robert Hawkins; ***Art Direction by*** Cedric Gibbons; ***Wardrobe by*** David Cox; ***Photography by*** Reggie Lanning; ***Film Editor:*** Frank Sullivan; ***Running Time:*** 75 minutes; ***Cast:*** ELMER, Buster Keaton (1895–1966); TRILBY DREW, Dorothy Sebastian (1905–1957); LIONEL BENMORE, Edward Earle (1882–1972); ETHYL NORCROSSE, Leila Hyams (1905–1977); NUSSBAUM, William Bechtel (1867–1930); SCARZI, John Byron

This was Buster Keaton's follow-up to *The Cameraman*, and also his last silent film. In it, he plays Elmer, who persistently asks Trilby Drew to marry him, who consistently refuses. However, one day she accepts—simply out of spite toward her boyfriend, whom she has broken off with.

Spite Marriage is perhaps best remembered for the famous sequences in which Trilby gets drunk, and Keaton as Elmer is struggling to get her home. This is a classic scene that has been often imitated since. The ironic thing about this sequence is that it came out during prohibition, thereby being a subtle stab at the much-ignored law of the time. Dorothy Sebastian is excellent in this sequence—possibly her most memorable performance.

In addition to leading players Keaton and Sebastian (who at the time this film was made reportedly had an off-screen romance), Leila Hyams is appealing as the new blonde girlfriend of Trilby's ex-boyfriend. Ms. Hyams would later gain immortal fame as the heroine of Tod Browning's *Freaks* (1932).

The finale of *Spite Marriage* has Buster on a ship in peril, borrowing heavily from his earlier films *The Navigator* (1924) and *Steamboat Bill, Jr.* (1928). He saves his wife's life, and she decides that she really loves him after all.

While *Spite Marriage* wasn't as strong a film as *The Cameraman* [owing in part to the fact that much of Keaton's own crew had been assigned to other projects on the MGM lot], it is still an excellent, solid marriage comedy.

627. Square Shoulders

Rating: ☆☆☆

Pathé; ***Directed by*** E. Mason Hopper; A Paul Bern Production; ***Adaptation by*** Peggy Prior; ***Continuity by*** George Dromgold and Houston Branch; ***Titles by*** John Krafft; ***Film Editor:*** Barbara Hunter; ***Art Direction by*** Edward Jewell; ***Production Manager:*** Richard A. Blaydon; ***Music Director:*** Josiah Zuro; ***Synchronization:*** R.C.A. Photophone; ***Running Time:*** 60 minutes; ***Cast:*** TAD COLLINS, Junior Coghlan (born 1916); SLAG COLLINS, Louis Wolheim (1880–1931); EDDIE CARTWRIGHT, Philippe De Lacy (1917–1995); MARY JANE, Anita Louise (1915–1970); MR. CARTWRIGHT, Montague Shaw; THE COOK, Maurice Black (1891–1938); DELICATE DON, Allen Morgan; COMMANDANT, Clarence Golden; A COMPETING CADET (BIT PART), Erich von Stroheim, Jr. (1916–1968)

Square Shoulders was Junior Coghlan's last silent film. In it, he plays an underprivileged orphan who goes by the name of Tad and dreams of going to military school. The only momento he has of his father is a World War I medal of honor, which inspires the younger son to make a goal of earning one himself. He conveys his dreams and hopes to a vagrant named Slag Collins, played by the prominent character actor Louis Wolheim. [This was a film role that Wolheim played just before starting work in the classic 1930 war film, *All Quiet on the Western Front.*] Tad even tells him, "I got six bucks saved up." Unbeknown to Tad, Slag recognizes him as his own son that he had abandoned years earlier. Collins robs a furniture store to pay for his son's tuition into the military school. On the day that Tad receives a letter from the school, all of the fellow orphans consider such to be a colossal event. The words "Tad got a letter!" flash bigger and bigger onto the screen as he is running to see what the letter says. The letter informs him that his military school tuition has been paid by an unknown benefactor, and that he is ordered to report to the school at once.

All goes well at military school. A girl named Mary Jane, daughter of the commandant of the school, attracts the attention of both Tad and his rival, Eddie Cartwright. Mary Jane is played by blonde child actress Anita Louise, who was also known as Anita Fremault in some of her earlier silents, including her debut in *Down to the Sea in Ships* (1922), *A Woman of Affairs* (1928), and *Four Devils* (1928). In talkies, she supported Will Rogers in *Judge Priest* (1934), played Marie Antoinette in *Madam DuBarry* (1934), and played Titania in *A Midsummer Night's Dream* (1935). Philippe De Lacy plays Eddie Cartwright. He grew up to be a successful advertising executive and refused to discuss his career as a child star when he got older.

A month later, Slag Collins shows up at the military academy working in the academy's horse stable. He tries his best to look out for his son and to make up for the years he neglected him. They develop a close relationship, looking out for each other. As Slag's battle with the bottle is ongoing, there are occasions on which Tad has to cover for him to keep him from losing his job. Eventually, Tad convinces Slag to try to give up the booze. Unfortunately, the father's past catches up with him. His two co-conspirators in the robbery demand their take of the money. A fight ensues, and Junior Coghlan as Tad joins in fending off the villains. The footage at the end of the film shows what is Coghlan's most heart-rending and compelling performance of his silent era career.

Be on the lookout for a cameo in the ice cream soda shop scene by none other than Erich von Stroheim, Jr. He plays the boy who steals Mary Jane's heart away from both Tad and Eddie. He bears a definite facial resemblance to his father.

Square Shoulders provides a good combination of comedic sequences, and also tells a powerful dramatic story. The way that this film deals with alcoholism reminds one a great deal of D.W. Griffith's final film, *The Struggle* (1931). It shows that although alcohol was prohibited by law in 1929, it was still ruining lives. This film shows what the director E. Mason Hopper was truly capable of, as it is the best of his directorial efforts that is available for evaluation.

As one of the later silents, *Square Shoulders* features an R.C.A. Photophone soundtrack with synchronized orchestra score and sound effects. Two different versions of the final reel were shot—one with music and sound effects, and the other with dialogue sequences. The silent version is the only one known to survive.

628. Tarzan the Tiger

Rating: ☆☆☆½

Universal; ***Directed by*** Henry MacRae; From Edgar Rice Burroughs'; *Tarzan and the Jewels of Opar*; ***Continuity by*** Ian McClosey Heath; ***Titles by*** Ford J. Bebbe; ***Film Editor:*** Malcolm Dewar; ***Art Direction by*** Charles D. Hall, David S. Garber; ***Photography by*** Wilfred Cline; ***Running Time:*** 290 minutes; ***Cast:*** EARL OF GREYSTOKE/TARZAN, Frank Merrill (1893–1966); LADY JANE, Natalie Kingston (1905–1991); ALBERT WERPER, Al Ferguson (1888–1971); LA [HIGH PRIESTESS], Kithnou; ACHMET ZEK, Sheldon Lewis (1868–1958)

This was the last of the silent *Tarzan* film adaptations, as well as the first in which the Tarzan yell was heard. As a silent with synchronized score and sound effects, the Tarzan yell was among the sound effects used.

Frank Merrill and Natalie Kingston, who played Tarzan and Jane in a previous serial *Tarzan the Mighty* (1928), played in this follow-up. Merrill, a champion gymnast, had doubled for Elmo Lincoln in *The Adventures of Tarzan* (1921).

In this adaptation, Al Ferguson plays a bogus scientist who kidnaps Jane and sells her into slavery. Tarzan, in his efforts to rescue Jane and the lost jewels of Opar, is caught in a torrential storm in which he is knocked out and loses his memory. La, the high priestess of sun worshippers, is infatuated with Tarzan, and intends to have Jane burned as a sacrifice so that she can have Tarzan. A number of action packed adventures occur before Tarzan regains his memory and defeats both La and villain Albert Werper, who tried to pass himself off as Tarzan's friend before his real motives were discovered.

Of all of the silent *Tarzan* adaptations evaluated, this serial has the best production values—featuring an elaborate storm sequence, excellent stunt work by Merrill, as well as lavishly staged religious ceremonies that feature dancing girls.

Tarzan the Tiger was both a critical and box-office success. Its enormous profits for Universal helped to finance their Academy Award winner, *All Quiet on the Western Front* (1930).

629. Trail of '98

Rating: ☆☆☆☆

MGM; ***Directed by*** Clarence Brown; ***Assistant Director:*** Charles Dorian; ***Art Direction by*** Cedric Gibbons and Merrill Pye; ***Continuity by*** Benjamin Glazer and Waldemar Young; ***Titles by*** Joseph W. Farnham and Benjamin Glazer; ***Story by*** Robert W. Service; ***Photographed by*** John F. Seitz; ***Costume Design by*** Lucia Coulter; ***Film Editing by*** George Hively; ***Running Time:*** 87 minutes; ***Cast:*** THE GIRL [BERNA], Dolores Del Rio (1905–1983); THE BOY [LARRY], Ralph Forbes (1896–1951); BERNA'S FRIEND, Doris Lloyd (1896–1968); BERNA'S GRANDFATHER, Cesare Gravina (1858–1954?); THE PREACHER, Otto Lederer (1886–1965); ***Supporting Cast:*** Karl Dane (1886–1934); Tully Marshall (1864–1943); George Cooper (1891–1943); Russell Simpson (1880–1959); Emily Fitzroy (1860–1954); Tenen Holtz (1887–1971); E. Allyn Warren (1874–1940); John Down; Ray Hallor (1900–1944); Ray Gallagher (1885–1953)

This production was filmed on a lavish scale, taking two years, $2 million, and thousands of extras to make. It is an epic on the migration to Klondike, Alaska, during the gold rush of 1898.

Dolores Del Rio plays Berna, who, with her grandfather, sails from San Francisco to Alaska in hopes of striking gold in the Klondike. On the voyage, she meets Larry and they fall in love and marry. The film portrays the hardships and disappointments faced by these and thousands of other gold prospectors.

Dolores Del Rio, star of *Trail of '98* (1929).

The sequence in which the prospectors are hauling food into Klondike was filmed during the winter in the Rocky Mountains. Many weather-related problems plagued the crew and caused seemingly endless delays in production. Among the perils endured were -60°F temperatures and several blizzards. It is reported that some extras died from hypothermia and/or pneumonia while these sequences were being shot, with three having drowned.

This epic ended up being over a year longer in production than was planned, as well as being several hundred thousand dollars over budget. Nonetheless, the sacrifices resulted in a spectacular and impressive epic that has stood the test of time. In many ways, this film is much like what this reviewer had expected from the overrated western epic, *The Covered Wagon* (1923). In addition to the blizzard sequence, there is an impressive sequence close to the film's finale which shows a man engulfed in flames falling into a crowd of people.

Unfortunately, the production delays caused *Trail of '98* to be released after the talkie era was in full swing. In 1929, the best of the silents simply could not compete with the worst of talkies. Even having a Vitaphone score with sound effects, music, and songs was not enough to save *Trail of '98* from being one of the biggest box-office flops of the silent era.

Turner Entertainment aired *Trail of '98* in the early 1990s, nearly 70 years after its production. It is, in this reviewer's opinion, the finest of Clarence Brown's (1890–1987) silent films, with the possible exception of *The Last of the Mohicans* (1920) which he co-directed with Maurice Tourneur.

630. Turksib

Rating: ☆☆☆½

Vostok-Kino/U.S.S.R.; ***Directed by*** Victor Turin; ***Photographed by*** Yevgeni Slavinsky and Boris Francisson; ***Running Time:*** 57 minutes

A scene from *Turksib* (1929).

This late silent documentary by Victor Turin (1895–1945) documents the hardships faced by the people of Turkestan and Siberia, and how some of these hardships were overcome by building a railway system to join the two regions. Turkestan's cotton crop is stifled, because valuable farming land has to be used to grow grain to feed the people of Turkestan. Siberia, which grows plentiful grain but needs the cotton grown in Turkestan cannot export grain for cotton due to lack of ability to transport the products between the two regions. The film goes on to show how the problem was solved by the construction of the Turkestan-Siberia railway.

This documentary is well produced, and grips the viewer's attention from the very beginning, holding it to the end of the film. Arthur Knight's 1957 book, *The Liveliest Art*, describes *Turksib* as "an early milestone in the development of the documentary film."

This reviewer concludes that *Turksib* is among the best of all silent documentaries, and will prove a fascinating addition to the collections of classic film enthusiasts.

631. Unaccustomed as We Are *Rating:* ☆☆☆½

Hal Roach/MGM; ***Directed by*** Lewis R. Foster; ***Photography by*** George Stevens, Len Lowers, John McBurnie, and Jack Roach; ***Edited by*** Richard Currier; ***Titles by*** H.M. Walker; ***Running Time of Silent Version:*** 18 minutes; ***Running Time of Talkie Version:*** 21 minutes; ***Cast:*** STAN, Stan Laurel (1890–1965); OLLIE, Oliver Hardy (1892–1957); MRS. KENNEDY, Thelma Todd (1905–1935); MRS. HARDY, Mae Busch (1901–1946); MR. KENNEDY, Edgar Kennedy (1890–1948)

This is a hilarious Laurel and Hardy comedy in which Ollie brings Stan as a surprise guest for dinner. Mrs. Hardy is furious that Ollie invited Stan unannounced, and refuses to cook for them, going to her mother's house. So, Ollie decides to cook dinner himself. Stan tries lighting the stove, with disastrous results. This is where Thelma Todd's character, Mrs. Kennedy, comes in. As Mrs. Kennedy, Ollie's neighbor across the hall and wife of police officer Kennedy, she offers to help with dinner. Then, Mrs. Hardy returns unexpectedly, and Mrs. Kennedy is hidden in a box. Pandemonium occurs when Mr. Kennedy, officer of the law, comes onto the scene.

This is one of two Laurel and Hardy vehicles in which Thelma Todd starred. She was 24 when she played in *Unaccustomed as We Are*. In 1935, she was found dead in her car from carbon monoxide poisoning under mysterious circumstances. Mae Busch was a highly popular character actress who starred in a number of Laurel and Hardy talkies. Her career in films began in 1912 with the Keystone Company. She rose to prominence in 1922 in Erich von Stroheim's *Foolish Wives*. Among her other notable silents were *Souls for Sale* (1923), *The Unholy Three* (1925), and *While the City Sleeps* (1928). This film was her first with Laurel and Hardy. She died at age 45 after a five-month illness in a San Fernando Valley hospital. Edgar Kennedy, a highly popular character comedian, was known for his mastery of the "slow burn." He died at age 58 from throat cancer.

Unaccustomed as We Are was filmed at the cusp of the silent and talkie eras. It was filmed in silent versions for the smaller theaters that were not yet wired for sound. The talkie version was distributed elsewhere. This film is among Laurel and Hardy's better shorts, and is highly recommended.

632. Where East Is East

Rating: ☆☆½

MGM; ***Directed by*** Tod Browning; ***Story by*** Henry Sinclair Drago and Tod Browning; ***Screenplay by*** Waldemar Young and Richard Schayer; ***Titles by*** Joe Farnham; ***Photographed by*** Henry Sharp; ***Film Editor:*** Harry Reynolds; ***Settings by*** Cedric Gibbons; ***Costumes by*** David Cox; ***Synchronized Sound by*** Western Electric Systems; ***Running Time:*** 66 minutes; ***Cast:*** TIGER HAYNES, Lon Chaney, Sr. (1883–1930); TOYO, Lupe Velez (1908–1944); MME. DE SYLVA, Estelle Taylor (1894–1958); BOBBY BAILEY, Lloyd Hughes (1897–1958); FATHER ANGELO, Louis Stern (1860–1941); MING, Mrs. Mong Wing; ANIMAL TRAINER, Richard R. Neil (1875–1970)

Where East Is East is the last of Lon Chaney's existing silents. *Thunder* (1929), released after this film and before *The Unholy Three* (1930), is among the four lost Chaney/MGM silents [the other three are *The Tower of Lies* (1925), *London After Midnight* (1927), and *The Big City* (1928)].

This is an intriguing, bizarre story of an unusual romantic triangle. Chaney plays Tiger Haynes, an animal trainer who has severe battle scars on his face from his work. His happy daughter, Royo, is engaged to fiancé Bobby Bailey. Haynes' estranged wife surfaces after many years of absence, and seduces her own daughter's fiancé. Despite Haynes' pleas with his ex-wife to leave Bailey alone, she continues the affair. Haynes unleashes a gorilla to attack her, but through a twist of fate, the plan goes awry.

With the similarity between the gorilla attack in this Chaney/Browning collaboration, as well as the gorilla attack in *The Unholy Three* (1925 and 1930 versions), these films could be said to have a similar formula. *West of Zanzibar* (1928) and *The Unknown* (1927), other collaborations between the two, also depict revenge plans going wrong and backfiring.

Despite the often-used formula, *Where East Is East* was a critical and box-office success. Like *West of Zanzibar*, it was released with a synchronized score of music and sound effects. Lupe Velez, the leading actress as the daughter, had just finished working in D.W. Griffith's *Lady of the Pavements* (1929) when she started work in this film. She gives a good performance and a radiant presence. She was highly temperamental in her private life, which led to her divorce from Johnny Weismuller in 1938 after five years of marriage. She committed suicide at age 35 in 1944 by taking an overdose of pills. Estelle Taylor made this film as her last silent. She was married to boxing champion Jack Dempsey, and the husband-wife team had appeared on Broadway together in 1928, just before she starred in *Where East Is East*. They divorced in 1931 after six years of marriage.

633. The White Hell of Piz Palu

Rating: ☆☆☆☆

Produced by Harry Sokal/Germany; ***American Distributor:*** Universal Pictures; ***Directed by*** G.W. Pabst and Arnold Fanck; ***Cinematographers:*** Sepp Allgeier, Richard Angst, Hans Schneeburger; ***Titles by*** Tom Reed; ***Film Editor:*** Edward Cahn; ***Music Score by*** Heinz Roemheld; ***Synchronization by*** David Broekman; ***Recording Supervisor:*** C. Roy Hunter; ***Running Time:*** 74 minutes; ***Cast:*** MARIA, Leni Riefenstahl (born 1902); JOHANNES KRAFFT, Gustav Diessl (1899–1948); MARIA'S HUSBAND, Ernst Petersen (died 1930); CHRISTIAN [A GUIDE], B. Spring; THE AVIATOR, Ernst Udet (1896?–1941)

This was the final silent film that Leni Riefenstahl starred in, but did not direct. It was originally planned as a production of Harry R. Sokal to be directed by Arnold Fanck, who specialized in nature films and photography. Riefenstahl convinced the producers to bring in G.W. Pabst to direct the acting scenes, as she had admired Pabst's work, and wanted to work under his direction. She also states in her memoirs that it was she who was responsible for getting world-renowned stunt pilot Ernst Udet to join the project. Udet was a highly decorated German war hero, and the world's most famous stunt pilot at the time.

Filmed on location in the Engadine Valley on the Morteratsch Glacier in the Swiss Alps, where temperatures were in the range of -50°F to -60°F, *The White Hell of Piz Palu* was one of the most popular of the mountain dramas that came out in Europe in the 1920s and early 1930s. Ms. Riefenstahl plays Maria, one of three members of a climbing expedition on Mt. Piz Palu. The opening shots show her frolicking in the snow in a short-sleeved shirt and knee-length skirt, making one wonder how she could stand the cold. The film goes on to show Maria and her husband in their cabin on their honeymoon when they hear the story of Dr. Krafft, who is looking for his wife, lost on the mountain. The couple decide to join him in the search, and this is where the drama really begins.

As the expedition conducts the search, a number of dangerous perils are braved, including an avalanche, creating a situation in which the rescuers must be rescued.

The footage in the blizzard sequence is phenomenal. One can see the ice forming on Riefenstahl's face as the icy wind blows. Her face is literally caked with ice, to an even greater extent than Lillian Gish's was in the blizzard sequence in *Way Down East*. Riefenstahl's memoirs state that she suffered frostbite on her upper thighs, and suffered a permanent bladder disorder. The ice on her face speaks for itself, and it is not difficult at all to believe that what she says is totally credible. It is a miracle that she came through this film alive and without losing body parts from frostbite.

The finale of the film has pilot Ernst Udet flying his plane perilously close to the glaciers, performing mind-boggling stunts as he attempts to rescue the stranded mountain climbers. It is doubtful that the modern day Blue Angels team would attempt some of the death defying stunts that Udet accomplished in this film.

The photography in the film is gorgeous. One can tell which scenes were done under Arnold Fanck's direction. The clouds are magnificent as they move in the path of the sun. The ice vapors are shown gracefully swirling up and around the mountains, as if to symbolize steam from the "white hell" in the valley of Mt. Piz Palu. This is some of the most artistic mountain or glacier photography ever committed to celluloid. With Fanck's knack for nature cinematography direction, and Pabst's penchant for dramatic direction, the combination is magnificent. *The White Hell of Piz Palu* is an artistic masterpiece, and remains an awe-inspiring film to watch today.

Leni Riefenstahl demonstrated with her later directorial projects *The Blue Light* (1931), *Triumph of the Will* (1934), and *Olympia* (1936) that she is the greatest female cinematographer, and possibly the greatest regardless of sex. In this film, she demonstrates that she was a remarkable and highly talented actress as well. She braved conditions that few of her male contemporaries would attempt. She is most definitely to German silent cinema what Lillian Gish was to American silent cinema.

Ms. Riefenstahl remains active today. At 95, she was presented an award at the recent 1997 Cinecon Convention in Hollywood. As the world's oldest ever licensed scuba diver, she still does underwater diving and photography.

Much of the flack that Riefenstahl gets is a result of her daring to be the best in what is typically a man's field. Sergei Eisenstein, a male director, did propaganda films for Joseph Stalin, who murdered far more people under his Communist regime than Hitler did during the Reich. Nobody condemns Eisenstein, but a Riefenstahl appearance still draws protest, which sounds like a bit of a double standard.

634. The Younger Generation

Rating: ☆☆☆

Columbia; ***Directed by*** Frank Capra; ***Adapted by*** Sonya Levien; ***From the Story by*** Fannie Hurst; ***Photography by*** Ted Tetzlaff; ***Dialogue by*** Howard Green; ***Recorded by*** Western Electric System; ***Music by*** Columbia Symphony Orchestra; ***Running Time:*** 84 minutes; ***Cast:*** BIRDIE GOLDFISH, Lina Basquette (1907–1994); MORRIS GOLDFISH, Ricardo Cortez (1899–1977); MR. GOLDFISH, Jean Hersholt (1886–1956); MRS. GOLDFISH, Rosa Rosanova (1869–1944); EDDIE LESSER, Rex Lease (1899–1966); A SOCIETY GIRL, Julanne Johnston (1900–1988); ***Supporting Cast:*** Sid Crossley (1885–1960); Martha Franklin (1868–1929); Julia Swayne Gordon (1878–1933); Jack Raymond (1886–1953); Otto Fries (1887–1938)

This is one of only two of Lina Basquette's silent era films known to survive. In *The Younger Generation*, she plays the daughter in a Jewish family of four on the poorer east side of town. Through the efforts of her brother, Morris, who is a financial wizard but a cold, arrogant snob, the family is brought out of poverty and into wealth and luxury. Basquette's character, Birdie, and her father both subscribe to the wisdom that money cannot buy happiness, but their mother is delighted to see her son bringing them out of poverty, and overlooks his arrogant transgressions.

Lina Basquette, delightful star of *The Younger Generation* (1929).

The trouble starts when Birdie, who loves Eddie Lesser, a longtime neighborhood friend, is told by her controlling brother that he is not allowed in the house that he paid for. The last straw comes when Eddie is unwittingly enticed into providing a cover for a group of jewelry store robbers. Birdie convinces Eddie to turn himself in, and marries him just before he goes to jail to pay his debt to society. Morris, furious over the marriage, orders Birdie out of the house.

The time comes when Morris pushes even his mother too far with his snobbery, and when Eddie gets out of jail, Birdie and her parents reunite as her father is on his death bed. The mother gives up the luxurious surroundings that Morris' wealth bought, and goes to live with Birdie and her family. Morris is left alone in his luxury home.

This Fannie Hurst story effectively gets across the point that money isn't everything if you alienate your loved ones in the process of making it. Director Frank Capra (1897–1991), although dealing with the new and primitive process of sound pictures, manages to get some good symbolic touches into the film. At the end, Capra photographs the shadows caused by the window venetian blinds in such a way that Morris is covered with shadows of horizontal bars—symbolizing the lonely prison he has made for himself with his arrogance.

Actress Lina Basquette graces this film with a charming and attractive presence. She was just starting to make real progress with her film career when her husband, Sam Warner (1887–1927), died unexpectedly at age 40 from pneumonia. She was working on this film at a time when there was a bitter legal battle with her in-laws in progress over the estate and over custody of Sam and Lina's daughter, Lita. The Warners, with their vast money and power, won their case, and made Ms. Basquette's life a living hell for some time to come. Having been blacklisted by the Warners, the only film work open to Ms. Basquette in the early 1930s was in westerns. Despite a number of further tragedies in Ms. Basquette's tumultuous life, she managed to hang on, and found happiness in later life by raising champion great danes and judging dog shows around the country until her death at 87 in 1994.

Among the other cast members in this film is Rex Lease, who would later go on to fame as a leading western star. Jean Hersholt plays an uncharacteristic role as the laid-back father with a sense of humor. Julanne Johnston, whose greatest success was in *The Thief of Bagdad*, has a bit part as one of the society ladies that Morris is trying to impress.

The Younger Generation has never been made widely available on video, although copies circulate in private collections. Lina Basquette's other surviving silent era film, *The Godless Girl* (1929), was also a part-talkie. Robert Gitt of UCLA restored it as a sound feature for UCLA, where it is archived.

1930

635. City Girl

Rating: ☆☆☆☆

Fox; ***Directed by*** F.W. Murnau; ***Based on*** *The Mud Turtle* ***by*** Elliott Lester; ***Adaptation/Scenario by*** Berthold Viertel, Marion Orth; ***Photography by*** Ernest Palmer; ***Settings by*** Harry Oliver; ***Costumes by*** Sophie Wachner; ***Edited/Titled by*** Katharine Hilliker, H.H. Caldwell; ***Running Time:*** 86 minutes; ***Cast:*** KATE, Mary Duncan (1895–1993); LEM, Charles Farrell (1901–1990); HIS FATHER, David Torrence (1864–1951); HIS MOTHER, Edith Yorke (1867–1934); A FARM WORKER, Guinn Williams (1899–1962)

For once, one of the films released in both silent and sound versions has had the right version to be the one to survive. The silent version of *City Girl* was F.W. Murnau's final film for Fox, before he went to Paramount to do *Tabu* (1931).

Completed in 1929 and released in early 1930, *City Girl* has Mary Duncan giving the performance of a lifetime as Kate, a Chicago waitress who meets and falls in love with farm boy Lem while he is in town selling his father's wheat crop. Kate is a sincere, hard working girl who aims to please. Unfortunately, when she and Lem arrive at the farm, she is greeted coldly by his father, who assumes that because of her occupation as a waitress and the fact that she is from the city, she is a gold digger out to get whatever she can out of Lem and his family. It seems that no matter how hard she tries to please, nothing she can do is good enough.

The time comes when the new wheat crop is ready to harvest, and workers are brought in. Mac, the foreman of the harvesters, makes a move on Kate as Lem's father is walking in the door. To force her to marry him, Mac calls on the workers to quit on a crucial night just before a hail storm is to strike, which has ruined the wheat crop in Canada. The father threatens to shoot whoever leaves the farm before the harvesting is completed, and unknowingly shoots at his own son. This close brush with death is what brings the father around to accepting his son's new wife.

City Girl is Mary Duncan's film all the way. She puts her heart and emotion into the role as the rejected girl from the city trying to fit into her new life in the country in which her father-in-law hates her, and has to deal with advances from crude men that she has no interest in. One really feels sorry for her as she tries so hard to be a good wife, with the efforts seeming futile.

Duncan was not chosen to play the role of Kate in the sound version of *City Girl*, reportedly because her voice did not match her looks. This is a shame, as Duncan was just really starting to come into her own as a wonderful actress who had talent to closely rival the abilities of Janet Gaynor. One wonders why Duncan's name did not come up in the Academy Award nominations for 1929–30. Duncan's performance in *City Girl* is at least as good, if not better, than Louise Brooks' performance in *Diary of a Lost Girl* (1929), for which Danny Peary awarded his "Alternate Oscar." Both Brooks' and Duncan's performances were many times better than Norma Shearer's Academy Award winning performance in *The Divorcee* (1930).

In addition, David Torrence gives what is probably the best performance of his career as the father who makes life miserable for his son and daughter-in-law. If Academy Awards for Supporting Actor had been given out for 1929–30, Torrence would have certainly deserved consideration in the nomination process.

There are some significant differences between the silent and sound versions of *City Girl*. The sequence in which Lem's father shoots at him does not appear in the sound version. Also, the sound version actually had Mac confessing to Lem that it was totally his doing when he made advances toward Kate, and that none of what happened was Kate's fault.

F.W. Murnau (1888–1931) was fired from Fox just before he completed work on *City Girl*. Director A.F. Erickson (1897–1956) finished the film, and another director directed the sound version.

City Girl stands the test of time as one of the last of the great silent romances, with top notch direction by F.W. Murnau and an award-worthy performance by Mary Duncan.

636. Ladies of Leisure

Rating: ☆☆

Columbia; ***Directed by*** Frank Capra; ***Adapted from a Stage Play by*** David Belasco and Milton Herbert Cropper; ***Produced by*** Harry Cohn; ***Adaptation by*** Jo Swerling; ***Titles by*** Dudley Early; ***Photography by*** Joseph Walker; ***Film Editor:*** Maurice Wright; ***Running Time:*** 85 minutes; ***Cast:*** "HOPE" ARNOLD, Barbara Stanwyck (1907–1990); HER ROOMMATE, Marie

Prevost (1898–1937); JERRY STRONG, Ralph Graves (1900–1977); ***Supporting Cast:*** Lowell Sherman (1888–1934); Nance O'Neil (1874–1965); George Fawcett (1860–1939); Juliette Compton (1899–1989); Johnnie Walker (1894–1949)

This film has historic importance as the earliest of Barbara Stanwyck's films that is widely available for evaluation. Stanwyck is best remembered for talkies such as *Stella Dallas* (1937), *Double Indemnity* (1944), and *Sorry, Wrong Number* (1948), all for which she received Academy Award nominations. She won an Emmy Award in 1961 for *The Barbara Stanwyck Show* and again in 1983 for the television miniseries *The Thorn Birds*. Before she hit it big, Stanwyck starred in four low budget silents for Columbia Pictures and Warner Bros. with *Ladies of Leisure* being the last of the four.

Barbara Stanwyck, who starred in *Ladies of Leisure* (1930) and three other low budget silents, in later years.

In *Ladies of Leisure*, she plays a coquettish model who is discovered by wealthy artist Jerry Strong. Strong believes in Hope Arnold, feeling that if given a chance, she could rise above the fast lane lifestyle that has brought her to the brink of being destitute. He takes her under his wing despite the objections of his friends and family, who believe Hope to be nothing but a gold-digging vamp.

This film is a potboiler that definitely was not among Frank Capra's better early films. It is possibly his worst. It is, however, interesting to watch to see Barbara Stanwyck as she was before she made it big. It is hard to believe when watching this film that its director would go on to win three Academy Awards, and that leading lady Stanwyck would receive multiple Oscar nominations, an honorary Academy Award, and two Emmys.

637. Salt for Svenitia

Rating: ☆☆

Goskinprom/U.S.S.R.; ***Directed by*** Mikhail Kalatozov; ***Photographed by*** M. Kalatozov and Sh. Geglashvili; ***Based on an Article by*** S. Tretlakov; ***Running Time:*** 30 minutes

This is the first major effort of Soviet director and cameraman Mikhail Kalatozov (1903–1973), whom international stardom eluded until 1958, when his *The Cranes Are Flying* (1957) won the Best Picture award at the 1958 Cannes Film Festival.

This is a highly controversial Communist propaganda film which has not widely circulated outside the Soviet Union until its 1997 video release. The first half is much like *Turksib* in that it demonstrates how Svenitia's isolation from other parts of the world created hardship for the hardworking people who resided there. The second half is where it gets to the part that makes it controversial even today. It depicts how the Svan people, in desperation, turn to the Judeo-Christian and Pagan religions, thinking that if they offer animal and human sacrifices, the Gods will be appeased. These sacrifice ceremonies are extremely graphic, showing animals having their throats cut with the blood dripping onto the grave of a previous sacrifice, as well as a horse literally being run to death. There was denial among the Svans that inhumane sacrifices of this sort actually took place. Considering the types of similar misdeeds committed in the name of religion even in today's world, it is likely that there was at least some truth in this portrayal.

Salt for Svenitia is a powerful film, but it may prove too graphic for some viewers.

638. The Silent Enemy

Rating: ☆☆☆½

Paramount; ***Directed by*** H.P. Carver; ***Story by*** W. Douglas Burden; ***Scenario by*** Richard Carver; ***Photographed by*** Marcel Le Picard; ***Animal Expert:*** Dr. Alan Bachrach; ***Titles by*** Julian Johnson; ***Running Time:*** 84 minutes; ***Cast:*** CHETOGA, Chief Yellow Robe

The Silent Enemy is a late silent epic of the plight of the Ojibway Indian tribe. It starts with a sound prologue by an Indian chief named Chief Yellow Robe. After giving the brief speech introducing the film, Chief Yellow Robe plays Chetoga, the chief of the Ojibway Indian tribe. The silent enemy which is the Indians' greatest obstacle is hunger and famine. Baluk is the highly respected Indian hunter of the tribe, who is designated as Chetoga's successor as chief. He and the chief's daughter, Neewa, are in love and hope to marry. Dagwan, the medicine man, is also covetous of Neewa, and will stop at nothing to win her hand in marriage. Neewa is somewhat afraid to say anything against Dagwan, as she believes that he as medicine man has magic powers that he can use to take revenge against her.

The Ojibway tribe is facing famine due to a decrease in the animal population of their current settlement. Dagwan, seeking to shake the tribe's confidence in Baluk, blames the famine on Baluk's ineptness as a hunter. To prove his point, Dagwan steals a deer from another tribe, "proving" that he was able to make a kill, and that Baluk was simply incompetent. Baluk asserts that the tribe needs to migrate northward to meet the crossing of the caribou stampede, which will bring plenty of game to hunt. Along the way northward, Chief Chetoga dies, and Baluk becomes the new chief.

Once the tribe reaches its destination, the caribou does not stampede from the north as expected. Dagwan sees this as an opportunity to remove the last obstacle that stands between him and Neewa. He asserts and convinces the tribe members that the failure of the caribou to show up is a sign that the gods above are angry at the tribe, and that it is necessary to sacrifice their chief to appease them.

The Silent Enemy serves as fascinating documentation of early Indian life. It is shown how they hunted and prepared their food, as well as some of their religious rituals. The way of life depicted in this film is virtually extinct 67 years later in the 1990s, and only a memory. The photography of the Indian tribe's naturalistic habitats in various seasons is beautifully done.

Of the Indian documentaries, this is by far the most interesting, showing us the old Indian way of life through an interesting story of one of the Ojibways' greatest struggles. This film is available from Milestone Video in a high quality video and laser disc version taken from an original 35 mm tinted nitrate print. The original organ score for the silent segment of the film is performed by John Muri.

639. Sweethearts on Parade *Rating:* ☆☆☆

Columbia; ***Directed by*** Marshall Neilan; ***Story by*** Al Cohn and Jimmie Starr; ***Continuity by*** Colin Clements; ***Supervised by*** F. McGrew Willis; ***Photography by*** Gus Peterson; ***Film Editor:*** Sidney J. Walsh; ***Running Time:*** 66 minutes; ***Cast:*** HELEN, Alice White (1907–1983); NITA, Marie Prevost (1898–1937); BILL, Lloyd Hughes (1897–1958); HANK, Kenneth Thompson

For the first time in nearly 70 years, it is now possible for the average person to

Alice White, the bubbly blonde star of *Sweethearts on Parade* (1930), her only silent known to survive.

watch a silent film starring Alice White. Until now, the only Alice White film accessible to the general public was an early talkie, *Show Girl in Hollywood* (1930), which is shown occasionally on Turner Classic Movies.

Some critics have said that Ms. White was a second-string Clara Bow. In actuality, Ms. White had her own type of charm, and was a delightful actress in her own, unique way. Whereas Clara Bow played the quintessential, flaming redheaded flapper, Alice White was more of a bubbly, vivacious blonde. Her most famous role was as Dorothy Shaw in the original *Gentlemen Prefer Blondes* (1928), a lost film. Although she was a natural blonde, she had her hair dyed dark for her role in the film which costarred Ruth Taylor (1907–1964) as Lorelei Lee. As brief as Ms. White's career was, she definitely made her indelible mark in motion picture history.

In *Sweethearts on Parade*, White portrays a country girl named Helen who has just moved to the city. She hooks up with a city girl named Nita. They are both looking for work, but have car fare to the job interview for one person. So, Nita tells Helen to wait on the park bench, and she will take care of getting their jobs. While on the park bench, Helen attracts two male admirers—one named Hank who is in the Navy, and a Marine named Bill. When Nita returns with the news that they got jobs at a local department store, Helen tells her that the two men got into a fight over her. A title card flashes onto the screen with Nita saying, "I leave you for one hour, and you upset the whole Navy!"

The following Monday, we find our girls working in a window display at Hyson's Department Store. Nita's job is to describe bath products, and Helen's job is to demonstrate the products—while actually taking a bath in a real bathtub for all to see. If this film had been released four years later when the strict Motion Picture Code went into effect, this scene would not have made it past the censors.

While on the job, our two military men arrive as part of the attracted crowd of onlookers. The two couples end up double dating with the Navy man paired up with Nita, and with Helen pairing up with the Marine. Complications arise when the men leave on military assignments, and Helen starts dating a rich millionaire.

Sweethearts on Parade was one of the earlier productions of Columbia Pictures, when the company was just starting to emerge from "poverty row" status. It was directed by the highly acclaimed director Marshall Neilan (1891–1958). By 1930, Neilan's alcoholism had ruined his reputation with the big studios. This enjoyable film demonstrates that despite his personal problems, Neilan was still doing good work. Another interesting historic aspect about *Sweethearts on Parade* is that in addition to showcasing Alice White at the height of her career, it featured Marie Prevost toward the beginning of the end of her career. She was actually better in this film than she had been in some of her earlier bedroom comedies that she did with Harrison Ford in the mid and late 1920s.

1931

640. The Blue Light

Rating: ☆☆☆☆

Leni Riefenstahl Studio-Film/Germany; ***Directed by*** Leni Riefenstahl; ***Screenplay by*** Bella Belaze; ***Photography by*** Hans Schneeburger, Heinz von Javorsky; ***Running Time of Silent Ver-***

sion Evaluated: 52 minutes; ***Running Time of Talkie Version:*** 70 minutes; ***Cast:*** JUNTA, Leni Riefenstahl (born 1902); VIGO, Mathias Waimann; TONIO, Bennie Fuhrer; LUCIA, Martha Mair; GUZZI, Frantz Maldacia; INN KEEPER, Max Ohlzboer

This film is historically important as Leni Riefenstahl's directorial debut, as well as the debut project of her production company. Ms. Riefenstahl financed the film herself using her personal savings, and had not originally planned to direct the film herself. She took on the directorial duties to save money, and discovered her talent for the directorial end of movie making as she progressed with this project.

In this film, Riefenstahl directed herself in the female lead as Junta, a peasant mountain girl who has come across crystals that emit a shimmering blue light when the moon is full. She is believed by the villagers to be a witch, and is later attacked by people who want her crystals, which only she knows how to get to on the mountain peak where they are to be found. All other men who have tried to reach the blue light have not lived to tell about it.

This film is highly acclaimed not only for its intriguing story, but its innovative cinematography—especially in the night time shots of the blue crystals. Riefenstahl was told by Arnold Fanck that the effect she wanted was simply impossible to do. Riefenstahl herself experimented with various color filters, inventing techniques and effects that were copied in later years by other directors. In short, Riefenstahl showed her male counterparts how to do the "impossible."

It was Riefenstahl's cinematography work in this film that so impressed Adolf Hitler (1889–1945) that he insisted on having her produce and direct his Nazi propaganda films. With *Triumph of the Will* (1934) and *Olympia* (1936), Riefenstahl showed the world the best photographed propaganda film and Olympic documentary footage ever filmed, which has yet to be surpassed in quality by any of her male counterparts in the years since.

The Blue Light is perhaps the best directorial debut of any director, and is a masterpiece of cinematography. In addition, Riefenstahl was never photographed more beautifully than she was in this film. *The Blue Light* contains the very best footage of Riefenstahl ever taken, bringing out her gorgeous facial features to their fullest potential.

641. City Lights

Rating: ☆☆☆

United Artists; ***Directed and Written by*** Charles Chaplin; ***Assistant Directors:*** Harry Crocker, Henry Bergman, Albert Austin; ***Photographers:*** Rollie Totheroh, Gordon Pollock; ***Settings by*** Charles D. Hall; ***Music Composed by*** Charles Chaplin; ***Running Time:*** 86 minutes; ***Cast:*** A TRAMP, Charlie Chaplin (1889–1977); A BLIND GIRL, Virginia Cherrill (1908–1996); HER GRANDMOTHER, Florence Lee (1888–1962); AN ECCENTRIC MILLIONAIRE, Harry Myers (1882–1938); HIS BUTLER, Allan Garcia (1887–1938); A PRIZEFIGHTER, Hank Mann (1887–1971)

When shooting began on *City Lights* in late 1928, the talkie era was in full swing. Charlie Chaplin believed that talkies were a passing fad, and that silents would prevail once the talkies ran a brief course. In effect, Chaplin was the one producer in Hollywood who held out against the talkies. It was a big gamble, but fortunately Chaplin was right in believing that American audiences would still be willing to see a silent film, and *City Lights* was a box-office and critical success.

City Lights has Chaplin playing a tramp, who falls for a blind girl who sells flowers. He uses the last money he has to his name to buy flowers from her, and resolves to help the girl finance an operation to restore her sight. He makes friends with an eccentric millionaire that he has stopped from committing suicide, who gives him a large sum of money as a gift, which he in turn gives to the girl for the eye operation. Once the millionaire sobers up, he does not remember giving the tramp the money, and Chaplin's character goes to prison for burglary.

Virginia Cherrill as leading lady gives a wonderful performance as the flower girl, and makes an impressive debut with her charm and beauty. At one point in production, Chaplin fired her and brought Georgia Hale in for screen tests on the part. A few scenes were shot with Hale, and these outtakes still exist. Chaplin ultimately brought Cherrill back to finish the film, and she used the opportunity to demand a raise from $75 per week to $150.

Among the supporting players, Harry Myers is the standout, giving an excellent performance as the drunken millionaire, and providing *City Lights* with its funniest scenes. This reviewer's favorite sequence would have to be the boxing match, in which Chaplin takes on a prizefighter in an effort to raise money. Charlie Chaplin deserves great admiration for realizing the superiority of silents over talkies and refusing to run with the pack until 1940, with *The Great Dictator*.

642. Tabu

Rating: ☆☆☆☆

Paramount; ***Directed by*** F.W. Murnau; ***Written by*** F.W. Murnau and Robert J. Flaherty; ***Photography by*** Floyd Crosby; ***Music Score by*** Hugo Reisenfeld; Recorded on RCA Photophone; ***Running Time:*** 82 minutes; ***Cast:*** THE BOY, Matahi; THE GIRL, Reri; THE POLICEMAN, Jean; THE OLD WARRIOR, Hitu

At the 1930–31 Academy Awards, *Tabu* won an Oscar for Best Cinematography. It was cinematographer Floyd Crosby's (1899–1985) first film, shot entirely on location in the lush tropical island of Tahiti. Crosby's later film credits include *High Noon* (1952), *Oklahoma* (1955), *The Pit and the Pendulum* (1961), and *X—The Man with the X-Ray Eyes* (1963). He was the father of singer-songwriter David Crosby (born 1941) of the popular 1960s music group Crosby, Stills, and Nash.

Tabu started out as a joint project between director F.W. Murnau (1888–1931) and documentary producer Robert J. Flaherty (1884–1951) of *Nanook of the North* (1922) and *Moana of the South Seas* (1926) fame. They collaborated on the script, but by the time production was ready to begin, they realized that their styles were totally different, and that they could not work together. So, Flaherty bowed out, and Murnau took sole charge of the directorial duties.

Told with the use of very few titles, *Tabu* is a simple love story reflecting the simple atmosphere of Tahiti at a time before modern civilization had touched the island. Reri, a beautiful native woman, is given the dubious honor of being chosen by the old warrior of the tribe as the tribe's choice to be consecrated with the gods of their native religion. With this "honor," she is declared "tabu"—off limits to the affection or love of any person. Reri does fall in love with Matahi, the leading man of the film, and their tale of unrequited love is magnificently portrayed.

The musical accompaniment for this film is just as impressive as the cinematogra-

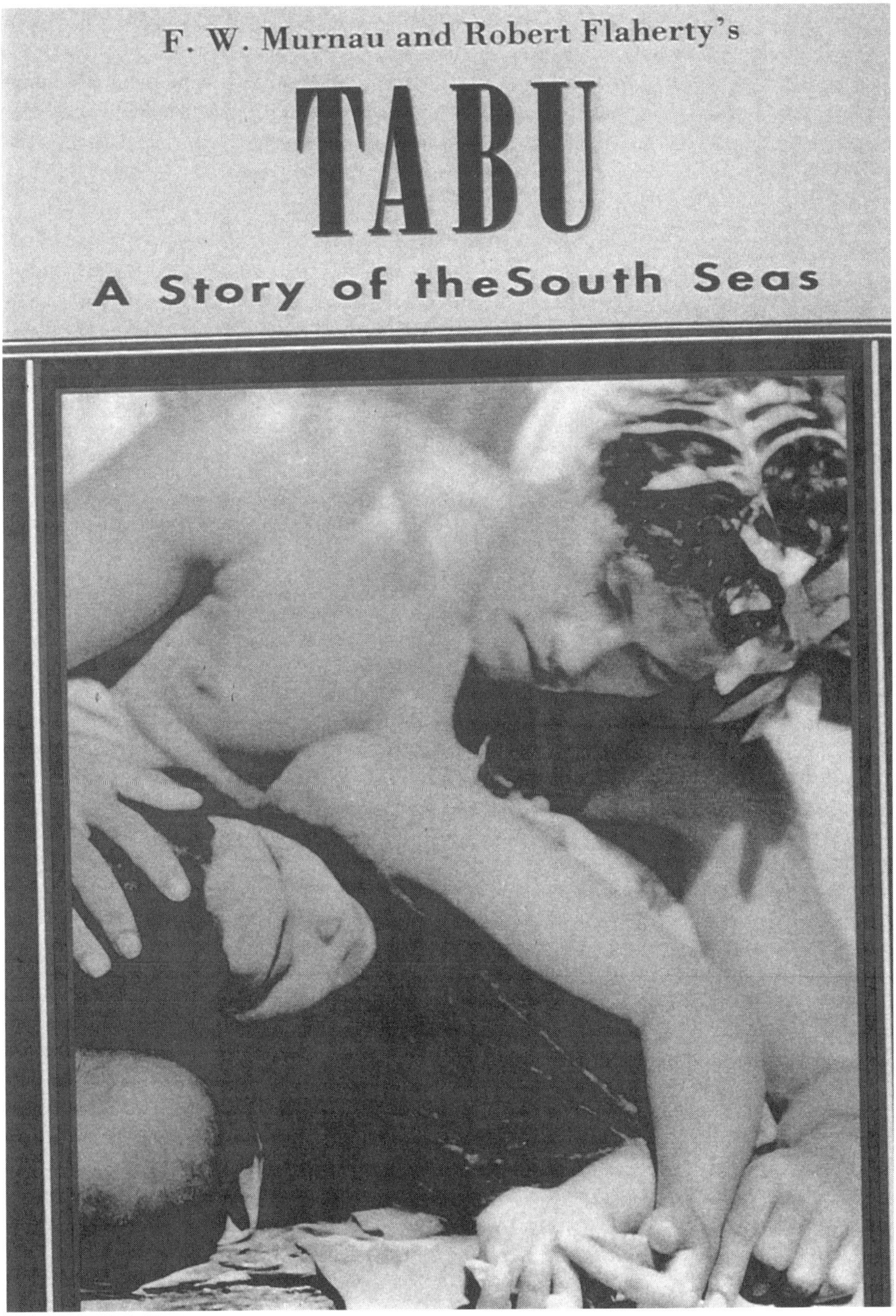
F. W. Murnau and Robert Flaherty's
TABU
A Story of theSouth Seas

Tabu (1931).

phy, including music appropriate for the South Seas atmosphere portrayed with vocal native chants during some of the dances.

In his 1959 book, *Classics of the Silent Screen*, Joe Franklin offers the following acclaim for Tabu: "*Tabu* was undoubtedly the greatest poetic-documentary that the American cinema ever produced, certainly a finer film even than *Nanook of the North*."

Sadly, *Tabu* would prove to be F.W. Murnau's final masterpiece. Just a few weeks before *Tabu* premiered in theaters, Murnau was killed at age 42 in a car accident.

For many years, *Tabu* was not available in its complete form, as some of the sequences featuring brief and partial nudity were censored. In 1992, Milestone Video restored these censored sequences and made the complete version available on video—the first time that the uncensored version was available to the public since its original release 61 years earlier.

The Post-Era Silents

1936

643. Modern Times

Rating: ☆☆☆☆

United Artists; ***Written and Directed by*** Charles Chaplin; ***Assistant Director:*** Carter DeHaven; ***Music Score Composed by*** Charles Chaplin; ***Photography by*** Rollie Totheroh, Ira Morgan; ***Settings by*** Charles D. Hall, Russell Spencer; ***Running Time:*** 87 minutes; ***Cast:*** A FACTORY WORKER, Charlie Chaplin (1889–1977); A GAMIN, Paulette Goddard (1911–1990); ***Supporting Cast:*** Henry Bergman (1868–1946); Stanley Sandford (1894–1961); Chester Conklin (1886–1971); Hank Mann (1887–1971); Stanley Blystone; Allan Garcia (1887–1938); Dick Alexander; Cecil Reynolds; Myra McKinney; Murdock McQuarrie (1878–1942); Wilfred Lucas (1871–1940); Ed Le Sainte (1870–1940); Fred Malatesta (1889–1952); Sam Stein; Juana Sutton; Ted Oliver (1892–1957)

This was both Charlie Chaplin's last silent, and the first film in which his voice was heard. In the sequence depicting Chaplin as a singing waiter, he can be heard singing a song. Otherwise, the film is silent with music, sound effects, and occasional dialogue emanating from machines, radios, television monitors, and other devices.

This was Chaplin's satire on the modern machine age, in which he plays a factory worker driven to insanity by the inhumanity of a modern technological age, in which the workers are seen merely as an extension of the machines. In one scene, Chaplin actually gets caught in the machine.

The best sequence in the film is when the factory boss tests out a new automatic feeding machine, with the hopes that the feeding machine will feed workers as they work, and thus eliminate the lunch hour. The machine starts off working fine, but then a glitch in the electrical system makes it go haywire, and Chaplin is a mess by the end of the demonstration.

Driven crazy, Chaplin ends up having a nervous breakdown. After his cure, he is mistaken for a leader of a Communist demonstration and thrown into jail. Paulette Goddard comes into the story as a waif who is struggling to support herself and is finally driven by starvation to steal bread from a bakery. After going through some trying ordeals, the two meet and try to support themselves as singing waiter and dancer in a fancy restaurant. Just as they are making progress and getting on their feet, the juvenile authorities come for Paulette, leading into the film's memorable ending.

Charlie Chaplin in *Modern Times* (1936).

This is a masterful portrayal of how the beginnings of the modern technological age dehumanized much of America, bringing high unemployment and the great depression. *Modern Times* was the first of Chaplin's overtly political films with its satire of modern technology and comments on capitalism, which certainly didn't endear him to the Red-baiting politicians who came to power in the late 1940s and early 1950s.

Paulette Goddard gives an excellent charm and is appealing as Chaplin's leading lady. She had previously had small roles in minor productions, and this was her first major role. She was catapulted to stardom in this film, and worked steadily in the industry through the 1960s. She had been the leading contender for the part of Scarlett O'Hara in *Gone with the Wind* (1939) but the part went to Vivien Leigh, as the executives felt that her live-in relationship with Chaplin before they were married would turn the public off of the film. Goddard and Chaplin were married the year that *Modern Times* was released, and divorced in 1942. She later married Burgess Meredith (1908–1997) in 1944, with the marriage lasting five years. Her third marriage to Erich Maria Remarque, a German novelist who wrote the novel *All Quiet on the Western Front* (1930), in 1958 lasted until his death in 1970. Goddard left her entire fortune of $20 million to New York University upon her death at age 78 in 1990.

Danny Peary's *Alternate Oscars* gives *Modern Times* its Best Picture of 1936 designation, and Charlie Chaplin the Best Actor designation. This praise is justified, as this reviewer, too, feels that this film should have swept the Academy Awards. Furthermore, Paulette Goddard should have received at least a nomination for Best Actress.

The theme song from the film, called "Smile," is an enduring pop classic that has been re-recorded many times over the years since its debut appearance in this film. Despite the fact that the Academy Awards snubbed this film, the National Board of Review named *Modern Times* one of the ten best films of the year.

1950

644. Un Chant d'Amour

Rating: ☆☆☆

Produced by Nico Papatakis/France; ***Directed by*** Jean Genet; ***Running Time:*** 24 minutes; ***Cast:*** A PRISONER, Lucien Senemaud

This late silent was the one and only film directed by the French writer Jean Genet, whose plays inspired a number of film adaptations. Among the films based on Genet's works are Joseph Strick's *The Balcony* (1963); actor Vic Morrow's one and only directorial effort, *Deathwatch* (1965); Christopher Miles' *The Maids* (1975); and the famous gay German film, *Querelle* (1982).

Un Chant d'Amour was a gay avant garde erotic film, which was artistically intended for presentation in complete silence—with no musical accompaniment. It is set in a French prison, and features three inmates acting out homoerotic fantasies. Two men share a cigarette by one man smoking and blowing the smoke through a hole in the wall into another man's mouth. A guard is shown watching one of the prisoners as he acts on sexual fantasies, and then storms into the cell and subjects the prisoner to brutality. A final erotic "dance of death" is also portrayed.

While this film has erotic and sexually suggestive poses and action, actual genitalia are seen only briefly as one of the men masturbates, classifying it as soft core pornography by today's standards.

Director Jean Genet intended this film to viewed by private collectors only. The film's producer sold prints to a few independent companies, and it was distributed "underground" for a time until it had its first public screening in 1954 at the Cinémathèque Française. The film was subjected to heavy censorship, and was not shown in France again for two decades.

A couple of American screenings of *Un Chant d'Amour* were attempted in the cities of Los Angeles and New York City. The Los Angeles courts banned it on the grounds of obscenity. A prominent theater exhibitor by the name of Jonas Mekas in 1964 ran the film in New York, and the screening was raided by the police, with Mekas ending up in prison on obscenity charges.

While *Un Chant d'Amour* has been frequently shown in Europe since the 1970s, it is still largely inaccessible in the United States. The only way to view it in the U.S. is to order it in SECAM video format from France, and have it converted to NTSC format.

While this film was daring and scandalous for the time it was produced, it is tame compared to the gay erotica that flourishes on the market today.

One of the actors was Lucien Senemaud, who was at the time Jean Genet's lover.

Un Chant d'Amour is widely regarded as the most famous gay themed short film produced in Europe. If erotica can be called "classic," this film is one of the erotic classics of the century.

1976

645. Silent Movie

Rating: ★★★½

20th Century-Fox; ***Directed by*** Mel Brooks; ***Story by*** Ron Clark; ***Screenplay:*** Mel Brooks, Ron Clark, Rudy DeLuca, Barry Levinson; ***Costumes by*** Patricia Norris; ***Choreography by*** Rob Iscove; ***Casting Director:*** Mary Goldberg; ***Photography by*** Ed Koons; ***Sets by*** Rick Simpson; ***Titles by*** Anthony Goldschmidt; ***Music by*** John Morris; ***Edited by*** John C. Howard, Stanford C. Allen; ***Running Time:*** 88 minutes; ***Cast:*** MEL FUNN, Mel Brooks (born 1926); MARTY EGGS, Marty Feldman (1933–1982); DON BELL, Dom DeLuise (born 1933); STUDIO CHIEF, Sid Caesar (born 1922); ENGULF, Harold Gould (born 1923); DEVOUR, Ron Carey; VILMA KAPLAN [THE VAMP], Bernadette Peters (born 1944); ***As Themselves:*** Paul Newman (born 1925); Liza Minnelli (born 1946); Burt Reynolds (born 1936); Anne Bancroft (born 1931); James Caan (born 1939); Marcel Marceau; ***Supporting Cast:*** PREGNANT LADY, Carol Arthur; NEWS VENDOR, Liam Dunn; MAITRE D', Fritz Feld (1900–1993); STUDIO GATE GUARD, Chuck McCann; INTENSIVE CARE NURSE, Valerie Curtin (born 1945); STUDIO CHIEF'S SECRETARY, Yvonne Wilder; ACUPUNCTURE MAN, Arnold Soboloff; MOTEL BELLHOP, Patrick Campbell; MAN IN TAILOR SHOP, Harry Ritz (1906–1986); BLIND MAN, Charlie Callas; FLY-IN-SOUP MAN, Henny Youngman; BRITISH OFFICER, Eddie Ryder; ***Executives:*** Al Hopson; Rudy DeLuca; Barry Levinson; Howard Hesseman; Lee Delano; Jack Riley; BEAUTIFUL BLONDE #1, Inga Neilson; BEAUTIFUL BLONDE #2, Erica Hagen; PROJECTIONIST, Robert Lussier

This was the first silent film produced in the United States since Chaplin's *Modern Times* (1936). In the 40 years between, Japan produced *The Island* (1962) and Jean Genet of France did *Un Chant d'Amour* (1950), as per the preceding review.

Mel Brooks, director and star of *Silent Movie* (1976).

This is a delightful parody of Hollywood's golden era, with witty titles and situations, as well as some funny situations and satire. Mel Brooks directs himself as the character of Mel Funn, a has-been director who has managed to kick the booze habit that destroyed his career, and proposes a last-ditch effort to save his old studio from being taken over by "Engulf and Devour" by making a new silent film. The boss rejects the idea—until Funn promises to get an all-star cast for the project. The boss is won over, and the next obstacle is to get the cast together, which Funn and crew go through outlandish measures to do. As Funn succeeds in rounding up Burt Reynolds and James Caan, Engulf and Devour see their chance to swallow "Big Pictures Studios" going out the window, and will stop at nothing to prevent Funn's silent movie from premiering.

There are some fun slapstick sequences in *Silent Movie*, which even has Engulf and Devour hiring Bernadette Peters to "vamp" Funn and stop him from completing the picture. There is also some recurring humor with gay overtones. One sequence has Mel and his crew posed in close positions, with women yelling "Fags!" Another sequence has Mel Funn temporarily falling off the wagon, progressing for a while from a wino to king of the winos and finally lord of the winos. During the binge, he ends up in a gay bar. He eventually gets back on the wagon again, and has what seems like thousands of cups of coffee to sober up so that work on the film can resume.

Ironically, the one major star who refuses to do the picture is Marcel Marceau, a pantomimist who utters the movie's one word of dialogue—a resounding "NO!" *Silent Movie* is in general a hilarious film which is chock full of good gags—going from one outlandish gag right into another.

Mel Brooks does justice to the art of silent cinema—making fun of it while flattering the art at the same time. What better plot to have for a new silent than the plot of doing the unconventional by making a new silent film? *Silent Movie* is cleverly done in typical Mel Brooks fashion, and is among his better efforts of the 1970s and early 1980s. It is one that every silent film enthusiast will get a lot of laughs out of.

The final title in the film states that it is a semi-autobiographical account of what Mel Brooks had to go through to complete this project. Among the supporting players is Fritz Feld, who started out in silents and had a part in *The Last Command* (1928), which was nominated for Best Picture of 1927–28 and reviewed elsewhere in this book. In addition, Valerie Curtin is the cousin of popular comedienne Jane Curtin. Harry Ritz was a part of the famous Ritz Brothers trio of the 1930s and 1940s.

While *Silent Movie* was snubbed by the Academy Awards, it was named by the National Board of Review as one of the ten best films of 1976.

1996

646. The Taxi Dancer

Rating: ☆½

Dalemans Brothers and Favourite Films/Belgium; ***Directed by*** Caroline Strubbe; ***Screenplay by*** Jan Dalemans, Gilbert Dalemans, Caroline Strubbe; ***Director of Photography:*** Paul Vercheval; ***Costumes by*** Isabelle Lhoas; ***Production Designer:*** Sergio Bigones; ***Running Time:*** 39 minutes; ***Cast:*** THE BELLBOY, Jeroen Williams; CHAMBERMAID, Delphine Roy; BARONESS, Vera De Mil; PAINTER, Jos Van Geldorp; MANAGER, Charles Martique

This is the most recent of silent film efforts, which was produced as a tribute to Rudolph Valentino, as well as homage to the silent era. Filmed and produced in Brussels, Belgium, *The Taxi Dancer* is set in 1926 in Paris, with Jeroen Williams playing a hotel bellboy who is mesmerized with Rudolph Valentino. The film progresses as the bellboy shares his thoughts on Valentino with a female coworker, giving an idea of what was going through his mind just before he committed suicide to follow in death the legendary star whom he idolized.

Director Caroline Strubbe won worldwide recognition with her 1993 short film, *Melanomen*, which was awarded the designation of Best Short Film at the Interfilmfestival of Berlin for 1993. While *The Taxi Dancer* seems like a sincerely motivated labor of love that a reviewer would love to be able to praise and recommend to others, it unfortunately is found to be lacking upon evaluation. As much as one would like to enjoy it, it just doesn't make the cut.

Basically, this film is 39 minutes of seeing a bellboy's work day, interspersed with some images of his carrying on with a coworker, listening to a record, and looking over his Valentino photos and memorabilia. One sequence has lead actor Williams dressed up in an outfit much like the one Valentino wore in stills from *The Young Rajah* (1922). Strangely, there are shots of centipedes crawling on the floor and on some of the Valentino memorabilia. The film is simply idle until the very end, when the news of Valentino's death is received, and the bellboy goes nuts. The final shot has the bellboy sitting in a room by himself—presumably getting ready to psyche himself up to commit suicide.

While *The Taxi Dancer* is a noble effort, it is a misguided effort that has little intellectual or entertainment appeal. In short, it's a solid bore.

Bibliography

Agee, James. *Agee on Film Volume One*. New York: Perigee, 1983 (reprint of 1958 book).

Amberg, George (editor). *The New York Times Film Reviews: A One Volume Selection, 1913-1970*. New York: Arno, 1971.

Anger, Kenneth. *Hollywood Babylon*. San Francisco: Straight Arrow, 1975.

_____. *Hollywood Babylon 2*. New York: E.P. Dutton, 1984.

Ankerich, Michael G. *Broken Silence: Conversations with 23 Silent Film Stars*. Jefferson, NC: McFarland, 1993.

Barry, Iris, and Eileen Bowser. *D.W. Griffith: American Film Master*. New York: The Museum of Modern Art, 1965.

Bellamy, Madge. *A Darling of the Twenties: Madge Bellamy*. Vestal, NY: Vestal, 1989.

Blum, Daniel. *A Pictorial History of the Silent Screen*. New York: Grosset and Dunlap, 1953.

Bodeen, DeWitt. *More from Hollywood: The Careers of Fifteen Great American Stars*. New York: A.S. Barnes, 1977.

Bohn, Thomas W., and Richard Stromgen. *Light and Shadows: A History of Motion Pictures*. Sherman Oaks, CA: Alfred Publishing, 1978.

Brooks, Louise. *Lulu in Hollywood*. New York: Alfred A. Knopf, 1982.

Brown, Karl. *Adventures with D.W. Griffith*. New York: Farrar, Strauss, and Giroux, 1973.

Brownlow, Kevin. *Behind the Mask of Innocence*. New York: Alfred A. Knopf, 1990.

_____. *Napoleon: Abel Gance's Classic Film*. New York: Alfred A. Knopf, 1983.

_____. *The Parade's Gone By*. Los Angeles: University of California Press, 1968.

_____, and John Kobal. *Hollywood: The Pioneers*. New York: Alfred A. Knopf, 1979.

Card, James. *Seductive Cinema: The Art of Silent Film*. New York: Alfred A. Knopf, 1994.

Carey, Gary. *All the Stars in Heaven: Louis B. Mayer's MGM*. New York: E.P. Dutton, 1981.

_____. *Doug and Mary: A Biography of Douglas Fairbanks and Mary Pickford*. New York: E.P. Dutton, 1977.

Carter, Joseph H. *Never Met a Man I Didn't Like: The Life and Writings of Will Rogers*. New York: Avon, 1991.

Cary, Diana Serra. *The Hollywood Posse: The Story of a Gallant Band of Horsemen Who Made Movie History*. Norman: University of Oklahoma Press, 1996 (reprint of 1975 edition).

_____. *Hollywood's Children*. Dallas: Southern Methodist University Press, 1997 (reprint of 1978 edition).

_____. *What Ever Happened to Baby Peggy?* New York: St. Martin's, 1996.

Chaplin, Charlie. *My Autobiography*. New York: Simon and Schuster, 1964.

Coghlan, Frank E. (Junior). *They Still Call Me Junior: Autobiography of a Child Star; with a Filmography*. Jefferson, NC: McFarland, 1993.

Conan Doyle, Sir Arthur. *The Lost World*. New York: Tom Doherty Associates, 1993 (reprint of original novel).

Cooper, Miriam. *Dark Lady of the Silents*. New York: Bobbs-Merrill, 1973.

Dardis, Tom. *Harold Lloyd: The Man on the Clock*. New York: Viking, 1983.

Davies, Marion. *The Times We Had*. New York: Ballantine Books, 1993 (reprint of 1975 Bobbs-Merrill edition).

Dixon, Thomas, Jr. *The Clansman*. Lexington: University Press of Kentucky, 1970 (reissue of original 1905 novel published by Doubleday and Page).

Doyle, Billy H. *The Ultimate Directory of the Silent Screen Performers: A Necrology of Births and Deaths and Essays on 50 Lost Players*. Metuchen, NJ: Scarecrow, 1995.
Drew, William M. *D.W. Griffith's Intolerance: Its Genesis and Vision*. Jefferson, NC: McFarland, 1986.
_____. *Speaking of Silents: First Ladies of the Screen*. Vestal, NY: Vestal Press, 1989.
Edmunds, Andy. *Frame-Up: The Untold Story of Roscoe "Fatty" Arbuckle*. New York: William Morrow, 1991.
Edwards, Larry. *Buster: A Legend in Laughter*. Bradenton, FL: McGuinn and McGuire, 1995.
Everson, William K. *American Silent Film*. New York: Oxford University Press, 1978.
Eyman, Scott. *Mary Pickford: America's Sweetheart*. New York: D.I. Fine, 1990.
Franklin, Joseph. *Classics of the Silent Screen*. Secaucus, NJ: Citadel Press, 1959.
Fussell, Betty Harper. *Mabel: Hollywood's First I-Don't-Care-Girl—The Life of Mabel Normand*. New York: Limelight Editions, 1992.
Gance, Abel. *Napoléon* (complete shooting script). London: Faber and Faber, 1990.
Genini, Ronald. *Theda Bara: A Biography of the Silent Screen Vamp, with a Filmography*. Jefferson, NC: McFarland, 1996.
Giroux, Robert. *A Deed of Death: The Story Behind the Unsolved Murder of Hollywood Director William Desmond Taylor*. New York: Alfred A. Knopf, 1990.
Gish, Lillian (1893-1993). *Dorothy and Lillian Gish*. New York: Charles Scribner's Sons, 1973.
_____, with Ann Pinchot. *The Movies, Mr. Griffith, and Me*. Englewood Cliffs, NJ: Prentice-Hall, 1969.
Golden, Eve. *Vamp: The Rise and Fall of Theda Bara*. Vestal, NY: Vestal Press Ltd., 1996.
Griffith, Linda Arvidson. *When the Movies Were Young*. Bronx, NY: Benjamin Blom, 1968 (reissue of original 1925 book).
Griffith, Richard, and Arthur Mayer. *The Movies*. New York: Simon and Schuster, 1970.
Jarvis, Everett Grant. *Final Curtain: Deaths of Noted Movie and Television Performers*. Secaucus, NJ: Citadel Press, 1996.
Karney, Robin (editor). *Chronicle of Cinema*. New York: Dorling Kindersley, 1995.
Karr, Kathleen (editor). *The American Film Heritage: Impressions from the American Film Institute Archives*. Washington, D.C.: Acropolis Books, 1972.
Katz, Ephraim. *The Film Encyclopedia*. New York: Harper-Perennial, 1994.
Kerr, Walter. *The Silent Clowns*. New York: Alfred A.Knopf, 1975.
King, Henry, interviewed by David Shepard and Ted Perry, edited by Frank Thompson. *Henry King, Director: From Silents to 'Scope*. Los Angeles: Director's Guild of America, 1995.
Kinnard, Roy. *Horror in Silent Films: A Filmography, 1896-1929*. Jefferson, NC: McFarland, 1995.
Kirkpatrick, Sidney. *A Cast of Killers*. New York: E.P. Dutton, 1986.
Klepper, Robert K. *Silent Films on Video: A Filmography of Over 700 Silent Features Available on Videocassette, with a Directory of Sources*. Jefferson, NC: McFarland, 1996.
Knight, Arthur. *The Liveliest Art*. New York: Macmillan, 1957.
Lahue, Kalton C. *Bound and Gagged: The Story of the Silent Serials*. South Brunswick, NJ and New York: A.S. Barnes, 1968.
Lambert, Gavin. *Nazimova: A Biography*. New York: Alfred A. Knopf, 1997.
Lamparski, Richard. *Whatever Became of...Eighth Series*. New York: Crown, 1982.
_____. *Whatever Became of...Ninth Series*. New York: Crown, 1985.
Long, Bruce. *William Desmond Taylor: A Dossier*. Metuchen, NJ: Scarecrow, 1991.
Loos, Anita. *Cast of Thousands*. New York: Grosset and Dunlap, 1977.
Maltin, Leonard. *Our Gang: The Life and Times of the Little Rascals*. New York: Crown, 1977.
Mapp, Edward. *Blacks in American Films: Today and Yesterday*. Metuchen, NJ: Scarecrow, 1971.
Marrero, Robert. *Dracula: The Vampire Legend—70 Years on Film*. Key West, FL: Fantasma, 1992.
Mast, Gerald. *A Short History of the Movies*. New York: Macmillan, 1986.
Medved, Michael and Harry Medved. *The Hollywood Hall of Shame: The Most Expensive Flops in History*. New York: Perigee, 1984.
Miller, Bettina (editor). *From Flappers to Flivvers...We Helped Make the '20s Roar*. Greendale, WI: Reminisce, 1995.
Morris, Michael. *Madam Valentino: The Many Lives of Natacha Rambova*. New York: Abbeville, 1991.
Murray, Raymond. *Images in the Dark: An Encyclopedia of Gay and Lesbian Film and Video*. Philadelphia: TLA, 1994.
Norden, Martin F. *The Cinema of Isolation*. New Brunswick, NJ: Rutgers University Press, 1994.
Norris, Frank. *McTeague: A Story of San Francisco*. New York: Doubleday and McClure, 1899.
Nunn, Curtis. *Marguerite Clark: America's Darling of Broadway and the Silent Screen*. Fort Worth, TX: Texas Christian University Press, 1981.

Oderman, Stuart. *Roscoe "Fatty" Arbuckle: A Biography of the Silent Comedian, 1887–1933*. Jefferson, NC: McFarland, 1995.
Peary, Danny. *Alternate Oscars*. New York: Delta (Bantam, Doubleday, Dell), 1993.
_____ (editor). *Close-Ups*. New York: Workman, 1978.
Pickford, Mary. *Sunshine and Shadow*. Garden City, NY: Doubleday, 1955.
Pratt, George C. *Spellbound in Darkness: A History of the Silent Film*. Greenwich, CT: New York Graphic Society, 1973.
Ramsaye, Terry. *A Million and One Nights: A History of the Motion Picture Through 1925*. New York: Simon and Schuster, 1926.
Riefenstahl, Leni. *Leni Riefenstahl: A Memoir*. New York: Picador USA, 1995.
Robinson, David. *Charlie Chaplin: Comic Genius*. New York: Harry N. Abrams, 1996.
St. Johns, Adela Rogers. *The Honeycomb*. Garden City, NY: Doubleday, 1969.
Schickel, Richard. *D.W. Griffith: An American Life*. New York: Limelight Editions, 1996 (reprint of 1984 book).
Schulberg, Budd. *Moving Pictures: Memories of a Hollywood Prince*. Briarcliff Manor, NY: Stein and Day, 1981.
Schulman, Irving. *Valentino*. New York: Simon and Schuster, 1967.
Shepard, David, and Nancy Dowd. *King Vidor*. Metuchen, NJ: Scarecrow, 1988.
Shipman, Nell. *The Silent Screen and My Talking Heart*. Boise, ID: Boise State University Press, 1987.
Sinyard, Neil. *Silent Movies*. New York: Smithmark, 1990.
Sklar, Robert. *Film: An International History of the Medium*. New York: Harry N. Abrams, 1993.
Slide, Anthony. *Early American Cinema*. New York: A.S. Barnes, 1970.
_____. *Nitrate Won't Wait: A History of Film Preservation in the United States*. Jefferson, NC: McFarland, 1992.
_____. *The Silent Feminists: America's First Women Directors*. Lanham, MD: Scarecrow, 1996.
_____. *Silent Portraits: Stars of the Silent Screen in Historic Photographs*. Vestal, NY: Vestal, 1989.
_____, and Edward Wagenknecht. *Fifty Great American Silent Films, 1912-1920*. New York: Dover, 1980.
Stenn, David. *Clara Bow: Runnin' Wild*. New York: Penguin, 1988.
Taylor, Deems. *A Pictorial History of the Movies*. New York: Simon and Schuster, 1943.
Thompson, Frank. *Lost Films: Important Movies That Disappeared*. New York: Citadel, 1996.
_____. *The Star Film Ranch: Texas' First Picture Show*. Plano, TX: Republic of Texas Press, 1996.
_____ (editor). *Henry King: From Silents to 'Scope*. Los Angeles: Director's Guild of America, 1995.
Truitt, Evelyn Mack. *Who Was Who on Screen*. New York: R.R. Bowker, 1983.
Vazzana, Eugene Michael. *Silent Film Necrology: Births and Deaths of Over 9,000 Performers, Directors, Producers, and Other Filmmakers of the Silent Era Through 1993*. Jefferson, NC: McFarland, 1995.
Von Stroheim, Erich. *Greed* (complete shooting script). London: Lorrimer, 1972.
Wagenknecht, Edward. *The Movies in the Age of Innocence*. Norman: University of Oklahoma Press, 1962.
Weaver, John T. *Twenty Years of Silents, 1908–1928*. Metuchen, NJ: Scarecrow, 1971.
Whitfield, Eileen. *Pickford: The Woman Who Made Hollywood*. Lexington: University Press of Kentucky, 1997.

Index